Mastering
Crystal Reports 9

Mastering™
Crystal Reports 9

Cate McCoy

Gord Maric

SYBEX®

San Francisco   London

Associate Publisher: Joel Fuggazzotto

Acquisitions and Developmental Editor: Tom Cirtin

Editor: Linda Recktenwald

Production Editor: Kylie Johnston

Technical Editor: Acey Bunch

Electronic Publishing Specialist: Jill Niles

Graphic Illustrators: Tony Jonick, Robin Kibbe

Proofreaders: Dave Nash, Laurie O'Connell, Nancy Riddiough

Indexer: Lynnzee Elze

Book Designer: Maureen Forys, Happenstance Type-O-Rama

Cover Designer: Design Site

Cover Illustrator: Tania Kac, Design Site

Library of Congress Card Number: 200211456

ISBN: 0-7821-4173-0

SYBEX and the SYBEX logo are either registered trademarks or trademarks of SYBEX Inc. in the United States and/or other countries.

Mastering is a trademark of SYBEX Inc.

TRADEMARKS: SYBEX has attempted throughout this book to distinguish proprietary trademarks from descriptive terms by following the capitalization style used by the manufacturer.

The author and publisher have made their best efforts to prepare this book, and the content is based upon final release software whenever possible. Portions of the manuscript may be based upon pre-release versions supplied by software manufacturer(s). The author and the publisher make no representation or warranties of any kind with regard to the completeness or accuracy of the contents herein and accept no liability of any kind including but not limited to performance, merchantability, fitness for any particular purpose, or any losses or damages of any kind caused or alleged to be caused directly or indirectly from this book.

Manufactured in the United States of America

10 9 8 7 6 5 4 3 2

Acknowledgments

NURTURING A PROJECT FROM the back of a paper napkin through to a book on a shelf has been an incredible adventure, and it makes this book project very special to me. My family and friends have stood by me yet again and let me do what I do. The comfort you special people provide to me cannot be measured with any tool known to (wo)mankind—thank you!

The team behind the writer includes family, friends, colleagues, and even the occasional kind stranger. The Sybex team is top notch: Richard Mills bought into my excitement early on, Tom Cirtin did a great job of keeping me calm and focused most of the time, Kylie Johnston pushed hard for the best possible material every step of the way, and Linda Recktenwald dotted all the *I*'s and crossed all the *T*'s with charm, grace, and wit. Without them, there would not be a book. Matt Tagliaferri contributed original material and deadline-saving expertise—thank you! Acey Bunch waded through thousands of bytes of our written material, and his technical edits helped fine-tune the message. My co-author, Gord Maric, shared my excitement early on and worked hard in pursuit of the goal.

I am forever indebted to my Dad, who can never properly be thanked for being the guy who did all things I couldn't do while this book was gestating and entering the world, including those oh-so-necessary life tasks like taking the garbage out, fixing the pool, whacking away at the lawn, and keeping Princess company. While you did not read a word, you made every word possible.
—*CM*

I want to thank Tom Cirtin, Kylie Johnston, and everyone at Sybex for all their help with this project. I would like to thank Cate McCoy, my co-author, for involving me in this project. Special thanks go to Tom Cirtin for his patience and creativity in dealing with time pressures when chapters took longer than anticipated and vendors changed their software unannounced. Special thanks also go to Acey Bunch for his technical editing and help with the RAS chapters and to Matt Tagliaferri for coming in at the eleventh hour and assisting with the .NET and ASP chapters. And Linda Recktenwald for her editing and amazing attention to detail in finding inconsistencies in the chapters.

I want to thank Nancy, my partner in life, for her patience with this project and reading and editing my raw material.
—*GM*

Contents at a Glance

Contents

Introduction

We're drowning in information and starving for knowledge.
—Rutherford D. Rogers

EVERY FAN OF COMEDY recalls with a smile the classic "Who's on first?" routine performed so well by Bud Abbott and Lou Costello. The comical confusion caused by ineffective communication of information between the two comedians can bring on a good belly laugh as you watch them try to make sense of the words they're sharing. This sense of comedy surrounding information sharing, however, may leave you shaking your head in despair instead of smiling if it involves the communication of information in your organization.

Have you ever been handed an assignment and told simply that you needed to "get the bottom line" for the boss but were given no idea on where the data that makes up that bottom line is stored, how to retrieve it, and how to synthesize the raw data in a way that represents a meaningful bottom line? Your boss might as well have been Bud Abbott and you the hapless Lou Costello trying desperately to fulfill a communication request but having very little help. *This book is the help you need.* It teaches Crystal Reports in great detail—entirely from a problem-solving perspective. You'll come away not only knowing the in and outs of the software, but more important, how to use its features and tools to provide *real-world reporting solutions.* In other words, when someone in your organization hands you an end-result request, you'll know how to retrieve the necessary data and produce an attractive report that conveys information people can use.

Crystal Reports is THE (yes, in capital letters) tool you need to help you get to your raw data, retrieve it, massage it, and present it in a way that answers business questions for people who need those answers. It may be you, the jack-of-all-trades, who needs the answers. You are master of the data and the techniques required to convert that data to solid information. Or perhaps it's a colleague, a boss, a business partner, or a customer who needs the information. They come to you with a business question, and your job is to provide an answer using that information. You are the middle man or middle woman, and Crystal Reports is the tool in your toolbox that helps you take the data from its murky storage location and present it in full light as an informational report.

This book is for you, the Crystal Reports developer. Use it to help create accurate, complete business answers to business questions using your organization's data.

Who Should Read This Book?

The book is arranged in a way that allows beginning Crystal Reports users and business people who rely on their data to "tell the truth, the whole truth, and nothing but the truth" to learn the product in a fun and easy way. This book begins where every good story should—at the beginning. We start with fundamental Crystal Reports 9 techniques and show you how to put easy-to-use features to work to retrieve, format, and synthesize data, transforming it into information.

Next, we move on to the fancy stuff by showing you how to incorporate graphics and grids and fine-tune performance-enhancing options. We then introduce intermediate skills to move you to the next skill level by explaining complex concepts in a straightforward manner so that you can really transform your data into *knowledge*.

Finally, we approach Crystal Reports from the perspective of a programmer to teach you how to use it as a platform for developing custom applications, including web services. Application developers new to Crystal will find information you need to know to integrate Crystal Reports and Crystal Enterprise into your Visual Basic, Visual Studio .NET, ASP, and Java programming environments.

The progression of topics is intended to get you going quickly with the basic features and move you forward just as quickly into the advanced areas of the software. The sections and chapters are laid in a way that allows you to jump to the area that you need at any given moment.

The Evolution of Crystal Reports

Crystal Reports is a Windows-based software tool used to retrieve stored data, organize it in a meaningful way, and present it as information used to solve business problems.

The company behind the software is Crystal Decisions, based in Vancouver, British Columbia, Canada. You can find them online at www.crystaldecisions.com. Their motto is "Access. Analyze. Report. Share." The people in the company are smart, vibrant, and anxious to showcase their product— and for good reason. Crystal Reports 9 is simply the best report-writing tool on the market.

How popular is this product? Over 11 million licenses have been shipped. The company has formed strategic alliances with both Microsoft and IBM, bundling their tool into the core software being delivered by both of these computer giants. Crystal Reports is the de facto report writer in use in today's software world, and as a company, Crystal Decisions is positioned for continued growth in the niche market of business intelligence, or BI as it is often abbreviated.

Crystal Decisions also has a set of enterprise tools, called Crystal Enterprise and Report Application Server (RAS), that allow you take and distribute your reports to your organization. Whether you work in a small company or a very large company, you will be able to distribute reports with the Crystal Enterprise tool and associated applications.

Simply put, every organization that has stored data needs this software product to positively influence the never-ending processing loop of turning a company's raw data into information and applied knowledge.

The Crystal Product Line

The Crystal Decisions product line consists of four major components, each addressing different tasks within the business intelligence market.

- Crystal Reports
- Report Application Server (RAS) and Crystal Enterprise
- Crystal Analysis
- Crystal Applications

CRYSTAL REPORTS

Crystal Reports is the flagship software product in the Crystal Decisions line. This tool is used to connect to a data source, retrieve data, and build a report. Crystal Reports 9 helps you organize, sort, filter, summarize, and format information. The report can be saved in a variety of formats including Crystal's RPT format, Microsoft Word and Excel formats, Adobe PDFs, and HTML, to name a few.

This book focuses on full coverage of Crystal Reports 9, including all its new features.

RAS AND CRYSTAL ENTERPRISE

Crystal Enterprise is the piece of the product line that allows for widespread report distribution and security. Delivery of reports with RAS or Crystal Enterprise is done in a web environment with users accessing reports from their web browser. Existing reports are stored on a web server and accessed through a portal application, ePortfolio, provided by Crystal Decisions. In addition, Crystal Enterprise provides for real-time report generation and automatic generation of scheduled reports.

Crystal Reports ships with an entry-level version of Crystal Enterprise called the Report Application Server (RAS). We'll cover RAS and Crystal Enterprise, explain the most recent product arrangements, and explain configuring, using, and developing applications.

CRYSTAL ANALYSIS

Crystal Analysis is a suite of products that addresses the analysis phase of problem solving. Analyzing data involves the ability to drill down from summarized data to detail data and the real-time slicing and dicing needed to answer questions about the business. The Crystal Analysis suite contains the following products:

- Crystal Analysis Professional
- Holos
- Crystal Analysis Server
- Crystal Analysis Developer

CRYSTAL APPLICATIONS

Crystal Applications are prepackaged applications built using Crystal Reports, Crystal Analysis, and Crystal Enterprise. We will see how we can build our own custom applications, using Crystal Reports and Crystal Enterprise, so that you can build similar applications specific to your business. However, you can also use these application to give you a jump. The set of prebuilt applications includes:

ePortfolio   A web application included with RAS and Crystal Enterprise for deploying reports using a web browser. We will examine this in detail in this book.

Balanced Scorecard   A key performance indicator measurement tool that provides company financial information as well as looking at setting objectives and measuring performance to provide a balanced view of the present and future performance of the company

Budgeting   A budgeting application to streamline planning and budgeting. The budgeting application integrates with SAP and Oracle Financials.

Customer Profiling   An analysis tool designed to help you better identify your customer. It can provide complementary products, cross-selling information, and statistics about your customers. Having more information about your customers will help you maintain them.

eTelecom   A tool that consolidates the data from numerous communication channels to provide information about utilization of your PDX, email, remote access, and other communication infrastructure. It breaks down costs by employee so that you can analyze usage and capacity of the communication infrastructure.

Product Development

Crystal Reports is a teenager in human years but a mature adult in computer years, having been around for fourteen years. What began as a DOS-based integration into a small accounting package has evolved to a Windows-based system of world-class stature. Behind the scenes, the company has maintained the same high standards and focus on data reporting even while undergoing changes in ownership and name.

Over the past fourteen years, the positioning of the product has changed from an end-user tool to a power user and programmer's tool. The goals for the tool are to meet both basic and advanced reporting needs for individuals and organizations.

Unlike most teenagers, Crystal Reports doesn't complain about things it can't control—like changing requirements. Instead, it adapts. The company is aggressive in keeping up and often outpaces the industry.

Crystal Decisions intends to stay indispensable in the business intelligence market. To do this, they are committed to staying on top of current technology trends, leveraging the ones that are widely adopted and using them to continually improve their product. The company vision includes a complete information infrastructure that allows *any* user to generate reports on *any* data source from *any* application for delivery to *any* device. A comprehensive and exciting vision!

What's New in Crystal Reports 9?

The focus of this version of Crystal Reports is on making the product easier to use, faster to both create and view reports, and extending its web functionality. Three simple words describe the changes: power, productivity, and usability. You'll find the following general changes to the product:

User Interface Changes   Crystal Reports has been a huge fan of wizards in the past, and the product continues this focus in the current release. Many of the wizards have been streamlined for usability and to clarify the purpose of the individual wizard.

Performance Enhancements   The core report engine has been rewritten from the ground up, providing positive performance results. Because the core engine has changed, reports created with Crystal Reports 9 cannot be opened with earlier releases of the product. Crystal Reports 9 can be used to open reports written in prior versions, and once saved, they are converted to the Crystal Reports 9 storage format.

There are also several specific changes:

Repository Explorer   The Repository Explorer is an anchored window in the Crystal Reports development environment that provides access to design elements that can be shared across reports. You can develop an element once—for instance, a formula or graphic—and use it in multiple reports. Changes in the repository will be reflected in the reports that use the elements.

Report Explorer   Also an anchored window in Crystal Reports, the Report Explorer provides easy navigation and drill-down access to the logical areas in a report. For example, a new report automatically has five logical areas: Report Header, Page Header, Details, Report Footer, and Page Footer. These five logical areas are directly accessible in the Report Explorer.

Field Explorer   The Field Explorer has evolved into an anchored window that is used to add database fields, formula fields, parameter fields, running totals fields, group name fields, and special fields to a report.

Templates   Templates provide the ability to create reports that contain design elements but do not contain data. A template can specify fonts, background colors, logos, graphs, and more that can be stored as a standard format and applied to any report.

SQL Commands   The SQL-savvy report creator can now directly use SQL commands as a data source. Any valid SELECT statement appropriate to the database being used can be typed into Crystal Reports and used to generate a data result set. This powerful feature expands Crystal Reports into areas that were impossible in the prior version—namely, unions; joins to the same table; having, order by, and group by clauses. This is a significant performance enhancement because SQL is executed on the database server, taking full advantage of that performance environment and freeing Crystal Reports for its main role: formatting, summarizing, and presenting information.

Text Objects   Text objects can now be identified with a name, making them reusable components in a report or within the repository.

Report Parts A subset of fields and formulas within a report can be associated with a name and used to export smaller, specific parts of the report as opposed to the entire report. Report parts have great utility for delivering data to smaller devices such as hand-held PDAs and cell phones, which are designed for smaller amounts of data.

Formula Workshop The formula-development environment in Crystal Reports 9 has been enhanced into the Formula Workshop, which contains both the older Formula Editor and a newer Formula Expert. The Formula Expert is a drop-down interface that provides guidance to building formulas and adding them to the repository.

Visual Reporting Elements Cross-tabs now allow multiple values to be displayed side-by-side in a cell. Gantt charts and gauge charts have been added to the built-in set of charting components.

Smart Linking Smart Linking in prior releases of Crystal Reports focused on matching field names to create a join on tables. In Crystal Reports 9, Smart Linking now takes advantage of linking driven by primary keys and foreign keys defined in the data source.

Data Sources Crystal Decisions has expanded the list of natively supported data formats in this release of Crystal Reports. The list includes:

Access/Excel (DAO)	Field definitions	ODBC (RDO)
ACT! 3	File system data	OLAP
ADO.Net	IBM DB2	OLE DB (ADO)
Borland Database Engine	Informix	Oracle
Btrieve	Java data	Outlook
CDO	Lotus Notes Domino	Public Folder ACL
COM data	Mailbox Admin	Public Folder Admin
Crystal queries	Message tracking log	Public Folder Replica
Database files	Microsoft IIS/Proxy log files	Sybase
Dictionary/Infoview	NT archived event log	Web/IIS log files
Exchange folders and Address Book	NT current event log	xBase

Visual Studio .NET Object Libraries Microsoft has shifted their software development focus from the Component Object Model (COM)–based development with Visual Basic, and C++ to Visual Studio .NET. In keeping pace with the industry, Crystal Decisions has developed an object model hierarchy for .NET so that Crystal Reports can be embedded directly in this new environment. The business relationship between Microsoft and Crystal Decisions is a close partnership, with Crystal Reports being the only third-party tool included in the Visual Studio suite of products. COM-based development with Visual Basic 6 and any tool that supports COM continues to be supported and enhanced. We will look at both in the application development sections of this book.

Java Object Libraries Java development for Crystal Decisions is the second big change in programming approach. RAS and the Crystal Enterprise servers can not only run in a Windows environment but can also run in a Unix environment and provide JAVA Application Programming Interfaces (APIs) for application development. Using the Java API, you can open or create existing Crystal reports and publish them on the web.

Downloading Materials

Everyone enjoys the prospect of going on a vacation, so to keep things fun while you're diving deep into the world of Crystal Reports, we'll be working with the VistaNations company. This fictitious organization specializes in the selling, renting, and trading of vacation villas around the world.

We've ported a version of their company's data to Microsoft Access for use in our example reports. The data and all sample reports created in this book are available for download from the Sybex website, www.sybex.com. We encourage you to download the materials and work through the samples provided.

How to Contact the Authors

We look forward to hearing tales of the wonderful feats you accomplish with Crystal Reports. You can reach Cate at cate@alphapointsys.com or through the AlphaPoint website at www.alphapointsys .com. Gord is equally accessible through e-mail at gmaric@ciram.com and www.ciram.com.

Enjoy your data adventures and thank you for taking us on your journey!

Part 1

Report Writing Fundamentals

Chapter 1

Building Your First Report

EVERY BUSINESS THAT STORES data has a need to retrieve that data and build good reports. Organizations don't typically store data without reason…business intelligence (BI) is the reason, and reporting is the process of creating that business intelligence.

The process begins with locating the stored data. Sometimes this is an easy task; sometimes it is not. Crystal Reports can help you easily connect to your data. The next part of the task is to identify and format the pieces of data you need to answer a business question. A data customer will never come to you and say, "Hey, can you build a report with five fields, a graph, and a title?" Instead, they'll ask you if you can build a report to answer a business question, for instance, "How many five-star resorts do we have in our inventory?" The focus for users of data is on the business intelligence it provides, not on the data itself.

This makes your job similar to that of a good detective. You piece together all the clues using data and tell your audience at the end of the process "whodunit" using summary information and visual elements. Your job as the report designer is to convert business requests into the nuts and bolts of a report.

Featured in this chapter:

◆ Using a wizard to choose a report gallery style

◆ Choosing a data source

◆ Adding and formatting fields

◆ Grouping information

◆ Sorting information

◆ Adding summary information

◆ Understanding the report design area

◆ Using the toolbars and menus

Setting Up the Right Report

In this first chapter, we have a simple goal: build a report. We'll take advantage of the built-in creation wizard in Crystal Reports and explain all the fundamentals along the way.

You can think of a report as the answer to a business question. Users, customers, and peers come to you with a question about their inventory, their sales, their competition, their expenses, and so on. Your answer gives a glimpse into the state of the business, and as a Crystal Reports developer, your job is to find the data and craft a report that answers their question.

To this end, whenever we build a report in this book, we'll first state the business question that the report you create will answer, as shown here:

> *Business Question: How many resorts does VistaNations have in each country and what are their names?*

Okay, we're ready to go! The VistaNations folks have a Microsoft Access database for us to use. To get started with Crystal Reports 9, you may have a desktop icon you can double-click or you can use the following menu sequence: Start ➤ Programs ➤ Crystal Reports 9.

NOTE   All menu sequences will be called out in this way. A Windows 2000 desktop environment is assumed, so your actual command sequences may vary slightly.

The Crystal Reports Welcome screen, shown in Figure 1.1, appears, and now you have to make your first decision.

FIGURE 1.1

Crystal Reports
Welcome screen

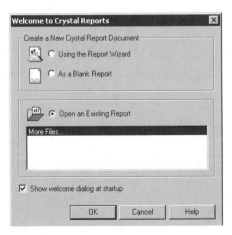

The top half of the screen provides radio buttons with choices on how to build your report:

- ◆ Using The Report Wizard
- ◆ As A Blank Report

The bottom half of the screen displays a radio button to open existing report files. When a report is saved in Crystal Reports, it is saved as an operating system file with the three-letter file extension .RPT for report. If you choose the radio button to open an existing report, you can choose from files shown in the file list directly below the radio button or you can click More Files to browse to any existing RPT file.

TIP   Notice the check box at the bottom of the window to show the Welcome dialog at startup. Uncheck the option to prevent this particular window from displaying in the future. You can access the window in the future by choosing the menu options Help ➤ Welcome Dialog.

At this point, we're going to use the Report Wizard, shown in Figure 1.2, by selecting the first radio button, Using The Report Wizard, and clicking the OK button. The Report Wizard provides a guide for adding key components to a report in a step-by-step manner. In later chapters, we'll revisit this screen and learn how to build a blank report.

FIGURE 1.2

Using the Report Wizard

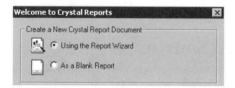

TIP   Well-designed applications for Microsoft Windows generally provide an OK button for you to click to acknowledge the acceptance of changes made to a dialog and to move forward in the application.

The bottom half of the Report Wizard screen is updated and presents a list of four typical report wizards in the Report Gallery shown in Figure 1.3.

FIGURE 1.3

Report Gallery

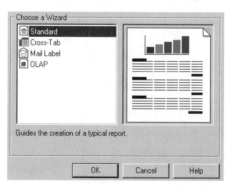

Choosing one of the report types tells Crystal the physical layout to use to present the information. The Standard Report Creation Wizard is the most commonly used report type. Each of the report types is described in Table 1.1.

TABLE 1.1: TYPES OF REPORTS

WIZARD	REPORT DESCRIPTION
Standard Report Creation	A report consisting of rows and columns of data
Cross-Tab	A report consisting of a table of summarized information
Mail Label	A report formatted to wrap data across multiple columns
OLAP	A report consisting of a summarized grid of data retrieved from an Online Analytical Processing database

For this example, we'll use a standard report, which is selected by default since the Standard Wizard is the first one in the list. Click OK to accept the options presented.

Choosing a Data Source

The next step in building a report is to select the data that will be used to *populate* your report. The Standard Report Creation Wizard dialog, shown in Figure 1.4, allows you to choose your data source.

FIGURE 1.4

Available data sources

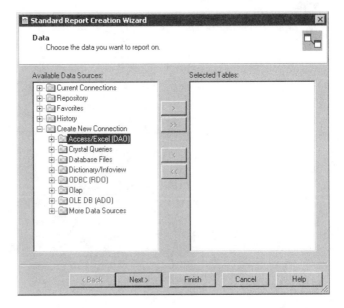

Available Data Sources

The Data dialog contains a list of available data sources on the left side of the window. Crystal Reports 9 supports a long list of data sources. There's a good chance the type of data you're using will be listed directly; if not, you can use the Create New Connection option to access the database. Table 1.2 describes the five general categories of data sources.

NOTE *Think of "available data sources" as being any database or data file located on your machine or accessible through a network connection from your computer.*

TABLE 1.2: CATEGORIES OF DATA SOURCES

SOURCE	DESCRIPTION
Current connections	Displays the databases to which Crystal Reports is currently connected.
Repository	Lists data stored in Crystal's common object repository.
Favorites	Displays a list of databases that you have manually added to your Favorites.
History	Shows data sources you have recently used; during the current Crystal session, all databases you access will appear; once closed and reopened, Crystal displays the most recent five data sources.
Create new connections	Allows a connection to any data source that you can access.

The process of specifying data for your report is to select a data source from the window on the left (Available Data Sources) and use the arrow in the middle to move your selected data source to the window on the right (Selected Tables).

NOTE *The + (plus sign) to the left of a word or phrase indicates that this is an expandable category that contains subcategories, as shown previously in Figure 1.4.*

The VistaNations organization uses a Microsoft Access database. In the collapsed format, the Standard Report Creation Wizard does not list the VistaNations database, so we need to go and find it. This will often be the case in your organization…finding the data can be an adventure!

Making a New Connection

Since we know the data source is a Microsoft Access database and we haven't worked with it before, the option to create a new connection sounds promising. In fact, whenever you start working with a database you haven't used previously in Crystal Reports, this is your starting point. Once you make a connection to a database, it appears directly in the list. Double-clicking the Make New Connection option opens the Connection dialog shown in Figure 1.5.

The Connection dialog provides an area to specify the database name, the type of database you're accessing, and whether you need to access the database with a user ID and password, in another words, a secure logon.

The options to add a database password, a session user ID, a session password, and a system database path become active and available only when the Secure Logon check box is marked.

Minimally, you can provide just the database name and its type to make the connection. You can enter this information directly, browse to it, or use a drop-down list to help you.

FIGURE 1.5

Connection dialog

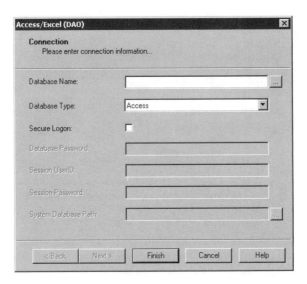

Let's find a database using the browse button (the button with three ellipsis points on it). The browse button brings up a dialog window to let you find and open any data file. In our example, the VistaNations database is located directly on the Local Disk (C:), as shown in Figure 1.6.

FIGURE 1.6

Open dialog

The VistaNations database is read-only and does not require any userID or password, so we'll leave the Secure Logon check box unmarked. Figure 1.7 shows the database name and database type properly filled in, so you're ready to click the Finish button to make the connection.

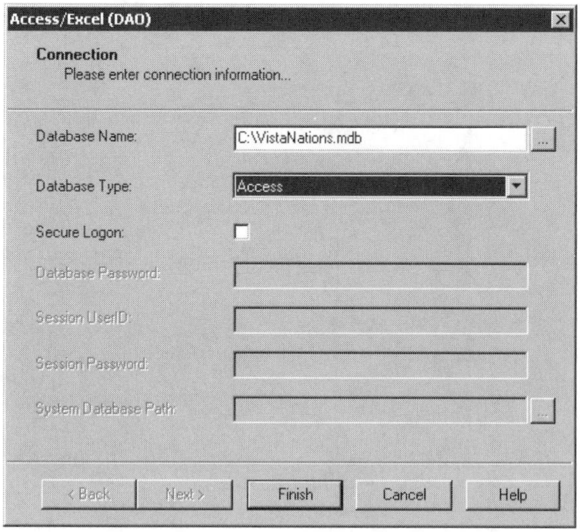

FIGURE 1.7

Connection settings

This completes the task of choosing a data source. The VistaNations data source now appears in your list of Available Data Sources, as shown in Figure 1.8, and you're ready to choose tables and fields.

FIGURE 1.8

An available data source

Choosing a Table

Database software (such as Microsoft Access) stores data in files that can contain any number of database tables. Within each table, any number of fields can be stored. The typical database components are depicted in Figure 1.9. Microsoft Access stores its data in a file that has an `.MDB` extension.

FIGURE 1.9

Database
components

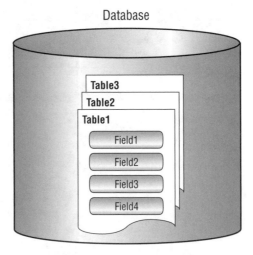

The Data dialog shown in Figure 1.10 shows a list of Available Data Sources on the left and a list of Selected Tables on the right: the tables you have selected to use in this particular report. When you begin a new report, this list is empty.

FIGURE 1.10

Data dialog

The VistaNations organization has several tables in its database; we'll build a report with one of them. By clicking a table, for instance, Resorts, you select that table from the list of Available Data Sources. With a table selected, the buttons in the middle become active. A single click on the first button copies the table to your Selected Tables list, as shown in Figure 1.11.

FIGURE 1.11

Selected table

DIALOG BUTTONS

Let's spend a moment discussing the Crystal-specific behavior of the five button options at the middle of the Data dialog. The first button, Back, is grayed out (disabled), signaling that moving to the previous dialog is not an option at this point. This is common practice in applications written for Microsoft Windows.

The Next button is available, and it is the button you use to move step-by-step through the Report Creation Wizard. So, the Back and Next buttons move you in either direction through the Report Creation Wizard. The nice thing about this is if you want to change one of the choices you've made during the creation process, simply use the Back button to go back and correct the option and the Next button to return to where you were and keep going.

The Finish button is also active and available. The behavior of the Finish button in Crystal is to stop the wizard at any point you choose, take the information collected up to that point, and use it to create and display the report. That means you don't have to use all the screens in the wizard in order to create a report! As a point of reference for when to do this, though, take note that if you were to click Finish at this point, you'd have a pretty dull report since you haven't chosen any field data.

The Cancel button also stops the wizard, halting the report-building activity completely and closing all open dialogs. The behavior of the Cancel button should be familiar to you Windows users out there!

The Help button opens a context-sensitive help window. An appropriate help window for the task you are doing will appear. Crystal Reports 9 has a very complete help file and provides a wealth of information. This feature has been vastly improved in Crystal Reports 9, so enjoy!

NOTE *After the wizard completes and you are in the Crystal Reports design environment, you can add additional tables or change your data source altogether using the toolbar. Notice the icon in the top-right corner of the Data dialog, shown in Figure 1.11. This icon will appear on the Crystal Reports toolbar later.*

Adding Fields

With a data source's table identified, the Report Creation Wizard next guides you to choose fields from the table to add to the report using the Fields dialog shown in Figure 1.12.

FIGURE 1.12

Choosing fields

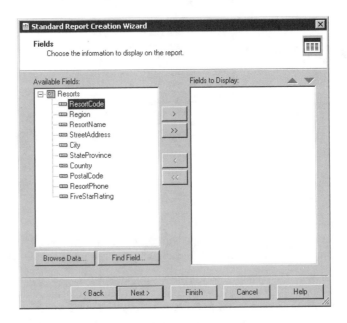

Choosing Fields

The Fields window should feel familiar since it is similar in design to the previous dialog we examined. Your job is to select fields in the list of Available Fields on the left side of the dialog and copy them to the right side of the dialog, Fields To Display, using the buttons between the two lists. Referencing the business question, we'll choose appropriate fields from the 10 available in the Resorts table.

> *Business Question: How many resorts does VistaNations have in each country and what are their names?*

To satisfy this business question, we'll need the following fields:

◆ ResortName

◆ Country

You can click each field individually to select it and then use the first button between the two lists to copy the field to the list of Fields To Display. When you've finished adding fields to the list of Fields To Display, you can click Next to move to the next step.

NOTE *The first two buttons shown in Figure 1.12 move fields to the list of Fields To Display; the second two buttons in Figure 1.12 (shown disabled here) remove fields from the display list.*

TIP *You can use the Microsoft keyboard shortcuts Ctrl or Shift while selecting fields to highlight individual or adjacent fields as a group.*

Browsing Data and Finding Fields

There are two buttons on the Fields dialog: Browse Data and Find Field. The Browse Data field is used to take a peek at the type of data that is stored in the field before adding it to your report. For instance, with the Country field selected in the Available Fields list, clicking the Browse Data button displays sample data and tells you what type of data is stored. Figure 1.13 shows the Browse Data window for the Country field. You can scroll through the list box to view the data that is stored in the field. Along the top, you can see that the field data type is String and its length is 50.

FIGURE 1.13

Browse Data window

The Find Field button is useful when a long list of fields is displayed and you want to avoid scrolling to find a particular field. You can type in the exact name of the field you're looking for or as much of the name, starting at the beginning, as you know, as shown in Figure 1.14.

FIGURE 1.14

Find Field window

Sequencing Fields

With a set of fields to display shown in the Fields dialog, you can determine the order in which the fields are added to the report. Click the upward- or downward-pointing triangle, visible here in Figure 1.15, to move the selected field higher or lower in the list of fields.

FIGURE 1.15

Sequencing fields

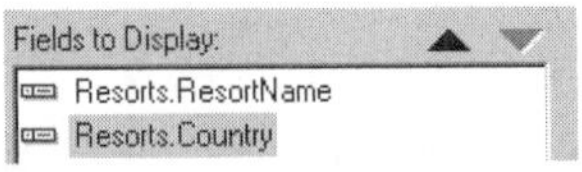

> **NOTE** *After the wizard completes and you are in the Crystal Reports design environment, you can still add fields using the toolbar. Notice the icon in the top-right corner of the Fields dialog, shown previously in Figure 1.12. This icon will appear on the Crystal Reports toolbar later.*

Grouping and Sorting Information

The Grouping dialog follows the same familiar approach of selecting items from the left and copying them to the right. On the Available Fields list, however, there are now two categories, as shown in Figure 1.16.

FIGURE 1.16

Grouping the information

> **TIP** *Navigate to the Grouping and Sorting dialog using the Next button or by clicking directly on the tab.*

Choosing a Field to Group By

The first category of fields is Report Fields. You can think of these as the fields you've already asked to be included in your report. The second grouping shows all the fields in the data source being used for the report, including the ones from your report, meaning there is inherent duplication.

If you choose a field to group by that is not represented by the Report Fields category, the new field will be automatically added to the list of fields that display in your report.

> *Business Question: How many resorts does VistaNations have in each country and what are their names?*

Our business question requires that we determine how many resorts are in each country, so we'll create a grouping based on the Country field. We select the Resorts.Country field from the list on the left and use the buttons in the middle to copy the field to the Group By list on the right, as shown in Figure 1.17.

FIGURE 1.17

Group By Country

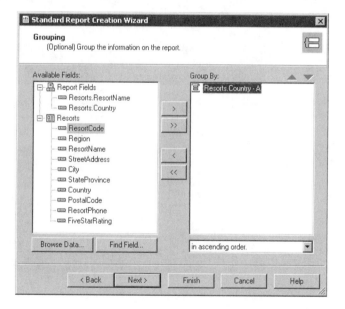

Sorting a Group

By default, a group is sorted in ascending order. The sorting drop-down box is located at the lower right of the Grouping dialog (see Figure 1.17). You can change the sort order to descending if you wish.

The -A to the right of the field name in the Group By list tells you that the Resorts.Country field will be sorted in ascending order; -D would appear for descending order.

NOTE   *After the wizard completes and you are in the Crystal Reports design environment, you can still add groups using the toolbar. Notice the icon in the top-right corner of the Grouping dialog, shown in Figure 1.17. This icon will appear on the Crystal Reports toolbar later. Notice also that this part of the screen identifies grouping as an optional step. This is the first time you've seen this feature in the Report Creation Wizard. The icon is a signal to you that you can expect reasonable results at any point when you click the Finish button.*

Summarizing Data

After grouping the fields, the Report Creation Wizard helps you summarize the data you've selected. If you've grouped the data, the fields involved in the grouping are automatically added to the Summarized Fields list. The Summaries dialog is shown in Figure 1.18. To summarize data, you choose a field to summarize and a summarization method.

FIGURE 1.18

Summaries dialog

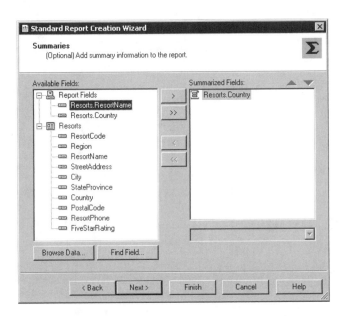

Business Question: How many resorts does VistaNations have in each country and what are their names?

Our business question requires that we count how many resorts are in each country. Count is a summarization method. We will summarize based on the Country field using a count summarization. We select the Country field from the list on the left and copy it to the list on the right using the buttons between the two lists.

A default summarization method will be automatically set for you, as shown in Figure 1.19, but you can change to another type of summarization method by selecting it from the drop-down list. The default method set is based on the type of data contained in the field you are summarizing. Table 1.3 describes each of the summarization methods.

FIGURE 1.19

Summarization
default

TABLE 1.3: SUMMARIZATION METHODS

SUMMARIZATION	DESCRIPTION
Maximum	Given a set of values, returns the largest value
Minimum	Given a set of values, returns the smallest value
Count	A number representing how many times the value appears in the field
Distinct Count	A number representing how many times the value uniquely appears in the field
Mode	Given a set of values, returns the value that occurs most frequently in the field
Nth largest, N is:	Type a value for N as an integer number (e.g., 5) and from a set of values in the report, Crystal returns the N largest values (in this case, the 5 largest values)
Nth smallest, N is:	Type a value for N as an integer number (e.g., 7) and from the set of all values, Crystal returns the N smallest values (in this case, the 7 smallest values)
Nth most frequent, N is:	Type a value for N as an integer number (e.g., 9) and from the set of values in the data source, returns the N most frequently occurring values; similar to Mode.

The summarization techniques available are determined by the data values stored in the field. To answer our business question, the Count summarization method makes the most sense, as shown in Figure 1.20. It allows you to summarize nonnumerical data by counting instances of a value.

FIGURE 1.20

Count
summarization
method

Notice that the sigma symbol appears indented under the grouping symbol in the graphic above. What this means is that the report will show a count for each unique grouping. For instance, if the Country is Canada, there will be a number representing how many resorts are in Canada. Likewise, if the Country is the United States, there will be a number representing how many resorts are in the United States. The indenting gives you a visual idea of how the summarization will be done in the report.

NOTE   *After the wizard completes and you are in the Crystal Reports design environment, you can summarize field data using the toolbar. Notice the icon in the top-right corner of the Summaries dialog, shown in Figure 1.20. This icon will appear on the Crystal Reports toolbar later.*

Creating the Reports

At this point you've done the following:

◆   Connected to a data source

◆   Chosen a table and fields to use in the report

◆   Created a group based on sorted field data

◆   Summarized data based on a field

You're ready to generate the report! To do this using the Report Creation Wizard, simply click the Finish button.

The Report Design Area

The result of the Standard Report Creation Wizard is the generation of a report that is opened in Preview mode in the Crystal Reports designer, as shown in Figure 1.21.

FIGURE 1.21

Previewing
the report

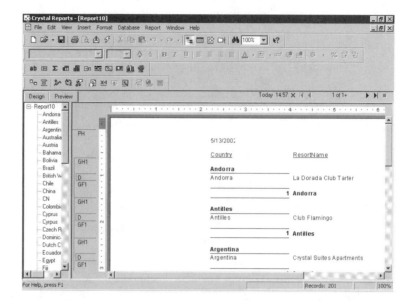

Navigating the Report

How can you tell you're in Preview mode? Well, the screen is quite busy, and we'll explore all of it, but let's focus our attention on a horizontal area a third of the way down the screen under the toolbars (see Figure 1.21). This horizontal area contains the following:

◆ Tabs for Design and Preview mode

◆ The current date and time

◆ An X button you can click to close this report but stay in Crystal Reports

◆ Forward and backward navigation buttons to move one page at a time through the report

◆ First and last navigation buttons to move to the first page or last page in the report

◆ An estimate of the number of pages in the report and the current page number

WARNING The page count estimate is usually incorrect until you navigate through the pages directly. For instance, the estimate in Figure 1.21 shows pages 1 of 1+. At this point, Crystal has made its best guess and knows that there is more data than will fit on a single page, but it does not yet know how many pages will be required to display it. Clicking the forward and backward buttons will update the page count estimator.

Using Preview Mode

The intent of Preview mode is to display the data as the user of the report will see it. From Figure 1.22, you can see that we have a column of data for Country and a column of data for ResortName, the two fields we chose using the Report Creation Wizard. We grouped the data based on Country and sorted it in ascending order, and sure enough our data is being displayed using these criteria.

FIGURE 1.22

Preview mode

```
5/13/200:

Country                          ResortName

Andorra
Andorra                          La Dorada Club Tarter

                              1 Andorra


Antilles
Antilles                         Club Flamingo

                              1 Antilles


Argentina
Argentina                        Crystal Suites Apartments

                              1 Argentina
```

Notice that Crystal took care of arranging the fields in the report automatically. While this was thoughtful, it might not be aestheticly pleasing, so rest assured that you can change it to your liking in Design mode.

GROUP TREE

Whenever you perform grouping in your report, a group tree is displayed in Preview mode in the Crystal Reports design area. The group tree is a vertical area that appears anchored to the left side of the screen, as shown in Figure 1.23. It is used as a navigation technique to let the user jump to a particular group within the report.

By clicking a group name in the group tree, the data that appears in the preview area changes to the data that references the chosen group. For instance, we clicked the text line Bahamas in the group tree, and the display area moved the Bahamas group to the top of the screen, indicating that there are two resorts in the Bahamas, as shown in Figure 1.24.

FIGURE 1.23

Group tree

FIGURE 1.24

Using the group tree

Design Mode

The Design mode layout area is where you'll do most of your work. In this area, you rearrange, add, and delete text, fields, and objects to create a visually appealing report. Notice in Figure 1.25 that we don't see actual data in Design mode; instead, we see placeholders for fields, group names, and summarization totals.

FIGURE 1.25

Design mode

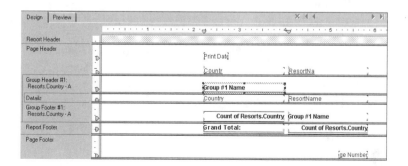

The wizard placed the following objects into appropriate places on the report:

Fields:

Country, ResortName

Groups:

Group #1 Name: This is the group created on the Country field.

Summary:

Count of Country: This is the summarization on the Country field.

Text Labels:

Country (field name), ResortName (field name), and Grand Total

Graphic Elements:

Single underline beneath each group name

Single underline beneath the last item in each group

Double underline beneath the Grand Total

AUTOMATIC FIELDS

Also notice in Figure 1.25 that Crystal added some additional information that you did not request while you were working through the Report Creation Wizard. Namely, the following two piece of information were automatically added to the report for you:

◆ Print Date

◆ Page Number

Print Date is a variable that shows the date the report was displayed on the screen or printed to a printer. Page Number is a variable that, as you would expect, displays the sequential page number currently being viewed.

Sections

How did Crystal know where to place the variety of elements it created during report generation? It followed some simple rules regarding section bands. Crystal Reports is known as a *banded report writer*. It has five basic *bands*, or sections, that information can be added to in a report. When you use the Report Generation Wizard, Crystal adds information to the appropriate band based on the element's type. Once the report is generated, you can make changes to the placement that Crystal set up for you.

The five basic bands represent physical layout areas on a piece of paper, and their purposes are described in Table 1.4.

TABLE 1.4: FIVE BASIC REPORT BANDS

BAND NAME	DESCRIPTION	EXAMPLES OF ELEMENTS
Report Header	Items placed in this section appear once per report; the information is placed at the very beginning of the report.	Report title
Page Header	Items placed in this section appear once per page and on every page of a report; the information is placed at the very beginning of the page.	Column headings, print date
Details	Items placed in this section repeat for each data record retrieved from the data source.	Fields
Report Footer	Items placed in this section appear once per report; the information is placed at the end of the Details section.	Grand totals
Page Footer	Items placed in this section appear once per page and on every page of a report; the information is placed at the end of the page.	Page number

From the above descriptions, you'll notice that the Page Footer appears after the Report Footer. This is indeed correct. The information placed in the Report Footer appears at the end of the data from the Details section. Imagine a page that has data only to about the one-third of the page mark. At that point, the Report Footer prints. The Page Footer, on the other hand, appears at the very end of the page in the last inch of the printable area. Figure 1.26 shows the bands as they relate to their physical layout on a piece of paper.

FIGURE 1.26

The five basic bands

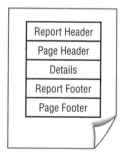

ADDITIONAL SECTIONS

In addition to the five basic bands, or sections, two additional sections are added for each group that you create. We added one grouping based on the Country field, so our report shows a header and footer band for that group:

◆ Group Header #1: Resorts.Country-A

◆ Group Footer #1: Resorts.Country-A

As with the other header and footer areas, items placed in the header area appear above the group, while items placed in the footer area appear below the group.

SECTIONS IN DESIGN MODE

In Design mode, the five basic section bands appear anchored to the left side of the screen and next to the design layout area. Additional header and footer bands appear for each group created, as shown in Figure 1.27.

FIGURE 1.27

Design mode sections

SECTIONS IN PREVIEW MODE

In Preview mode, a section band appears to the right of the group tree and to the left of the actual data in the preview area. The names of the band may appear abbreviated, such as PH for Page Header and GH1 for Group Header #1, or will display with their complete names.

For each group added, an incrementing number identifies the group. The report we're creating has only one group, so you see GH1 and GF1 for Group Header #1 and Group Footer #1 repeated for each new country. Remember that Country was the field upon which we based our group.

Toolbars and Menus

Good Windows applications are consistent, and Crystal Reports is a good Windows application. It conforms to the standards of having a title bar at the top, a menu beneath the title bar, and toolbar icons below the menu. Table 1.5 describes what each of these areas do for you, and Figure 1.28 displays them.

TABLE 1.5: GOOD WINDOWS CONVENTIONS

AREA NAME	PURPOSE
Title bar	Every window should have a title; it displays the name of the application, in this case, Crystal Reports, and the name of the current object, in this case, the report name.
Menu	Contains drop-down text-based navigation to the tasks that can be performed in the application; the first two and last two menus are standard in most applications: File, Edit, Window, and Help.
Toolbar	Contains shortcut icons to menu items; moving the mouse slowly over the icon displays a short tool tip in text to describe the task performed by the icon.

Crystal Reports follows the typical Windows convention for changing the menu options and toolbar options available at any given point by displaying context-appropriate options.

FIGURE 1.28

Toolbars and menus

TIP   You can drag and drop the toolbar sections alongside one another and reorder them; click very near the left edge of the section you want to move to select it.

Putting On the Finishing Touches

At this point, the report we created answers the business question of how many resorts VistaNations has in each country and the names of the resorts. We can make the report a little more visually appealing by making some simple changes and using some basic graphic elements. This will also give you a chance to use the design interface, toolbar, and menus a bit.

Indenting Groups

One of the first and easiest enhancements to make is to indent the detail data beneath a group name. By default, Crystal left-aligns the group name and the data. You can easily change this by doing the following:

1. Click the Design tab.
2. Click the Country field in the Details section.
3. Press the right arrow key twice to indent the field data.
4. Click the Preview tab to see the effect of your change.

The group data should now display indented, as shown in Figure 1.29.

FIGURE 1.29

Indented group data

Country	ResortName
5/13/2002	
Country	ResortName
Andorra	
Andorra	La Dorada Club Tarter
	1 Andorra
Antilles	
Antilles	Club Flamingo
	1 Antilles
Argentina	
Argentina	Crystal Suites Apartments
	1 Argentina

Boxes and Lines

Lines and boxes can be added around text labels and fields to call attention to a particular area of the report. In our report, we'll draw a box around the two column headings, Country and ResortName, by doing the following:

1. Click the Design tab.

2. Choose Insert ➤ Box.

3. Use the pencil drawing tool to draw an outline box around the two column headings in the Page Header.

The result is shown in Preview mode in Figure 1.30.

FIGURE 1.30

Drawing boxes

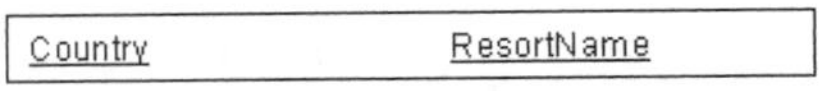

Country	ResortName

TIP   *Another simple visual effect is to add a line by choosing the menu options Insert ➤ Line.*

Pictures

One of the easiest ways to make your reports look more professional is to add a picture image. Let's add the VistaNations logo to the Page Header so that it appears at the top of every page in the report.

The VistaNations logo exists in a TIF image file. To add a graphic to the page header, do the following:

1. Click the Design tab.

2. Choose Insert ➤ Picture.

3. Locate and select the image using the Open menu.

4. Click the mouse inside the Page Header section to anchor the image.

Table 1.6 shows the types of graphics that can be placed in a Crystal report.

TABLE 1.6: TYPES OF GRAPHICS

FILE EXTENSION	MEANING
.BMP	Microsoft Windows bitmap format
.WMF	Microsoft Windows Metafiles
.TIF	Tagged Information File format; also known as TIFF images
.JPG	Joint Photographic Expert Group format; also known as JPEG images
.PNG	Portable Network Graphics format

The result of adding the graphic can be seen by previewing your work, as shown in Figure 1.31.

FIGURE 1.31

Adding a graphic

Resizing and Moving Objects

When Crystal adds fields and text to a report, it adds them in a default size that may or may not completely display the object. Notice the Print Date variable that was automatically added, as shown in Figure 1.32. You can see that the last letter appears to be cut off in Design mode and would display truncated in Preview mode as well.

FIGURE 1.32

Print Date variable

Print Date

You can fix this by manually resizing the field area using the object resize handles shown in Figure 1.33. These handles are shown as very small squares centered on each border of the object. Moving your mouse over the square displays a two-headed arrow, signaling that you can drag and drop the border to resize the object.

FIGURE 1.33

Object resize handles

With an object selected and the object resize handles visible, you can reposition the object in the design or preview windows using drag-and-drop techniques. The resize symbol is an intersection set of two double-headed arrows. When you see this symbol, you can drag and drop the object to move it any place in the report, including to different sections.

Saving a Report

We've done a good deal of work on this report. Let's save what we've done so that we can use it later. Saving a Crystal Reports file in the Windows environment is like saving any other type of file. Reports are saved in a file with an .RPT extension. To save a report, use the menu sequence File ➢ Save. A Save As dialog opens to prompt you to provide a filename and automatically sets the type as Crystal Reports. We'll save this report as **CH01.RPT**. You can save it to any location accessible to your computer.

WARNING   *Files created with Crystal Reports 9 cannot be opened with older versions of Crystal Reports.*

A WORD ABOUT REPORT NAMING CONVENTIONS

Small companies may have just a few reports, while large companies may have hundreds of reports. It is a good investment of your time to sit down with the IT (Information Technology) folks in your organization and agree on some report naming conventions.

Each Crystal report is stored in an operating system file that has an .RPT extension. Some companies embed information in the name of a report; for instance, D582-CM.RPT is a report created in Department 582 by someone with the initials CM. Another convention might involve the content of the report, for instance, Employee Sales.RPT or MonthlyProjections.RPT. (Check with your operating system rules before using blank spaces in filenames.)

Before you decide on conventions, consider the operating systems and devices to which you will be deploying reports. Many operating systems, including Microsoft's, allow long filenames, which means that you can make the portion of the filename that comes before .RPT very robust and meaningful and include spaces. Other operating systems, such as Unix, prefer the 8.3 (pronounced *eight-dot-three*) naming convention, or short filename, where the number of characters that comes before the period should be eight or fewer. Similarly, small handheld devices, such as cell phones, can store less information and have smaller output displays, so short filenames might be easier to manage.

Agreeing on a good naming convention early in the process will help you find your reports more easily later on!

The Business Questions Answered

The simple report shown in Figure 1.34 and created in this chapter shows that there are a total of 201 resorts in VistaNations' inventory, with 94 of them being in the United States and the remainder spread out in smaller groups around the world. The report has a total of 9 pages. Further, it's an attractive document that is easy to read.

FIGURE 1.34

Last page of the report

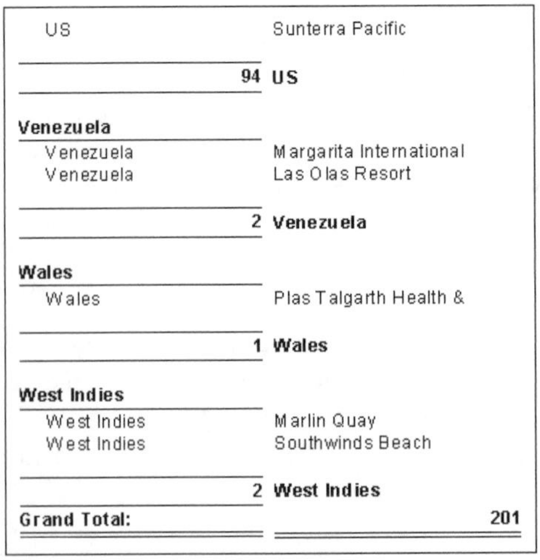

US	Sunterra Pacific	
	94 US	
Venezuela		
Venezuela	Margarita International	
Venezuela	Las Olas Resort	
	2 Venezuela	
Wales		
Wales	Plas Talgarth Health &	
	1 Wales	
West Indies		
West Indies	Marlin Quay	
West Indies	Southwinds Beach	
	2 West Indies	
Grand Total:		**201**

Summary

As you've seen in this chapter, creating a report with Crystal Reports is easy. Creating a good report, however, requires that you understand how to connect to the data, retrieve the pieces you need, and lay them out in an aesthetically pleasing and meaningful way. A solid understanding of your report-writing tool is essential.

The five basic sections, or bands, of a Crystal Report play a large role in the ultimate look, feel, and behavior of a report. The report wizard places fields and text automatically in appropriate sections, and with a little background information on why the wizard does what it does, you can confidently move data around to make the layout work for you. The Standard Report Creation Wizard helps you perform summarization and grouping during the first stages of report writing, which is where you start the process of converting raw data into meaningful information.

Beyond the wizard approach to building a report, you can add visual elements to a report, which can go a long way in delivering quality reporting. While you can't change the news the data delivers, sometimes the news is easier to swallow if it at least looks organized and neat in the report! We'll continue working with this report in the next chapter as we move beyond the Report Creation Wizard to additional Crystal Report features.

Chapter 2

Modifying a Report

IN THE LAST CHAPTER, we used the Standard Report Creation Wizard to create a basic report, and this got us going very quickly. Much of your time as a report builder, however, will be spent modifying an existing report to meet additional requirements. One of the reasons for this is that iterative development keeps the users involved on a continual basis; you build something, show it to them, they critique it, and you change it. This is a nice way of saying that users don't really know what they want until they see something they don't want. Then, with something in front of them, they can tell you specific changes they'd like you to make. Report building is an ongoing cycle to perfection.

The skills you need in order to modify an existing report are very similar to the ones you use when you build a report from scratch. The Report Creation Wizard is a good starting point when you're new to Crystal Reports, but very quickly you will find that you can do the layout yourself and make equally good time at it with better control.

Featured in this chapter:

◆ Opening and enhancing existing reports

◆ Working with database fields

◆ Managing groups

◆ Changing sort options

◆ Working with basic summary fields

◆ Getting help

Locating and Using an Existing Report

If you already have Crystal Reports open, you can locate and open the report using the standard Windows File ➢ Open command, then browse to the file's location and open it. Crystal supports the normal Windows keyboard shortcuts as well, like Ctrl+O for opening a file.

TIP *A very handy keyboard shortcut is Ctrl+S, which saves your current work and leaves you in Editing mode. Save early and save often so you always have a recent copy of your report to return to should anything unexpected happen!*

On the other hand, if you are just starting up the Crystal Reports software, you will see the Welcome dialog unless you disabled this feature. The Welcome screen, shown in Figure 2.1, lists in the scrollable area at the bottom of the window the most recent reports you've worked on. By clicking the Open An Existing Report radio button, you can select the report you want from the list and open it.

FIGURE 2.1

Open An Existing Report

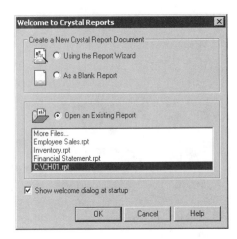

You'll recall that the report you built in Chapter 1, "Building Your First Report," answered the business question of how many resorts the VistaNations company has and what their names are. The boss was thrilled with the report you built (most likely because she had no idea how to do it), and when she looked at it said, "This is exactly what I need! But. . . ." In the world of developers and customers, the word *But* always means they need *something* changed! The new business question is a bit more complex.

> *Business Question: We need the resort region, resort code, and mailing information for all the resorts sorted by resort name, with totals grouped by region and showing which ones are in North America.*

To satisfy this business question, we'll need a few more fields, a few changes in the sort order, and some additional summarization.

Working with Database Fields

The Report Creation Wizard can be used only during the creation stage of report building. Once you have a report to work with, you add additional fields using the Field Explorer, shown in Figure 2.2.

Several additional fields were specified in the business question:

- ResortCode
- StreetAddress
- City
- StateProvince
- PostalCode
- Region

FIGURE 2.2

Field Explorer

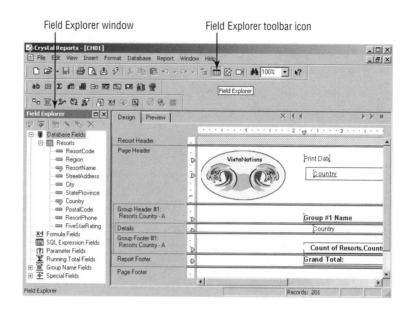

Field Explorer window   Field Explorer toolbar icon

While you can use the Field Explorer and other design objects in both Preview mode and Design mode, there is more help available to you as a report creator in terms of layout in Design mode than there is in Preview mode. Preview mode is ideal for seeing the visual effect as the user might see it.

WARNING   *In Crystal Reports 9, you can no longer add fields using the Insert menu.*

The Field Explorer has been updated in Crystal Reports 9 and works as a kind of home base for all the work you do with fields while designing a report. When you click the Field Explorer toolbar icon, the Field Explorer window becomes anchored, or *docked*, to the left side of the design window, as shown in Figure 2.2. The Field Explorer icon works like a toggle switch: Click it once and the Field Explorer displays; click it again and the Field Explorer disappears. The Field Explorer window can also be detached from its docked position by dragging and dropping its title bar window. Once detached, the Field Explorer becomes a floatable window that you can leave floating over the design window or redock to the left, right, or bottom of the design screen.

The seven categories of fields listed in the Field Explorer are described in Table 2.1. We'll go into more details on how to use each of the fields in subsequent chapters, and for now, we'll focus on database fields.

TABLE 2.1: TYPES OF FIELDS

FIELD TYPE	DESCRIPTION
Database Fields	Fields that are stored in a data source table
Formula Fields	Calculated fields that evaluate to a result

Continued on next page

TABLE 2.1: TYPES OF FIELDS *(continued)*

FIELD TYPE	DESCRIPTION
SQL Expression Fields	Fields that perform a SQL calculation or expression
Parameter Fields	Fields that prompt users for values at runtime
Running Total Fields	Counting fields that increment in special ways
Group Name Fields	Custom named references for groups created in a report
Special Fields	Fields generated by Crystal that can be added to any report

Adding a Database Field

With the Field Explorer visible on the design screen, you can add any number of additional fields to your report. If you had created a report using the As A Blank Report radio button visible in Figure 2.1, you would use the technique about to be described to add fields to the report instead of using the Report Creation Wizard.

The Database Fields option is the first item in the Field Explorer. This is handy because a good deal of what you add to a report is field data from a database. Figure 2.3 shows the Field Explorer as a floating window and with the Database Fields option expanded. You can collapse both the Database Fields option and the Resorts table option by clicking the minus sign.

FIGURE 2.3

Database Fields

Figure 2.3 shows that this report uses the Resorts table as a data source and currently makes use of the ResortName and Country fields. The green check mark next to each field signals that the field is placed somewhere on the open report, which is nice information to know. You can reuse fields as many times as you need to, so the green check mark will not stop you from adding the field to the report again.

FIELD EXPLORER BUTTONS

At the top of the Field Explorer are six icon buttons that perform the following tasks on the selected (highlighted) field:

◆ Insert the field into the report

◆ Browse the data in the data source for the field

◆ Create a new field

◆ Edit the field

◆ Rename the field

◆ Delete the field

In the case of a database field, the only options available are to insert the field or browse its data; the remaining icons are grayed out because they don't apply to the field.

CONTEXT MENUS

We can also get more information about an individual field by using the context menu. Right-clicking an item displays an item-specific menu. For instance, right-clicking the ResortCode field (which is selected in Figure 2.3) displays the context menu shown in Figure 2.4. The context menu also shows the keyboard shortcuts for the mouse-oriented menu tasks.

FIGURE 2.4

Field Explorer
context menu

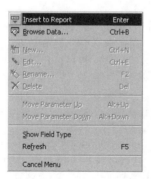

Insert to Report	Enter
Browse Data...	Ctrl+B
New...	Ctrl+N
Edit...	Ctrl+E
Rename...	F2
Delete	Del
Move Parameter Up	Alt+Up
Move Parameter Down	Alt+Down
Show Field Type	
Refresh	F5
Cancel Menu	

TIP   Crystal Reports is very fond of context menus; whenever you're wondering what you can do at a given point in the application, right-click the object of interest to see what's available.

DRAG AND DROP

The most popular way to add fields to your report still makes use of the Field Explorer but does so in a drag-and-drop operation (see Figure 2.5). You can select a field from the Field Explorer (including non-database fields) and drag it to the position on the report where you want it placed.

FIGURE 2.5

Dropping a field
into position

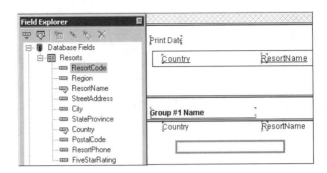

As you're dragging a field from the Field Explorer to a section in your report, a thick gray rectangle representing the field placement floats over the report until you let go of the mouse. Once you do, the field is positioned at the point where you let go of the mouse and the gray positioning rectangle disappears. During this drag-and-drop activity, the mouse pointer changes from a pointer to a circle with a diagonal line through it; the pointer is telling you whether or not it's valid to drop the field at the position the mouse is on currently. A pointing arrow means that you've found a legal place to put the field; the circle with the line through it means that it's illegal and you won't be allowed to drop the field.

You can also use drag and drop to reposition any field, moving it to another location within the same section or into a different section entirely.

Field Placement

As you add fields to a report, you need to think about where you're placing the fields. Two issues become very important in field placement: section management and visual aesthetics, or your ability to make fields look good on the piece of paper or screen on which it will ultimately be viewed. You can think of aesthetics in terms of physical placement, and there are several utilities to help you with that task, such as guidelines, grids, and rulers.

SECTIONS

The primary concern in field placement involves in which section to place a field. The section you place it in can actually affect how the field behaves. As an example, recall that fields placed in report headers or footers display only once per report. If you dragged the ResortCode field into the Report Header section, then the resort code for the first resort in the database would appear as the only Resort Code value in the entire report. Hang on, though, weren't there over 200 resorts? What about the other 199+ values that ResortCode has in each record of the database? Well, if you place the field in the Report Header, then only the first value in the database will display and all other values will be ignored.

The only section that guarantees that a value for every record in the database will appear in your report is the Details section. So if your goal is to list all the resort codes and resort names in the database, then you must position these two fields in the Details section. When the Report Creation Wizard generated the report for you in Chapter 1, it automatically put all database fields in the Details section so that a value would appear for each record in the database. When you don't use the wizard for field selection, the burden is on you to make sure the field is placed in a section appropriate to its purpose.

WARNING   *Crystal will not stop you from putting a field in any section; that part of the job is up to you.*

GUIDELINES

Each time you place a field on the report, guideline positioning markers are added to the rulers that border the design area. These guideline markers, visible on the ruler in Figure 2.6 as downward-pointing triangular shapes, can be used as both vertical and horizontal alignment aides. The ones in this figure are vertical placement guides.

FIGURE 2.6

Vertical guideline markers

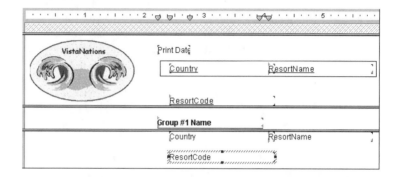

If you click a downward- or right-pointing icon marker on the ruler, a dotted line temporarily appears that represents the alignment line; this is a guideline. You can permanently show the guidelines by right-clicking the report background and selecting Guidelines ➢ Design or Guidelines ➢ Preview from the context menu, as shown in Figure 2.7. The guidelines themselves appear as dotted lines, which are visible later in Figure 2.11. You can drag the guideline markers to new positions on the ruler, which moves the dotted lines and all fields connected to the guideline to a new position uniformly.

FIGURE 2.7

Activating guidelines

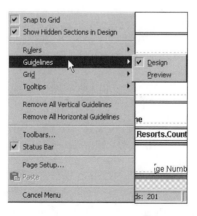

TIP   *Guidelines can also be turned on by choosing View ➢ Guidelines and its submenu.*

Vertical Guidelines

When a field is added to the report, a vertical positioning guideline marker is added to the ruler at the top of the design area. If you move the guideline marker, all fields anchored to the guideline move with it. Newly added fields automatically have their own guideline. You can add fields to a vertical guideline by dragging and dropping a field close to the vertical alignment guideline. This can be handy when you're trying to line fields up accurately beneath one other. If you move a field without using its guideline marker, it detaches from its guideline.

Since Crystal automatically generates a new vertical alignment guideline for every field you add to the report, the guidelines can result in clutter instead of clarity. Also, once you detach a field from a guideline, the guideline marker remains in place. You can remove unwanted vertical alignment guidelines by selecting them and sliding them off the ruler to the left or right. Since it is easy to remove guidelines, you could guess that it is also easy to add new ones; simply click in the ruler area to add a new guideline.

TIP   Be sure to use vertical guidelines for reports that will be displayed in a Web browser; they are essential in helping report fields line up in a browser.

Horizontal Guidelines

Unlike vertical guidelines, Crystal generates horizontal guidelines only when the Report Creation Wizard is used. When you add fields individually to a report using the Field Explorer, no horizontal guidelines are created for you. You can manually add them, however, by clicking the ruler along the left edge of the design area. Removing them is done as before—slide the guideline marker off the end of the ruler.

THE ALIGNMENT GRID

Horizontal and vertical guidelines can be used in conjunction with another alignment aide, the grid. The grid is made up of dots aligned vertically and horizontally that you can use to eyeball where you should place a field. As you place fields on the report, you can manually line them up at a grid position, or you can rely on the Snap To Grid option to automatically move a field onto the nearest grid line after you drop it onto the report. When you use grids and guidelines together, if the Snap To Grid option is enabled, shown as the first menu item in Figure 2.7, guidelines can be positioned only on top of grid lines.

TIP   The grid can also be turned on by choosing View ➤ Grid and its context submenu.

For fine-tuning changes in alignment, use the arrow keys for very detailed and specific movement of selected objects one grid mark at a time. You can move fields up, down, left and right using the arrow keys on the keyboard and the mouse.

THE RULERS

You've seen that having rulers along the top horizontal edge of the report and along the left vertical edge of the report can help you visually place fields. While alignment grids and guidelines don't require the rulers to be visible, they are more useful when rulers are displayed. For guidelines, the hexagon at the border of the guideline does not show without rulers enabled. You can toggle the rulers off using either the context menu options Rulers ➤ Design and Rulers ➤ Preview or the menu sequence View ➤ Rulers and its submenu.

PHYSICAL PLACEMENT

The grid, guidelines, and rulers can give you a good idea of how a field will ultimately look in relation to other items in the report. Switching to Preview mode frequently will also help you make good decisions on where to move fields and text. Crystal Reports allows you to place one field over the top of others in Design mode. When you take a peek at your work in Preview mode, check to make sure that you've adhered to all the following placement practices:

- Fields are not overlapping.

- Fields are horizontally aligned.

- Fields are big enough to display their data.

TIP   *For help with fixing these problems, try the menu options Format ➤ Move, Format ➤ Align, and Format ➤ Size.*

Deleting Fields and Labels

Deleting a field or a column label from a report is a simple matter in either Design mode or Preview mode:

1. Click the field to select it.

2. With the square resize blocks on the field visible, press the Delete key on the keyboard.

You can delete multiple selected fields as well. You select multiple fields by holding down the Ctrl key and selecting each individual field with a mouse click, or you can draw an expanding selection rectangle around the fields to capture all fields inside of it. To draw a selection rectangle within a section, hold down the left mouse button and draw a border on the outside of all fields you want to capture. (This technique does not work across sections.)

TIP   *If column titles are self-explanatory with the label, deleting them can reduce the cluttered look of a report.*

Visual Checkpoint: Fields

At this point, we'll assume that the additional fields for ResortCode, StreetAddress, City, StateProvince, PostalCode, and Region have been added to the report and positioned in a visually appealing way, as in Figure 2.8.

FIGURE 2.8

New fields added

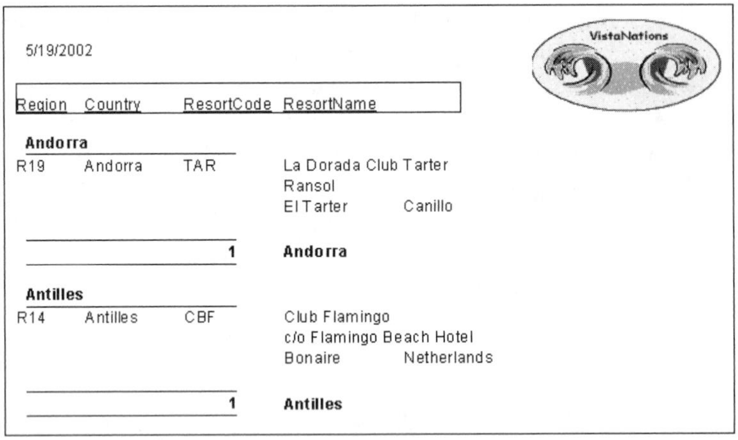

Several design techniques were used in the field placement visible in Figure 2.8:

◆ The StreetAddress and City fields were dragged beneath the ResortName field and dropped on the guideline for the ResortName; when you drag the guideline, the three fields will move as a group.

◆ The column labels for StreetAddress, City, StateProvince, and ZipCode were deleted.

◆ The column labels for Country, ResortName, and ResortCode were selected as a group, and the menu sequence Format ➤ Align ➤ Bottoms was used to force all three to be horizontally aligned with one another.

◆ The Region field was added to the left of Country.

◆ The logo was moved to the right.

◆ The PrintDate field was moved toward the left margin.

◆ The Group field was left-aligned on the margin.

TIP *You can activate the Align menu by right-clicking a set of selected objects.*

Adding fields to a report can go a long way in satisfying changing business requirements, as it has in our case. We've satisfied the additional database field requirements of the business question and cleaned up the report along the way.

Managing Groups

Revisiting the business question, we can next turn our attention to the requested changes in the grouping component of the report. Groups are created to help you view data in smaller segments and are created based on field values and calculations. Currently the group in our report splits the resort information into smaller bits of data based on the country in which the resort is located.

Business Question: We need the resort region, resort code, and mailing information for all the resorts sorted by resort name, with totals grouped by region and showing which ones are in North America.

We need to create an additional grouping of data showing the countries organized by region code.

Creating New Groups

When you were using the Report Creation Wizard, the way you added a group was through the Group Expert after choosing fields. The toolbars shown in Figure 2.9 give you a quick way to work with a whole series of experts, including the Group Expert. In Figure 2.9, the Group Expert icon is second from the left on the Expert toolbar. You can click this toolbar icon or choose Report ➤ Group Expert to open the Group Expert.

FIGURE 2.9

Grouping toolbar icons

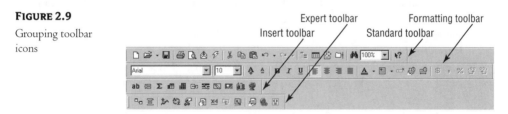

TIP   Turn on toolbars by choosing View ➤ Toolbars and select which toolbars to display and whether to show ToolTips text.

THE GROUP EXPERT

The Group Expert is useful for creating new groups and visualizing how groups are hierarchically related to one another. In Figure 2.10, the Region field has been added to the grouping using the techniques you learned in Chapter 1.

FIGURE 2.10

Group Expert

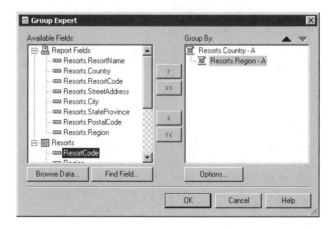

In the hierarchy shown, the Country field appears in the list before the Region field. This is not what we want. Adding a new field using the Group Expert simply copies an item from the list on the left to the list on the right, and you control the hierarchy grouping after the field exists in the list on the right. At this point, you can use the upward- and downward-pointing triangles above the Group By list on the right, visible in Figure 2.10, to reorder the fields so that Country more correctly comes below Region. How did we decide on this order?

The questions to ask yourself in order to create correct group hierarchies have to do with one group being a part of or a subset of another. For instance, in our case, the questions were "Can a country be part of a region?" or "Can a region be part of a country?" The correct answer is that countries are part of regions; therefore, regions are at the top of the hierarchy and countries are listed below.

When Crystal adds a new group, it adds it to the design area based on the hierarchy you specified in the Group Expert. You'll recall that all groups are automatically left-aligned, and each group has its own header section and footer section. This is where manually indenting will help you out again. In Figure 2.11, Group #2 was indented manually under Group #1. Ideally, you should indent all lower groups, in this case, Country, as well as the data in the Details section for the groups. The group names are given incrementing numbers based on their hierarchical position, so we now have Group Header #1, Group Header #2, Group Footer #1, and Group Footer #2.

FIGURE 2.11

Group alignment

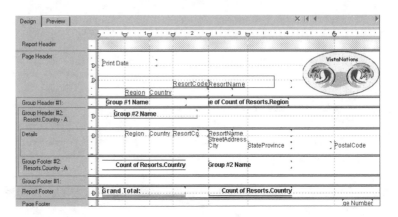

TIP   You can rearrange the hierarchy of the groups directly in Design mode using a drag-and-drop technique; drag the gray section area for a group up or down to reposition it and then drop it. The icon changes to a hand during the drag-and-drop process.

INSERT GROUP ICON

In addition to the Group Expert, the toolbar bar has an icon specifically for adding a new group, as shown previously in Figure 2.9. Using this icon is the equivalent of choosing Insert ➤ Group and results in the dialog shown in Figure 2.12.

In the first drop-down list box, you choose the field on which the new group will be based. You can choose from any of the fields currently in the report and any of the fields in the data source but not on the report.

This dialog window also allows you to choose a group sort option from the second drop-down list. The default sort option is ascending order.

FIGURE 2.12

Inserting a group

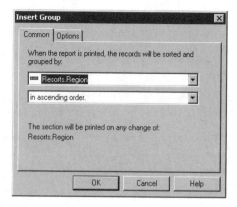

TIP   This dialog window can be opened from the Group Expert as well by clicking the Options button, visible in Figure 2.10. The only difference on the dialog is that the title bar label is Change Group Options.

The Options tab visible behind the Common tab in Figure 2.12 allows you to set the following options:

♦ Customize a group name field by typing your own or using data from another field in the database.

♦ Keep the group together to print on the same page in case it would have started midway through one page and finished on a second page.

♦ Repeat (display) the group header on every page in your report.

When you add a group with the Group Expert or the Insert Group technique and base the group on a field not already in the report, the group is added to the report but the field that you're grouping on is not added to the Details section. This is true whether you group on a report field or choose a field that's in the database but not already on the report. The benefit of this option is it that it doesn't clutter up the Details section.

If, on the other hand, you add a group based on a field that's already on the report, the field is not removed from the Details section. Rather, the data is now represented in both the Details section and the grouping area. If you want to remove the field from the Details section, just select the field and press the Delete key as discussed earlier. For our sample report, the data for the Region field and the Country field is represented in the group sections, so these fields are unnecessary in the Details section.

GROUP ORDER

There are four sort orders for groups: ascending (the default), descending, specified order, and original order:

Ascending Order   Data is sorted lowest to highest; alphabetic characters sort from A ascending to Z, numbers sort from 0 ascending to 10 and higher, and Boolean values sort False before True (which applies to 0 before 1 as well).

Descending Order   Data is sorted highest to lowest; alphabetic characters sort from Z descending to A, numbers sort from 10 or higher descending to 0, and Boolean values sort True before False.

Specified Order   Data is sorted based on a customized criterion that does not exist in the raw data. This is also known as creating a custom group.

Original Order   Data is sorted in the order in which it was added to the data source, with the oldest data appearing at the top and the most recently added data appearing at the bottom.

The data in a field, and therefore the grouping component, is subject to rules unique to its data type. Date and time values sort in chronological order, while text fields sort non-alphabetic characters before alphabetic characters and uppercase letters before lowercase letters. Sort order does not apply to large text fields like memo, binary large object (BLOB), and character large object (CLOB).

> *Business Question: We need the resort region, resort code, and mailing information for all the resorts sorted by resort name, with totals grouped by region and showing which ones are in North America.*

Hmmmm.… North America is a continent, and that is not a field that is being captured directly in the database. However, we can derive a rule that defines North America based on other stored data; namely, if the resort's country is the United States or Canada, then the continent is North America. At any time, the custom North America group could be expanded to include countries like Mexico, the countries of Central America, Greenland, the island countries, and the dependencies of the Caribbean if the data in the database referenced these places. The point is that your custom group definition may change over time, and that is perfectly okay. This ability to state a rule that uses existing fields is the essence of specified order custom groupings.

Okay, let's take this part step at a time since it's not very intuitive and see how to turn our business rule into Crystal Reports functionality. First, you need to do a specified order grouping on the Country field since it's the Country field that will determine whether the data belongs in the custom group. When you select this option on the Common tab on the Insert Group dialog, the Specified Order tab becomes visible, as shown in Figure 2.13.

FIGURE 2.13

Insert Group dialog

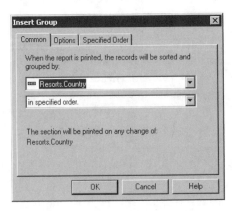

On the Specified Order tab, you begin your new business rule by clicking a button labeled New. This opens the Define Named Group dialog shown in Figure 2.14. The first thing you do here is type the name of the group as you want it to be known; it can be anything you like but should add meaning to the process and generally describe the business rule. The phrase "North America" describes the group we're building, so that's what we've used.

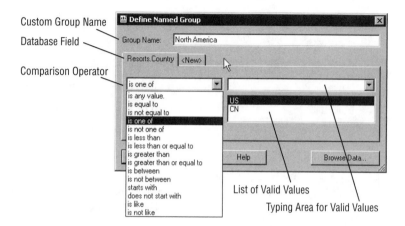

FIGURE 2.14
Define Named
Group dialog

Custom Group Name
Database Field
Comparison Operator

List of Valid Values
Typing Area for Valid Values

There are two tabs below the group name; one represents the database field you are using to create the custom group and the other lets you add additional fields. Referring to the business question we're answering, the field of interest here is Country since it is the country that will determine whether the value is in North America. On this tab, you specify that the United States and Canada, for example, are countries in North America.

Using the valid values typing area, you can type valid values or use the drop-down list to pull values from the database. The values you choose then appear in the list below as the set of all valid values. A comparison operator is chosen to compare the database field to the list of valid values. The available comparison operators are described in Table 2.2.

TABLE 2.2: COMPARISON OPERATIONS

OPERATION	DESCRIPTION
is any value	Allows any value (basically has no effect, which is the default)
is equal to	Checks to see if field value is exactly equal to a value you provide
is not equal to	Checks to see if field value is *not* equal to a value you provide
is one of	Checks to see if field value is one of several values you provide
is not one of	Checks to see if field value is *not* one of several values you provide
is less than	Checks to see if field value is less than a value you specify
is less than or equal to	Checks to see if field value is less or equal to a value you specify
is greater than	Checks to see if field value is greater than a value you specify

Continued on next page

TABLE 2.2: COMPARISON OPERATIONS *(continued)*

OPERATION	DESCRIPTION
is greater than or equal to	Checks to see if field value is greater than or equal to a value you specify
is between	Checks to see if field value is between two other values; very useful for dates
starts with	Checks to see if field value starts with a particular letter
does not start with	Checks to see if field value *does not* starts with a particular letter
is like	Checks to see if field value is similar to a value you specify
is not like	Checks to see if field value is *not* similar to a value you specify

The data stored in the Country field in the database does not contain the full names United States or Canada. Instead, the Country value for these two countries is stored as US and CN, respectively, so it is US and CN that need to appear on the valid value list. How would you know how the data was stored? You can click the Browse Data button to peek inside the field identified on the tab to see the actual stored data.

WARNING *If you were to type United States or Canada in the valid value list, there would be no data in the database that matched your business rule, so you should click the Browse Data button to be sure you're right.*

Now the moment is here to create a custom group and use values from the database to define whether a record will fit into the group. You need to consider what will happen on your report to the values that don't fit your criteria. This is exactly what the Others tab, shown in Figure 2.15, is intended to do.

FIGURE 2.15

Data that doesn't meet the custom group criteria

On this tab, you can specify that any data outside the value list be discarded and not shown in the report. Another option is to group all the values that don't fit into the custom group and show them under a general title; Others is the default, but names like Miscellaneous and Extra make sense too. The label is up to you, so you can type something meaningful to you. For our example, if the custom group label is North America, values that don't fit into the group could be labeled Outside North America. This tab also provides the option to simply represent the data in whatever group it was already in and display it after the custom group.

TIP   The Others tab is not visible unless you create a Specified Order custom group since it does not apply to any other sort order.

Deleting Groups

To delete a group, you need to delete the group header and group footer. To do so, right-click the gray section for either the group header or group footer to display the context menu. Both sections contain the Delete Group menu option, as shown in Figure 2.16.

FIGURE 2.16

Group header context menu

NOTE   Notice also in this context menu the Change Group option. Selecting this option opens a window similar to the one shown previously in Figure 2.10 titled Change Group Options.

It is not sufficient to select and delete the group field from the report in either the group section itself or the totaling field, if one exists, in the group footer. This will delete the data from the report but will not stop the grouping from taking place. To delete the group, you must use the section menu shown in Figure 2.16.

Sorting Data

We've shown that groups can be sorted, which will arrange one group of data before another group. What about the data, or detail records, within each group? For instance, in our report we've created groups based on the Country field, but in the group for each country, we haven't specified whether resorts or resort codes that start with the letter *A* should come before those that start with the letter

Z. To do this, we need to use explicit sort options that are not related to grouping; instead, the sort order is related to the records as a whole.

Record-sorting options are available using the menu sequence Report ➤ Record Sort Expert or its equivalent toolbar icon. The Record Sort Expert displays the hierarchy of the groups implemented in the report and lets you select a field to use to sort the records. Figure 2.17 shows that there are three groups in the report and their sort order (*S* for specified order and *A* for ascending). The records within each country within a region will be sorted in ascending order.

FIGURE 2.17

Sorting records

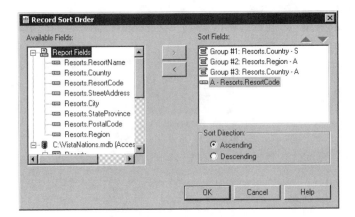

As mentioned with sorting groups, the data type of a field contributes to the sorting rules. Date and time values sort chronologically; text fields sort nonalphabetic characters before alphabetic characters, and uppercase letters sort before lowercase letters.

You can also specify multiple record-sorting fields. For instance, in data for North America, you might sort by state first and then by city. Each field that you sort on can be sorted in ascending or descending order. The upward- and downward- pointing triangles shown at the top right of Figure 2.17 can be used to prioritize the sorts in a way that makes sense for the data. There is no limit to how many fields can be sorted.

Basic Summarization Techniques

Each time you add a group, you have the opportunity to do some quick and easy summarization on the data being grouped. In Chapter 1 we listed the basic summarization techniques for character data, including Count. The design result of using Count on the Country field can be seen in Figure 2.18.

FIGURE 2.18

Group and summarize

Group Header #3: Resorts.Country - A	ᴅ	**Group #3 Name**		
Details	ᴅ	ResortCo	ResortName StreetAddress City	StateProvince	PostalCode
Group Footer #3: Resorts.Country - A	·	**Count of Resorts.Country**		

Summary information is automatically added to a footer section area. However, there is nothing preventing you from dragging and dropping the summary field Count of Resorts.Country into the Group Header area. Many reports look better with the summary information presented before the detail data.

It would make sense in this report to add a summary based on the region information we added earlier. You can use Insert ➤ Summary or the Insert Summary toolbar icon to add summary information based on field data if it was not specified in the Report Creation Wizard or if no wizard was used to build the report. Figure 2.19 shows the Insert Summary dialog. In this case, for each group of regions a percentage will be displayed showing what part of all the regions it comprises.

FIGURE 2.19

Percentage summary

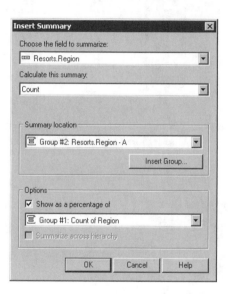

Visual Checkpoint: Groups, Sorts, and Summaries

The data has been finessed in a way that not only answers the business question but also presents it in an organized way that is pleasing to the eye. Figure 2.20 shows the North America group, the region code group beneath that, the country group within the region group, and the records within the country group sorted according to the ascending order of the resort code and summarized on group values.

> *Business Question: We need the resort region, resort code, and mailing information for all the resorts sorted by resort name with totals grouped by region and showing which ones are in North America.*

Notice that the group tree on the left displays the specified group for North America and all of the region groups within North America. From examining the data, you can tell that Region 14 has properties in both North America and other territories. You can click each of the group tree items to jump to that group of information.

FIGURE 2.20

Groups, sorts, and summaries

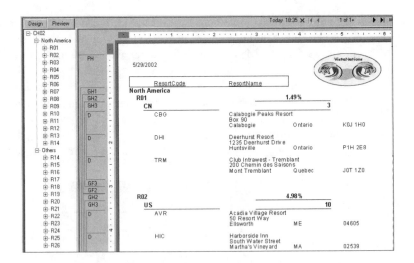

Finally, you can see that the sections of the report are represented in their entirety, showing the section hierarchy, even in Preview mode. The following abbreviations should help you figure out exactly what is in each section:

PH	Page Header
GH1	Group Header 1
GH2	Group Header 2
GH3	Group Header 3
D	Details
GF3	Group Footer 3
GF2	Group Footer 2
GF1	Group Footer 1

Getting Help

The Crystal Decisions team has put together an excellent support structure for Crystal Reports. In addition to the searchable help file and the context-sensitive help available from the menu and the F1 key, three additional help files are provided with information specific to the version of Crystal Reports you purchased:

- Standard edition
- Professional edition
- Developer edition

All of the installed help files and even the web-based help are available from the Help menu, as shown in Figure 2.21.

FIGURE 2.21

Help file main menu

TIP   The help file opens in its own window in Stay-On-Top mode. To continue working in the report designer with the help file open, minimize it to return to the Crystal Reports designer.

You can find the Crystal Decisions support online as well at `support.crystaldecisions.com`, where you'll find a wealth of information in their knowledge base. Before calling the support team or searching the knowledge base, check to see what version of Crystal you're running since many of the help documents are categorized by version. You can find this information at Help ➤ About Crystal Reports; the product version is listed at the top of the dialog, as shown in Figure 2.22.

FIGURE 2.22

About Crystal Reports

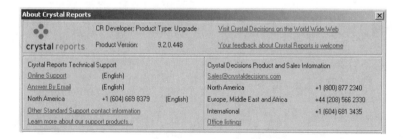

In addition, you can click the More Info button in the Help area to display information on modules currently loaded into memory at runtime. This may be useful when you're talking online or on the phone with the Crystal Care support team.

Summary

The goal of a good report is to present in a pleasing way any information that will answer the business question. Database fields that are grouped, sorted, and summarized are the heart of a good report.

You can use the Field Explorer to add fields to a report either after running the Report Creation Wizard or creating a report from scratch. Remember that you must take care in placing the fields since the sections will determine the behavior of the data when it displays in the report. To help with placement, you take advantage of guidelines, rulers, and alignment grids.

The goal of grouping and sorting data is to organize it in a way that is easily digested by whomever is reading the report. The sorting options for groups range from the simple to the complex, culminating in custom groups that are not based on values actually stored in the database. Instead, you write business rules to derive a meaning for the data. As you've seen, sorting isn't limited to groups. Sorting data values within a group can help organize information as well.

Finally, summarizing data adds information to a report that wasn't part of the stored data. The simple summaries performed in this chapter help to answer the business question.

Chapter 3

Formatting Fields and Objects

A SOLID REPORT IS built by choosing and arranging the appropriate database fields in an organized way on an area that represents a piece of paper. Your job doesn't stop there though! Once you have the mechanics of the data and the story it tells correctly represented in a report, the next step is to format the fields and all the objects in a way that is pleasing to the eye and focuses the reader's attention on the important parts of the report. For instance, bolding summary numbers and outlining or underlining them makes them jump out at the reader and say "Look at me first!" Attention paid to the aesthetic details can transform a solid data report into a great information report.

In Chapter 2, "Modifying a Report," the business question focused on retrieving, grouping, and summarizing field data:

> *Business Question: We need the resort region, resort code, and mailing information for all the resorts sorted by resort name, with totals grouped by region and showing which ones are in North America.*

In this chapter, the business question is still valid, and we have a data answer already, so what needs to be done next is to format the report in a way that does justice to the data, the intent of the report, and your skills as a designer.

Featured in this chapter:

- Adding report summary information
- Adding text objects to a report
- Formatting common attributes
- Working with borders
- Setting font attributes
- Formatting paragraphs
- Adding hyperlinks
- Defining report parts
- Working with OLE objects

Report Summary Information

Summary information at the report level is *metadata* that describes the report as a whole but that is not part of the report when it is viewed. In essence, this becomes nonprinting information that can help a report designer add comments to the report for documentation purposes. To create report summary information, choose File ➤ Summary Info to display the Summary tab of the Document Properties dialog shown in Figure 3.1. On this dialog, you can add the following types of report information:

- The name of the report author
- Keywords that describe the report
- Comments
- A report title
- A brief subject
- A template alias name

You can also set an option to display the first page of the report in a thumbnail preview when opening the report.

FIGURE 3.1

Report summary information

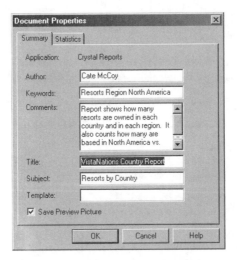

Through the use of special fields in Crystal, three of the report summary values can be included in the actual report. Table 3.1 identifies these summary values and the name of the special field used to add the value to a report.

NOTE   *Only the first 256 characters of the Comments value display in a report.*

TABLE 3.1: REPORT SUMMARY FIELDS

SUMMARY VALUE	REPORT FIELD NAME
Author	File Author
Comments	Report Comments
Title	Report Title

To add a summary value special field to a report, use the Field Explorer, expand the Special Fields category, and drag the File Author, Report Comments, or Report Title fields into a section on the report. For our business problem, adding a report title sounds like a good idea. After dragging the Report Title special field into the Report Header section, notice from Figure 3.2 that what displays in Design mode is the phrase Report Title as a placeholder instead of the actual value from the field. In Preview mode, however, the value typed in the dialog in Figure 3.1 appears. A report title is generally placed in the Report Header section of a report since it is best that it display only once in the report and at the top of the report.

FIGURE 3.2

Report Title placeholder

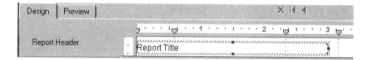

The Statistics tab of the Document Properties dialog, visible but not displayed in Figure 3.1, gives you additional read-only information:

- Name of the author who last saved the report
- Revision number
- Total editing time
- Date and time the report was last printed
- Date and time the report was created
- Date and time the report was last saved

Report summary information can also be accessed outside of Crystal Reports. If you've worked recently with a word processing file, like a Microsoft Word document, you might recall being able to access the document properties with the document selected in a list before it is open using the Microsoft menu options File ➢ Properties. The report summary information you enter in Crystal is a part of the overall document properties; take a peek back at Figure 3.1 and you'll notice that the title bar actually says Document Properties. For a Crystal report, the information displayed externally by Microsoft using File ➢ Properties includes a Summary tab that displays Crystal's information, as shown in Figure 3.3. This information is viewed without opening the report in Crystal Reports. This includes a preview of the first page of the report if you enable the Save Preview Picture option on the Summary tab of the Document Properties dialog. All this external information can be valuable when you're trying to figure out what a report is all about but don't have Crystal Reports installed on the machine.

FIGURE 3.3

Document Properties

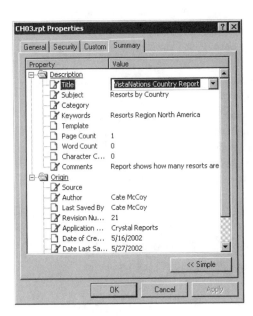

Formatting Report Objects

Are you ready to spice up the report with a little color and some visual elements? Imagine a report that consisted of only columns and columns of Times Roman 12 point black text pulled from a data source with no textual information to describe what you're looking at. Sounds like a fairly ugly report. Let's learn some techniques to get beyond the basics.

Inserting Text Objects

When you created a report and added database fields to the Details section, text objects containing the field name were automatically added to the Page Header. These became the column headings to describe the fields in the report. So, without intentionally doing it, you've already used text objects! Text objects are elements that you add to a report to do one of two things for you:

◆ Add descriptive text information to a report

◆ Combine multiple objects for formatting purposes

To add a text object directly, choose Insert ➤ Text Object. The gray placement rectangle appears, and you can then drop the text object into any of the sections. In Chapter 2, we introduced the visual aides of alignment markers, grids, and rulers to help place database fields in a report. These same visual aides can be used with text objects as well.

Once you've placed a text object in a report, you can add several types of content to it:

◆ Interactively typed text

◆ The contents of an external file

◆ A combination of typed text and report fields

◆ A combination of report fields

Figure 3.4 shows a combination of typed text and a report field. Here, we added a text field to the report, inserted the text "Printed: ", including the blank space after the colon, into the text object, and then dragged and dropped the special field PrintDate into the text object. The result is a text string, followed by a space, and then the print date all being treated as a single object. Whenever a database field is added to a text object, its field name is enclosed by a set of parentheses to signal that this is no longer a direct field on the report but rather part of another object.

FIGURE 3.4

Text objects

The benefit to creating text object combinations is that you can treat a set of objects as a single object for formatting purposes. Text objects can be added to any section in a report.

WARNING   *Text objects are limited to a size of 32K.*

The Format Editor

The Format Editor, shown in Figure 3.5, is used to change the appearance, including color, of an object in a report. There are two basic ways to open the Format Editor after selecting an object: Choose Format ➤ Format Field or right-click and select the Format Field menu option.

TIP   *Whenever you're trying to locate an option for an object, try right-clicking after selecting it to see if there is a shortcut menu.*

The tabs on the Format Editor vary based on the type of data contained in the field. The field being formatted here is the Report Title mentioned in the first section, so it is a text field and the tabs visible are specific to working with character data. We'll explore these tabs first and then describe tabs you will encounter with other data types.

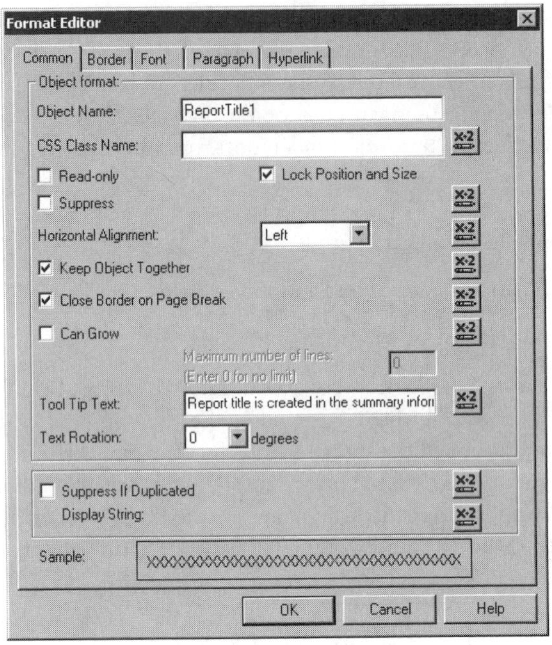

FIGURE 3.5

Format Editor -
Common tab

Formatting Text Objects

The Format Editor is used to make text information look good on a report. You do this with the use of color, font type and size, and other visual effects. The Sample area at the bottom of the Format Editor gives you a visual idea of how the object will look once it is displayed. The tabs described here are visible in Figure 3.5.

COMMON

The formatting options found on the Common tab are there for one of two reasons: Either they are frequently used and made it to the Common tab for ease of use, or they don't quite fit into the categories defined by the rest of the tabs so the Common tab becomes the catchall. Either way, this is a good starting point.

Object Name One of the new features in Crystal Reports 9 is the ability to associate an object name to a text object. Here, ReportTitle1 is the programmatic name used to identify the text object. The use of an object name makes it easier to manipulate the object programmatically and to use it in drop-down box choices throughout Crystal Reports.

CSS Class Name Another new feature in version 9 is the ability to use cascading style sheets (CSS) by associating an object with a CSS class name. Cascading style sheets are rules used with HTML and web browsers to add formatting information (color, font type, font size, etc.) to web pages. If your Crystal Report will be used on the Web as part of a website, the use of style sheets lets you make use of the web page's styling features so that it appears more closely integrated with the rest of the site.

Read-only The check box option to enable or disable Read-only mode for the object prevents you from accidentally changing format options later on. When Read-only is enabled, all other options in the Format Editor are grayed out and cannot be changed. This option is not related to a user's ability to change a value on a report if they receive it in an editable format, for instance, as a Microsoft Word document.

Suppress You will have many occasions where you'll want to add a field to a report but not display it. Instead, it may be used for sorting or grouping or as part of a combination of other fields. The Suppress check box hides a field value from view but leaves it available in Design mode.

Lock Position And Size The option to lock the position and size of an object prevents you from accidentally moving an object. This is great option to turn on after you have the object placed exactly where you want it.

Horizontal Alignment The Horizontal Alignment option provides choices to align left, centered, right, justified, or use the default identified for this type of data. Default settings for data types are globally set using the menu sequence File ➤ Options and choosing the Fields tab. It is important to remember that the data values are being aligned within the dimensions of the object in the report. For instance, referring back to the Report Title placeholder shown in Figure 3.2, the ruler at the top of the screen shows that the text object is three inches wide. Using the Horizontal Alignment option and choosing Left moves the value all the way to the left side of the three-inch area. Likewise, if you chose Right alignment, the text would appear right-aligned at the three-inch mark. So, before using the Horizontal Alignment option, stretch or shrink the object to the size you want and then choose an alignment style.

Keep Object Together When a report is viewed or printed, the values of an object may span more than one page. If an object is small enough to print on one page, selecting this option will prevent the values from starting on one page and finishing on another page. The object will be forced to a new page so that it appears on a single page. If the object is too large to fit on a single page, this option has no effect.

Close Border On Page Break Border boxes can be placed around objects. If the object doesn't fit on a single page, this option controls whether the border appears with the top and sides on one page and the bottom and sides on the second page, or whether each piece of the object is surrounded by a complete rectangle border.

Can Grow When a field or text object is placed in a report, it is positioned with a default size. The data value in the field or text object may be shorter or longer than the object size. Crystal's default behavior to handle this is to display only as much of the value as can be seen in the default object size. You have two options for changing this behavior: preview the report and resize the object so that it displays contents in their entirety or enable the Can Grow option. With the latter option activated, the size of an object can grow vertically (lengthwise) to accommodate the object contents. You can specify a maximum number of lines you want the contents to grow to before being truncated or leave the setting at 0 to let the field grow to the size of the contents. The Can Grow option is especially useful when working with fields from a database that were defined as variable lengths; for instance, memo fields in Microsoft Access and text fields in Lotus Notes Domino.

Tool Tip Text   Any text you type here will appear in Preview mode as black text in a yellow box as you move the mouse over the object in Preview mode. There is no limit to the amount of text you can type in the field, but there is no way to add a carriage return to the tool tip area, so 70 characters is a practical limit since that much text appears on exactly one line.

Text Rotation   Your options here are 0, 90, and 270 degrees, so the only way text can't appear is upside down. Zero degrees is normal left-to-right text; 90 degrees is readable when you tilt your head to the left with the start of the text at the bottom and moving toward the top. If you tilt your head to the right, 270 degrees appears as starting from the top and moving downward. The 90 degree and 270 degree options are often used as column headings if the width of the column heading exceeds the width of the data column.

Suppress If Duplicated   When you format field values retrieved from a database, it is common to come across duplicate values in the data. For instance, a field named FavoriteColors might contain 27 instances of red, 41 instances of blue, 12 instances of green, and 26 instances of purple. Activating the option to suppress duplicates would result in values displaying the values red, blue, green, and purple exactly one time each.

Suppress If Embedded Field Blank Lines   This option is available only if you are formatting a text object that contains a combination of text and report fields. The effect of the option is to hide any blank lines in a text object if the only value on that line is empty. As an example, you might use this option if you were printing address labels and the address was formatted as a text object in your report. If the address consisted of an AddressLine1 and an AddressLine2, and the AddressLine2 was on its own line but had no value, using this option would prevent the blank line from printing.

Display String   You can place any valid formula here to programmatically format an object; formulas are discussed in Chapter 4, "Adding Business Logic with the Formula Workshop." The buttons labeled "X+2" that appear in various areas in the Format Editor are places where you can write formula code.

BORDER

Borders are lines drawn around an object. Using the Border tab in the Format Editor, shown in Figure 3.6, you can control the how the border looks.

Line Style   Line styles include single, double, dashed, and dotted. Notice that you independently set the left, right, top, and bottom border line styles.

Tight Horizontal   Enabling the Tight Horizontal option automatically sizes the border to the width of the contents of the object. When this option is used in the Details section, which displays records from the data source, the size of the border will vary to match the size of what is stored in the field. Again using the color values of Red, Blue, Green, and Purple, the borders associated with these values would range in size from smallest for the value Red to largest for the value Purple since "Red" is three characters in length while "Purple" is six characters in length; the difference in border sizes is created because of the different character widths of the two text strings.

Drop Shadow   The Drop Shadow option adds definition to a border by adding some thickness to it on the right side and the bottom.

Color   You can set the border color and the interior background color for a border. A nice formatting technique is to use a dark drop shadow and a light background color. Standard colors are predefined, such as Silver and Maroon, but the entire color spectrum is available using either RGB values or choosing from a color wheel.

FIGURE 3.6

Border options

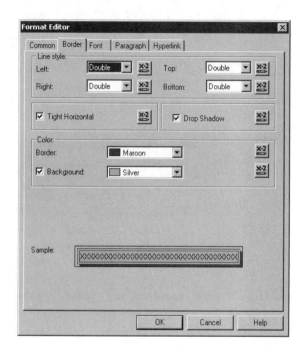

FONT

The Font, Style, Size, and Color can be set on the top portion of the Font tab, shown in Figure 3.7. All available fonts installed on the computer are available as choices through the Font drop-down box, and the one currently being used appears in the box itself. Styles are limited to either Regular or Bold. Font size can be typed directly or chosen from the drop-down list. Font color refers to the color the text will be and should be chosen with the background color in mind; use a color that can be easily read and avoid pastels and lighter colors unless you have a very dark background color. The default font color is black.

FIGURE 3.7

Font options

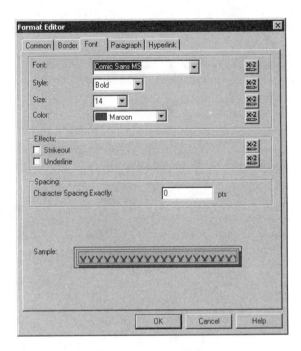

Effects   The Strikeout option draws a line through the contents of the object, while Underline draws a line beneath an object.

Spacing   When you choose a font size, it has a default point value used to separate one character from the next. For instance, a 12-point font separates its characters by exactly 12 points. The measurement is taken from the beginning of one character to the beginning of the next character. You can change this default spacing by typing a different number to tell Crystal exactly how many points apart to space each character. Choosing a smaller number will have the appearance of moving the characters closer together, while choosing a larger number will spread the characters out. The font size itself remains the same and controls the height of the characters.

Notice the Sample area at the bottom of Figure 3.7. It appears that the font size selected may have the affect of cutting off part of the object contents. You should take care to size the object back in Design layout mode after changing font formatting to ensure that the contents display correctly. In Figure 3.8, which shows the Preview mode for the Report Title object, the text object needs to be resized so that the full height of the contents can be displayed.

FIGURE 3.8

Font problem

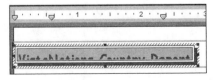

WARNING   *Crystal Reports will not automatically resize an object to accommodate font changes.*

PARAGRAPH

Large text objects and database fields that contain varying-length data need to be formatted so that the text will fit it into the report in an eye-pleasing way. For instance, you might format a text object like a newspaper column and place it alongside the right or left border in a report. The Paragraph tab of the Format Editor, shown in Figure 3.9, lets you specify the indentation, spacing, reading order, and text interpretation methods for the contents of an object. The presence of a carriage return line feed character (a hard return) determines when one paragraph ends and a new one begins.

FIGURE 3.9

Paragaph options

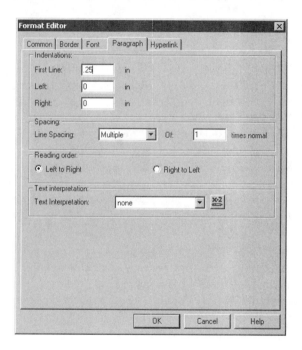

Indentations   The options for First Line, Left, and Right specify the number of inches text should be indented from the borders of the object. The first line is often indented more than other lines to help it stand out.

Line Spacing   Line Spacing is the space placed vertically between each line of text. There are two options: Exact and Multiple. Choosing Exact lets you specify the exact number of points to leave between two lines. When you select Multiple, the base number involved in the multiplication is the font size. So if a 12-point font size was in effect, a multiple of 1 would be 12-point vertical spacing between lines, while a multiple of 2 would be 24-point vertical spacing, and so on.

Reading Order   Reading Order is specified as Left To Right, as with the English language, or Right To Left.

Text Interpretation   Most text typed directly into a Crystal Report or retrieved from a data source is typed or stored as plain text, meaning text without any formatting attributes associated with it. Some text, however, is already preformatted and needs to be treated differently. You can change how Crystal Reports interprets text by selecting None for plain text, RTF Text for data stored in rich text format, or HTML Text for text stored with HTML tags and ready for display in a browser.

When choosing HTML tags, only a subset of the entire set of tagged language statements is supported. While the list of supported tags includes those that are the most important and most often used, be sure to check the help file to see if the ones in your text field are valid in Crystal Reports.

HYPERLINK

Hyperlinks are clickable links that move you to another part of the current report or to a destination outside the current report. The Hyperlink tab in the Format Editor is used to set the destination for a hyperlink. This topic is discussed fully in the "Creating Hyperlinks" section of this chapter.

Formatting Non-Text Data Types

In addition to text objects and text fields, there can be many other data types in a Crystal Report. The Format Editor is still the centralized place to format the object, and in addition to many of the tabs found with text objects, non-text objects have formatting options specific to the data type or object type. Each new data or object type has its own tab in the Format Editor, which is visible only if the object being formatted is of that data type. For instance, if you're formatting a Boolean field, you'll see a Boolean tab but not a Number tab.

BOOLEAN DATA

Boolean data is a data type that says a value is either True or False. There are many ways to represent these two different states in stored data, and no two products or data sources are guaranteed to store them the same way. Boolean values can be stored as any of the following:

◆ True or False

◆ T or F

◆ Yes or No

◆ Y or N

◆ 1 or 0

Use the Boolean tab in the Format Editor, shown in Figure 3.10, to choose how the values will display in your report regardless of how they are stored in the data source.

DATE AND TIME DATA

Crystal provides an enormous number of options for formatting date and time data. The standard set of date options, shown in Figure 3.11, provides a long list of easy-to-use styles for setting the year, month, and day formats.

FIGURE 3.10

Formatting
Boolean data

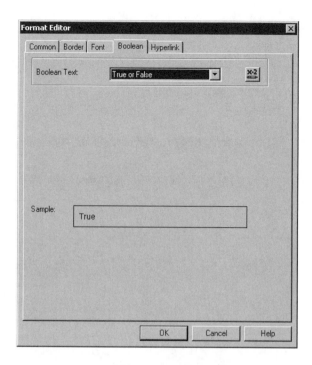

FIGURE 3.11

Standard date
formatting

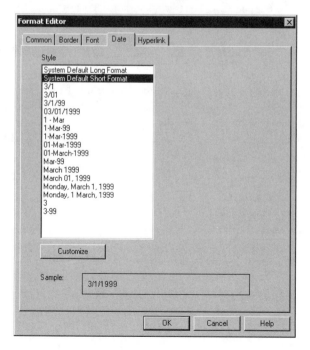

If the style you need isn't on the list of standard styles, click the Customize button to display the Custom Style dialog for date data, shown in Figure 3.12. As you can see, there is quite a lot going on in this settings window. Options on Date/Time fields include all possible date options as well as time options, letting you fine-tune year, month, and day formats on one tab and time specifications on a separate tab. In addition, you can format dates so that they appear within square brackets or parentheses using the Encl (enclosure) setting located in the Day Of Week section of the dialog.

FIGURE 3.12

Custom date formatting

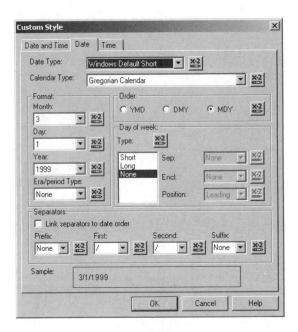

Time formatting also has a standard list of styles that let you set the hour, minute, and second components and whether the A.M. and P.M. values should display. These options are shown in Figure 3.13.

In addition to the standard Style list for time, clicking the Customize button displays the Custom Style window for time, shown in Figure 3.14. Here you can set a 12 hour or 24 hour clock, select whether to use one or two digits for the hour, minute, and time components, and also choose a separator character.

FIGURE 3.13

Standard time formatting

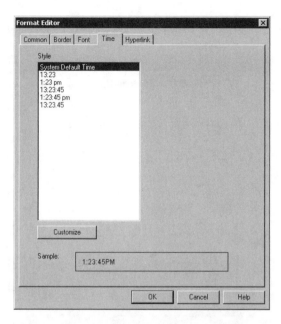

FIGURE 3.14

Custom time formatting

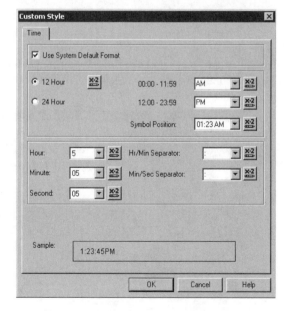

NUMBER DATA

Numeric data can be formatted in many styles, as shown in Figure 3.15. The choices in the Style list determine how the numeric values in your report display. The two things that change are whether a minus sign or a set of parentheses will be used for values less than zero and how many decimal places should be used. Beyond these two options, everything else is a customized number style.

FIGURE 3.15

Standard number
formatting

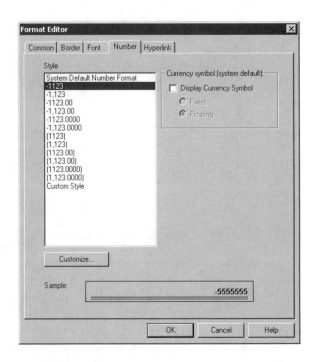

Choosing the Display Currency Symbol check box shown in Figure 3.15 automatically switches you into Custom Style mode. You can also choose Custom Style directly from the Style list. The Custom Style dialog for numbers is shown in Figure 3.16.

FIGURE 3.16

Custom number
formatting

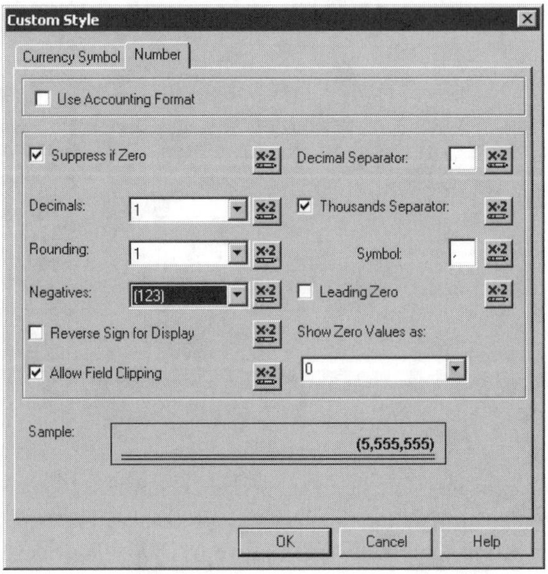

The Use Accounting Format option sets a negative symbol based on your operating system's settings, displays a dash for data values that are zero, and positions the currency symbol to the left of the data value. Enabling this option changes the values in the bottom half of the dialog; likewise, changing a setting on the bottom to a value that doesn't match the accounting settings disables the Use Accounting Format option.

If you opt not to use the accounting format, you have granular control over how currency values appear in a report. You can do all of the following to your currency data:

◆ Specify the number of decimal places.

◆ Round values to the nearest whole number, tenth, hundredth, and so on.

◆ Display negative values with a minus sign or parentheses.

◆ Allow field clipping to truncate large numeric values.

◆ Specify a decimal separator character.

◆ Choose whether to display a thousands separator, and if so, what character it should be.

◆ Include leading zeros for data values.

◆ Substitute a hyphen for a zero data value.

On the Currency Symbol tab, visible but not displayed in Figure 3.16, you can specify the following display options:

◆ Show the currency symbol in a fixed position for all data values.

◆ Show the currency symbol as close to the data value as possible (float).

◆ Show only one currency symbol per page with the first number on the page.

◆ Show the currency symbol on the left or on the right.

Formatting Visual Objects

Visual objects can be added to a report and include boxes, lines, and pictures. Once they exist in the report and are selected as the active object, you can format these object types with the Format Editor.

WORKING WITH BOXES

You can draw boxes around text objects and field objects by choosing Insert ➤ Box. A pencil mouse pointer appears and assists you in drawing a rectangle of any size. With the object selected, right-click and select Format Box to open the Format Editor or choose Format ➤ Format Box from the menu bar. This displays the Box tab of the Format Editor, as shown in Figure 3.17.

FIGURE 3.17

Formatting boxes

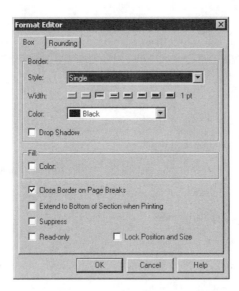

You can vary the style, width, and color of a box border as well as add a drop shadow. The width can be set for only the single line style, not dotted or dashed. Enabling the Fill Color option displays the standard predefined color choices and the RGB (red, green, blue) color wheel.

Choosing to close the border on page breaks guarantees that your box will have four sides even if the contents get split between pages; otherwise, the box will have a left, right, and top on one page and a left, right, and bottom on the next page. The Suppress option hides a box from view. The Read-only option disables all other formatting, and the Lock Position And Size option prevents the box from accidentally being moved during your design work.

The Extend To Bottom Of Section When Printing option is specific to the box object, and it allows the box to stretch to the end of a section. When used in the Details section around a field value, this option can be used to make check boxes in your report or to give you a writing area associated with a field value. Figure 3.18 shows how this option looks around the ResortCode field in our report.

WORKING WITH LINES

A line is added to a report by choosing Insert ➤ Line. A pencil mouse pointer appears, and it helps you draw a straight line up, down, to the left, or to the right. Once you've positioned a line in the report, the Format Editor lets you change the style, width, and color of the line, as shown in Figure 3.19. The Format Editor is displayed by selecting the object and then either choosing Format ➤ Format Line or right-clicking and choosing the Format Line option.

TIP *To show a double line below a field, add a border instead of a line, and set the top, left, and right of the border to "None" while setting the bottom of the border to "Double."*

For line styles, you can choose from Single, Dashed, and Dotted. There is no option for a double line style as there is with formatting a border. The width can range from less than .5 points (known as a hairline) up to 3.5 points. You choose the width by clicking the desired button; the point size of the selected button appears to the right of the row of buttons. The Color drop-down list contains a set of predefined colors and also lets you specify RGB values.

FIGURE 3.18

Extending boxes

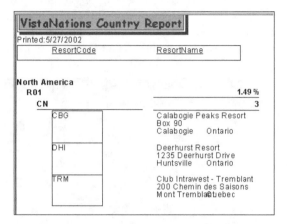

FIGURE 3.19

Formatting lines

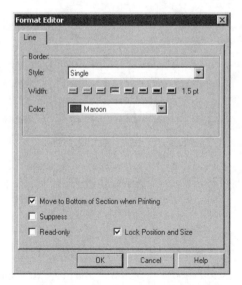

The check box options to suppress a line, mark it as read-only, and lock its position and size behave in the same manner as these same options described for text objects earlier.

The Move To Bottom Of Section When Printing option is specific to the line object. Enabling this option sizes the line according to the size of the section. This option is useful for creating a line in a section with a varying-length field (e.g., a memo field) so that the line is the same length as the data. When this option is disabled, which is the default, the line remains a constant size in each section.

WORKING WITH PICTURES

A picture is added as an OLE object (discussed later in the section "Working with OLE") to a report. You have some limited formatting control over the object once it exists in your report; however, you should do any fine-tuning to the graphic in a graphics software package and not in Crystal Reports. With the picture selected, choose Format ➤ Graphic or right-click and choose Format Graphic to display the Format Editor, which now includes a Picture tab, as shown in Figure 3.20.

FIGURE 3.20

Formatting pictures

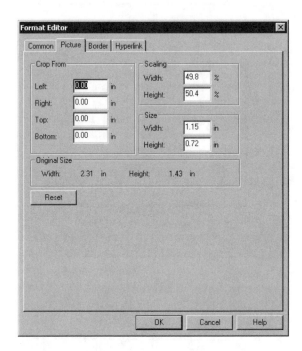

There are three things you can do to format a picture:

◆ Crop it.

◆ Scale it.

◆ Size it.

Cropping a picture lets you choose a portion of the image to display. You can remove parts of the picture in rectangular fashion, cropping from the left, right, top, or bottom.

Scaling a picture geometrically resizes the image to display the whole picture in a fraction of its original size. To shrink the picture in half, you would set the Width and Height values to 50%. You can scale the picture in one dimension only, such as by height, if you need to, but the results will resemble the Hall of Mirrors at a carnival, so be careful. You can also size the picture exactly using inch measurements. The Size measurements affect the Scaling measurements and vice versa.

TIP   *If you change your mind at any point, click the Reset button to restore the picture settings to their original values.*

Pictures often have hyperlinks associated with them, so now's a good time to discuss how to create hyperlinks.

Creating Hyperlinks

Hyperlink is one of those words that conjures up images of space travel and fancy transport mechanisms…a cool word indeed. In Crystal, hyperlinks move you quickly from one place in your report to an alternate destination. A hyperlink is attached to a Crystal object, so when a user views a report and clicks the object, the user travels to the destination associated with the hyperlink. Hyperlinks in Crystal are often connected to picture objects or text objects, but they can be attached to any Crystal object. To add a hyperlink to an object, select the object, and then choose Format ➤ Hyperlink to display the dialog shown in Figure 3.21. The Hyperlink tab of the Format Editor is where you create and maintain hyperlinks.

FIGURE 3.21

Hyperlink options

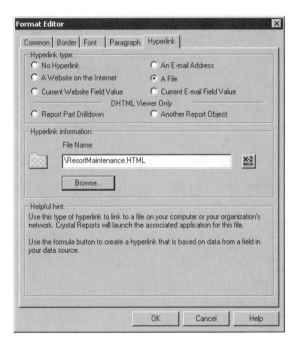

There are several types of destinations that you can jump to using a hyperlink, and the idea behind each of them is to allow the report to integrate other types of information so that Crystal is used as a launch point for gathering or reacting to information relevant to the report. The types of hyperlink destinations are described here:

A Website On The Internet   Any valid Uniform Resource Locator (URL) can be used as a destination. Crystal supplies the `http://` component of the web address, and you type the rest. Although the radio button mentions the Internet specifically, any valid URL will work whether it is on the company's intranet, an extranet, or the public Internet. The rule of thumb is that if you can get to the destination with a web browser, you can use it as a Crystal hyperlink destination.

Current Website Field Value   Database tables that store information about companies, for instance phone numbers and street addresses, often include a field for the company's website. If you add this field to a report, its value will appear as an active link when the appropriate hyperlink options are enabled. To use this feature, be sure to select the field containing the web address before choosing Format ➢ Hyperlink; otherwise, the radio button option itself is unavailable and cannot be selected.

An E-mail Address   Choosing the radio button for an e-mail address lets you type in any e-mail address. No validity checking is done on what you enter, so be sure to type carefully. When the user clicks this type of link in a report, a mail client (such as Outlook Express) opens and a traditional e-mail composition window is displayed, where you can enter text in the Subject line, type the text of your message, and click the Send button.

A File   Any file can be a link destination. You can use the Browse button to find it on your hard drive or a network drive. The only caveat in using this option is that the person viewing the report must also have appropriate access to the file for the link to work. Things that might prevent this access are security or the location of the file.

Current E-mail Field Value   If the database you're working with for a report contains an e-mail field, you can place the field in your report and then use its value as a link. This will be useful if the report you're building will be web-deployed and needs to show an e-mail address for each record in the Details section. In our business scenario, this might be to the e-mail address for the sales staff at each of the member resorts.

Report Part Drilldown   A new feature in Crystal Reports 9 is the Report Part Viewer, which is used to display detail data associated with summarized parts of a report. Compared to a traditional report drilldown, which jumps to a page within a report, the part drilldown identifies and displays only a specific object within a report. Using the Hyperlink tab in the Format Editor, you define a report part, which prepares it for use in report part navigation. Basically, you define the destination with a hyperlink and then use the Report Part viewer to navigate between reports and report parts. Report part drilldown is available for only the following summary object types:

- Group charts
- Group footer fields
- Group header fields
- Group maps
- Summary fields

To define a report part, select the summary object type and then choose Format ➢ Hyperlink to display the dialog shown in Figure 3.22. The report part is automatically given an object name that represents what the summary operation was in the report; in this case, CountofCountry1 is a grouping established in our CH02.RPT in Group Header #2.

FIGURE 3.22

Defining a
report part

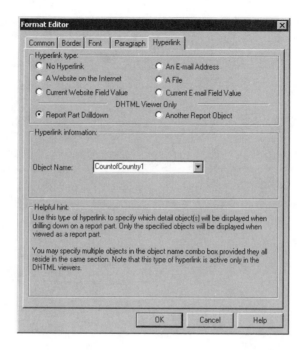

Dynamic Hypertext Markup Language (DHTML) is a version of HTML that is installed as part of your web browser. It is not a part of older web browsers such as Internet Explorer 3.0 and Netscape 3.0. If you have a more recent web browser installed on your machine, it likely supports DHTML and the Crystal Report Part Viewer will work correctly.

WARNING *If your browser does not support DHTML, hyperlinks using Report Part Drilldown and Another Report Object will not work.*

Another Report Object You can link from one Crystal Report to a specific part of another Crystal Report using the Report Part Viewer by selecting the Another Report Object radio button, as shown in Figure 3.23. To do this, first open the destination report and select the specific object to which you want to jump. Copy the location to the Windows clipboard using Ctrl+C (or any of the other Microsoft paste methods you know). Then return to the report in which you want to create the hyperlink starting point, and with Another Report Object selected, position the mouse in the Select From area and paste the destination location into the dialog (Ctrl+V is the keyboard combination to do this). The Data Context area tells you which field value will be the first one viewed and jumped to in the report part.

FIGURE 3.23

Linking to another report object

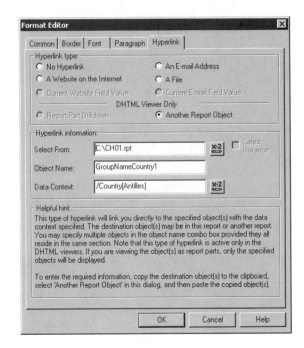

Working with OLE

Do you have a Microsoft Excel spreadsheet that you've been perfecting and maintaining for years that perfectly represents a piece of your business? And now you've been asked to do the same thing in Crystal Reports? There is no need to start from scratch and rebuild all the same capabilities into a report. Instead, object linking and embedding (OLE) might be just what you need.

OLE is a technical standard that allows one software application to share its information with other software applications. The goal is the integration of technologies, for example, Microsoft Excel and Crystal Reports, while allowing each application to do what it does best. In this case, Crystal Reports is a great report-writing application and Microsoft Excel is a terrific spreadsheet application. The most effective way to include spreadsheet capabilities in Crystal Reports is not to build this functionality into Crystal but instead to make use of the existing Microsoft Excel spreadsheet technology. The result is a Crystal Report that contains a Microsoft Excel spreadsheet.

OLE Components

OLE technology can be broken down into five components working together to create a shared information environment. The five pieces are shown in Figure 3.24. Let's look at each one separately.

OLE server application This is a software application that allows its information to be used in OLE container applications. Examples include Microsoft Excel, Microsoft Paint, and Microsoft Word.

OLE container application   This is a software application that uses information from OLE server applications. Crystal Reports is a container application.

Server document   This document is a file created and stored using the OLE server application, e.g., an Excel spreadsheet stored in an XLS file.

Container document   This document is a file created and stored using the OLE container application, e.g., a Crystal Report. A container document can contain OLE objects. A container document is also known as a *compound* document.

OLE object   This is an item that becomes a part of the container document but retains a connection to or relationship with the server document.

FIGURE 3.24

OLE components

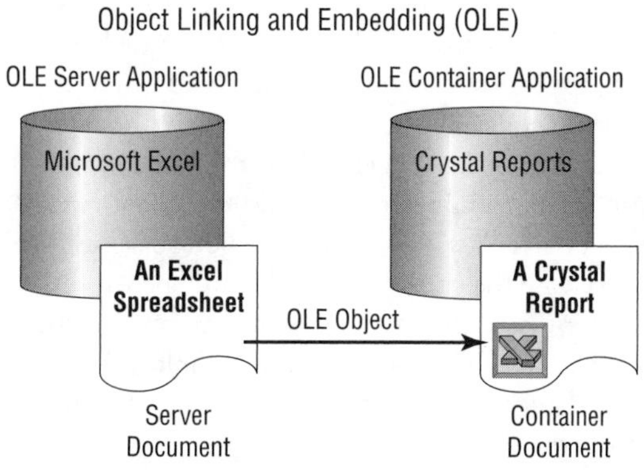

Object Linking and Embedding (OLE)

Adding OLE Objects to a Report

An OLE object can be added to a Crystal Report by linking it, embedding it, or creating a copy of it. The choice of which method to use is often driven by the availability of the OLE server application and runtime performance considerations.

LINKING

Linked items placed in a Crystal Report maintain a connection or reference to the original source document. If you edit the OLE object from within Crystal, the changes you make are actually being made back in the original file outside of Crystal. Any other applications that are linked to the same object would automatically detect and display any updates to the source document. So, if one spreadsheet was embedded in several reports, using the link method would guarantee that each Crystal Report always contains the most up-to-date spreadsheet information.

The process of creating an OLE link begins with the menu sequence Insert ➢ OLE Object. The next choice is whether to create a new OLE object in this report or to link to an existing external object by selecting an object type. The list of object types is unique to each computer because the information is pulled from the software registry of installed products. For this example, we'll choose to create a new Microsoft Excel Worksheet inside of Crystal, as shown in Figure 3.25.

FIGURE 3.25

Linking to Excel

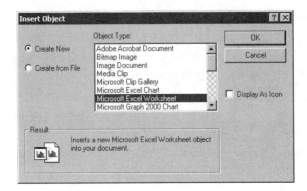

When you click the OK button on the Insert Object dialog shown in Figure 3.25, the familiar gray placement rectangle appears in Design mode, and you can drop the embedded object in whichever section of the report makes sense for your purposes.

At this point, a new worksheet labeled with the name of your report is created as Crystal opens the Excel application. Figure 3.26 shows the file `Worksheet in CH03.rpt`, and you can see Excel open behind it with Crystal open on the task bar at the bottom. This gives you the full power of all the Excel menu commands to create the spreadsheet. After we opened this particular spreadsheet in Crystal, we entered the column for CostBasis and its values. You can also choose Insert ➢ Name ➢ Define from the Excel menu to name a cell. Named cells can be linked directly to a report field in Crystal Reports so that when the cell changes in Excel, the update is reflected in the report's field value. In Figure 3.26, cell A2 has been given the name CostBasisA2.

FIGURE 3.26

Linking to a cell

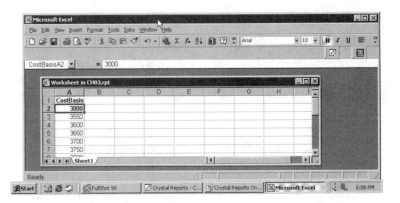

There are two types of links that can be included in a report:

◆ Automatic

◆ Manual

When an automatic link is used, when the report is opened, the most recent information stored in the source document is retrieved and added to the report. By comparison, a manual link provides an icon that you click in the report to retrieve the most recent information on demand. A linked OLE object is an automatic link by default. To modify this setting, select the OLE object and choose Edit ➤ Links to display the Links dialog shown in Figure 3.27.

FIGURE 3.27

Editing links

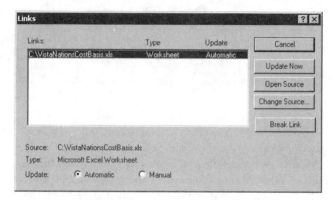

The radio buttons at the bottom let you choose between automatic or manual updating. The buttons along the right side of the dialog give you the opportunity to force an immediate refresh of the object, open the object in the source application, change the object source, or break the link entirely. Breaking the link converts the OLE object to an embedded object.

EMBEDDING

When you embed an OLE object into Crystal Reports, the original document is displayed in your report. Embedding does not maintain a link back to the original document for purposes of data refreshes. This means that if something changes in the original, the Crystal report will reflect the information as it existed at the time it was embedded and not how it exists after being updated. You can, however, edit the version of OLE object stored in the report. This is called *in-place editing*, and the source application must exist on the computer being used to view the report. The original object used to create the embedded object is not modified by the editing process; only the version of it that exists in the report is modified.

Let's take the example of embedding a Microsoft Paint BMP graphic into our report. You begin by choosing Insert ➤ OLE Object from the menu as you did with linking. You can choose to create a new object directly in your report or create the object using an existing file. For our example, the difference between these in practical terms is that you can either draw the picture inside Microsoft Paint, which is included in Crystal Reports, or you can use an existing BMP file that was created previously with Microsoft Paint. Figure 3.28 demonstrates the latter type of embedding.

FIGURE 3.28

Embedding a
BMP file

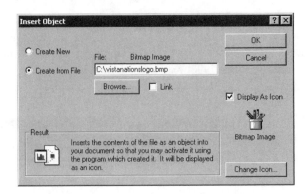

Notice also that in Figure 3.28 the check box to Display As Icon is checked; this option will display Microsoft's Paintbrush icon in your Crystal Report as a clickable icon. The icon that you will see in the report is actually shown on this dialog; you can replace this icon with another using the Change Icon button. When a user clicks the icon in the report, the Paintbrush application opens and the image you embedded is displayed. The technique of using an icon can preserve initial real estate in your report, effectively displaying the embedded object only if the person using the report wants to see it.

WARNING   *To embed the object, be sure to leave the Link check box unchecked.*

If you leave the Display As Icon check box in Figure 3.28 unchecked, the BMP image is displayed directly in your report. Right-clicking the image gives you the opportunity to edit, open, or convert it using the Bitmap Image Object menu. The menu option Bitmap Image Object is specific to OLE objects that are of the BMP type. If the OLE object was of another type, the menu item would refer more specifically to that type of object. For instance, if the object was an Excel spreadsheet, the menu item displayed would be Worksheet Object. The options to edit and to open are self-explanatory; the option to convert allows you to display the OLE object as an icon or in its entirely on initial opening of the report.

NOTE   *The OLE object and its edit, open, and convert tasks are also directly accessible from the main Edit menu in Crystal Reports.*

COPYING

Copying an OLE object is also referred to as working with *static* OLE objects. The idea behind a static OLE object is that the item is placed in the report in its entirety with no connection to the original stored version. This completely suppresses the ability to edit the object inside Crystal Reports. An example of inserting a static OLE object is choosing Insert ➤ Picture to add a graphic to a report.

The static OLE technique expands the list of external data objects that can be added to a report, especially in the area of graphics, since Crystal does not have to provide a way to edit the object. With Insert ➤ Picture, all of the following image types are supported: BMP, TIFF, JPEG, PNG, and Windows Metafiles.

In some cases, a static OLE object can be converted to an editable OLE object using a variation of the Convert menu option discussed earlier. By right-clicking the static object or by choosing the Edit menu with the object selected, the Convert Picture Object option is available. After conversion, the ability to actually edit the object from a report is dependant on the presence of the underlying application. For instance, to convert a static BMP object to an editable BMP object, the Microsoft Paint application needs to be present on the computer that is attempting the edit process.

Summary

In addition to the information a report gives to its user, it leaves a visual impression as well. In fact, it's an error to think of content and presentation as separate matters in the finished report. Marshall McLuhan became famous over three decades ago for his observation "The medium is the message." In other words, your presentation both conveys and manipulates your content; the two have a symbiotic relationship. While a wonderfully formatted report hits the eye and is easily accepted, it's the badly formatted information that really gets attention—negative attention. Formatting the text and data objects so that they are visually pleasing is a key part of the report design process, and you should take time to explore all the visual options available in the Format Editor as well as the judicious use of text objects.

The ability to integrate external information and external applications using hyperlinks and OLE either by linking, embedding, or copying objects allows a report to be a starting point of information gathering. The idea is to capitalize on the product features in external software and make those features available in Crystal Reports.

Part 2

Putting Report Elements to Work

In this section you will find:

Chapter 4

Adding Business Logic with the Formula Workshop

FORMULA LANGUAGE PROGRAMMING IS an adventure of the best kind: It's creative and fun, and there's no risk of hurting yourself! Programmers from the end-user level through the professional-developer level and all the levels in between write code to add functionality where none initially existed. Some write code because it's their hobby and they like making a computer do new and interesting things. Most, however, write code to fulfill a business need.

The most powerful person in report writing is one who has personal understanding of the meaning of the data from a business perspective, has the ability to write formula code to manipulate it, and has the skill to lay out the report in an organized and visually pleasing way. In this chapter, we'll build the foundation you need to master the formula languages built into Crystal and use them effectively in a report to do tasks such as adding a calculated value directly to a report, coding record-selection criteria to affect data retrievals, creating group-selection formulas, formatting sections and other report elements based on conditions, searching for data in a previewed report, building a running total field, and adding alert messages to reports based on condition criteria.

Featured in this chapter:

- ◆ Understanding core concepts in formula programming
- ◆ Using formulas in Crystal Reports
- ◆ The Report Explorer
- ◆ The Formula Workshop and Workshop Tree
- ◆ The Formula Expert and the Formula Editor
- ◆ Writing code using Basic Syntax and Crystal Syntax
- ◆ Using operators and built-in functions
- ◆ Programming custom functions
- ◆ Understanding evaluation time issues
- ◆ Troubleshooting formulas

Setting the Foundation

The core concept in formula programming is that you write an equation that performs a calculation using data available through the report. Sometimes a formula involves math, sometimes it involves dates, and other times it involves processing text data. For instance, you can have the first name field and the last name field print on your report with combined labels of either "Name" or "Last Name, First Name" or "Last Name, First Name Initial" by processing text data with a formula.

A formula calculates a value and returns that value as a result to the report at the end of its processing. Some values are used to directly display values in a report, while other calculated values may be used as interim results needed in turn for other formulas. Formulas add meaning to a report that wasn't a part of the natively stored data.

Components of a Formula

An example of a formula is a calculation to convert a Fahrenheit temperature to a Celsius temperature. Imagine that your data source contains the field of Celsius temperatures by day for the past month and that you've been asked to provide the average temperature for the month in Fahrenheit. Although the data does not exist in the data source, you can write a formula to calculate the value. There are two basic equations needed to calculate this result:

```
Fahrenheit = (Celsius * 9 / 5) + 32
Average = TotalTemperatures / NumberOfValues
```

Both formulas represent a calculation that will return a result. The first is a calculation performed for each new day; the second is a summary calculation that takes place after all values for the days of the month have been calculated. This example of direct single-record calculations and summary calculations is typical in report writing. Each part of a formula is identified by a component name; Table 4.1 identifies and describes the key components of a formula.

TABLE 4.1: IDENTIFYING FORMULA COMPONENTS

COMPONENT NAME	FORMULA REFERENCE	DESCRIPTION
Variable	Fahrenheit, Celsius, Average, TotalValue, NumberOfValues	A variable is a placeholder whose value can change; a variable references a storage location in a computer's memory.
Constant	9, 5, 32	A constant is a value that does not change; a constant also references a location in a computer's memory.
Operator	=, *, /, +	An operator specifies the type of calculation to be performed on the values to either side of the operator. The names associated with the operators in the example are assignment operator (=), multiplication operator (*), division operator (/), and addition operator (+).

In Crystal, the "Last Name, First Initial" formula idea combines two text values from a database by *concatenating* them with a comma and a space (concatenate means to connect or link in a series). Code to do this would look something like the following:

```
"Name: " + {table.LastName} + ", " + {table.FirstName}
```

where `"Name: "` represents a constant (it never changes), `{table.LastName}` and `{table.FirstName}` represent variables (which change for each record in the database), and + is an operator (which operates on the variables on either side of it). This is a direct calculation that would execute for each record in a database; there is no summarization here. To do summarization, temporary values need to be stored in computer memory for further processing.

Computer Memory

Storing information in computer memory is analogous to storing things in post office boxes at your local post office. Inside a post office, there is generally a wall devoted to small, uniquely numbered boxes. Each of the boxes has a particular size and shape to accommodate small or large envelopes. You can store and retrieve items from a post office box by knowing the number on the box, and the storage is strictly temporary. Map your knowledge of the wall of post office boxes to computer memory.

A variable or a constant is like the number on the outside of the post office box. The post office box itself is like a memory location in a computer. Knowing the name (also known as the *identifier*) of a variable or a constant allows you to store and retrieve information from the memory location simply by using its name.

Most memory locations store a single value (also known as a *discrete* value), although some storage locations allow multiple values to be stored. Like a post office box, values in computer memory are temporary, and in terms of Crystal Reports, storage used by a report is recycled at several points and definitely when a report is closed.

A storage location in memory is also associated with a specific data type. Once associated with a data type, it can store only values of that type. You can think of the data type as the size and shape of the post office box; certain values will fit into the slot while others will not. The formula languages in Crystal Reports require that all variables and constants be associated with a data type, and, generically, they support the following types:

◆ Boolean values (`True` and `False`)

◆ Date and time values

◆ Numeric data

◆ Text (string) data

Later in this chapter we'll look at the specifics of coding variables and associating them with data types in the two formula languages: Basic Syntax and Crystal Syntax.

Functions

Functions are code statements that are grouped together to perform a task and return a result. Crystal Reports supports both built-in functions and user-defined (custom) functions. A function is written as a generic routine that can be invoked over and over again by passing in new values each time the function is invoked; values passed to a function are known as *arguments* to the function. An argument is a value that exists only while the function is doing its processing; when the function ends, it returns a value to the report (or the calling function) and all computer memory associated with the function arguments goes away. A function has four parts:

◆ A function name

◆ A list of arguments (optional)

◆ The body of the function, which contains coded statements

◆ A return value

An example of a familiar function is the Sum function. The primary purpose of a function like Sum is to take several values, add them together, and return a single result. This describes the purpose of a function fairly well: Process values and return a result.

To invoke a function, you code a function call. You can invoke built-in functions or custom functions in Crystal. When one function calls another, which calls another, and so on, we say that we have a *stack* of function calls. Using this stack, we can trace back to all the previous code statements that were involved in generating a particular result. A function call to the function Sum might look like this:

```
myValue = Sum(x, y)
```

The identifiers myValue, x, and y are storage locations in memory. To calculate a value to store in myValue, the value of x is retrieved from its storage location, the value of y is retrieved from its storage location, the two values are added, and the result of the calculation is placed into the storage location identified by the variable myValue. X and Y are said to be *arguments* to the function Sum and represent the values to be used within the function.

Control Structures

Control structures in a programming language are used to directly influence the processing of information using logic. Control structures include the following:

◆ If-Then-Else single-selection constructs

◆ Multi-way selection constructs

◆ Loop constructs

◆ Keywords that interrupt normal processing

If-Then-Else constructs compare values and force a programmed action based on the result of the comparison. Multi-way selection statements (case or switch statements) compare multiple values and provide actions for each comparison. Loop constructs use a logical True or False comparison as a condition to trigger processing a set of code statements. Keywords like Break and Continue change the normal processing of a formula and force a change in the processing flow.

Arrays

An array is a storage structure that exists in memory and allows multiple values to be stored and referenced by a single identifier name. Although an array can store multiple values, all of the values must be of the same data type. As an example, a string array containing the values Sunday, Monday, Tuesday, Wednesday, Thursday, Friday, and Saturday might be known by the single name, DaysOfTheWeek. The elements in the array are all text (string) data and the array is said to have seven elements; Crystal contains a built-in function named UBound that will return the number of elements in an array. For example, UBound(DaysOfTheWeek) returns 7.

Setting and retrieving values for an array requires knowing the single name of the array as well as interacting with a particular slot or element number in the array. The DaysOfTheWeek array has seven slots, each of which can store a single value. Arrays can contain a maximum of 50 elements.

WARNING   *Crystal Reports allows one-dimensional arrays only.*

Using Formulas in Crystal Reports

There are many areas in Crystal that make use of formulas: from retrieving the data to adding calculated values to grouping and sorting creatively right through custom formatting for presentation purposes. The Formula Workshop is a completely new area in Crystal Reports, and its goal is to make writing formulas easy for the novice report designer as well as to address the needs of the veteran formula creators. As we present examples in this chapter, we'll point out where in Crystal you might use the finished formula and provide some examples to get you coding! We'll be using some new user interface objects in Crystal Reports 9 as well as some familiar ones from prior releases:

- ◆ The Report Explorer (new in Crystal Reports 9)
- ◆ The Field Explorer
- ◆ The Formula Workshop (new in Crystal Reports 9)
- ◆ The Workshop Tree (new in Crystal Reports 9)
- ◆ The Formula Editor
- ◆ The Formula Expert (new in Crystal Reports 9)

The Report Explorer

The complete structure of a report is available in an abbreviated, easy-to-navigate format using the Report Explorer. The five standard report sections and any additional sections added form leaves on a drill-down tree that can be used to navigate to any part of a report. Formulas are no exception; an entry is made in the Report Explorer showing where report formulas are used. Figure 4.1 shows the Report Explorer in floating format in its own window; it can also be docked to either side of the Crystal development environment (the left side definitely makes more sense because otherwise you obscure the Preview area). The Report Explorer can be opened from the toolbar or by choosing View ➤ Report Explorer.

FIGURE 4.1

The Report
Explorer

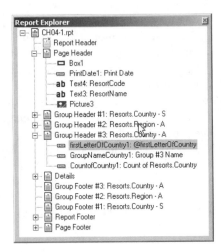

In Figure 4.1, the Page Header Tree is expanded and you can see that it contains a box report element, the special field PrintDate, two text objects, and a picture. Group Header #3 is also expanded and shows the use of a formula field in addition to a group and a summary field. Formula fields in Crystal Reports are given names prefixed with an @ symbol; you invent the name, Crystal adds the @ symbol. Using the Report Explorer, you can easily see what is going on in each section right down to where formula fields are being used. Writing code for a formula is done in the Formula Workshop.

There are two ways to open the Formula Workshop in Crystal Reports. The easiest way is to use its toolbar icon. You'll find this icon on the Expert toolbar with the label X+1. If your Expert toolbar is not displayed, open it by choosing View ➤ Toolbars and enabling its check box.

There is a second formula icon used throughout Crystal Reports that is very similar to the Formula Workshop icon; the second icon has the label X+2. While the X+1 icon opens the complete Formula Workshop, the X+2 icon opens the Format Editor, which is a part of the Formula Workshop. Figure 4.2 shows the Format Editor for a field that contains many opportunities for coding formulas, as is apparent from the X+2 icons.

The Field Explorer

The second path into the Formula Workshop is one that will be familiar to all Crystal Reports 8 and 8.5 users: the Field Explorer. The Field Explorer can be opened from the toolbar or by choosing View ➤ Field Explorer. With the Field Explorer displayed, shown in Figure 4.3, select the Formula Fields category and click the New button near the top of the dialog or right-click to display the submenu and choose New. Pressing Ctrl+N from the keyboard will also work.

After you select New for a new formula field, the dialog shown in Figure 4.4 displays to allow you to name the formula. At this point, Crystal Reports 9 preens a little, showing off its new features. The buttons along the bottom expect you to choose between using the Formula Expert or the Formula Editor. Both choices open the Formula Workshop, albeit with very different screens.

FIGURE 4.2

Using formulas in
the Format Editor

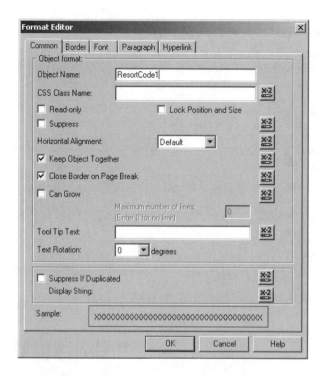

FIGURE 4.3

The Field Explorer

FIGURE 4.4

Naming a formula

The Formula Workshop

The Formula Workshop is a new feature of Crystal Reports 9. It is the master container for all other formula-related activities. Figure 4.5 shows the Formula Workshop displayed with the Workshop Tree and New button options visible. Some features of the Formula Workshop are as follows:

◆ The gray background is the default display; if a formula is selected, the Formula Editor displays in place of the gray background.

◆ The Workshop Tree is initially docked to the left border of the Formula Workshop and is not labeled.

◆ All windows in Formula Workshop are dockable or floatable.

◆ The Workshop Tree can be dragged off the border to float anywhere on the screen.

FIGURE 4.5

The Formula
Workshop and
the Workshop Tree

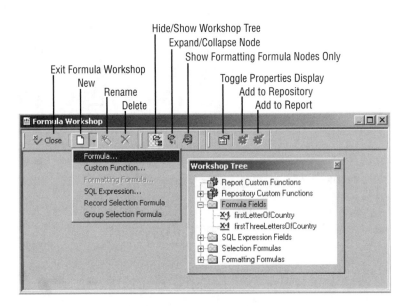

The buttons at the top of the Formula Workshop help you navigate and customize the Formula Workshop interactively.

Close   This button exits you from the Formula Workshop and all open windows within it. If there are unsaved changes, you'll be asked if you want to save the changes before exiting. If you elect to save your changes and are editing a formula, the code is checked for *syntax* errors. If there is an error in the code, Crystal notifies you that there is an error and asks if you want to save it anyway; this is a great new feature of Crystal Reports 9. In prior releases, if there was an error in the code, you had to correct it before exiting or delete the code before exiting. Now you can save your work as is and come back to it later.

NOTE *The word* syntax *refers to the rules of a programming language that govern the structure of statements and commands.*

New   Use this option to create new formulas, custom formulas, formatting formulas, SQL expressions, record selection formulas, and group selection formulas. When you click the New button directly, a window for a new object of the type that is selected in the Workshop Tree opens. If you click the drop-down arrow to the left of the button, a menu displays and lets you choose the type of Formula object to create at that point. Right-clicking the selected object in the Workshop Tree also displays a menu that contains the New menu item.

Rename   This option opens the Formula Name window and allows you to rename the currently selected Formula object. You can also right-click the selected object in the Workshop Tree to rename an item.

Delete   Use this option to delete the currently selected Formula object. You can also right-click the selected object in the Workshop Tree to delete it.

Hide/Show Workshop Tree   This toggle button option displays or hides the Workshop Tree window. If you click the button to show the Workshop Tree, it displays in whatever docked or anchored position it was in when it was hidden.

Expand/Collapse Node   This option expands and collapses selected nodes or multiple selected nodes in the Workshop Tree. This option has no effect if no category or element in the Workshop Tree is selected.

Show Formatting Formula Nodes Only   This option toggles the expansion of the Report objects in the Formatting Formulas category in the Workshop Tree. Notice the difference between Figure 4.6 and Figure 4.7. When the nodes are expanded, you can select a node and click the New button to create a formatting formula; this option appears grayed out in Figure 4.5 and becomes available when a report node is selected.

When you click the New button with a report node selected, the New Formatting Formula dialog displays. The options in the list of formatting commands vary depending on which section or report element was selected when the New button was clicked. Figure 4.8 shows the dialog for the formula coding opportunities for the Report Header section, and specifically the New Page After option is selected. Any code written here is also accessible through the X+2 button in the application area of Crystal, which in this example is the Section Expert X+2 New Page After check box shown in Figure 4.9. See Chapter 8, "Customizing Sections," for more ideas on how to control section behavior and use the Section Editor.

FIGURE 4.6

Formatting Formula
folder without all
nodes displayed

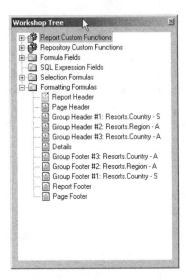

FIGURE 4.7

Formatting Formula
folder with all nodes
displayed

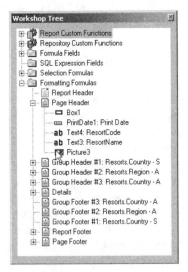

FIGURE 4.8

New Formatting
Formula

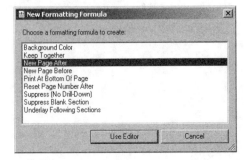

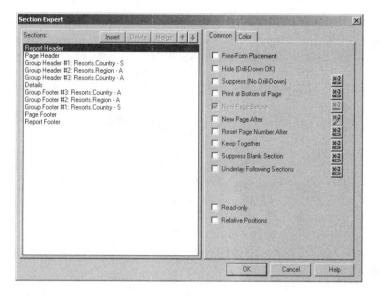

Selecting the Use Editor button on the New Formatting Formula dialog opens the Formula Editor window; at this point, you code a conditional formula that evaluates to True in order to force the behavior selected in the formatting option list.

Toggle Properties Display   When you are working on a custom function, this button toggles between the editor and the Properties windows. See the section "Crystal Custom Functions" for more information on working with custom functions.

Add to Repository   Use this option to add the currently selected object to the centralized Crystal Repository. For more information on how the repository works, see Chapter 5, "Working with the Crystal Repository."

Add to Report   This option is available when you select an object in the Repository Custom Functions category of the Workshop Tree. Selecting this option adds the selected function to the report. This results in a change in the Workshop Tree to copy the function from the repository into the Report Custom Functions area. Figure 4.10 shows the SixSigma Repository function after being added to the report. Notice the symbol to the left of the function name; in the report, it has the gear symbol plus a connection pipe symbol, while in the repository it has only the gear symbol.

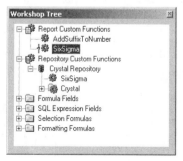

The Workshop Tree

Within the Formula Workshop, the Workshop Tree is a centralized area to access code for any existing Report objects as well as code new Formula objects. Figure 4.11 shows the completely expanded Workshop Tree with access to Report Custom Functions, Repository Custom Functions, Formula Fields, SQL Expression Fields, Selection Formulas, and Formatting Formulas.

FIGURE 4.11

The complete Workshop Tree

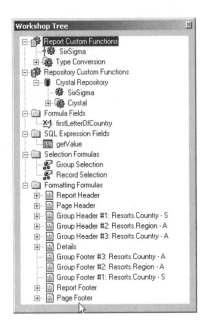

FORMULAS ACCESSED FROM THE WORKSHOP TREE

The category folders for formulas in the Workshop Tree represent most of the formulas you'll use in Crystal Reports. You can think of the Workshop Tree as a central portal to help keep you organized and quickly edit formulas. Let's take a quick look at what the general category of formulas does in Crystal Reports.

Report Custom Functions   Custom functions are code modules that can be stored at the report level and called by any other formula within the report. Custom functions are a new feature to the Crystal family. The functions are reusable within a single report.

Repository Custom Functions   Custom functions can be stored in the Crystal Repository. This enables them to be shared with other reports. The functions are reusable across multiple reports. The Crystal Repository is a new feature in Crystal Reports 9.

Formula Fields   Formula fields are fields that exist in the report, are given a name, and calculate a value that is used within the report for display purposes or as interim values for use in other calculations.

SQL Expression Fields   SQL expressions are calculations performed at the database level using the functions and commands of the Structured Query Language. In the Formula Editor, the Function Tree and the Operator Tree display SQL-related functions and operators instead of Crystal functions and operators. For a background on the components of a SQL command, refer to Chapter 11, "Using SQL in Crystal Reports."

Selection Formulas   Selection formulas in Crystal refine the data brought back from the data source or displayed in the report. Record-selection formulas limit the set of data that is available to Crystal, while group-selection formulas suppress groups of data at a time.

Formatting Formulas   Do you want to set alternate line colors for every record in the Details section? How about forcing a new page before each group? These kinds of things are done with formatting formulas. Formatting formulas can change the look and behavior of a report element. A new feature in this release of Crystal Reports is the ability to access all formatting formulas from a central place in the Workshop Tree.

NOTE   *In earlier releases of Crystal Reports, all formatting was done through the report element editors (e.g., the Field Editor).*

FORMULAS NOT ACCESSED THROUGH THE WORKSHOP TREE

While access to many formulas in Crystal Reports is provided through the centralized Workshop Tree, there are still a few formula areas that are not in the Workshop Tree.

Running Total Fields

Running total fields are used to accumulate values that aren't captured in Crystal's built-in summary operations. These fields are created from the Field Explorer, not the Workshop Tree. Let's say, for instance, that you wanted to count all five-star resorts in Canada with sales figures that meet a specified threshold value. Since this involves multiple fields and business logic to determine which resorts to include, none of the built-in summarization or methods will work and a running total would be used instead. Refer to Chapter 6, "Summarizing Information," for more information on running totals.

Searching for Data in a Report

There is one additional place where formulas can be coded in Crystal Reports that is not accessible from the Workshop Tree: the Search Expert. This expert is used to find data in a report and is therefore available only in Preview mode. You can access it through a toolbar icon or by choosing Edit ➤ Find on the menu. A simple Find dialog is shown in Figure 4.12, with the word "Cancun" being looked for in the report. To open the Search Expert, click the Advanced Find button.

FIGURE 4.12

The Find dialog

The Search Expert opens in a rather dreary mode, as shown in Figure 4.13, but once you click the New button, you have access to all the fields in the report and group information to build a condition clause. You can build criteria to search for a value in a particular field, for instance, checking to see if a City field contains "Cancun," which is a more refined search than simply looking for it generally in the report. Figure 4.14 shows a search involving "Cancun" once again, but this time the search is limited to looking for data values in the City field. The formula used to generate the search appears at the bottom of the dialog (or is hidden until you click a Show Formula button). You have full access to the Formula Editor at this point to write a customized data search.

FIGURE 4.13

The Search Expert

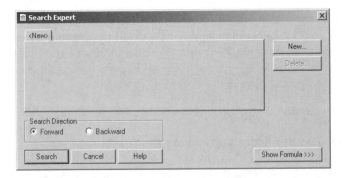

FIGURE 4.14

Using conditions in the Search Expert

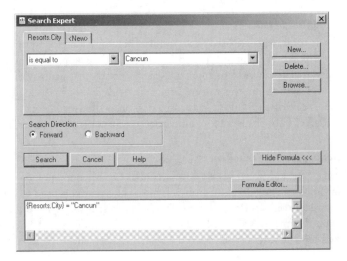

WARNING   *The Search Expert is not available in Design mode.*

Creating Formulas in Crystal Reports

Crystal Reports 9 provides three ways to create formula code:

- The Formula Editor
- The Formula Expert
- The Formula Extractor

The Formula Editor will be familiar to veteran users of Crystal Reports and provides a complete environment for coding a formula. The Formula Expert is a new feature in Crystal Reports 9 that adds a non-coding interface to the creation of formulas by basing a new formula on an existing custom function. Likewise, the Formula Extractor builds a new function based on an existing function in a fill-in-the-blanks type of screen. (Crystal doesn't actually call the Extractor tool "the Formula Extractor," but we'll take a leap here and refer to it by that name as all the window labels use wording like "Extract Custom Function from Formula.")

We'll introduce each interface in this section, and then later we'll code a custom function from scratch in the Formula Editor and revisit that function with the Formula Expert and the Formula Extractor.

THE FORMULA EDITOR

The Formula Editor, shown in Figure 4.15, is a place to type code, check it, use built-in functions and operators, and access fields on the report or in the data source. All code is written in the bottom part of the window. The buttons along the top, described below, help perform the tasks involved in creating and editing formulas.

FIGURE 4.15

The Formula Editor

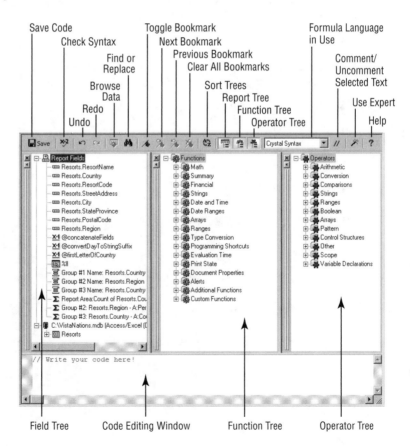

Save Code
Check Syntax
Find or Replace
Browse Data
Redo
Undo
Toggle Bookmark
Next Bookmark
Previous Bookmark
Clear All Bookmarks
Sort Trees
Report Tree
Function Tree
Operator Tree
Formula Language in Use
Comment/ Uncomment Selected Text
Use Expert
Help

Field Tree   Code Editing Window   Function Tree   Operator Tree

Save Code   After making code changes in the editing window, use this button to save the changes. If there is an error in the code, a dialog message will prompt you to see if you want to save the code anyway. Saying "Yes" saves the code even though there is an error in it so that you can come back and figure out the problem later. Saying "No" leaves you in Edit mode for the formula and displays a message providing general information about the error.

Keyboard shortcut: Alt+S

 Check Syntax   This button checks the syntax of the code in the editing window for correctness. Any typing errors related to language syntax will be caught at this point; logic errors in your code, however, will not be caught. If Crystal finds an error, it attempts to put the cursor in the vicinity of the error. If it finds no errors, a dialog happily reports this wonderful event.

Keyboard shortcut: Alt+C

 Undo   This button reverses any typing recently performed in the editing window.

Keyboard shortcut: Ctrl+Z

 Redo   Reapplies any typing that was previously reversed using the Undo button in the editing window.

Keyboard shortcut: Ctrl+Shift+Z

 Browse Data   This option is active when a report field or database field is selected in the Field Tree, and it displays a scrollable dialog showing sample values in the field.

Keyboard shortcut: Alt+B

 Find or Replace   Use the Find option to search for and/or replace words and phrases within the Field Tree, Function Tree, Operator Tree, or edit code window. Figure 4.16 shows a search for the word "If" in the edit code window.

Keyboard shortcut: Ctrl+F

FIGURE 4.16

Finding things in the Formula Editor

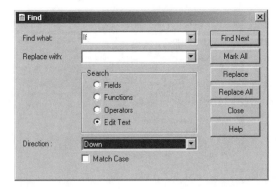

Toggle Bookmark   Bookmarks are small, blue, rounded rectangle markers that can be placed to the left of a line of code in the edit code window. Use the bookmark feature to mark an area of code that you want to come back to later in the editing session of a long formula. All bookmarks are automatically cleared when the editing window is closed.

Keyboard shortcut: Ctrl+F2

Next Bookmark   Use this option to navigate to a bookmark that appears below the line of code that currently has the focus. This option is unavailable when bookmarks are not being used.

Keyboard shortcut: Ctrl+Alt+F2

Previous Bookmark   Use this option to navigate to a bookmark that appears above the line of code that currently has the focus. This option is unavailable when bookmarks are not being used.

Keyboard shortcut: Shift+F2

Clear All Bookmarks   This option removes all bookmarks interactively. This option is unavailable when bookmarks are not being used.

Keyboard shortcut: Ctrl+Shift+F2

Sort Trees   When one of the three tree windows at the top of the Formula Editor has focus, using this option sorts the category list in alphabetical order or back to their original order.

Keyboard shortcut: Alt+O

Field Tree   This option toggles the Field Tree window open or closed. You can also right-click the background of the Tree window to display a submenu from which you can select the Hide option to close the window.

Keyboard shortcut: Alt+F

Function Tree   This option toggles the Function Tree window open or closed. You can also right-click the background of the Tree window to display a submenu from which you can select the Hide option to close the window.

Keyboard shortcut: Alt+U

Operator Tree   This option toggles the Operator Tree window open or closed. You can also right-click the background of the Tree window to display a submenu from which you can select the Hide option to close the window.

Keyboard shortcut: Alt+P

Syntax   Use the drop-down list shown in Figure 4.17 to choose between Crystal Syntax or Basic Syntax. The code in the edit window is checked for correct syntax against whichever language is chosen in this drop-down box. You can set a global default for your formula language choice by choosing File ➢ Options, choosing the Reporting tab, and setting the Formula Language at the bottom of the tab.   Keyboard shortcut: Ctrl+T

FIGURE 4.17

Choosing the formula language in the Formula Editor

WARNING   Switching from one language to another in the Formula Editor does not automatically update the code in the edit window; you must correct the lines of code manually for the formula language chosen.

Comment/Uncomment Selected Text   After selecting a block of code (one line or multiple lines) in the edit code window, use this button to comment or uncomment the entire block. If Basic Syntax is the formula language in effect, each commented line of code is prefixed with a single quote ('), while when Crystal Syntax is being used, each line of commented code is preceded with two forward slashes (//) to signal that the code following the symbols will not execute. Use this option when you have a block of code that is not working properly and you want to debug it but leave it intact.

Keyboard shortcut: Alt+M

TIP   You can also use this button to comment out blocks of code as a formula changes during its lifetime; it's a good idea to preserve old versions of the code by commenting out but never deleting the original code.

Use Expert   This button toggles from the Formula Editor to the Formula Expert when a custom formula is being edited.

Keyboard shortcut: Alt+X

WARNING   If the current formula is not a custom function, using this option will delete all the code in your Formula Editor editing window and then open the Formula Expert.

Help   This option opens the Crystal Reports help file to an area that provides help specifically for the Formula Editor. If the help file is already open and minimized, clicking this button will redisplay the help file. If the help file is open but not minimized, nothing will happen onscreen, so you'll need to switch on the help window manually to give it focus.

Keyboard shortcut: Alt+H

Earlier in this chapter in Table 4.1 we provided definitions for three components of a formula:

Variable   A named placeholder whose value can change; a variable references a storage location in a computer's memory.

Constant   A named placeholder whose value does not change; a constant references a storage location in a computer's memory.

Operator   Specifies the type of calculation to be performed on the values to either side of the operator.

With these abbreviated definitions in mind, examine the three windows at the top of the Formula Editor in Figure 4.15 and map the above definitions to the windows and what is being provided in each window:

- Field Tree
- Function Tree
- Operator Tree

You can drag and drop each of the Tree windows to reposition it as well as close it using the X button in its window. The Tree windows can be free-floating, by right-clicking on the window and unselecting allow docking, or they can be docked to the top, bottom, or sides of the Formula Editor, if the Allow Docking Option is selected (which it is by default). Click the arrow button in each Tree window to toggle that window to full-screen mode or back to its opening size.

The Field Tree

The Field Tree represents the field variables currently in the report. The value of a field variable can change for each record in the database. The Field Tree also provides access to all of the fields within the data source, not just the ones on the report. In Figure 4.15, shown previously, the Report Fields branch is completely expanded while the `C:\VistaNations.mdb` branch is collapsed. You can tell from the latter branch what type of connection was made, and you can expand it to access all tables and fields available to the report through the data source. Report fields and database fields are variables in a Crystal report. You can also create one more kind of variable in Crystal: a *temporary variable*. Temporary variables are named values in your code that are used within a block of code and discarded when the code returns its final value to the report. As we discussed earlier, in reporting average temperatures when converting from Fahrenheit to Celsius, the following code uses temporary variables:

```
Average = TotalTemperatures / NumberOfValues
```

`TotalTemperatures` and `NumberOfValues` are both temporary in the sense that they collect values during the life of the formula, and when the `Average` value is returned to the report, computer memory for storing `TotalTemperatures` and `NumberOfValues` is released and the variables no longer exist.

There is an additional concept relevant to variables, and that is the concept of *scope*. The scope of a variable determines when and where the variable can be used. Crystal Reports supports three types of variable scope:

Local   The variable and its value exist only during the life of the function and then go away. The computer memory associated with the variable is given back to the general memory pool for reuse.

Global   The variable and its value exist for the life of the report; when a report is closed, all computer memory associated with the variable is returned to the general memory pool for reuse.

Shared   Shared variables allow data values to be passed between a Crystal subreport and a Crystal main report. This is the only mechanism for sharing data between a subreport and a main report. For more information on subreports, refer to Chapter 6.

The Function Tree

The Function Tree provides categorized access to all the built-in functions in Crystal Reports as well as any custom functions that are stored in the report; the lists are slightly different for Crystal Syntax versus Basic Syntax. Double-clicking a function name in the Function Tree adds it to the code editing window. Each category in a tree can be expanded or collapsed, and the calling syntax for the function is shown as well. Figure 4.18 shows a few of the Math functions with the `Truncate` function expanded to display two ways to call the function: with one argument or with two.

FIGURE 4.18

Expanding and collapsing categories in the Function Tree

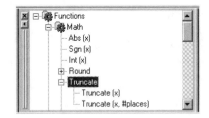

In addition to double-clicking a function name to add it to the editing window, the new Keyword Auto Complete feature in Crystal Reports 9 lets you quickly add functions while typing in the code editing window. Press Ctrl+spacebar to activate the Keyword Auto Complete tool, which shows a list of function names that match what you're typing. Type as little or as much of the function name as you know, and then press Ctrl+spacebar to see similar functions based on what you typed. Figure 4.19 shows the result of typing the characters "Le" and then pressing Ctrl+spacebar; the selection window shows the built-in functions `Left` and `Length`. If nothing is typed when you press Ctrl+Space, an alphabetized list of applicable functions displays, as shown in Figure 4.20.

FIGURE 4.19

Function Keyword Auto Complete with a typed value

FIGURE 4.20

Function Keyword Auto Complete without a typed value

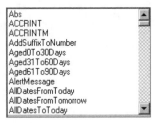

Double-clicking an item in the list presented by Keyword Auto Complete copies the function name into the code editing window.

NOTE   *Examples of how to use the function are found in the help file, but you do need to search on the function name to find them. There are no F1 or context-sensitive help jumps based on function names.*

The Operator Tree

The Operator Tree, shown previously in Figure 4.15 in the top-right window, is a categorized list of operations that can be performed on data. Operators can be mathematical, such as addition, or string-based, such as concatenation, or even logically based, such as the operators AND and OR. The categories of operators determine the type of data that will be processed by the operator. Operators are known as either *unary* operators or *binary* operators. A unary operator works on one piece of data; a binary operator works on two pieces of data, one on either side of the operator. The concatenation operation we mentioned earlier uses the plus sign as a binary concatenation operator; it joins the two strings on either side of it, as shown here:

```
"Name: " + {table.LastName} + ", " + {table.FirstName}
```

A special operator used in all programming languages is the *assignment* operator. Its purpose is to take the value from the expression on the right and store that value in the memory location referenced by the identifier on the left; here's an example in Basic Syntax that takes the text string Miller and stores it in the memory location referenced by the identifer lastName:

```
lastName = "Miller"
```

The syntax for the assignment operator is slightly different in Crystal Syntax, with a combination of a colon and an equal sign being used in place of the single equal sign:

```
lastName := "Miller"
```

Table 4.2 lists the operators and the syntax for each. As with functions, the list of operators supported and their syntax may differ slightly from Crystal Syntax to Basic Syntax. Neither language is case-sensitive, so the syntax is shown using the same case for both languages.

TABLE 4.2: CRYSTAL REPORTS OPERATORS

OPERATOR NAME	CRYSTAL SYNTAX	BASIC SYNTAX
Assignment	:=	=
Add	x + y	x + y
Subtract	x - y	x - y
Multiply	x * y	x * y
Divide	x / y	x / y
Integer divide	x \ y	x \ y
Percent	x % y	Not supported

Continued on next page

TABLE 4.2: CRYSTAL REPORTS OPERATORS *(continued)*

OPERATOR NAME	CRYSTAL SYNTAX	BASIC SYNTAX
Modulus	x mod y	x mod y
Negate	-x	-x
Exponentiation	x ^ y	x ^ y
To currency	$x	Not supported
Equal	x = y	x = y
Not equal	x <> y	x <> y
Less than	x < y	x < y
Greater than	x > y	x > y
Less than or equal to	x <= y	x <= y
Greater than or equal to	x >= y	x >= y
Concatenate	x + y	x + y
Concatenate	x & y	x & y
Subscript	x[y]	x(y)
In string	x in y	x in y
Insert Empty String	" "	" "
In range	x in y	x in y
Make range	x to y	x to y
Left endpoint excluded in range	x_to y	x_to y
Right endpoint excluded in range	x to_y	x to_y
Both endpoints excluded in range	x_to_y	x_to_y
Up to	upTo x	upTo x
Up to but not including	upTo_x	upTo_x
Up from	upFrom x	upFrom x
Up from but not including	upFrom_ x	upFrom_ x
Range less than	Is < x	Is < x
Range greater than	Is > x	Is > x
Range less than or equal	Is <= x	Is <= x
Range greater than or equal	Is >= x	Is >= x

Continued on next page

TABLE 4.2: CRYSTAL REPORTS OPERATORS *(continued)*

OPERATOR NAME	CRYSTAL SYNTAX	BASIC SYNTAX
Not (logical)	Not x	Not x
And (logical)	x and y	x and y
Or (logical)	x or y	x or y
Xor (logical)	x xor y	x xor y
Eqv (logical)	x eqv y	x eqv y
Imp (logical)	x imp y	x imp y
Make array	[x,…]	Array (x,…)
Subscript array	x[y]	x(y)
In array	x in y	x in y
Redim array	Redim x[n]	Redim x(n)
Redim preserve array	Redim preserve x[n]	Redim preserve x(n)
Starts with (text pattern)	x startsWith y	x startsWith y
Like (text pattern)	x like y	x like y

NOTE   The Crystal documentation states that while an operator might be supported in both languages, one syntax might be preferred when using Crystal Syntax and another might be preferred when using Basic Syntax. We believe that you should try to keep things simple when writing code and if an operator works the same in both languages, use the common operator for better compatibility should you someday decide to switch languages. Besides, remembering one operator is just plain easier than remembering two!

The Editing Window

The editing window appears on the bottom half of the Formula Editor, as shown in Figure 4.15. In this free-form typing area, you can directly type code as well as use the Field Tree, Function Tree, and Operator Tree to copy and paste the objects listed within into the editing window. When you select an object in one of the trees and double-click it, the code necessary to reference the field, function, or operator is added to the editing window wherever the cursor is currently.

Formulas consist of variables, operators, and constants combined with control structures and statements of the programming language being used. All of these statements are written in the code editing window.

THE FORMULA EXPERT

If writing code is new to you, you might want to start with the Formula Expert. Using the Formula Expert lets you create a new formula by using an existing custom function as a pattern. The Formula Expert opens when you do any of the following in Crystal Reports:

◆ Create a new formula field in the Field Explorer and click the Use Expert button (see Figure 4.4).

◆ Edit an empty formula from the Formula Fields category in the Field Explorer.

◆ Click the Use Expert toolbar icon in the Formula Editor.

Code created using the Formula Expert converts to code viewable (and editable) in the Formula Editor. The purpose of the Formula Expert shown in Figure 4.21 is to provide a point-and-click approach to creating formula code.

FIGURE 4.21

The Formula Expert

Choose a custom function to use as a starting point.

Data type returned by function

Summary information from function properties; use the More Info button to see all function properties

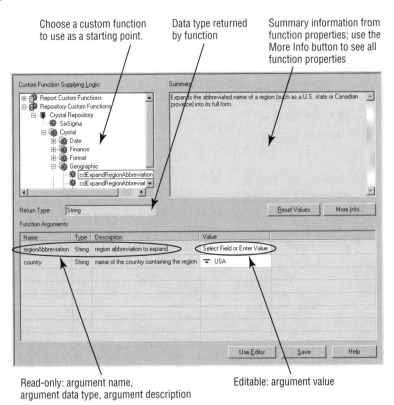

Read-only: argument name, argument data type, argument description

Editable: argument value

In the top-left corner of the Formula Expert, choose the custom function to use as the basis for your new function. The list shows the custom functions that exist in the current report as well as those that are stored in the repository. Choosing a function from the list sets three values for the function you are creating:

Summary   This area contains the comments written by the programmer of the custom function to describe the purpose and use of the function. The summary is a read-only value.

Return Type   This area is set to the type of data that will be returned by the new function. The return type is a read-only value.

Function Arguments   Arguments are the values passed from a calling function to the function that is going to do a calculation. The names of the arguments are determined by the underlying custom function as are the data types and descriptions of the parameters. Each row in the bottom half of the dialog represents one argument to the function and all its identifying information. The name, data type, and description are read-only.

The value of each function argument can be interactively set at this point. You can type values directly or use the drop-down list choices provided. In the formula shown in Figure 4.21, for example, the `regionAbbreviation` parameter has its initial value set to `Select Field or Enter Value`; it does not contain an initial default value. For the formula to run correctly, a valid value is required for this parameter; to be valid, it must be the correct data type defined for the argument. Clicking this field reveals the drop-down list shown in Figure 4.22; the bottom half of the list of choices is shown in Figure 4.23 and includes all field values in the report, group names, SQL commands, running totals, and constants.

FIGURE 4.22

Populating a
parameter value in
the Formula Expert

FIGURE 4.23

Additional choices

Once you've set values for each argument to the function, save it to the report by clicking the Save button. When the function is saved, two things happen:

- The function is added to your report's custom functions.

- Any custom functions that your new function uses are also added to your report's custom functions.

As the function is being saved, you'll see dialog boxes similar to those shown in Figure 4.24 and Figure 4.25 telling you which functions are being added to your report.

FIGURE 4.24

Saving a formula created with the Formula Expert

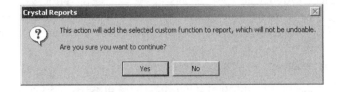

FIGURE 4.25

Dependencies on other custom functions

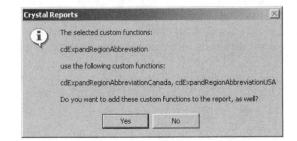

The result is the inclusion of all the custom functions involved in the one you created showing up in the Workshop Tree under the Report Custom Functions area, as shown in Figure 4.26.

FIGURE 4.26

The Workshop Tree after using the Formula Expert

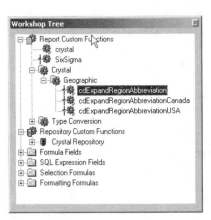

If you want to start over again with new values after making modifications to the arguments, click the Reset Values button. For fields that have default values, the first valid default value in the list of all default values is placed in the input box when you choose Reset Values. If the field doesn't have a default value, the generic Select Field or Enter Value message displays.

When you click the More Info button, the complete properties of the custom function display; this is where the summary information originated. From here, you can also see what category it falls into in the Function Tree, where it is stored, what version of editing it is using, who the author is, and any help text associated with the function. Figure 4.27 shows the properties for the built-in Crystal function cdExpandRegionAbbreviation.

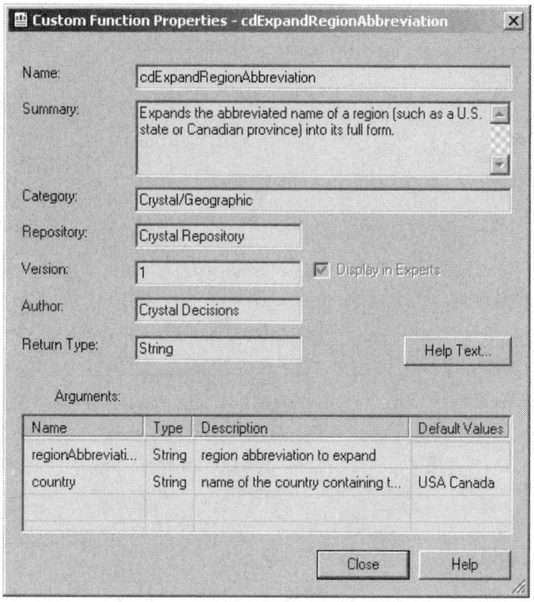

FIGURE 4.27

Viewing properties of custom functions

You can click the Use Editor button to view the code that the Formula Expert created and continue working on it in the Formula Editor. The Save button saves the currently open formula and leaves you in Edit mode in the Formula Expert. The Help button activates help specific to working with the Formula Expert.

Coding Formulas

The purpose of creating a formula or writing code is to solve a problem. Now that you've seen where the code goes in Crystal Reports and you have some background on variables, constants, and operators, let's take a look at how to program in the two formula languages built into Crystal Reports: Crystal Syntax and Basic Syntax.

Choosing a Language

Your choice of language will be determined by a few factors:

◆ Your personal preference

◆ Your experience with other programming languages

◆ The existence of required language constructs for the problem at hand

Either language can be used. Neither language is case sensitive. You can code one function in Crystal Syntax and code a different one in Basic Syntax. As long as you don't try to combine the two languages within one formula, you'll be fine. Table 4.3 shows quick list of key syntactic point differences for the two languages.

TABLE 4.3: CRYSTAL SYNTAX VERSUS BASIC SYNTAX

TASK	CRYSTAL SYNTAX	BASIC SYNTAX
Assignment operator	`:=`	`=`
Comment operator	`//`	`'`
End of a statement	`;`	Carriage Return / Linefeed (Enter Key)

Data types	`stringVar x;`
	`numberVar y;`
	`dateVar z;`
		`Dim c as String`
		`Dim x as Number`
		`Dim y as Date`

Variable scope	`Local numberVar x;`
	`Global numberVar x;`
	`Shared numberVar x;`
	(Global if not specified.)
		`Dim x as Number`
		`Local x as Number`
		`Global y as Number`
		`Shared z as Number`
		(Local if not specified;
		[Dim and Local are equivalent.])

Array declaration	`stringVar Array x;`
	`Redim x[2];`
	`x[1]:="Hello";`
	`x[2]:="World";`
		`Shared x() as String`
		`x = Array("Hello", "World")`

Returning a value to the report	`Value`	`Formula = value`
Closing keyword on block statements	No	Yes

WARNING *The Variant data type supported in the Visual Basic language is not supported in Crystal's Basic Syntax formula language.*

Control Structures

Both languages support the use of variables, constants, and operators as well as standard programming language control structures such as these:

◆ Condition-based statements

◆ Iteration statements

Control structures are used to force the execution of an action based on conditional values. Figure 4.28 and Figure 4.29 show the Control Structures category of the Operator Tree for Crystal Syntax and Basic Syntax.

FIGURE 4.28

Control Structures for Crystal Syntax

FIGURE 4.29

Control Structures for Basic Syntax

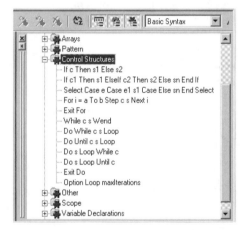

CONDITION-BASED STATEMENTS

Conditional statements test a condition and then take an appropriate action based on whether the condition is true or false. Conditions always return `True` or `False`, where a `True` result triggers an action and a `False` result either triggers no action or an alternate action. Parentheses are used in code statements to both isolate and prioritize the execution of a statement; by default, code statements execute in a left-to-right order within a statement except when parentheses are used and the statements within them are processed first.

If-Then-Else

The basic structure of an `If-Then-Else` statement is

```
If (condition) Then (action) Else (alternate action)
```

Conditions, actions, and alternate actions often involve fields from the report, built-in functions, and built-in operators. This is one of the most powerful structures in a programming language and it's one you'll use all the time in Crystal Reports. An `If-Then-Else` statement can simply be expressed as an `If-Then` statement; the `Else` (alternate action) is implied to be "do nothing." You can also nest `If-Then-Else` statements within one another as well as test multiple conditions within the condition clause by using logical `AND` and logical `OR` operators.

```
If (condition) then
  (If (condition) then
    action
  else
    alternate action)
else
  alternate action
```

Crystal Syntax and Basic Syntax use slightly different syntax for the `If-Then-Else` statement. Crystal Syntax does not use closing block keywords like `End If` for its executable statements, while Basic Syntax does use them. Also, values are returned to a report only through the use of the keyword `Formula` in Basic Syntax, while no keyword is required in Crystal Syntax.

Basic Syntax:

```
If {Resorts.StateProvince} = "New York" Then
  Formula = "The Big Apple"
Else
  If {Resorts.StateProvince}="Rhode Island" Then
    Formula = "The Ocean State"
End If
```

Crystal Syntax:

```
If {Resorts.StateProvince} = "New York" Then
  "The Big Apple"
Else
  If {Resorts.StateProvince}="Rhode Island" Then
    "The Ocean State"
```

Both Basic Syntax and Crystal Syntax also support the shorthand `IIF` notation for the full `If-Then-Else` statement:

```
IIF(condition, action, alternate action)
```

Condition Only

In several areas in Crystal Reports, you'll have occasion to simply use the condition part of the `If-Then-Else` statement; the context of where the statement is located determines the action. Here are examples of using pure conditions without the `Then-Else` components in formula fields and selection formulas. The formatting formulas show the use of an `If-Then` example.

Formula Field   A formula field is given a name and can then be placed into any section on a report. If you want one column of data to represent the last name separated by a comma and a space from the first name, you would create a formula similar to the following formula, making sure to use the appropriate table name and field names:

```
{Owner.LastName} + ", " + {Owner.FirstName}
```

Selection Formula   A selection formula needs only to use a condition; when the condition is met (meaning it is `true`), the records selected from the database meet the criteria defined by the condition. A condition clause can contain multiple conditions as long as it is connected with the logical `AND` operator or the logical `OR` operator. The following condition looks for data in the VistaNations Owners table and returns a list of resorts owned by Cate McCoy:

```
{Owner.LastName}=McCoy" and {Owner.FirstName}="Cate"
```

Formatting Formulas   Formatting formulas change the way information looks or behaves in a report. Figure 4.8, shown earlier in this chapter, showed how to create a formatting formula using the Workshop Tree. If you selected the Details section and the Background Color formatting option, the Workshop Tree and Formula Editor would appear as in Figure 4.30 and allow you to type a formatting formula. In this example, we've coded a Crystal Syntax formula that formats the background to be the color green if the value of `Country = "US"` and white otherwise.

FIGURE 4.30

Using a formula to format a background color

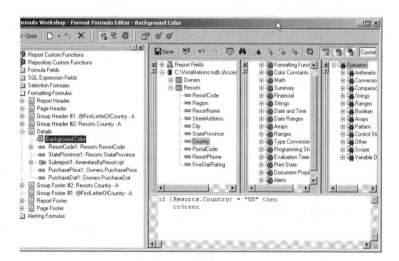

Multi-Way Selection

Both Crystal Syntax and Basic Syntax provide for a clear, concise statement for multi-way selection called the `Select` statement. Instead of nesting one `if` statement inside another, it is usually easier to write, read, and maintain code if you use a `Select` conditional statement instead. In the following two code examples, the value of the variable *lastTwo* is inspected. If its value equals 01, the value of the variable suffix is set to st, and the other statements do similar assignments. The beauty of the Select statement is that when the first true condition is encountered, the statement associated with it executes and then remaining conditions are not executed; control passes to the end of the statement. Notice the following differences about the code:

◆ Basic Syntax closes the code block with an End Select statement, while Crystal Syntax does not.

◆ Crystal Syntax ends the statement with a semicolon, while Basic Syntax does not.

◆ The assignment operators for the two languages are different.

Basic Syntax:

```
Select Case (lastTwo)
  Case "01"
    Suffix = "st"
  Case "02"
    Suffix = "nd"
  Case "03"
    Suffix = "rd"
  Case Else
    Suffix = "th"
End Select
```

Crystal Syntax:

```
Select lastTwo
  Case "01" :
    Suffix := "st"
  Case "02":
    Suffix := "nd"
  Case "03":
    Suffix := "rd"
  Default:
    Suffix := "th";
```

We'll make use of this code in just a bit when we build a custom function.

ITERATION (LOOPS)

A *loop* is a programming statement that moves you through a set of data one element at a time and takes an action that applies to the element. You can use a loop to do such things as create a count of records as they're being read from the database, apply functions to a record in the database, and compare one value to another, taking an action based on the comparison. The concept of a loop is that you test a condition, and if the condition is true, an action is taken; the process of testing and taking an action continues, repeating the code, until the condition proves to be false. A loop has three parts:

◆ Initial value of a loop control variable

♦ Condition to test to determine if the loop should continue or stop

♦ Increment of a loop control variable

A loop essentially allows a program to repeat pieces of the code. Figure 4.31 depicts this process.

FIGURE 4.31

How a loop works

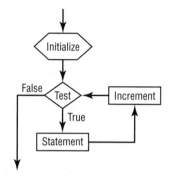

Crystal Reports provides for several types of loops in each of the formula languages. Loops take the following structures:

FOR loops   Process a specified number of times.

WHILE loops   Test a condition and process it if it is true.

UNTIL loops   Process and then test a condition to see if it is true.

Crystal Syntax and Basic Syntax both support the spirit of these three types of loops with slightly varying syntax:

Crystal Syntax:

```
For I := 1 to 100 Do
  (
    fiveStarCount = fiveStarCount + 1;
  );

While ({Resorts.FiveStarRating = "Yes"}) Do
  (
    fiveStarCount = fiveStarCount + 1;
  );

Do
  (
    fiveStarCount = fiveStarCount + 1;
  )
While ({Resorts.FiveStarRating = "Yes"});
```

Basic Syntax:

```
For I = 1 to 100
  If {Resorts.FiveStarRating = "Yes"} then
    fiveStarCount = fiveStarCount + 1
Next I

Do While ({Resorts.FiveStarRating = "Yes"})
  fiveStarCount = fiveStarCount + 1
Loop

Do Until ({Resorts.FiveStarRating = "Yes"})
  fiveStarCount = fiveStarCount + 1
Loop

Do
  fiveStarCount = fiveStarCount + 1
Loop While ({Resorts.FiveStarRating = "Yes"})

Do
  fiveStarCount = fiveStarCount + 1
Loop Until ({Resorts.FiveStarRating = "Yes"})
```

NOTE   *The* Exit Do *statement immediately exits the loop at whatever point it is placed.*

Coding and Using Functions

Okay, you've been reading about a good many of the syntax rules associated with Crystal Syntax and Basic Syntax and have identified some of the operator and function differences. Crystal supports the use of two kinds of functions:

◆ Custom functions

◆ Built-in functions

Functions can be written in either Crystal Syntax or Basic Syntax. As with operators and control structures, there are some syntactic differences between the functions in Crystal Syntax and those in Basic Syntax. One of the key differences is in how a value is returned to the calling function or the report in the two languages. In Crystal Syntax, returning a value requires only that the name of the variable that contains the value be the last line of code in the formula. In Basic Syntax, the keyword formula is used to return a value. In both of the following examples, a value that represents a 25 percent increase in unit price is returned to the report:

Crystal Syntax:

```
{Owners.UnitPrice} * 1.25
```

Basic Syntax:

```
formula = {Owners.UnitPrice} * 1.25
```

One of the best ways to truly absorb the differences between the two formula languages and learn how to use functions is to code a formula or a function in one language syntax and then convert it to the other language syntax. We'll begin our coverage of functions by building a custom function that will make use of some built-in functions. We'll finish with a look at the built-in functions in Crystal from the perspectives of what functions are available, what kinds of control they offer, and when they should be used.

Crystal Custom Functions

Custom functions are modules of code that can be called by name and that can be passed parameters. These are functions are coded once in a report in either Crystal Syntax or Basic Syntax and used over and over again. In addition to being stored in a report and reused throughout the report, custom functions can be added to the Crystal Repository. This gives them two additional important features:

◆ The ability to share functions across many reports

◆ One central place to make code changes in shared functions

You can write your own custom function and store it in the report or in the repository. You can also use over 25 custom functions that ship with Crystal Reports 9 that you'll find ready-to-use in the repository. You can even customize the custom functions that ship with Crystal Reports.

CODING A CUSTOM FUNCTION

Are you ready to try your hand at coding and using a custom function?

> *Business Question: VistaNations wants to add a tag line to the bottom of every report to display the date it was printed using the general format "This report was printed on the 3rd day of September."*

To solve this business question, we could start with the special PrintDate field available from the Document Properties category of the Function Tree or from the Special Fields area of the Field Explorer. However, there are no functions built into Crystal Reports that will add a text-based suffix to a number or a date, so we'll need to code our own.

The first step in writing any code is to think about the problem and come up with a solution as if you were going to solve it by hand without a computer just using your good old brain. Remember, the only reason we write code is to solve a problem. A solution to a problem is called an *algorithm* in programming terminology.

Designing the Algorithm

For the problem we're trying to solve, the first step is to identify what the suffix will be for each number in a month. Our function is a formatting function. Here are the results we need to create:

1st, 2nd, 3rd, 4th, 5th, 6th, 7th, 8th, 9th, 10th,

11th, 12th, 13th, 14th, 15th, 16th, 17th, 18th, 19th, 20th,

21st, 22nd, 23rd, 24th, 25th, 26th, 27th, 28th, 29th, 30th

31st

The next step is to look for and identify any patterns that exist. The way the numbers are arranged on this page makes it easy to pick out a few rules or patterns:

Numbers that end in 1 use "st" except for the teens.

Numbers that end in 2 use "nd" except for the teens.

Numbers that end in 3 use "rd" except for the teens.

Numbers in the teens use "th."

Numbers that end in 4, 5, 6, 7, 8, 9, or 0 use "th."

Were you able to identify all these patterns? Did you find others? These patterns represent the business logic we'll code into our custom function. Let's call the function AddSuffixToNumber, and begin the coding.

Coding the Algorithm

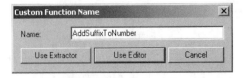

To begin, open the Formula Workshop by clicking its toolbar icon. When the Workshop Tree displays, highlight the Report Custom Functions category in the Workshop Tree and click the New button, as shown in Figure 4.32. We'll build and test this function in the report and send it to the repository after we're sure it works correctly.

FIGURE 4.32

Starting a new custom function

When the Custom Function Name dialog displays, type the name of the new function, as shown in Figure 4.33.

FIGURE 4.33

Naming a custom function

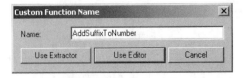

At this point, you have the choice of using the Extractor or going directly to the Formula Editor. Since we are not basing this new custom function on any other function, we'll go directly to the

Formula Editor to code our algorithm by clicking the Use Editor button. The Workshop Tree and the Custom Function Editor display; notice in Figure 4.34 that the new function has been added to the Report Custom Functions category in the Workshop Tree. The function name is highlighted and the typing cursor is positioned in the bottom editing window. The keyword `Function ( )` is provided, and you can begin typing your code.

FIGURE 4.34

A new function in the tree

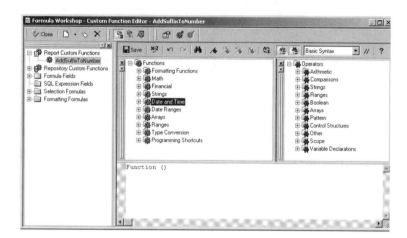

NOTE *The Workshop Tree will display in whatever size and format (docked or floating) that you left it last.*

Let's break the writing of the function down into smaller steps for identification and clarity:

1. Name the function, identify the arguments, and set the return type.

2. Declare all temporary variables and assign data types.

3. Convert the number passed to the function to a string value.

4. Test the length of the string value; if the length is greater than or equal to 2, set the last two characters aside in their own variable; if the length is less than 2, prefix the number with a 0 in the two-character temporary variable.

5. Inspect the last two characters and for each pair, determine whether to suffix it with `st`, `nd`, `rd`, or `th`.

6. Return a string value as the last step of the function.

Figure 4.35 shows the completed code using Basic Syntax, while Figure 4.36 shows the same function written in Crystal Syntax. See if you can identify the built-in functions and operators being used as well as the control structures.

FIGURE 4.35

AddSuffixToNumber function in Basic Syntax

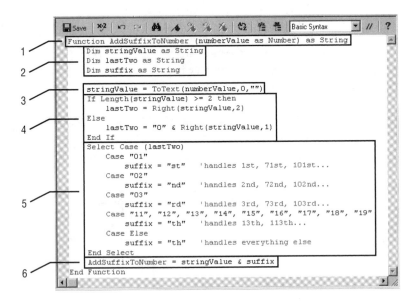

```
Function AddSuffixToNumber (numberValue as Number) as String
    Dim stringValue as String
    Dim lastTwo as String
    Dim suffix as String

    stringValue = ToText(numberValue,0,"")
    If Length(stringValue) >= 2 then
        lastTwo = Right(stringValue,2)
    Else
        lastTwo = "0" & Right(stringValue,1)
    End If
    Select Case (lastTwo)
        Case "01"
            suffix = "st"    'handles 1st, 71st, 101st...
        Case "02"
            suffix = "nd"    'handles 2nd, 72nd, 102nd...
        Case "03"
            suffix = "rd"    'handles 3rd, 73rd, 103rd...
        Case "11", "12", "13", "14", "15", "16", "17", "18", "19"
            suffix = "th"    'handles 13th, 113th...
        Case Else
            suffix = "th"    'handles everything else
    End Select
    AddSuffixToNumber = stringValue & suffix
End Function
```

FIGURE 4.36

AddSuffixToNumber function in Crystal Syntax

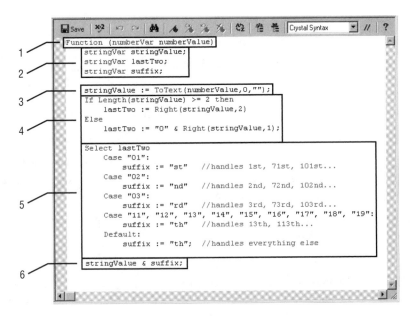

```
Function (numberVar numberValue)
    stringVar stringValue;
    stringVar lastTwo;
    stringVar suffix;

    stringValue := ToText(numberValue,0,"");
    If Length(stringValue) >= 2 then
        lastTwo := Right(stringValue,2)
    Else
        lastTwo := "0" & Right(stringValue,1);

    Select lastTwo
        Case "01":
            suffix := "st"    //handles 1st, 71st, 101st...
        Case "02":
            suffix := "nd"    //handles 2nd, 72nd, 102nd...
        Case "03":
            suffix := "rd"    //handles 3rd, 73rd, 103rd...
        Case "11", "12", "13", "14", "15", "16", "17", "18", "19":
            suffix := "th"    //handles 13th, 113th...
        Default:
            suffix := "th";   //handles everything else

    stringValue & suffix;
```

The following language features were used in this custom function:

Built-in functions:

- ◆ `ToText`: Truncates a number to zero decimals and converts to a text string; this is a very useful function when presenting number data within text strings.

- ◆ `Length`: Returns the number of characters in a text string.

- ◆ `Right`: Returns the rightmost part of the string for the number of spaces specified.

Control structures:

- ◆ `If-Then-Else`

- ◆ `Select`

Operators:

- ◆ `Assignment`

While most built-in functions, control structures, and operators can be used in custom functions, there are a few limitations imposed because of the need to guarantee reusability across a report and, if added to the repository, across multiple reports. When coding custom functions, avoid using the following in the body of the function:

- ◆ Built-in functions in the Evaluation Time, Print State, or Document Properties categories

- ◆ Calls to user function libraries

- ◆ Database fields

- ◆ Formula fields

- ◆ Global variables

- ◆ Recursive function calls (functions that call themselves)

- ◆ Shared variables

- ◆ Summary fields

Setting Custom Function Properties

The Toggle Properties display button at the top of the Formula Workshop is used only when working on a custom function. Use the button to display the Formula Editor and the code for the custom function or toggle it to display and edit the properties for the function. Figure 4.37 shows the properties for the `AddSuffixToNumber` function.

FIGURE 4.37

Custom function
properties

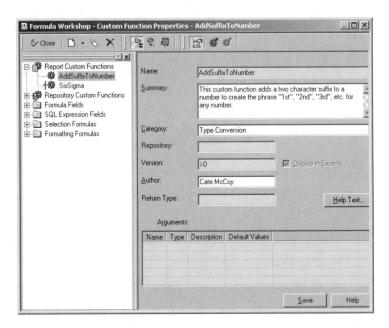

The text typed in the Category area displays in both the repository and the Function Tree, which is shown in Figure 4.38. If you discipline yourself to using a few meaningful categories, this text can help you easily find the functions later on.

FIGURE 4.38

Categorized custom
functions

The Help Text button visible in Figure 4.37 opens a window for free-form typing. Use this area to type helpful hints and how-to steps for using the custom function.

Using the Formula Extractor

You can create a custom function based on any existing formula. The Extractor tool pulls out the executable code and replaces key values with variables and arguments. The arguments are generically named (v1, v2, v3...) and can be directly renamed to more meaningful names. After extracting a custom function, you must save it with a new name before using it in the report. The option to use the Extractor appears when you are creating a new function; it is a button choice in the dialog shown previously in Figure 4.33.

Calling a Custom Function

Calling a custom function is identical to calling a built-in function: Use the function name and provide values for the arguments to the function as well as a place to use the value returned from the function. One of the easiest ways to do this is to create a formula field, double-click the function name in the Custom Functions category to add it to the code editing window, and type a valid value for the argument. In Figure 4.39, a call is being made to the `AddSuffixToNumber` custom function through the formula field `callAddSuffixToNumber`, passing in the integer value 13; the expected result of the function is the string 13th. To see this value in a report, drag and drop the formula field `callAddSuffixToNumber` onto your report and then preview it.

FIGURE 4.39

Calling a custom function

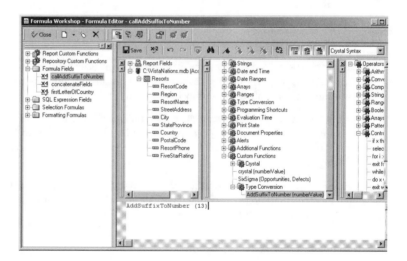

So, to summarize, calling any function requires the following steps:

1. Type the name of the function.

2. Provide valid arguments to the function.

3. Use the return value.

Storing a Custom Function in the Repository

Adding a report custom function to the repository is an easy matter of clicking an icon in the Formula Workshop. With the function displayed in the Formula Workshop, click the Add To Repository toolbar icon, or right-click the formula name in the Workshop Tree and choose Add To Repository from the submenu that appears.

USING CRYSTAL'S CUSTOM FUNCTIONS

The Crystal Decisions team took a look at the most popular User Function Libraries (UFLs) in use for Crystal Reports 8.5 earlier and came up with four groups of custom functions that ship with the Crystal Repository. These functions may replace some of the UFLs in use in your organization. The groups are date functions, financial functions, formatting functions, geographic functions, and math functions. Each of the functions is prefixed with the characters cd to identify them as Crystal Decisions functions. You can use these functions as a starting point and customize their code to your needs. To customize a function in the repository, you must first disconnect it from the repository and then add it back to the repository after making your changes. Refer to Chapter 5 for more information on the repository.

Refer to Appendix D, "Crystal Reports Custom Functions," for a complete list and description of custom functions.

USER FUNCTION LIBRARIES

Custom functions in Crystal Reports may replace many user-defined function libraries in use in prior versions of Crystal Reports. UFLs are code routines typically written in languages such as C, C++, and Visual Basic and compiled into dynamic link libraries (DLLs).

Crystal Reports ships with several UFLs that you'll find listed under the Additional Functions category of the Function Tree. When deploying a report that uses UFLs, you need to distribute the DLL file that represents the UFL in addition to the RPT file for the report. The UFL DLL files can be found in the system folder `C:\Program Files\Common Files\Crystal Decisions\2.0\bin`.

Because UFLs require the distribution of a DLL in addition to the RPT that calls the function, custom functions and the Crystal Repository might provide an easier reusability path and distribution path as they are contained within an RPT file.

Crystal Built-in Functions

In building our custom function, we used Crystal Build in function. Please refer back to Figure 4.34 and notice the Functions tree. Crystal Reports provides an enormous number of built-in functions to help make writing formulas easier. The Function Tree splits the functions into categories based on data type and usage type. If you need to do mathematical calculation, refer to the math branch for available functions. If you need to work with dates or strings (characters), refer to the appropriate function branch. As with any long list of function you only need to know about twenty percent of the functions and this will cover eighty percent of your work—the rest you can learn about as the need arises. All the functions are called using the same syntax discussed in this chapter, so all you need to do is familiarize yourself with the groups and functions available in the groups to be able to build custom business logic for your reports.

Refer to Appendix E, "Crystal Reports Built-in Functions," for a complete list and description of the built-in functions.

NOTE *Refer to the help file for the calling syntax and return type associated with built-in functions.*

Crystal Built-in Constants

The value of a constant never changes, so Crystal takes advantage of this fact to define several formatting and calculation values for you. You can use these constants in code or in drop-down boxes to make choices in the various Expert dialogs provided.

◆ Boolean Conditions: `on any change`, `on change to yes`, `on change to no`, `on every no`, `on next is yes`, `on next is no`

◆ Colors: Color constants appear in the Function Tree when a formatting formula is being coded; this is shown in Figure 4.40. To use any of the colors in code directly, preface the color name with a `cr`, for example, `crRed`.

FIGURE 4.40

Color constants for formatting

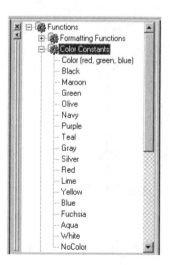

◆ Date Conditions: `for each day`, `for each week`, `for each two weeks`, `for each half month`, `for each month`, `for each quarter`, `for each half year`, `for each year`

◆ First Day of Week: `UseSystem`, `Sunday`, `Monday`, `Tuesday`, `Wednesday`, `Thursday`, `Friday`, `Saturday`

◆ First Week of Year: `UseSystem`, `FirstJan1`, `FirstFourDays`, `FirstFullWeek`

◆ Fonts: `crRegular, crBold, crItalic, crBoldItalic`

◆ Time Conditions: `for each second, for each minute, for each hour, for AM/PM`

SQL Expression Fields

Structured Query Language has its own set of functions and operators. You cannot pass Crystal Syntax or Basic Syntax functions to a database for processing. Any record selection formulas that reference Crystal Syntax or Basic Syntax formulas will be processed in Crystal and not in the database. Since a database is tuned for performance for large records sets, it is more advantageous to process data at the database level whenever possible. SQL expressions are one of the mechanisms you can use to pass processing off to the database. When a statement is coded completely using SQL, it can be passed directly to the database for processing and the resulting data set returned to Crystal Reports. Figure 4.41 shows the Function Tree and Operator Tree for SQL expressions.

FIGURE 4.41

The Function Tree and Operator Tree for SQL expressions

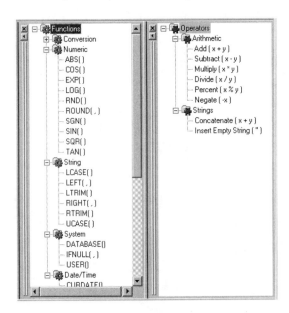

NOTE   *The Formula Expert cannot be used to create SQL expression fields.*

Troubleshooting Formulas

It can definitely be a challenge to write good code, and in fact, you'll never get it right the first time. Programmers call the process of finding the errors in their code *debugging*, a phrase attributed to Grace Hopper, a twentieth-century military computer programmer. There are several things you can do to help yourself write good code and help find errors when they do occur.

Call Stack

The Formula Workshop contains a feature known as the *call stack*. If there is a problem in your code, the call stack will automatically appear with a drill-down path to show where the error occurred. It returns interim values as part of a call stack, with the line of code on the bottom of the stack being the line that actually encountered the error.

Performance Issues

Crystal Reports provides built-in information on how your report is performing. From the menu, select Report ➤ Performance Information to open the dialog shown in Figure 4.42. Use this dialog to choose between report definition information, saved data specifications, processing time information, and grouping information. You also have the option to save the data to a file, which allows you to return to it at any point.

FIGURE 4.42

Finding performance information

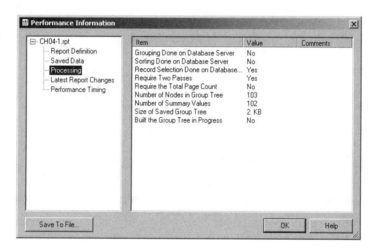

Writing Good Code

The following are a few tips and techniques that will improve the quality of your code and help you become an efficient programmer:

♦ Space and format your code well; the easier it is to read, the easier it is to troubleshoot (debug).

♦ Code a little, test a little, debug a little, then repeat; it is much easier to debug a little bit of isolated code than a huge set of code statements that might contain multiple errors.

♦ Break large coding tasks down into smaller ones, using a function for each task. This will help organize your work and keep you from creating overly complex single functions.

♦ Create a special section at the top of your report to use to test values as you're working on new formulas.

♦ Comment your code—you want to be able to read it in a few days!

◆ If the code isn't working, take a break from the computer and write the steps down in English to try to make sense of what you're doing; often it's our logic that is at fault, not the code.

◆ Finally, have fun with what you're doing! Writing code is a creative process; sometimes it's a painful process, but ultimately, you'll be proud of your work.

Summary

Programming formulas in your reports lets you create calculated results that can add meaning to a report beyond the data values retrieved from a data source. The two flavors of formula programming built into Crystal Reports are Basic Syntax and Crystal Syntax. Both languages provide access to a wide variety of built-in functions plus the ability to create custom functions. A formula consists of variables, constants, operators, and keywords. In addition to creating formula fields and searching for information in a previewed report, which were covered in this chapter, you can code formulas in additional places in Crystal Reports, including the following:

◆ Record selection formulas (Chapter 7, "Selectively Refining a Report Using Data Values")

◆ Group selection formulas (Chapter 6, "Summarizing Information")

◆ Formatting sections and other report elements based on conditions (Chapter 8, "Customizing Sections")

◆ Running total fields (Chapter 6)

◆ Creating conditional report alert messages (Chapter 7)

Use the information from this chapter together with the rest of Part 1, "Report Writing Fundamentals," to put formulas to work and add business logic to a report.

Chapter 5

Working with the Crystal Repository

THE CRYSTAL REPOSITORY IS a major new feature of Crystal Reports 9. It adds to the product the ability to extract report elements for reuse in other reports. The potential for reusable code in the Crystal environment increases further when the repository is combined with another new Crystal Reports 9 feature, custom functions, introduced in Chapter 4, "Adding Business Logic with the Formula Workshop." Imagine being able to reuse a complex formula in multiple reports, and if you change the formula, propagate the change automatically to all reports that use the formula. This is exactly what the repository can do.

Featured in this chapter:

◆ Using the Repository Explorer

◆ Managing repository objects

◆ Working with custom functions in the repository

◆ Deploying reports that use the repository

◆ Understanding the structure of the repository

◆ Creating and linking to a repository

Using the Crystal Repository

The repository in Crystal is a database in which certain report objects can be stored independently of their RPT files. Figure 5.1 depicts the concept of sharing a report object by extracting it from one report and adding it to different report. As a centralized resource, it can be used by any report you write.

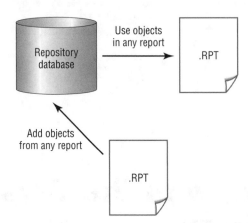

FIGURE 5.1

Sharing report objects

In Crystal Reports 9, the repository is implemented as a Microsoft Access 2000 database. You can use this database exactly as it is installed (the default behavior), or you can create your own repository database. Crystal Reports manages direct interactions with the database through a drag-and-drop interface in the Formula Workshop and several action buttons on Crystal dialog windows. The basic idea of the repository is twofold:

- Add objects to the repository from a report.

- Add repository objects to a report from the repository.

NOTE *You do not need to have Microsoft Access installed on your machine to use the Crystal Repository; all that is required is the presence of the repository database in a location known to Crystal Reports and an ODBC connection to it. The information for the default sample database is configured for you when Crystal Reports is installed.*

Opening the Repository

The Crystal Repository can be opened by choosing View ➤ Repository Explorer from the menu or by clicking the toolbar icon.

The repository can store and share the following types of report objects:

- Images (bitmaps)

- Text objects

- Commands (SQL commands)

- Custom functions

Images, text objects, and commands can be accessed through the Repository Explorer shown in Figure 5.2. Custom functions are accessed through the Formula Workshop, which can be opened with the Formula Workshop toolbar icon.

FIGURE 5.2

The Repository
Explorer

The Repository Explorer can be docked into position along the edge or can be dragged and dropped as a free-floating window. The images, text objects, and commands visible in Figure 5.2 are supplied with Crystal Reports. You can add objects to this list as well as delete the ones that are not useful to you.

There are two parts to the repository for viewing purposes. Notice in Figure 5.2 that no custom functions are visible in the repository. To see custom functions stored in the repository, you need to access the repository using the Formula Workshop and view the formula portion of the repository through the Workshop Tree. Figure 5.3 shows the Workshop Tree containing a custom function called SixSigma, which exists in the repository.

FIGURE 5.3

The Workshop Tree

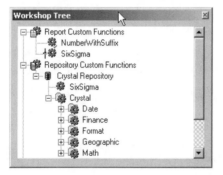

The SixSigma custom function is currently in use by the open report; the vertical line connector symbol to the left of the function name denotes this.

Managing Repository Objects

The Images, Text Objects, and Commands folders that display by default in the repository are created automatically for you. You can add folders of your own to sort and manage the objects for your projects. To add a folder, select the name of the repository in the Repository Explorer; when the menu displays, choose New Folder and give the folder a name. Figure 5.4 shows the default set of folders, a custom folder named VistaNations as well as subfolders, and the menu used to create new folders. Folders can be nested in a hierarchy, one beneath the other, by selecting a folder and right-clicking to display the New Folder menu from the folder level.

FIGURE 5.4

The folders in the repository

You can also delete the default folders by right-clicking the folder and choosing the Delete option from the menu. Deleting a folder from the repository deletes the objects contained in the folder; in other words, the objects are deleted from the repository.

WARNING *Once an object is deleted from the Repository, there is no undo command to reverse the deletion. You can, however, re-create the object using the same name.*

ADDING OBJECTS TO THE REPOSITORY

Objects are added to the repository in one of three ways depending on the object type. Use one of the following areas in Crystal Reports to add an object:

◆ The report's Design or Preview window

◆ The Formula Workshop

◆ The Database Expert

NOTE *The name you give an object should be meaningful enough to give an idea of the purpose of the object.*

You can drag text objects and bitmap images directly from their position in a report into a folder in the Repository Explorer window. After you drop the object into a folder, the Object Information dialog shown in Figure 5.5 displays. You can give the object a meaningful name, provide the author's name, and type a description of the object. Selecting the object in the report and right-clicking it also displays a menu from which you can choose Add To Repository.

FIGURE 5.5

Adding text and bitmap objects

Object Information
Please provide information to be associated with this object
Name:
Information Disclaimer Text
Author:
Cate McCoy
Description:
Company disclaimer regarding the accuracy of the information presented.
OK   Cancel

Custom functions are added to the repository from the Formula Workshop. Select the function in the Workshop Tree, right-click it to display the submenu, and choose the Add To Repository option. You can also click the Add To Repository toolbar icon in the Formula Workshop after selecting the custom function.

Once a custom function is added to the repository, it is said to be "connected" to the repository; the vertical bar icon to the left of the function denotes that it is connected. The Add Customs Functions To Repository dialog displays at this point, as shown in Figure 5.6.

FIGURE 5.6

Adding custom functions

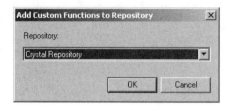

Adding SQL commands to the repository begins at the point when you select a data source using the Database Expert. When you choose a data source, the Add Command icon is an available option.

When you choose Add Command as a data source, the dialog shown in Figure 5.7 displays so that you can code a SQL command directly. To add the SQL command to the repository, enable the Add To Repository check box at the bottom left of the dialog.

FIGURE 5.7

Adding a SQL command to the repository

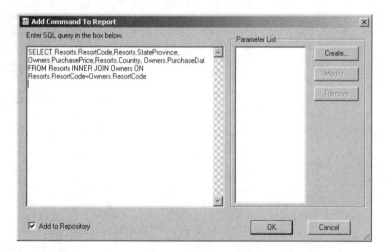

The Add Item dialog, shown in Figure 5.8, displays; type a name for the object, set the name of the author, type a description, and choose a folder location in the repository to place the object. The default description is the SQL command itself.

When you use a SQL command as a data source, it displays in the Database Expert with a "connected" icon to the left of its name. This is shown in Figure 5.9.

FIGURE 5.8

Describing a SQL
command object

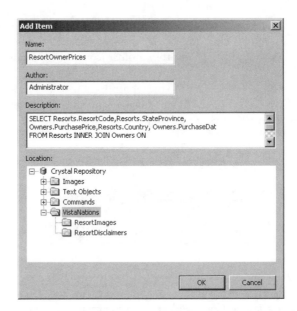

FIGURE 5.9

A SQL command as
a data source

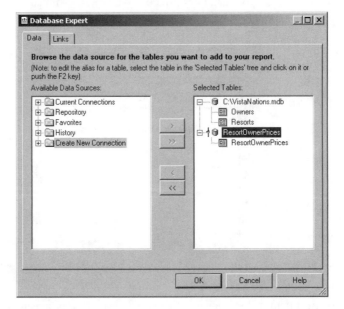

MODIFYING REPOSITORY OBJECTS

Modifying an object that is stored in the repository requires a few steps to accomplish the complete task. Objects in the repository are stored in Read-only mode; they cannot be changed directly in the repository. In addition, once an object has been added to a report, it is connected to the repository and therefore cannot be changed. To modify a repository object and update it in the repository, do the following:

1. Drag the object from the repository into the report.

2. Right-click the object and choose Disconnect From Repository.

3. Modify the object.

4. Right-click the object and choose Add To Repository.

Whenever you add an object to the repository, a dialog will appear asking you to give it a name. If you save it back into the repository using the same name it had previously, a confirmation dialog will appear to verify that you want to complete the task.

After a repository object is modified, a global report setting controls whether the change will be made available to the reports that use the object. All reports that use the repository object and are connected to it can potentially be affected by the changes you make, including changes to the object's name and its contents. Report objects not connected to the repository are not affected. You can control whether repository changes are propagated to connected reports in two ways:

♦ Use a global report setting to force updates to all report using it.

♦ When the report is opened, choose to update the report.

To set a global option that will be in effect for all reports created that contain repository objects, choose File ➢ Options, go to the Reporting tab, and enable the Update Connected Repository Objects When Loading Reports option shown in Figure 5.10.

FIGURE 5.10

Setting a global option to update connected repository objects

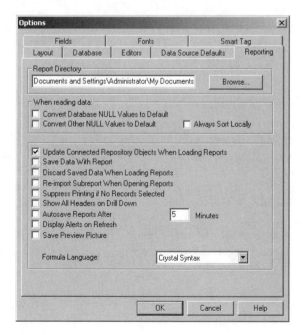

Alternatively, you can make the decision to refresh from the repository when opening an individual report. When you open a report using the File ➢ Open method, the dialog in Figure 5.11 displays. Notice the Update Repository Objects check box at the bottom of the dialog. This option is automatically enabled when the global report option is set and automatically disabled when it is not set. Use this option to override the global setting.

FIGURE 5.11

Updating connected
repository objects
when a report is
opened

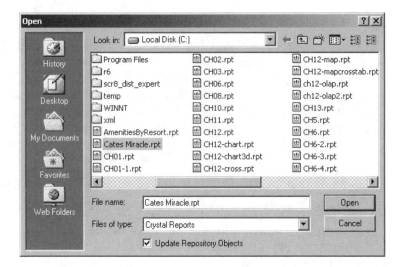

NOTE   *The option to update repository objects is not available from the Crystal Reports welcome dialog (Welcome To Crystal Reports), which is often set to display automatically when Crystal Reports opens. You can choose to cancel out of this dialog and use the File ➢ Open menu option.*

DELETING REPOSITORY OBJECTS

To delete an object from the repository, select the object in either the Repository Explorer (for images, text objects, and SQL commands) or the Workshop Tree (for custom functions), right-click the object, and choose the Delete option from the menu. You can also use the Delete key on the keyboard to delete a selected item.

Deleting an object from the repository does not affect the reports that previously used the object. This is true for both linked and unlinked repository objects. If an object is linked from a report to the repository and then deleted from the repository, the link is broken and a copy of the object remains in the report in editable mode. Likewise, if a linked repository object is deleted from the report, the link is broken, the report object is deleted, and the repository object remains intact.

Building a Report Using Repository Objects

Objects stored in the repository are globally available to all report designers using the repository. When an object is added to a report, the original object remains in the repository; a copy of the object is placed in the report. A link exists between the object in the report and its original in the repository. Linked objects have the advantage of being able to be automatically updated when you make a change to the object in the repository. When the object is in the report and linked or connected to the repository, however, the object is read-only and cannot be modified. Refer to the earlier section, "Modifying Repository Objects," to learn how to update repository objects.

ADDING A REPOSITORY OBJECT TO A REPORT

A repository object can be added to a report in several ways depending on the object's type. Text objects and bitmap image objects can be added directly to a report from the Repository Explorer. Select the object and drag and drop it into position on the report.

Custom functions stored in the repository are added to a report from the Workshop Tree of the Formula Workshop. Expand the Repository Custom Functions Tree, select the custom function you want to use, and then click the Add To Report toolbar icon, as shown in Figure 5.12, or right-click and choose Add To Report from the menu.

FIGURE 5.12

Adding a repository
custom function to
a report

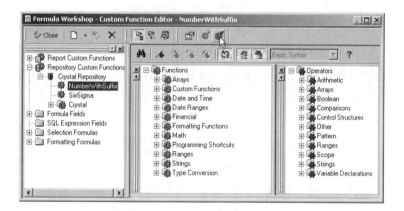

The repository contains a set of prebuilt custom functions that may replace many of the User Function Libraries (UFL) in use in earlier versions of Crystal Reports applications. These custom functions have been coded for you and can be called from any report. They also make great examples to demonstrate how to code your own custom functions! You can also disconnect the function from the repository, modify it for your own purposes, and place it back in the repository. Table 5.1 lists the built-in custom functions in the repository and the folder category where they are located. The names of the functions are fairly descriptive and give you an idea of what each function does.

TABLE 5.1: PREBUILT REPOSITORY CUSTOM FUNCTIONS

CATEGORY	FUNCTION NAME
Date	cdDateAddSkipHolidays
Date	cdDateAddSkipWeekends
Date	cdDateDiffSkipHolidays
Date	cdDateDiffSkipWeekends
Date	cdEasterDate
Date	cdFirstDayOfMonth
Date	cdFirstDayOfQuarter
Date	cdLastDayOfMonth
Date	cdLastDayOfQuarter
Date	cdSpecialDateRange
Date	cdStatutoryHolidays
Finance	cdConvertUSToCanadian
Format	cdFormatCurrencyUsingScaling
Format	cdFormatDateRange
Format	cdFormatDateRangeArray
Format	cdFormatNumberRange
Format	cdFormatNumberRangeArray
Format	cdFormatNumberUsingScaling
Format	cdFormatStringRange
Format	cdFormatStringRangeArray
Format	cdFormatTimeInterval
Geographic	cdExpandRegionAbbreviation
Geographic	cdExpandRegionAbbreviationCanada
Geographic	cdExpandRegionAbbreviationUSA
Math	cdIncreaseCurrencyByAPercentage
Math	cdIncreaseNumberByAPercentage
Math	cdPercentageDifference

SQL commands are added to a report by using the Database Expert to use a SQL command as a data source for a report; see the earlier discussion on this topic in the "Adding Objects to the Repository" section.

DISCONNECTING A REPOSITORY OBJECT FROM A REPORT

Report objects that are linked to the repository cannot be edited. To edit them, they must first be disconnected from the repository. To do this, select the object in the report and right-click it. When the submenu displays, choose the Disconnect From Repository option. At this point, the disconnected report object can be edited.

DEPLOYING REPORTS

An object in a report that has been added from the repository is a copy of the original object. As a copy, it is stored in the RPT file directly. The repository database is not needed when the report is opened for display. However, if the repository is available and the object is connected to the repository, it is available to be updated by the repository if any changes have been made to it since the time it was added to the report.

The Structure of the Repository

When Crystal Reports 9 is installed, a sample Microsoft Access database named `Repository.mdb` is installed in a directory accessible to all program files. This database is ready to go and does not need anything done to it before being used. The directory path for Crystal Reports is shown in Figure 5.13, while the directory path for the repository is shown in Figure 5.14.

TIP   If you plan on customizing the Repository database, make a copy of the .mdb file so that you always have an original version to go back to without needing to re-install Crystal Reports.

FIGURE 5.13

Crystal Reports installation directory

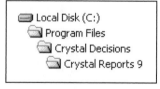

FIGURE 5.14

Repository installation directory

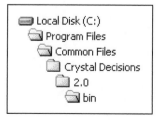

Repository Database Tables

Although it is not necessary to ever open the repository through Microsoft Access, if you plan to replace the sample repository with your own repository database, you'll need to be familiar with its structure.

If you open and view the Crystal Repository through Microsoft Access, you will see that it contains six tables: or_objectdetails_30, or_objectdetails_31, or_objectdetails_32, or_objectdetails_33, or_objects, and or_type_schema. The tables, the column names, and the column attributes are shown in Figure 5.15, Figure 5.16, Figure 5.17, Figure 5.18, Figure 5.19, and Figure 5.20. The first four table names are strikingly similar; they store object repository detail information for each of the four types of objects allowed in the repository.

FIGURE 5.15

or_objectdetails_30 table

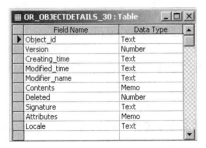

FIGURE 5.16

or_objectdetails_31 table

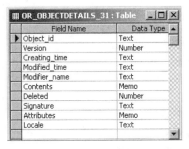

FIGURE 5.17

or_objectdetails_32 table

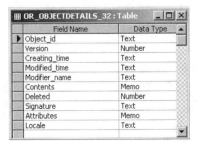

OR_OBJECTDETAILS_33 : Table

Field Name	Data Type
Object_id	Text
Version	Number
Creating_time	Text
Modified_time	Text
Modifier_name	Text
Contents	Memo
Deleted	Number
Signature	Text
Attributes	Memo
Locale	Text

FIGURE 5.18
or_objectdetails_33 table

OR_OBJECTS : Table

Field Name	Data Type
Object_id	Text
Object_name	Text
Parent_id	Text
Owner_id	Number
Type	Number

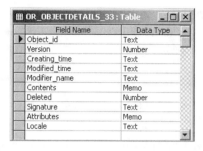

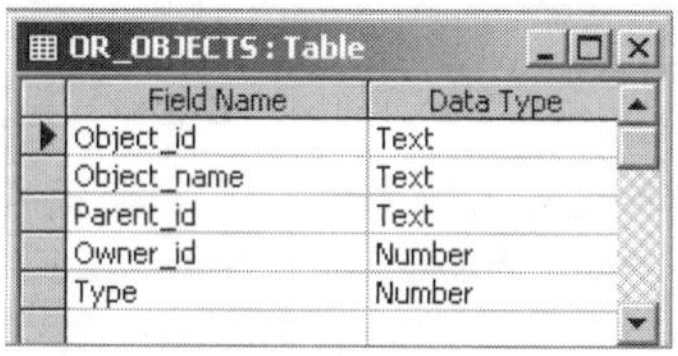

FIGURE 5.19
or_objects table

OR_TYPE_SCHEMA : Table

Field Name	Data Type
Type	Number
Type_name	Text
Table_name	Text
Meta_info	Text

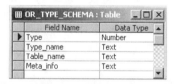

FIGURE 5.20
or_type_schema table

When creating a new database to be used as the repository, use an identical table-naming convention and design as the sample repository database. The name of the actual database is less important, as it will be associated with an ODBC data source name that is actually used by Crystal. However, avoid the use of the seven following special reserved characters when naming the database or when naming objects being added to the repository through Crystal: ", -, #, {, }, ;, and /.

SECURITY PERMISSIONS

Crystal Reports does not provide security for the repository database. This should not be a surprise; Crystal doesn't supply the security for any of the databases it connects to during the reporting process. Nor should it have to. Security is one of the more powerful features provided by a database management system, so it makes sense to rely on the database to enforce data security.

Database-level security generally involves granting privileges to users or groups to specific tables in a database or to a database as a whole. In order for the user to be able to add, delete, or modify objects in the repository, the permissions on the database have to be set appropriately. As an example, if a report designer does not have Delete privileges on a repository table, the report designer will not be allowed to delete objects from the repository.

The Microsoft Access Repository database shipped with Crystal Reports does not have any initial security applied to it. If you have Microsoft Access, you can add security to the default Repository.mdb; however, all reports that reference the linked repository would then require a user id and password in order to be refreshed.

Creating and Linking a Repository

The Microsoft Access Repository database installed during the Crystal Reports installation process is accessible to and used by Crystal automatically. You can, however, store the database in a different location or create a completely different database using another type of database software. Here are the steps required to integrate a new repository with Crystal Reports:

1. Create a blank database using the table names and design covered earlier in the section "Repository Database Tables."

2. Configure an ODBC System data source name (DSN) connection to the new database. System data sources are accessible to all users on a computer while user data sources are available only to the user who created the data source.

3. Update the ODBC data source name in the ORMAP.INI file.

By default, the repository database is installed on the local machine with Crystal Reports. You may want to move the repository to a shared network drive so that multiple report designers can access it simultaneously in a shared way. To change the location of the repository, use the ODBC Manager to update the data source's location information. Figure 5.21 shows the ODBC Microsoft Access Setup dialog that is used to specify the data source and give it a data source name. The exact steps to access the ODBC data source setup area vary by operating system; for Windows 2000, you can use Start ➤ Control Panel ➤ Administrative ➤ Data Sources (ODBC), switch to the System DSN tab, and either add or configure the data source from this point.

FIGURE 5.21

ODBC data source setup

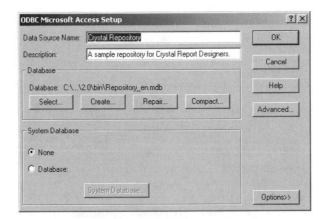

The data source name from the ODBC setup is used in the object repository initialization file, ORMAP.INI. This file is located in the same directory as the repository (see Figure 5.14). INI files are ASCII text files that can be modified with any word processing tool. Figure 5.22 shows the ORMAP.INI file opened using Notepad. The last line of the file is the one that needs to be updated if you change the ODBC data source. On the left of the equal sign, the phrase Crystal Repository needs to be left as is. On the right side of the equal sign, the phrase Crystal Repository represents the sample Microsoft Access database's data source name. To update the location or name of the repository, replace the text on the right side of the equal sign with the ODBC data source name used in the ODBC Microsoft Access Setup dialog (see Figure 5.21).

FIGURE 5.22

ORMAP.INI

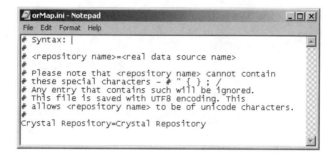

NOTE *There can be only one repository associated with the phrase Crystal Repository; creating a different database replaces the one that was installed with Crystal Reports.*

Summary

The repository is a major new feature in Crystal Reports 9. It adds to the product something report developers have had on their wish list for a long time: a central place to store reusable report objects. Crystal Reports ships with a default sample Microsoft Access database to use as the repository; this is ready to use directly after installing Crystal Reports. You can add, delete, and modify objects in the repository. When an object is modified, all reports that use the object will automatically have the opportunity to inherit the modification the next time the report is opened. The repository can be moved from its default location or replaced with a different type of ODBC database, allowing maximum flexibility to an organization.

Chapter 6

Summarizing Information

Rows AND ROWS OF raw data records from a data source do not make for a very interesting or informative report. To impart information, a report takes the original stored data and arranges it in ways that tell a story about the business. The most popular techniques of processing raw data for report purposes involve sorting the data, then grouping it, and finally deriving summary information for the groups based on the originally stored data values. Along the way, the data is transformed into information.

In Chapter 1, "Building Your First Report," and Chapter 2, "Modifying a Report," the concepts of sorting, grouping, and summarizing were introduced through the use of the Standard Report Creation Wizard and through simple modifications to the report created by the wizard. In this chapter, we'll fully explore Crystal's sophisticated sorting, grouping, and summarizing capabilities. In addition, we'll look at the subreport design element and use it to segment and manage data within a report.

Featured in this chapter:

- ◆ Creating groups with the Group Expert

- ◆ Using the Group Sort Expert

- ◆ Applying special fields to grouped data

- ◆ Selecting the top or bottom records only

- ◆ Adding subtotals and grand totals to your report

- ◆ Using running totals to move beyond grand totals and subtotals

- ◆ Creating subreports

- ◆ Linking subreports to main reports

- ◆ Sharing data values between subreports and main reports

Grouping Data

Grouping data means to organize it around a key value found in the data itself, for instance, grouping resorts by the country they are in or by the amenities they include. Groups do not exist as stored entities in a database, but instead Crystal or the database itself can perform the processing needed to associate a data record with a group for a more organized look at the data. By its very nature, grouped data is also data sorted either in ascending order (lowest to highest), descending order (highest to lowest), specified order (custom grouping), or original order (database storage order).

NOTE   *For more information on the four types of sort order, refer to the "Managing Groups" section in Chapter 2.*

As an example in this chapter, we're going to work with a VistaNations report that shows the resort code, state or province, country, purchase price paid by owners for a unit in the resort, and the purchase date. In the VistaNations database, a resort code may be listed more than once if more than one resort unit has been sold. Figure 6.1 shows the beginning of this report, which is currently sorted alphabetically on resort code.

FIGURE 6.1

A sorted report

Creating Groups

Once a report is created in Design mode, there are several ways to add groups. Use any of the following methods:

- ◆ Choose Insert ➢ Group from the menu.

- ◆ Click the Insert Group icon on the toolbar.

- ◆ Choose Report ➢ Group Expert from the menu.

- ◆ Click the Group Expert icon on the toolbar.

The Group Expert and the Insert ➢ Group approaches start out with slight differences but ultimately end up at the same dialog screen. With the Group Expert, you pick a field to group on using a list of available fields, as shown in Figure 6.2. This is the same dialog used to create groups using the Standard Report Creation Wizard.

After you pick a field to group on, the Options button becomes available. When you click the Options button, the dialog used with the Insert ➢ Group command or toolbar icon opens with one minor difference: With the Group Expert, the title bar says "Change Group Options" while with the Insert Group command, the title bar says "Insert Group." So here you are, at the same place anyway! Figure 6.3 shows the Insert Group dialog.

FIGURE 6.2

Group Expert

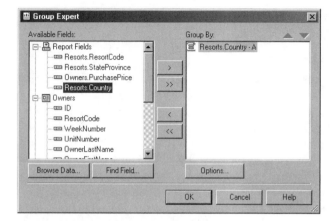

FIGURE 6.3

Inserting a group

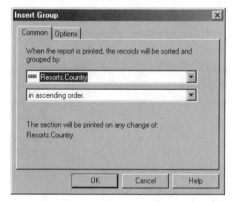

The first drop-down box lets you choose or change the field on which the group will be based. If you selected a field in Design mode first and then used the menu or toolbar icon to insert a group, the field you chose is automatically placed in the first drop-down box. You can group on a field that exists in the report, a field from any of the tables available to the report, or a formula field that was previously created.

The sort order is specified in the second drop-down box, and you can choose from ascending, descending, specified, or original order.

Ascending Order   Data is sorted lowest to highest; alphabet characters sort from A to Z, and numbers sort from 0 to 10 and higher.

Descending Order   Data is sorted highest to lowest; alphabet characters sort from Z to A, and numbers sort from 10 or higher to 0.

Specified Order   Data is sorted based on a customized criterion that does not exist in the raw data. This is also known as creating a custom group.

NOTE   *For a complete discussion of specified order, refer to Chapter 2.*

Original Order   Data records are presented in the order in which they were added to the database.

GROUPING ON A FIELD

The easiest way to create a group is to use a field in the report. Just select the field, insert the group, choose a sort order, and you're done! You can group on the field only once directly; however, by using a formula you can get creative if you need to group on the same field additional times. If you group on a field, you may want to delete the field from the Details section since the value from the field will now be a part of the group name.

The group name shown in a report defaults to the value of the field, and since the value of the field can change for each record, the name of the group is a variable and will change. For instance, if we group on Resorts.Country, the group name shown in the report will be the name of each country and a set of resorts belonging in that country will appear in the group. The group name will change from Andorra to Antilles to Argentina, etc. Crystal refers to this as a *live header* since the value changes according to the content of the data. The Options tab of the Insert Group dialog, shown in Figure 6.4, lets you control this default behavior by allowing you to choose another field as a group name or use a formula to hard-code a value for a group name or conditionally set a name with a formula.

FIGURE 6.4

Setting group options

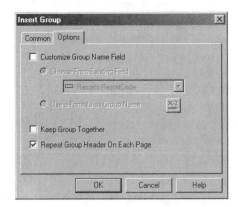

By default, the Group Header (which contains the group name) will not repeat on each new page if the group spans more than one page. You can override this default by enabling the Repeat Group Header On Each Page option. Since the Group Header is its own section, you can add and delete text, fields, images, etc., in it as you would with other sections. If the variable group name is not what you want, you can use a simple text object to create a group name that doesn't change from record to record.

In addition, you can enable the Keep Group Together option if the data spans more than one page; this option forces a new page before starting a new group if the data in the group will take up more than one page. Figure 6.5 shows the result of the grouping based on the Resorts.Country field. Since grouping was done on a field in the Details section, that field has been manually deleted from the Details section to save screen real estate and clean up the report a bit.

FIGURE 6.5

A report grouped
on a field

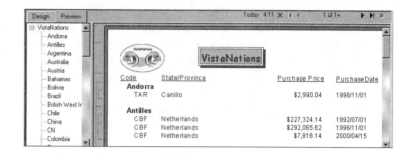

GROUPING ON A FORMULA

A formula returns a value that can be used in a report. One of the purposes for the value is to group on it. Earlier we mentioned that you can be creative with formulas in order to group on a single field more than one time. To do this, just create a formula that returns the value of the field. For instance, if you already have a group created on the Country field, you can create a second group on the Country field by creating a formula with the following code:

```
WhileReadingRecords;
{Resorts.Country}
```

This formula simply returns the value of a field for each record in the database as it is being read from the database. More complex formulas will process the value in some way before returning the value. In our example report, we have a formula named @FirstLetterOfCountry that processes the Country field using the following code:

```
{Resorts.Country}[1]
```

This single line of code returns the first letter of the value stored in the Country field by using the array subscript [1] (an array subscript of [2] would return the second letter in the field, [3] the third, and so on). You can insert a group based on this field, as shown in Figure 6.6.

FIGURE 6.6

Choosing a formula
for a group

Crystal automatically adds new groups below the existing groups; however, you can rearrange their order. Use a drag-and-drop technique in the Design tab to drag one group above or below the other by clicking its gray area section name.

Groups are also automatically left-aligned with the left margin. This is fine when there is only one group; with more than one group it is more aesthetically pleasing to indent groups slightly from one another to create a visual hierarchy. Since Crystal does not do this for you, you need to do it manually by selecting the group name and moving it to the right using the arrow keys on your keyboard one or two clicks; you can also use your mouse for the same task.. You may have to indent the field in the Details section as well. Figure 6.7 shows two groups in a nesting structure that have been manually indented. A Group Header and a Group Footer have been added for each group; in this depiction, the sections are showing short names instead of the complete section name.

FIGURE 6.7

Manually indenting groups

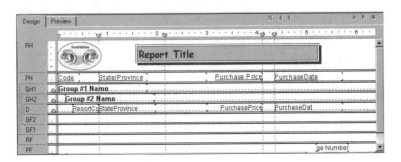

Figure 6.8 shows the result in Preview mode. Notice that the group tree on the left clearly shows the hierarchy of data and allows you to navigate to a specific group very easily.

FIGURE 6.8

A report grouped on a formula

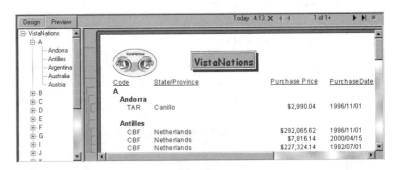

WARNING   Although formulas provide endless grouping possibilities, because the formulas are entirely evaluated and processed within Crystal, the performance aspect of your report may suffer. Crystal must first retrieve all the records from the database and then internally run the formula to group the data; this can be an intensive processing operation. As an alternative for better performance, consider using a stored procedure, SQL functions, or a SQL Command in the database to return data already grouped if the performance of your report suffers when Crystal does the formula grouping. The rule of thumb is to use the capabilities of the database whenever possible for complex processing.

GROUPING AND DATA TYPES

Since a group is created based on a field or a formula, the underlying field or formula has a data type that will affect the behavior and attributes of the group. The grouping dialog will automatically detect what type of data is in the field or being returned by the formula that you are using for grouping.

Text Data   In prior releases of Crystal Reports, you could not sort or group on text fields larger than 255 characters. This restriction has been lifted in the newest release of Crystal Reports. Large text fields can now be used for grouping and in formulas.

Number Data   Grouping directly on number fields (like AnnualSalary or AnnualSales) can be tricky because the data records may each contain unique, nongroupable values. Consider using a specified grouping to create a custom group that can help you group on a range or set of numbers instead of a specific number value.

Date or Date/Time Fields   When you group on a date, time, or date/time field, Crystal presents additional grouping options specific to this type of data. Figure 6.9 shows the additional drop-down box provided for date data. The additional date options allow you to group the records in the report into meaningful buckets of dates.

FIGURE 6.9

Grouping on a
date field

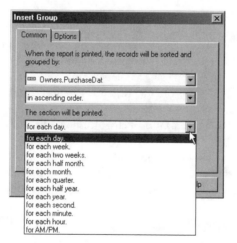

MODIFYING A GROUP

An existing group can be modified, moved, or deleted. You modify a group in Design mode by right-clicking the group section name (gray part of screen) to display the context menu. From the menu, choose the Change Group option. This will open the same dialog shown in Figure 6.3, except that instead of inserting a new group you are modifying an existing group, so the title bar changes to Change Group Options. A group can be moved up or down in the list of sections in Design mode. Figure 6.10 shows the Group Header 2 and Group Footer 2 sections about to be dragged before Group Header 1. This will reorder the groups; however, if you manually indented the groups (as was done in this report), you'll need to reindent manually after the groups are moved to their new positions.

FIGURE 6.10

Moving or
reordering a group

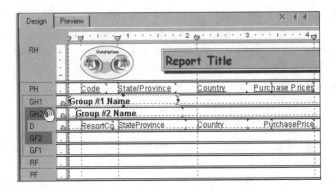

FIGURE 6.10

Moving or
reordering a group

To delete a group, right-click the group's section name and select the Delete Group option from the context menu. Again, any manual indenting that you added to the report will stay as it was, so you may want to reindent after deleting a group that was a part of a nested hierarchy.

Hierarchical Grouping

Some business relationship rules in a data source can exist within a single table. In the relational model, it is more typical to have relationships between fields in different tables rather than between fields within a single table. Crystal can report on both types of relationships. A typical example of a single table having this type of unique relationship between two fields in a table within the same data record is one that lists employee information using a unique EmployeeID for each record. In each record, one of the columns (attributes) of the record identifies the EmployeeID of the person's manager, while this manager is also listed in the same table as an employee with a unique EmployeeID. This type of data is used to build an employee organizational chart to show who works for whom, and it is known as *hierarchical data*.

Hierarchical data exists when two fields within a single data record share a parent-child relationship with each other. The VistaNations report contains an example of hierarchical data in the RegionAreas table with a geographic relationship between ResortRegion and ResortArea, as shown in Figure 6.11.

FIGURE 6.11

Hierarchical table

ResortRegion	ResortArea
NA	CN
NA	MX
NA	US
CN	BC
CN	QU
US	CA
US	NY
US	FL
NY	ALB
NY	NYC

The data in the ResortArea column has a hierarchical or parent-child relationship to the data in the ResortRegion column; this is illustrated in Figure 6.12.

FIGURE 6.12

Hierarchical
relationships

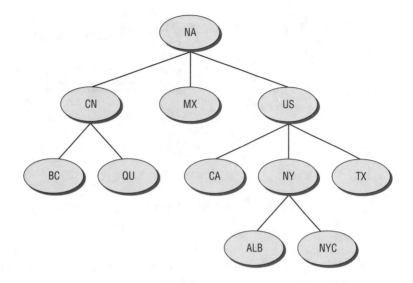

Crystal Reports has a built-in facility to help you build a report using this type of specialized data. The first step in displaying the hierarchy relationship in Crystal is to create a group based on the data that contains the relationship. In the case of ResortArea and ResortRegion, it is ResortArea that links back to ResortRegion, so the group is created on ResortArea. This group should be sorted in ascending order. After the group exists, you can choose Report ➤ Hierarchical Grouping Options to create the hierarchy; the Hierarchical Options dialog appears, as shown in Figure 6.13.

FIGURE 6.13

Hierarchical Options

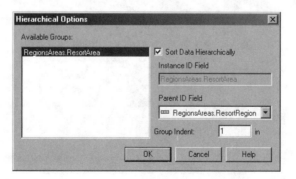

Using this dialog, select a group from the set of groups that exist in the report. When you enable the checkbox option to Sort Data Hierarchically, the Parent ID Field area becomes available. Here, you choose the field that the grouped data (the child) is related to (the parent). You can also choose an indent size in inches for display purposes. The data is then sorted and indented based on the parent-child relationship between the two fields. The result of this type of data association is a visual representation of the hierarchical information, including the easy-to-read group tree representation. Figure 6.14 shows the start of a report with this type of grouping and the group tree to the left.

FIGURE 6.14

Hierarchical report with group tree

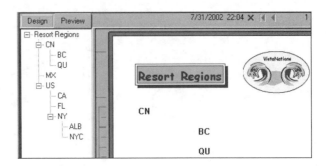

NOTE *If a parent-child relationship doesn't exist in the data for a record in a group, the record is sorted to the top of the hierarchy.*

Once the data is grouped hierarchically, you can add summary fields like subtotals and grand totals based on the hierarchy groups. For this type of summarization, you should choose the Summarize Across Hierarchy option, as shown at the bottom of Figure 6.15.

FIGURE 6.15

Summarize Across Hierarchy

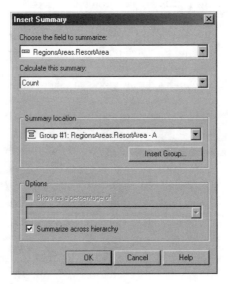

Group Selection Formulas

Crystal contains two types of selection formulas: record selection and group selection. A group selection formula eliminates groups from a report based on a formula. To create a group selection formula, choose Report ➢ Selection Formulas ➢ Group. This opens the Formula Workshop - Formula Editor, where you can then type any formula that evaluates to a TRUE value. When the value of the formula is TRUE, then the group is included in the report; a value of FALSE eliminates the group from the report.

In Figure 6.16, the formula returns a TRUE value if the first letter of the Resorts.Country field is not equal to the letter *A*. This will eliminate all countries from the report that start with *A*.

FIGURE 6.16

Coding a group selection formula

The statement does not have to be wrapped in a properly formatted IF-THEN-ELSE statement; all that needs to be present in a group selection formula is the condition clause of the IF portion of the IF-THEN-ELSE. When the clause is TRUE, the group is included in the report, and when it's FALSE, the group is excluded. The result of this particular group selection formula on the VistaNations report is displayed in Figure 6.17.

FIGURE 6.17

Group selection formula applied

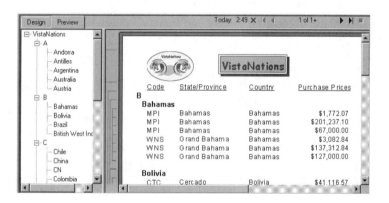

Notice that the group tree still includes a reference to the countries that begin with the letter *A*. Clicking any of the *A* entries in the group tree, however, will not take you anyplace. The records do not exist in Crystal's data set, but the group tree was created *before* the groups were filtered out of the report. The group tree is created during Crystal's first pass through the data, while the group selection filter is applied in Crystal's second pass through the data. Similarly, grand totals and group totals on groups are processed before the group selection filter is applied, which can throw off your totals; see the "Running Totals" discussion later in this chapter on how to deal with totals in a group when a group selection filter is being used.

NOTE *For more information on Crystal's processing engine passes, refer to Chapter 14, "The Report Engine Processing Model."*

Special Fields for Grouped Data

As a part of the Field Explorer, the Special Fields category contains two fields specifically targeted to working with groups: Group Number and Group Selection Formula. Adding these fields to a report imparts information about the group's position and value in the report. The special fields are shown in the Field Explorer in Figure 6.18.

FIGURE 6.18

Special grouping fields

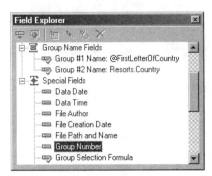

Also notice in the Field Explorer that any groups that have been added to the report appear in a special category called Group Name Fields. A green check mark next to the field name denotes that it has been used in the current report.

GROUP NUMBER

As a part of the Group Header or Group Footer, the {Group Number} field is placed into a report to display a unique number for each group. The {Group Number} field increments from 1 to the last number for the group. It defaults to an integer value and can be further formatted using the Format Editor. This field can be placed multiple times into a report, once for each group in the report.

TIP   For a variation on group number uniqueness, insert a text object and type a few text prefix characters (for instance, A-) and then add the Group Number field to the text object. This will result in group numbering like A-1, A-2, etc.

GROUP SELECTION FORMULA

This special field provides a way for the group selection formula being used in the report to be displayed as part of the information in the report. You create and use the group selection formula itself by choosing Report ➤ Selection Formulas ➤ Group. You can display in your report the text of the formula coded in the formula window to create the selection criteria so that you can easily know which criteria are in effect. Since items placed in the Report Header and Report Footer appear only once in the report, these sections are a good place to position the special Group Selection Formula field to display the value in your report. If no group selection criterion is in effect, the value of the field is empty and nothing will display.

Summarizing Data

Grouping and summarizing data often go hand in hand, but in fact you can add summary information to a report without building it into a group. You can think of a summary as a display of a main point in the data records. In a report of total sales by salesperson, for instance, a summary point might be the total sales for all salespeople.

Creating Summaries

A summary can be created on a field or a formula in the report or a field in the data tables being used by the report. To add a summary to a report, use any of the following techniques:

◆ Choose Insert ➤ Summary from the menu.

◆ Click the Insert Summary icon on the toolbar.

◆ Right-click a field and select the Insert ➤ Summary menu item.

All of the above actions display the Insert Summary dialog shown in Figure 6.19. When you choose the field to summarize on by right-clicking in the Design tab and then choosing Insert ➤ Summary, the field is automatically placed in the first drop-down box as the field to be summarized. If this is not what you want, just use the drop-down box to pick a different field from the report, the formula list, or the tables in the report.

FIGURE 6.19

Inserting a summary

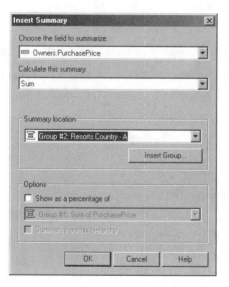

TYPES OF SUMMARIES

The second drop-down box in Figure 6.19 determines the kind of summarization that will take place. For selected fields of text or date types, the default is the Maximum function. For numeric fields, the default is the Sum function. Crystal provides a wide and powerful selection of summarization techniques, which are described in Table 6.1. If the summary you need to do is not listed in this table, you can write a formula to perform the specialized calculation using one of Crystal's built-in formula languages. The data type of the field determines the list of summarization methods displayed for a field. The table contains the complete list of summarization techniques; the data types for Text, Boolean, date, and time values each present a pick list of techniques specific to the summarization methods valid to the data type.

TABLE 6.1: TYPES OF SUMMARIES

SUMMARIZATION	DESCRIPTION
Sum	Adds all record values for the selected field.
Average	Calculates an average for the record values for the selected field.
Sample variance	Calculates a variance, which is the mean of the absolute values of the deviations from the mean for a selected sample of data; variance is the value of the standard deviation squared, which is $[(Ex*Ex - n*m*m) / n]$ where n is the number of samples, Ex is the sum total of the samples, and m is the mean value of the samples where $m = Ex / n$.
Sample standard deviation	Calculates the standard deviation on a sample of data, which is a measure of the spread or dispersion of data using the formula square root $[(Ex*Ex - n*m*m) / n]$ where n is the number of samples, Ex is the sum total of the samples, and m is the mean value of the samples where $m = Ex / n$.
Maximum	Given a set of values, returns the largest value.
Minimum	Given a set of values, returns the smallest value.
Count	A number representing how many times the value appears in the field.
Distinct count	A number representing how many times the value uniquely appears in the field.
Correlation with	Calculates the degree to which the values of a field vary.
Covariance with	Measures the relationship between two values and reports on how much they vary as a pair from the other values in the fields and how they track/trend together.
Median	Calculates the middle value in a distribution, below and above which lie values with equal total frequencies.
Mode	Given a set of values, returns the value that occurs the most frequently in the field.
Nth largest, N is:	Defines N as a number (e.g., 5), and from a set of values, returns the N largest values (in this case, 5 largest values).
Nth smallest, N is:	Defines N as a number (e.g., 7), and from a set of values, returns the N smallest values (in this case, 7 smallest values).
Nth most frequent, N is:	Defines N as a number (e.g., 9), and from a set of values, returns the N most frequently occurring values; similar to Mode.
Pth percentile, P is:	Displays the percentage of the calculation rather than the numerical value of the calculation.

Continued on next page

TABLE 6.1: TYPES OF SUMMARIES *(continued)*

SUMMARIZATION	DESCRIPTION
Population variance	Estimates the variance, which is the mean of the absolute values of the deviations from the mean for the entire population of data.
Population standard deviation	Estimates the standard deviation on the entire population of data, which is a measure of the spread or dispersion of data.
Weighted average with	Calculates the average of one field and multiplies it by the value of another field.

PLACEMENT OF THE SUMMARY VALUE

After choosing a summarization method, you must specify the location to place the summary in the report in the Insert Summary dialog. Figure 6.19, shown previously, shows that the summary will be added to the Report Footer; this is the default location. Summaries placed in the Report Footer are grand total values and will incorporate all data records in the report. The following summarization methods are considered grand total calculations and generally involve all the data records in the report:

Average

Count

Distinct count

Maximum

Minimum

Population standard deviation

Standard deviation

Sum

Variance

If you don't want the summary placed in the Report Footer, you can add it to a Group Footer using the drop-down list to choose from the list of existing Group Footers in the report. Summaries placed in a Group Footer are subtotal values and incorporate only the values within the group.

You can also create a group on the fly using the Insert Group button and add the summary you're building to the new group. When the summary value is placed in a Group Footer, the check box option to show the value as a percentage of the whole becomes active. The default behavior is that the summary calculation displays as an actual number; the percentage option displays it as a percentage and compares it against the other values in the report.

Figure 6.20 shows the VistaNations report summarized with subtotals on the sum of purchase prices for each group and a grand total of all purchase prices at the end of the report. The text labels describing the summary values as well as the single and double-line separators were created manually in Design mode with text objects and line objects.

FIGURE 6.20
Summarized number fields

GRAND TOTALS AND SUBTOTALS IN PRIOR RELEASES

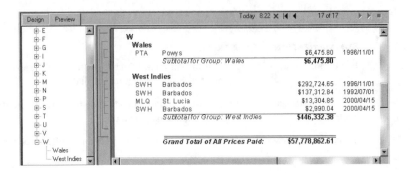

In prior versions of Crystal Reports, you could insert grand totals and subtotals directly from menu choices. In this release of Crystal Reports, both types of summaries are created somewhat more generically using the Insert ➢ Summary approach. What determines whether they are grand totals or subtotals is in which section they are placed. To create a grand total, place the summary in the Report Footer; to create a subtotal, place the summary in the applicable group's footer. The values are added to the footers without Grand Total or Subtotal labels, so be sure to add your own descriptive text describing the summary value.

Group Sorts

Once you've grouped and summarized data in a report, the Group Sort Expert becomes available to you for refining the data shown in the report. With this expert, you can reduce the number of records being shown in the report to concentrate on the important ones. Group sorts include Top N, Bottom N, Top Percentage, and Bottom Percentage. Choosing Report ➢ Group Sort Expert opens the dialog shown in Figure 6.21.

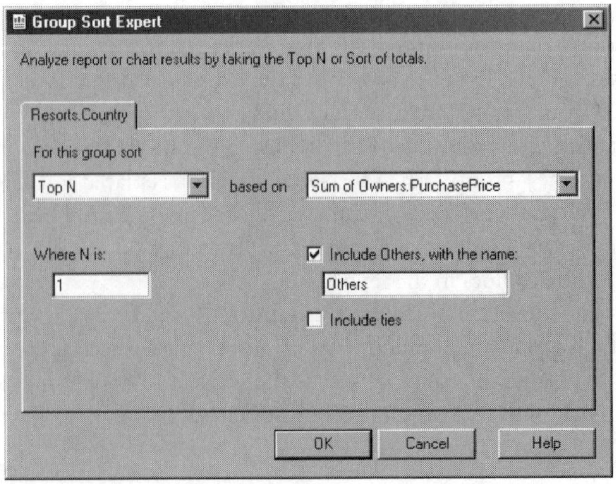

FIGURE 6.21
Group Sort Expert

Note the check box labeled *Include ties*. Enable this option to tell Crystal that when multiple groups have exactly the same summary value, include all the equal groups in the report. This may mean that more than the *N* number of values you asked for will display, but the advantage is that the tied values will all be present in the report. Figure 6.22 depicts the process of selecting out the top set of records or bottom set of records from the data that exists in Crystal. All the records still exist in Crystal; they are just being concealed in this report.

FIGURE 6.22

Top and Bottom N
reporting

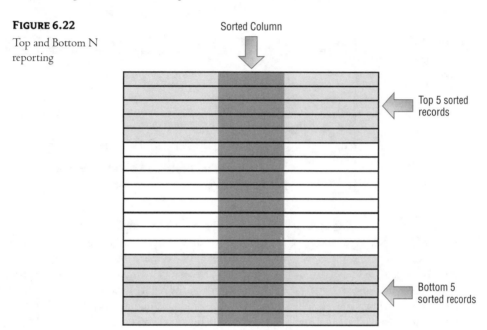

Sorted Column

Top 5 sorted
records

Bottom 5
sorted records

Using the dialog shown in Figure 6.21, you can set the N value to determine how many of the groups should display. N is a number that is specified by the report designer and can be any positive integer value. For the report in Figure 6.23, an N value of 1 was chosen. Compare Figure 6.23 to Figure 6.20. Both figures present the group of resorts that start with the letter *W*.

FIGURE 6.23

Top 1 with Others

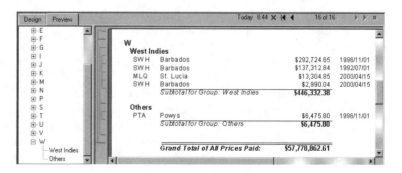

Notice that the Others designation has replaced the specific reference to the Wales data. A Top N sort with the value of N set to the integer 1 displays the group with the highest total purchase prices only, which was the West Indies. The Others category was included in the report based on the *Include Others with the name* check box visible in Figure 6.21. Checking this option pushed all non-Wales data into a group called Others; unchecking the option will still filter the non-Wales data out of the W category and will additionally exclude it completely from the report. This is demonstrated in Figure 6.24; the Others group is not in report.

FIGURE 6.24

Top 1 without Others

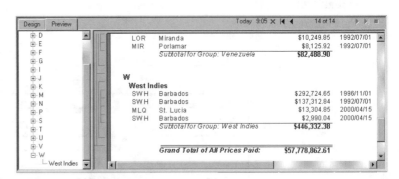

Hang on! We're leading up to a very interesting plot twist. Compare the grand totals shown in Figure 6.20, Figure 6.23, and Figure 6.24. They are all identical: $57,778,862.61. However, we just finished discarding the groups that weren't in the Top N. Why are the numbers the same? Shouldn't the grand total have updated? The grand total was calculated *before* you eliminated the groups, so its value remains unchanged; it is totaling all the records in the report including the ones that were eliminated with the Others option. The built-in summarization techniques provided by Crystal are working as designed; the nuance is that summaries process before many other steps in the report are complete. Basically what we have here is a timing problem involving when summaries are processed as compared to other report elements. The solution to this timing problem lies in a different type of summary object, running total fields. The grand total summary added here totals all records; what you need is a running total that summarizes only the groups being displayed in the report.

Running Totals

Grand total and subtotal fields are the perfect solution to coming up with a number to represent summarized report data; the calculations are preprogrammed for you and are easy to use. Sometimes, though, you need the ability to create totals on fields or calculations that are beyond the built-in summarization formulas. To go beyond the built-in routines, running totals are the answer.

Running totals are formulas that you create to accumulate values, counting up as records are processed by the formula. Since you code the formula yourself, you control how the total is calculated as well as what triggers it to reset to zero and start incrementing anew. An example of a running total that ties into our VistaNations resort-tracking database is building a total to count the number of five-star resorts in a particular place, like the New York State, while still displaying the entire list of resorts. To do this, you need a conditional formula that tests the value of the fields {Resorts.StateProvince} and {Resorts.FiveStarRating}, incrementing a variable by one whenever the fields equal NY and True, respectively. This type of conditional counting is impossible with the built-in summarization fields provided by Crystal.

Running totals provide the flexibility and power of formula language to allow any combination of logic to be used in an increment calculation. Among the things that running totals can be used to do are:

♦ Increment a variable by examining records as they are read

♦ Total values within a grouping but separate from the group total

♦ Perform conditional incrementing of a variable to add to a total

♦ Create a total after a group selection formula filters the data

WHEN TO USE RUNNING TOTALS

You'll know its time to use a running total when you preview a report and the result of a grand total or subtotal just doesn't make sense given the data being displayed. This was the case earlier in this chapter when you compared the grand totals in Figure 6.20, Figure 6.23, and Figure 6.24 and realized that they shouldn't be the same but were. Crystal's built-in summarization formulas return results based on evaluating all the records that were returned from the database for the report. There are several cases, however, when this will return misleading totals:

♦ Top and Bottom N sorts

♦ Group selection formulas

♦ Custom groups that exclude Others from the report

A Top N report conceals records that were returned by the data query but that are not part of the top or bottom slices of data. The entire data set still exists in Crystal, but Crystal is displaying only the ones you want to see. Top N is a great example of a report that needs running totals in order to calculate totals for just the displayed records rather than relying on the grand total built into Crystal. Crystal's grand total, subtotal, and summary fields build totals based on the data set in memory. For Top N, that includes all the records, not just the displayed ones. So if you do a grand total on the sorted sales figures for the year and put it on a Top N report showing the sales for the top five sales people, the grand total field will display the grand total for *all* salespeople and not just the top five. In order to show a total number for just the top five people, a running total is needed to create a meaningful subtotal to accumulate just the values you specify. To correctly arrive at summary information just for the records in the Top N, you need to create separate totals, or running totals, in Crystal. Running totals are values that are arrived at by incrementing a counting variable based on criteria you define.

Group selection is another example of a type of data reduction that conceals data, creating the need for running totals. Group selection prevents groups of records from displaying in a report. The records that are concealed, however, are still included by Crystal in the set of records on which grand totals, summaries, and subtotals are based.

Custom groups can exclude data records that do not fit into the criteria for the custom groups. If you choose not to display the records that are outside the custom criteria, totaling fields can be misleading. Running totals should be used in place of built-in totals to correctly reflect the summarization numbers.

CREATING RUNNING TOTALS

To create a running total field, use the Field Explorer to highlight the Running Total Fields entry and then click the New button, or right-click to expose the submenu that contains the New option. Figure 6.25 shows the Field Explorer as you're about to create a new running total field.

FIGURE 6.25

Creating a running total field

After you select New, the Create Running Total Field dialog shown in Figure 6.26 displays. This dialog is also known as the Running Total Expert. At the top right of the dialog, you type a name for the running total formula; this name will later appear in the Field Explorer's list of formulas and fields.

TIP   It is handy to leave the prefix set as `RTotal` *on the front of the formula name so that you can easily identify it as a running total field when looking at a report.*

FIGURE 6.26

Running Total Expert

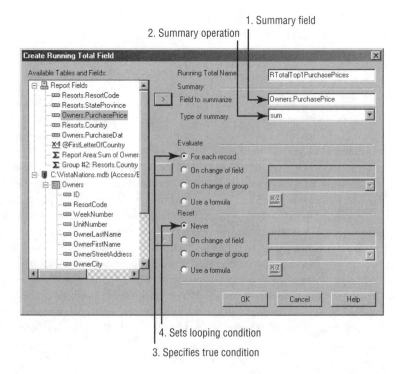

1. Summary field

2. Summary operation

4. Sets looping condition

3. Specifies true condition

The dialog allows you to specify the criteria needed to calculate the running total by using the following steps:

1. Select the field on which to base the summary.

2. Choose the summary operation to apply.

3. Specify the true condition that determines when the summary should be applied.

4. Set a looping condition to tell Crystal when to reset the evaluation within the criteria.

When you specify a true condition for the evaluation, you can simply choose to evaluate for every record, field, or group, or you can use a formula. You would require a formula for the example mentioned earlier to count five-star resorts in NY; here's the code you would put behind the formula button:

```
{Resorts.StateProvince} = "NY" and
{Resorts.FiveStarRating} = True
```

Once the Create Running Total Field dialog is filled out properly and closed, the field is available in the Field Explorer under the Running Total Fields category. From here, you can drag and drop it into the report in an appropriate position. As with all fields in a report, the section in which the field is placed affects how the field is evaluated. For Figure 6.27, the RTotalTop1PurchasePrices field has been placed in the Report Footer just above the grand total field so that the difference between the two numbers is clearly visible.

FIGURE 6.27

A running total result

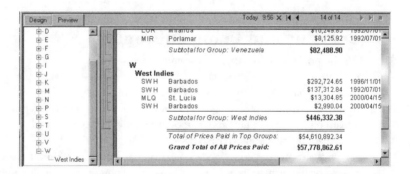

The RTotalTop1PurchasePrices field needs to examine every record in the Details section, so it needs at the minimum to be placed in a section that follows the Details section. The Report Footer is an appropriate place for the new field since the Report Footer section immediately follows the Details section and comes before the Page Footer. If the field was placed in the Report Header, only first record in the report would be evaluated, which would return an incorrect total since the remaining records would not have been processed by the formula. Table 6.2 describes the effect of placing a running total in a given section and uses the assumption that the running total is not reset at any point in the report.

TABLE 6.2: RECORD EVALUATION BY SECTION

SECTION	RECORDS EVALUATED BY RUNNING TOTAL FIELDS
Report Header	Running Total is comprised only of the value in the first database record.
Page Header	For each page, the Running Total includes all records processed on prior pages plus the first record on the current page.
Group Header	For each group, the Running Total includes all records in prior groups plus the first record in the current group.
Details	For each record, the Running Total includes all records in prior to and including the current record.
Group Footer	For each group, the Running Total includes all records in prior groups plus all records in the current group.
Report Footer	Running is comprised of all the records in the report.
Page Footer	For each page, the Running Total includes all records processed on prior pages plus all the records on the current page.

Running total fields are processed early in the report-processing cycle; refer to Chapter 14 for a detailed explanation of the order of evaluation of report elements.

Creating and Using Subreports

A subreport is a report that can be embedded within another report. This design element is used to separate and organize information, promote reusability in data reporting, and in some cases, enhance the performance of a report. The full complement of insert options are available for subreports including summary objects, groups, lines, boxes, charts, etc. Subreports can contain any element that a main report can contain and support the same drill-down capabilities and suppressing options as their main report counterparts.

Once a subreport is embedded, the original report is referred to as the main report, the container report, or the primary report. Once saved, the subreport becomes a part of the main report and is stored within the same RPT file. A subreport can be directly created within a main report or it can be created from an existing separate RPT file, which is then embedded in a main report. Multiple subreports can be inserted into a single main report, and depending on which sections they are placed into, the subreports may display once per report, once per page, once per group, or once per detail record.

Choosing Insert ➤ Subreport opens the dialog in Figure 6.28, and you can then choose to retrieve an existing report by clicking the Browse button or create an internal subreport and give it an alias name.

If you create an internal subreport with an alias name, clicking the Report Wizard button (shown grayed out in Figure 6.28) opens the Standard Report Creation Wizard to help you choose a data source and fields and perform grouping and record selection. The fact that the Standard Report Creation Wizard is used here should further convince you that a subreport is nothing more than a report within a report!

FIGURE 6.28

Inserting a subreport

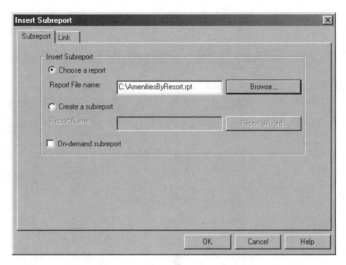

NOTE *Refer to Chapter 1 for more information on the Standard Report Creation Wizard.*

Types of Subreports

The information contained in a subreport may or may not be related or relevant to the information in its main report. When there is a relationship between the two, Crystal calls this a *linked* subreport. Conversely, when there is no relationship between the data in the subreport and the data in the main report, the *unlinked* subreport is used.

Unlinked Subreports Using the subreport approach, a main report can display a variety of data that may or may not be related. There is no requirement that the data in a subreport have any relationship to the data in the main report. For instance, if you typically generate a report called The Daily Report, it can contain information about the sales part of the business, the newest employees hired, and the company picnic. The main report is simply the vehicle used to contain all this information as a unit. When the subreport does not contain any information that is connected to the data in its main report, it is known as an unlinked subreport.

Linked Subreports The data in a subreport may be very relevant to the data in the main report and will share a common field value. This type of subreport is known as a linked subreport. A typical example of a linked subreport is to create customer invoices where one-time-only information is positioned on the main report to show the customer's name, address, and order number while the subreport contains the line item details of items within each order. When you connect a subreport to a main report, you choose a database field or a formula to use as the connecting value. The field or formula's value is used as a dynamic runtime parameter in the subreport to build a secondary record selection formula to retrieve data into the subreport. Data is retrieved into the subreport only when the link field's value equals the parameter's value. In the invoice example, the link field and dynamic parameter in the subreport is the order number that connects the main report to subreport's invoice line items.

Figure 6.29 demonstrates the creation of a link from a field in the container report to a field in the subreport; this Link tab is available from the Insert ➤ Subreport option. The tab is visible but not open in Figure 6.28. In this subreport, the link is being made on the ResortCode field, which exists in the main report and in the subreport.

FIGURE 6.29

Creating a link in a subreport

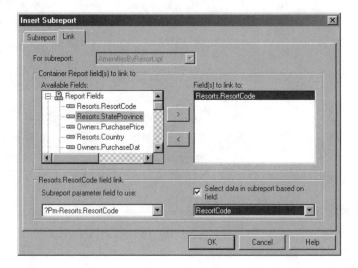

Figure 6.30 shows the result of a linked subreport; the Amenities report displays within the main report. The design tab for the `AmenitiesByResort.rpt` file is visible behind the previewed report.

FIGURE 6.30

An embedded subreport

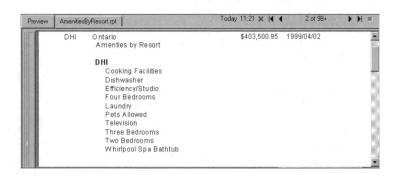

In addition to the concept of linked and unlinked subreports, a subreport can be evaluated either as an in-place subreport or as an on-demand subreport.

IN-PLACE SUBREPORTS

An in-place subreport is one that loads and displays at the same time as the main report. To a person looking at a report that contains an in-place subreport, the subreport may appear to be inside a black-outlined rectangle. Depending on which section the subreport is placed inside, the subreport will be visible a variable number of times.

ON-DEMAND SUBREPORTS

At the bottom of the Insert Subreport dialog box, shown previously in Figure 6.28, the On-Demand Subreport check box option is visible. This option is disabled by default. When enabled, the subreport is not viewed by the user or evaluated by Crystal's runtime process until the user clicks a link to display the subreport. This can help a report load and display on a computer screen very quickly since some of the processing is being deferred until later if and when the user wants to see the subreport.

Once the on-demand option is chosen, no further configuration is required to embed the link; however, you can add formatting that will make the link a little more pleasing to the eye. By default, the link appears as the name of the subreport, whatever you may have called it, with a simple hyper-link underline. You can modify the appearance of the text link using the Format Editor submenu, which is described in the next section. You can also suppress the text altogether and use a graphic as a link instead. To do this, suppress the subreport text link with the Format Editor, bring in a picture by choosing Insert ➢ Picture from the main menu, and then position the graphic *behind* the subreport text link by right-clicking to show the context menu and selecting Move To Back.

Placement of a Subreport

Elements in a report are evaluated positionally from left to right and from top to bottom, and since a subreport is an element, it will be evaluated and displayed after any fields that come before it and before any elements that follow it. The positional placement is especially important when working with linked subreports. When working with data linked by group, you can position the linked subreport in the Group Header or Group Footer so that each time the group field value changes, the subreport changes to display data specific to the current group of data records. You'll also want to make sure to place linking fields in the main report in sections that precede the subreport. This will allow the link fields to be evaluated and have a value that can then be used to connect to the subreport. If the subreport is placed before the linking field, no connection can take place because the link field will have no value in the main report until after the evaluation of the subreport.

Formatting a Subreport

Once a subreport is embedded in a report, you can right-click the subreport object to open a context menu, as shown in Figure 6.31. The items on the menu assist you in customizing the look and behavior of the link from formatting its appearance to editing the placement of the fields in the subreport.

FIGURE 6.31

Subreport menu

Subreport: AmenitiesByResort.rpt
Format Subreport...
Edit Subreport...
Save Subreport As...
Change Subreport Links...
Re-import subreport
Move   ▶
Size and Position...
Paste
Delete
Cancel Menu

As a standard convention in Crystal, the top item in the menu tells you the object type you're working with and its name. The menu here shows us working with the object type of subreport whose name is `AmenitiesByResort.rpt`. This particular subreport was created by embedding a previously created RPT file in the main report. Table 6.3 describes the behavior of the menu options.

TABLE 6.3: SUBREPORT MENU DESCRIPTIONS

MENU OPTIONS	PURPOSE
Format Subreport	Displays the Format Editor with options specific to changing the visual affects on a subreport or its behavior; see the discussion below for more information.
Edit Subreport	Opens the subreport in Design mode in its own tab with all sections and fields visible and available for normal report formatting.
Save Subreport As	Allows the subreport to be saved as an external RPT file; this option can be used whether the subreport was an internal one using an alias name or imported as an RPT file from the beginning.
Change Subreport Links	Modifies or creates a field link between a subreport and its main report; the dialog that displays is the same as the Links tab that is used when a subreport is first created.
Re-import Subreport	Interactively refreshes the data in the subreport and displays the most current data and its formatting.
Move	Allows an on-demand subreport link to be moved behind or in front of another object in the report, creating a layered effect.
Size And Position	Sets the height and width allotted to the subreport in Design mode as well as the x and y offset value positions in inches from the top-left corner of the section containing the subreport.
Delete	Deletes the subreport from the main report.
Cancel Menu	Closes the subreport menu.

EDITING A SUBREPORT

When you edit the subreport, the layout of the design elements is shown in its own tab, as shown in Figure 6.32. The particular subreport shown here includes a group and a formula. Unlinked subreports can be previewed directly from Design mode by clicking the Refresh toolbar icon or choosing View ➤ Other Views and choosing the subreport to display. If you click the Refresh button while viewing the layout of a linked subreport, you'll be prompted to provide any values required by the subreport that are normally provided by its main report; you can avoid this parameter-prompting approach by viewing the subreport through the main report's Design tab instead.

The subreport displays as part of the main report on the Preview tab, and when you click the subreport itself, you can drill down to display the subreport in its own tab. Figure 6.32 also shows a second `AmenitiesByResort.rpt` tab, which is the drill-down display of the subreport; notice its jagged right edge and the left and right arrows beside the tab. Whenever Crystal can't display the tab or additional tabs in their entirety, the jagged edge signals that there are unseen areas on the screen. Use the left and right arrows to navigate between tabs, and use the close button (X) visible at the top-right corner of a displayed tab to close the tab when desired.

FIGURE 6.32

Subreport in
Design mode

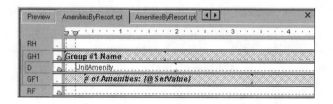

At its creation, a subreport contains several sections of its own: a Report Header and Footer and a Details section. It will not and cannot contain Page Headers and Footers; the concept of a page does not apply to subreports. The remaining sections, however, are identical in behavior and function to their main report counterparts. If you add a group to a subreport, a Group Header and Group Footer are inserted into the sections. When working with linked subreports, there may be times when there is no data in the subreport to match the main report's linking value; in this case, summaries and group totals may appear onscreen as zeros or be otherwise blank. You can modify this behavior by condition-ally suppressing the Details section of a subreport using a formula in the Section Editor. The formula would test to see whether the field has a value, and if it does not, it would hide the section or the detail row. You can also conditionally suppress the Report Header and Report Footer as well as add additional sections.

NOTE   *Refer to Chapter 8, "Customizing Sections," for more information on how to add additional sections and con-ditionally suppress a section based on a field or formula value.*

THE SUBREPORT FORMAT EDITOR

Selecting the Format Subreport menu option described in Table 6.3 opens the Format Editor shown in Figure 6.33. From here you can do things like changing the default look of an on-demand subreport to spice it up a bit beyond the blue underline hyperlink. While the majority of the settings in the Format Editor, such as the Common, Border, and Font tabs, should be familiar from Chapter 3, "Formatting Fields and Objects," there are new settings that directly affect subreports. Subreport settings are found on the Subreport tab.

Subreport Name   The subreport name will be either the alias you gave it for an internal subreport or the name of the RPT file retrieved into the report from a stored location. This name can be used for programmatic purposes for code-based interactions with the report. The subreport name should not be changed after you initially set it because only the first name assigned will ever be known or displayed inside Crystal on the Preview tabs.

On-Demand Subreport   If an on-demand subreport was created when you inserted the subreport, this option is automatically enabled. It can be enabled or disabled to change from on-demand to in-place reports and vice versa.

On-Demand Preview Tab Caption   This option is associated with a programming button that lets you write a formula to determine what the text for the hypertext link will be. The formula may be as simple as a manually typed text string or may be a complex calculation that results in a text string. If a subreport caption is not specified, the subreport name is used; this is the default. This option is not available if the subreport being formatted is not using the on-demand opening style.

Subreport Preview Tab Caption   When a subreport is opened in Crystal, it displays on its own tab or in its own web browser window. The value set for the tab caption displays on the Preview tab itself or on the title bar in a web client. You can code a formula to dynamically set the Preview tab caption or hard-code a value like `Amenities` instead of settling for the default name of the subreport.

Re-Import When Opening   This option forces Crystal to rerun the data query and refetch the data into the subreport when it is opened for use.

Suppress Blank Subreport   Even when a subreport contains no data, it still takes up placement space in your report. To minimize the amount of space devoted to Crystal for this purpose when the subreport has no records, enable the Suppress Blank Subreport option.

FIGURE 6.33

Formatting a subreport

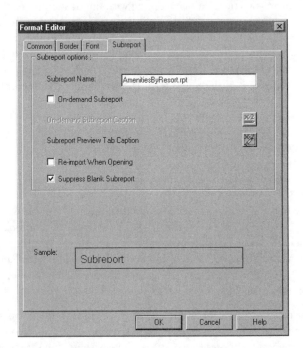

Subreport Data Sources

A subreport can use the data source of the main report or it can have an entirely independent data source. A data source can be different tables or different databases or even databases of different types. This makes a subreport a handy device for incorporating data from different places and presenting it within one report. The subreport can be either a linked or unlinked subreport as well as an in-place or on-demand subreport.

If your report makes use of more than one type of database, for instance, IBM DB2 and Microsoft SQL Server, subreports are recommended as a way to pull the data into a single report. Using this approach, you gain the following benefits:

♦ Each subreport can use a database driver specific to the data source for enhanced performance.

♦ Each subreport can use its own SQL statement for data retrieval.

♦ Each subreport connects to its data source separately without knowledge of the other data source.

♦ Nonindexed tables can be linked in a subreport to a main report.

Tables that do not have an index can benefit from being embedded in a linked subreport because, in general, nonindexed tables cannot be joined with any other table. A subreport that contains a field in common with the main report can superimpose a link into the report that did not exist in the data source or data sources. While it will not be as fast and efficient as a table join performed inside a database using an index, subreport linking can provide an alternative to an otherwise unlinkable data situation. In this case, performance is sacrificed for functionality. Whenever possible, it is best to link a subreport to a main report using an indexed field in the subreport to optimize the speed at which records are retrieved into the subreport.

Passing Values between a Subreport and a Main Report

Crystal allows data to be passed from a subreport to its main report using variables that are defined with a scope of Shared. These are known as *shared variables* and were introduced conceptually in Chapter 4, "Adding Business Logic with the Formula Workshop." Shared variables are used to pass values between a subreport and a main report and, to be effective, require the use of two formulas:

♦ One formula to initially store a value in the shared variable

♦ A second formula to retrieve and use the value in the shared variable

As you might have guessed, you need to store the value before you can use it, so the placement of the formulas matters in relation to where the subreport is placed. The formula that stores the value is placed in the subreport; the formula that uses the value is placed in the main report.

Let's demonstrate the sharing of values with two generically named formulas called @SetValue and @GetValue. If you were creating these types of formulas in your report, you might want to use more descriptive names like SetValueMyCount and GetValueMyCount, building the name of the variable being worked on into the name of the set and get formulas; this would make it easier to maintain the report over time. In the following formulas, we want to count the number of five-star resorts and display it with the grand total at the end of the report. The placement of the @SetValue formula field is visible in Figure 6.32. In this example, the field has been formatted to be suppressed so that no interim values will be displayed for this formula but the value will be available to pass to the main report.

```
//@SetValue…place formula in subreport
WhilePrintingRecords;
Shared numberVar myCount;
if {Resorts.FiveStarRating} = True then
    myCount := myCount + 1;
```

With this field in the subreport (which has been positioned in the Details section), the field to retrieve the value can be placed anywhere in the report below the subreport. In Figure 6.34, you can see that the `@GetValue` formula has been placed in the Report Footer to display the total number.

FIGURE 6.34

Placing a value retrieval formula

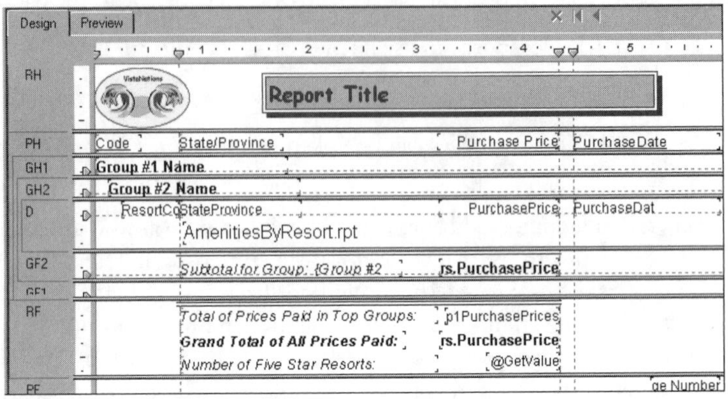

```
//@GetValue … place formula in main report
    WhilePrintingRecords;
    Shared numberVar myCount;
    myCount;
```

In this formula, the second line of code retrieves the value of the `myCount` variable, while the final line of code returns that value for printing in the report. For the formulas to work together between a subreport and a main report, the following rules must be followed:

♦ The keyword SHARED must be used to define the variable in both formulas.

♦ The variable name must be identical in the two formulas.

♦ The formula that sets the value must appear in the report before the formula that retrieves the value.

♦ Shared variables can be used only while records are being printed to the screen; therefore, the `WhilePrintingRecords` formula statement is required.

NOTE *For more information on the* `WhilePrintingRecords` *formula, refer to Chapter 14.*

In the code example for `@SetValue` and `@GetValue`, if the `@GetValue` formula had been positioned in the report in a section above the subreport, the value displayed would be zero since myCount would not exist until after the subreport was evaluated. A common technique to guarantee that the subreport sets the value before the main report uses the value is to create a new section and place the subreport in that section prior to the section that contains the retrieval formula. To create a new section, right-click the section name in Design mode and choose Insert ➢ Section Below, and then place the subreport in the first section and the retrieval formula in the second section.

Once retrieved, the value from the subreport can then be used in the main report in any formulas that appear after the subreport.

WARNING *Because the evaluation time of an on-demand subreport is determined by the user of the report, variables cannot be shared between on-demand subreports and main reports. If the sharing of values is a requirement of your report, use in-place subreports.*

Subreport Caveats

Subreports are very much like ordinary reports in that you can add all the usual design elements to a subreport in the same way you would do it in a main report. However, because of their embedded nature, there are a few limitations put on subreports:

♦ Subreports do not get assigned their own `.rpt` file extension but instead are saved as a part of the main report's RPT file unless intentionally and explicitly stored as an RPT using the Save Subreport As menu option (see Table 6.3).

♦ A subreport created internally inside an existing RPT file cannot be viewed or accessed independently of a main report (unless saved separately).

♦ Subreports cannot contain other subreports.

♦ A subreport can't link to another subreport.

♦ Options set for the main report using File ➢ Report Options apply only to the main report; to set options for the subreport, select the object in Design mode and choose File ➢ Report Options for the selected object.

♦ Subreports do not have their own Page Header and Page Footer sections.

♦ If a subreport is placed in the Page Header or Page Footer of a main report, the subreport must be small enough to fit on a single page.

Page Headers and Footers cannot span multiple pages since, by their very definition, they are placed at the top and bottom of a page. If you embed a subreport that is too large for a Page Header or Footer, you'll see a warning message similar to that shown in Figure 6.35.

FIGURE 6.35

Page size warning

Summary

Grouping data organizes it for human consumption. We understand data better in smaller chunks. Crystal Reports can group data on fields, on formulas, and hierarchically. Summarization methods built into Crystal include grand totals and grouping summaries with a wide range of operations that can be applied to the data. Operations include summing, counting, and taking the top five or so values. These summaries can be easily added to a report. When a simple summarization won't work for you, you can write your own running total for more complex and conditional summarization. In addition to summarizing data, subreports provide a powerful way to synthesize information by combining data that might normally be in two separate reports and that can be linked in a single report.

Chapter 7

Selectively Refining a Report Using Data Values

THE REPORTS WE'VE LOOKED at so far consist of selecting all the records from a table and including specific fields from the table in a report. We've sorted and grouped this data, used formulas to manipulate the fields to create new values, and used the Crystal Repository in our reports. For all this, though, we've taken a relatively simple approach to retrieving data.

Many data retrievals use complex conditions to compare one data value to another data value or pick and choose data based on comparison values. To do this, we need to move beyond the Database Expert and Field Explorer and investigate the additional mechanisms built into Crystal Reports for building more complex data retrievals and filters. In addition, once the data is in Crystal, you can selectively modify how Crystal handles the data using built-in features like the Highlighting Expert and report alerts.

Featured in this chapter:

◆ Coding a WHERE clause with the Select Expert

◆ Modifying selection formulas

◆ Filtering data based on user input with parameter fields

◆ Suppressing information with conditional statements

◆ Highlighting data values with color

◆ Coding and activating conditional report alerts

Selection Formulas

In a report, the Database Expert lets you choose the data tables and the Field Explorer helps you pick the fields to place in your report. If you were using a structured query language (SQL) command to retrieve the data, these two pieces would comprise the SELECT fields FROM tables part of the SQL statement. For instance, a VistaNations report that selects the resort code, its state or province, its purchase price, its country, and its purchase date would generate a SQL statement like this behind the scenes to send to the database:

```
SELECT Resorts.ResortCode,Resorts.StateProvince,
Owners.PurchasePrice,Resorts.Country, Owners.PurchaseDat
FROM Resorts INNER JOIN Owners ON Resorts.ResortCode=Owners.ResortCode
```

This type of statement retrieves all the rows in the two tables that match on the ResortCode field. How would you go about creating a statement that restricted the selection of data to only those records where the resort was located in Canada or the United States? We have no way to do this with the Database Expert and the Field Explorer; we need something more. We need the Select Expert.

The Select Expert

The job of the Select Expert is to generate the WHERE clause in a complex SELECT statement. The WHERE clause is ideally passed to the database for processing as a part of the SELECT statement. There are cases when it is not possible to pass the WHERE clause to the database, specifically, when Crystal formulas are used as part of the WHERE clause.

To retrieve only records for resorts located in Canada or the United States, here's the type of SQL that needs to be generated:

```
SELECT Resorts.ResortCode,Resorts.StateProvince,
Owners.PurchasePrice,Resorts.Country, Owners.PurchaseDat
FROM Resorts INNER JOIN Owners ON Resorts.ResortCode=Owners.ResortCode
WHERE
    (Resorts.Country="CN" or Resorts.Country="US")
```

 To open the Select Expert, choose Report ➢ Select Expert or click the Select Expert icon on the toolbar. Either method opens the dialog shown in Figure 7.1.

FIGURE 7.1

The Select Expert

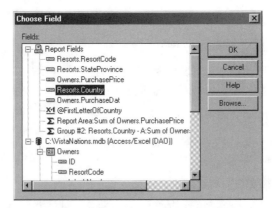

To begin, you choose the field that will be used to compare against a value. To generate the SQL we have above, the field to choose is the Country field in the Resorts table. With the field chosen, the Select Expert displays a dialog to help you choose the comparison operation, which is presented in the drop-down list shown in Figure 7.2. Table 7.1 describes the comparison operations and describes how the WHERE clause would be constructed for each operator.

FIGURE 7.2

Comparison operators

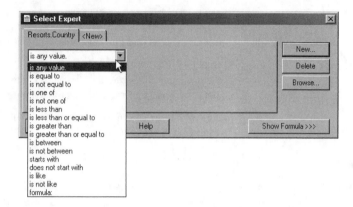

TABLE 7.1: SELECT EXPERT COMPARISON OPERATORS

COMPARISON OPERATOR	WHERE CLAUSE CONSTRUCTION
is any value	Does not generate a WHERE clause.
is equal to	WHERE field = value
is not equal to	WHERE field <> value
is one of	WHERE (field in [value1, value2, …])
is not one of	WHERE not (field in [value1, value2, …])
is less than	WHERE field < value
is less than or equal to	WHERE field <= value
is greater than	WHERE field > value
is greater than or equal to	WHERE field >= value
is between	WHERE (field >= value1 AND field <= value2)
is not between	WHERE NOT (field >= value1 AND field <= value2)
starts with	WHERE field LIKE 'C*' Here, C is any character or sequence of characters, and the asterisk is a wild card character matching against any characters that follow.
does not start with	WHERE field NOT LIKE 'C*' Here, C is any character or sequence of characters, and the asterisk is a wild card character matching against any characters that follow.

Continued on next page

TABLE 7.1: SELECT EXPERT COMPARISON OPERATORS *(continued)*

COMPARISON OPERATOR	WHERE CLAUSE CONSTRUCTION
is like	WHERE field LIKE 'C?CC*' Here, C is any character, the ? is a wild card to match on any single character, and the asterisk is a wild card character matching against any characters that follow.
is not like	WHERE field NOT LIKE 'C?CC*' Here, C is any character, the ? is a wild card to match on any single character, and the asterisk is a wild card character matching against any characters that follow.
formula	Any valid Crystal formula that compares a field to a value and returns a discrete result.

WARNING   If the Formula *option is chosen, a Crystal formula can be coded in place of the* WHERE *clause. However, this may negatively affect Crystal's performance for any formula that can't be passed to the database for equivalent processing. A Crystal formula can be evaluated only within the Crystal environment, meaning that all data will be retrieved from the database and processed locally in Crystal by the formula. It is generally a better idea to process complex* WHERE *clauses in the database environment and return a subset of data to Crystal rather than return all the records and have Crystal do the processing.*

To limit the records in a VistaNations report to the countries of Canada and the United States, the is one of operation is ideal. The is one of operation expects you to choose the values that it should allow for the report. To do this, use the drop-down arrow to the right of the is one of drop-down box or click the Browse button. Each time you choose a value in the list box, it is added to the area below the list box. Figure 7.3 shows the inclusion of CN and US for Canada and the United States, respectively.

You can also type values directly in the value area of the drop-down box and then click the Add button; the Add button is active only when you've typed a new value in the drop-down box. However, using the drop-down list to choose the values is preferred since it helps to eliminate typing errors and the occurrence of those not-quite-right values. For instance, if you typed *Canada* as the value, it would not match against anything in the database since the value is actually stored only as CN.

FIGURE 7.3

An *is one of* selection

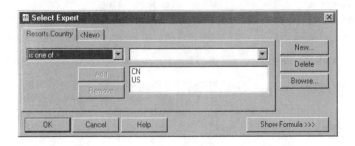

NOTE   You can remove a value from the list after you add it by selecting it and clicking the Delete key on the keyboard or using the Remove button to the left of the value list. The Remove button becomes available only when a value is selected.

DATA TYPE CONSIDERATIONS

The type of data available in the value drop-down box is determined by the data type of the field represented by the tab name. The example above is a record selection based on a text field. If the data is numeric or date/time, both the operations and the value choices are different. The `starts with`, `does not start with`, `is like`, and `is not like` options are specific to text data and therefore do not appear as options when numeric fields or date/time fields are being used in the condition.

TIP   Crystal uses an internal format for its date and time values. When you type a date as a value rather than picking it from the drop-down list, surround it with # signs to force Crystal to convert it properly to its internal format. For instance, type #9/3/1985# to allow the value you supply to be converted to a Crystal date. You could also use the built-in Date function for the same purpose using the format `Date(1985,9,3)`.

The following two additional options are added for date and time data to allow for flexible and powerful combinations within date ranges:

`is in the period`

`is not in the period`

When you choose either of these date range options, a large list of preprogrammed ranges is presented in the drop-down box. The list below shows the range names, which are reasonable enough names to be able to figure out each one's purpose just from reading the names:

WeekToDateFromSun	MonthToDate	YearToDate
Last7Days	Last4WeeksToSun	LastFullWeek
LastFullMonth	AllDatesToToday	AllDatesToYesterday
AllDatesFromToday	AllDatesFromTomorrow	Aged0To30Days
Aged31to60Days	Aged61to90Days	Over90Days
Next30Days	Next31To60Days	Next91to365Days
Calendar1stQtr	Calendar2ndQtr	Calendar3rdQtr
Calendar4thQtr	Calendar1stHalf	Calendar2ndHalf
LastYearMTD	LastYearYTD	

NOTE   Crystal Reports is bundled with many of the top-selling accounting systems, and the standard date range selection criteria are used to create financial reports and aging reports.

FORMULA EDITOR

Using the drop-down boxes in the Select Expert generates a formula representing the Crystal equivalent of the `WHERE` clause condition(s). The Show Formula button visible at the bottom of Figure 7.3 opens an editing window where you can directly type a formula or edit the formula created by the Select Expert. From within the editing window, a Formula Editor button provides direct access to the Formula Workshop and all of Crystal's built-in functions and operators. When the formula is showing, the Show Formula button disappears and is replaced by a Hide Formula button so that you can toggle between the two.

TIP *Changes made to the selection criteria directly in the Formula Editor go into effect after the settings have been saved by closing the Select Expert.*

MULTIPLE CONDITIONS

A SQL WHERE clause can contain multiple conditions. For instance, if we wanted to use only records for resorts in Canada and the United States where the resort code starts with the letter C, we would need two conditions in the WHERE clause. The Select Expert has a separate tab for each condition in the WHERE clause. In Figure 7.3, the Country field has its own tab and a second tab is labeled as <New>. To add additional conditions, click the <New> tab or the New button; the current <New> tab moves to the right and a new condition tab slips in to its left. In Figure 7.4, we see that the ResortCode field has been set to allow only resort codes that start with the letter C.

FIGURE 7.4

Additional
conditions

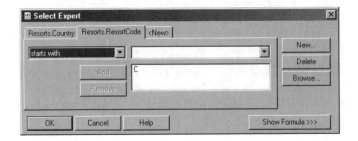

For each condition added (meaning each tab added), Crystal performs a logical AND operation to connect one condition to the next. For Figure 7.4, the default behavior of Crystal is to look for a Country code equal to either CN or US AND Resort codes that start with the letter C. There will be cases when you don't want to do an AND but instead want to code an OR. While Crystal will allow this, the Select Expert is not capable of generating this code, so you'll need to use the Show Formula button to directly edit the generated code to replace the AND with an OR.

CONTROLLING PRECEDENCE AND DETERMINING A RESULT

AND and OR clauses are of equal precedence and therefore calculate in left-to-right order as they appear in a formula. To modify this default behavior, use parentheses around the condition that you want to execute first. Conditions within parentheses can be nested, with innermost sets of parentheses evaluating first and then moving out to the next innermost set of parentheses. Figuring out how a sequence of multiple logical ANDs and ORs will combine and what result will be returned can be tricky. Here are the two rules a computer uses to evaluate pairs of ANDs and ORs:

```
(condition AND condition)
    returns TRUE if both conditions are TRUE, otherwise returns FALSE
(condition OR condition)
    returns TRUE if either condition is TRUE, otherwise returns FALSE
```

Conditions, and therefore the tabs associated with the conditions, can be removed from the WHERE clause using the Delete button.

VIEWING THE SQL

When a SQL-capable database is used as the data source, you can look at the SELECT clause and the WHERE clause generated by choosing Database ➤ Show SQL Query. Figure 7.5 shows the SQL generated by the Select Expert for records with resorts located in Canada or the United States.

FIGURE 7.5

Generated
SQL query

Record Selection

The Select Expert generates a record selection that can be edited directly without using the Select Expert dialog. The Record Selection option is available on the menu by choosing Report ➤ Selection Formulas ➤ Record. This opens the Formula Workshop directly, as shown in Figure 7.6. The formula shown here is the one that was generated from the Select Expert example visible in Figure 7.4. Notice that the drop-down choice of "starts with" has been converted to a Crystal Reports formula keyword "startswith." This translation was done automatically by Crystal Reports.

FIGURE 7.6

Record selection
formula

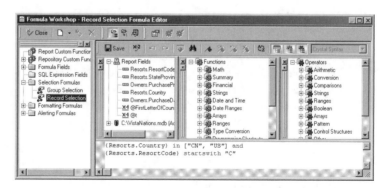

The complete power of the Formula Workshop, including access to fields, groups, functions, and operators, is available to create a record selection formula. Crystal will generate generic SQL statements based on the Crystal formula coded if possible or pass as much of the SQL to the database as possible, leaving Crystal to process locally only what cannot be processed by the database.

Group Selection

In Chapter 6, "Summarizing Information," we took a good look at how to create and manage groups. In addition, we introduced group selection formulas as a way to filter groups of data out of a report. To create a group selection formula, a report must first be grouped on a field in the report, a formula, or a field in a database table. With a group created, you can choose Report ➤ Selection Formulas ➤ Group to code a statement that will evaluate to TRUE or FALSE to filter out group data. This opens the Formula Editor, where you can then type any formula that evaluates to a TRUE value. When the value of the formula is TRUE, then the group is included in the report; a value of FALSE eliminates the group from the report. In Figure 7.7, the formula returns a TRUE value if the first letter of the Resorts.Country field is not equal to the letter *A*. This will eliminate all countries from the report that start with *A*.

FIGURE 7.7

Coding a group
selection formula

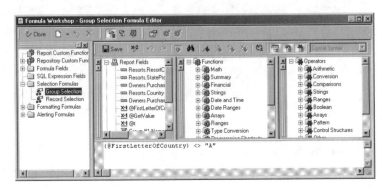

The condition statement is all that is needed in the formula edit box; it does not need to be a complete IF-THEN-ELSE statement. When the clause is TRUE, the group is included in the report, and when it's FALSE, the group is excluded.

Filtering Data Using Parameters

Do you have a report that you need to run periodically with exactly the same data format except that each time you run it, you go into Design mode and change the query to use a different date range? This is a great example of when using a parameter field in a report makes sense. The idea behind a parameterized report is that you can write a general report, prompt the user to provide a value, and pass that value into the report where it is used as a variable in the request for data, filtering out data that doesn't meet the criteria. This makes the report very adaptable since the user is in control of the input used to retrieve the data.

Earlier we discussed using the Select Expert to create the WHERE clause for a SQL statement, and we presented the following SQL statement as a way to limit the data in the report to those resorts located in Canada or the United States:

```
SELECT Resorts.ResortCode,Resorts.StateProvince,
Owners.PurchasePrice,Resorts.Country, Owners.PurchaseDat
FROM Resorts INNER JOIN Owners ON Resorts.ResortCode=Owners.ResortCode
WHERE
    (Resorts.Country="CN" or Resorts.Country="US")
```

While this is a great approach to refining the data, it is entirely dependent on the fact that the report designer knows which countries to include in the report when the report is being built rather than when the report is being run. The report would be more flexible for the user, and ultimately require less maintenance for the programmer, if the report user could decide and vary which countries to include at runtime rather than design time. The idea is to let the user choose a value for the country in an ad hoc and on-the-fly manner. Parameter fields can help you accomplish this task.

Creating a Parameter Field

Parameter fields can be created and used directly from the Field Explorer, as shown in Figure 7.8. With the Parameter Fields category selected, you can use the New button or right-click and select New from the menu in order to create the parameter field. If there are existing parameter fields, they appear indented under the category like Purchase Date does, and from here, you can edit the parameter by clicking the Edit button beneath the Field Explorer's title bar or right-clicking the parameter itself and selecting New from the submenu that displays.

FIGURE 7.8

Parameter fields in the Field Explorer

PROMPTING THE USER

Any time you use a parameter field, you are doing so with the goal of asking the user to provide information. That means that a dialog will pop up for the person using the report and, with the question you provide, ask them to type or choose a value for a field in the report. The question should be meaningful and concise. To create a parameter field in Design mode, three key pieces of information are required:

1. A name for the parameter field

2. A question or prompting text the user will see and need to answer

3. The data type allowed for the expected answer

Let's create a parameter that will ask the user for the country to be used in the query above instead of hard-coding values in the Select Expert. This will let the user decide at runtime which countries to use. Figure 7.9 shows that the initial information of name, prompting text, and value type is added to top portion of the Edit Parameter Field dialog. Valid data types are Boolean, Currency, Date, DateTime, Number, String, and Time.

FIGURE 7.9

A new parameter field

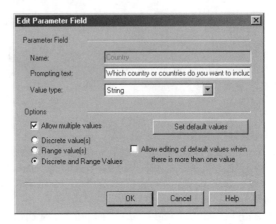

The bottom half of the Edit Parameter Field dialog asks for additional details needed for the new field. When the user is asked to provide a data value, they may want to specify one value or multiple values. For instance, you can have the user provide one country or multiple countries for the parameter. To let the user provide more than one value as an answer to a question, enable the Allow Multiple Values check box option. The set of three radio buttons for Discrete Values, Range Values, or Discrete And Range Values tells Crystal whether the user will be choosing or typing a single value (which is known as a *discrete value*) or providing a starting range and ending range for data values. The option to do both provides ultimate flexibility to the user, letting them choose to add a single value at a time as well as ranges of data and to intermix the two ways of choosing values.

You can provide a list of values for the user to choose from; this is known as a *default value list* in Crystal. If a list is provided for a user and the value desired doesn't appear in the list, the Allow Editing Of Default Values When There Is More Than One Value option (which appears below the Set Default Values button) can be used. This lets the user add additional values for the report being run but does not permanently add values to the set of value choices.

CREATING A LIST OF VALID VALUES

It's possible to generate a default list of choices for a parameter that is to be used interactively. This gives the person using the report a bit of a head start on choosing valid values. You can create the list of valid values in three ways:

- Manually by typing individual values

- Using a field from a database table

- Importing a pick list from an external file

When you click the Set Default Values button, the dialog shown in Figure 7.10 or one similar to it will appear. The options available on the Set Default Values dialog are dependent on the value type of the parameter. To manually add a valid value, type it into the Select Or Enter Value To Add box and then use the right arrow button to move the value to the Default Values list. This is useful for adding values like None or Type something here. In Figure 7.10, we typed the word *None* and we can move it to the list of default values by clicking the button with the > symbol on it.

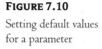

FIGURE 7.10

Setting default values
for a parameter

To present a list based on values stored in a database column, use the Browse Table and Browse Field drop-down boxes at the top-left corner of the dialog. These drop-down boxes let you choose the table and field to use to populate the list of values available on the left side of the screen; then you can add valid values to the list on the right by using the arrow buttons between the two lists. It is the list on the right that is seen by the person using the report.

If you already have the values stored externally in a text file, you can use the Import Pick List button to retrieve the values from the file directly into the Default Values list on the right side of the dialog. You can also export the values of a Crystal Default Values list and store it in an external file using the Export Pick List button.

The Define Description button can be used to add descriptive text for the user to see that might better explain the value that they are choosing. Values in the list can be sorted using the Display, Order, and Order Based On drop-down boxes.

WARNING   *The Default Values list is what the user will see when prompted for a parameter value. Crystal will not change or automatically update the list of values even if you chose the option to browse a table and a field. Adding values or deleting values is done manually in the Set Default Values dialog.*

ALLOWING THE USER TO TYPE VALUES DIRECTLY

A default list of values is definitely the best way to get input from a user, since there's less chance of input error if all that has to happen is a click of the mouse on a valid value. Sometimes, though, you need to allow direct editing. To help prevent errors in this case, you can use a set of options at the bottom left of the Set Default Values dialog to do the following:

◆ Set a length limit on the typing

◆ Set a minimum length

◆ Set a maximum length

◆ Specify an edit mask for validity of input on string data

For edit masking, Crystal uses characters to represent valid values in specific positions. For instance, an edit mask of ###-###-#### would require that the user type three numbers then a dash then three numbers and a dash and finally four numbers, like this: 800-555-1212. Edit masking helps prevent bad data by checking the values for validity and commonsense values. Table 7.2 describes the edit mask characters.

TABLE 7.2: EDIT MASK CHARACTERS

CHARACTER	POSITION RESTRICTION
A	Alphanumeric character required.
a	Alphanumeric character allowed but not required.
0	Digit required.
9	Digit or a space allowed but not required.
#	Digit, space, plus/minus sign allowed but not required.
L	Alphabet character required.
?	Alphabet character allowed but not required.
&	Any valid character or space required.
C	Any valid character or space allowed but not required.
. (period)	Separator character.
, (comma)	Separator character.
: (colon)	Separator character.
; (semicolon)	Separator character.
– (dash)	Separator character.
/ (slash)	Separator character.
< (less than)	Converts subsequent characters to lowercase.
> (greater than)	Converts subsequent characters to uppercase.
\ (backslash)	Escape character used to allow A, a, 0, 9, #, L,?,&,C in the text being typed by the user; e.g., type the value as \A to allow an A in the data.

DATA TYPE VARIATIONS

The options available on the Set Default Values dialog are dependent on the value type of the parameter. For example, string data allows edit masking while number fields do not. Boolean data (TRUE or FALSE values) presents a dialog that lets you group values into a dialog box from which you can choose one value (exclusive) or multiple values.

Using a Parameter Field

With a parameter field created, you can now put it to work in a report. Since parameter fields appear in the Field Explorer beneath the Parameter Fields category, you can treat the field like any other field, even dragging and dropping it into your report. Parameter fields can be used in any of the following ways:

- ◆ Select Expert to create a WHERE clause
- ◆ Formulas to suppress values or sections
- ◆ Highlighting Expert
- ◆ Sorting criteria
- ◆ Grouping criteria
- ◆ Directly on the report to print the parameter's value

THE SELECT EXPERT AND PARAMETERS

One of the main purposes of using a parameter field in a report is to ask the user a question so that data can be fetched based on the criteria they specify. To get a parameter field to ask for a value from the person using the report, you need to enter it in the Select Expert. This makes the parameter value a part of the WHERE clause to query the database. In the WHERE clause, a field value is compared to the value provided by the user. The example we're building uses the Country field, and we want to ask the user to supply a value, so we're building a WHERE clause whose structure resembles this:

```
WHERE Country = {value specified by the user}
```

In order to get the report to ask the user for a value, select the field you're matching in Design mode of the report, and then open the Select Expert by choosing Report ➤ Select Expert. The dialog in Figure 7.11 appears, and you can put the skills you learned earlier in the chapter on using the Select Expert to use here. In this dialog, one parameter has already been added to the report, {?Purchase Date}. To add the first or additional parameters, click either the <New> tab or the New button.

FIGURE 7.11

Adding a parameter to a report query

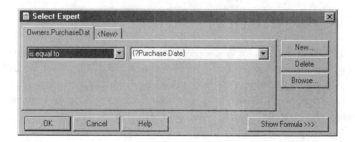

When you click the New button, the Choose Field dialog shown in Figure 7.12 opens. From the list of fields, choose a field to compare against in the WHERE clause. In this example, we're going to compare against the Country field in the Resorts table.

FIGURE 7.12

Choosing a comparison field

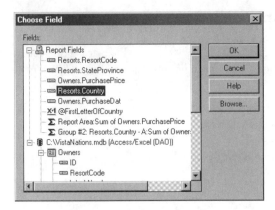

After choosing a field, you must then choose the comparison operation. Comparison operations like less than, greater than, and equal to appear in the first drop-down box in the Select Expert. For a complete discussion of the options here, refer back to Table 7.1. Figure 7.13 shows the second tab added for Resorts.Country and the list of comparison operations available for the data type of the field.

FIGURE 7.13

Choosing a comparison operator

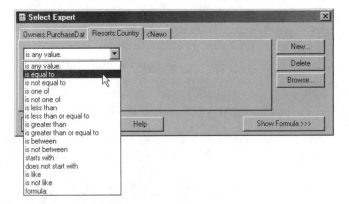

A second drop-down box will appear after choosing the comparison operator. In this second drop-down box, the parameter field shows up on the top of the list of available values. Parameter field names display with a question mark as the first character and then whatever you named the field. The list of values in the Select Expert sorts parameter fields to the top since the question mark sorts alphabetically before the letter A. Figure 7.14 shows the approach taken to choose a parameter field. Clicking the {?Country} item will add it to box above the list of values.

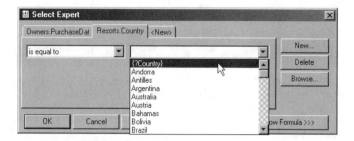

FIGURE 7.14

Choosing a comparison value

That's all you need to do to get Crystal to ask the users for a value! When the report is opened or refreshed, you'll first see a dialog asking whether you want to use the current parameter values or prompt for new values. If you prompt for new values, a dialog similar to that shown in Figure 7.15 displays.

FIGURE 7.15

Ask the user a question or two.

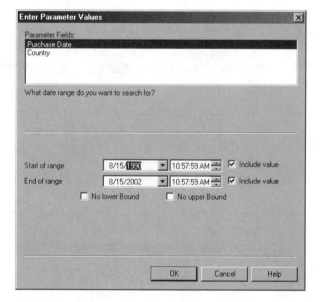

THE SINGLE-SCREEN INPUT APPROACH

Crystal uses a single-screen approach to asking for all parameter input. It uses this single screen regardless of how many parameters the report requires. The input screen has three distinct areas, starting at the top:

◆ List of parameters interactively requiring a value

◆ Prompting text asking a question for the selected parameter

◆ Value area to answer the question and provide the value

The example shown in Figure 7.15 asks for two parameter values: Purchase Date and Country. The parameters are listed in the order they were added to the Select Expert. In the top part of the screen, the user must select with the mouse the parameter for which they are providing input. With a parameter selected, the prompting text and value area change to be specific to the question. For the Purchase Date, a date range is required and drop-down boxes are provided for the starting and ending date and time values. After you select values for the Purchase Date parameter, it is very important that you *not* click the OK button yet. There is a second parameter for this report that needs a value before you click OK.

WARNING   *If the user clicks OK before providing values for all parameters, the report will have unexpected results since the remaining parameters will not have valid values.*

Once a value is provided for the Purchase Date parameter, the user selects the Country parameter in the list. Figure 7.16 shows this second input dialog. When it was created, the Country field used the Discrete Value and Range Value (refer back to Figure 7.9). This allows either single values or a range of values to be added as answers to the parameter prompt. It also makes the dialog a bit more complex!

FIGURE 7.16

Single and range value parameter

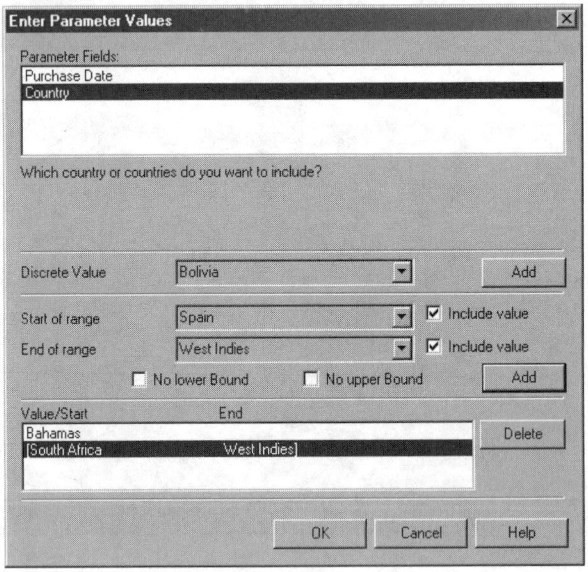

In the Discrete Value area of the screen, use the drop-down box to select a single value from the list. After selecting the value, click the Add button to its right to add the value to the list of values at the bottom of the screen. This list at the bottom of the screen is used in the WHERE clause of the query when the report runs.

In the Start Of Range and End Of Range area of the dialog, use the two drop-down boxes to pick a starting value and an ending value from the lists. After picking both values, click the Add button to add them to the list at the bottom of the screen. Optionally, you can use the check box to the right to include the value itself in the range; not checking the box excludes the value from the range.

Below the specific range setting area are two checkboxes that can be used to avoid needing to provide specific ranges. Enabling the *No lower Bound* option effectively tells the query to retrieve all data earlier than the end of the date range. Likewise, enabling the *No upper Bound* option retrieves all data later than the starting date range. Only one of these options can be enabled at any one time.

When all parameters have valid values, it's time to click the OK button to create the query that is sent to the database, and the report is then displayed.

Suppressing Data

Another way that you can filter, control, or refine what the user of a report sees is to suppress (meaning to hide) data and text objects. You can suppress items based on whether a condition is true or unconditionally suppress it at all times. There are several places in Crystal Reports to suppress information. In some cases your knowledge of formula language will be required; in others, you just need to enable a check box. Let's take a look at how to hide individual field objects, text objects, and embedded fields within text objects as well as how to hide entire sections.

Field Objects

The Format Editor can be used to enable the suppression of individual fields of data in several different scenarios:

◆ Suppress unconditionally

◆ Suppress if duplicated

◆ Suppress conditionally based on a formula

Any field can be unconditionally suppressed using the Common tab of the Format Editor, shown in Figure 7.17. With the Suppress check box enabled, the field will be hidden at all times. This is particularly handy if you're coding temporary fields or formulas that are needed for interim calculations whose results do not need to appear in the actual report.

At the bottom of Figure 7.17, the Suppress If Duplicated option is visible. When this option is enabled, if the field encounters a value that it has had in a previous record, the value will not be printed in the report or shown onscreen. Space is still reserved for the suppressed duplicate value and an empty space will be substituted.

The dialog shown in Figure 7.17 can also be used to conditionally suppress a field by writing a formula. To the far right of the Suppress check box and on the same horizontal line, there is a Formula button that you can click to open the Formula Workshop. Coding a condition in the editing area that will evaluate for each record in the database will suppress the field when the condition is true. Crystal will not display the value for the field; however, the space allocated for the field will remain visible. An example of a formula to conditionally suppress a field is shown here:

```
If {Resorts.PurchasePrice} < 100000 Then
   formula = True      'suppress the value
Else
   formula = False     'do not suppress it
End If
```

Alternatively, you can code just the condition portion of the statement, which will directly return a TRUE or FALSE value to suppress the field:

```
{Resorts.PurchasePrice} < 100000
```

If the field exists in a section by itself and you do not want to see the empty space left by suppressing the field, you can suppress the entire section.

FIGURE 7.17

Unconditionally suppress fields

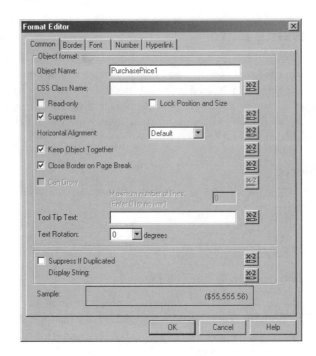

NUMBER FIELDS

If the field being suppressed is a number field, you can apply an additional level of suppression by hiding the number only if the value is zero. Figure 7.18 shows this option.

Accessing this option is a little tricky in the interface, so here's how to do it:

1. Select the field in the Design pane.

2. Open the Format Editor for the field by right-clicking and choosing the Format Field menu option, or choose Format ➤ Format Field.

3. Click the Customize button.

4. On the Number tab, select the Suppress If Zero option.

FIGURE 7.18

Suppress zero values

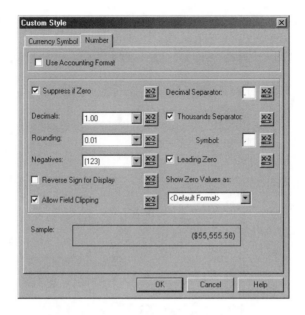

DATE FIELDS

Date fields can be formatted to suppress dates unconditionally, suppress a date value if it duplicates a date value in a previous record, or suppress conditionally based on a formula. Use the Common tab on the Format Editor for all of these actions.

Text Objects and Embedded Fields

The Format Editor can be used to suppress text objects as well as field objects. To open the Format Editor, select the text object and then right-click it and choose the Format Text menu option, or choose Format ➤ Format Text from the main menu. The Common tab for a text object is very similar to the Common tab for field objects, containing the same first three suppress options plus a fourth option specific to text objects:

- Suppress unconditionally
- Suppress if duplicated
- Suppress conditionally based on a formula
- Suppress embedded field blank lines

You can refer to the discussion of unconditionally suppressing, suppressing on duplicate values, and suppressing conditionally in the "Field Objects" section above. Let's look at the new option, suppressing on embedded field blank lines.

Oftentimes you'll embed a field or series of fields inside a text box. For instance, when you build a name and address block for a form letter, you might put all the fields inside a text object so that you can format them as a single unit. This technique is shown in Figure 7.19.

FIGURE 7.19

Text object with embedded fields

Since a text object of this type consists of several other fields and sometimes typed text, you may want to hide parts of the text object but not the entire thing. Anything placed on its own line within a text object can be hidden. In the example of the name and address block, if Address2 has no value and is on its own line, you can suppress the line using the Suppress Embedded Field Blank Lines option on the Common tab of the Format Editor. This option is shown in Figure 7.20.

FIGURE 7.20

Suppressing embedded blank fields

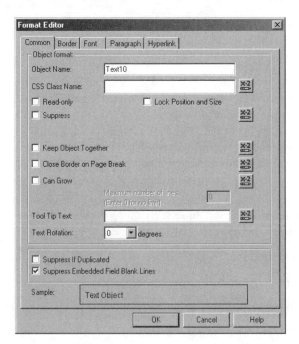

With this option enabled, when no value is retrieved from the database for a field embedded in the text object, the blank line that would normally be left as a placeholder will be suppressed and no space will be reserved for the embedded field.

Suppressing Sections

Sections act as a container for report elements. You can hide sections to force an entire container of elements to be hidden at any given time. Like fields, sections can be suppressed conditionally, unconditionally, or not at all. A section can be suppressed in the following ways:

◆ Suppress a section initially and allow drill-down later

◆ Suppress and do not allow drill-down (unconditional and conditional)

◆ Suppress blank sections

Suppress and allow drill-down   Drill-down refers to the capability to click a topic and open the detail data for that topic in a separate window tab. For instance, if you click a grand total, you can drill down and see the detail data that contributed to the grand total. Hide (Drill-Down OK) is a section property that you set by using either the Section Editor or by right-clicking the gray section title in Design mode and choosing the Hide (Drill-Down OK) option from the menu, as shown in Figure 7.21. You'll know a section is drill-down-capable by the change in the cursor; a magnifying glass appears over the top of drill-down-capable areas.

FIGURE 7.21

Section

Suppress and do not allow drill-down   In Figure 7.21 the section option to Suppress (No Drill-Down) is visible. When you select this menu option, the entire section, including all report elements, is suppressed completely and not visible at any time. When used from the submenu, this option is unconditional. When you select it from the Section Editor, you can click a Formula button to conditionally enable or disable the option to suppress and not allow drill-down. For more information on using the Section Editor, refer to Chapter 8, "Customizing Sections."

Suppress a blank section   A blank section is one that does not contain any text objects or fields that contain values. The Section Editor contains a check box option to Suppress Blank Section, which can be enabled either unconditionally so that the section will always be suppressed when blank or conditionally based on a formula value that, when true, will suppress a blank section.

Bringing the Message to Life

When a report first opens, the person viewing the report takes it in as a visual specimen, examining it, absorbing it, and assimilating the information. The process involves reading the information on the report and figuring out what its main message is. Have you ever wanted to have a particular part of the overall message jump out at the reader? Crystal Reports provides two features that will help you bring the data to life for the report reader and really focus their attention on its message:

◆ The Highlighting Expert

◆ Report alerts

The two differ from each other in that the Highlighting Expert uses color to focus a user's attention on records that meet a criterion, while report alerts use text messages in a dialog box to display data that meets a coded condition.

The Highlighting Expert

If the report you're designing will be viewed on a color monitor or printed on a color printer, it might be nice to add a splash of color to a data value to make it stand out. The Highlighting Expert can help call attention to specific information within a report by allowing you to code conditions that, when true, will force the font style, font color, background color, and data border to change.

CREATING A HIGHLIGHT CONDITION

To get started, select a field in the report whose value changes during the course of the report. This can include group names or fields in the Details section. With a valid field selected, you can choose Format ➢ Highlighting Expert to open the dialog shown in Figure 7.22.

TIP *You can also select the field and right-click to access the Highlighting Expert from the context menu.*

We selected the field PurchaseDat (our badly named database field that contains the resort unit's purchase date) prior to opening the Highlighting Expert. While there is nothing in the dialog itself that tells you which field was selected, you can determine the data type of the selected field by observing the type of data shown in the Sample box at the bottom right of the dialog.

FIGURE 7.22

The Highlighting Expert

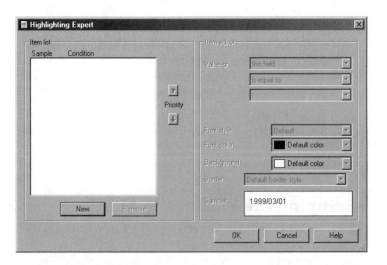

The dialog is split into two sections. The area on the left is the Item List, which shows all the conditions being processed by the Highlighting Expert. The Item Editor, on the right of the dialog, is where you set the conditions and visual attributes that will change if the condition is true. Notice that we're not going to write any formula code here; instead, the Highlighting Expert dialog provides drop-down boxes and buttons to automate the process for you.

When you click the New button below the Item List, a value is automatically added to the Item List, representing a new condition. When multiple conditions appear in the Item List, you can order them in the priority that you want them to be run. The up and down Priority arrows are used to move a condition up in priority so that it is considered before conditions listed below it or move a condition down in priority so that it is evaluated after conditions above it. Conditions execute in a top-to-bottom order in the Item List, and all conditions will execute. If you have conflicting settings in different conditions, the last one executed will set the format, so be careful not to override a condition with a different condition.

Clicking the New button also activates the Item Editor. This part of the screen is organized into two parts. At the top, you set the condition criteria, and at the bottom, you set the visual characteristics that will change when the condition is true. In Figure 7.23, the current field (signified by the phrase *this field*) has been set to change to italic maroon font with a double-lined border if the date is less than or equal to 12:00 a.m. on January 1, 1993. In business terms, this will highlight in maroon any resorts that were purchased prior to 1993. With the condition coded, it appears in the Item List on the left.

FIGURE 7.23

Coding a highlight

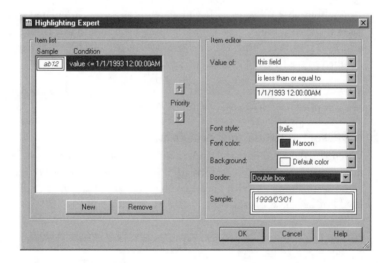

The top of the Item Editor uses three drop-down boxes to specify the three parts of a condition statement:

♦ Field value

♦ Operation

♦ Threshold value

You selected a field value on the report in order to open the Highlighting Expert. The selected field is the one that will be formatted (highlighted) or visually changed. You can choose to set a condition based on this same field or on a different field. All report fields, formulas, group names, and database fields are accessible through this list. This means that you can change the formatting of the selected field based on the value of a different field. For instance, if the country is Bahamas, you can set the Purchase Date field to display in italics with a maroon font and double-border box.

The operator drop-down box lets you compare a field to a value using the following comparison operations:

```
is equal to
is not equal to
is less than
is less than or equal to
is greater than
is greater than or equal to
is between
is not between
```

NOTE   *Table 7.1 describes the behavior of the comparison operators.*

The threshold value drop-down box is automatically populated with sample data from the database for the field value chosen. You can pick a threshold value from the list or type one directly. If a field is of type date/time, the time component defaults to 12:00 a.m. and will be automatically included in the threshold value by Crystal.

NOTE   *You can add as many conditions to the Item List as you need, giving you the ability to set multiple fields in the same data record based on the same or differing criteria.*

THE RESULT OF A HIGHLIGHT OPERATION

When you open a report that contains a highlighted condition, the group name or variable data that meets the criteria will be formatted with the visual settings coded in the Highlighting Expert. Figure 7.24 shows the MPI and WNS resorts in the Bahamas in italic maroon font with a double-lined border; these resorts were purchased prior to 1993.

FIGURE 7.24

A highlighted field

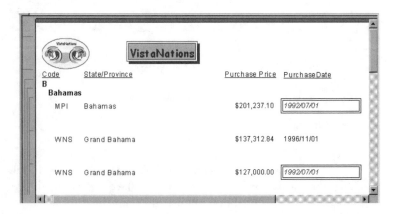

NOTE   *The Highlighting Expert can also be used to format cells in cross-tabs or OLAP grids by setting conditions on row and column heading values.*

Report Alerts

A report alert is a custom message that you program to display when certain conditions are met by the data contained in the report. For instance, if there is a trend that shows a decrease in sales prices for resorts, an informational message can point this out instead of leaving it to the report reader to deduce. To create a report alert, you write a formula with a condition statement in it. To trigger the alert, the condition must be true. A true condition causes a text string message to be displayed onscreen in a prompt window with an OK button. The informational message and alert appear when the report is opened or the data in the report is refreshed.

CODING AN ALERT

To create an alert, choose Report ➤ Alerts ➤ Create Or Modify Alerts to open the Create Alerts dialog shown in Figure 7.25. In this example, an alert named SalesPriceBelowAverage has already been created. Modifying and creating an alert are done from the same dialog, and the New, Edit, and Delete buttons guide you in the task you want to do.

FIGURE 7.25

Creating an alert

When you create a new alert or edit an existing one, the Create Alert or Edit Alert dialog displays. The dialogs are identical with the exception of the word *Create* or *Edit* in the title bar. In Figure 7.26, an alert is being edited.

FIGURE 7.26

Editing an alert

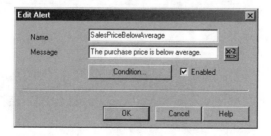

You should give an alert a meaningful name in the Name box and type a meaningful text message for the alert to display into the Message box. Notice the Formula icon located to the right of the

Message box. You can use this to code a formula that will dynamically create the text string message rather than hard-coding (typing it directly) it into the Message box area. Below the Message box is a check box to enable or disable the alert. The Condition button is where you actually write the logic that will trigger the alert. Clicking the Condition button opens the Formula Editor, as shown in Figure 7.27. Here, you code only the condition portion of an IF-THEN-ELSE statement, not the full code. The condition itself must be coded in a way that its value results in either TRUE or FALSE; no other value is valid for a report alert. In this example, the PurchasePrice field is being checked to see if it is less than $200,000; if it is, the alert will trigger.

FIGURE 7.27

Coding an alert

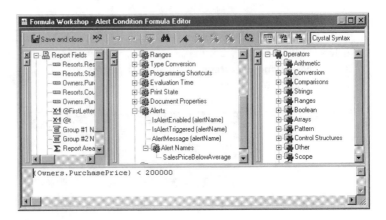

RUNNING AN ALERT

A report alert will run automatically if its trigger condition is true. It will activate only when a report is first opened or if the data in the report is refreshed. When an alert is triggered, the dialog shown in Figure 7.28 displays, and you have the option of viewing the records that meet the trigger criteria or simply clicking the Close button and dismissing the dialog without viewing the records.

FIGURE 7.28

A triggered alert

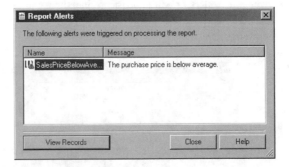

If you click the View Records button, a separate tab in the report is displayed, showing only the records that meet the alert condition. The Preview tab displays the report in its entirety. The name of the alert, for instance, SalesPriceBelowAverage, becomes the tab label for the alert data, so it is a good idea to give your alerts meaningful names. Figure 7.29 shows a set of data that generated a true condition for the alert shown in Figure 7.28.

FIGURE 7.29

Alert results

CHECKING PAST ALERTS

Once you view a report onscreen, you may want to go back and see which alerts were triggered for this report, if any. To do this, choose Report ➤ Alerts ➤ Triggered Alerts. This is a handy thing to do if you simply closed the Report Alerts window earlier rather than viewing the records. The dialog shown in Figure 7.28 redisplays and gives you the chance to once again view the records that meet the alert criteria.

FORMULAS AND ALERTS

You can write formulas in the Formula Workshop that refer to report alerts to check whether an alert is enabled or was triggered or to display a text message for the alert. Any formula that references a report alert is evaluated after Crystal Reports has retrieved the data from the database and as it is being written to the screen for display. The Function tree in the Formula Workshop, shown in Figure 7.30, shows the built-in formulas that are provided to work with alerts.

FIGURE 7.30

Alert function tree

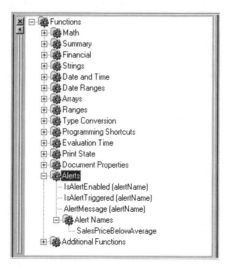

The three formula language functions are available in both Crystal and Basic syntax, and each take as their single parameter the name of the report alert being referenced. Table 7.3 describes the functions.

TABLE 7.3: REPORT ALERT FUNCTIONS

FUNCTION NAME	DESCRIPTION
IsAlertEnabled("*alertname*")	Returns TRUE if an alert is in effect for the report
IsAlertTriggered("*alertname*")	Returns TRUE for a record that triggered the alert
AlertMessage("*alertname*")	Displays the text message when the alert condition is true

In addition to the built-in functions for alerts, notice in Figure 7.30 that each existing alert is also displayed in the Function tree beneath a category called Alert Names. An alert is listed in the Function tree whether it is enabled or disabled. Double-clicking the alert name simply copies its text name surrounded by double-quotes to the editing window. This lets you use the alert name in a formula without needing to type it manually, for instance, as the parameter to one of the functions described in Table 7.3.

Summary

The best way to refine the data returned to a report is to create a WHERE clause for a SQL statement, which is exactly what the Select Expert does. Creating combinations of conditions and understanding how to AND or OR them together in the Select Expert helps you create succinct reports.

Reports that can run based on user input are powerful ways to tailor the data needs to the user's requirement; you can use parameters to ask users for values, filter data, and suppress data. Suppressing field data, entire lines, and even sections is another way to refine the information a report is showing.

The Highlighting Expert can clarify the message being imparted by a report through the use of color on fields or rows of data, while report alerts can separate out records that meet certain criteria so that you can examine them as a unit.

Chapter 8

Customizing Sections

IN CHAPTER 1, "BUILDING Your First Report," we introduced the concept of Crystal Reports being a banded report writer that contains five basic bands, or sections, that are initially created for every report. In this chapter, we want to dig deeper into customization options that allow you to control both the appearance and behavior of sections and the information contained in a section area.

Sections allow you to control a group of report elements in a common way. Changing how a field or text label looks one at a time is easy enough, but if you had to manually change the font on every field, it would quickly become a tedious endeavor. You can think of a section as a container for the fields, images, and labels placed in the section during report design. A single report can have many of these containers that group and style the information they hold. That container, or section area, can be formatted to behave according to rules that you design, forcing all of the report elements in that section to have the same behavior and visual attributes.

Featured in this chapter:

◆ Hiding sections completely

◆ Using drill-down sections for groups

◆ Creating underlays

◆ Using formulas to control visibility

◆ Creating columns within sections

◆ Sizing a section to fit your data

◆ Changing spacing options

Section Areas

When you first create a report, five section bands are automatically added to your layout area as if it were an 8 1/2" by 11" piece of paper.

◆ Report Header

◆ Page Header

- ◆ Details
- ◆ Report Footer
- ◆ Page Footer

TIP   *The bands are also referred to as* areas *in the Crystal Reports help file.*

These bands are depicted in Figure 8.1 as if they were laid out on a piece of paper and in Figure 8.2 as they would appear in Crystal's design area. When the report is previewed or printed, the information in the Report Header and Report Footer will each appear once in the report: at the very top of the report and at the very end of the report. Page Headers and Footers will appear once per page. Notice in the layout that the Page Footer is the last section, not the Report Footer. The information in the Page Footer prints in a very small margin at the bottom of each page; this puts it visually below the Report Footer, which will print directly after the last bits of data in the Details section. The Details section is where each record or row of data from the data source will be placed; its size is determined by the number of records retrieved from the data source.

FIGURE 8.1

Band layout

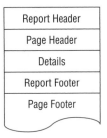

FIGURE 8.2

Bands in
Design mode

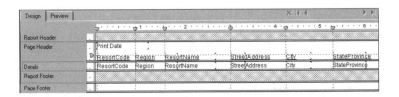

The simple report in Figure 8.2 was created with the Standard Report Creation Wizard. The wizard automatically suppresses the Report Header and Report Footer. The fact that these two sections are currently hidden is reflected in the different background markings: The two sections are cross-hatched with gray lines.

NOTE   *The Report Header and Report Footer are not automatically hidden when you build a blank report manually instead of using the Standard Report Creation Wizard.*

Sections that are not hidden have a plain white background. This is the designer's visual clue that a section has been hidden. If you prefer, you can change this feature so that hidden sections do not display in your report at all, regardless of the hatch marks. To set a report option to control whether the section displays during your design work, choose File ➤ Options, and on the Layout tab, shown in Figure 8.3, and select the Show Hidden Sections option. With this option enabled, the gray hatch marks appear; with it disabled, the section will not display at all in Design mode.

FIGURE 8.3

Designer settings

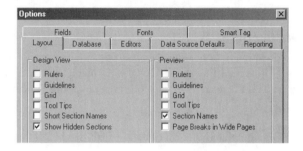

Hiding Sections

To the left of a section's design layout is the section's name or abbreviation. Right-clicking this area displays the submenu for sections, shown in Figure 8.4. From here, you can choose to unilaterally hide or display an entire section and all the information it contains.

FIGURE 8.4

Section submenu

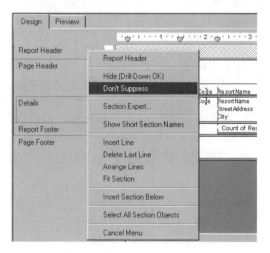

TIP   The first option in a submenu is always the name of the report object that currently has focus.

The Don't Suppress option displays a hidden section, making it visible and eliminating the gray hatch marks on the section's background. The opposite of Don't Suppress is Suppress (No Drill-Down). Only one of these two options will ever appear on the submenu; click the option to change the behavior and the next time you view the pop-up submenu, the opposite action is listed.

TIP   If you need more room for your design, try using the short section abbreviations (RH, PH, D, RF, PF) by choosing the Show Short Section Names option in the menu shown in Figure 8.4.

Drill-Down Sections

User-controlled section hiding is called drill-down, and its purpose is to hide detail data until the user asks to see it. Notice the Hide (Drill-Down OK) menu option directly above the Don't Suppress option in Figure 8.4. There are two ways to prevent an entire section of information from displaying:

◆ Hide it but allow drill-down into detail information.

◆ Suppress it completely and do not allow drill-down.

Both options hide the section and its contents. The difference between the two is that the person viewing the report can display a section at runtime using the first option, while with the second option the user never sees the section.

Drill-down is frequently used with group sections and detail data; the detail data section is hidden with drill-down capability, and all that is visible when the report opens is the summary information in the group section. For instance, in our example, we have a report that lists resorts by country. A simplified list would show just the country names, and if you wanted to see which resorts were in that country, you could expand the section to display the detail information. A double-click (a drill-down) on a summary item in the group section displays the detail data.

The net effect of the hiding in this case is to initially hide the data but still make it available interactively on demand when a user wants to view it. This type of report conserves real estate when the report first opens. As the user moves the mouse over a hidden drill-down-capable section, the mouse cursor changes into a magnifying glass. This signals that a double-click can be used to reveal detail data. Figure 8.5 shows a list of resorts by country, and the magnifying glass is visible when the mouse is over the top of the country name.

FIGURE 8.5

Drill-down sections

7/15/2002

Country

Andorra

Antilles

Argentina

Australia

Austria

When the user double-clicks the summary line, the detail information for that particular summary item is displayed in its own tab in the Crystal Reports designer, as shown in Figure 8.6. The group tree also displays with only the single entry in the new tab. In the original Preview tab, the group tree still contains an entry for all groups in the report. The drill-down section can be closed by clicking the **X** on the tab.

FIGURE 8.6

Drill-down tabs

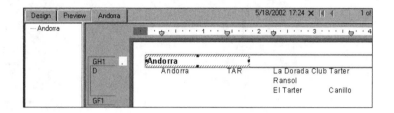

SECTION NAMES

Notice in the gray label area for the section in Figure 8.6 that only a single detail section (D) and its group header (GH1) and group footer (GF1) are being displayed. These are the abbreviated section names. In Design mode, you can choose to show just these short names using the option Show Short Section Names from the section pop-up submenu. This option is visible in Figure 8.4. In Preview mode, you can choose to prevent all section labels from displaying by disabling the Section Names option in the Preview section of the report's options. Refer back to Figure 8.3, where the option is enabled; you could click the option to disable it and prevent the section short names from displaying in Preview mode. You control the displaying of section names in Preview mode independently of the settings in Design mode.

Conditionally Hiding Sections

The options to hide and suppress sections using the pop-up menu for sections hide the section entirely. Drill-down allows the person viewing the report to display the section. There is one more way to hide sections and that is *conditionally*, meaning that if certain conditions are true, the section will not be displayed. To conditionally hide sections, you'll use the Section Expert with a formula to control when the section displays.

The Section Expert

The Section Expert, shown in Figure 8.7, is used to customize the behavior of sections beyond what is accessible through the pop-up section submenu. To open the Section Expert, choose that option from the pop-up submenu shown previously in Figure 8.4 or choose Report ➤ Section Expert.

FIGURE 8.7

Section Expert

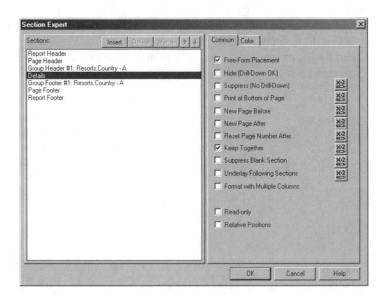

The left side of the Section Expert lists all sections currently in the report. Here we have the standard set of five plus Group Header and Group Footer sections. Along the top edge of the list of sections are five action buttons:

Insert   You can add a new section below the currently selected section. The type of section (Group Header, Page Header, Details, etc.) is based on the type of the currently selected section. For example, if the Details section is highlighted and you click the Insert button, a new Details section is added after the current Details section. The Section Expert adds the new section and assigns a new alphabet character to it in ascending order. Figure 8.8 shows that a new Group Header section was inserted as well as a new Details section. The Group Header #1 now consists of two components: Group Header #1a and Group Header #1b. #1a is the original and #1b is the one that was added. At this point, you can no longer configure Group Header #1 as it is just a title that contains the other two; it is the two subcomponents that can be configured. You can do things like move #1a below #1b and Crystal will automatically renumber them.

FIGURE 8.8

Inserting sections with the Section Expert

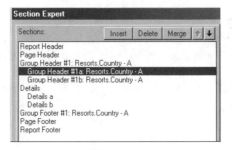

When adding sections, they do not have to be added in balanced pairs. Above, only a Group Header was added; no Group Footer was added. In Design mode, shown in Figure 8.9, the effect is a blank section added below the original section.

FIGURE 8.9

New sections in Design mode

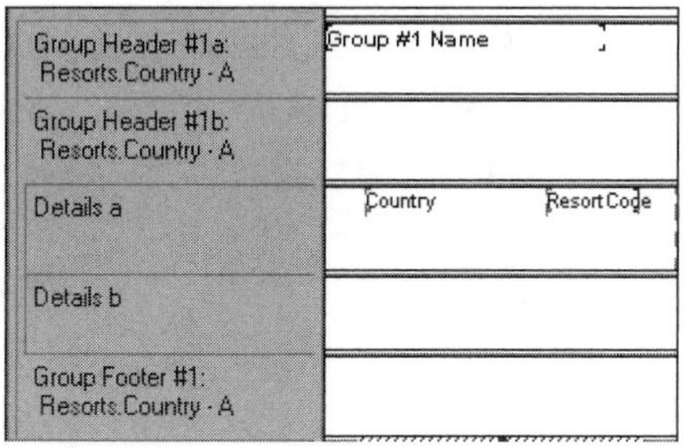

TIP *New sections can also be added with the pop-up submenu, shown in Figure 8.4, using the Insert Section Below menu choice.*

Multiple sections of the same type can help add to the flexibility in displaying information. For instance, perhaps you want to print one set of heading information on the front side of a report page, like Phone Listing, and a different heading on the back side of the page, e.g., Phone Listing - Continued.

Delete   Deleting an unwanted section is easy! Select it from the list, and click the Delete button. There is a caveat, though. You can delete only sections that you have added. In other words, the five basic sections that Crystal placed cannot be deleted.

Merge   If you created two sections of the same type, for instance, two Details sections, you can use the Merge button to consolidate the two sections into one. This button is active only for multiple sections of the same type. For instance, the Group Header #1a and Group Header #1b shown in Figure 8.8 could be merged together; the result would be a single line once again labeled Group Header #1. The contents of the two sections are preserved and merged.

Up Arrow   This button repositions a section by moving the selected section up one section at a time through the list of identical section types. You cannot change the order of the five original sections placed in a report by Crystal.

TIP *You can also reposition sections of the same type directly in Design mode using a drag-and-drop technique. Single-click the gray area containing the section name, hold the mouse down, and watch as the mouse pointer changes to a hand, and then drag the hand to an alternate section position to move it.*

Down Arrow   This button repositions a section by moving the selected section down one section at a time through the list of identical section types. As with the up arrow button, the order of the five original sections placed in a report by Crystal is static and cannot be changed.

With one of the sections selected in the list on the left side of the Section Expert, the options on the right can be used to customize the look and behavior of the selected section (refer back to Figure 8.7 for details). Table 8.1 shows the options available and to which sections they apply.

TABLE 8.1: OPTIONS AVAILABLE BY SECTION

OPTION	RH	PH	GH	D	GF	PF	RF
Free-Form Placement	X	X	X	X	X	X	X
Hide (Drill-Down OK)	X		X	X	X		X
Suppress (No Drill-Down)	X	X	X	X	X	X	X
Print At Bottom Of Page	X		X	X	X		X
New Page Before			X	X	X		X
New Page After	X		X	X	X		
Reset Page Number After	X	X	X	X	X	X	X
Keep Together	X		X	X	X		X
Suppress Blank Section	X	X	X	X	X	X	X
Underlay Following Sections	X	X	X	X	X	X	X
Format With Multiple Columns				X			
Reserve Minimum Page Footer						X	
Read-only	X	X	X	X	X	X	X
Relative Positions	X	X	X	X	X	X	X

Section Options

Along the right side of the Section Editor are check box options that you can enable or disable. Any combination of options can be used, and in addition, formulas can be associated with the option to conditionally enable or disable it.

Free-Form Placement   With this option enabled, fields and labels placed in the section reference absolute x- and y-coordinates and placement for printing purposes. This means that what you see on the screen will very closely match what prints. If the option is disabled, then the printing position of fields and labels is governed by the individual printer driver used at the time of printing. The printing of graphics, boxes, and lines drawn in a section always abides by free-form placement and uses x- and y-coordinates from the top left to the bottom right of a page. As you might guess, this can cause some undesirable results when you enclose text labels or field values inside graphics elements such as boxes. In this case, it is recommended that free-form placement be enabled. It is also desirable that all sections within a report use the same setting for free-form placement for consistency.

Hide (Drill-Down OK) The option to hide with drill-down hides a section until a user double-clicks to drill-down and reveal detail data. The Hide (Drill-Down OK) option in the Section Expert is a duplication of and is connected to the identical setting discussed above in the pop-up submenu for sections. When you choose that menu option, the check box here is enabled. Likewise, disabling it in the section submenu or in the Section Expert disables it in both places.

Suppress (No Drill-Down) The option to suppress a section completely hides it at runtime. Like the Hide (Drill-Down OK) option, the Suppress option in the Section Expert is a duplicate of and is connected to the menu option with the same name in the pop-up submenu for sections. When you choose that menu option, the check box here is enabled, and disabling it in the section submenu or in the Section Expert disables it in both places.

Print At Bottom Of Page For grouped information, using this option prints the summary value at the bottom of a page even if the information would normally have printed only halfway down the page. This option is useful for pages of documents where a summary value needs to be the last piece of information displayed, for instance, with invoice totals. When used with the Details section, this option prints/displays the detail records at the bottom of the page. This option is useful if you want data to appear below a chart or graph and consistently be anchored to the same ending place on a page.

New Page Before Use this option to place a page break before printing and displaying the section. This starts each new grouping of information on its own page when used with a Group Header section. When used with the Details section, each individual record (row) retrieved from the data source prints on a new page.

New Page After Use this option to place a page break after printing and displaying a section. This also starts each new grouping of information on its own page when used with a Group Header section. When used with the Details section, each individual record (row) retrieved from the data source prints on a new page.

Reset Page Number After When you're printing batches of reports, for instance invoices, this option allows you to restart the numbering with each new group. Consider that the group may be based on a customer number; for each new customer number, the page counter is reset to 1. Even if there are 10,000 invoices to print, each one is guaranteed to be page numbered based on the group rather than showing "Page 741" at the bottom of a customer's one-page invoice.

TIP *Using the Reset Page Number After and Print At Bottom Of Page section options together gives the best results for printing groups of information that need to be considered as stand-alone units.*

Keep Together An 8 1/2" by 11" piece of paper consists of about 66 lines, with around 55 of those lines dedicated to the Details section. In general, a page break will occur at its fixed place regardless of your data; the break is based on the line count. Use the Keep Together option to force Crystal Reports to keep the entire contents of a section on the same page. For instance, the Report Footer section ordinarily begins printing directly after the last record in the Details section. If you have a large amount of information displayed in the Report Footer section and you mark the Keep Together option, Crystal will insert a page break before printing the Report Footer so that the entire section appears on one page. The Page Header and Page Footer options always print at the top and bottom of a report, which means that they "Keep Together" by default.

WARNING *The Keep Together option for sections is not intended to keep groups of detail data rows together; for that purpose, use the Keep Group Together option associated directly with a group.*

Suppress Blank Section If a formatted section ends up having no data in it at runtime based on filter criteria, use this option to prevent the entire section from displaying. Some sections take up a default and reserved amount of space regardless of whether they are suppressed, like the Page Footer, but using this option will minimize the amount of space devoted to blank sections.

Underlay Following Sections A section underlay is the layering of one section under another. The underlay technique can be used to place information under other information, for instance, place an image under text so that the image appears as a background. In our example scenario, we want to use the company logo as a background for every page in a report. To do this, you begin with the Page Header section and create a second Page Header. On the second Page Header, enable the Underlay Following Sections option in the Section Expert, and then place the graphic in the section in Design mode. With this option activated, the logo will appear to be under all sections up to the Page Footer section, which acts as the Page Header's boundary. You should suppress the Page Footer (absolutely, not conditionally) since the Page Header can't underlay the Page Footer. This technique is also known as using a watermark and can be used to place words like "Internal Use Only" and "Confidential" behind the contents of a report.

Format With Multiple Columns A simple list of names with phone numbers may take up many pages if Crystal prints only one record per line in a report. It would be handy to print this data as two columns to more effectively use the screen and paper real estate. Since this is an option that affects the rows of data being retrieved from a data source, it is available only for the Details section. When the option is enabled, an additional tab appears in the Section Expert to specify the size of the columns and the amount of space to leave between columns. Figure 8.10 shows the Layout tab with spacing information.

FIGURE 8.10

Formatting multiple columns

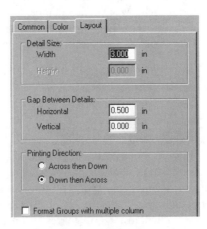

The Printing Direction option in Figure 8.10 determines whether the data in the Details section is reflowed from top to bottom and then to the next column or from left to right from the first column to the second column and then back to the first column. The Format Groups With Multiple Column option determines whether group headers and footers should be associated with the reflowed data in the Details section. With this option enabled, the data reflows and the groups stay intact and reflow as well. Figure 8.11 shows a phone listing report formatted with two columns based on the Layout information.

FIGURE 8.11

Data displayed in multiple columns

ResortName	ResortPhone		
Acadia Village Resort	207-667-6228	Residence la Piana	0324-93543
Harbor Ridge	207-244-7000	Villa Rubinacci	818-781909
The Ponds at Foxhollow	413-637-1469	Villagio Torre Macuada	0925-968111
Marriott's Custom House	617-310-6300	Club Dolmen by the Sea	581510
Harborside Inn	508-27-4321	Sunquest Gardens	05-321132
The Mountain Club on Loon	800-229-STAY	Hever's Harbour Beach	90-392-378900
The Newport Bay Club	401-849-8600	Villea Village	0843-51697
Neptune Vacation Club	401-466-2100	Elani Bay	037-424245
Trapp Family Lodge	802-253-8511	Club Patara	24208443920

NOTE *The Format With Multiple Column option reflows the data in the Details section; it does not do anything to the column headers. To repeat column headers above the multiple columns, you need to manually copy and paste the headings from the original columns into an aesthetically pleasing position above the additional columns.*

Reserve Minimum Page Footer Crystal Reports reserves space at the bottom of each page for the information to appear on a footer. This space is reserved whether or not there is information in the footer, whether multiple footers are used, or whether the footer is suppressed, conditionally or absolutely. Enabling the Reserve Minimum Page Footer option can minimize the amount of space set aside for a footer by using the height of the single largest footer. If this option is not enabled, Crystal adds together the combined sizes of all Page Footers and reserves that amount of space at the bottom of each page regardless of whether the footers have been suppressed or not.

Read-only If a section's Read-only option is enabled, all other section options are disabled. Report elements in the section cannot be moved, resized, or formatted in any way. You can think of this option as a way to prevent yourself from accidentally changing things once you have the report formatted exactly as you like it.

Relative Positions The repositioning of elements in a section is generally done by dragging and dropping elements. With the Relative Positions option enabled, report elements are repositioned using the Object Size And Position dialog shown in Figure 8.12. This dialog positions the report object relative to the top-left corner of the report. The X value is used to change the position of the object horizontally from the left margin. The Y value is used to change the position of the object vertically from the top margin.

FIGURE 8.12

Object Size And
Position

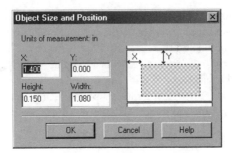

Conditionally Applying Options

In the Section Expert, the formula formatting button appears to the right of many of the section options. This means that you can use a formula to determine whether the option is applied to the section. Table 8.2 describes the three states that a button may be in. The result of the formula coded to control a section must have a value of True in order for the section to be affected. As with other formulas in Crystal Reports, you can write your code in either Crystal Syntax or Basic Syntax; see Chapter 4, "Adding Business Logic with the Formula Workshop," for more information on formula syntax.

TABLE 8.2: SECTION FORMULA ICONS

ICON IMAGE	ICON DESCRIPTION
	Formula formatting allowed; none currently in effect
	Formula formatting allowed and currently in use
	Formula formatting not allowed

TIP   *If the section option is selected outright with a check mark and a formula is coded to conditionally control the option as well, the formula overrides the check mark.*

CONDITIONAL FORMULAS FOR PAGE HEADERS

You can also use formulas to place different headings on odd and even pages. Again you'll make use of two similar sections, this time Page Header sections. In one of the Page Header sections, a formula is used to suppress the section if the page number is an odd number; on the other Page Header section, a formula is used to suppress the section if the page number is even. The formula in the Suppress option section on one of the Page Header sections would be

```
Remainder(PageNumber,2) <> 0
```

While the other Page Header Suppress option section would use

```
Remainder(PageNumber,2) = 0
```

These two formulas may appear to be incomplete at first glance since they are not wrapped in an if-then-else clause. Formulas written in the Formula Workshop need only to return a True or False value when used to conditionally control sections. Here, the built-in function, Remainder, is used to divide the current page number (accessed through the special variable PageNumber) by 2 and return the remainder from the division. For instance, if there are seven pages, Remainder(7,2) returns 1 because 2 divides into 7 three times with a remainder value of 1. The final test is whether 1 = 0; this returns False with the number 7 as it would with all odd-numbered pages.

CONDITIONAL FORMULAS FOR GROUP HEADERS

You can use formulas to add great flexibility to the sections and their behavior in Crystal. For instance, imagine that you're printing a large report that contains groups in Duplex mode on the printer. You'd like each new group to start on a new page, but you also want that new page to always be the front side of a piece of paper. In Duplex mode, the page numbers in this situation would have odd page numbers on the front side of a paper and even page numbers on the back side of a paper. To force your group data to always start printing on the front side, you can combine the following section options that test odd and even numbers:

♦ Group Footer section: Enable the New Page After section option.

♦ Group Header Section: Insert a second group header (A and B).

♦ Group Header A Section: In the New Page After section option, code the formula
  `Not onFirstRecord`

♦ Group Header A Section: In the Suppress section option, code the formula
  `Remainder(PageNumber,2) <> 0`

The combination of these settings suppresses a blank page on the first page of the report, forces a new page for every group, and places the new group on only the odd-numbered pages through the use of the Suppress option.

CONDITIONAL FORMULAS FOR DETAIL SECTIONS

The Suppress option for sections is very powerful, especially when you use multiple Details sections. Again using the Suppress option, you can conditionally hide or display a section based on the value in a field. For instance, with our Resorts table, we can selectively display a section if the value of the FiveStarRating field is Yes. To do this, in the Details section, code the following formula in the Suppress option:

```
isnull({Resorts.FiveStarRating}) or {Resorts.FiveStarRating} = "No"
```

If either condition is True, the section will not display. This means that if there is no value for the FiveStarRating field or if its value is No, the section is suppressed, which prevents that line of detail data from displaying in the report.

Multiple detail sections are used to conditionally control the appearance of the rows of data retrieved from a data source. In addition to suppressing the section as the formula above does, you can conditionally add blank lines based on field values, conditionally add boxes and graphics based on comparing values, and add color shading based on the record numbers.

Getting complex section formatting to work is a matter of thinking through in Crystal section terminology what you want to have happen, then testing and combining individual options to get the results you desire. The list of built-in functions in the Print State area of the Formula Workshop will be of great use to you in conditionally formatting sections.

Adding Color to a Section

The Color tab in the Section Expert lets you set a background color for a section. This can be done absolutely or conditionally using a formula. In Figure 8.13, you can see that you can either set the color absolutely by enabling the check box and selecting a color or set the color conditionally by writing a formula and choosing a color in the formula.

FIGURE 8.13

Setting a section background color

The background color is in effect for the entire section, and the objects (fields, labels, images, etc.) appear on top of the background color. You can control the color of each section independently of the other sections, so the Report Header can be one color while the Report Footer is an entirely different color.

A typical formula used to set a background color for a section is one to alternate the line shading in the Details section for easier reading of rows and rows of data. If you want every other row to be white and the alternate row to be another color, the following formula will work (where RecordNumber is the number of rows retrieved from the data source):

```
If Remainder(RecordNumber,2) = 0 Then
    Aqua
Else
    White
```

White is actually the default color, so you don't have to specify it, but it makes your code much more readable if you completely express your intentions in a formula. In this formula, you could eliminate the `Else` clause entirely or write it as `Else NoColor`. If you want blocks of every three rows to be shaded a different color, a formula like this will do the trick:

```
WhilePrintingRecords;// Controls evaluation point
numberVar x;          // Create a record counter
x:= x + 1;            // Initialize counter value
If x = 6 Then
      x:= 0; // Reset to zero at 6 records
If x < 3 Then         // Test counter's value
   Aqua               // first 3 records are aqua
Else
   White;             // second 3 records are white
```

The keywords `Aqua`, `White`, and `NoColor` are placeholder names that represent RGB (Red, Green, Blue) values. Figure 8.14 shows the Color dialog.

FIGURE 8.14

Color spectrum

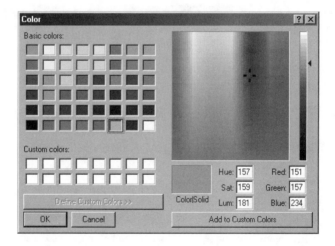

The entire RGB (Red, Green, Blue) color spectrum of the computer world is available to you. This is handy if you need to match a specific color on your company's website or marketing material to keep your company information styled consistently. You can set a color directly using the RGB values with Crystal syntax using the following type of statement:

```
If CurrentFieldValue < 2741 Then
   Color(151, 157, 234)      // Lavender
Else
   Color(255, 255, 255)      // White
```

In Basic syntax, you can use the `RGB` function call instead of the `Color` function. They do exactly the same thing; the `RGB` function name is standard in Microsoft Visual Basic and other languages.

TIP   You can use Microsoft Paint to determine the exact RGB value of a color in a computerized image. Display the image on your computer screen, copy it to the Clipboard using Ctrl+C, paste it into Microsoft Paint using Ctrl+V, and then use the eye dropper tool to select a color from the image. The color is now stored in the primary color box and you can look up its RGB value. To do this, choose Colors ➤ Edit Colors in Paint to open the color wheel, click the Define Custom Colors button, and the RGB value of the color you selected displays at the bottom-right corner of the Edit Colors window.

Controlling Spacing in a Section

Have you thought that you might want to print your report in Double Space mode? Or perhaps add or remove space between lines as the detail rows display? These sound like options you should be able to set when printing a report. In Crystal Reports, however, these are section-controlled options. The Section Expert handles quite a bit in terms of formatting and conditional section options; a combination of Design mode changes and the Section Expert pop-up submenu control line spacing in a report. Take a look at the partial report in Figure 8.15.

FIGURE 8.15

Section spacing

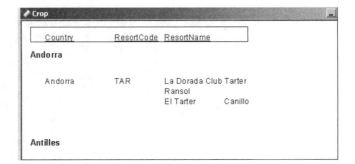

Notice that there is quite a bit of space between the detail data and the group name below it. There is no option in the Section Expert to control line spacing; this is done in Design mode. In Figure 8.16, you can see a double-lined arrow sitting on the section divider at the bottom of the Group Header #1 section. This means that the section divider can be dragged to resize it. Dragging it up so that it fits just under the [Group #1 Name] element will eliminate the extra white space visible in Figure 8.15 below the group name.

FIGURE 8.16

Resizing a section

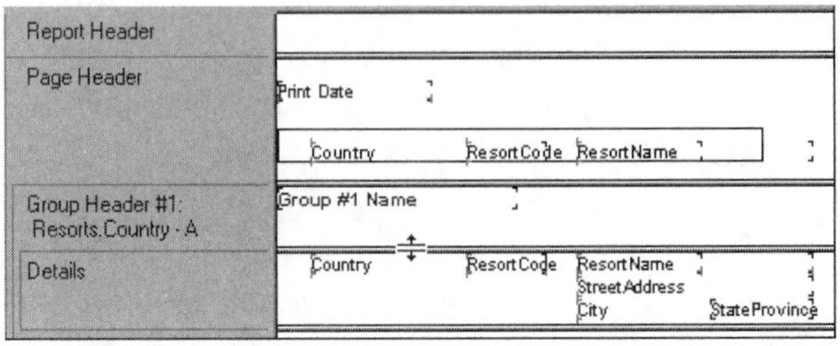

The quickest and surest way, however, to resize a section to fit the contents without including any extra blank vertical space is to use the Fit Section option from the Section Expert pop-up submenu. Refer back to Figure 8.4 and you'll see this option in the fifth area. Selecting this option shrinks a section vertically, leaving no extra white space between sections.

The line control options available in the submenu and visible in Figure 8.4 are:

- Insert Line

- Delete Last Line

- Arrange Lines

- Fit Section

Fit Section removes vertical white space from the bottom of a section. Insert Line adds one line to a section while Delete Last Line removes the bottom-most line from the section. You can use the Insert Line option to create a double-spaced section; you can also drag the section divider down slightly to create more space below the detail record. This forces the next detail record to print with a little space between it and the prior detail record. If the View ➤ Guidelines option is enabled in Design or Preview mode, a guideline is added to the horizontal (left side) margin for each new line added to the section; these guidelines can be used for snap-to-grid purposes. When the last line is deleted from a section, the bottom-most horizontal guideline is removed as well as the line. The Arrange Lines option removes white space between lines rather than from the top or the bottom of the section and evenly spaces the horizontal guidelines.

Selecting All Section Objects

We learned earlier that we can completely hide a section and its contents. We can also use the section container to format an entire section by selecting all the elements it contains it so that global formatting can be applied. This is a new timesaving feature in Crystal Reports 9. To access the option, right-click the gray section label and choose Select All Section Objects (visible in Figure 8.4). This will add selection handles to each of the objects in the section, including text, fields, and graphics, as shown in Figure 8.17.

FIGURE 8.17

Select All Section Objects

Whenever more than one object is selected, right-clicking any of the objects displays a Multiple Selection submenu, as shown in Figure 8.18. Items of the same data type can be formatted using the Format Objects option to open the Format Editor with tabs appropriate to the type of data represented by the selected objects.

FIGURE 8.18

Multiple selection
of objects

WARNING   *To format multiple objects, they must be the same data type. If the selected objects are not all of the same type, a Multiple Selection submenu will appear but will not have any options that can be selected, and the Format Editor is not accessible.*

Summary

Areas and sections in a Crystal Report contain and organize the fields, labels, images, and all other design elements. Their placement in a report controls where the information displays and how frequently. Custom section options allow both the report designer and the report user to choose to hide or display information either conditionally or completely. Conditional formatting can be applied using the Section Expert to add formulas that force behavior based on the content or characteristics of the section. Print State formulas come in handy for customizing the behavior of multiple sections of the same type as well as controlling how the sections look.

Part 3

Advanced Reporting

In this section you will find:

Chapter 9

Working with Multiple Tables

ONE OF THE JOBS of the report designer is to understand the meaning of the stored data and its inherent relationships. People who design and build a database are generally a different set of people than those who ultimately need to retrieve data from it. Database designers and programmers focus on capturing the right information and creating a storage facility to efficiently hold it. Business people, on the other hand, focus on the intelligence and sleuthing needed at the other end of the process to retrieve and synthesize the data in order to answer business questions. Because the two groups inherently have different purposes, bridging the gap between understanding the storage and knowing how to use the data to answer questions can be frustrating.

As a report designer, you play a powerful role sitting in between the two groups and providing a context for the data in order to transform it into information. This puts the responsibility of accurately representing the data on your shoulders. Nothing brings this to the forefront any clearer than the need to work with multiple tables in a way that generates correct information. To build a good report, it is an absolute requirement that you understand the data relationships behind the report and how they can safely and accurately be combined.

Featured in this chapter:

◆ Understanding essential database concepts

◆ Working with multiple tables

◆ Creating database schemas

◆ Defining business rules

◆ Using the Database Expert Links dialog

◆ Understanding the types of links

◆ Creating an inner join

◆ Creating a left outer join

◆ Creating a right outer join

◆ Creating a full outer join

Essential Database Concepts

Crystal Reports can retrieve data from a variety of data sources. The most popular is a relational database, depicted in Figure 9.1, and indeed, even when Crystal is not interacting with a relational database, it treats most data sources as if they were relational.

FIGURE 9.1

Database components

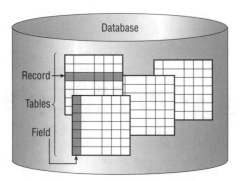

The most universal definition of a database is that it is a collection of related or themed data. In non-technical terms, the phone book found in most homes can be considered a database because all the information in it shares a theme; the theme is the name, address, and phone number of an individual or a business. In electronic terms, a database is a collection of related information that is stored in a file on a computer.

Tables are used to store data about major topics, and the majority of databases consist of multiple tables. The tables themselves share a context and are therefore related. Business rules defined by database designers specify these relationships. For instance, in a database that tracks customer information, a business rule would define how many phone numbers would be tracked for each customer and whether a customer would be allowed to be added if their phone number was not known. These business rules form the basis for understanding how the database should be used for reporting.

Let's take a brief look at the components that are important in understanding the database world:

DBMS Database management system. The term RDBMS is also common, where the R stands for relational. A DBMS can consist of many databases as well as the security and system information required to manage the data.

Database A container for storing tables that are related to one another. The container is stored as a single operating system file or set of files in a proprietary format specific to the database vendor. For example, a Microsoft Access database is stored in a file that has an `.mdb` file extension; these types of files can only be opened in Microsoft Access or using an access mechanism that Microsoft has provided.

Table A table is a two-dimensional (row and column) conceptual representation of how data is stored. Each table represents data elements that are closely related. For instance, in a table of customers, all the information in the table relates to customers; extraneous information about today's weather in Hawaii would not be included.

Record   A record is an individual row of data within a table. In the customer example mentioned earlier, in a table of all customers, each customer would be represented as a row of data; if there were five customers, there would be five records in the table, one for each customer.

Field   A field is a column or attribute of data in a database record. In the customer example, for each customer, attributes such as first name, last name, and phone number would each be stored in columns and represent attributes of the customer.

Index   An index is an optimized access path used to quickly retrieve information from a table. For instance, if the customer number is always retrieved when you access customer data, an index that sorts and manages the customer number will help retrieve the data in the most efficient manner.

OLAP   Online Analytical Processing servers organize stored data into multidimensional hierarchies for real-time, high-speed data analysis. Key features of an OLAP approach to data include being able to slice and dice information by comparing one parameter to another in real time with drill-down and "what if?" analysis. The hierarchy, or cube, provides top-down analysis of data.

A database must ultimately store its data in an operating system file; however, each type of DBMS stores its information differently. Some databases store an entire database that consists of many tables as a single operating system file; Microsoft Access databases were mentioned earlier as an example of this. In contrast, a dBASE database is stored as a set of multiple operating system files where each table is stored in an individual file.

Crystal Database Interactions

When you use Crystal Reports to connect to a database and work with its data, Crystal is being used as a data access mechanism into the database. Since Crystal supports so many different kinds of databases, it becomes a generic front end to almost any data. The process involves Crystal Reports requesting data from the database, the database returning that data, and then Crystal arranging the data in an .rpt file according to the report designer's layout. Crystal sits outside the database and pulls the data into the reporting world, as depicted in Figure 9.2.

FIGURE 9.2

Pulling data

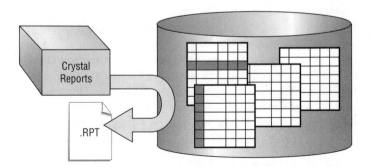

Read-Only Reporting

Basic database functionality includes the ability to insert, update, delete, and read rows of data. These operations can be done with tools internal to the database or with third-party tools. As a third-party tool, Crystal Reports is used to read data from databases. In this sense, it is a read-only tool. You can retrieve data, but you cannot update or delete it or use Crystal to insert new records into a table.

This should be a comforting thing to know, since a common worry is making a mistake with a software tool and hurting the data in the process. If you build a report, export it to Microsoft Word, and then give it to someone to work with where they change data values manually, they have not changed the data stored in the database itself. If you were to rerun the report, you'd again see the original numbers.

Security

One of the services provided by a full relational database management system is data security. Crystal Reports, in contrast, provides no security. If you can retrieve data from its data source, you can use the data in Crystal Reports. There is no facility built into Crystal Reports to prevent users from opening a report.

Security needs to be applied at the database level or at the operating system level. A database administrator typically grants access to databases or tables for individuals and groups. From a Crystal perspective, if a user encounters security on a database when attempting to retrieve data to pull it into a report, a login dialog should appear prompting for a user ID and password. This dialog is being presented by the database system, not Crystal Reports.

NOTE   *Crystal Enterprise can be used with Crystal Reports to provide secure access to a report from a web browser.*

Beyond a Single Table

Some business questions cannot be answered by pulling data from just a single table. Database designers build tables to follow a series of rules in a process called *normalization*. In addition to this, they build in relationships to represent business rules. For example, if a company was tracking information about its inventory and used part numbers to identify the products they built and sold, a business rule might be that each part number must be unique and identify only one specific part. This business rule makes logical sense outside the database world, because we wouldn't want to go looking for part number 2741 and find that it was associated with both a chair and a refrigerator in our inventory. To code the business rule, a database designer builds constraints into the database tables to prevent duplication of part numbers.

An example of a business rule in the VistaNations database is that one three-character region code corresponds to one textual description of the region. With this in mind, let's take a look at a business question that will help demonstrate how to work with multiple tables.

Business Question: In addition to the region code, please display the region description on all reports.

To answer a question like this, you first need to identify which tables hold the data you want to use in your report. To do this, you generally use a *database schema*, which is a visual representation of the tables, usually printed on a piece of paper, showing how all the tables in a database are related to one another. If a database schema exists for your database, you are truly leading a charmed life. In many cases, however, one doesn't exist, and you need to reverse-engineer one to identify the business relationships built into the table design. When a database designer creates the schema, they are defining the relationships between tables as well as the business rules. Relationships between tables are made by linking, or joining, fields that are common to a set of tables.

Visually Linking Tables

Crystal Reports has a mechanism for helping you visualize the tables and view or create relationships between them called the Links dialog, shown in Figure 9.3. When multiple tables are selected with the Database Expert, a tab for Links is added. When you're working with a single table, this tab does not display.

NOTE *The Database Expert and Data Explorer dialog windows are very similar in look and in purpose. It is the Database Expert that contains the Links tab. The Database Expert opens when you choose Database ➤ Database Expert from the menu. The Data Explorer opens when you choose Database ➤ Log On or Off Server from the menu. Both show a tree-like approach to Current Connections, Repository, Favorites, History, and Create New Connection options. The Data Explorer provides the additional capability to log onto and off of a server. Crystal remains connected to a database it connects to until you log off of it.*

FIGURE 9.3

Database Expert - Data tab

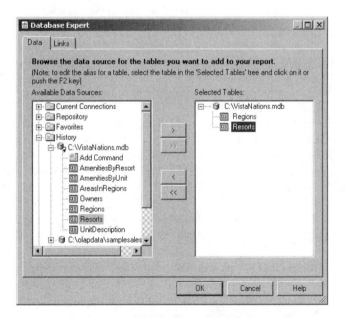

You can see in Figure 9.3 that two tables have been selected for use in this report, the Resorts table and the Regions table. You can add as many tables as you need to the report. When you switch to the Links tab, shown in Figure 9.4, the Links dialog presents visual representations of all the tables being used in the report.

FIGURE 9.4

Database Expert -
Links dialog

NOTE *The Links dialog replaces the Visual Linking Expert present in prior releases of Crystal Reports.*

From a visual look at the tables, you can see the table names and all the field names. The rectangles that represent the tables can be resized to show more or less data, and vertical and horizontal scroll bars automatically appear when they're needed. You can also reposition the tables and line them up horizontally instead of vertically.

This peek at the links between the tables is telling you that there is apparently no relationship between the Regions table and the Resorts table. If the Links dialog noticed a relationship between any fields, you would see a line from the field in one table to a field in the other table. While there actually is a relationship between the two tables, the Links dialog didn't have enough information available to figure it out. The Links dialog isn't as smart as a human who has knowledge of the data, so it did the best it could.

The Links dialog uses the following two items to figure out if there is a relationship between tables:

♦ Identical match on field name

♦ Primary and foreign keys that exist in the tables themselves

Field Name Matching If a field with an identical name exists in two tables, Crystal creates a link between the two fields if the data types also match.

Key Matching Some databases allow for the option of creating primary keys and foreign keys in a table. If these keys exist, Crystal Reports can use them to link the tables. This is the preferred way to do linking because it ties directly back to the business relationships intended in the tables when the database designer built them. The design purpose of a primary key is to guarantee a unique identifying value for every record in a table. Foreign keys are specifically used in joins, and they link from one table (often called a secondary table) back to another table (called a primary table). Primary keys and foreign keys work together to define the business relationships between tables.

Take a peek back at Figure 9.4. No links were created. In this case, there were no matching field names between the two tables and there were no keys defined in them. Hang on, that doesn't mean there isn't a relationship! All it means is that the Links dialog could not help build the links. The Links dialog may not have enough information to build the links at all or it could make false assumptions and build the links incorrectly.

TIP   Whenever the Links dialog is used, assume that you need to verify the accuracy of what it is showing you. The Links dialog is not infallible, and its link choices must be validated by the report designer.

The buttons along the right side of the dialog shown in Figure 9.4 will help you verify, validate, and correct the links. Table 9.1 describes what each of the buttons does.

TABLE 9.1: LINK OPTIONS

BUTTON	DESCRIPTION
Auto-Arrange	Repositions the tables within the white area using link information; you can maximize the screen in order to provide the most amount of room for viewing purposes.
Auto-Link	Creates links between fields either by name or based on primary/foreign keys.
Order Links	Chooses the order in which the links will be processed, from first to last. This option is not available if there is only one link between tables.
Clear Links	Removes all links. This option is not available if there are no links between tables.
Delete Link	Deletes a specific link that you select. This option is only available when a link is selected.
Link Options	Changes the type of join and link type between the tables.
Index Legend	Identifies the five-sided geometric shape to the left of fields that are indexed.

VALID LINKS

The Links dialog makes an initial attempt at automatically creating links using either the field name or database keys as a guide. If database keys are used, the links will be accurate and will follow the design rules of the database schema. If just the name is used, however, the links have a reasonable chance of either not being created or being invalid for the intention of the data. Why? Let's start with the name. In Figure 9.4, there is a field called RegionCode in the Regions table and a field called Region in the Resorts table. The Links dialog will not connect these two as a link because the field names are different.

As someone who works with the data, a report designer would browse the data, figure out that it was the same, and declare that the two fields should be linked regardless of the difference in names. You can browse the field data from the Links dialog by right-clicking the field and choosing Browse Field, as shown in Figure 9.5. Also visible is an index marker on the PostalCode field.

FIGURE 9.5

Browse Field

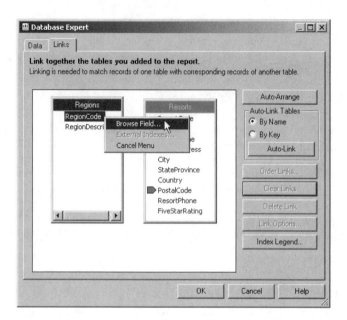

Browsing field data lets you inspect the actual data stored in the table for that column, as shown in Figure 9.6. If the data in two fields in different tables is the same, then a link can be made. There is no requirement in the world of relational tables that fields from two different tables must share the same name just because they share the same purpose. That is the case here. The purpose, or intent, of the RegionCode and Region fields is identical; they both contain a three-character code that identifies a region where resorts are located around the world.

FIGURE 9.6

Sample data

To create a valid link between two fields, the data type of the two fields must match one another. The RegionCode field has a data type and can only be linked to a field of this same data type.

The other very important concept in creating a valid link is that the intent of the two fields involved in the link must be the same. As an example, assume that in one table you have a field called PostalCode that is defined as String with a length of 5. In another table, you have a field called CompassDirections, which is also defined as String of length 5. The Links dialog in Crystal Reports will allow you to create a link between these two fields because the data type matches; however, the intent and purpose of the data do not match. The PostalCode field will contain values like 12508 and 06644, while the CompassDirections field will contain values like North and South. Clearly, the intent of the data is different, yet Crystal allows a link to be made between the two fields.

This is where knowledge of the data and the business rules that the data is modeling is crucial. It is also the human element involved in report designing. There is no way to build a good report if you've linked fields incorrectly. So, there are two ways you can potentially end up with bad links: You, the report designer, create them because you don't understand the data, or the Links dialog creates them because fields are named the same but are used for different purposes.

WARNING   *The toolbar icon used to identify the Database Expert in this version of Crystal Reports was previously used to enable the Visual Linking Expert. The Visual Linking Expert has been replaced by the Links dialog on the Database Expert.*

MANUALLY BUILDING LINKS

Manually building links is the surest way of guaranteeing that the linking respects the business relationships intended by the data, given that you are knowledgeable of the meaning of the data. To create a manual link, use a drag-and-drop technique: Click the field you want to link *from* and drag it to the field you want to link *to*. It is generally easiest if the tables are arranged in left-to-right order with the links flowing from left to right as well. As you drag from the starting field, the mouse pointer will change to a circle with a line through it when you are over a place where you cannot link and will change to a shortcut arrow, shown in Figure 9.7, when you are over a valid drop point.

FIGURE 9.7

Creating a manual link

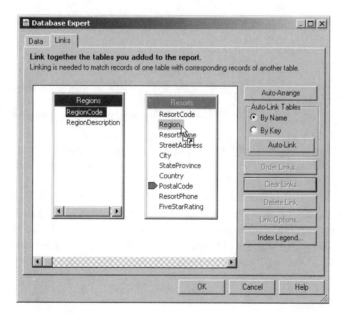

In Figure 9.7, a manual link is being created between the RegionCode field in the Regions table and the Region field in the Resorts table. Once the link is created, a black line with an arrow from one field to the other field appears between the tables.

AUTOMATICALLY BUILDING LINKS

Crystal defaults to building automatic links between tables whenever possible. When two tables are added in the Database Expert that share a common field name, the Links dialog will automatically show a link between the two tables. In Figure 9.8, the Resorts table and the UnitDescription table both contain the field ResortCode, and the Links dialog has connected the two tables using this field. Also notice in Figure 9.8 that the ResortCode and PostalCode fields have an index associated with them. Since one of the indexed fields is involved in the link, you are guaranteed of having the fastest possible data retrieval.

FIGURE 9.8

Automatic links

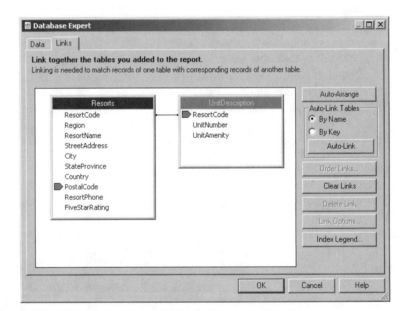

After adding new tables to the report, attempt to update the links using the Auto-Link button and associated radio button choices. If no keys are defined on the tables, enabling the By Key radio button will have no effect.

When a set of tables is linked by more than one common field, the Order Links button (shown as unavailable in Figure 9.8) lets you set the order in which the links should be carried out first, then second, etc. The Order Links option is also available when three or more tables are linked and can be used to control which set of links between tables are evaluated before the others. Changing the link order of tables may result in a change to the data that is returned from the database.

NOTE   *Crystal Reports does not allow Crystal queries (a feature of the product for releases 8.5 and earlier) to link to other database tables, views, stored procedures, and other Crystal queries. To work around this constraint, use a linked subreport embedded in a main report where the subreport and main report have separate data sources. See Chapter 7, "Selectively Refining a Report Using Data Values," for information on how to link subreports to a main report.*

INDEXED FIELDS

Linking to a field in a table that has an index will speed the retrieval of data from the database, so if an indexed field is available, try to use it. An index is created by a database designer or database administrator and can involve a single field or a group of fields. Crystal denotes an index in the Links dialog with a five-sided geometric shape (a sideways doghouse?) that we'll call an index arrow. Index arrows are pentagons that are color-coded; the color tells you whether it was the first index created, second index created, etc., if there are more than eight indexes, or if there are multiple indexes. The color relationship is described in Table 9.2.

TABLE 9.2: INDEX LEGEND

COLOR	MEANING
Red	First index
Yellow	Second index
Blue	Third index
Green	Fourth index
Pink	Fifth index
Orange	Sixth index
Dark Grey	Seventh index
Light Grey	Eighth index
White	More than eight indexes
Black	Multiple indexes on same field

NOTE   *It is important to note that indexes are created at the database level and not in Crystal Reports. Crystal can use only existing indexes.*

LINK TYPES

When a join between tables is created using a field, the field value in both tables must match. For instance, if the value in the ResortCode field in the Resorts table is TRM and the value in the ResortCode field in the UnitDescription table is also TRM, a join can be performed. This is referred to as an *equal* link. Once a link is created, however, the link type can be changed using the Link Options button visible in Figure 9.8. There are six link types, which are depicted mathematically in Crystal, as shown in Figure 9.9, and which are explained below.

FIGURE 9.9

Link types

Equal   The values in the two fields involved in the link are identical. For instance, `"TRM"` = `"TRM"`.

Greater Than   The value in the first field (the from field) is greater than the value in the second field (the to field). For instance, `"TRM"` > `"RCB"` for string data and 30 > 25 for numerical data.

Greater Than or Equal   The value in the first field (the from field) is greater than or equal to the value in the second field (the to field). For instance, `"TRM"` >= `"RCB"` for string data and 30 >= 25 for numerical data.

Less Than   The value in the first field (the from field) is less than the value in the second field (the to field). For instance, `"TRM"` < `"ZEN"` for string data and 25 < 30 for numerical data.

Less Than or Equal   The value in the first field (the from field) is less than or equal to the value in the second field (the to field). For instance, `"TRM"` <= `"ZEN"` for string data and 25 <= 30 for numerical data.

Not Equal   The value in the first field (the from field) is not equal to the value in the second field (the to field). For instance, `"TRM"` != `"ZEN"` for string data and 25 != 30 for numerical data. The symbol <> may also be used if the underlying database does not support the != symbol.

NOTE   *If a data source was created using a SQL statement that used inequalities on the linking field, the default link type will match the inequality used in the SQL statement. The link type is determined by the* **WHERE** *clause in a SQL statement. SQL statements and* **WHERE** *clauses are covered in Chapter 11, "Using SQL in Crystal."*

Table Relationships

Building appropriate links between two tables not only requires knowledge of the data, it also requires knowledge of what is actually happening to the data during the linking process and what kind of result is desired. The relationship achieved between tables based on linking a field will be one of four types: one-to-one, one-to-many, many-to-many, or no relationship.

One-to-One   When linking Table A with Table B, for each record in Table A, there is exactly one matching record in Table B. In Figures 9.10 and 9.11, the Resorts table and the ResortFinance-Company table both contain a ResortCode field. For each unique record in the table identified by the ResortCode, there is exactly one match in the other table. The business rule that this is enforcing is that each resort has exactly one finance company; you would combine the tables to create a report that contained the finance company name and the resort name.

FIGURE 9.10

Resorts

ResortCode	ResortName
AML	Amara Lifetime Resort
ARE	Holiday Club Are
ART	Holiday Club Airisto
ASC	Tenerife
ATB	Peppertree Atlantic Beach
ATO	Club Peurto Atlantico
AVP	The Avenue Plaza Hotel and Spa
AVR	Acadia Village Resort
BAY	The Bay Club
BDC	Bluebeards
BEA	The Beacons
BLK	Club Intrawest - Blackcomb
BRM	Banff Rocky Mountain Resort
BSH	Bona Sweden Hotel
BST	Balisani Beachside Suites
BYN	Hawaiian Sun

FIGURE 9.11

Finance companies

ResortCode	FinanceCompany
AML	Azzolin & Sons
ARE	German Holdings Ltd.
ART	Mercer
ASC	German Holdings Ltd.
ATB	Mercer
ATO	Azzolin & Sons
AVP	Schuyler Securities
AVR	The Royal Group
BAY	The Royal Group
BDC	Mercer
BEA	Swiss International
BLK	The Royal Group
BRM	Dutchess Enterprises
BSH	Azzolin & Sons
BST	Jenda Inc.
BYN	Jenda Inc.

One-to-Many   When linking Table A with Table B, for each record in Table A, there are multiple matches in Table B. This is the most common type of table relationship. In Figures 9.12 and 9.13, you can see that for each RegionCode listed in the Regions table, there are multiple entries in the Resorts table. The business rule in effect in this situation is that one region can contain many resorts.

FIGURE 9.12

Regions

RegionCode	RegionDescription
▶ R01	Eastern Canada
R02	New England, USA
R03	Middle Atlantic, USA
R04	South, USA
R05	Central Florida
R06	Florida Coast
R07	Midwest, USA
R08	Southwest, USA
R09	Rocky Mountains, USA
R10	Canadian Rockies & Western Canada

FIGURE 9.13

Region resorts

Region	ResortCode
▶ R01	TRM
R01	CBG
R01	DHI
R02	HRB
R02	PAF
R02	MCU
R02	HIC
R02	MCL
R02	NBC
R02	NVC
R02	TFL
R02	WAT
R02	AVR
R03	BAY
R03	CPM
R03	LAR

Many-to-Many The concept is that in linking Table A with Table B, multiple entries in Table A match multiple entries in Table B. In reality, many-to-many tables cannot be involved in a Crystal linking activity nor are they a good idea for a database table due to poor performance issues. When a database designer creates a database schema, many-to-many relationships are generally split into multiple one-to-many relationships.

No Relationship There is no business rule that states that a table has to be related to another table. Sometimes, a table is simply used to store information that is referenced in lookups or by applications. A standalone table not involved in a linking relationship is said to be a reference table.

Types of Joins

When two tables are joined, the process that takes place is that the first table's rows and columns are retrieved and then the second table's rows and columns are retrieved. This means that the linking field appears twice in the resulting data set, once for each table that it appeared in. This is shown in Figure 9.14 with the results of a query joining resort names with finance company names by linking on the ResortCode field.

FIGURE 9.14

Joining data

ResortCode	ResortName	ResortCode	FinanceCompany
AML	Amara Lifetime Resort	AML	Azzolin & Sons
ARE	Holiday Club Are	ARE	German Holdings Ltd.
ART	Holiday Club Airisto	ART	Mercer
ASC	Tenerife	ASC	German Holdings Ltd.
ATB	Peppertree Atlantic Beach	ATB	Mercer
ATO	Club Peurto Atlantico	ATO	Azzolin & Sons
AVP	The Avenue Plaza Hotel and Spa	AVP	Schuyler Securities
AVR	Acadia Village Resort	AVR	The Royal Group
BAY	The Bay Club	BAY	The Royal Group
BDC	Bluebeards	BDC	Mercer
BEA	The Beacons	BEA	Swiss International
BLK	Club Intrawest - Blackcomb	BLK	The Royal Group
BRM	Banff Rocky Mountain Resort	BRM	Dutchess Enterprises
BSH	Bona Sweden Hotel	BSH	Azzolin & Sons
BST	Balisani Beachside Suites	BST	Jenda Inc.
BYN	Hawaiian Sun	BYN	Jenda Inc.

When a table join is being performed, the temporary result set is stored in memory. The result set is dependent on the type of join; there are four types:

◆ Inner join

◆ Left outer join

◆ Right outer join

◆ Full outer join

In many cases, you can change the type of join by clicking the Link Options button to open the Join Type area, shown in Figure 9.15.

FIGURE 9.15

Join types

Inner Join

Inner joins are performed by default in the Links dialog of the Database Expert. An inner join assumes two tables and a common field between them. The result of an inner join returns all the database records in both tables where the common field is an exact match between the two tables. The resulting virtual table contains all the records in both tables where a match was found between them.

Using a Venn diagram, we show the visual representation of the inner join operation in Figure 9.16. Venn diagrams are used to describe mathematical sets of information that are logical; these diagrams were popularized by John Venn in England during the 1800s. The overlapping area depicts the result set that contains only records that matched from the first table and the second table. As an example, if the Resorts table is inner joined with the ResortFinanceCompany table, linking on the ResortCode field, only those resorts that actually have a finance company will be returned. Refer back to Figure 9.14 for data results for this type of join.

FIGURE 16

Inner join

Left Outer Join

A left outer join returns all the rows from the table on the left plus any rows from the table on the right that match the link field. Using a Venn diagram, we show the visual representation of the left outer join operation in Figure 9.17. The overlapping area depicts the result set that contains only records that matched from the first table and the second table.

FIGURE 9.17

Left outer join

For an example, if the Resorts table is left outer joined with the ResortFinanceCompany table, the result returns all the rows from the Resorts table plus data for matching Resorts found in the Resort-FinanceCompany table. Figure 9.18 shows the data results for a left outer join on the Resorts table and the ResortsFinanceCompany table. Notice that all rows were returned even if no finance company exists because there was an exact match on the ResortCode; nulls are placed in the FinanceCompany field.

FIGURE 9.18

Left join data

ResortCode	ResortName	ResortCode	FinanceCompany
AML	Amara Lifetime Resort	AML	Azzolin & Sons
ARE	Holiday Club Are	ARE	German Holdings Ltd.
ART	Holiday Club Airisto	ART	Mercer
ASC	Tenerife	ASC	German Holdings Ltd.
ATB	Peppertree Atlantic Beach	ATB	Mercer
ATO	Club Peurto Atlantico	ATO	Azzolin & Sons
AVP	The Avenue Plaza Hotel and Spa	AVP	Schuyler Securities
AVR	Acadia Village Resort	AVR	
BAY	The Bay Club	BAY	
BDC	Bluebeards	BDC	Mercer
BEA	The Beacons	BEA	Swiss International
BLK	Club Intrawest - Blackcomb	BLK	The Royal Group
BRM	Banff Rocky Mountain Resort	BRM	Dutchess Enterprises
BSH	Bona Sweden Hotel	BSH	Azzolin & Sons
BST	Balisani Beachside Suites	BST	Jenda Inc.
BYN	Hawaiian Sun	BYN	Jenda Inc.

Right Outer Join

A right outer join returns all the rows from the table on the right plus any rows that match in the table on the left based on the link field. Using a Venn diagram, we show the visual representation of a right outer join operation in Figure 9.19.

FIGURE 9.19

Right outer join

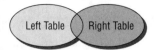

Full Outer Join

A full outer join returns all the rows from the table on the left and all the rows from the table on the right. Using a Venn diagram, we show the visual representation of a full outer join operation in Figure 9.20. Null values are placed in fields where no match existed.

FIGURE 9.20

Full outer join

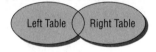

Beyond Two Tables

The examples and discussions of multiple tables up to this point have all involved two tables, one on the left and one on the right. What happens if you decide to use three tables in a report? Or four? Or more? Which table is the table on the left? Is there one? Do we need to think about things from a whole other perspective? Not really!

When tables are combined, they combine left to right. In the Database Expert, the order in which you add the tables determines the concept of left to right. Add the first table, and it is the left table; add the second table, and it is the table on the right. For more than two tables, the process of combining tables moves from left to right, pairing as it processes. This is graphically depicted in Figure 9.21.

FIGURE 9.21

More than two tables

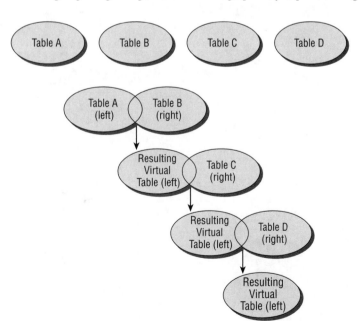

In this diagram, four tables are being linked. Table A was the first table added in the Database Expert. The second table, Table B, was added next. Table C was the third table added using the Database Expert. Finally, Table D was the last table added using the Database Expert.

NOTE *The left-to-right order is determined by the order in which tables are added to the Database Expert.*

The processing of the links combines the first two tables, A and B, and comes up with a temporary result that is saved in memory until it's needed in its next calculation. The next calculation happens to be a link to a third table. So the result of the first join is treated as a virtual table itself and is then joined to the third table, C. Once these two are joined, the result of this operation is joined to the final table, D. The entire process results in a virtual result set of data that meets the criteria specified in the joins.

Summary

Database designers build tables that form relationships with other tables through the use of linking fields, primary keys, and foreign keys. Knowledge of the data relationships that tie tables to one another is essential in creating a good report. Understanding database terminology such as records and fields becomes critical when working with table linking. To do the linking, four table relationships and five link types can be combined in various ways to create unique data result sets.

The decision to involve multiple tables creates a left-to-right relationship between them, which Crystal Reports facilitates through the Database Expert. Working from left to right with linked tables, report designers choose among inner joins, left outer joins, right outer joins, and full outer joins to achieve the blending of data that answers their business questions.

Chapter 10

Data Sources and the Database Expert

ORGANIZATIONS SPEND A GREAT deal of time and money building databases and storing enormous amounts of data in them. For new and old development projects alike, resources have often focused on creating database structures that capture the essential data needed by the company. Today, that data is plentiful and it is spread all over the organization. The days of a single database containing a company's data came and went in the blink of an eye. Most, but not all, stored data exists in databases. Some exists as simple text files. This is why we use the phrase *data source* more universally than the word *database*. Crystal Reports can report on data from almost any data source, whether it is a text file or a complex database. Companies have data stored in a wide variety of formats coming from storage locations that weren't even dreamed of ten years ago.

One of the problems with having data stored in multiple places is that the people who need to connect to and retrieve the data are generally not the people who stored the data in the first place. This can mean a large learning curve for those attempting to figure out how to retrieve data from each different kind of data source. As people come and go from an organization, it can impact the organization's ability to harvest its information in a productive manner. Crystal Reports can play a key role in addressing this issue. The connectivity capabilities built into Crystal Reports are designed to make it as easy as possible to connect to a wide variety of data storage locations.

Featured in this chapter:

- ◆ Understanding Crystal connectivity
- ◆ Configuring and using ODBC data sources
- ◆ Working with OLE DB
- ◆ Connecting to OLAP data sources
- ◆ Using native data sources

Crystal Connectivity

Crystal Reports is known as a third-party software tool because it sits as an outside application apart from the stored data and the other applications that created the original data. Its role is to retrieve and synthesize the data. The Database Expert is the mechanism used in Crystal to connect to data.

When you create a new report by choosing File ➤ New, you can either use a Report Creation Wizard or create a blank report to start your report. Right up front, you need to connect to your data source to give Crystal some data to chomp on. The Database Expert is the mechanism by which Crystal connects you to your data. The Database Expert, shown in Figure 10.1, is invoked automatically when you build a new report.

FIGURE 10.1

The Database
Expert

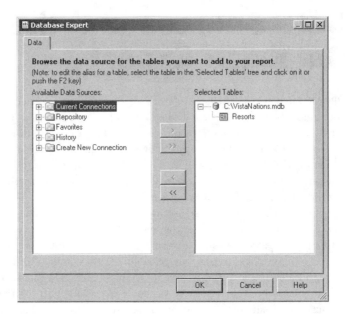

In addition, you can open the Database Expert manually on demand after you've begun building your report. This is useful if you want to change to a different data source or add additional data sources to the report. You can open the Database Expert from the Experts toolbar or choose Database ➤ Database Expert.

The five categories of data sources in the Database Expert are described in Table 10.1.

TIP   You can right-click any of the options in the Database Expert to display a context menu. The menu lets you accomplish the following tasks: Add To Report, Add To Favorites, Remove From Report, Properties, Rename Favorite, Delete Favorite, Remove From Repository, Rename Repository Object, and Refresh.

If you open and close more than five databases within a single Crystal Reports session (meaning without exiting Crystal Reports), the list of databases in the History category will include them all. When you reopen Crystal Reports, the most recently opened five will appear in your History list.

TABLE 10.1: DATABASE EXPERT CATEGORIES

DATA SOURCE FOLDER	DESCRIPTION
Current Connections	Contains a list of all data sources to which Crystal Reports has a current connection.
Repository	Provides a list of data source connections stored in the common repository.
Favorites	Holds a manually maintained list of commonly used data sources; you can drag and drop sources from within the Database Expert to add them to the Favorites folder.
History	Shows the five data sources most recently used within Crystal Reports.
Create New Connection	Holds the master list of all available data sources, as well as generic mechanisms to connect to new data sources.

Three-Tiered Data Architecture

The Database Expert dialog accounts for wide variety of data sources through one simple interface. To achieve this simplicity, Crystal Reports takes a three-tiered information approach to all data sources, which streamlines the model of retrieval and reporting. The three tiers in Crystal's data architecture are the Crystal Reports software application itself, the database translation layer, and the database storage container layer. These are depicted in Figure 10.2.

FIGURE 10.2

Data access
architecture

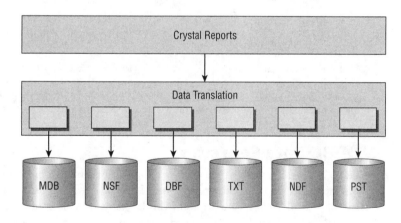

Database (a subset is shown)

As you've seen in prior chapters, as a report-writing tool and the starting layer, Crystal Reports provides a front end for retrieving data as well as all the essentials needed to present, group, and summarize it. Once a data source is attached to Crystal, requests for data when the report opens are passed to the database translation layer.

At the database translation layer, Crystal Reports makes use of a series of *dynamic link libraries* (DLLs) that ship and install with the product to provide access to virtually any database. By using a different

DLL for each database that it supports, Crystal solves the problem of accessing and retrieving data from any database. A DLL is a program used by other programs to perform a specific task. In this case, the task is to access a database for reading, updating, inserting, and deleting data.

At the data storage level, Crystal treats data as relational entities obeying the laws of the relational world. The core concept is that data is treated as rows and columns in tables, and that combining multiple tables creates relationships between the elements. Therefore, understanding relational terms such as tables, rows, and columns is helpful to the Crystal designer even if the data being retrieved comes from a text file data source.

Creating New Connections

Are you ready to put the alphabet soup on the stove and figure out what it all means? There are quite a few acronyms involved with data access, and since they appear on many of the dialog windows in Crystal Reports, we have some natural interest in them. The implementation of Crystal's database translation layer utilizes any of several connection strategies based on how you choose to access the data. They include:

◆ Open Database Connectivity (ODBC) connections

◆ Object Linking and Embedding Database (OLE DB) connections

◆ Native database connections

◆ Crystal queries

◆ Database files

◆ Dictionary/Infoview

◆ Programmatic access

Each strategy plays a different role, and your goal is to understand and know enough about each one in order to be able to choose the one that makes the most sense for your situation.

ODBC Data Sources

ODBC (Open Database Connectivity) is a well-known methodology for connecting to a database that was introduced in 1992. Structured Query Language (SQL) is used as ODBC's data access language, and while there are many variations of this language, the core commands are somewhat universal.

At a very high level, ODBC can be described as middleware that sits between a data source and an application. In our case, it can be used as the go-between for a data source and Crystal Reports. As depicted in Figure 10.3, there are four layers in the ODBC model.

From this diagram, you should get the sense that a single application like Crystal Reports can access a variety of different data sources as long as they are registered and managed by the ODBC driver manager. The driver manager's job is to respond to Crystal's request for data from a configured data source, locate the correct DLL to use to fulfill the request, and then pass the request down to the DLL layer. At that point, the DLL layer interacts with the data source layer, retrieves the requested data, and returns it to the Crystal Reports application.

FIGURE 10.3

ODBC layers

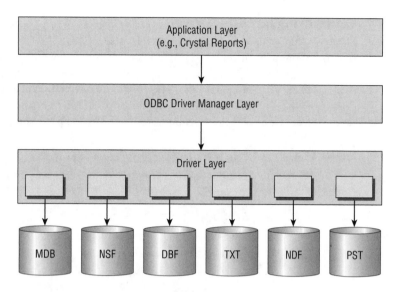

Data Source Layer

If you were to ask a roomful of people who have worked with ODBC to give you a one-word description of it, you would hear words like easy, slow, cumbersome, reliable, mandatory, functional, free, and probably many others. The gist of the message is that, yes, ODBC access is slower than being in the database directly, but it sure does simplify the job of getting to the data. This is no surprise. Take a second look at Figure 10.3 and you'll realize that it is slow(er) because of the two layers between the application (Crystal Reports) and the data source. The trade-off for this slower access (by the way, we're talking milliseconds slower, not hours slower) is consistent, reliable access that doesn't have to be coded anew each time a different application wants to get to the data. Tried, true, tested code. Sounds like a good trade against fast any day.

ODBC also offers the advantage of providing an upgrade path for a report. Many reports start out life retrieving data from a smaller database like Microsoft Access and then get promoted to official duty in a larger database like Microsoft SQL Server. If the table structures between the two databases are identical, the process of converting a Crystal Report from one data source to another is easy. The goal is to not have to start from the beginning again on a new report.

WARNING   *If table structures are not identical, changing an ODBC data source may render a Crystal report unusable.*

Putting ODBC to work for you in Crystal Reports is a two-step process:

1. Install and configure a data source using the appropriate ODBC driver at the operating system level.

2. Use the Database Expert to connect to the data source from within Crystal Reports.

Configuring an ODBC Driver

Database vendors have done a very good job of supplying ODBC drivers to access their product from other products. It is rare that a database doesn't come with an ODBC mechanism to use it. In order to use an ODBC data source in any application, including Crystal Reports, the data source has to be installed and configured at the operating system level. In Microsoft Windows systems, this is done using the ODBC Data Source Administrator, shown in Figure 10.4. In Windows 2000, you'll find this from Control Panel ➢ Administrative Tools ➢ Data Sources (ODBC).

FIGURE 10.4

ODBC Data Source Administrator

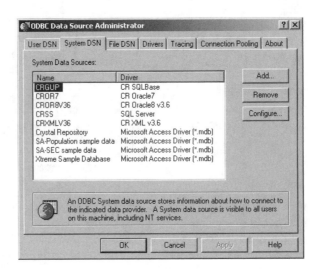

NOTE *If the ODBC driver you want to use is not installed on your computer, you would need to do that first using the installation program provided with the driver. Many drivers are available for downloading directly from the Internet.*

From here, you configure an individual data source name (DSN) to represent the database you want to access. What you are doing is telling the operating system (Microsoft Windows) how to physically find the database on the computer. You can think of a DSN as an alias or nickname that an application uses to request a connection to an ODBC data source rather than using the full filename and path of the database. Table 10.2 shows what each tab of the ODBC Data Source Administrator is used for.

TABLE 10.2: ODBC DATA SOURCE ADMINISTRATOR

DATA SOURCE TAB	DESCRIPTION
User DSN	Contains a DSN created for a specific user and usable only by this logged-in user. The DSN connection parameters are stored in the Registry.
System DSN	Contains a DSN created for all users of a system and usable by any user who logs into the system. The DSN connection parameters are stored in the Registry.

Continued on next page

TABLE 10.2: ODBC DATA SOURCE ADMINISTRATOR *(continued)*

DATA SOURCE TAB	DESCRIPTION
File DSN	All parameters needed to connect to a data source are stored in a text file with a `.dsn` extension. The DSN name is configured to point to the file, e.g., `C:\ program files\ common files\ODBC\Data Sources\vistanations.dsn`.
Drivers	Lists all ODBC drivers installed on the computer.
Tracing	Traces system calls to ODBC for debugging purposes.
Connection Pooling	Optimizes performance by setting several options.
About	Determines what versioning of ODBC is in use.

If multiple users will be logging into the same physical computer, a system DSN is your best choice and is probably the one you will use the most frequently. Figure 10.4 depicts the ODBC Data Source Administrator. When it opens, it defaults to a user DSN, so you need to change tabs to create a system DSN.

FILE DSNs

File DSNs can be used to create connections across systems. Since all of the connection information is stored in a file, you can store it in a drive that is network-accessible by users in an organization. When a file DSN is created, the file extension must be `.dsn` and is generally stored in the `\program files\common files\ODBC\Data Sources` directory.

Here's an example of what a file DSN to the `VistaNations.MDB` database might look like using standard connection parameters.

```
[ODBC]

DRIVER=Microsoft Access Driver (*.mdb)
UID=
PWD=
ReadOnly=0
UserCommitSync=Yes
Threads=3
SafeTransactions=0
PageTimeout=5
MaxScanRows=8
MaxBufferSize=512
ImplicitCommitSync=Yes
FIL=MS Access
DriverId=25
DefaultDir=c:\ program files\common files\ODBC\Data Sources
DBQ=c:\vistanations.mdb
```

Each database is its own data source; to create a new one, click the Add button shown in Figure 10.4 to display a setup screen similar to the one shown in Figure 10.5; the setup screen is specific to the type of database. Here, an ODBC data source is being configured for the Vista Nations database, vistanations.mdb, which is visible as the database just above the Select button. Click the Select button to browse the current computer or any network resources to locate a database. Notice that the Data Source Name area allows you type in a meaningful alias or nickname to identify the database.

FIGURE 10.5

Setting up a DSN

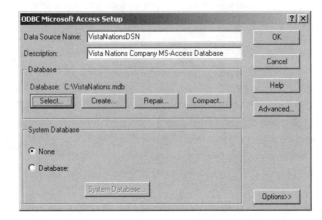

Using an ODBC Driver

Once an ODBC driver is installed, you can use it in Crystal Reports via the Database Expert by selecting the ODBC (RDO) folder beneath the Create New Connection folder, as shown in Figure 10.6. RDO is an abbreviation for the Microsoft data access methodology, Remote Data Objects.

FIGURE 10.6

Database Expert ODBC connections

The list displays all the built-in ODBC connections that were installed either with your computer or with subsequent software installs as well as any DSNs that you created using the ODBC Data Source Administrator. When you double-click the plus sign (+) to the left of the ODBC (RDO) folder, the Data Source Selection window shown in Figure 10.7 appears. Notice that the VistaNationsDSN data source that was created previously is in this list. Notice also that just above it is a data source called VistaNations.dsn. This data source was created using the File DSN tab in the ODBC Data Source Administrator, as denoted by the file extension .dsn, and it is indeed a different data source than the VistaNationsDSN, although the names are perhaps a little too similar for comfort.

FIGURE 10.7

Data Source
Selection

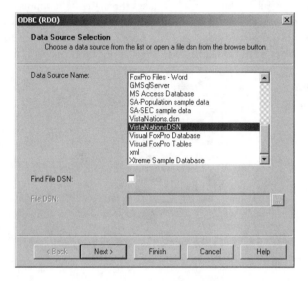

Earlier we mentioned that Crystal Reports provides no security to the data, but rather the database itself provides the security. When you connect to an ODBC data source in Crystal Reports, you'll be prompted to supply a password, as shown in Figure 10.8. That doesn't mean you have to provide one! For instance, the VistaNations database has no security applied to it in Microsoft Access, so there is no password. On the other hand, if the database requires a password, you are required to provide it at this point.

FIGURE 10.8

Connection
Information

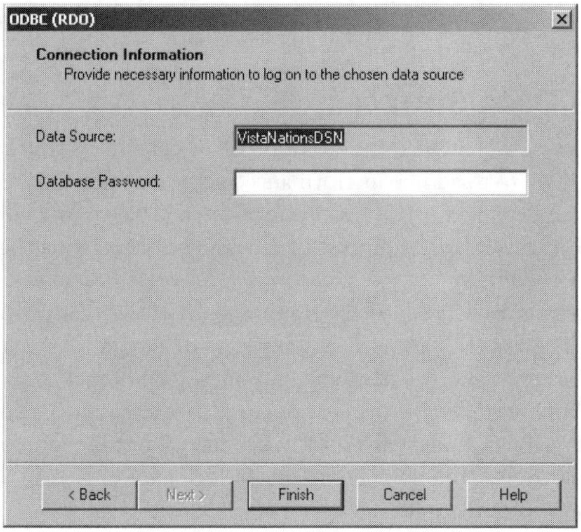

When you've completed the connection, the new data source and all its tables will show up in the ODBC (RDO) folder of the Available Data Sources, as shown in Figure 10.9. In Chapter 1, "Building Your First Report," we used a different method to connect to VistaNations. That method is called DAO and is described a bit later. This makes three ways that you have now learned to connect to the `vistanations.mdb` database: file DSNs, ODBC using RDO, and DAO. DAO is an abbreviation for the Microsoft data access methodology, Data Access Objects. The point here is that you can have multiple connection types to the same database. Each connection creates a distinct data source.

FIGURE 10.9

VistaNations ODBC connection

As a mature technology, ODBC is a powerful data access tool, especially because software products such as Crystal Reports ship with it built-in and ready to go. Virtually any database can be treated as an ODBC data source even if it is not a relational data source. This greatly expands the types of databases that Crystal can service.

NOTE   *ODBC and OLE DB are specification guidelines detailing how applications (such as Crystal Reports) can communicate with data sources (such as Microsoft Access). ODBC and OLE DB are not software products.*

OLE DB Data Sources

In 1996, Microsoft continued the evolution of its data access strategy (which is "Make it easy!") from ODBC to OLE DB to address performance and extensibility concerns left unaddressed by ODBC. There are a large number of ODBC installations and this trend will continue, but the option to look to OLE DB is attractive. The process of accessing a database has been simplified even further with this newer methodology.

OLE DB consists of a set of programming interfaces that provide applications such as Crystal Reports with consistent, fast access to any kind of tabular (row/column) data. This includes and then goes beyond traditional relational data and expands data access possibilities to OLAP (Online Analytical Processing) data, e-mail containers, file systems, text, and graphics. Figure 10.10 depicts an application's interactions with an OLE DB interface that connects to a data source. Since no driver manager is involved in the transaction, the performance of OLE DB is positioned to be better than that of ODBC from the start.

FIGURE 10.10

OLE DB

The core component of OLE DB is known as a *provider*, representing a provider of data or services to the data. There are two categories of providers:

◆ Data providers

◆ Service providers

The data provider component connects a data source to an application that needs to access it. Service providers do a slightly different task by interacting between an OLE DB data provider and a software application for extended functionality such as query processing. In other words, a service provider goes beyond the retrieval of the data.

In the Database Expert, the OLE DB option appears two entries down from ODBC (this is an alphabetical list!). When you select OLE DB, the Crystal Reports process mirrors the one for connecting to an ODBC source. The difference, however, is that you do not have to configure an OLE DB connection to a database at the operating system level as you did with ODBC. Figure 10.11 displays a list of OLE DB providers.

FIGURE 10.11

OLE DB Provider

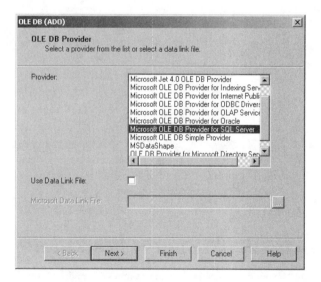

The list includes an OLE DB driver for every type of database installed on the system as well as several built-in ones. Notice that the list has providers for popular databases like SQL Server and Oracle. The OLE DB driver is provided by the database manufacturer. After you choose the OLE DB provider, the next step is to provide the connection information required to access a specific database. In Figure 10.12, a connection is being made to a server that requires a user ID but no password.

FIGURE 10.12

OLE DB connection

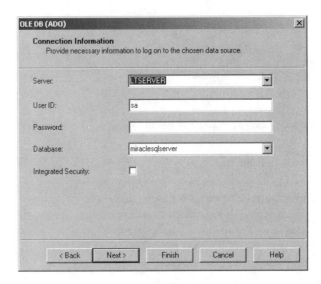

After the connection is made, the server name and the individual database are added to the list of Available Data Sources in the Database Expert, as shown in Figure 10.13.

FIGURE 10.13

SQL Server
OLE DB

RULES OF THUMB FOR CHOOSING BETWEEN ODBC AND OLE DB

◆ Use ODBC if your data is relational and in a non-OLE environment.

◆ Use OLE DB to access non-SQL data.

◆ Use OLE DB if you're writing code to access data in an OLE environment.

◆ Use OLE DB to build interactions between multiple database components.

NOTE   *If the Current Connections folder in the Database Expert was opened at this point, the SQL Server connection just accomplished with OLE DB would be listed. Likewise, the History folder would capture it automatically as well. The Favorites folder, on the other hand, is manually updated, so the connection would not automatically appear in this folder.*

OLAP Data

OLAP (Online Analytical Processing) involves real-time interactions with data that is represented in multiple dimensions. OLAP data is depicted as a cube, which is three-dimensional. OLE DB has a major advantage over ODBC in that it can handle *n*-dimensional tabular data. While row and column data is two-dimensional and represents the typical table we think of in a relational database, once you move to three dimensions or beyond, ODBC has no way to interact with the data. OLE DB, on the other hand, can handle any number of dimensions. Version 2.0 of the technical specification for OLE DB includes OLE DB for OLAP and details the programming methodology required to interact with this type of data.

Crystal Reports can report on OLAP data sources, and the first step is, not surprisingly, connecting to it. The Database Expert contains a folder for OLAP, which makes use of OLE DB behind the scenes for its data access methodology. When connecting to an OLAP data source, you have the option of connecting directly to an OLAP server (a server dedicated to this type of data) or using a *cube file*. Cube files are OLAP data that has been saved to a file rather than generated in an OLAP server in real time. An HTTP cube is OLAP data that can be accessed through a web browser. Figure 10.14 shows an OLAP connection configuration dialog.

FIGURE 10.14

Connecting to OLAP data

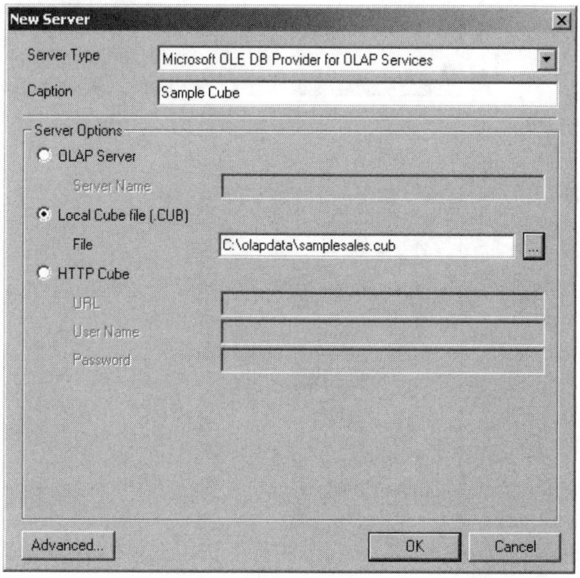

The process of working with OLAP data in Crystal Reports is to use cubes of data. The representation of the information is in three dimensions initially; think of it in terms of length, width, and depth. The intersection of the three dimensions is a single cell of data, just as the intersection of a row and column in relation data is a single cell of data. In retrieving the data, each dimension consists of an aggregation (summarization) of a data item to allow drilling up to a higher summary level or drilling down to a more specific data level. The OLAP Connection Browser can connect to an OLAP server, a stored cube of data that was previously generated, or an HTTP cube of data. After you connect by clicking the Add Server button in Figure 10.15, the OLAP data source appears in the list of Available Data Sources, as shown in Figure 10.16.

FIGURE 10.15

Adding an OLAP server

FIGURE 10.16

OLAP cubes

Once the OLAP Connection Browser is connected to the data source, the OLAP Expert in Crystal Reports is used to build a report using OLAP data. For more information on using the OLAP Expert, refer to Chapter 12, "Analyzing Data Visually."

Native Connections

A *native* connection is one made from Crystal to a data source using a DLL that is specific to the database itself and that is sometimes provided directly by the database manufacturer. Native drivers are used for these connections and are the preferred way to access a database using Crystal, if one is available, because they have been optimized for fast, efficient direct access to data for that type of database. Figure 10.17 depicts the close relationship between the native driver and the database itself.

FIGURE 10.17

Native drivers

Crystal ships with a long list of native driver DLL files. The following table shows a partial list of native drivers that are placed on a computer during the installation of Crystal Reports. The driver itself, however, is not actually installed until you connect to it for the first time in Crystal Reports.

p2bact3.dll	P2ctbtrv.dll	p2irdao.dll	p2molap.dll	p2sfs.dll
p2bbtrv.dll	P2ctbtrv.dll	p2ixbse.dll	p2sdb2.dll	p2solap.dll
p2bdao.dll	P2ctdao.dll	P2ldb2.dll	P2smon.dll	p2soledb.dll
p2bxbse.dll	P2iract3.dll	p2lodbc.dll	p2sNote.dll	p2soutlk.dll

When you read the filenames, the characters to the left of the period give you a hint as to what type of data the driver retrieves. For instance, the `p2bact3.dll` retrieves data from Act! 3.0 databases, and `p2soutlk.dll` retrieves data from Outlook databases.

In the Crystal Reports interface, you select the native drivers through the Create New Connection folder and its More Data Sources option in the Database Expert, as shown in Figure 10.18.

FIGURE 10.18

Native drivers in Database Expert

When you expand the Create New Connection folder in the Database Expert, a list of friendly names describing the DLLs that were found on the computer is shown. The friendly version of the name tells you what database it is rather than showing the actual DLL filename. On the initial install of Crystal Reports, the following databases can be accessed with native drivers stored on your computer:

◆ ACT! 3.0

◆ ADO.NET

◆ Borland Database Engine

◆ Btrieve

◆ CDO

◆ COM Data

◆ Dataset Consumer

◆ Exchange Folders/Address Book

◆ Field Definitions

◆ File System Data

◆ IBM DB2

◆ Informix

◆ Java Data

◆ Lotus Domino

◆ Mailbox Admin

◆ Message Tracking Loc

◆ Miracle Systems IIS/Proxy Log Files

◆ NT Archived Event Log

◆ NT Current Event Log

◆ Oracle

◆ Outlook

◆ Public Folder ACL

◆ Public Folder Admin

◆ Public Folder Replica

◆ Sybase

◆ Web/IIS Log Files

◆ xBase

To install the driver for any of the additional data sources, you double-click it and Crystal Reports installs the driver. Once the driver is installed, that type of data source is moved out of the list of More Data Sources and added to the list of data sources directly under the Create New Connection folder.

A connection to an Oracle server, for instance, would use a native connection making use of software provided by Oracle. If an Oracle client exists on a computer, the Net8 Easy Config utility would configure the client for communication with an Oracle server. The process of using the configuration utility installs the necessary native drivers to the computer, therefore making them available to Crystal Reports.

Crystal Queries

The Crystal SQL Designer is a separate, and free, product that was installed with earlier versions of Crystal Reports. Its purpose is to allow you to build a SQL query, preview the data in rough form, and then save the query for use as a data source. In Crystal Reports 9, you can still use the Crystal SQL Designer, but it is not shipped with the product. You can download it as part of a set of Crystal Reports 9 Data Compatibility tools that includes the Crystal SQL Designer and a second tool we'll talk about momentarily, the Crystal Reports Dictionary tool. To download these free tools, go to the support.crystaldecisions.com site, choose the option to download updates and samples, and search for the file named cr9_data_tools.zip.

To activate the Crystal SQL Designer, choose Start ➢ Crystal Reports Tools ➢ Crystal SQL Designer. The Create SQL Expert uses a tabbed query builder interface, shown in Figure 10.19, and takes a tab-by-tab approach to building a SQL query.

FIGURE 10.19

Crystal SQL Designer

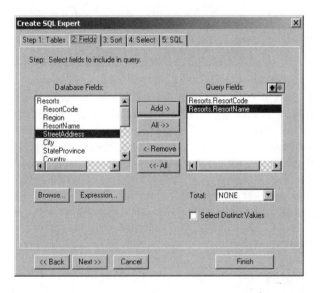

The first step is to connect to the data on the Tables tab, which is done the same way you've seen with the Database Expert, but with a slightly different dialog window. Next, choose the fields to include in the query.

NOTE *If multiple tables are involved in the query being built, a tab labeled Links appears directly to the right of the Tables tab. On the Links tab, you can add links manually or click the Smart Linking button to link based on primary and foreign keys, which were discussed in Chapter 9, "Working with Multiple Tables."*

Once you've selected the data on the Fields tab and chosen a sort order on the Sort tab, then you can click the SQL tab to display the resulting SQL query based on your criteria. An example is shown in Figure 10.20. You can modify the query using the SQL tab at this point by applying any SQL statements valid in a SELECT clause. In addition, you can go directly to the SQL tab and type a valid SQL statement without using the tabbed interface at all.

FIGURE 10.20

SQL query

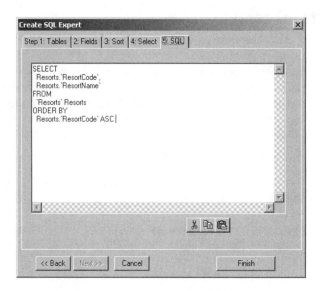

When you click the Finish button, you have the option of processing the query immediately or saving it to a file. Running the query displays the results of the field selection along with its data and any other SQL statements. The behavior is reminiscent of working with a database interactively, running a query, and seeing the tabular results immediately. An example of this is shown in Figure 10.21. This is a great tool to use if you want to have a quick look at the data in its raw format.

Choosing File ➢ Save As provides a way for you to save the query in a file that can then be used as a Crystal Reports data source, as shown in Figure 10.22. The file automatically gets a .qry extension, and you can save it to any location on your computer or attached network drive. When you choose this option as the data source, each time the report opens, the query will be run anew and data generated for use in the report.

The File menu also contains the Save Data With Query option. This option prevents Crystal from running the query when a report is opened and instead uses the data that was generated with the query when it was created and saved. This means that the query itself is not rerun when the report opens. An example of how a Crystal query will be displayed in the Database Expert is shown in Figure 10.23.

FIGURE 10.21

Query results

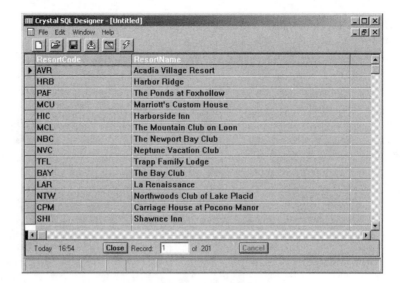

FIGURE 10.22

Saving a .qry file

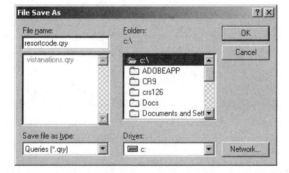

FIGURE 10.23

Crystal queries in the
Database Expert

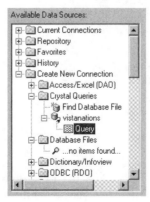

Dictionary/Infoview

Have you ever worked with a database table that was so massive that you cringed doing a query? Especially if, on a regular basis, all you ever worked with in the table was a set of five fields out of the 300 being stored. Crystal Dictionary files (known in earlier versions of Crystal as Infoview files) can help manage the data source in a way that presents only the fields of interest to the Database Expert. Like the Crystal SQL Designer, the Crystal Dictionary tool can be downloaded from the Crystal Decisions website as part of the Crystal Reports 9 Data Compatibility tools. Once installed on your computer, you can start this free tool by choosing Start ➢ Programs ➢ Crystal Reports Tools ➢ Crystal Dictionaries. Figure 10.24 demonstrates that choosing a data source involves the familiar technique of picking an ODBC or other data source from a list.

FIGURE 10.24

Crystal Dictionary data source

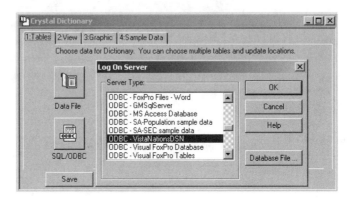

The tabs walk you through the essential steps needed to create a subset of visible data to be used in Crystal Reports. You begin by picking a table in the Tables tab after connecting to the data source. One of the strengths of a Crystal Dictionary is the ability to shield the end user from unwieldy table and field names. Throughout, you can specify alias names that you want users to see. Figure 10.25 shows that you're given the opportunity to name a table whatever you want. Doing so renames the table in the dictionary file only and has no effect on the stored table or its data.

FIGURE 10.25

Setting an alias

NOTE *As in the Crystal SQL Designer tool, if the dictionary being built involves multiple tables, a tab labeled Links appears directly to the right of the Tables tab, allowing you to build links manually or by using the Smart Linking button to link based on primary and foreign keys.*

The View tab is the core of creating a Crystal Dictionary. Here you create aliases for field names and choose the fields that become part of the dictionary. No other fields will be visible to the report designer, so the View tab determines the view of the data that will be seen by the dictionary users. The column on the left in Figure 10.26 shows the table name and all the field names, while the column on the right shows the fields that will be included in the view and the alias names (if any) that will be displayed.

FIGURE 10.26

Determining the view

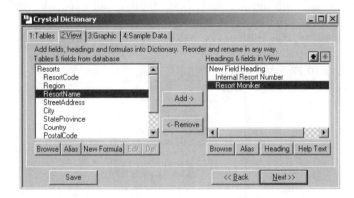

In this example, the ResortCode field was given an alias of Internal Resort Number, the Resort-Name field was given the alias Resort Moniker, and the Country field was added but no alias was assigned. When you click the Save button, a dictionary file will be created that allows access to only these three fields through the Database Expert in Crystal Reports.

Dictionary files can help you accomplish two major goals:

◆ Limit the fields that are accessed in a table.

◆ Display field and table names that are more meaningful to the report designers.

NOTE   *Dictionary files are saved with the file extension* `.dc5` *and can be stored anywhere on a computer or a network. Infoview files have a file extension of* `.civ`.

Database Files

Crystal Reports has the ability to work with certain types of databases directly through the use of a single data access layer with no reliance on SQL or ODBC. In other words, if Crystal Reports is installed on your computer, you can get to certain kinds of databases without doing any connectivity work at all. These databases are referred to as *PC databases* or *direct-access databases*. They do not come under the client/server model of databases.

PC databases are typically used to build databases that will be used by a single user at a time and are generally not used to store enterprise-wide data. The list of PC databases includes:

◆ Clipper

◆ dBASE

◆ FoxPro

◆ Microsoft Access

◆ Paradox

◆ Pervasive

To work with any of these types of databases, all you need to do with the Database Expert is locate the file on the computer using the built-in browse window. The database is then added below the Database Files connectivity folder in the Database Expert, as shown in Figure 10.27.

FIGURE 10.27

Database Files connectivity

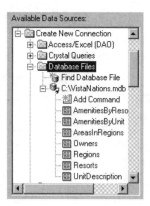

There is a limitation on PC databases: You cannot switch from one type of data source to another regardless of whether the database table and fields are identical or not. If you predict a need to switch database types down the road, using ODBC to make the connection is a safer choice.

NOTE   *When you use multiple tables with direct access connectivity, if non-SQL native drivers are used, all linking is performed as left outer joins.*

Programmatic Access

If you're a programmer, you'll be happy to hear that you have full programmatic access to Crystal Reports and many of the databases used with Crystal. Collaboration with Microsoft has provided a path to that company's concept of Universal Data Access to data in the business enterprise. Acronyms abound here and include methodologies such as DAO, RDO, and ADO. Luckily, they all accomplish the same task—access to stored data from external programs. Here's a quick overview of each:

DAO   Data Access Objects (DAO) is an older technology that uses the JET Engine and ODBC to connect to a data source. Although Microsoft is phasing out this programmatic methodology, you will notice at the top of the list of available data sources in the Database Expert shown in Figure 10.28 that one of the ways you can connect to Microsoft Excel and Microsoft Access is using DAO. The Database Expert shows the programming technology in parentheses, while the name of the supported database application appears to the left and is the focus. This architecture is sometimes referred to as a one-tier architecture based on its simplicity and lack of ability to be extended to other types of data sources.

RDO Remote Data Objects (RDO) is more recent than DAO and is sometimes referred to as a two-tier architecture. Programmers can use RDO with the Enterprise Edition of Visual Basic to connect to remote databases using ODBC. In the list of data sources shown in Figure 10.28, note that about two-thirds of the way down you'll find ODBC (RDO) data sources listed. Microsoft is also phasing out this programmatic methodology, but Crystal Reports fully supports existing applications and databases that use it, especially since it is so prevalent in today's business world.

FIGURE 10.28

DAO in the
Database Expert

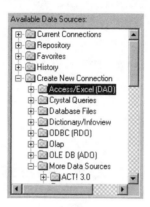

ADO ActiveX Data Objects (ADO) is a programming interface into the world of Microsoft's OLE DB data access methodology. Its goal is to provide programmatic access to a wide variety of data while minimizing the complexity of dealing with different databases. A standard set of objects provides fast, easy access to underlying databases. ADO is fairly lightweight and can be used for desktop programming and Internet programming. Take a look back at Figure 10.27 and notice that just short of the bottom you'll see an option to connect to an OLE DB (ADO) data source. This is the currently blessed Microsoft methodology for accessing databases from within code.

Part 4 of this book, "Application Development with Crystal Reports," goes into depth on the topic of programming Crystal Reports without using the user interface. It provides everything you need to know to use code to manipulate Crystal Reports and its data for report delivery on the desktop and the Web.

XML and ODBC

Extensible Markup Language (XML) files are becoming a popular medium for transferring data from one system to another. These files have a hierarchical structure that allows the data to be treated relationally as rows and columns through an ODBC interface. Crystal Reports can both read from and export to an ODBC XML data source. Figure 10.29 shows the structure of a typical XML file as viewed through Internet Explorer. This particular example file is a set of books. In relational terms, here's how such a file will be interpreted:

♦ Table: The set of all books represented in the file

♦ Row: An individual book within the file

♦ Column: The information used to describe the book, such as title and author

FIGURE 10.29

An XML file structure

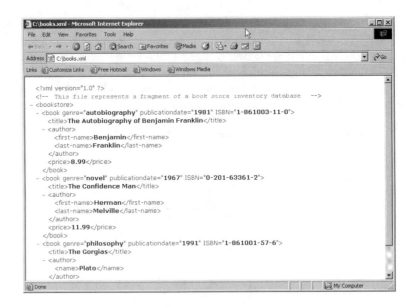

Using XML As a Data Source

Crystal Reports 9 ships with the Crystal Reports XML ODBC driver that can be used to access an XML document. A single document or set of XML documents is a valid Crystal Reports data source. Configuring the connection requires choosing the driver as a system DSN as well as installing the XML driver on your system. Although Crystal ships with the driver, it is not actually installed on your system until the first time you create a data source that uses the driver. To install the driver, refer back to Figure 10.4 and you'll see the Add button. After clicking this button, choose the CR ODBCXML Driver 4.10 from the list of drivers, and then click Finish, as shown in Figure 10.30.

FIGURE 10.30

Installing the XML ODBC driver

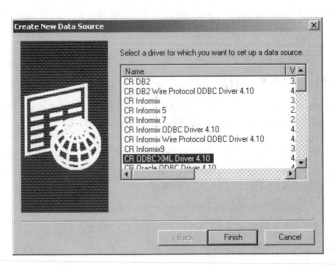

On the General tab of the ODBC XML Driver Setup dialog, do the following:

1. Type a meaningful data source name.

2. Add an optional description.

3. Click the Add button to find the XML file.

Clicking the Add button displays the Configure Location dialog shown in Figure 10.31. Enter the Location Name field in the free-form typing area. Choosing the location itself, on the other hand, involves clicking a Location Type radio button and then clicking the Location browse button (an ellipsis appears on the button). The location can be a URL pointing to a folder containing the XML documents (choose the Folder radio button), a single XML file, or a single HTML document. You can either type the path for a file use or the browse button to locate it. Figure 10.31 shows this task completed.

TIP *When you use a URL, the Location field needs to specify the name of the folder containing the XML file(s) and not the XML file(s) themselves.*

FIGURE 10.31

Configuring an
XML location

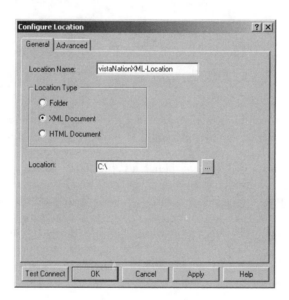

You can test the ODBC connection from this dialog by clicking the Test Connect button. If all goes well, you should see a message that the test connect succeeded. After testing the connection, you can click the Advanced tab, shown in Figure 10.32, to configure additional options if required for your application. The Advanced options include thefollowing:

◆ Adding an Extensible Stylesheet (XSL) reference for the table (table hint)

◆ Adding an XSL reference for the row (row hint)

◆ Validating the schema (business rules) found in the XML document against another file that contains the business rules

◆ Requiring a user ID and password to use the data source

FIGURE 10.32

Advanced options for XML configuration

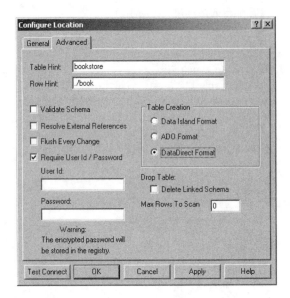

The table and row hints will be required if the XML document contains a hierarchy that is more than one level deep because the CR ODBCXML driver supports only one hierarchy level. The sample XML file shown in Figure 10.29 is only one level deep, with the hierarchy being **bookstore**. You can add this to the Advanced tab even though it's only one level deep, and if you had more levels, you would simply add a forward slash before typing the next level name after the previous level name. The table hint identifies the **<bookstore>** hierarchy as the table, while the row hint identifies the **<book>** tag as the row within the table. In Figure 10.32, the row hint contains a period before the forward slash; this indicates that the **book** is an element in the XML file (as opposed to an attribute). When you change a table or row hint, you are essentially changing the structure of the data source, so you'll need to log out of the data source and log back in before the new hints will be applied to the data. To log on or off a data source, choose Database ➢ Log On Or Off Server.

TIP *XML is a case-sensitive language, therefore the text of table and row hints must match the case used in the XML document exactly.*

Once the data source is configured at the ODBC level, back in Crystal Reports you simply choose to connect to an ODBC (RDO) data source and select the DSN you created to point to the XML documents. Figure 10.32 shows the Database Expert with an XML ODBC source selected.

FIGURE 10.33

The Database
Expert with an
XML data source

Creating XML from an RPT File

Crystal Reports can also be used to create XML documents. To do this, choose File ➤ Export to export data from the Details section of an RPT file to an XML ODBC data source. There are three formats that Crystal can use to create XML documents, and these are visible as radio button choices in the Table Creation area in Figure 10.32. These three choices represent the three different types of XML files that Crystal knows how to read as well to write. Table 10.4 describes these three choices.

TABLE 10.4: VALID XML FORMATS FOR CRYSTAL REPORTS

TABLE CREATION CHOICE	DESCRIPTION
Data Island Format	Choosing this option means that you have an XML document that represents the data as well as a second document that specifies the structure. The second file is a Data Definition document. Both files must be stored in the same file directory folder.
ADO Format	Choosing this option means that you have an XML document(s) that contains data, but within that same file a schema structure is also stored.
DataDirect Format	Choosing this option means that you have an XML document (or set of documents) that contains the data, and no external data definition document exists.

If your report is intended to be XML output, you can use the XML Expert (Report ➤ XML Expert) to format the XML element tags and attributes. The expert allows you to specify the Crystal ML schema used to identify the components of an XML document as well as apply external XSD (XML Schema Definition) or DTD (Document Type Definition) validations.

NOTE *XSD is an XML-based grammar that describes the structure of an XML document and can therefore be used to validate it. Likewise, DTDs do the same thing, but a DTD is not based on XML grammar.*

Summary

It's a fact: Building a report requires data, and the Database Expert is the heart of the action for Crystal connectivity. The access strategies used to connect to the data, while hidden behind the simple dialog interface of the Database Expert, go a long way to making Crystal Reports a universal database-reporting tool.

Your options for connecting to data using Crystal Reports are wide and varied. At one end is the very easy-to-use Crystal Dictionaries and local PC databases. In the middle of the complexity spectrum are ODBC access and OLE DB. At the high end of the range, you can use OLAP cubes and servers for data sources as well as programmatically access a variety of data sources.

In choosing a connectivity path, we showed that you can connect to the same data source using a variety of connection types. There are advantages and disadvantages to using each, and your decision will be based on your computing environment and growth needs.

Chapter 11

Using SQL in Crystal Reports

Do you wonder exactly what goes on between the time you choose a data source and the time the data appears in your report? The Database Expert is a powerful interface for connecting to a wide variety of data sources. When you build a new report, one of the very first decisions you need to make is which data source to use. From there, Crystal does the rest of the legwork to retrieve the data you specified. The wizard approach provided by the Database Expert hides the entire complex nature and the gory details of database connection and data retrieval from you. While this may be a good thing most of the time, we all know that too much of a good thing can also cause some grief. In this case, choosing one data source over another may work against you when optimum data retrieval performance is your goal.

To help you achieve the best retrieval speeds, you can use Structured Query Language (SQL) within Crystal Reports. In Chapter 10, "Data Sources and the Database Expert," we touched on the concept of personal computer (PC)–type databases versus client/server databases. We will continue this discussion in this chapter so that you may better understand the role that SQL plays in Crystal Reports. SQL is a command syntax used exclusively with relational databases. Some databases support this language; others do not. If a report designer chooses a SQL-capable database, Crystal can use a subset of this language to retrieve data efficiently from SQL-capable databases. To this end, you need to get a good handle on the structure and use of SQL statements and where in Crystal Reports you can make use of this knowledge.

Featured in this chapter:

- ◆ Choosing client/server databases versus PC-type databases

- ◆ Understanding Structured Query Language

- ◆ Using SQL expression fields

- ◆ Using SQL commands as a data source

- ◆ Creating stored procedures

- ◆ Creating views

- ◆ Using Crystal Reports database utilities

Database Types

Do you remember the last time you bought a car? If not, just think of one that you own or a friend owns. For a moment, we'll use car terminology so that we can explain a new database concept. Let's say you were buying a Honda Civic sedan. Just from that name, you know at least three pieces of information: the make, the model, and the type. You actually know more than that, though. You know that you are buying a durable, reliable car from which you expect certain performance characteristics. The type combined with the make and model allows you to deduce this information. Now let's apply this theme to databases.

When you work with a Microsoft Access database, you know the make (Microsoft) and the model (Access). The type of database is said to be a file-based database or a PC type, meaning it runs on a standalone personal computer or a set of connected workgroup computers. Based on the type, you also know that you are using a database from which you expect low-end performance characteristics. Sound familiar?

What if you're working with an Oracle 8i database or a Microsoft SQL Server database? Again, you know the make (Oracle or Microsoft) and the model (8i or SQL Server). The type for these databases is client/server. Based on this information, you know that you are using a database that has high-end performance characteristics.

So the distinction being drawn here is that there are generally two types of databases:

- PC databases
- Client/server databases

Like a car, the model of database used determines data retrieval performance. Depending on which type of database you use, you can expect different performance levels and behavior in Crystal Reports.

PC Databases

A PC database is generally one that is stored in a single operating system file and sits on a personal computer for use by one person at a time. Examples of this are Microsoft Access, Btrieve, and Clipper DBF formats. There are certainly exceptions to the single operating system file. For example, DBF files each store exactly one table so when you're working with a database, or collection of tables, you're working with several operating system files. There are also exceptions to the single-user guideline. The point is that PC databases tend to handle low-volume and low-transaction data requests and are not scalable for use by large numbers of simultaneous users.

When Crystal Reports interacts with a PC database, it uses built-in utilities to open and retrieve data for a report; this can make the access to the data very fast. On the other hand, all of the processing takes place from within the confines of Crystal Reports, which may have the effect of slowing down the processing. Figure 11.1 demonstrates that the processing steps all take place in Crystal's memory: requesting data, finding the data, and retrieving the data from the files.

FIGURE 11.1

Standalone PC database

Crystal requests data, pulls all records, creates data results internally

Personal Computer

All of this processing happens when Crystal opens a report and needs to refresh its data supply. A performance delay, therefore, is apparent to the person opening the report. Will you always experience a delay? Not necessarily. Imagine the difference in how long it would take to retrieve 100 records of data from a database versus 100,000 records. The performance impact will more readily be felt as the number of rows being retrieved increases. This is because all the data has to be pulled into Crystal Reports and then processed in terms of filtering, sorting, and grouping. The performance hit is also directly related to the amount of memory the personal computer has available to process the data.

Another variation on the PC type of database is the use of a set of personal computers that act as a workgroup in a local area network. In this scenario, a group of computers are connected together and can share information in a peer-to-peer manner. One of the computers is often designated as a file server, meaning that it holds all the important files that multiple users want to access. This centralized file server is generally the only one on which a nightly backup routine is run. This type of computer environment is often found in small-to-midsize office organizations. Figure 11.2 demonstrates what happens when Crystal opens a report and retrieves data from a nearby computer.

FIGURE 11.2

Workgroup PC database

Crystal requests data, pulls all records, creates data results internally

Personal Computer   LAN-connected computer or file server

The net effect of using PC databases is that all of the data processing is being handled by Crystal Reports. How do you know when you're using PC databases in Crystal Reports? You choose Database Files in the Database Expert! Figure 11.3 shows the Database Files option below the Create New Connection folder in the Database Expert. Whenever you connect to a database using the Database Files folder, you are working with a PC database.

FIGURE 11.3

Database Files

NOTE *PC databases are also known as* direct access *database files in Crystal Reports.*

Client/Server Databases

In contrast to PC databases, client/server databases tend to involve multiple operating system files and tend to be used by large groups of users simultaneously. The heart of a client/server database is a database server as opposed to a file server or personal computer. A database server is a much more sophisticated piece of software than a database file and it takes into account high-volume transactions and multiple simultaneous users. It often sits on a physical server that is dedicated to running just that piece of database software; it has been loaded with the maximum amount of memory, hard drive space, and processing units.

NOTE *The use of the word* server *in the computer world has two meanings depending on its context. One meaning refers to the physical computer hardware and its operating system, usually in a network environment. The other meaning refers to a software application that runs on top of the operating system of a physical server. A database server is the latter of these types.*

When Crystal Reports interacts with a client/server database, Crystal is the client. The client makes a request for data to the server. The server then processes the request in its entirety and sends a result back to the client. In essence, the client delegates a task to the server and sits and waits for the finished result.

Can you remember the last time you delegated a task to someone? The experience goes best if the person you delegated to doesn't come back and ask you a hundred interim questions before giving you a result. In a client/server environment, the client asks for something and doesn't do any work on the report until the server hands back the requested data. During this time, the client computer can be doing other tasks, thus managing its workload more effectively. Figure 11.4 depicts this situation.

FIGURE 11.4

Client/server
databases

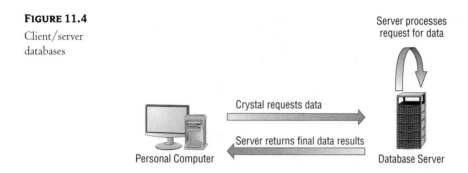

The database server's memory and processor are put to use processing the data. The memory and the processor on the Crystal Reports computer are responsible for building the report on the set of data that was returned by the server.

SQL-Capable Databases

To interact with a client/server database, software as well as people generally use a SQL approach. This means that you can use SQL commands to interact with the database for the purpose of retrieving data, updating data, deleting data, and even defining the tables and columns. PC databases, on the other hand, are accessed directly by Crystal Reports using built-in utilities with vendor-specific, proprietary syntax. This is how they get their reputation for fast access; they use a proprietary access language optimized for that specific database.

SQL STANDARDS

There are hundreds of different database products available today as third-party products, shareware, and freeware. While each of them may support the use of SQL statements, it is not a requirement that they each support the *same* set of SQL statements. Each database vendor tends to have its own dialect that conforms to but is not identical to the standards specified by the two groups which formalize such standards in the United States and internationally: American National Standards Institute (ANSI) and International Organization for Standardization (ISO). The most recent ANSI and ISO SQL standard is SQL3, also known as SQL99. Prior SQL standards were set in 1986, 1989, and 1992. This means that if you're working on more than one type of database, there's a good chance that among them they're using a different set of SQL standards and subset of the SQL language.

Beyond the different ANSI and ISO standards, database vendors typically create extensions in their language to handle interactions that are specific to their own product. Each of the major database manufacturers has its own SQL dialect, including Oracle's PL/SQL, Microsoft SQL Server's Transact-SQL, and IBM's DB2 SQL, to name a few. Figure 11.5 gives you a feel for the concept of supersets and subsets of standard SQL; ODBC, IBM, Microsoft, and Oracle all implement the SQL-99 Standard, and indeed all go beyond to varying degrees with extended or extra capabilities.

FIGURE 11.5

SQL dialects

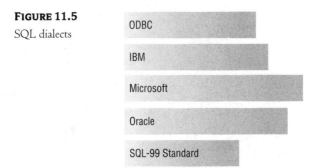

Vendor-specific extensions create differences in the SQL dialects used in the database products. This is the purpose that the database driver (usually a .DLL file) fulfills when Crystal Reports needs to interact with a database: using the correct dialect to interact with the database.

ODBC

Notice also in Figure 11.5 that ODBC is listed. While not a vendor-specific SQL, it does provide a standard way to interact with multiple databases that are being treated as ODBC data sources. In the last chapter, ODBC (RDO) was discussed as a method to connect to a data source. We showed that you could connect to the same database multiple ways. This is true of PC databases as well. As an example, if you choose to connect to a Microsoft Access database as a database file, there's a built-in driver to accommodate that. Or you can choose to connect to a Microsoft Access database as an ODBC data source.

There is a trade-off involved, depending on your decision. When you access a PC database directly as a direct access database file, you have only the vender-specific DLL between you and the data source. When you use ODBC, you have several layers between Crystal and the data source. So the advantage of the PC database, which we mentioned earlier, is optimum speed. The disadvantage is the lack of SQL support from within Crystal Reports.

The result of using an ODBC access mechanism with a PC-style database is that the world of SQL is now open to you while you're using that data source from Crystal Reports. This includes being able to push some of the processing workload off Crystal Reports and onto the PC database in terms of sorting, filtering, and grouping.

A Structured Query Language Primer

As the name implies, SQL is used to query a database to ask for specific data to be returned. As a database interaction language, SQL provides other features as well. Here's a summary of what a generic SQL interface provides:

♦ Data retrieval through the query facility

♦ Calculations (SQL expressions) on stored data

♦ Filtering, sorting, and grouping of data

♦ Creation of the database structure itself

- Definition of relationships between data elements

- Insertion of new data

- Update of existing data

- Deletion of existing data

- Enforcement of data-integrity constraints

- Granting of security through privileges assigned to groups and individuals

Retrieving Data

Crystal Reports and report designers focus on the data-retrieval component of SQL, which is performed by the SELECT statement. This statement is read-only in the sense that executing a SELECT statement does not make any changes to the data or the database. A SELECT statement finds and retrieves columns of data from a database by searching for rows that meet criteria you specify. The basic syntax of a SELECT statement is

```
SELECT <column(s)> FROM <table>
```

where column(s) is the actual column name from the database and table is the actual table name. Let's look at how to use the SELECT statement by working with several business questions on the VistaNations database, which is being accessed as an ODBC data source.

Business Question: In which cities does VistaNation have resorts?

To retrieve the names of all the cities that have resorts in them, the SELECT statement would look like this:

```
SELECT City FROM Resorts
```

This statement returns a set of records, also known as a result set, that resembles Figure 11.6. SQL statements are *not* case-sensitive; the mix of casing used here is for stylistic purposes only. The results in Figure 11.6 were generated using the Crystal SQL Designer add-on tool described in Chapter 10, "Data Sources and the Database Expert."

NOTE   *All the queries and results shown in this chapter were generated using Crystal SQL Designer, an add-on utility that is part of the Crystal Reports 9 Data Compatibility toolset. You can download the Data Compatibility tools from Crystal Decisions using* http://support.crystaldecisions.com/communityCS/ FilesAndUpdates/cr9_data_tools.zip.asp *as the URL address.*

A few things should jump out at you when you view the results of this simple query. First, there are duplicates in the list, and second, the results are not sorted. Also, the bottom of Figure 11.6 shows that we retrieved 201 records. By default in a SELECT statement, records are returned in the order in which they were entered into the database. There are several keywords you can use with a SELECT statement to refine both the number of rows that are returned and the order in which they are returned. Let's use the DISTINCT keyword to see what difference it makes. The new query is presented below and its results are displayed in Figure 11.7:

```
SELECT DISTINCT City FROM Resorts
```

FIGURE 11.6

Selecting cities

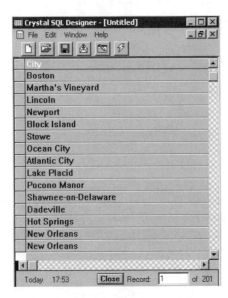

FIGURE 11.7

Selecting distinct cities

The number of records returned has been reduced to 171 and the list has been sorted. The DISTINCT keyword picks out the first occurrence of a value so that the list contains no duplicates; in addition, it automatically sorts the records in ascending order. This answers the business question a bit better. So the DISTINCT keyword is one way to reduce or refine the number of records returned by your query.

Refining a *SELECT* Statement

Without the use of keywords to modify the behavior of the SELECT, a query returns every row that matches your criteria. The DISTINCT keyword is one way to limit the rows returned, but it works on only one column. The most powerful way to fine-tune a query is to write a good WHERE clause, which has the general format of

```
SELECT <column(s)> FROM <table>
WHERE column <operator> value
```

A WHERE clause filters out data records that do not meet the specified condition, which has the potential to reduce the number of records returned by a query. It sets up a condition that must be true in order for the record to be retrieved from the database. The condition is formulated by comparing a column value to either another column value or a specific value that you provide. A WHERE clause can contain multiple condition statements each separated by the logical conditions AND and OR. Table 11.1 lists the operators that are valid in a WHERE clause.

TABLE 11.1: OPERATORS VALID IN A WHERE CLAUSE

OPERATOR	DESCRIPTION
=	Column value is equal to a value you specify.
<>	Column value is not equal to a value you specify.
>	Column value is greater than a value you specify.
<	Column value is less than a value you specify.
>=	Column value is greater than or equal to a value you specify.
<=	Column value is less than or equal to a value you specify.
BETWEEN	Column value is greater than or equal to one value that you specify while at the same time being less than or equal to a second value that you specify.
IN	Column value is one of a set of values that you specify.
AND	Both conditions must be true to satisfy the criteria.
OR	Either condition can be true to satisfy the criteria.

As an example of a WHERE clause, let's try to answer a business question for the VistaNations folks.

Business Question: How many five-star resorts does VistaNation have in the United States?

The query makes use of two conditions that must be met in order for a row to be returned in the result set. The results of the query are shown in Figure 11.8.

```
SELECT COUNT(ResortCode) FROM Resorts
WHERE FiveStarRating = True AND Country = 'US'
```

FIGURE 11.8

Using a WHERE clause

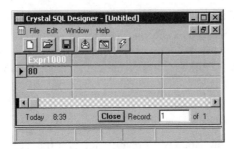

This query uses a built-in function called COUNT to operate on the ResortCode column. The result of this query is a single number representing how many rows meet the criteria, in this case 80. Notice in Figure 11.8 that the column name for the result is provided as Expr1000; this is called a SQL expression. Since a SQL expression is a calculation and not an actual column in the table, the column header reflects this. The general syntax for using a built-in SQL function in a SELECT is

```
SELECT function(column) FROM table
```

Table 11.2 describes several other popular SQL functions that can be used on column data.

TABLE 11.2: SQL FUNCTIONS VALID WITH COLUMN DATA

FUNCTION	DESCRIPTION
AVG	Returns the average of a column of numeric data.
COUNT	Returns a whole number representing how many rows meet the WHERE criteria for the column being counted.
COUNT(*)	Returns a whole number representing how many rows meet the WHERE criteria for the entire query.
MIN	Returns the smallest value in a column of numeric data.
MAX	Returns the largest value in a column of numeric data.
SUM	Returns the sum of all the values in a column of numeric data.

GROUPING AND SORTING

The result of a SELECT statement is a set of data records. This result set is held in memory in the database until processing is complete and then returned to Crystal Reports. While this temporary result set is in memory, it can be grouped, sorted, and filtered using SQL SELECT keywords. Let's vary the business question just a little and see how these keywords work.

Business Question: How many five-star resorts are within each state and zip code in the United States? Create the list in reverse order by state.

To following query answers this business question and its results are shown in Figure 11.9:

```
SELECT COUNT(StateProvince), StateProvince, PostalCode
FROM Resorts
WHERE FiveStarRating = True AND Country = 'US'
GROUP BY PostalCode, StateProvince
ORDER BY StateProvince DESC
```

FIGURE 11.9

Grouping and sorting

Expr1000	StateProvince	PostalCode
1	WV	26505
1	VT	05672
1	VA	23451
1	UT	84060
1	UT	84092
1	TX	78205
2	TN	37738
1	SC	29577
1	SC	29928
1	OR	97365
1	NV	89109
1	NV	89118
1	NV	89449
1	NV	89450
1	MT	59711
1	MN	56359

In this query, two actual columns are retrieved from the table and one aggregate function or SQL expression is used. The results are grouped by state and presented in reverse order by state, but within the state the zip codes are sorted in ascending order. Things are getting pretty complex! Having complete control over the SQL statement generating the data helps you guarantee that you're answering the business question correctly.

SQL JOINS

In Crystal Reports, the Database Expert is used to create joins by visually linking one column to another column. In a SELECT statement, keywords are used to perform joins except for the default join type.

In Chapter 9, "Working with Multiple Tables," we discussed the concept of inner joins, left outer joins, right outer joins, and full outer joins. Depending on which join types are supported by the data source, join conditions can be included in a SELECT statement. If you don't specify a join condition when using multiple tables with a SELECT statement, a default inner join is performed, meaning that every record in the first table is joined with every record in the second table if the WHERE clause condition is true.

The use of keywords in a SELECT statement pushes a good deal of processing back onto the database and results in fewer data records being sent over the network wires into Crystal Reports.

WARNING   *Left and right outer joins performed by ODBC will return different results than left and right outer joins performed by native database drivers due to implementation differences and generic assumptions made in ODBC.*

A summary of the keywords and the syntax for using them is described in Table 11.3.

TABLE 11.3: SQL KEYWORDS

SQL KEYWORD	SYNTAX
DISTINCT	`SELECT DISTINCT column FROM table`
COUNT	`SELECT COUNT(column) FROM table`

WHERE	`SELECT column1, column2, column3`
	`FROM table1, table2`
	`WHERE table1.column1 = table2.column2`

IN	`SELECT column1, column2, column3 FROM table` `WHERE column1 IN (value1,value2)`
BETWEEN	`SELECT column1, column2, column3 FROM table` `WHERE column1 BETWEEN value1 AND value2`
AND	`SELECT * FROM table` `WHERE ((column1<value) AND (column2=value))`
OR	`SELECT * FROM table` `WHERE ((column1<value) AND (column2=value))`
ORDER BY	`SELECT * FROM table` `ORDER BY column`
ASC	`SELECT * FROM table` `ORDER BY column ASC`
DSC	`SELECT * FROM table` `ORDER BY column DESC`
GROUP BY	`SELECT function(column1), column2 FROM table` `GROUP BY column2`

HAVING	`SELECT column, SUM(column) FROM table`
	`GROUP BY column`
	`HAVING SUM(column) condition value`

INNER JOIN	`SELECT column1, column2, column3`
	`FROM table1`
	`INNER JOIN table2`
	`ON table1.keyfield = table2.foreign_keyfield`

LEFT OUTER JOIN	`SELECT column1, column2, column3`
	`FROM first_table`
	`LEFT OUTER JOIN second_table`
	`ON table1.keyfield = table2.foreign_keyfield`

RIGHT OUTER JOIN	`SELECT column1, column2, column3`
	`FROM first_table`
	`RIGHT OUTER JOIN second_table`
	`ON table1.keyfield = table2.foreign_keyfield`

UNION	`SELECT * FROM table2`
	`UNION`
	`SELECT * FROM table2`

ODBC and SQL Statements

ODBC is a middle layer between a requesting application and a data source. The data source has its own proprietary SQL dialect. ODBC has its own version of SQL as well. With each call made to an ODBC data source, ODBC makes data requests using a generic version of SQL that has been designed to work in tandem with the data source being queried. This often results in translations from the SQL statements that you would use directly in the data source versus those that ODBC will use. For instance, in the query that counted resort codes with five-star ratings in the United States, the following two SQL syntaxes should be considered:

Query in Microsoft Access directly:

```
SELECT COUNT(ResortCode) FROM Resorts
WHERE FiveStarRating = "Yes" AND Country = "US"
```

Query using ODBC driver to Microsoft Access:

```
SELECT COUNT(ResortCode) FROM Resorts
WHERE FiveStarRating = True AND Country = 'US'
```

While both queries return the same result of 51 resorts meeting the criteria, note the syntactic differences that the ODBC driver used, namely:

◆   The FiveStarRating field was treated as a Boolean data type instead of character data.

◆   The string comparison on Country required single quotes instead of double quotes.

The syntax and conversions required depend on the software tool being used, the version of the ODBC driver, and the ODBC support provided by the database vendor. Do not be surprised by syntactic differences like the ones shown here; an ODBC driver is a different access mechanism into the database than the native SQL drivers. Most of the differences are explained by the need for ODBC to service a multitude of data source types while individual native SQL drivers are tuned for exactly one data source.

NOTE   *Boolean data is represented with the keywords* True *and* False. *It is equivalent to the character values of "Yes" and "No" as well as the numeric values of 1 and 0.*

SQL Expression Fields

The COUNT function was introduced earlier as a keyword used with a SQL SELECT statement and resulted in a SQL expression. Referring back to Figure 11.8, you'll recall that a SQL expression is a derived value based on other database fields or attributes and that the result displays in a column with a placeholder column name. So the idea behind a SQL expression is that it is a calculation based on stored values but is not a stored value itself.

Within a report, Crystal Reports provides this type of calculated value in the design environment through the use of SQL expression fields in the Field Explorer. If the database is SQL-capable and has been connected to using ODBC, OLE DB, or SQL native drivers, then the SQL Expression Fields category displays in the Field Explorer, as shown in Figure 11.10; otherwise, this category does not exist.

FIGURE 11.10

SQL Expression
Fields

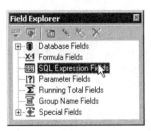

This type of field is a calculation written using SQL functions, not formula language. These database functions are passed to the database server for processing and return a result to Crystal Reports through the SQL expression field.

To create a new SQL expression field, right-click to display the context menu and choose New, or click the New icon at the top of the Field Explorer. After giving the field the name of your choice, the Formula Workshop - SQL Expression Editor opens and displays only the database functions that apply for the type of database you are using. It builds the list of functions dynamically after detecting the database type and connection type. Figure 11.11 shows a partial look at the database functions that are present when you connect to SQL Server using OLE DB.

FIGURE 11.11

SQL Expression
Editor

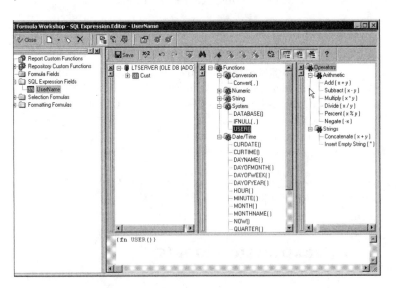

One of the database functions available in a SQL Server database allows you to pick up the name of the currently logged-in user from the operating system. Figure 11.11 shows the coding of this expression in the coding area of the editor. Note that all you need to provide is the function call itself; even though it looks incomplete, it is an expression that returns a result, and that is exactly what is needed here. As with other areas of the Formula Workshop, double-clicking the User() function in the list above adds it to the editing area below. Once the function is written, check and save it as you do with other code, and then drag and drop it onto your report to display its value.

You use SQL expression fields to perform calculations that are a native part of a database's language but that would take a great deal of coding effort to re-create in Crystal Reports.

NOTE *There is no built-in help in Crystal Reports to assist you with these functions; they are database functions, not Crystal functions. To learn more about how to use database-specific functions and which ones are available in which database, refer to the database documentation provided by the software vendor.*

SQL Commands

If you're using an ODBC, OLE DB, or SQL native driver connection, a new feature built into Crystal Reports 9 lets you type a SQL SELECT command directly to create a result set to use as a data source. The result of the query appears to Crystal as a table object complete with fields of data that can be added to a report.

To begin the process of creating a new SQL command in Crystal, first choose the type of connection you want to make and then double-click the Add Command option in the Database Expert. Figure 11.12 displays this option for the VistaNations database using an ODBC connection.

NOTE *If you do not see an Add Command option for your data source, it is most likely not an ODBC, OLE DB, or SQL native driver data source.*

FIGURE 11.12

Adding a SQL command

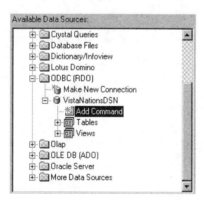

Choosing this option opens the Modify Command dialog window, shown in Figure 11.13. Here, you can type directly the SQL SELECT command to use as the basis of the report.

NOTE *At the bottom left of this dialog is the Add To Repository option. Enabling this option allows you to save this SQL command to the Crystal Reports repository for use in other reports.*

FIGURE 11.13

Modify Command
dialog

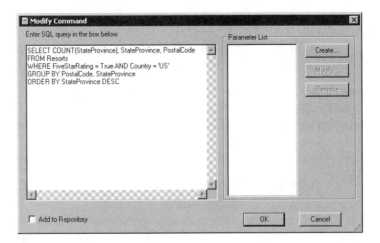

After typing the SQL command, click the OK button save it and use in this report. Closing the Modify Command dialog returns you to the Database Expert and places the new command in the list of Selected Tables, as shown in Figure 11.14. You can modify the SQL command at any time by double-clicking the Command table object in the Selected Tables list to reopen the Modify Command dialog.

FIGURE 11.14

Selected Tables

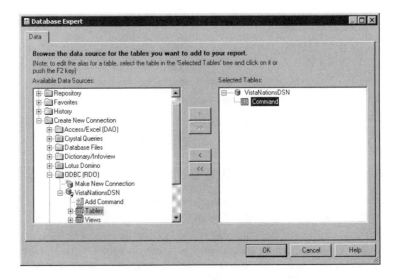

The Field Explorer treats the result of the SQL command as a table object and provides access to its fields, as shown in Figure 11.15. Notice that the SQL expression name remains since this calculation was performed in the query and doesn't tie back to an actual field stored in the table. The resulting report using the three fields is shown in Figure 11.16.

FIGURE 11.15

Field Explorer

FIGURE 11.16

Report based on a
SQL command

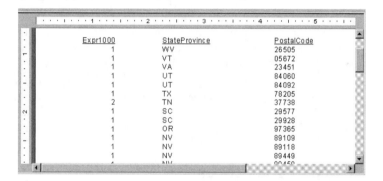

Wasn't that simple? If you have a good grasp of creating SELECT statements, you have the power of SQL commands at your fingertips for bringing data in Crystal Reports.

Parameterized Queries

The more generic a query is, the more reusable it becomes. One way to make a query reusable is to pass parameters to the query at runtime instead of hard-coding the values at design time. A SQL command can use a parameter list in which you provide the following:

◆ A name for the parameter

◆ The text you want to display for a user to ask for a data value

◆ The data type of the value you're expecting the user to provide

◆ A starting default value for the parameter

Take a peek back at Figure 11.13. On the right side of the screen is a Parameter List. To create parameters to pass to this query, we'll use the Create button, which is next to the Parameter List. Clicking the Create button opens the Command Parameter dialog, where you provide all the necessary information for the parameter. We're going to convert the earlier query to a parameterized query that prompts the user to indicate whether they want to look for five-star resorts or not. Figure 11.17 shows the Command Parameter screen filled out and ready to go.

FIGURE 11.17

Query parameter

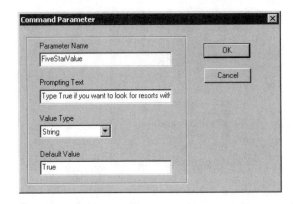

From this point, all you need to do is modify the SQL query to reference the name of your parameter. SQL Command parameter fields are referenced with their name preceded by a percent sign (%). When the report is opened and before the query is sent to the database, the person opening the report is prompted to supply a data value using the prompting text you supplied. The query is then formulated using the values specified by the user, and the query is sent to the database.

The Modify and Remove buttons in the Modify Command dialog shown in Figure 11.13 can be used to make changes to a parameter field after it has been created.

Stored Procedures

Stored procedures are a series of SQL commands that are stored in the database under a name that can be referenced by a calling application. The SQL commands execute sequentially on the server whenever the stored procedure is called by name. So you can think of a stored procedure as a code module.

These code modules are typically created by a database administrator or programmer and stored in a table in the database itself. Stored procedures run on the database server in server memory after being invoked by a client application. The result set is then sent back to the calling client application, in our case, Crystal Reports. Typical uses of stored procedures in a database include:

◆ Joining large tables and sorting and grouping the data

◆ Performing a series of queries

◆ Combining the results of one query with another

◆ Generating statistics based on stored data

Programmers generally decide to create a stored procedure if they find themselves coding the same or similar SQL queries over and over again. Writing a parameterized query can simplify their jobs. The main advantages to using stored procedures from Crystal Reports are security, performance, reusability, and maintainability.

Security

Stored procedures are stored in a table in a database. Since permissions are granted on a table-by-table basis, security can be put in place to control who can run stored procedures. This centralizes the administration of security, moving it away from the plethora of applications that use the data and placing it closer to the data itself.

Performance

If Crystal Reports is processing large amounts of data but ultimately displaying only a subset of that data due to filtering and other formulas, it can generate a lot of network traffic because all of the data has to be present in Crystal before final processing. A stored procedure does this processing on the server, which sends only the required end result data back to the client, therefore reducing network traffic. In addition, once a stored procedure has been run, it becomes a compiled module and is cached in server memory so that future calls to it will be faster than the first. A client application takes advantage of the superior processing capabilities of a server without impacting its own processing resources. Also, the more individual SQL statements a database has to handle, the more database locks are used; stored procedures can process SQL statements in groups and reduce the number of database locks being used, which helps overall database performance for other applications as well.

Reusability

Once you've written a very complex SQL SELECT statement, you'll find that you'll copy and paste it, tweak it, and fine-tune it for years to come for a variety of applications. A good use of a stored procedure is to group together SQL statements that can be called in a block to return results. The goal is to write a stored procedure once, test it exhaustively until it's perfect, and then call it frequently instead of writing the SQL statements from scratch every time.

Maintainability

In any organization, it is typical to have multiple people who need to execute the same queries over time. By saving the queries as stored procedures, you increase the reliability of the results as well as having only one place to look for problems or to make a programming change. For example, if the stored procedure is being called from multiple web pages and something changes in the query, you can change it once rather than changing it in every web page, because the web page is simply invoking a routine that is stored on the server.

Stored Procedures As a Crystal Data Source

The result of executing a stored procedure in a database is the return of a result set of data. The result set is a virtual table held in the database's memory. Since this is a virtual table, and it is represented in row and column format, it can be used as a data source in Crystal. If the database being connected to has stored procedures, they will be listed as a data source below the Tables option. Figure 11.18 shows stored procedures that are accessible in the miracleSqlServer data source that has been connected to using OLE DB.

Choosing a stored procedure from the list of Available Data Sources in the Database Expert identifies the result of the stored procedure to be the data set Crystal Reports will process. The result set is treated as a table object in Crystal Reports.

FIGURE 11.18

Stored procedures as a data source

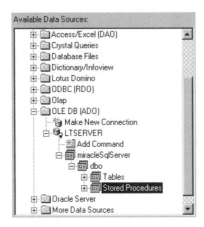

The stored procedure is actually executed and run on the server when the finished Crystal Report is opened. Figure 11.19 shows that the stored procedure named EmpDeptJob was run and the result was that the fields DeptDesc, JobTitle, FPTime, Salary, FName, and LName were returned to Crystal for use in the report.

FIGURE 11.19

Stored procedure results

TIP   *If a database's stored procedures do not automatically appear in the Database Expert, you can verify that Crystal Reports is set to display them by choosing File ➢ Options, selecting the Database tab, and enabling the Stored Procedures check box.*

Stored procedures are very powerful in that they offload a good deal of processing onto the server. However, there are some guidelines that limit how stored procedures can be used within Crystal data sources:

◆ The stored procedure cannot change data in the database, meaning it needs to use SELECT statements only.

◆ If a stored procedure is used, it is the only data source allowed.

- ◆ A report can use only one stored procedure as a data source at a time.
- ◆ Any joins on tables must be part of the stored procedure code.

Views

Views are another type of database object that can used as a data source when you're using a SQL-accessible database. Like stored procedures, views are treated as table objects in Crystal Reports. You can think of a view as presenting a particular perspective of the underlying data. For instance, in a table called People, a view built based on that table might be called Women. Its contents would be only those records where the gender field was equal to Female. This new Women view could then be reported on directly.

In a relational database, a view is the dynamic creation of a new relation, or virtual table, as a result of mathematical combinations involving other tables. Since a view is virtual, its definition exists in the database but does not exist as an actual stored table structure. The view is built at runtime by retrieving the view definition from a table, executing, and storing the temporary results in memory. The view definition has a name, and this is what is accessed to produce a table object in memory. Since views are dynamic entities, any change to an underlying table is automatically reflected in the view. In the example of the Women view, if a new person was added to the People table, and that person happened to be female, the Women view would reflect the addition of the new person.

As data sources, if views exist in the database, they display in the Database Expert together with tables and stored procedures. If they exist but are not visible, you can enable them to be visible by choosing File ➢ Options, selecting the Database tab, and enabling the Views check box.

SQL Database Utilities

Crystal Reports provides several database utilities when working with ODBC, OLE DB, and SQL native driver data sources. You can access these utilities using the Database option on the main Crystal menu. The submenu is shown in Figure 11.20. Let's look at each option separately.

FIGURE 11.20

SQL database utilities

Database Expert   This option opens the familiar Database Expert for adding and removing data sources from a report in Design mode. This option is available for all data sources and is not limited to ODBC, OLE DB, or SQL native drivers.

Set Datasource Location   This option can be used to point Crystal to a different set of tables to report on as long as their database structure is identical to the one currently in use. An example of when this option can be used is in developing reports on a test machine that will be ported to a production machine; the table names, fields, and attributes are all identical, but the name of the server and database are different. For example, you might use this when scaling a Microsoft Access database up to a SQL Server database for use as an enterprise data source. Figure 11.21 demonstrates changing a data source from a SQL Server connection to an ODBC connection, which you might do to build a test database.

FIGURE 11.21

Changing a database

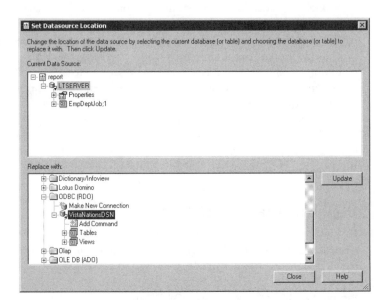

Log On Or Off Server   When you connect to an ODBC, OLE DB, or SQL native driver data source, you have effectively logged on to a database server. A connection to this server is maintained until you either log off or close Crystal Reports. Use this option to log onto or off data sources as you need them or finish with them.

Verify Database   Select this option to interactively check whether the data being used by the report is the most current data available in the database.

Verify On First Refresh   This option is set to either on or off. When this option is enabled (denoted by a check mark to the left of its name in the menu), it will automatically perform the Verify Database task before a report is printed.

Show SQL Query   Use this option to view in read-only mode the actual SQL query being sent from Crystal Reports to the data source.

Perform Grouping On Server   Select this option to tell the database management system to group the data before returning it to Crystal Reports, thereby off-loading work to the server that would normally be done in Crystal. Using this option will have a positive effect on the speed of data retrievals between Crystal and a server.

Select Distinct Records   Using this option is the equivalent of adding the `DISTINCT` keyword to the Crystal Reports SQL query before it is sent to the server. The net effect of using `DISTINCT` is that duplicate values are suppressed. This option cannot be used if a stored procedure is being used as the data source.

Summary

The ability to use SQL as a data source for Crystal Reports extends the reach of the product as well as its appeal to seasoned SQL developers. There is nothing that makes a true SQL person happier than being able to code exactly the right `SQL SELECT` statement that meets their needs. Add to this the ability to push workload onto the server and off Crystal, and SQL becomes a winning situation for users as well. SQL expression fields are an additional way to pass some work off to a database server.

The SQL data-manipulation language command that is used in Crystal Reports is the `SELECT` statement. There are many keywords that can be added to a simple `SELECT` to refine the values returned by the columns as well as the rows that meet the criteria for your report. In addition to using SQL commands as a data source in Crystal Reports, you can use both stored procedures and views in a database management system to provide data sets for use in a report.

With all the power of SQL and databases behind you, you'll also need to work with some of the built-in database utilities that Crystal provides. Tasks include changing from one database to another, viewing the SQL generated by Crystal Reports and sent to a database, and telling the database to do the grouping of data sets rather than Crystal Reports. The utilities are geared for use with SQL-capable databases that have been connected to using ODBC, OLE DB, or SQL native drivers.

Chapter 12

Analyzing Data Visually

NEED CHARTS? NEED GRAPHS? Need spreadsheet-like analysis? You've got the right tool! While tabular data presented as rows and columns in a report imparts essential detail information, the analysis of the data is left to the person reading the report. After combing through row after row of data values, an employee can analyze the data and come up with a summary statement like "Our sales are slipping in the Caribbean sector." Charts, graphs, maps, and cross-tabs can be used to sift through the data to graphically depict a trend or major points faster than a human could do it. Many people also find it easier to understand graphical information than detailed data. At many management meetings, all the boss wants to see is a chart summarizing the point of the meeting. Visual analysis can summarize data to answer business questions in a more absorbable format than detail data values. In this chapter, we'll explore the visual analysis capabilities for representing detail and summarized data.

Featured in this chapter:

- ◆ Creating charts with the Chart Expert

- ◆ Understanding the integrated chart types

- ◆ Placing a chart effectively in a report

- ◆ Using built-in and user-defined chart templates

- ◆ Finessing a chart with in-place editing and chart options

- ◆ Creating maps for geographic data using the Map Expert

- ◆ Adding geographic layers to report maps

- ◆ Creating two-dimensional cross-tabulation reports

- ◆ Customizing cross-tabs with percentage values and groups

- ◆ Understanding OLAP grid options

- ◆ Using Analyzer to interact with OLAP data

Charts and Graphs

Crystal Reports contains a completely integrated graphic module that can quickly chart the data in your report. There are 14 standard chart types like bar, line, and pie as well as variations within each chart type like side-by-side bar chart, stacked bar chart, and percent bar chart, which, provide a wide variety of graphing capability within a compact interface dialog.

The presence of groups and summarized values in a report is the starting point for using charting, mapping, and cross-tabs. Figure 12.1 shows the first page of a report that's suitable for charting, which answers the business question with data and summarization.

Business Question: Create a report that shows resort unit purchase prices by resort and country and is split into regions of North America, Caribbean, Europe, and Others.

FIGURE 12.1

First page of report

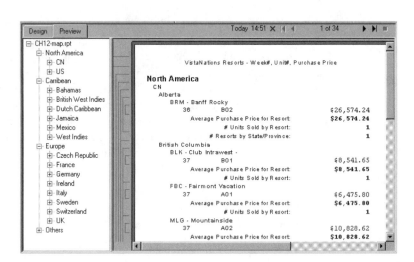

Figure 12.2 shows the same report with a chart of the report data placed in the Report Header. Notice that the graphic very quickly lends itself to answering the business question without having to scan all of the pages of the report and add up the numbers. Charts can be used in combination with detail data to completely provide the information and as well as the ability to compare and contrast summary values.

FIGURE 12.2

A bar chart in a report

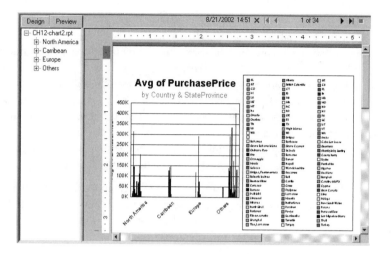

Creating a Chart or Graph

The Chart Expert in Crystal is used to create both charts and graphs; a graph is considered to be a type of chart. You can open the Chart Expert from the menu by choosing Insert ➤ Chart.

Once open, the Chart Expert displays tabs for configuring the key information for a chart. Figure 12.3 shows the Chart Expert and five tabs: Type, Data, Axes, Options, and Text. Not all chart types use all five tabs. In addition, the options available on each tab are based on the type of chart chosen on the Type tab. The Axes and Options tabs are suppressed when the Automatically Set Chart Options check box is enabled.

FIGURE 12.3

Chart Expert

CHOOSING A CHART TYPE

Use the Type tab to choose the chart visual that will best represent the story your data is trying to tell. Each chart type represents the data a bit differently. Pie charts are good for showing data values as they relate to 100 percent, while bar charts can easily show data that doesn't reach 100 percent. Use a chart that gets your point across. Configuration includes choosing the type of chart to create and, within that type, the visual effects particular to that chart. Crystal is smart enough to know whether the data in your report supports a particular type of chart. For instance, if you have no date/time values in your report, the Gantt chart option is unavailable.

Each chart type has a number of variations as to how it can be presented. Use the buttons on the right side of the dialog (Figure 12.3) to choose a chart variation.

Bar   Solid rectangular bars and stacked rectangular bars display in side-by-side mode to display individual data items, groups, and subgroups. Using this type of chart, you can visually compare one set of values to another based on the size of the rectangles and their component rectangles and present percentage information.

Line   Individual data points are connected inside an X/Y coordinate system to form lines representing data trends.

Area   Within an X/Y coordinate system, lines are drawn to represent data points, and the area beneath the line is shaded to represent the volume of data for the area being covered. This chart type can show trends over time.

Pie   Pie charts are most useful when 100 percent of the data (values, groups, or subgroups) is to be charted and each of the contributing parts is significant enough to display in the pie. For instance, a pie chart that shows data with a 30–30–40 percent split creates a nice visual, while a pie chart showing data with a 2–2–2–4–10–10–70 percent split might not be as helpful to the user visually. There is no time component to a pie chart, so no X/Y coordinate system is used.

Doughnut   A doughnut chart does exactly what a pie chart does; however, it has the additional capability of showing a data value in the center hole. For example, the total sales for the year can be included as a text value in the center of the doughnut, while the doughnut slices each show a relative percentage for each resort's sales.

3D Riser   3D riser charts are three-dimensional blocks, pyramids, cylinders, and rectangles. The data is represented in three dimensions instead of the normal two for X/Y coordinate systems. Time is usually one of the three dimensions. This type of chart is useful with grouped data and spreadsheet data.

3D Surface   Three dimensions are used to show trends over time in a surface analysis chart. The topology depicts the lows and the highs in data values over time.

XY Scatter   Using an X/Y coordinate system for bivariate analysis, XY scatter charts plot data points representing discrete or grouped data values for two variables. The data is scattered across the plane, showing patterns and density of data.

Radar   Data is presented in a grid of concentric circles, showing patterns of data.

Bubble   Using an X/Y coordinate system for trivariate analysis, bubble charts plot data points representing discrete or grouped data values for three variables. The data is scattered across the plane, showing patterns and density of data.

Stock   Floating bar charts show limit values together with plotted data value points. This type of chart is useful for showing trends over time within limits, such as minimums and maximums.

Numeric Axis   The numeric axis chart changes values for each data value plotted on the X-axis. It combines a visual representation of the data with a numeric data representation. Numeric axis charts can be bar charts, line charts, or area charts.

Gauge   Showing a gauge that goes from a low value to a high value, left to right, the gauge chart presents a dial that incorporates colors to show values in acceptable or dangerous ranges. Single categories of data are good candidates for this type of chart as it shows values as they relate to the 100 percent mark. This chart type is new in Crystal Reports 9.

Gantt   Gantt charts represent time-based milestones as horizontal bar charts in an X/Y coordinate system. This type of chart is popular for project management and forecasting. Date fields are required in the data in order to create Gantt charts. This chart type is new in Crystal Reports 9.

CONFIGURING DATA OPTIONS

Use the Data tab to configure options specific to the data points being plotted or charted. There are three areas on this tab: Placement, Layout, and Data. Within the Placement area, you choose where the chart will be placed in the report and the frequency of occurrence. Choosing Once Per Report means it will be placed in the Report Header or Footer; choose the Header or Footer radio button to indicate where to place the chart. Additional choices in the drop-down box map directly to the presence of groups in the report. In Figure 12.4, the phrase "For each" represents the groups that exist in the report.

FIGURE 12.4

Data options

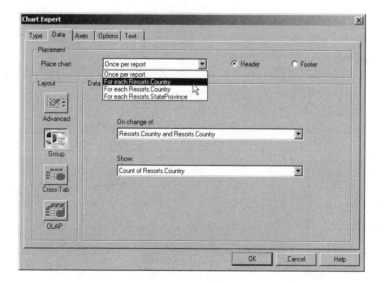

After choosing the placement option, you must next decide what kind of chart layout best matches your data. There are four layouts: Advanced, Group, Cross-Tab, and OLAP. If a layout button is available, then the appropriate type of data is present in the report, so if the report does not contain groups, cross-tabs, or OLAP data, these buttons are unavailable. If a group is available, the Group button is the default; otherwise, the Advanced option is preset. Charting group data is the simplest method to create a chart because the on-change events in the Data area within this tab correspond to the groups. It is reasonable to assume that if the report segments the data into groups, then the charts in the report will display information relative to these groups.

The Advanced option gives you the opportunity to work with detail data and any field contained in the report or the data source underlying the report. Figure 12.5 shows the Data tab with the Advanced option selected. In this chart, the average purchase price of a resort is being graphed relative to the country and state or province in which it is located.

FIGURE 12.5

Advanced layout option

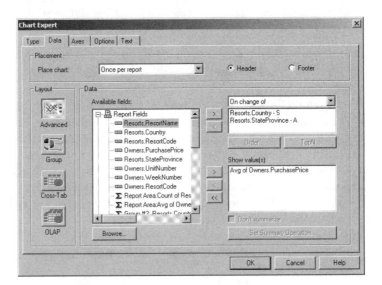

You can set the frequency of the chart in the report using the drop-down box in the Data area of the dialog, which has three choices:

◆ On Change Of

◆ For Each Record

◆ For All Records

The setting you choose will determine the frequency or periodicity of the data being graphed. To help decide between the options, ask yourself the question, "What kind of segmentation do I want to see in the data?" When you choose On Change Of, the values in the field of your choice will be summarized each time the value changes. For a field like Country in the VistaNations data, this means that a data point will be created for each country that has a resort, and the X-axis will show the set of countries found in the data. Figure 12.6 illustrates the X-axis and the Y-axis.

FIGURE 12.6

X-axis and Y-axis

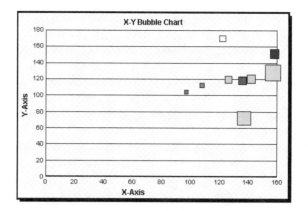

The On Change Of drop-down list is directly related to the field you place in the box just below it; you add a value by selecting it from the Available Fields list on the left and using the arrow key in the middle to copy it over to the list on the right. You can add multiple fields to this area, creating groups and subgroups on the X-axis. Selecting (highlighting) one of the fields in this area will enable the Order and TopN buttons; otherwise, they are disabled. The Order button lets you change the chart sort order using the dialog shown in Figure 12.7. Here, you can resort and regroup the data in the report, and if the chosen field was a specified order group, the options for adding members, deleting members, and managing others in the custom group are available as well. The TopN button lets you add a TopN filter to the data at this point.

FIGURE 12.7

Chart Sort Order

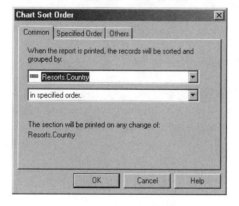

Choosing the option For Each Record or For All Records in the frequency drop-down box shown in Figure 12.5 will create a chart directly based on the detail data in the report. There is no need to select a field for these two frequencies because all data in the report is considered and summarized for chart purposes.

TIP   *Selecting the For Each Record or All Records option clears out the value in the field area below the drop-down box.*

In the Show Value(s) area at the bottom right of the Data tab shown in Figure 12.5, you choose the summarized data value to be plotted in the chart. The values for the Y-axis are derived from the plotted data. For instance, if you choose to summarize the average purchase price for a resort, the lowest purchase price will be the value shown at the bottom of the Y-axis and the highest purchase price will be the value shown at the top of the Y-axis. The data points are then graphed against these low and high values to show the data distribution. The Summarized field that is added to this part of the Data tab determines what the bar, pie, or scatter chart actually plots as data values. Clicking the Set Summary Operation button opens the Edit Summary dialog, shown in Figure 12.8, allowing you to change the statistical operation being performed to any valid Crystal summary. In addition, you can enable the option to show the data values in the chart as percentages in place of the summary value.

FIGURE 12.8

Edit Summary

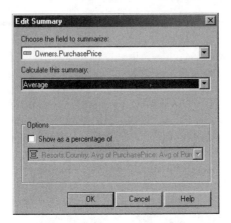

Enabling the Don't Summarize check box option shown in Figure 12.5 will prevent Crystal from summarizing the value and will instead present the raw data points in the chart.

MODIFYING AXES INFORMATION

Using the Axes tab, you can configure options to control how the label data on the axes appears. You can set minimum and maximum values and enable automatic segmenting of the axes. An option exists to AutoScale the labels so that if there are too many labels to display, fewer labels will be placed on the chart, enabling the remaining ones to be clearly displayed. The Axes option appears only for charts that use an X-, Y-, or Z-axis; pie charts, doughnut charts, and Gantt charts do not use axes. Crystal can use default values for all of these settings if you enable the Automatically Set Chart Options check box on the Type tab (shown previously in Figure 12.3).

NOTE   *If the Automatically Set Chart Options check box on the Type tab is enabled, the Axes tab will not be visible.*

CONTROLLING ADDITIONAL OPTIONS

The Options tab of the Chart Expert, shown in Figure 12.9, controls the settings for a chart's color, the labeling format used, background color and behavior, and data legend configuration. You can change the colors a chart shows or display it in black and white to save color ink on those printers! The Marker Size field refers to how large the shapes representing data in the chart will appear. When working with pie data (not shown in Figure 12.9), additional options exist to detach the pie slices, set the pie size, and show data values as percentages or actual numbers. Crystal can use default values for all of the settings on the Options tab if you check the Automatically Set Chart Options check box on the Type tab (see Figure 12.3).

FIGURE 12.9

Setting chart options

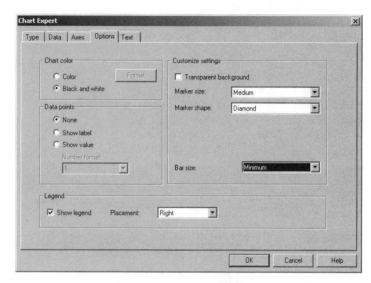

NOTE   *If the Automatically Set Chart Options check box on the Type tab is enabled, the Options tab will not be visible.*

Customizing a Chart

Once you've created a chart and placed it in a report, you can go back and revise it as well as add more formatting to it. When a chart is selected, the Chart menu becomes visible on the main menu, or you can right-click the chart to open the submenu specific to charts. The three main configuration options for modifying a chart available from the menu are Chart Expert, Chart Options, and Format Chart.

Choosing the Chart Expert reopens the dialog that was used to originally create the chart. You can change all or any of the original settings. Usually you'll build a quick chart, see what it looks like, and then reopen the Chart Expert to fine-tune the data distribution choices and grouping choices based on how well your initial attempt fit your needs. Since building charts can be more of an art than a science, an incremental approach to the process is very helpful. Make a change, and then preview the result to see what happened.

USING CHART OPTIONS

A new feature in Crystal Reports 9 is the ability to modify the chart using an "in-place" approach to formatting. The changes you make using the Chart Options menu item are immediately applied to the underlying report, changing it in-place with no need to delete it and re-create the chart. A chart consists of many internal items; each item can be selected and edited in place. Figure 12.10 shows the submenu from the Chart Options menu with all items active; depending on the type of object selected, a menu option may be grayed out and unavailable.

FIGURE 12.10

Chart menu options

NOTE *Custom chart options are not available if the typical install of Crystal Reports was performed; the custom install allows the addition of Custom Charting functionality.*

Template

Chart templates are a way to apply user-defined styles or built-in styles to a chart. In the Gallery of chart templates, shown in Figure 12.11, you can choose from a standard chart type and then change the layout, size, and other settings using options specific to the chart type.

FIGURE 12.11

Chart templates

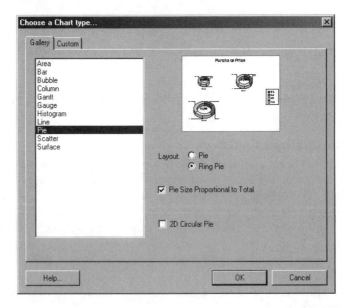

The Custom tab behind the Gallery tab provides access to several sets of custom chart templates, including those that are user-defined. For user-defined chart templates, the idea is that you find a chart type that you like, customize it, and save the result as a template that can be reused. Any chart you build can be saved as a chart template file by choosing Chart ➤ Save As Template. User-defined chart templates are saved with the filename of your choice and a .3TF extension. The 3 is there as an indirect reference to the third-party company that created all the built-in chart templates, Three D

Graphics, Inc. Prebuilt chart templates are stored beneath the Crystal Decisions installation directory in the `C:\Program Files\Common Files\Crystal Decisions\2.0\ChartSupport\Templates` directory, while user-defined chart templates can be found in the `C:\Program Files\Common Files\Crystal Decisions\2.0\ChartSupport\Templates\User Defined` directory. Figure 12.12 shows the set of custom charts available. You can see thumbnail sketches of the variations of a chart category by selecting its name. If you have stored any charts in the User Defined subdirectory for custom charts, they too will have thumbnails.

FIGURE 12.12

Custom chart templates

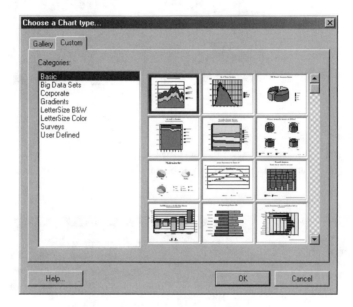

The Help button in the chart template area is especially useful to a report designer as it is an entire help resource dedicated to working with the custom charts provided by the Three D Graphics folks.

NOTE *Chart templates are available only if you installed the complete version of Crystal Reports or chose the Custom Charting option during a custom installation.*

General

Choosing the General option from the Chart Options menu opens a dialog that is also labeled Chart Options; this can be a little confusing. Here, six tabs of information let you customize a chart, as shown in Figure 12.13: General, Layout, Data Labels, Numbers, Look, and Display Status. You can set general formatting and layout options for a chart in this dialog. The options available change based on the type of chart chosen. For instance, on the graphics side of the story, pie charts can be tilted, rotated, exploded (really!), compared to other pies, have their size set proportional to their data, or turned into doughnut charts. On the value side of the pie chart, data labels can be changed or suppressed, percents shown as values, and legends positioned or suppressed. All in all, a great bit of fun awaits when you start playing with the General options and discovering the granular control you have over your charts.

FIGURE 12.13

General chart
commands

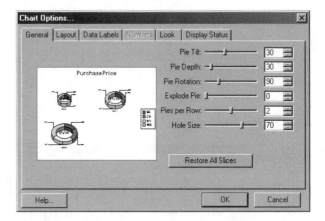

Titles

A chart is labeled with several descriptive titles. Crystal generates default titles automatically based on the groups and data values chosen to be part of the chart. Figure 12.14 shows the Titles configuration dialog.

FIGURE 12.14

Customizing
chart titles

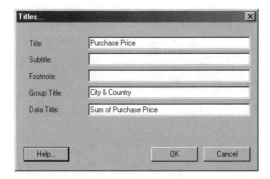

You can override the values by any of the titles by typing a new value; the default position of the title relative to the chart is noted here:

Title   The Title value appears above the chart.

Subtitle   The Subtitle appears below the Title but above the chart in a smaller font and lighter shade than the Title.

Footnote   The Footnote appears at the bottom of a chart in the lower-right corner.

Group Title   The Group Title appears below the chart along the X-axis.

Data Title   The Data Title appears on the left side of a chart on the Y-axis and rotated 90 degrees.

Grid

When charts with X/Y or X/Y/Z axes are selected (bar charts, scatter charts, etc.), you can choose the Grid menu item to finesse formatting options on the chart axes, grid lines, and scales. You can set such options as the size and location of labels in relation to the axes. Figure 12.15 shows the Numeric Axis Grids & Scales dialog box with its assorted tabs. Notice that there are tabs located along both the side and the top.

The majority of charts are arranged within two dimensions. Two of the possible tabs along the left side deal with detail data versus group data, or the X and Y coordinate planes. The tabs along the top (General, Scales, Labels, Numbers, and Grids) may or may not apply to the detail or group data. For instance, in Figure 12.15, the Data Axis tab is chosen along the left. Along the top, the General, Labels, Numbers, and Grids tab are not grayed out and therefore have settings that can be changed. Not all of the top tabs apply to the tabs at the left; for instance, when the Group Axis tab is active, the Numbers tab is grayed out since detail data numbers do not appear (numbers are not used as group values on a chart axis).

FIGURE 12.15

Grid customizations

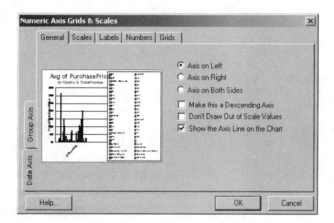

For three-dimensional charts, like 3D risers, a third tab appears along the left side of the dialog showing the Series dimension, or Z coordinate plane. The General, Labels, and Grids tabs are available for customizing this information dimension.

Selected Item

In this release of Crystal Reports, each component of a chart is an individual item that, when viewed with the set of all items, forms the chart. Individual items include titles, background graphic components, axis labels, and data object representations. When selected, they can be repositioned and resized within the chart as part of the in-place graphics editing capabilities of Crystal. Choosing the Selected Items command opens the Formatting dialog shown in Figure 12.16. The tabs available in this formatting window are dependent on the type of item (object) selected. Here you can set fonts, lines, and fill colors for each item. This granular level of control gives you complete flexibility in the chart's visual presentation.

FIGURE 12.16

Changing chart
item fonts

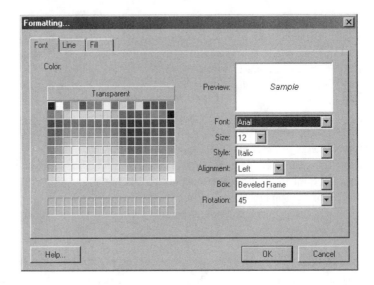

Viewing Angle

You can change the viewing angle of a chart to highlight different aspects of the data. Thumbnail pictures of standard viewing angles appear on the left side of the dialog shown in Figure 12.17; simply click a thumbnail to select that viewing angle. Alternatively, you can maneuver the chart three-dimensionally using the Rotate, Pan, Walls, and Move tabs found at the bottom-right corner of the dialog. This part of the screen is made visible when you click the Advanced Options button on the starting screen; clicking the Presets Only button on this dialog returns you to the starting screen.

FIGURE 12.17

Changing a chart's
viewing angle

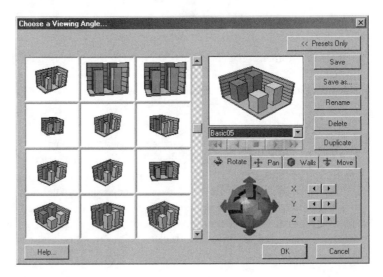

Series

The Series menu option is available only when three-dimensional charts are being used and when a series item is selected. Series represents the third dimension, or Z coordinate plane, in a three-dimensional graph. Figure 12.18 shows that you can manipulate general items and data labels for the selected series item.

FIGURE 12.18

Z coordinate series settings

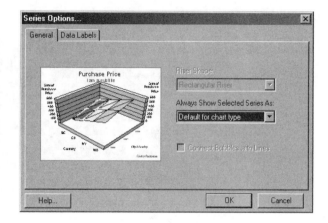

FORMATTING A CHART

The Format Editor is the familiar control area used with all Crystal objects to set basic options. To open the Format Editor for the chart, select the chart on the page and then choose Format ➤ Format Chart, or right-click the selected chart to directly choose Format Chart from the submenu. The Format Editor contains tabs that allow you to format the current object of focus (the chart) for page and layout issues. As with other objects in Crystal, you can use the universal Format Editor to format the chart with options such as conditionally suppressing based on a formula, drawing a border around the chart, and adding a hyperlink to another destination. Every object in Crystal is also given a unique object name, like Graph1, so that it can be manipulated programmatically through languages such as Java and the languages used with the .NET platform; the programmatic name for the object is set using the Format Editor.

The Map Expert

The Map Expert analyzes summarized geographic data by creating visual representations of the information using stored map files. To use it, your data must contain fields that reference geographic locations such as cities, states, countries, and regions. A third-party vendor, MapInfo Corp., provides mapping capability to Crystal Reports. Because of the tight integration, map-creation experts in Crystal utilize externally stored maps and combine them with summarized and grouped data to present visual data as a bitmap within a report. This approach to mapping was introduced in Crystal Reports 7.0 as an easy-to-use map-charting facility for all kinds of geographic data, and it continues to be a solid feature of the product.

When Crystal Reports is installed, the mapping program is also installed in its own subdirectory. Maps and layers that can be added on top of the maps are installed beneath this directory. Figure 12.19 lists the files that are used to create maps, while Figure 12.20 shows files that can be used to add layers to the maps once they are in Crystal. From the filenames, you can get a good idea of the kinds of maps that are included in the product.

FIGURE 12.19

Map files

FIGURE 12.20

Map layer files

Creating a Map

To begin the process of creating a map, the data must have geographic significance. The best data to map on is data that has an inherent geographic hierarchy to it, for instance, Country, then State, then City. Groups should be created in this order as well, with the largest geographic region acting as the container for all other regions. The region also should be fairly well-populated in order to provide the best statistical summaries. The sample report referred to earlier in Figures 12.1 and 12.2 contains geographic data, which makes it a good candidate for mapping. Figure 12.21 shows a map created to model the number of resorts contained in the Others category of the resort area report, which shows resorts located in areas outside North America.

> *Business Question: Create a report that shows where the resorts not in North America, the Caribbean, or Europe are actually located.*

FIGURE 12.21

Geographic map

TIP   *If the map appears in the report as an empty rectangle, the data in the report is unable to fulfill the map option settings chosen in the Map Expert.*

The map tool can be used to visually show data points, such as where the resorts in North America are located. To open the Map Expert, choose Insert ➤ Map. The dialog shown in Figure 12.22 displays the tabbed interface of the Map Expert.

CONFIGURING DATA OPTIONS

The first tab of the Map Expert is the Data tab, which is used to identify the data that will be mapped in the report; this dialog is shown in Figure 12.22. The screen is arranged into three areas: Placement, Layout, and Data. In the Layout area along the left side of the screen, four buttons roughly identify the four types of data that maps can be built upon:

- Advanced (detail data)
- Group
- Cross-Tab
- OLAP

FIGURE 12.22

Map Expert

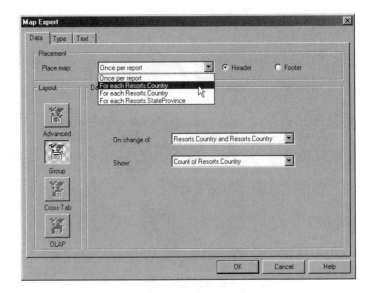

Figure 12.22 shows how to create a map based on group data. Group data is the easiest type of data to work with for summary purposes because the bulk of the formatting decisions are predetermined just by the data being in the group. If a button is grayed out and unavailable, it is a signal that your report does not contain that type of data; for instance, if no groups are contained in the report, the Group button is not available. Whenever a report contains groups that have summarized values, the Map Expert opens with the Groups option already highlighted; otherwise, the Advanced option is highlighted. Use the Advanced layout option, shown in Figure 12.23, to map data summaries based on specific field values.

FIGURE 12.23

Advanced map
layout

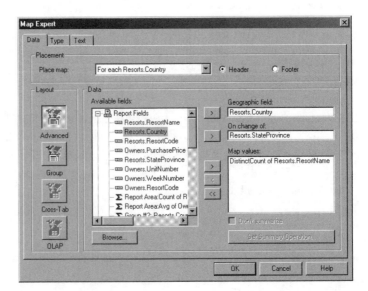

The summary information cells in a cross-tab grid or OLAP grid can also be used as mapping values for a map object. If the report contains this type of grid, geographic map information can be generated based on it. The summarized values in the cells of cross-tabs can be used as data points on a map. Figure 12.24 shows the Map Expert with the Cross-Tab option selected. The choices for the geographic mapping field, the subdivision field to be mapped, are taken directly from the rows, columns, and intersection cells defined in the cross-tab grid that exists in the report. For the example shown in Figure 12.24, the Region field is the column value in a grid, the Country field is the row value, and the cross-section where the two meet stores the distinct count of the FiveStarRating field.

FIGURE 12.24

Maps based on cross-tab grids

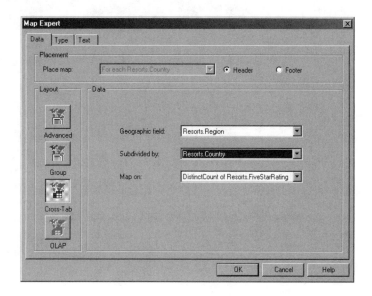

Since maps work with summarized data, a map can be placed in the header and footer sections of a report. The drop-down list at the top of the Data tab in the Placement area lets you choose a section in which to place the report, and then radio buttons let you choose between the header or footer area. Each of the groups in a report will display as drop-down box choices. Referring back to Figure 12.22, for instance, Resorts.Country appears twice since there are two groups using this field: one in specified order and the other in ascending order.

In the Data area (the middle section of the dialog), you specify the field values to show and the frequency when it should change. The values available in the drop-down box are directly related to the placement location chosen for the map. This is reasonable; think of the Placement area as defining the outer group and the Data area as defining the inner group in a parent-child relationship.

CONFIGURING TEXT OPTIONS

On the Text tab of the Map Expert you can define the following:

- A title for the map
- The type of map legend to be created (full, compact, or none)
- The legend title and subtitle (automatically generated or typed by you)

CHOOSING A MAP TYPE

The Type tab of the Map Expert, shown in Figure 12.25, is used to select the type of data arrangement and analysis strategy to integrate with a map. There are five types, and depending on the context of the data being mapped, one or more of the buttons for choosing the type will be available. Field-level data can be mapped with Ranged, Dot Density, and Graduated maps, while grouped data is well served by Pie Chart and Bar Chart maps.

FIGURE 12.25

Map types

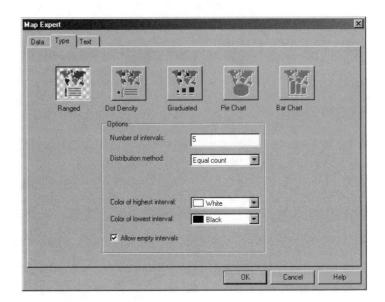

Ranged

In this type of map, you segment the data into ranges and associate a color to each range. You then create a legend associating the range to a color and set the geographic area on the map to the color. In the VistaNations data, you could create a map to display the resort sale prices last year by region, where region is a geographic boundary. Numerical values for sales range from zero to the highest price, and you can break these ranges into smaller chunks of dollar intervals by choosing a number of intervals that will then create ranges of 0–$50,000, $50,001–$100,000, and so on. Intervals such as prices less than $100,000 and prices more than $500,000 can also be useful for either end of the range. By associating a color code with the price interval, you can use the map to depict where (geographically) sale prices were the highest. You set the color using drop-down boxes to assign colors to the highest interval and the lowest interval. Within a ranged map, there are four options for assigning distribution methods to data: Equal Count, Equal Ranges, Natural Break, and Standard Deviation.

Equal Count   The number (count) of values in a range within an interval is relatively constant across all intervals.

Equal Ranges   The value of each summarized data point in a range interval is relatively uniform within the range.

Natural Break   A statistical algorithm is used to distribute values such that the difference between the summary values and the average of all the values is as small as possible.

Standard Deviation   The range interval centers data on the mean value and includes data that is one standard deviation on either side of the mean.

Dot Density

With dots representing the data summary value, a Dot Density map shows the distribution of data geographically. For example, you could show one dot for each resort in North America. This option is best used with the Group type of layout on the change of a value within a group.

Graduated

Graduated maps are similar to ranged maps in that they show a colored circle for each instance of a value. The size of the symbol represents the relative size of the data value being mapped; for instance, a circle representing $50,000 would be smaller than a circle representing $100,000. The circle can be changed to another symbol by using a drop-down list that includes such symbols as arrows, diamonds, and boxes.

Pie Chart

Given a geographic area, a Pie Chart map is constructed to represent the area as a whole, with different slices colored to represent different proportions of values in geographic areas. This type of map lends itself well to comparing the distribution of values in a geographic area. A pie chart inherently represents 100 percent of the geography.

Bar Chart

Like a pie chart, a Bar Chart map can be used to represent a geographic area, where the segments in the bar chart represent areas in the geographic entity, and each segment itself can relay information about a part of that geographic entity. A bar chart can be used to represent 100 percent of a geographic area or parts of a geographic area that do not equal 100 percent of the geographic region.

Customizing a Map

Once you've created a map and placed it in a report, you can modify its original settings or you can insert additional formatting. When you select a map, the Map option appears on the main menu, or you can right-click the map to open the submenu specific to maps. You can reopen the Map Expert at any time to display the dialog originally used to create the chart. You can then change all or any of the original settings.

USING MAP TOOLS

Maps created in Crystal Reports and displayed in Preview or User mode are active maps. You can add a title, zoom in, zoom out, pan, or center the map in the area provided. When a map is selected, the Map menu shown in Figure 12.26 lists the options at your disposal. Two very powerful features are adding layers to a map and resolving field name mismatches.

FIGURE 12.26

Map menu

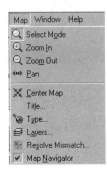

Adding Map Layers

Using the menu shown in Figure 12.26, the person viewing the map can add layers to it. A layer is placed on top of a map element to represent features like cities, oceans, rivers, highways, and other geographic details. Figure 12.27 shows a layer control that has been opened from the Map menu. The geographic elements available in the layer control vary based on the map being displayed. For instance, adding a highway layer would not be an option when the continents of the world is the underlying map currently being displayed because the level of detail does not match (granular to global).

FIGURE 12.27

Layer Control

Resolving a Mismatch

The maps built into Crystal have names associated with the countries, cities, and so on. The geographic names for data in your database may not match the geographic names used for the standard built-in maps. For instance, the built-in map of the world refers to the United States and Canada as "USA" and "Canada," respectively. The field data in the tables for your report may have stored the values as "US" and "CN." Unless the mapping tool recognizes the data names, the map will not display properly. In anticipation of this data problem, the mapping tool contains a utility to resolve mismatches of field names; it allows you to associate the names of fields in your tables with the names of fields in the built-in map facility.

Click the Resolve Mismatch menu item to open the utility. The first step in resolving the mismatch is to pick the map to associate names with. All maps are listed as choices, and the one you choose will depend on the granularity of your answer. For instance, choose the World map to resolve country name field problems or a country map to resolve city name field problems. After choosing the correct map, choose the Resolve Mismatch tab shown in Figure 12.28. The fields from your data appear in the Assign This Field Name list, while the fields from the map appear in the To This Map Name list. Select a field on the left, choose its matching field on the right, and click the Match button to add it to the Matched Results list in the bottom of the screen. In this figure, the field name US has been matched with USA, and the field CN is about to be matched with the value Canada.

FIGURE 12.28

Resolving a mapping mismatch

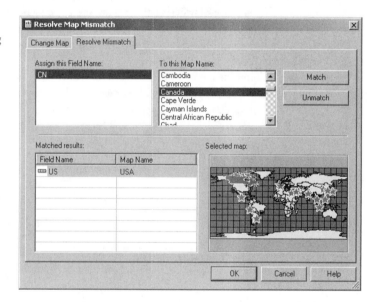

FORMATTING A MAP

Basic options like closing borders on page break and locking position and size come under the purview of the Format Editor. This editor is used to set popular options for the currently selected object, and in this case, it is a map. To open the Format Editor for a chart, select the map on the page and then choose Format ➤ Format Map, or right-click the selected map to directly choose Format Map from the sub-menu. The Format Editor contains tabs that allow you to format the current object of focus (the map) for page and layout issues. As with other objects in Crystal, the universal Format Editor can be used to format the map with options such as conditionally suppressing based on a formula, drawing a border around the map, and adding a hyperlink to another destination. Every object in Crystal is also given a unique object name, like Map6, so that it can be manipulated programmatically through languages such as Java and the languages used with the .NET platform; the programmatic name for the object is set using the Format Editor.

Cross-Tabs

A cross-tabulation (cross-tab) object is a two-dimensional grid that helps users quickly analyze data by comparing two variables against each other. Cross-tabulation is a popular basic bivariate and multivariate statistical process whose goal is to identify interdependency between two variables. The business question being asked when a cross-tab is used is whether there is a relationship between the two variables being compared.

Cross-tabs can compute frequency counts and summary statistics for pairs of variables. The intersection cell values are always numerical. As an example, consider that a cross-tab could present data showing how gender and salaries are related. Or in the case of the VistaNations company, a cross-tab can help answer the question of whether there is an interdependency between five-star resorts and the regions in which the resorts are located. The business question answered by a cross-tab involves comparing one parameter to another: gender versus salary and five-star status versus region location. Reports can contain as many cross-tabs as you need.

The row and column format of a cross-tab lets a user see large quantities of summarized data in an easy-to-digest spreadsheet-like fashion, with numerical values displayed in row/column intersecting cells. The row and column data are the parameters to the grid, e.g., five-star status and region location. The results of the comparison are presented in tabular format, and the intersection of a row and a column answers a question that involves both parameters. Figure 12.29 depicts row and column data intersecting, with a numerical value in their intersection; this cross-tab shows the average purchase price by resort in Canada.

Business Question: Create a report that compares the average unit purchase price of resorts in the Canadian provinces.

FIGURE 12.29

Cross-tab example

North America

CN	CN					Total
	Alberta	British Columbia	Ontario	Quebec	Total	
BLK	$0.00	$8,541.65	$0.00	$0.00	$8,541.65	$8,541.65
BRM	$26,574.24	$0.00	$0.00	$0.00	$26,574.24	$26,574.24
CBG	$0.00	$0.00	$67,291.83	$0.00	$67,291.83	$67,291.83
DHI	$0.00	$0.00	$62,827.95	$0.00	$62,827.95	$62,827.95
FBC	$0.00	$6,475.80	$0.00	$0.00	$6,475.80	$6,475.80
MLG	$0.00	$10,828.62	$0.00	$0.00	$10,828.62	$10,828.62
TRM	$0.00	$0.00	$0.00	$71,434.59	$71,434.59	$71,434.59
Total	$26,574.24	$8,615.36	$65,054.64	$71,434.59	$66,847.68	$66,847.68

The intersection cell of a cross-tab displays summary data. The cross-tab grid can therefore be placed in any header or footer section in a report. When you drop the cross-tab into place, it will be outlined with a gray border; position the top-left corner where you want the grid to be placed. Since each section has access to different information, the data displayed by a cross-tab changes based on the section into which it is placed.

WARNING   A cross-tab cannot be placed in the Details section. The Details section contains individual rows of data retrieved from a database; no summarization is allowed in this section.

Creating a Cross-Tab

The process of creating a cross-tab object begins with thinking about and identifying the three or more fields that will participate in the cross-tab:

- Field for the column headings
- Field for the row headings
- A summary data item relating the column field to the row field

A report may consist entirely of a cross-tab object or it can also contain the detail that supports the summarization. To add a cross-tab object, choose Insert ➤ Cross-Tab or click the Insert Cross-Tab toolbar icon. This opens the Cross-Tab Expert, shown in Figure 12.30.

FIGURE 12.30

Cross-Tab Expert

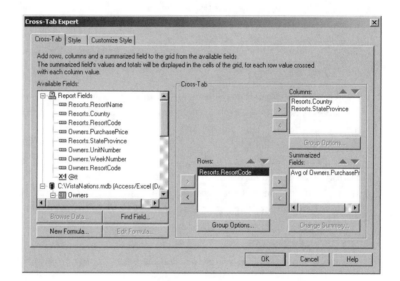

CONFIGURING DATA OPTIONS

The goal of setting options for a cross-tab is to choose appropriate rows and columns first and then select a field to summarize that is related to the chosen rows and columns. The Cross-Tab Expert takes the familiar approach of listing values on the left that you choose from and areas on the right to which the chosen fields are added. On the right, three distinct areas are provided to hold fields from the Available Fields list: Columns, Rows, and Summarized Fields. The arrow buttons to the left of these areas let you copy fields to or remove fields from the grid or drag a field from the list on the left and drop it into one of the areas on the right. This Available Fields list contains all report fields, all fields in the attached data source, and all formula fields.

TIP   In Crystal Reports 9, you can use memo fields in a cross-tab grid by first creating a formula in the Formula Workshop, setting the formula's value to the memo field, and then using the formula field in the cross-tab. For display purposes, the formula containing the memo field should make use of string functions such as LEFT, MID, *and* RIGHT *to control which text in the field displays in the cross-tab or use an array subscripting technique to display parts of the field (e.g.,* {Database.MemoField} [27 to 41]*).*

For the cross-tab being created in Figure 12.30, resort codes will be used as row data, and resort countries with a subcategory of StateProvince will appear as columns. In the intersecting cells, the average purchase price for the resort will be displayed. The intersecting cell can display any of the following and can display multiple values at the same time:

- A single numerical value

- Multiple numerical values

- Percentage value

Above each of the row, column, and summary areas, an up and down arrow pair appears. Use these buttons to reorder the way fields are categorized and subcategorized in the cross-tab. For instance, you could select the Resorts.Country option in the Columns area and use the up and down arrows to position the Country field below the StateProvince field.

TIP   The cells of the cross-tab can be resized by selecting the field in the cell and resizing just as you would any other field in a Crystal report. It is the field size that controls the size of the cross-tab cell.

Below each of the row, column, and summary areas, a Group Options or Change Summary button is visible. When you select the row, column, or summary data item, the associated button becomes active. For the row and column data, the Group Options button opens a Cross-Tab Group Options dialog. From the dialog, you can control the sort and grouping order for the data in the row or column; it can be sorted in ascending, descending, or specified (custom) order. The Change Summary button affects the data in the intersecting cell and allows you to choose a different summary method from the full range of those available in Crystal. Refer to Chapter 6, "Summarizing Information," Table 6.1, for a complete list and description of the summary methods available in Crystal Reports.

STYLING A CROSS-TAB

Crystal Reports 9 makes it easy to create a great-looking cross-tab. Built-in styles give you quick and slick reports, while customized styles give you formatting control down to a very detailed level.

Built-In Styles

The Styles tab contains a list of built-in styles that can spruce up your cross-tabs with color schemes, font combinations, and cell border variations. From the Original style (simple grid) to the Custom style (any combination of formatting features you can think of), you can quickly give the cross-tab a professional look. Figure 12.31 shows the Basic - Gray Scale style (after all, this is a black and white book!).

The Custom style at the bottom of this list can be used to completely define a cross-tabs style. To use it, select the Custom option and then switch to the Customize Style tab.

Customizing a Style

The Customize Style tab, shown in Figure 12.32, uses the style specified on the Style tab as a starting point, and from there, you can change the look of just about everything.

FIGURE 12.31

Cross-Tab Styles

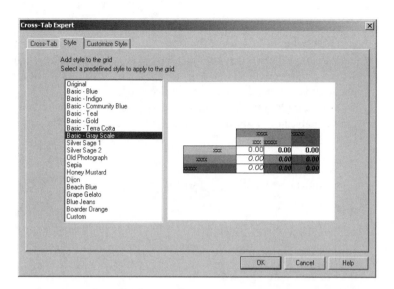

FIGURE 12.32

Customizing a style

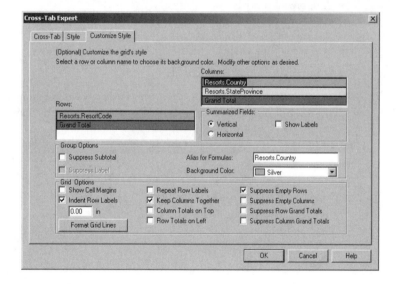

To customize options for a row or column, first select it in the appropriate area on the top half of the screen. Then use the options in the Group Options area to modify the look and behavior of the selected row or column. All options are not available at all times; the selected row determines the available options. The customizations you can make for rows and columns include the following:

◆ Suppress a subtotal

◆ Suppress a label

◆ Assign an alias to a row or column that can be used in a formula

◆ Change the background color of each row independently of the other rows and columns

For the data values in the Summarized Fields area, you can choose to display text labels for the summary values. The text for the labels can be edited like any text object in Design mode. When more than one field is being summarized, you can determine how the values display inside the intersection cell: Horizontal (side-by-side) mode or Vertical (one below the other) mode. If there is only one summary value, this option is disabled.

The Grid Options area contains settings that affect the cross-tab as a whole. The following options can be enabled or disabled using the associated check box, and any combination of these options is allowed:

◆ Show Cell Margins

◆ Indent Row Labels (and set the indent size in inches)

◆ Repeat Row Labels

◆ Keep Columns Together

◆ Column Totals On Top

◆ Row Totals On Left

◆ Suppress Empty Rows

◆ Suppress Empty Columns

◆ Suppress Row Grand Totals

◆ Suppress Column Grand Totals

The Format Grid Lines button opens the dialog shown in Figure 12.33. Here, you can control the visibility, color, style, and width of each grid line in the cross-tab.

FIGURE 12.33

Formatting grid lines

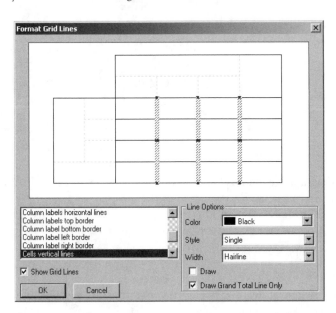

Customizing a Cross-Tab

After creating a cross-tab grid and placing it in the report, you can continue to customize all aspects of the grid as well as perform additional tasks on it. With the cross-tab grid selected, the Format menu provides access to the Format Cross-Tab option, the Cross-Tab Expert, and the Pivot Cross-Tab option. Right-clicking a selected cross-tab provides additional choices, as shown in Figure 12.34. From here you can select Insert Chart or Insert Map to directly add a chart or map to the report based on the summarized data in the cross-tab. You can also use the Group Sort Expert option to limit the data reported in the cross-tab to the Top N, Bottom N, Top Percentage, or Bottom Percentage values.

FIGURE 12.34

Cross-tab options

The Cross-Tab Expert can be reopened at any time to display the dialog originally used to create the cross-tab. You can change all or any of the original settings.

TIP When you right-click a cross-tab to display its submenu of options, be sure to right-click the upper-left corner of the cross-tab and not in any of the individual cells. Clicking an individual cell will display a formatting menu specific to the field in the cell.

PIVOTING A CROSS-TAB

A cross-tab in a report can be pivoted to swap the row and column axes. This is helpful if, after previewing the cross-tab, you decide that the descriptions and data would fit more successfully on the screen by converting wide columns to rows. To pivot a cross-tab, select the cross-tab and use the Pivot Cross-Tab menu command shown in Figure 12.34.

INTERACTIVE ANALYSIS WITH CROSS-TABS

When viewed in Preview mode in Crystal Reports, a cross-tab is an active in-place editing object. You can select any of the column headings and drag and drop it to a different column heading location in order to analyze the data in different ways. This gives the user the ability to think through a problem interactively by comparing one value against another in real time. When a column title is selected, dragging it to a new location converts the mouse pointer to an icon that resembles a piece of paper. Figure 12.35 shows the cross-tab columns repositioned from their original locations, shown in Figure 12.29.

FIGURE 12.35

Cross-tab after

interaction

CN	BLK	BRM	CBG	DHI	FBC	MLG	TRM	Total
Alberta	$0.00	$26,574.24	$0.00	$0.00	$0.00	$0.00	$0.00	$26,574.24
British Columbia	$8,541.65	$0.00	$0.00	$0.00	$6,475.80	$10,828.62	$0.00	$9,615.38
Ontario	$0.00	$0.00	$67,291.83	$62,827.95	$0.00	$0.00	$0.00	$85,054.64
Quebec	$0.00	$0.00	$0.00	$0.00	$0.00	$0.00	$71,434.59	$71,434.59
CN	$8,541.65	$26,574.24	$67,291.83	$62,827.95	$6,475.80	$10,828.62	$71,434.59	$66,847.69
Total	$8,541.65	$26,574.24	$67,291.83	$62,827.95	$6,475.80	$10,828.62	$71,434.59	$66,847.68

NOTE   Data cells cannot be repositioned to column locations; selecting a data cell and attempting to move it will result in repositioning the entire cross-tab object.

FORMATTING A CROSS-TAB

Basic formatting options for any report object are set with the Format Editor. For a cross-tab, the options include setting tool tip text, conditional controls over suppressing the cross-tab, and adding hyperlinks. To open the Format Editor for the cross-tab, select the cross-tab on the page and then choose Format ➤ Format Cross-Tab, or right-click the selected cross-tab to directly choose Format Cross-Tab from the submenu. The Format Editor contains tabs that allow you to format the current object of focus (the chart) for page and layout issues. As with other objects in Crystal, the universal Format Editor can be used to format the cross-tab with options such as conditionally suppressing based on a formula, drawing a border around the cross-tab, and adding a hyperlink to another destination. Programmers who write in languages like Java or use the .NET software platform can manipulate a cross-tab object in code using the unique object name that is set in the Format Editor; CrossTab1 is the default and it can be changed.

OLAP

Online Analytical Processing (OLAP) is an approach to processing information that helps an organization look at its stored data from a wide variety of possible information perspectives or views. Its goal is to put data for multiple variables of a problem at a user's fingertips so that they can perform what-if analysis and variable combinations without programmer intervention or the resources of the Information Technology (IT) department. OLAP is both a data storage technique and a data analysis methodology.

NOTE   To use Crystal's OLAP features, you must have the Professional, Developer, or Advanced version of Crystal Reports 9.

Understanding OLAP

OLAP combines multidimensional analysis of data with the ability for users to navigate through the data and make parameter changes during the analysis for maximum flexibility. This specialized type of data analysis can be used in the following ways:

◆ Compare analyses of historical and projected data

◆ Model "what-if" data scenarios

◆ Analyze trends over a time period

◆ Summarize data while allowing drill-down for further analysis

◆ Interact with data to change comparisons while viewing the data

Figure 12.36 displays an OLAP grid that compares the sales of products in a company over the course of two years, showing store cost, store sales, unit sales, and profit numbers.

FIGURE 12.36

An example of an
OLAP grid

		Store Cost	Store Sales	Unit Sales	Profit
		All Yearly	All Yearly	All Yearly	All Yearly
All Product	1997	225,627.23	565,238.13	266,773.00	339,610.90
	1998	432,565.73	1,079,147.47	509,987.00	646,581.74

BUSINESS USES FOR OLAP

The business question asked for an OLAP approach is typically more complex than for the basic summarization methods used on numerical data. For example, you might want to know the effect on resort prices if the cost of liability insurance went up by 10 percent and labor costs went down by 2 percent. For OLAP support and answering this type of question, Crystal provides basic navigation and browsing of data (fondly known as "slice and dice") and interactive analysis capability. The business uses of OLAP include the following:

◆ Budgeting

◆ Cost allocations

◆ Customer analysis

◆ Financial analysis

◆ Financial modeling

◆ Market research analysis

◆ Sales analysis

◆ Sales forecasting

OLAP data is characterized by multidimensional views of data, complex calculations, and time (period)-based data. Complex calculations include percentage of total or share calculations, trend analysis, and allocations of values from a top-down perspective. Table 12.1 describes the typical types of data analysis and the tools used to model them.

TABLE 12.1: EXAMPLES OF MULTIDIMENSIONAL ANALYSIS

ANALYSIS TYPE	SAMPLE SCENARIOS	TOOL
One-Dimensional	Total sales	Simple data rollups in a report
Two-Dimensional	Profit = sales − expense	Cross-tab or spreadsheet
Multidimensional	Profit for all products, for all regions, for all time periods, etc.	OLAP grid
Cross-Dimensional	Advertising expense attributed to one business unit for a particular product based on the product's projected sales as compared to the company's total sales and advertising expense	OLAP grid

OLAP Client-Server Technology

Like sophisticated relational database management systems, high-end OLAP involves sophisticated data storage techniques, including an OLAP server and an OLAP client.

OLAP Server   An OLAP server is a specialized database that stores and serves multidimensional data. The storage structure stores a data item using a reference to the dimensions (parameters) that define the item; in essence, the intersection is stored by virtue of the existing row and column.

OLAP Client   The concept of an OLAP client is a software product or application that requests data from an OLAP server. The client provides the ability to analyze the multidimensional data. Crystal Reports is an OLAP client; it can retrieve data from OLAP servers, process it, and present it in a report for real-time manipulation.

Creating an OLAP Grid

Crystal Reports 9 works with OLAP data cubes. OLAP cubes are not created in Crystal Reports, but Crystal Reports can access data stored in a cube in the same conceptual way that it accesses data stored in a relational table. There are two ways to bring cube data into Crystal:

◆ Using the OLAP Report Creation Wizard

◆ Using the OLAP Expert

When you're building a new report and select the option to use the Report Wizard, OLAP is a wizard choice. Using the wizard presents the same screens as using the OLAP Expert, except that the OLAP Expert displays the screens in a single tabbed dialog while the OLAP wizard walks you through one screen at a time.

To use the OLAP Expert to create an OLAP grid in an existing report, select Insert ➤ OLAP Grid from the main menu in Crystal Reports; this displays the OLAP Expert shown in Figure 12.37. Using one tab a time, this expert walks you through the process of selecting data, arranging it in the grid, and styling it. We'll use the OLAP Expert dialog in this chapter.

Configuring Data Options

Selecting the data source is the first step. Click the Select Cube button to bring the OLAP data into Crystal Reports for processing. You can use an existing cube or a CAR file. CAR files are OLAP analysis files created by Crystal Analysis Professional. Connections to OLAP data through Crystal are done with either a direct connection to an OLAP server or through an OLAP gateway accessible through the Internet. Crystal Reports supports a wide spectrum of OLAP data sources, including:

◆ Microsoft's OLE DB Provider for OLAP Services

◆ IBM DB2 OLAP Server

◆ Holos Live Server

◆ IBM Informix MetaCube

◆ Hyperion Essbase

FIGURE 12.37

Starting the OLAP process

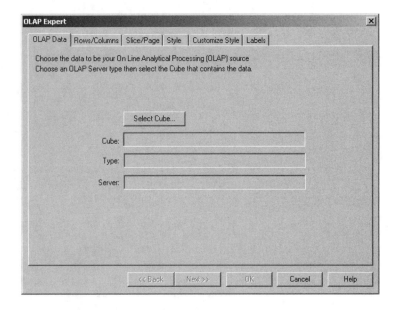

When you click the Select Cube button, the Crystal OLAP Connection Browser shown in Figure 12.38 appears. Here you can open the type of OLAP data source for the report from the list of those already known to Crystal.

FIGURE 12.38

Choosing an OLAP data source

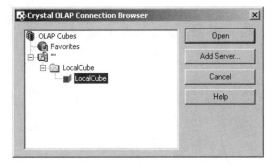

If the data source you want to use is not listed, click the Add Server button to open the New Server dialog shown in Figure 12.39. From here, you can choose an OLAP server, a local cube file (.CUB), or an HTTP cube accessed with a URL, username, and password.

The Advanced Settings button lets you specify how to make the connection to the data. Connecting directly to an OLAP server (or bypassing it for local cube files) is the default option; there are three options in total:

◆ Direct to OLAP server (the preselected default)

◆ Using Crystal Enterprise Automated Process Scheduler (APS)

◆ Choosing Open OLAP with a named service host and service port

FIGURE 12.39

Adding an OLAP server

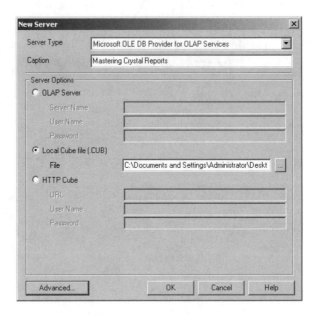

With an OLAP data source chosen, the OLAP Expert opens and the data source is shown directly on the OLAP Data tab, as shown in Figure 12.40. The Rows/Columns and Slice/Page tabs are used to configure data.

FIGURE 12.40

The OLAP Expert

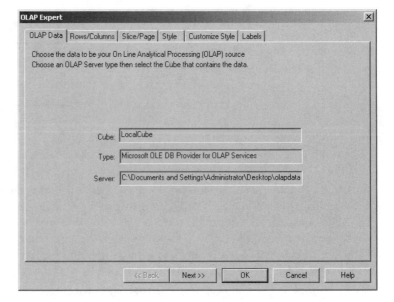

Rows/Columns

On the Rows/Columns tab, Crystal creates the initial list of dimensions on examination of the underlying data source. The data for the example in Figure 12.41 has four dimensions: Time, Measures, Product, and Yearly Income. We added Time to the Rows area by selecting it in the list of Dimensions and using the arrow key to move it to the row. Likewise, we've already moved Measures to the Column area.

FIGURE 12.41

Adding rows and columns

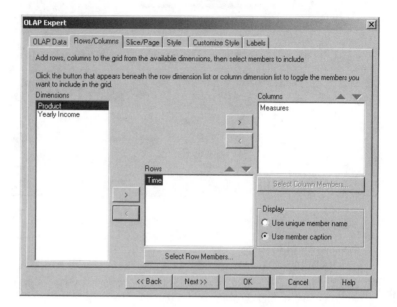

Moving Product to the Rows area and Yearly Income to the Columns area will configure the grid as it appears in Figure 12.36, shown previously.

When choosing values to add to the Columns area, keep in mind that Crystal processes information one page at a time. Using a large number of columns may force the grid to be wider than 8.5 inches (for an 8 ½ × 11 ″ piece of paper), which means that Crystal has to evaluate all the data in the cross-tab before it can display the columns of data. For better performance, try using rows as the dimension that takes up the most space, since this will benefit from the page-at-a-time evaluation. For more information on Crystal's evaluation process, see Chapter 14, "The Report Engine Processing Model."

Slice/Page

The Slices area is for dimensions that will not initially be shown in the grid as rows and columns. If the Dimensions list has any items remaining, they are carried over onto the Slice/Page tab, as shown in Figure 12.42. The slices can later be interactively added to the grid using a drag-and-drop technique.

FIGURE 12.42

Adding slices

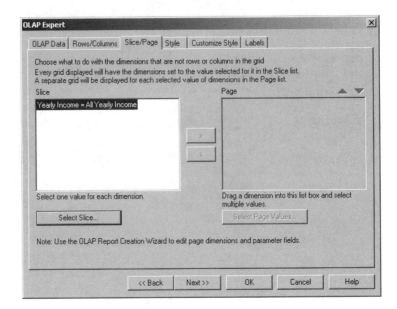

STYLING AN OLAP GRID

The Style, Customize Style, and Labels tabs in the OLAP Expert add formatting controls to the grid. In the same way that you can apply built-in styles or customized styles to cross-tabs, you can add the same styling capabilities to OLAP grids.

Built-In Styles

The Styles tab contains a list of built-in styles that you can use to spruce up your cross-tabs with color schemes, font combinations, and cell border variations. Styles range from the Original style, a simple grid with a white background and black text, to the Custom style, which can be any combination of formatting features. Figure 12.43 shows the Old Photograph style.

You can use the Custom style at the bottom of this list to completely define an OLAP style. To use it, select the Custom option and then switch to the Customize Style tab.

Customizing a Style

The Customize Style tab, shown in Figure 12.44, uses the style specified on the Style tab as a starting point and then allows individual changes to rows and columns.

FIGURE 12.43

OLAP grid styles

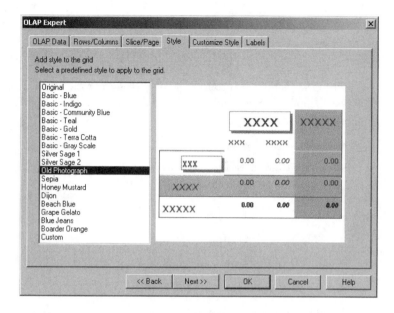

FIGURE 12.44

Customized
OLAP styles

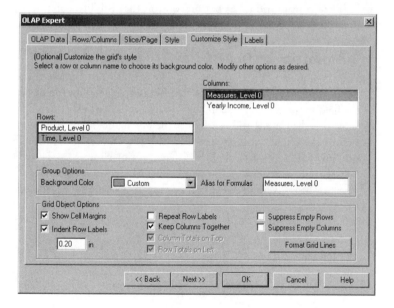

To customize options for a row or column, first select it in the appropriate area on the top half of the screen. Then use the options in the Group Options area to assign an alias to a row or column that can be used in a formula and to change the background color of each row independently of the other rows and columns.

The Grid Options area contains settings that affect the OLAP grid as a whole. The following types of options can be enabled or disabled using the associated check box, and any combination of these options is allowed:

- Show Cell Margins
- Indent Row Labels (and set the indent size in inches)
- Repeat Row Labels
- Keep Columns Together
- Column Totals On Top
- Row Totals On Left
- Suppress Empty Rows
- Suppress Empty Columns

The Format Grid Lines button controls the visibility, color, style, and width of each of the grid lines in the OLAP grid in the same manner as was done for cross-tabs (see Figure 12.33).

Customizing an OLAP Grid

After creating an OLAP grid and placing it in the report, you can continue to customize all aspects of the grid as well as perform additional tasks on it. The cells of the grid can be resized by selecting the field in the cell and resizing just as you would any other field in a Crystal report.

When the OLAP grid is selected, the Format menu provides access to the Format OLAP Grid option, the OLAP Grid Expert, and the Pivot OLAP Grid option. Right-clicking a selected OLAP grid provides access to a slightly different set of choices, as shown in Figure 12.45. The difference between this submenu and the Format menu on the main screen is that from here you can select Insert Chart or Insert Map to directly add a chart or map to the report based on the summarized data in the OLAP grid.

FIGURE 12.45

OLAP menu options

You can reopen the OLAP Expert at any time to customize the options selected while the grid was being built. You can change all or any of the original settings.

TIP   When you right-click an OLAP grid to display its submenu of options, be sure to right-click the upper-left corner of the OLAP grid and not any of the individual cells. Clicking an individual cell will display a formatting menu specific to the field in the cell.

PIVOTING AN OLAP GRID

Like a cross-tab, an OLAP grid can be pivoted to swap the row and column axes. Switching rows to columns and vice versa can help size the grid more appropriately on a page based on its content. To pivot an OLAP grid, select it, right-click to open its menu, and select Pivot OLAP Grid. Alternatively, with the grid selected, choose Format ➢ Pivot OLAP Grid.

INTERACTIVE ANALYSIS WITH OLAP GRIDS

OLAP data lends itself to interactive processing that gets the user involved in analysis while looking at the grid. Crystal provides two mechanisms for this interactive analysis:

◆ In-place editing

◆ Analzyer utility

In-Place Editing

When viewed in Preview mode in Crystal Reports, the OLAP grid is an active in-place editing object. You can select any of the column headings and drag and drop them to a different column heading location to analyze the data in different ways. This lets the user think through a problem interactively by comparing one value against another in real time. When a column title is selected, dragging it to a new location converts the mouse pointer to an icon that resembles a piece of paper. Figure 12.46 shows a single OLAP grid whose columns were repositioned in Preview mode by dragging and dropping column headings; the original grid appears in Figure 12.36.

FIGURE 12.46

OLAP grid after interaction

		Store Cost		Store Sales		Unit Sales		Profit
		1997	1998	1997	1998	1997	1998	1997
		All Yearly	All Yearly	All Yearly	All Yearly	All Yearly	All Yearly	All Yearly
	All Product	225,627.23	432,565.73	565,238.13	1,079,147.47	266,773.00	509,987.00	339,610.90

NOTE   Data cells cannot be repositioned to column locations; selecting a data cell and attempting a move operation will result in the table repositioning as a unit.

Analyzer

Crystal includes a built-in analysis tool specifically for OLAP grids. With a grid built and selected, choose the Launch Analyzer option from the OLAP menu visible in Figure 12.45. This opens the Cube View of the Analyzer, as shown in Figure 12.47. This is the same data that was seen earlier in non-interactive mode in Figure 12.36.

FIGURE 12.47

Analyzer's
Cube View

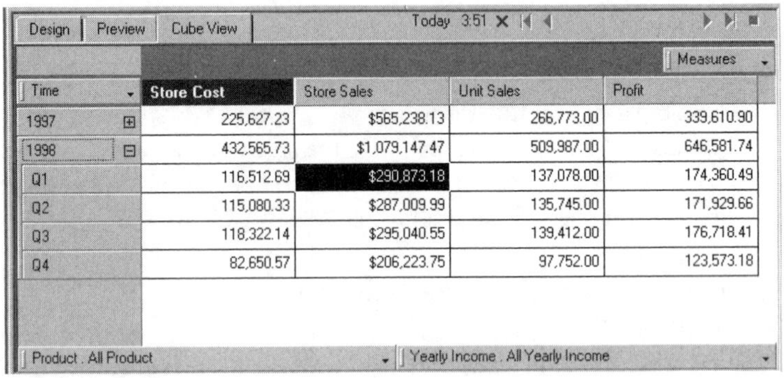

OLAP data is three-dimensional:

◆ Row

◆ Column

◆ Slice

The row dimension in Figure 12.47 is Time. The column dimension is Measures. The slice dimension contains both Product and Yearly Income. To interact with the cube data, drag and drop columns, rows, and slices to different positions to show different views of the data. Alternatively, you can right-click an area to display a submenu specific to that area. The main Crystal Reports menu is not used to interact with cube data.

While data on the Cube View cannot be changed, it can be selected to show additional information as well as perform operations on the data. Right-clicking a piece of data in an intersection cell (such as $290,873.18, the intersection of Store Sales and the Q1 in 1998) brings up a submenu containing the Show Cell Properties option, which can give you information on the formatted value of the field and the field's actual value. This is handy when cells have been formatted to round or truncate values. Right-clicking a dimension displays a submenu with options to swap the position of the dimension with another dimension or to swap rows with columns. The bulk of the menu interactions for a cube, however, are done on the category and subcategory titles displayed in the row dimension. In Figure 12.47, right-clicking the title 1997 in the row displays the menus shown in Figure 12.48.

FIGURE 12.48

Row menus

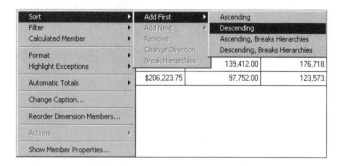

Each of the menu items allows you to perform an analysis action on the data. For instance, choosing the Highlight Exceptions option opens the dialog shown in Figure 12.49, which is used to add colors to the grid based on threshold values in the data. Each cell can be turned a series of colors (green, then yellow, then red, for example) depending on which threshold range the data value falls into.

FIGURE 12.49

Highlighting threshold values

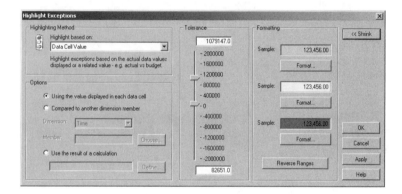

The rows in Figure 12.47 present the Time dimension, which consists of the years 1997 and 1998, with each year having four subcategories for the quarters. The drop-down arrow and plus signs indicate that a category is expandable. When you click the drop-down arrow for a dimension, its Member Selector window opens. This window lets you select any or all of the subcategories for display in the OLAP grid. For this example, there are four dimensions: Time, Measures, Product, and Yearly Income. Time and Measures are currently open in the grid; Time is on the row axis and Measures is on the column axis. Product and Yearly Income are sitting on the bottom of the cube, an area called the slice area. Figures 12.50, 12.51, 12.52, and 12.53 show the Member Selector windows for the Time, Measures, Product, and Yearly Income dimensions.

FIGURE 12.50

Time - first
dimension

FIGURE 12.51

Measures - second
dimension

FIGURE 12.52

Product - third
dimension

FIGURE 12.53

Yearly Income -
fourth dimension

TIP   To open a Member Selector as a free-floating window, click the down arrow on the right edge of the dimension identifier, use the mouse to highlight the gray line in the window's title bar, and when it changes to a blue line, select it and drag it to the middle of the screen.

To interact with the data and compare variables against one another for different views (or slices) of the data, drag and drop the dimensions from the bottom of the cube up to the row or column heading area. In Figure 12.54, the Measures dimension has been dragged to the row position and both Yearly Income and Product have been dragged to the column position to show the sales for the different years by product and income generated. The bottom of the cube no longer contains any dimensions, and the message "Drop dimensions here to display as slices" is shown.

FIGURE 12.54

Dimensions rearranged

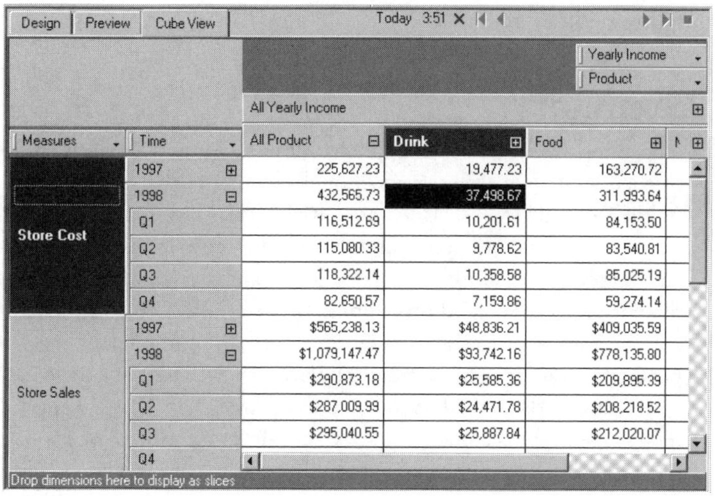

WARNING   The Edit Undo option and Undo icon are disabled in Cube View mode. You cannot undo a dimension rearrangement in this way. Instead, you must reposition the dimensions by dragging and dropping them on their original positions.

The Analyzer is a powerful interactive OLAP client, and the features in this section have introduced you to its use. The best way to learn to use this tool, though, is to grab some cube data from your own company and start playing with it. Enjoy!

NOTE   The Analyzer tool included in Crystal Reports is a subset of the Crystal Decisions' Crystal Analysis Professional (CA Pro) software. CA Pro is a separate product in the Crystal Decisions line of business intelligence tools and is specifically designed to work with OLAP data in a desktop, network, or Web environment.

FORMATTING AN OLAP GRID

In Design and Preview modes, you can use the Format Editor to set basic options for how the grid looks in these modes. To open the Format Editor for an OLAP grid, select the OLAP grid on the page and then choose Format ➢ Format OLAP Grid, or right-click the selected OLAP grid to directly choose Format OLAP Grid from the submenu. The Format Editor contains tabs that allow you to format the current object of focus (the OLAP grid) for page and layout issues. As with other objects in Crystal, the universal Format Editor can be used to format the OLAP grid with such options as conditionally suppressing based on a formula, drawing a border around the cross-tab, and adding a hyperlink to another destination. Every object in Crystal is also given a unique object name, like OLAPGrid1, so that it can be manipulated behind the scenes using programming languages. The object name is preset in the Format Editor, or can be changed to reflect something more meaningful to the application.

Summary

The company motto of Crystal Decisions is "Access. Analyze. Report. Share." The analysis portion of their strategy is well served through the use of charts, graphs, maps, cross-tabs, and OLAP capabilities. Visually representing data with charts, graphs, and maps can help you answer business questions in an easy-to-understand manner, and Crystal's built-in tools make it simple to do so. Charts and graphs are ideal for visualizing any quantifiable data, while geographic maps add a graphical dimension to data based on regions and locations. Cross-tab data presents information in row and column format, with summarization information in intersecting cells; single parameters and group parameters can be used in cross-tabulation as well as percentage data.

As an OLAP client, Crystal Reports provides analysis capabilities for working interactively with multidimension data and complex data calculations. To these tools, Crystal adds the ability to perform in-place editing and on-the-fly variable comparisons; it also provides the built-in Analyzer, making visual analysis an easy and powerful way to work with an organization's data.

Report Templates

MANY OF THE REPORTS you'll create as a report designer will begin with an existing report. It's a logical first step to speed up development. Often when you are asked to develop a custom report, you'll notice that what one customer is asking for is very similar to what you've done for another customer. And so you'll open that report, save a copy of it with a new name, and then start modifying it to fit the new situation. Report developers have been using this approach for years. With the new version of Crystal Reports, the team at Crystal Decisions acknowledges this need for quick starts and has built it in as a new feature in the product. Crystal Reports now allows you to save and apply report templates, which makes it even easier to reuse existing report elements.

Featured in this chapter:

◆ Creating a template

◆ Applying a template to your report

◆ Working with template field objects

◆ Using an existing report as a template

Template Files

A template in Crystal Reports is simply an RPT file that is intended to be reused. It is stored in a special directory that allows it to be used as a formatting structure to easily style other reports. The idea is to set the format once and then create many reports off the same template; this reduces code maintenance headaches. Any report can be used as the basis for a template. Storing it in a separate template directory using Save As preserves the original report and makes the template easy to locate.

Built-In Templates

The goal of a template file is to standardize a set of formatting options for implementation in many reports. Crystal Reports ships with a set of built-in templates that have been preformatted in popular styles. Each file is an .RPT file in its own right and is stored in the Templates subdirectory beneath the Crystal Reports installation directory. The list of template .RPT files is shown in Figure 13.1 and described below. The file names shown are the actual operating system file names. Each operating system file name is also known with a more readable alias inside of Crystal Reports. In Crystal dialog windows, templates are listed by alias name with the actual operating system file name in parentheses.

NOTE *If you saved an image preview of the first page of the report using File ➤ Summary Info and the Save Preview Picture option, the image displays alongside the list of templates. The built-in reports all have preview images.*

FIGURE 13.1

Template files

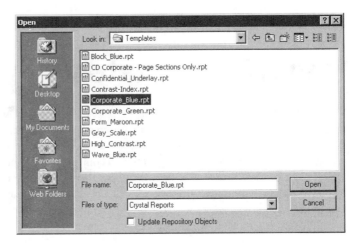

Block_Blue (Block_Blue.rpt)   This template uses blue fonts and blue drop shadows on boxes and borders. The detail data displays inside a light-gray-bordered box. The report title appears at the top in blue, while beneath is a drop-shadowed rectangular box that contains the report comment that was created from the File ➤ Summary Info area. The Powered By Crystal logo appears at the top right in a Page Header.

CD Corporate - Page Sections Only (Crystal Decisions Corporate _ Page Sections Only.rpt)   This template formats the Page Header and Page Footer only; it uses Crystal logos to demonstrate image placement. The report title appears at the top in black. A text object with a three-line company address appears at the bottom in black.

Confidential_Underlay (Confidential_Underlay.rpt)   This template uses black and gray fonts and rounded border boxes. The word *Confidential* appears as a background image in light gray; the text is arranged on a 45-degree angle. The detail data displays on a white background with a dashed black underline beneath each detail line. The report title appears at the top in black. The Powered By Crystal logo appears at the top right in a Page Header.

Contrast Index Sample (Contrast-Index.rpt)   This template takes a reverse color approach with a black background and blue solid boxes separating groups of data. Text font is white.

Corporate_Blue (Corporate_Blue.rpt)   This template uses blue fonts and light blue boxes with borders. The detail data displays on a white background with a blue underline beneath each detail line. Chart development is accounted for in a report header. The report title appears at the top in blue, while beneath is a simple rectangular box containing the report print date, the last modified date, and a report comment that was created from the File ➢ Summary Info area. The Powered By Crystal logo appears at the top right in a Page Header and at the bottom-left corner.

Corporate_Green (Corporate_Green.rpt) This template uses dark green fonts with light green and gradient green boxes. The detail data displays on a white background with a green underline beneath each detail line. Chart development is accounted for in a Report Header. The report title appears at the top in green, while beneath is a simple rectangular box containing the report print date, the last modified date, and a report comment that was created from the File ➢ Summary Info area. The Powered By Crystal logo appears at the top right in a Page Header.

Form_Maroon (Form_Maroon.rpt) This template uses maroon fonts and dark pink boxes and borders. The detail data displays inside a dark-pink-bordered box. Group names appear along the left margin rotated 90 degrees as vertical text. The report title appears at the top in maroon, while beneath is a drop-shadowed rectangular box containing the report comment that was created from the File ➢ Summary Info area. The Powered By Crystal Logo appears at the top right in a Page Header.

Gray Scale (Gray_Scale.rpt) This template uses thick black and gray rectangular borders to delineate groups. The report title is placed in a rectangular box and drop-shadowed. The Powered By Crystal logo appears at the top right in a Page Header.

High_Contrast (High_Contrast.rpt) This template uses a black background with colorful blue, maroon, and green solid rectangles separating the headers, groups, and data. The detail data prints in a white font in blue boxes. The Powered By Crystal logo appears at the top right in a Page Header.

Wave_Blue (Wave_Blue.rpt) This template uses quite a few colors! Black borders, blue borders, white letters, black letters, peach boxes with blue drop shadows, and, oh yes, light and dark green charts. It demonstrates the use of rounded rectangular boxes to create a portal look and feel.

Creating Templates

In addition to the built-in templates provided with Crystal Reports, you can create your own templates or modify the built-in ones. Creating a template is easy! All you have to do is create a report and save it to a special directory. Templates are stored in their own directory beneath the Crystal Reports installation directory. Figure 13.2 shows where they are stored in a computer in which Crystal Reports was installed on the C: drive.

FIGURE 13.2

Storage location

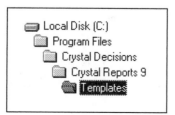

Any file located in the Templates directory is automatically available as a template. It is important that the report be given a title; its title acts as a descriptive name showing up in the list of all Crystal Reports templates built-in or user-created. To give the report a title, use the menu sequence File ➤ Summary Info to open the Document Properties window as shown in Figure 13.3, and type a meaningful and descriptive name into the Title box. The phrase "VistaNations Country Report" is the name that would display in the list of templates; for an example of this, refer to Figure 13.9 later in this chapter.

FIGURE 13.3

Document
Properties

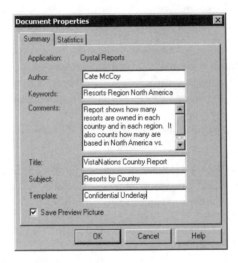

The Document Properties dialog also includes a text field where you can enter the name of the template being used for the current report. This additional box labeled "Template" is for informational purposes only; it is not used by Crystal Reports to identify the template. This is a free-form text area and you have no obligation to fill it out, but it is a good place to make a comment as to which template is in use by the currently open report.

There are three approaches to creating new templates:

◆ Modify a prebuilt template and save it with a new template name.

◆ Create a new blank template without a data source and use template fields.

◆ Save an existing report as a template with a new name.

MODIFYING A PREBUILT TEMPLATE

If you want to modify one of the built-in templates, simply change the component you don't like and resave the template to the same location under the same name or a new name. For instance, you can delete the Crystal Decisions logo and embed a logo for your organization. Since the templates are report files themselves, the full complement of report-formatting options is available to you.

USING TEMPLATES AND DATA SOURCES

A traditional report file contains a data source and the formatting required to make the fields from the data source look good. A template, however, doesn't require a data source. Since it is a structure that will be applied to other reports (which contain their own data source), having a template without a data source is an appealing approach to report design. A data source–less template is created using a blank report. To get started, here's what you do:

1. Create a new report by choosing File ➤ New.

2. From the Crystal Reports Gallery, choose to create a report with the As A Blank Report radio button.

3. On the Database Expert, click the Cancel button.

The effect of these three steps is to open a blank report in Design mode with a Report Header, Page Header, Details section, Report Footer, and Page Footer and without any data source identified or fields in the report. Clicking the Cancel button on the Database Expert leaves the report without a data source.

Now that you have a blank report and no data source, the next step is to place template fields in the report. Template fields are report objects that do not reference a database field or contain any data; essentially, they are placeholders for field data that will be filled in when the template is applied to a report. The net effect is to display the report's data items with the formatting specified in the template field.

To create a template field on a blank report with no data source, choose Insert ➤ Template Field Object. A gray rectangle appears to help you position and drop the field in the section of your choice. In Figure 13.4, a template field has been dropped into position in the Details section; a placeholder for the field name has been added to the Page Header as the column title.

FIGURE 13.4

Template field placement

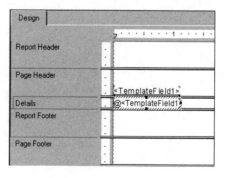

To format the template field placeholder, right-click the field to display the formatting menu shown in Figure 13.5.

FIGURE 13.5

Template menu

The Format Template Field option, shown in the above menu, opens the Format Editor shown in Figure 13.6, which provides access to the full set of field formatting options that were described in Chapter 3, "Formatting Fields and Objects."

FIGURE 13.6

Format Editor

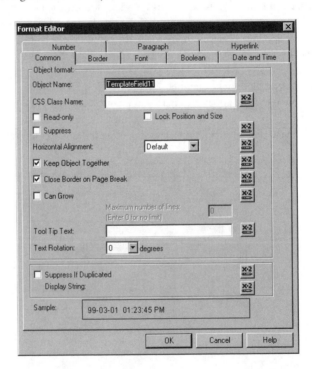

Since you cannot know what kind of data will be displayed using the template, the concept here is that you set the formatting options in anticipation of handling any data types. For example, perhaps you want to format the numbers in the first column of a report to have two decimal places and the numbers in the fourth column to have four decimal places. Formatting is applied positionally, top to bottom and left to right, based on field placement. You can apply any formatting that is valid at the field level to a template field.

If the data in the report field is a number, the formatting specified on the Number tab will be applied; for instance, you can determine whether to display the currency operator, set it as fixed or floating, or create a customized number style. The formatting tabs call out Number, Boolean, and Date and Time values. Note also that a CSS Class Name can be set on the Common tab to enable the use of HTML and XML with Crystal Reports data.

TIP *You can select multiple template fields simultaneously and use the Format Editor to format attributes that appear on every field.*

The following types of report fields, known as *result* fields, are mapped positionally by a template field; fields not of the following types are skipped by template formatting:

◆ Database fields

◆ Formula fields

◆ Parameter fields

◆ SQL Expression Fields

After you add a template field to a report, it appears in the Field Explorer as a formula field. From here, you can edit it in the Formula Workshop, as shown in Figure 13.7.

FIGURE 13.7

Formula Workshop

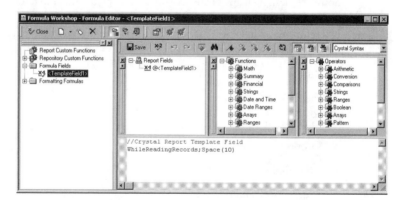

REUSING EXISTING REPORTS AS TEMPLATES

Do you have the perfect report already written and want to use it over and over again? No problem. From the menu of the report, choose File ➢ Save As to save a new version of the report to the Program Files ➢ Crystal Decisions ➢ Crystal Reports ➢ Templates subdirectory. This preserves the original report and does not modify it. Once saved to this directory, the file can be used as a Crystal Reports template.

TIP *After saving the report, go to the Document Properties by choosing File ➢ Summary Info and set the Title field to an appropriate name for the template file.*

Although any report can be used as a template, not every design element that you used in the report will be valid for use as a template element. If you choose to use an existing report as a template rather than creating a template using template field objects, the following design elements are not valid and will not be applied to your report:

◆ Cross-tab grids

◆ Custom-created groups (specified order)

◆ Detail charts

◆ Embedded OLE objects

◆ Fields that contain audio, video, images, or other rich text or binary large object (BLOB) data

◆ Maps

◆ OLAP grids

◆ Percentage summaries

◆ Running total summaries

◆ Subreports

◆ Top N summaries

So which design elements are actually able to be included in a template when an existing report is the starting point? In general, all field-level, group-level, and summarization information carries over from a template to an existing report. The following report objects can be defined in a template and applied to a separate report file:

◆ Bitmaps

◆ Fields

◆ Group charts

◆ Groups

◆ Hyperlinks

◆ Lines, boxes, and borders

◆ Static OLE objects

◆ Summary fields

Template Actions

The Template Expert is used to apply, remove, and reapply templates to the currently open report. Open the expert by choosing Report ➤ Template Expert, which opens the Template Expert dialog shown in Figure 13.8.

FIGURE 13.8

Template Expert

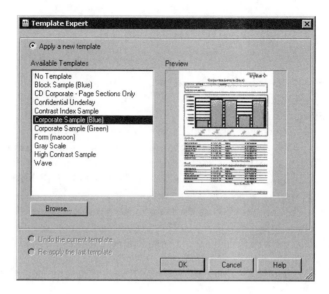

Applying a Template

You can apply a template to a report as the report is being created using the Standard Report Creation Wizard. You can also apply a template at any point after the report has been created. If you choose to use the wizard approach, applying a template is the last step in the wizard; it follows choosing a data source, selecting fields, and setting group options. Figure 13.9 displays the screen that you'll see when using the wizard. Notice the icon at the top right corner of the dialog. This icon appears on the toolbar in Crystal Reports so that you can choose or change the template during report design.

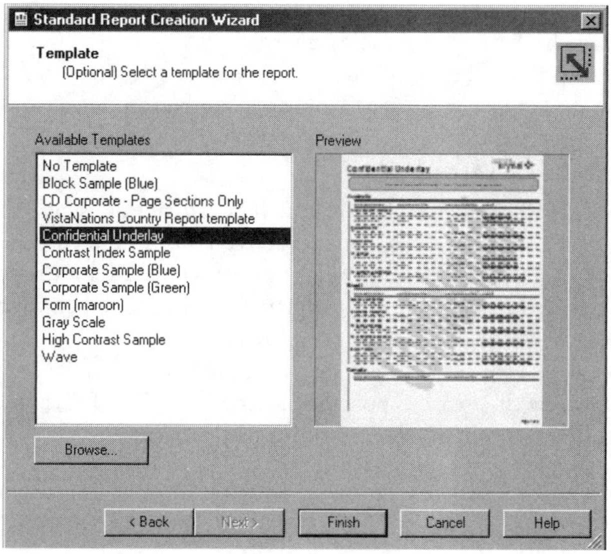

FIGURE 13.9

Standard Report Creation Wizard— Optionally Applying A Template

NOTE *Notice that the custom template created as an* `.rpt` *file and stored directly in the template directory appears in the list just above Confidential Underlay. This value displays in the list as a result of the report title field in the document's properties.*

As in other steps in the wizard process, the Template Expert icon is displayed in the top-right corner. This icon is available on the toolbar at any time from within a report once you're inside the design environment.

Crystal ships with several built-in template styles that can be applied to your report. At the top of the list is the No Template option, which means that no special formatting has been added to your report. If the template you want to use is not in the list, you can find it using the Browse button. Clicking the Browse button displays the standard File Open dialog for locating a file on your computer or a network-attached computer.

When a template is applied, the fields in the report are matched up positionally, top to bottom, left to right, to the template fields. The formatting from the matching position field in the template is applied to the report field for as many field positions as are available and match positionally.

NOTE *If a report contains more fields than are accounted for in the template, all extra fields are placed in a secondary Details section, for example, Details B.*

The design elements in a template are applied to the report you're building and will override any settings that are in conflict.

You can also apply multiple templates to a single RPT file providing that the objects within the template do not collide with one another.

Removing a Template

You can tell that a template has been applied to a report by opening the Template Expert and observing the radio buttons. If the Apply A New Template radio button is marked and both radio buttons below the Browse button are grayed out (Undo The Current template and Re-apply The Last Template), no template has been applied to this report.

If a template has been applied, you can remove it from a report by using the Template Expert and selecting the Undo The Current Template radio button. This is visible in Figure 13.10.

Reapplying a Template

In Figure 13.10, the Re-apply The Last Template option is visible below the Undo The Current Template option. Since the template is an RPT file, you might have occasion to change the template itself. For example, if the company logo changes or you want to add additional fields to the template, you can make the changes to the template RPT file, save them, and then come back to your report and select the Re-apply The Last Template radio button.

Changes to a template are not automatically reflected in the reports that use them. Instead, you have to actively choose to reapply the modified template. This approach to template modifications prevents older reports from being inadvertently updated.

TIP *Refresh your report's data after making any change to template field formulas.*

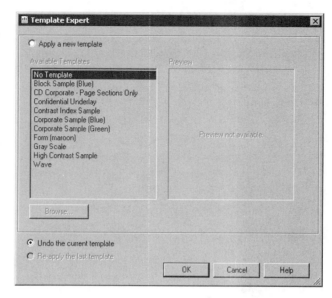

Summary

The ability to reuse formatting options and apply them to multiple reports is a new feature in Crystal Reports that has been implemented as templates. Some templates are prebuilt from Crystal Decisions; others can be created from scratch using template field objects or sourced off an existing report file. All templates are stored in one location, and their title alias is displayed as a template name to apply to a report. Templates can be removed from a report, refreshed, and reapplied.

Chapter 14

The Report Engine Processing Model

DESPITE THE MULTITASKING CLOAK that surrounds the world of computers, the typical personal computer is inherently a sequential processing device. In computer time, each task is carried out incredibly fast, which gives you the feeling that things are all happening at the same time; but way down deep in the internals, the processor ultimately executes one task after another to fulfill your requests. This is true of your Crystal report as well. At the point that a page of a report displays on a computer screen, it has gone through a processing cycle that involves several sequential steps. Crystal combines its report engine processing with a page-on-demand approach to displaying information.

The order in which the processing steps take place affects the outcome of the report. As a good report designer, you must understand the processing cycle so that you know which report elements are available to you and when and where to place elements to maximize their effectiveness. The placement of report elements and in which sections they are placed matters a great deal. The focus of this chapter is on helping you understand the evaluation process of the report as a whole and the individual report elements it contains so that you can use the elements correctly.

Featured in this chapter:

- ◆ Multi-pass report processing
- ◆ The three evaluation passes defined
- ◆ Order of report element evaluation
- ◆ Subreport evaluation
- ◆ Page on demand architecture
- ◆ Evaluation time formulas

Multi-Pass Processing Model

To fully evaluate design elements and build a report, the Crystal Report engine goes through the actual report three times before the final result appears on screen. During each pass, different design elements come to life and their values become available in the report. Figure 14.1 depicts this process from the starting point at the data source to the ending point on a user's screen or printed report.

FIGURE 14.1

Three-pass processing

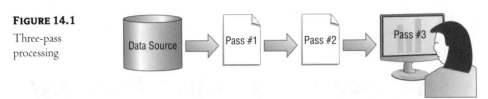

Pass 1 focuses on the data source and field-oriented portion of the report cycle, while Pass 2 concentrates on complex processing of data that is now in Crystal's memory. Pass 3, the smallest of the passes, can almost be considered a post-processing step.

TIP   *The Crystal Reports help file contains a visual flowchart of the three pass-processing steps. The easiest way to locate it is to search the help file using the phrase "Multi-pass reporting flowchart."*

Pass 1 Processing

Visualize what happens when you preview a report in Crystal Reports: The data is retrieved, processed, formatted, and written to the screen. The process, therefore, begins with data. The list presented here shows the sequential tasks that take place in Pass 1; a discussion of each task follows the list.

◆ Set values for all constants.

◆ Retrieve the data from the data source.

◆ Evaluate formulas that return a direct result and that contain database fields.

◆ Perform any additional record selection needed using Crystal elements locally on the data returned from the initial query.

◆ Sort the data.

◆ Group the data.

◆ Calculate group subtotals.

◆ Calculate group summaries.

◆ Generate cross-tabs that contain database fields or formulas that contain database fields.

◆ Generate charts that contain db fields or formulas with database fields.

◆ Generate maps that contain db fields or formulas with database fields.

◆ Store data records and interim values (such as totals) in memory or temporary files.

CONSTANTS

The first data values initialized in a Crystal report don't actually come from an external data source; instead, the values are internal to the report. The very first thing Crystal does is initialize values for any constant formulas that were used in the report. These data values are completely internal to the report. There are several predefined constants that may have been used, such as Pi (3.14 when rounded to two decimal places). In addition, you may have created formulas that have static values, for instance, a variable called TaxRate that was assigned the value 8.06 and is never changed by any other formula. While Crystal does not have a keyword that identifies a constant, the fact that it is not used in another assignment formula tells Crystal that it is a constant. Here's an example of some typical formulas that are considered constant values using Crystal syntax:

```
DaysInTheWeek := 7;
GolfDay := "Wednesday";
TaxPercentage := 8.07 / 100;
OurStandardValue := PI * 100;
```

Some of these values are direct assignments and the others are calculated results. The key to being evaluated in the constants portion of the processing model is that the assignment does not involve any database values.

NOTE   *The evaluation of constant formulas is referred to as Pre-Pass 1, or the Before Reading Records pass, because formula evaluation is taking place prior to the retrieval of data from a data source.*

DATA RETRIEVAL AND SERVER-BASED RECORD SELECTION

After constants are initialized, Pass 1 officially begins. During this pass, the result data set from the data source is initiated and data is retrieved and loaded in your computer's memory. Depending on how you asked for the data and what data source you're accessing, the data set may come back sorted and grouped with much of the processing done on the server, or it may come back as a complete block of data that will be sorted and grouped locally within Crystal.

The data to be retrieved is specified in three places in Crystal Reports, and what is retrieved is outlined in Table 14.1. As a result of the mechanisms used, Crystal generates a SQL (Structured Query Language) statement that is passed to the data source for processing.

TABLE 14.1: SPECIFYING DATA

CRYSTAL REPORTS MECHANISM	SQL QUERY COMPONENT	PURPOSE
Field Explorer	SELECT	Identify fields to retrieve
Database Expert	FROM	Specify data source and tables
Select Expert	WHERE	Filter data based on field-level comparisons

If the Standard Report Creation Wizard was used to create the report, much of the information in the above three areas could be specified through the wizard, but the query can be modified using the mechanisms described above. Also, SQL commands can be directly used in Crystal Reports 9 to generate the query for the data source, which replaces the mechanisms in Table 14.1.

Information in the SELECT and FROM portions of a query is always sent to the data source for processing. The WHERE clause, however, may be processed by the data source or by Crystal Reports after the data is received from the data source. Pass 1 deals with retrieving all possible data from the server based on the query. Here's an example of a query that can be completed executed by the data source:

```
SELECT `Resorts`.`ResortName`,`Resorts`.`ResortCode`
FROM   `Resorts` `Resorts`
WHERE  `Resorts`.`FiveStarRating`=TRUE
```

Since no internal Crystal functions were used in the WHERE clause, it can be sent to the data source for processing. All record selections that are created with Crystal's Select Expert dialog window and that avoid Crystal formulas can be sent to the server. Oftentimes a Crystal formula can be replaced with a direct SQL-supported function, which would therefore enable the data source to process it in its entirety. For example, the following criterion for the Select Expert specifies a user-created function:

```
{@TaxPercentage} < .08
```

where the code for the @TaxPercentage formula is (TaxRate / 100). If the statement is rewritten in the Select Expert to use a database function instead of a Crystal formula, it can be passed directly to the data source as part of the initial data query:

```
WHERE {Orders.TaxRate}/100 < .08
```

The benefit of server-side record selection is smaller data sets returned from the server and therefore better performing reports. Your report will perform better when Crystal processes 100 records returned from the data source rather than 10,000 records!

SIMPLE FORMULA EVALUATION

Once the query has been passed to the data source and data retrieval begins in the report, the evaluation of formulas for Pass 1 can take place on each record being read. This formula pass is known as the While Reading Records phase because the formulas are being processed as the data records are being read from the data source. The formulas that are evaluated in this pass are ones that do either or both of the following:

◆ Return a direct result

◆ Contain a single database field

These formulas do not reference subtotals or summarizations because that would require access to database fields outside the current data record. The formulas evaluated in this pass are generally in the Details section and apply to a single detail data record that will recur for each detail data record in the data set. Because they recur for each detail record, they are also known as *recurring formulas*. Here's an example of three simple recurring formulas using Crystal syntax:

```
FirstInitial := (left{Cust.FName},1);
FullName := ({Cust.FName}) + " "+ ({Cust.LName});
RefID := "REF" + ({Cust.CustID}) + ({Order.OrderNum});
TaxAmount := ({Order.TotalPurchase}) * TaxPercentage;
```

Notice that although some of the examples reference more than one database field, because they stay within the same record in the Details section and do not reference subtotals or summaries, they are considered simple recurring formulas. Simple formulas, therefore, must require only the current record of data in order to calculate a result.

LOCAL RECORD SELECTION

After Crystal receives the data and simple formulas are carried out at the record level, local record selection for the record is performed. This is record selection that cannot be performed on the server and is therefore processed directly in Crystal.

The following are examples of when local record selection will take place (versus being passed to the data source with the original query):

- A Crystal function is used in the Select Expert (WHERE clause).

- No index is available on the data source.

- For non-ODBC and non-OLE data sources, WHERE clauses uses OR logical operator.

SORTING

Following record selection, the data is sorted. Unsorted data is displayed in the Details section in the order in which it was originally added to the database (known as *original order* in Crystal Reports).

GROUPING

Sorted data can optionally be grouped. For ODBC, OLE, and other SQL-capable databases, grouping can take place on the server; for non-SQL data, Crystal does the grouping.

To enable server-side grouping for SQL-type data sources for the current report, choose File ➤ Report Options and enable the Perform Grouping On Server option. To enable server-side grouping of SQL-type data sources for *all* reports you design, choose File ➤ Options, switch to the Database tab, and in the Advanced Options section, enable the Perform Grouping On Server option.

GROUP SUBTOTALS

The records within groups can be subtotaled for each occurrence of a group. This happens after the sorting and grouping because it involves more than one record of data. If a subtotal is based on a field that involves a formula, the formula must be a simple recurring formula (see above) so that it already has a value.

GROUP SUMMARIES

After processing all the detail records one at a time and creating subtotals where required, Crystal can summarize the groups. To do this, it sorts the data, places each item into a group, and then creates a summary of all the values in each group. If a summary is based on a field that involves a formula, the formula must be a simple formula (see above) so that it already has a value.

CROSS-TABS

After Crystal builds grouping summaries, it can build cross-tabs, charts, and maps since all of these rely on summarized data. The cross-tabs constructed during this pass can contain database fields or formulas that reference database fields but cannot contain any grouping and summary information. If a cross-tab cell summary is based on a field that involves a formula, the formula must be a simple formula (see above) so that it already has a value.

CHARTS

After creating cross-tabs, Crystal adds chart components. The charts constructed during this pass can contain database fields or formulas that reference database fields but cannot contain any grouping and summary information. If chart summary data is based on a field that involves a formula, the formula must be a simple formula (see above) so that it already has a value.

MAPS

After all charting in the report is complete, Crystal adds geographic maps and any data points populating the map to the report. The maps constructed during this pass can contain database fields or formulas that reference database fields but cannot contain any grouping and summary information. If a map uses fields involving formulas, the formulas must be simple formulas (see above) so that values already exist.

STORING THE DATA

At the end of Pass 1, the data set is saved in memory and other interim values including grouping, summaries, and formula results are stored in local temporary (TMP) files. This combination represents preprocessed data, which is used as the starting point for Pass 2 evaluation.

Pass 2 Processing

The following tasks are carried out sequentially in Pass 2 processing:

- Sort any groups created if Top/Bottom N or Hierarchical Grouping is used.
- Execute group-selection formulas.
- Calculate running totals.
- Calculate formulas that contain the formula `WhilePrintingRecords`.
- Generate cross-tabs that contain running totals or `PrintTime` formulas.
- Generate charts that contain running totals or `PrintTime` formulas.
- Generate maps that contain running totals or `PrintTime` formulas.
- Generate OLAP grids.
- Generate in-line subreports.
- Generate pages on demand including on-demand subreports.

COMPLEX SORTS

The sorting of data for Top and Bottom N reports as well as hierarchical reports takes place in a pass that is officially known as Pre-Pass 2. It uses the in-memory data set and any group information calculated during Pass 1, reorders it for top, bottom, or hierarchical slicing, and then makes it available for the complex processing in Pass 2.

GROUP-SELECTION FORMULAS

After completing Top N and Hierarchical sorting, Pass 2 officially begins with the execution of group-selection formulas. Group selection applies only when groups exist in the report. In the following group-selection criterion, for instance, the report will show only data where the count of the Country field is not equal to one, meaning not to count any country that contains only one resort.

```
Count ({Resorts.Country}, {Resorts.Country}) <> 1
```

Since group-selection formulas occur in Pass 2, they execute after subtotals, grand totals, and summaries, which were generated in Pass 1. This means that if you want to use subtotals, grand totals, and summaries to calculate groups, you should use running total fields instead of the normal subtotaling, totaling, and summarizing methods. In the above example, to get a total for how many countries have more than one resort, you would add a running total field instead of a total or subtotal field.

RUNNING TOTALS

Running totals calculate after group selection and in a completely different processing pass than summaries, totals, and subtotals. This allows them to access and count all information available in the report.

WHILEPRINTINGRECORDS FORMULAS

The `WhilePrintingRecords` formula is one of four formula statements that you can use to specify exactly in which pass to process data. Any formula in the Details section that includes the `WhilePrintingRecords` statement is evaluated during the second pass through the report. For more information, see the discussion later in this chapter in the "Specifying Execution Time" section.

COMPLEX CROSS-TABS

A cross-tab that contains group information is generated after the group selection formula filters out unwanted groups. The cross-tabs built in this pass can contain grouping and summary information as well as cells that use complex formulas such as running totals and `PrintTime` formulas.

COMPLEX CHARTS

In this pass, charts that contain grouping and summary information are generated. All formulas are valid at this point for inclusion in the charts, including running totals and `PrintTime` formulas. Charts that are based on complex cross-tabs can also be built.

COMPLEX MAPS

Geographic maps based on summary and group data are built during this pass. As with charts and cross-tabs, any valid formula can be used at this point in the process to generate mapping data points.

OLAP GRIDS

After cross-tabs, charts, and maps have been created, Crystal creates OLAP grids. OLAP grids by their very nature are more complex than traditional row and column-analysis grids, requiring therefore the sophistication of powerful formulas. All formulas are available at this point to juxtapose one variable against another for analysis.

IN-LINE SUBREPORTS

An in-line subreport is one that appears in a main report and opens with the main report as opposed to opening when a user clicks a link (an on-demand subreport). These subreports undergo their own two-pass evaluation process (which excludes the third pass for calculating the total page count). Since a subreport can contain any element that a traditional main report can contain (with the exception of a subreport), the Crystal Reports engine processes it according to all the same rules.

PAGES ON DEMAND

Crystal evaluates page formatting only when it is about to display that particular page; this is known as the *page on demand architecture*. When evaluating a page, the following two issues come into play:

- The sequence of sections as they appear top to bottom

- The physical placement of elements within a section

The elements located in the Page Header are evaluated after the elements in the Report Header, the elements in the Details section are evaluated after the elements in the Page Header, the elements in the Page Footer are evaluated after the elements in the Details section, and so on. In addition, the physical placement of the elements matters since elements are evaluated from the top-left corner of a report from left to right and top to bottom (in the same way you're reading this page). Where you place formulas, therefore, matters a great deal in their correct evaluation.

As a part of the on-demand architecture, on-demand subreports are not processed until the user clicks their link. If you use on-demand subreports instead of in-line subreports, your report will be a single-pass report until the user clicks the link to open the on-demand subreport. At that point, the Crystal Report engine takes its second pass through the subreport. This will shorten the time it takes to open the initial report, thereby improving performance when the report first opens.

Pass 3 Processing

Imagine that you have just clicked the Refresh key in Crystal Reports to go from the Design tab to the Preview tab to view a report that includes 500 detail records. When the report displays, you are viewing the first page. In the page navigation area of the Preview tab located at the upper-right corner of the report, the text "1 of 1+" appears, as shown in Figure 14.2.

Have you ever wondered why it doesn't just put the correct page number in there instead of using the "1+" placeholder? The reason is that the report engine doesn't know how many pages the report has at this point of the processing. All it knows regarding page numbers when it displays the first page is that it is not displaying the last page.

FIGURE 14.2

Page count indicator

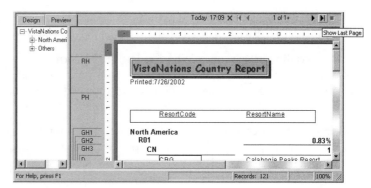

The calculation of the total page count occurs in Pass 3. When you click the Show Last Page button, visible in Figure 14.2, (a right-pointing black arrow immediately followed by a short vertical black line), you're forcing the immediate evaluation of the last processing phase. If you instead click the Show Next Page button, which is to the left of the Show Last Page button, the counter would increment to "2 of 2+" demonstrating Crystal's page on demand architecture and reaffirming that the total page count is not yet available.

You can force the full evaluation of a report by using any of the following fields any place in your report:

Print state formulas:

♦ `TotalPageCount`

♦ `PageNofM`

Special fields:

♦ `Page N of M`

♦ `Total Page Count`

When one of these formulas appears in a report, previewing the report shows the page count in the page navigation area; instead of "1 of 1+," you will see something like "1 of 11."

Specifying Execution Time

Crystal Reports provides four formulas that you can use to force the evaluation of a processing block at a specific time. The four formulas are `BeforeReadingRecords`, `WhileReadingRecords`, `WhilePrintingRecords`, and `EvaluateAfter`. These can be found in the Execution Time category of the Function Tree in the Formula Editor.

BeforeReadingRecords Using this keyword phrase in a formula has the result of forcing the statements that follow it to execute before Crystal sends the query to the data source. This means that it is valid only on processing constant formulas that do not reference anything else. You might use this formula to force Crystal to calculate a value on a parameterized field in your report to ask the user for a value before fetching records from the database.

WhileReadingRecords　The WhileReadingRecords formula is used as the first statement in a group of formula statements in order to force them to be evaluated during Pass 1 by the processing engine. You might use this statement to populate an array with record data during the reading of records from the database.

WhilePrintingRecords　Use this formula statement to force a group of statements to execute during Pass 2, which is after the data is retrieved from the data source. You might use this formula when you need to share data across sections of a report or when accumulating values in a variable based on data stored in a field.

EvaluateAfter()　This function forces one formula statement to execute after the completion of another. Use this function when the value of one formula depends on the presence and value of another formula. The parameter to the EvaluationAfter function is the name of another function; e.g., EvaluateAfter(CalculateSalesSaturation).

Summary

Underlying all the processing that takes place in Crystal Reports to display or print a report is the concept of evaluation time. Everything takes place in a predetermined order. From section order to field order to page on demand architecture to using evaluation time formulas, the report-processing engine determines the outcome of the hard work you put into the report design. If you take the time to understand the report-processing model, you will find yourself on the top of the pyramid of Crystal Report writers.

Configuring Your Design Environment

NOW THAT YOU KNOW how to build reports in Crystal Reports, you most likely have plenty of questions on how to finesse the design environment for your own needs. Each time you build a new report, you start with a clean slate in the Crystal design client. There are global settings that you can configure that will be remembered from report to report, which will make your report building go even smoother. There are also settings that you can configure at the report level to apply to the elements within a single report. These can also override the global settings you make on a report-by-report basis. In this chapter, we'll take the approach of a Frequently Asked Questions (FAQ) forum to help you figure out what design elements you can fine-tune and where to find the settings.

Featured in this chapter:

◆ Understanding data source options

◆ Tuning database options

◆ Configuring the design layout environment

◆ Grouping and sorting options

◆ Setting options for field and text objects

◆ Saving a report

Data Sources and Databases

There are some data sources and databases that you work with frequently and others that you'll never use. You can configure Crystal Reports to focus on the ones that you do use. In addition, you can tune database performance for your environment. Many of the database options are globally set; Figure 15.1 shows the global database options area accessed through the File ➢ Options menu. Data source defaults are set on the Data Source Defaults dialog shown in Figure 15.2.

FIGURE 15.1

Global database options

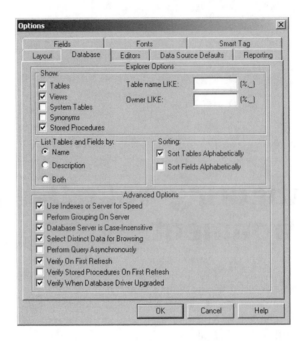

FIGURE 15.2

Global data source settings

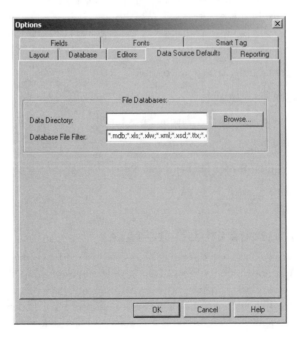

I work only with Excel data files. Can I force Crystal Reports to look for only XLS data files? Choose File ➤ Options, Data Source Defaults tab, Database File Filter area, and remove any unwanted file types.

All my database files are stored in a specific drive. Can I set a default to have Crystal Reports look there first for my databases? Choose File ➤ Options, Data Source Defaults tab, Data Directory area, and use the Browse button choose a directory.

I've connected to the right data source, but I do not see my tables in the Database Expert. Choose File ➤ Options, Database tab, Show area, and enable the Tables check box.

I do not see any stored procedures in the Database Expert, yet I know the database contains stored procedures. Is there a setting I need to know about? Choose File ➤ Options, Database tab, Show area, and enable the Stored Procedures check box.

I do not see any views in the Database Expert, yet I know the database contains views. Is there a setting I need to know about? Choose File ➤ Options, Database tab, Show area, and enable the Views check box.

The table names I'm seeing in Database Expert do not match the table names when I look at them through the actual database. Choose File ➤ Options, Database tab, Show area, and disable the Synonyms check box.

I need to write a report using the database's system tables, but these do not appear in the Database Expert. Choose File ➤ Options, Database tab, Show area, and enable the System Tables check box.

I work only with payroll tables. How can I show only tables that start with the letters *PAY* in the Database Expert? Choose File ➤ Options, Database tab, Show area, and in the Table Name LIKE area, type **PAY%**. The percent symbol will match any letters from where you use it to the end of a word. The underscore character will match on a specific character. For instance, the filter PAY% will find tables named PAYROLL, PAYEE, PAYMENTS, etc.

The database I work with contains an enormous number of tables. How can I show only the tables I created in the Database Expert? Choose File ➤ Options, Database tab, Show area, and in the Owner LIKE area, type the name of the table owner. The percent symbol will match any letters from where you use it to the end of a word. The underscore character will match on a specific character. For instance, the filter _il% will find tables created by BILL and DILBERT.

Tables in the Database Expert are appearing with a hyphen and a comment after the table name. I'd like to see just the table names. Choose File ➤ Options, Database tab, List Tables And Fields area, and enable a suitable combination of the Name, Description, or Both radio buttons.

The tables listed in the Database Expert are not in alphabetical order. Is this right? Choose File ➤ Options, Database tab, Sorting area, and enable the Sort Tables Alphabetically option.

When I look at a list of fields in a database through Crystal Reports, they are not in alphabetical order. Is this right? Choose File ➤ Options, Database tab, Sorting area, and enable the Sort Fields Alphabetically option.

The database I'm working with is indexed. How can I be sure Crystal Reports will use the indexes?   Choose File ➢ Options, Database tab, Advanced Options area, and enable the Use Indexes Or Server For Speed option.

For the current report only, choose File ➢ Report Options and enable/disable the Use Indexes Or Server For Speed option.

I'm working with a SQL-capable database on a database server. Can I push some of the processing off Crystal and onto the database?   Choose File ➢ Options, Database tab, Advanced Options area, and enable the Use Indexes Or Server For Speed option.

For the current report only, choose File ➢ Report Options and enable/disable the Use Indexes Or Server For Speed option.

I'm working with a SQL-capable database on a database server. Can I force the server to group the data so that Crystal Reports doesn't have to?   Choose File ➢ Options, Database tab, Advanced Options area, and enable the Perform Grouping On Server option.

For the current report only, choose Database ➢ Perform Grouping On Server.

For the current report only, choose File ➢ Report Options and enable/disable the Perform Grouping On Server option.

When I search for data in a SQL database, I don't care about the differences between upper- and lowercase letters; after all, green is still GREEN. Can Crystal ignore case for searches?   Choose File ➢ Options, Database tab, Advanced Options area, and enable the Database Server Is Case-Insensitive option.

For the current report only, choose File ➢ Report Options and enable/disable the Database Server Is Case-Insensitive option.

When I connect to a SQL database server, my machine is tied up for a long time. Can I break out of this without crashing my machine?   Choose File ➢ Options, Database tab, Advanced Options area, and enable the Perform Query Asynchronously option.

For the current report only, choose File ➢ Report Options and enable/disable the Perform Query Asynchronously option.

My database structure changes from time to time. How can I make sure Crystal picks up the changes whenever I open a report that uses the database?   Choose File ➢ Options, Database tab, Advanced Options area, and enable the Verify On First Refresh option.

For the current report only, choose Database ➢ Verify Database.

I've upgraded from a Microsoft Access to a Microsoft SQL Server database. How can I make sure Crystal picks up the changes whenever I open a report that uses a changed database?   Choose File ➢ Options, Database tab, Advanced Options area, and enable the Verify When Database Driver Upgraded option.

For the current report only, choose Database ➢ Verify On First Refresh.

I need to tell Crystal Reports that the database has changed locations.   *For the current report only,* choose Database ➤ Set Datasource Location.

I have finished using one SQL database server and need to use a different SQL database server, but Crystal Reports still thinks I'm using the first one. How do I change this?   *For the current report only,* choose Database ➤ Log On Or Off Server.

Can I see the SQL query that was sent by Crystal to a SQL data source?   *For the current report only,* choose Database ➤ Show SQL Query.

I want to prevent Crystal from retrieving duplicate records into my report from a SQL data source.   *For the current report only,* choose Database ➤ Select Distinct Records.

For the current report only, choose File ➤ Report Options and enable/disable the Select Distinct Records option.

I want to use XML as a data source in Crystal. Where do I go to start this process?   Open the XML Expert by choosing Report➤ XML Expert. This allows you to create a custom format for an XML schema as well as create validation by associating XSD and DTD files. Figure 15.3 shows the XML Expert.

FIGURE 15.3

XML Expert

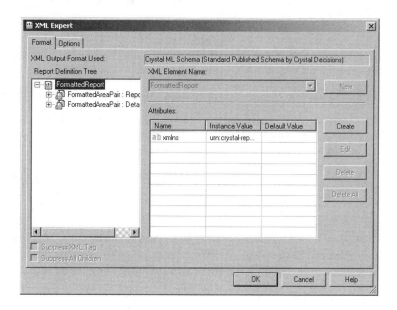

Configuring Design Aides

Do you always turn the grid off because it annoys you? Or always use the guidelines? You can customize your layout area so that it defaults to your favorite settings.

When I start Crystal, I always need to make the Preview area show in a bigger screen. Is there a global setting for this? Choose File ➤ Options, Layout tab, Preview area, and click a radio button to have the page start with full size (100%), shrink your report to the width of the margins, or shrink/expand your report to the size of the page.

For the current report only, choose File ➤ Report Options, Preview Pages Start With area, and choose a size option from the drop-down list.

How do I turn the design grid on or off for all reports in Design mode? Preview mode? Choose File ➤ Options, Layout tab, Design View area, and enable/disable the Grid option.

Choose File ➤ Options, Layout tab, Preview area, and enable/disable the Grid option.

Can I control the size of the grid? Choose File ➤ Options, Layout tab, Grid options area, and type the inch measurement for the grid box size.

How can I force objects to line up on the design grid? Choose File ➤ Options, Layout tab, Grid options area, and enable/disable the Snap To Grid option.

Will objects always need to be on the grid or can they be dragged to a position not aligned with the grid? Choose File ➤ Options, Layout tab, Grid options area, and enable/disable the Free-Form placement option.

Can I decide to show the horizontal and vertical rulers on or off as a global setting in Design mode? How about Preview mode? Choose File ➤ Options, Layout tab, Design View area, and enable/disable the Rulers check box.

Choose File ➤ Options, Layout tab, Preview area, and enable/disable the Rulers check box.

Can the hints that appear when I roll my mouse over a button icon below the menu be turned off or reenabled in Design mode? Preview mode? Choose File ➤ Options, Layout tab, Design View area, and enable/disable the Tool Tips option.

Choose File ➤ Options, Layout tab, Preview area, and enable/disable the Tool Tips option.

Can I set the zoom percentage to always be 150%? Choose Zoom from the menu and set the percentage of magnification desired.

Can I use keyboard shortcuts in Crystal Reports? Yes, all the menu items can be accessed using keyboard shortcuts. For instance, to toggle the Field Explorer on or off, use press ALT+V then F. The keyboard shortcut keys are noted in the menu with an underline character. Another example is to use CTRL+D or ALT+V then N to switch to Design mode.

How can I move, align, and size my fields? Choose File ➤ Move, File ➤ Align, and File ➤ Size from the menu.

Controlling What Happens When a Report Opens

As a report is read from its storage location, read into memory, and then displayed, you have the opportunity to control some of what happens to fields and information on the report. Many of the options discussed here are set on the Reporting tab of the global options area shown here in Figure 15.4.

FIGURE 15.4

Global reporting options

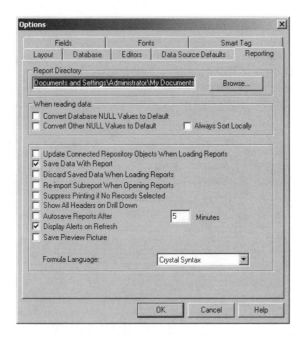

When my report was saved, the data was saved with it. How can I get rid of the data for all the reports when I open them?   Choose File ➢ Options, Reporting tab, and enable the Discard Saved Data When Loading Reports option. Resave the report.

I have a subreport that needs to retrieve data every time I open the report.   Choose File ➢ Options, Reporting tab, enable the Re-import Subreport When Opening Reports option.

I used the repository in my report and want to make sure I always have the most recent repository information in my report. How can I do this?   Choose File ➢ Options, Reporting tab, and enable the Update Connected Repository Objects When Loading Reports option.

I am using Report Part Navigation. Where do I set the initial report part and data context to be used when the report first opens?   *For the current report only*, choose File ➢ Report Options, Initial Report Part Settings area, and use the Object Name and Data Context input boxes.

Customizing Section Settings

The five default sections in Crystal Reports can be formatted for display purposes. In addition, you can modify the behavior of a data value that appears in Group Header sections and Page Header sections. Many of the options discussed here are set on the Layout tab of the global options area as shown here in Figure 15.5.

FIGURE 15.5

Global layout options

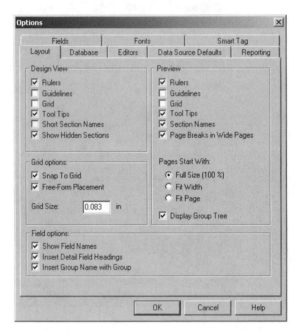

The names of the sections take up too much space in Design mode. Can I change this? Choose File ➤ Options, Layout tab, Design View area, and enable Short Section Names.

For the current report only, right click on the gray area containing the name of the section and select Show Short Section Names from the menu.

Can I display the names of the sections in Preview mode? Choose File ➤ Options, Layout tab, Preview area, and enable Section Names.

Can I completely hide the names of the sections in Preview mode? *For the current report only*, right-click on the gray area containing the name of the section and select Show Short Section Names from the menu.

I want the titles for all fields to always display and print with the same font in the Page Header area. Choose File ➤ Options, Fonts tab, click the Field Titles button, and set the appropriate font information.

Can I select all of the report objects within a section?   Yes, right-click on the gray area containing the name of the section and choose the Select All Section Objects option.

Grouping, Sorting, and Filtering Options

Grouping, sorting, and filtering are performance-intensive operations. Crystal Reports has several settings available to help you fine-tune the performance settings to meet the requirements and capabilities of your database server.

I create groups but I don't see the group tree in my reports. Why not?   Choose File ➢ Options, Layout tab, Preview area, and enable Display Group Tree.

For the current report only, choose File ➢ Report Options and enable/disable the Create Group Tree option.

How can I prevent group names from being added to a Group Header when I create new groups?   Choose File ➢ Options, Layout tab, and disable the Insert Group Name With Group check box.

Can I tell Crystal Reports to sort any data it retrieves using my own computer's memory resources?   Choose File ➢ Options, Reporting tab, When Reading Data area, and enable the Always Sort Locally check box.

For the current report only, choose File ➢ Report Options and enable/disable the Always Sort Locally option.

I don't want the Group Headers to show when I create drill-down areas.   Choose File ➢ Options, Reporting tab, and disable the Show All Headers On Drill Down option.

For the current report only, choose File ➢ Report Options and enable/disable the Show All Headers On Drill Down option.

When a report doesn't have any records that meet my filtering or selection criteria, can I prevent it from returning or printing a blank report?   Choose File ➢ Options, Reporting tab, and enable the Suppress Printing If No Records Selected option.

For the current report only, choose File ➢ Report Options and enable/disable the Suppress Printing If No Records option.

Field Object and Text Object Defaults

Companies often standardize on a particular format for data in reports. Setting field type defaults can go a long way in preserving a consistent look for all your reports. Many of the settings discussed are set in the global options area using the Fields and Fonts tabs. These are shown in Figure 15.6 and Figure 15.7.

FIGURE 15.6

Global field formatting

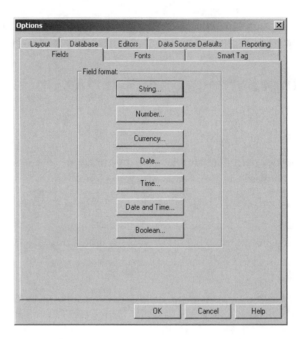

FIGURE 15.7

Global font formatting

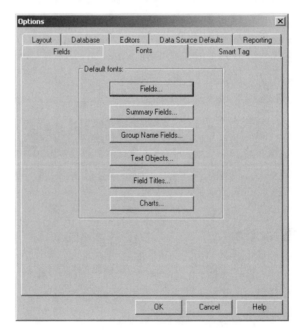

When I look at a list of fields in a database through Crystal Reports, they are not alphabetical. Is this right? Choose File ➤ Options, Database tab, and enable the Sort Fields Alphabetically option.

When browsing field data using the Crystal Reports Browse button, I see data for 500 unique records but I'd rather see unique field values. Choose File ➤ Options, Database tab, Advanced Options area, and enable the Select Distinct Data For Browsing option.

For the current report only, choose File ➤ Report Options and enable/disable the Select Distinct Data For Browsing option.

How can I prevent field headings from being added to the Page Header section whenever I add a field to the Details section? Choose File ➤ Options, Layout tab, and disable the Insert Detail Field Headings check box.

How can I prevent field names from displaying in Design mode? Choose File ➤ Options, Layout tab, and disable the Show Field Names check box.

Some fields in my report show a question mark or asterisk instead of a value. I've been told this is because the database is storing a null value in this field. I'd prefer to see zeros or blanks. Can I do this? Choose File ➤ Options, Reporting tab, When Reading Data area, and enable the Convert Database NULL Values To Default check box.

For the current report only, choose File ➤ Report Options and enable/disable the Convert Database NULL Values To Default option.

My company's standard is to use a cascading style sheet for formatting all our report fields. Where can I set the style sheet Class name reference as the default for all my reports? Choose File ➤ Options, Fields tab, and choose the type(s) of data the setting applies to; then on the Common tab, use the CSS Class Name input box.

When I add fields, I want to anchor them into position so they can't be moved accidentally. Choose File ➤ Options, Fields tab, and choose the type(s) of data the setting applies to; then on the Common tab, enable the Lock Size And Position option.

Can I prevent field formatting options that I want to be universal from being overridden for individual reports? Choose File ➤ Options, Fields tab, and choose the type(s) of data the setting applies to; then on the Common tab, enable the Read-only option.

The data values for fields on my reports have to be centered at all times. Can I set this is as default instead of setting it for each field? Choose File ➤ Options, Fields tab, and choose the type(s) of data the setting applies to; then on the Common tab, choose the Horizontal Alignment option.

I'd like to always start a new page to prevent a field's worth of data from being split at the bottom of one page and continuing at the top of another. Choose File ➤ Options, Fields tab, and choose the type(s) of data the setting applies to; then on the Common tab, enable the Keep Object Together option.

I work with borders quite a bit and don't like how Crystal splits a border, partially printing it at the bottom of one page and completing it on the next page.   Choose File ➤ Options, Fields tab, and choose the type(s) of data the setting applies to; then on the Common tab, enable the Close Border On Page Break option.

Can I universally enable the Can Grow option so that any field that has more data than will fit in the field can grow in size vertically?   Choose File ➤ Options, Fields tab, and choose the type(s) of data the setting applies to; on the Common tab, enable the Can Grow option and choose zero or more lines.

If a field value is a duplicate, I do not want it to appear on my report.   Choose File ➤ Options, Fields tab, and choose the type(s) of data the setting applies to; then on the Common tab, enable the Suppress If Duplicated option.

All numeric values in my reports need to print in a specific format.   Choose File ➤ Options, Fields tab, and click the Number button; then on the Number tab, choose the appropriate style for numbers or use the Custom Style option.

My company likes the currency symbol to appear immediately to the left of a number value with no spaces in between.   Choose File ➤ Options, Fields tab, and click the Number button; then on the Number tab, enable the Display Currency Symbol option and select the Floating radio button.

Choose File ➤ Options, Fields tab, and click the Currency button; then on the Number tab, in the Currency symbol area, select the Floating radio button.

Currency symbols need to appear in a fixed and aligned way and should not depend on the width of the number in the field.   Choose File ➤ Options, Fields tab, and click the Number button; then on the Number tab, enable the Display Currency Symbol option and select the Fixed radio button.

Choose File ➤ Options, Fields tab, and click the Currency button; then on the Number tab, in the Currency symbol area, select the Fixed radio button.

I need to use a fixed format for all date fields in all reports.   Choose File ➤ Options, Fields tab, and click the Date button; then on the Date tab, choose a formatting style for dates or customize your own.

I need to use a fixed format for all time fields in all reports.   Choose File ➤ Options, Fields tab, and click the Time button; then on the Time tab, choose a formatting style for times or customize your own.

I need to use a fixed format for all date/time fields in all reports.   Choose File ➤ Options, Fields tab, and click the Date And Time button; then on the Date And Time tab, choose a formatting style for dates and times or customize your own.

For Boolean data, I want the values to print with standard values regardless of what the database field actually contains.   Choose File ➤ Options, Fields tab, and click the Boolean button; on the Boolean tab, choose a text format using the drop-down list for True Or False, T Or F, Yes Or No, Y Or N, 1 Or 0.

Can I set universal font attributes for all data fields in all my reports?   Choose File ➤ Options, Fonts tab, click the Fields button, and set the appropriate font information.

Can I set universal font attributes for all summarized fields in all my reports?   Choose File ➤ Options, Fonts tab, click the Summary Fields button, and set the appropriate font information.

I want all text fields to always display and print with the same font.   Choose File ➤ Options, Fonts tab, click the Text Objects button, and set the appropriate font information.

I want the titles for all fields to always display and print with the same font in the Page Header area.   Choose File ➤ Options, Fonts tab, click the Field Titles button, and set the appropriate font information.

Can I set a default font to be used with charts?   Choose File ➤ Options, Fonts tab, click the Charts button, and set the appropriate font information.

I am using Office XP Smart Tags. Can I set default information to tell Crystal Reports where to link?   Choose File ➤ Options, Smart Tag tab, and use the Web Server Name, Virtual Directory, and Viewing Page options.

Working with Formulas

The Formula Workshop programming area can be modified to help you see your code better and to visually pick out color references for the different aspects of writing code. Several of the options discussed here are set using the global settings for editors; this dialog is shown in Figure 15.8.

FIGURE 15.8

Global formula editor settings

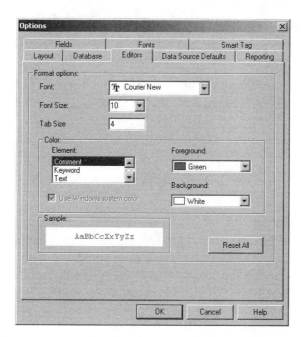

Can I control the font used in the Formula Workshop Editor?   Choose File ➢ Options, Editors tab, Format options area, and choose a font type and point size for individual elements like keywords, text, and comments.

I like to indent my code with tabs every two spaces. Where can I set the tab size in the Formula Editor?   Choose File ➢ Options, Editors tab, Format options area, and type a value for Tab Size.

Can I set different colors for formula comments, keywords, text, and highlighted text?   Choose File ➢ Options, Editors tab, Color area, choose one of the elements, and set the foreground and background colors individually or use the Windows system color.

I always use Basic Syntax for my formulas. Can I set this as a default?   Choose File ➢ Options, Reporting tab, and set the Formula Language to Basic Syntax.

Saving Reports

The default behavior for saving reports includes identifying a directory to save all reports in and making a decision about whether to save data with the report.

What is the default directory for saving new reports and can I change it?   Choose File ➢ Options, Reporting tab, the Report Directory setting, and use the Browse button to change the directory.

Can I set Crystal to autosave my report while I'm designing it?   Choose File ➢ Options, Reporting tab, enable the Autosave Reports After option, and type a number for the repeat frequency in minutes.

I like working with thumbnail images to figure out what is inside a file. Can Crystal Reports provide a thumbnail of the first page of the report?   Choose File ➢ Options, Reporting tab, and enable the Save Preview Picture option.

I do not save the data from the database in the report when I save the report and am always unchecking this Crystal Reports option. Where can I set this as my preference?   Choose File ➢ Options, Reporting tab, and disable the Save Data With Report option.

For the current report only, choose File ➢ Report Options and enable/disable the Save Data With Report option.

For the current report only, choose File ➢ Save Data With Report.

Summary

Crystal Reports provides a set of global options that can be set using the Options submenu off the main File menu. You can override many of these settings on a report-by-report basis using local settings in the Report Options area. In this chapter, we've presented the questions you might be asking as you're trying to figure out where a default or option can be set or overridden.

Part 4

Application Development with Crystal Reports

Chapter 16

Deploying Your Report

CONGRATULATIONS! YOU JUST CREATED a wonderful report in the previous chapter. But now you need to get that report to your end user before you are finished. In this chapter, we take all your hard work in creating a Crystal Report and look at options for delivering the report to the end user.

You will need to choose how best to deploy the report, because depending on the choices you make, the end user will be able to either review the latest information from the database, view the report offline, or use a web browser to view the report. With the last option, the user will require only a web browser and you will not need to install any software on the user's computer. You need to answer the following question to make this decision.

> *Business Question: I have users who need the latest information, users who need to view the report offline, and users who want to view the report from a web page. How can I satisfy all these needs with Crystal Reports?*

In this chapter, you will learn how to:

◆ Choose a report-deployment technique

◆ Deploy a Crystal Report with and without data

◆ Export your report to various formats

◆ Export your report to HTML and a web server

◆ Compile your Crystal Report

◆ Install a compiled report on your user's computer

Choosing a Report-Deployment Technique

Crystal Reports offers many report-deployment techniques. Each has its pros and cons. To help you to identify the best deployment technique for the report, we've listed some questions you should ask yourself and explained them below. Remember to ask yourself these questions for each report and each end user because they may all have different requirements.

Will the user be happy with a fax or printed report?   In the world of sophisticated Internet technology and desktop tools, we may forget that sometimes the simplest solution is best. Does the user merely want a monthly sales report? If so, then printing the report or faxing the report may meet your user requirements.

Does your end user have Crystal Reports?   If the end user has a copy of Crystal Reports installed, then deploying the report may be as simple as sending the user a copy of the RPT file or providing access to the RPT file on a shared network server. You will need to verify that the end user's computer has the same connectivity configured as the computer where the report was developed. See the section "Deploying the Crystal Report" below.

Can the report be static, that is, a snapshot of the database?   If the information the end user requested is not time-sensitive, such as a monthly sales report, your deployment choices are these:

- Printing or faxing the report
- Exporting to a different format such as Word (DOC), Excel (XLS), or Adobe's Portable Digital Format (PDF)
- Sending the RPT file with data to the end user
- Exporting the report to HTML format

Should the report contain real-time information?   If the information the end user requested is time-sensitive, such as current sales data or stock market information, you will need to deploy the report in a way that lets the user run the report. In this case the report will require a live connection to the database. The report can be deployed on the user's computer, and the user can refresh the report as needed.

You can also deploy the report on a web server, and the user can request the current report. Crystal Reports 9 includes the Report Application Server, which is an entry-level version of Crystal Enterprise. The Report Application Server allows you to deploy the report to a web server and users can run the report to view real-time information. In addition, the Report Application Server provides a Software Development Kit that can be used to provide users with the ability to create, modify, and view reports. The Report Application Server is discussed in Chapter 24, "Report Application Server."

You can also develop a custom windows or web application to allow users to view reports. These options are discussed in Part 4, "Application Development with Crystal Reports," and Part 5, "Enterprise Reporting."

How often will the report need to be updated?   How often will the RPT file need to be changed? If the users will frequently ask for changes in the report, such as adding fields or changing the report structure (of course this never happens!), you must keep in mind how many places you will need to update the RPT file to deploy it. If the report is going to be changed often, it might be better to deploy the report to a central server or a web server.

How big is the report?   The answer to this question will impact the processing time of the report, the load on your database when the report runs, or even how much paper it needs to print. If the report is too large, you may want to think about splitting the report into several smaller reports and a summary report.

Do I want the user to retrieve the report?   If you have a large user base, you may be able to ease your deployment task by placing the report in a shared network location where the users can pick up the report themselves. Using a web server also makes this task easier; when the user requests the web page, the report is displayed.

Is the report developed with objects from the Crystal Repository?   The Crystal Repository is a new feature in Crystal Reports version 9. The repository is a database that can contain report objects such as images, text objects, report functions, and SQL commands. These are copied into the report when they are included in the repository. However, when you make a change to the repository, you want the reports that are using those objects to reflect those changes. The objects in the reports can be updated only if the report has access to the repository. If the report does not have access to the repository, then the changes will not be reflected in the report. The report will still run, but this defeats the purpose of the repository.

Do you need to schedule or archive reports?   Scheduling a report allows you to run the report during off-peak hours, such as when the database is not busy. If the users don't require up-to-the-minute information and they can view the last-run report, this will save a lot of traffic on the database server—especially if the report is large. Unfortunately, in version 9 of Crystal Reports, Crystal Decisions did not include any tools for scheduling and archiving reports. You will need to purchase another Crystal Decisions product called Crystal Enterprise for scheduling and archiving reports. In Part 5 of the book we discuss what Crystal Enterprise is so you can decide if you need this tool for report deployment. Or you can develop your own application; in Part 4 we cover Visual Basic, ASP, and .NET development.

By answering the preceding questions, you can get a good idea of your deployment requirements. You can break the requirements into two major categories:

◆ Users who need real-time data

◆ Users who are happy with a static report

But these are only broad requirements. There are many other factors that need to be considered before you can decide on the proper method of deployment. Using Crystal Reports, you have many options for delivering these reports to the users. Further, you also have at your disposal other Crystal Decisions products, such as Crystal Enterprise and ePortfolio, which are designed for report deployment. Table 16.1 is a summary of the types of deployment, based upon end-user requirements.

TABLE 16.1: SUMMARY OF DEPLOYMENT METHODS

TYPE OF DEPLOYMENT	USER REQUIREMENTS	COMMENT
REAL-TIME DATA		
Crystal Report File (RPT) on each user's computer	Each user must have Crystal Reports installed.	Developer can use e-mail to distribute RPT file to many users. Each user must have access to database. Crystal Report savvy users can change the report. May need to train users how to work with Crystal Reports.
Crystal Reports running on a web server, using ASP (Active Server Pages) or .NET technology	User must have a web browser.	Covered in Part IV.
Crystal Reports deployed via Report Application Server, or Crystal Enterprise	User must have a web browser.	Covered in Part V. Use Crystal Enterprise when performance or administration using ASP or .NET is an issue, or you have a large user base.
STATIC DEPLOYMENT		
Crystal Report with saved data	Each user must have Crystal Reports installed.	User can refresh the report to get real-time data.
Compiled reports with saved data	User needs compiled report to be installed.	Currently not available for version 9, see "Compiled Reports" later in this chapter.
Print or fax report	Simple Paper Deployment	User can print report manually if user has Crystal Reports.
Export to an application format such as DOC, XLS, PDF, etc.	User without Crystal Reports can use a different application to view the report.	Developer can export report manually if user does not have Crystal Reports. Depending on export format some report formatting will be lost.
Export to HTML	User must have web browser.	Loss of report formatting
Crystal Enterprise archived reports	User must have web browser.	Must purchase a copy of Crystal Enterprise.

We've addressed many of these types of deployment in this chapter, but we've saved others to discuss with more advanced topics later in this book. For example, custom desktop application, or web server deployment, requires Visual Basic, ASP, or the .NET platform, all of which are covered later in Part 4. Then, in Part 5, we'll cover the Report Application Server, and ePortfolio lite, which is a packaged web-based application that uses Crystal Enterprise services to provide report deployment. Now let's start deploying a Crystal Report.

Deploying the Crystal Report

When you save a Crystal Report, you save it in an RPT file. This file is your complete report; it contains everything you used to create this report. An easy deployment technique is simply to provide your customers with the RPT file. You can e-mail this file to them as an attachment, and they can copy the file to their hard drive. The pros and cons of this deployment method are shown below:

Pros	Cons
Easy to deploy.	User requires a licensed version of Crystal Reports to open the report.
Deploys to a shared networked drive for easy access.	Requires connectivity set up on the user's computer so they can access the shared drive.
Users can change the report.	Users can change the report.
Developer can send report via e-mail as an attachment.	User requires a database ID and password to the database.
User can refresh report to gain access to most current data.	

WARNING *Keep in mind that when you deploy the RPT file to the end user, their computer must have the same database connectivity set up as the report developer's computer before the user will be able to refresh the report.*

Deploying the Report without Saved Data

The RPT file without saved data is small enough that it can be e-mailed to the end user or placed on a shared network drive for the user to access. As a report developer, you can do the sophisticated report development and the user can make any minor changes they may need.

WARNING *If you are placing a report on a shared network drive for multiple users, you can run into trouble with users making changes to the shared copy. It is best for the users to copy the report to their computer and open it from there.*

To save a report without data, click the File menu, deselect Save Data With Report, and save the report. This will not save the data for this report.

Alternatively, you can create a global setting so that all reports by default have no data by choosing the File ➤ Options ➤ Reporting and deselecting Save Data With Report.

Deploying the Report with Saved Data

Deploying the report with data is useful when having the latest data is not necessary. Saving data in a report and distributing it to multiple users also minimizes the number of hits on the database server.

Reports with saved data can be large files. Before deploying the report, decide on the best way to send a large file in your organization.

To save a report with data, choose File ➤ Save Data With Report and save the report. This will include the data in the report.

Alternatively, you can create a global setting so that all reports by default save the data by choosing File ➤ Options ➤ Reporting and selecting Save Data With Report.

REPORT BURSTING INDEXES

Report Bursting Indexes are a new feature in Crystal Reports 9. When a report is saved with data, the data in the report is just a blob of data. When the report viewer requests a particular field from the report, the Crystal reporting engine must search all the stored data to find the required information. It is like searching for a particular reference in a book without a table of contents.

Report Bursting Indexes act like a table of contents in a book; they help the Crystal Report engine find the data you are looking for more quickly.

Once you create Report Bursting Indexes, they are completely transparent to the end user viewing the report. They make navigating through the report faster, but the end user does not know the indexes are being used.

Consider using Report Bursting Indexes on large reports with saved data.

CREATING REPORT BURSTING INDEXES

To create a Report Bursting Index, choose Report ➤ Report Bursting Indexes. The Saved Data Indexes dialog will appear, as shown in Figure 16.1. The Available Fields list contains a list of fields on the report. Move fields that are commonly referred to in the report's record-selection formulas or record selection into the Indexed For Bursting list, by highlighting the field and clicking the arrow button.

FIGURE 16.1

Creating Report
Bursting Indexes

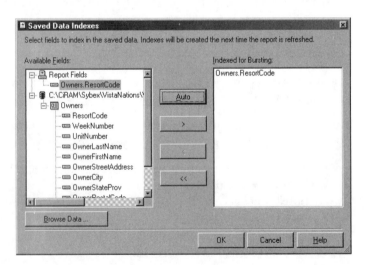

You can click the Auto button to automatically add fields that are used in the record-selection formulas. When the report is refreshed, the indexes will be built.

WARNING   *You may think that it would be advantageous to index all the fields in the report. Do not do this, as it will increase the size of the report and will actually slow the retrieval.*

Switching Data Sources

Reports are often created on a sample database or test database. When it is time to deploy your report to the end users, you must switch the data source to the production data. Choose Database ➤ Set Datasource Location. The Set Datasource Location dialog will appear, as shown in Figure 16.2.

FIGURE 16.2

Switching databases

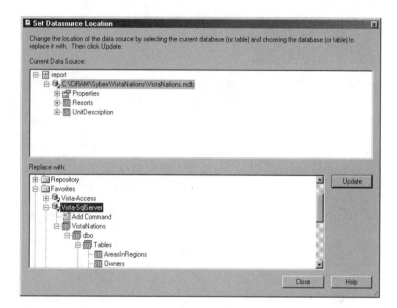

The top window displays the current connection to the database. The bottom window allows you to select the alternative data source. You establish a connection to the alternative data source in the bottom window.

You can switch tables individually or switch the entire database. If your report contains tables from only one database, in the top window select the current database, and in the bottom window select the database you want to switch to. Then click the Update button.

If your report contains tables from various databases, select the tables individually and then click the Update button.

If the two databases contain the same structure, your report is now pointing to the same new data source.

TIP   When we develop reports, we like to make a copy of the client's database in Microsoft Access. Then we do all our report development in Access, and then back at the customer's office we switch databases to move the reports to production.

When switching data sources, remember that you are changing the underlying program (data access DLL, or Dynamically Linked Library) that queries the data source. It is important to verify the data in your report after making the switch. When Crystal Reports is reporting from a data source that it can read directly, it is processing the retrieval of records. However, when Crystal is reporting through a driver, such as ODBC or OLEDB (Object Linking and Embedding for Databases, a special DLL for database connectivity), it is passing a SQL statement to the driver, telling the driver what it wants. This difference can lead to inconsistencies in how tables are joined and queries are resolved and what data is displayed in your report.

The problem can be resolved by changing the order in which the tables are joined or changing the join from an equal join to a left or right outer join. Choose Database ➤ Database Expert and click the Links tab to show the linking information for the report. The Database Expert dialog will appear, as shown in Figure 16.3. Select the links between the tables, and then click the Link Options button to change the linking information. This step is not always necessary, but if you do run into problems, this can help.

FIGURE 16.3

Link Options

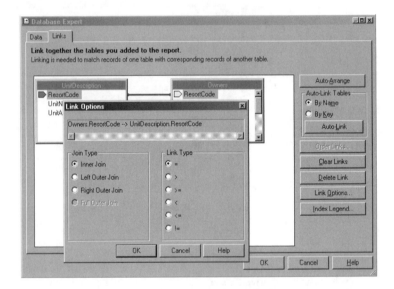

TIP   *To avoid the linking issues, create an OLEDB connection to Access. That way, Crystal Reports is always passing a SQL statement to the database and not directly processing the record. This avoids potential differences in how data is accessed.*

MAPPING DATABASE FIELDS

If the two data sources are not the same, then the Map Fields dialog will be displayed, as shown in Figure 16.4. Notice that the Report Fields list expects a UnitNumber field, but in the GMARIC database, the fields have been renamed to UnitNum. Select the fields that you need to map and click the Map button.

The Match Type check box can be used to tell the Map Fields dialog to display only unmapped fields that match the data type in the Unmapped Fields list. For example, if UnitNumber is a character field, it will display only unmapped character fields. If the Match Type check box is deselected, all the unmapped fields will be displayed.

The bottom part of the window displays the files that are currently mapped. If necessary you can unmap the fields by selecting them and clicking the Unmap button.

FIGURE 16.4

Mapping fields

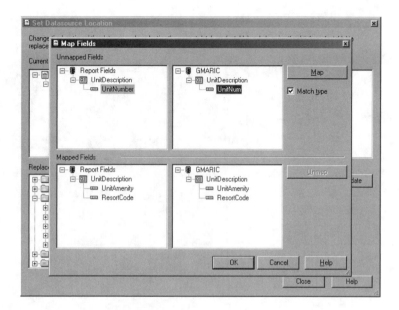

VERIFYING DATABASES

When you first create a report with Crystal Reports, it copies the structure of the data source and uses that structure to build the Field Explorer dialog box. If there is a change to the database structure, such as a new field being added, the Field Explorer will not reflect the change until you choose the Database ➢ Verify Database menu. If the data source has changed, then you will be prompted by a Map Fields dialog, and you will need to remap the fields as described above. If everything is okay, Crystal Reports will tell you that the database is up to date, as shown in Figure 16.5.

FIGURE 16.5

Database verified

You can choose File ➢ Options ➢ then the Database tab and choose further verify options, as shown in Figure 16.6. By default Crystal Reports will verify your report on the first refresh; you can choose to turn this feature off. Or you can choose to verify stored procedures on the first refresh, which is off by default, and then choose whether to verify when the Database driver is upgraded, which is on by default.

FIGURE 16.6

Database verification
options

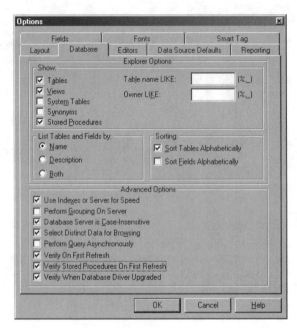

Deploying Reports and the Crystal Repository

The Crystal Repository is a new feature with Crystal Reports 9. The repository is a database that contains objects, such as images, text objects, and report functions, that you can add to any Crystal Report.

You can think of the repository as a shared, global Field Explorer. All report writers have access to it and they can share the report objects. This makes report writing faster because you can reuse components that are added to the repository. Also, if an object changes in the repository, all the reports that use the object can be refreshed to reflect the new object. For example, if a company logo changes, all reports that use the company logo can be refreshed to show the new logo.

Before version 9 of Crystal Reports, the entire report was self-contained in the RPT file. With the repository, parts of your report can be stored in a remote database.

When you add an object from the repository to the report, Crystal copies the object from the repository to the report. It also keeps track of the object from the repository by keeping a connection to the object in the repository. It is important to keep this in mind when deploying reports if you want the end user to have access to the repository and to be able to retrieve updates.

You can disconnect repository objects if desired. If you added an object to your report from the repository and you want to disconnect it from the repository so you cannot receive future updates of that object, right-click the object and choose Disconnect From Repository.

To update your report with changes that are made to the repository, choose File ➣ Options, choose the Reporting tab, and select Update Connected Repository Objects When Loading Reports to refresh the repository objects when the report is loaded (see Figure 16.7). If the database is secure, the user will be prompted for a user ID and password.

FIGURE 16.7

Updating repository objects

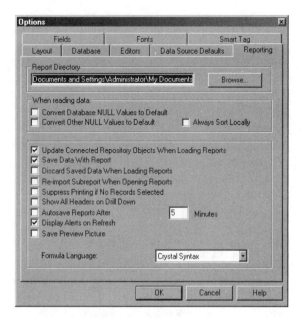

Exporting Your Report to Different Formats

A very powerful feature of Crystal Reports is the ability to export the report to various formats or destinations. That means that you can use Crystal Reports to create a report but your end user does not need to have a copy of Crystal to view your report. The pros and cons of this deployment are shown below:

Pros	Cons
Crystal Reports is not required for end user.	User cannot refresh report data.
End user can use office tools such as Excel, Word, or generic applications to view reports. Refer to export list below.	User can change exported data.
Original report can't be modified.	Original report can't be modified.
Report can be exported to HTML and viewed through a web browser.	

To export a report, select File ➤ Export (see Figure 16.8). Crystal supports all the export formats in the following list and the destinations shown in Table 16.2:

TABLE 16.2: EXPORT FORMATS

EXPORT FORMAT	COMMENTS
Acrobat PDF	Very accurate rendition of the original report. User will require Adobe Acrobat Reader to view reports. You can download the reader at www.adobe.com.
Crystal Report	Exports the report in version 9 format, but does not save it in a previous version. This is the same as saving the report.
HTML 3.2	Some formatting is lost; this HTML format is compatible with most browsers.
HTML 4.0	Retains more report formatting but will not support all browsers. User will require at minimum a version 4 compatible browser to view report.
MS Excel 97–2000	Graphics and report data are exported; the Excel file will closely resemble your report.
MS Excel 97–2000 Data Only	Exports data only. This format is good if you want to do further Excel calculations on the data.
MS Word	Exports report data and graphics. The Word document will closely resemble the report.
ODBC	Enters the data of your report to a specified table in an ODBC data source. The tables must be configured so column names and field names in the report match.
Record Style (Columns, no Spaces)	Your report data is export-to-text format, with no spaces between fields.
Record Style (Columns with Spaces)	Same as Record Style (Columns, no Spaces), except a single space is included between fields.
Report Definition	Creates a report of the formulas, formatting, and settings of a Crystal Report. The exported text file is intended to be read by the developer of the report for an overview of the report setup. This is similar to a source code listing of a computer program.
Rich Text Format (RTF)	Saves data and graphics of a Report. Similar to Word, except other word processors can read an RTF file.
Separated Values (CSV)	Similar to Record Style, except fields are separated by commas.
Tab-Separated Text	Similar to Separated values (CSV), except values are separated by tabs.
Text	Converted to straight text with no formatting.
XML	Converted to an XML file structure.

Some of the export formats, such as PDF, Word, or Excel, will be very close to the Crystal Report formatting. Other export formats will lose some formatting. Limitations you may encounter include the following:

◆ Graphics may not export.

◆ The group tree may not export.

◆ Sub-reports may not export as expected.

◆ Hyperlinks in the report many not work.

Make sure you verify your exported report. If you plan to deploy your report by exporting it, it is a good idea to know the limitations of the export format and design your report with those limitations in mind. Table 16.3 shows the format and the export destination.

FIGURE 16.8

Export options

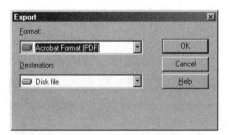

Some of the reporting export formats are not meant for human consumption, such as ODBC, Tab Separated, XML, and Record Style and Separated Values. These formats are designed so another computer program can read your Crystal Report as input for its data processing. In this case, you are using Crystal Report as data-conversion utility.

TABLE 16.3: SUPPORTED DESTINATIONS

FORMAT	EXPORT DESTINATION
Application	Crystal will open the application and the application will contain the exported report in the application's native data format. For example, if you choose MS Word, the report will be exported to Word format and Word will open automatically.
Disk File	File on the hard drive.
Exchange Folder	Microsoft Exchange folder.
Lotus Domino	Notes Database.
Lotus Domino Mail	Notes Mail.
MAPI (Messaging Application Program Interface)	Exports the report to a mail message as an attachment. Your e-mail program will open and a message will contain the attached exported file.

Exporting to HTML

Exporting the report to HTML format provides a very simple way to deploy the report to your end users. All the end users require is a web browser, such as Internet Explorer or Netscape Navigator, installed on their computer. It also provides an easy way to publish your reports to the Internet or an intranet.

Crystal Reports supports two HTML formats, HTML 3.2 and HTML 4. HTML 3.2 is best used when your users have older browsers, such as Netscape 3 or Internet Explorer 3, installed. It is also advantageous when you have a large user community and you are not sure which version of the browser they have. Using HTML version 3.2 guarantees that your report will be viewable with most browsers. The downside to using version HTML 3.2 is that some report formatting is lost in the export. HTML version 4.0 does a better job of maintaining the original report format, but older browsers do not recognize HTML 4. See Figure 16.9 and Figure 16.10, which compare the same report exported to HTML 3.2 and HTML 4.

TIP *Most computers now have version 5 or 6 of Netscape or Internet Explorer installed. We tend to think that in most cases you should be fine with HTML 4.*

FIGURE 16.9

Export HTML version 3.2

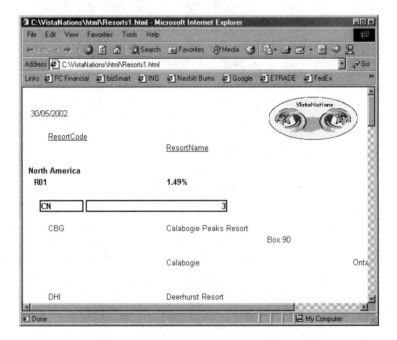

FIGURE 16.10

Export HTML
version 4

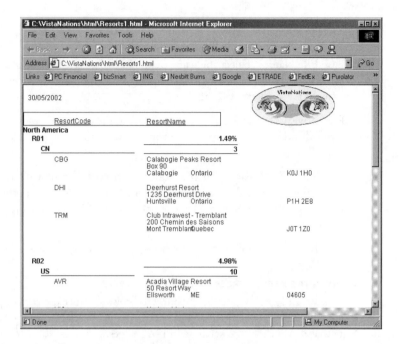

Choose HTML 4 or HTML 3.2 in the Export dialog, shown previously in Figure 16.8, and click OK. The Select Export File dialog is displayed (see Figure 16.11). In this dialog, you can configure the HTML export files as described below.

FIGURE 16.11

Export HTML
Version 4

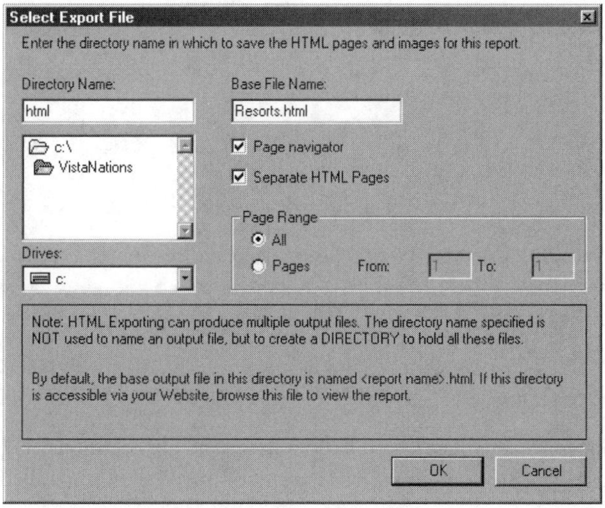

Directory Name The export converts your report to multiple HTML files. Choose a name for the directory, and select the drive and directory where you want this directory to be created.

Base File Name Select the name of the HTML file to export to. If you check the Separate HTML Pages option, Crystal will append a page number to the end of each filename, such as `Resorts1.html`, `Resorts2.html`, etc.

Page Navigator This option creates a link at the bottom of each report page so users can navigate forward and backward through the pages. This option is applicable only if you choose Separate HTML Pages.

Separate HTML Pages If this option is selected, Crystal will create a separate HTML file for each report page. If the report is small, one HTML file is fine; otherwise, choose separate pages. If the report is large and you choose one HTML file, then the browser must download the entire report.

Page Range Your choice determines whether to export the whole report or just a page range.

VIEWING THE REPORT FROM A NETWORKED DRIVE

To view your HTML report, start your web browser, either Internet Explorer or Netscape Navigator, and in the Address line type the path and report name selected in the Select Export File dialog box. Note that if you choose to separate HTML pages, you must add "1" to the report name. Your report will be displayed in the browser window (see the address bar in Figure 16.10, shown previously).

Using this technique you can copy the HTML files to a shared network drive to easily deploy your report. Instead of entering the C: drive on the Address line, you would replace it with the drive letter assigned to your shared network drive, such as P:.

PUBLISHING TO A WEB SERVER

A web server is a file server that publishes HTML files. You can think of a web server as a globally accessible shared networked drive.

NOTE   A web server can do more than publish web pages. However, its basic functionality is to serve up HTML files.

A web server consists of two directory types:

Virtual Directory A virtual directory is a directory that is accessible by users through a web browser. To access this directory, users type a web address such as `HTTP://ServerName/Directory/HTMLFileName.html`. The web address is broken down as follows:

◆ `HTTP://` is the protocol used to communicate to the web server. HTTP is a standard protocol to request web pages.

◆ `ServerName` is the name of the web server. On the Internet this usually starts with www. It can also be a private web server in your company; then it is called an intranet web server.

◆ `Directory` is the name of the directory that contains the file you are requesting.

◆ `HTMLFileName.html` is the name of the report (HTML file) you are requesting.

Physical Directory   The physical directory is the actual directory on the computer where the web server is running, where the web server can find the requested HTML file. When a request is made to a web server, such as `HTTP://ServerName/Directory/HTMLFileName.html`, the web server translates this directory to a physical directory.

In the case of Internet Information Server (IIS), Microsoft's web server, the default physical directory is `C:\inetpub\wwwroot`. Any directories or files off `C:\inetpub\wwwroot` would be accessible by a web browser.

In our example, the requested file `HTTP://ServerName/Directory/HTMLFileName.html` would be located at `C:\inetpub\wwwroot\Directory\HtmlFileName.HTML`.

To publish our report to Microsoft's IIS web server, we created a directory named `VistaReports` off the web server's main directory, `C:\inetpub\wwwroot\VistaReports`. Then we copied all the exported files to the new directory. You can now access the report via a web server, as shown in Figure 16.12. Notice the address line in the browser.

FIGURE 16.12

Accessing a report on a web server

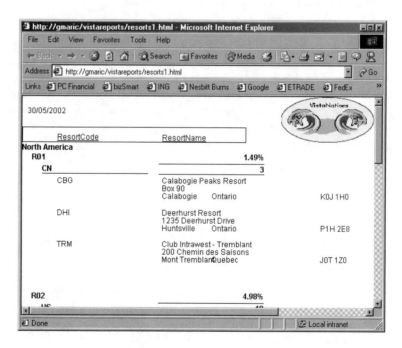

NOTE   *We covered one way to publish your report to a web server, using Microsoft's IIS. However, HTML files can be published to various web servers. Each web server is slightly different, but the principles discussed here are the same. See your network or web administrator to learn which web server your company is using and what procedure to use to publish the reports (HTML files).*

You might be wondering when you would publish a report using the hard drive technique versus using the web server. Use the hard drive if all your users are internal to your company and all of them have access to the same shared network drive. If they cannot access the same network drive, then you will need to publish to a web server. Publishing your report to a shared hard drive also removes you from the complexity of web servers.

Compiled Reports

Compiled reports are reports that are compiled into an executable program that can be installed on the end user's computer. The end user does not need a copy of Crystal Reports to view the report and will be able to view, refresh, and schedule running the report on a desktop.

Crystal Reports contains a Distribution Expert that guides you through the steps to create a setup package for the end user's computer. The Compiled Report utility and Crystal Report Distribution Expert are part of Crystal Reports 7. In version 8 and 8.5 it is a separate add-on utility that you need to download from the Crystal Decision website.

WARNING   *As of this writing, the compiled deployment utility is not available for Crystal Reports 9, and the version 8 utility does not work with Crystal 9. Crystal Decisions indicated to the Crystal Decisions User Group of North America,* http://www.cdugna.org, *that they will make compiled reports available for version 9. Crystal Decisions have also indicated that their preferred choice for deployment is web based using the Report Application Server or Crystal Enterprise, and as a result we don't expect functionality to be added when the compiled report utility for Crystal Reports 9 is released. If you have version 7 or 8 of Crystal Reports, you can follow our examples. If you have version 9 this will give you an overview of the capabilities of the compiled report utility so you can decide if you would like to wait for it to be released or use one of the alternative deployment techniques discussed.*

TIP   *The Crystal 8 compiled distribution tool,* SCR8_distr_expert.exe, *can be downloaded from* http://support.crystaldecisions.com/updates. *Also, keep an eye on this Internet support database for the version 9 compiled deployment tool.*

The pros and cons of this type of deployment are shown below:

Pros	Cons
Easy to deploy.	Less functionality than Crystal Enterprise.
Free distribution of report.	Requires files to be installed on the end user's computer.
Users cannot change report.	Requires a Crystal Developers license to compile reports.

The remaining chapters in Part 4, "Application Development with Crystal Reports," reveal how you can create a customized application to deploy Crystal Reports using VB 6 or VB.NET. You can duplicate the compiled report's functionality and add your own functionality. Creating and compiling a report using the Crystal Reports compiled report utility is a multistep process:

1. Download and install the Compiled Report utility if you're using Crystal Reports 8 or greater.

2. Compile the report.

3. Create a setup program to install on the end user's computer.

4. Install the Compiled Report package on the end user's computer.

We expect the functionality of version 9.0 to be identical because Crystal Decisions has stated that they want customers to migrate to Crystal Enterprise and their web-based technology. However, they don't want to abandon customers that still want to use this older technology. They will continue to support them.

Installing the Compiled Reports Utility

Once you download `scr8_distr_expert.exe`, copy it to a directory on your computer and double-click it. `Scr8_distr_expert` is a self-extracting zip file, and it will extract itself into three files:

◆ `Compiles_reports.pdf`: contains program documentation.

◆ `Rdwiz.exe`: contains the setup program.

◆ `Readme.txt`: contains licensing information and indicates what versions of Crystal this utility is for.

NOTE   *Crystal Licensing requires that you have the Developer Edition to use Compiled Report utility.*

Double-click the `rdwiz` file to start the installation process. When the installation is done, start Crystal Reports and click the Report menu. Notice that Compile Report and Report Distribution Expert have been added to the bottom of the menu (see Figure 16.13).

FIGURE 16.13

New items added to the Report menu

Compiling a Report

Once your report is complete and you are ready to give the report to the end users, save the report and choose Reports ➢ Compile Report. You will see the Compile Report dialog, as shown in Figure 16.14.

FIGURE 16.14

Compile Report
dialog

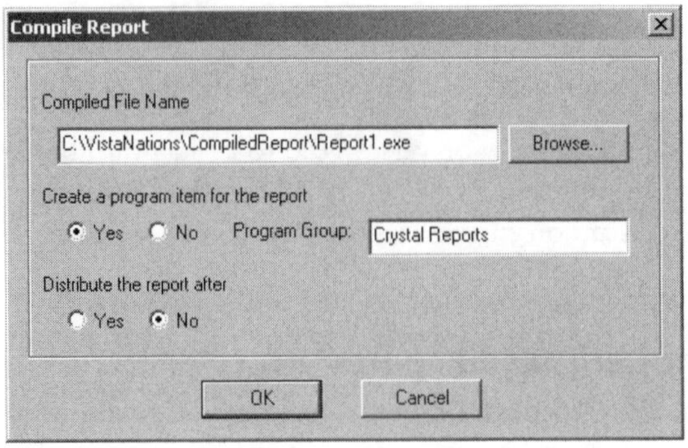

In the Compiled File Name text box, specify the directory and report name for the compiled report. Crystal reports will provide a default filename the same as the report name.

TIP   *To avoid confusion, we recommend that you keep the compiled filename the same as the report name.*

After this step is finished, Crystal will create three filenames in the directory you specified:

◆ RPT file: report file

◆ EXE file: program to run and view the report

◆ CRF file: configuration file required by the EXE file

It is important that all three files have the same name, and the name cannot be `setup.exe`.

To determine whether a program group will be created off the Start menu, choose one of the Create A Program Item For The Report options. If you choose Yes, an icon link to your compiled report will be placed in the program group specified. If a program group does not exist, it will be created. If the program group does exist, an icon link will be added to the program group.

TIP   *If you choose not to create a program link, then you can create a shortcut using Windows.*

Choose Yes under Distribute The Report After to run the Distribution Expert, which will build the necessary setup files to install the compiled report on the end user's computer. If you choose No, you can run the Distribution Expert at a later time by choosing Report ➤ Report Distribution Expert.

Distribution Expert

The Distribution Expert creates the `Setup.exe` program and installs all the required files to view and run Crystal Reports on the end user's computer.

After you have compiled the report, the Distribution Expert will start automatically if you selected Yes in the Distribute The Report After options in the Compile Report dialog (see Figure 16.14). Otherwise, you can start the Distribution Expert by choosing Report ➤ Report Distribution Expert.

The Distribution Expert consists of four tabs that must be completed before the distribution files are created. These tabs are detailed in the following sections.

1. OPTIONS

The Reports field contains a list of reports that will be added into this distribution (see Figure 16.15). Click the Add button to add other reports to this distribution if you are going to deploy multiple reports.

FIGURE 16.15

Report Distribution
Expert - Options

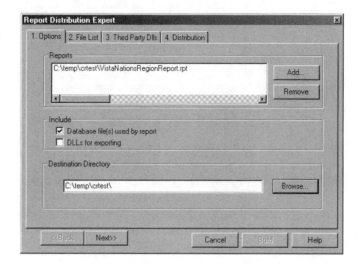

NOTE   *Make sure each report is compiled before adding it to the Reports list.*

Select a destination directory where the setup programs and reports will be placed.

If this is the first time you are installing a compiled report on the end user's computer, we recommend selecting both Include Database Files(s) Used By Report and DLLs For Exporting. These options will ensure that the end user has all the necessary files to run the report.

NOTE   *Crystal Reports requires many support programs in order to run and view reports. Those programs are called Dynamically Linked Libraries (DLLs). They are automatically installed when you install Crystal Reports. However, because we want to view reports on a computer where Crystal Reports is not installed, we need to include them in our distribution. You will see a list of these files in the File List tab.*

WARNING   *Be careful about distributing third-party DLLs without first checking the license agreement with the vendor that created them. Crystal Decisions has a royalty-free license agreement.*

2. FILE LIST

The File List tab provides a list of all the files that will be included in your distribution, including the export DLLs and database files mentioned above (see Figure 16.16). In this screen you have the option of adding and removing any DLLs in your distribution.

FIGURE 16.16

Report Distribution
Expert - File List

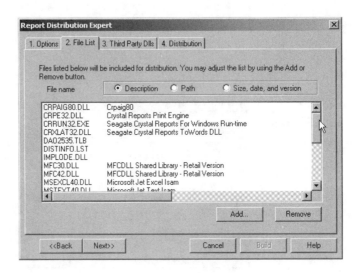

TIP   *This list can be very intimidating because you may not know which files to touch. We recommend leaving the files alone and clicking the Next button. Refer to the section below on testing the deployment for how to deal with these files if necessary.*

3. THIRD PARTY DLLS

This list is similar to the File List tab's list above, except that it is a list of required files that are not from Crystal Decisions but from other vendors (see Figure 16.17). These files can include files such as database drivers.

FIGURE 16.17

Report Distribution
Expert - Third
Party DLLs

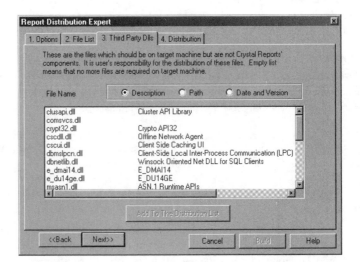

TIP   *Again we recommend leaving the files alone and clicking the Next button. Refer to the section below on how to test the deployment for how deal with these files if necessary.*

4. DISTRIBUTION

The Distribution tab is the final step in your distribution (see Figure 16.18). The Distribution Expert should display a screen saying it is ready to build the distribution program. At this point all you need to do is click the Build button, and the Distribution Expert will package up all the DLL, RPT, report EXE, and CRF files and create a `Setup.exe` file that you can run on the end user's computer.

FIGURE 16.18

Report Distribution
Expert - Distribution

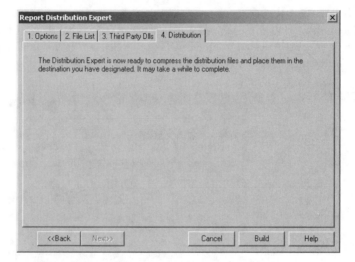

Installing the Compiled Report on the End User's Computer

At this point, the Crystal Decisions Distribution Expert has created an installation program called `Setup.exe` in the destination directory you specified in the Options tab above. This directory also contains all the DLLs and files that your report will require.

WARNING   *Before you roll out your newly created installation program to your entire organization, we suggest testing it on one user's computer to make sure everything works as expected.*

To install the compiled report on the end user's computer, run the `Setup.exe` program from the end user's computer. If your destination directory was on a network drive and your user also has access to this destination drive, then run the installation in the distribution directory from the end user's computer.

TIP   *If you have a CD burner, it might be easier to burn a CD with the contents of the distribution directory and run* `Setup.exe` *from the CD on the end user's computer. This will also provide a backup disk.*

The installation program is a standard Windows-type installation program. You will be asked to do the following:

◆ Specify the installation directory. The default directory is `C:\Program Files\Seagate Software\ Distributed Reports`. If this is okay, click Yes to continue; otherwise, choose an appropriate directory.

◆ Choose the program group that will be created off the Start menu for Windows. If the program group exists, the report will be added to it. Otherwise, the group will be created and the report added. The default program group name is Seagate Crystal Reports Distribution.

Running a Report

From the Start menu, select ➢ Programs ➢ Seagate Crystal Reports Distribution and select the name of the report you would like to view. The compiled report viewer allows you to view, export, or print your report immediately or at a scheduled time in the future (see Figure 16.19).

FIGURE 16.19

End-user report viewer

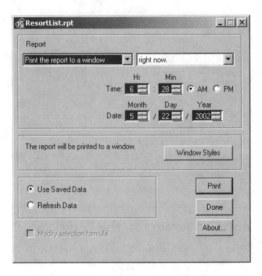

In the Report drop-down list, select where you would like the report to be displayed. You must choose from viewing the report in a window on your computer, exporting it to a different format, or exporting it to a printer. Depending on the output destination you choose, the button in the middle of the screen will change and allow you to format your destination:

◆ If you choose the Print The Report To A Window option, you will be able to customize the report view (see "The Report Viewer" section below).

◆ If you choose the Export The Report option, choose which format you want to export the report in and the destination. These are the same export options as discussed earlier in the chapter.

◆ If you choose the Print The Report To A Printer option, the report will be sent to a printer of your choice.

The unlabeled drop-down list beside the Report drop-down allows you to select when you would like to run the report. The default is Right Now. Click the Print button and the report will run right away.

Notice beside the Print button the Use Saved Data and Refresh Data buttons. If your report contains saved data, you will be able to view the saved data. The report will access the database source when you refresh to get the latest information.

SCHEDULING THE REPORT

By selecting Right Now in the drop-down box, you can see your options to run the report in the future. Crystal has created some standard future times, such as in one hour, at midnight, at two in the morning, etc. If none of these meets your requirements, you can choose At A Specific Time and enter the time and date when you want to run the report.

When you click the Print button, the report viewer will minimize and wait for the time indicated to run the report.

NOTE *Keep in mind that the report is running on the computer where the report viewer is installed, so the computer must remain on.*

CHANGING THE REPORT SELECTION CRITERIA

If your report contains selection criteria, you may choose Modify Selection Formula. The report viewer will display a Record Selection dialog (see Figure 16.20), allowing you to choose how you would like to filter the report.

FIGURE 16.20

Changing the
selection criteria

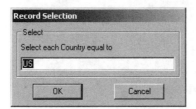

THE REPORT VIEWER

When you choose the Print The Report To A Window option, the report is displayed in a report viewer (see Figure 16.21). The report viewer is similar to the report viewer in Crystal Reports, but it does not allow you to change the report.

The toolbar at the top of the viewer allows you to navigate through the report, print the report, or export it to another format. You can customize the toolbar in the report viewer by clicking the Window Styles button to bring up the Window Style Options screen (see Figure 16.22). This will allow you to choose which viewer options you want to make available.

FIGURE 16.21

Report viewer

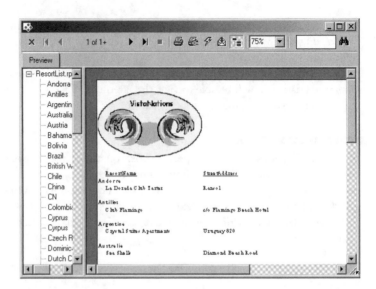

FIGURE 16.22

Report viewer
Window Style
Options screen

Testing and Troubleshooting the Installation

If you are deploying your report to many users, it is best to test your installation package on *one user's computer* until it works. If the installation package works on your computer, there is no guarantee it will work on the end user's computer. There are two main things that can go wrong:

Database connection   The connection information is contained in the report. When you move the report to the end user's computer, that computer must have the same access setup as the computer where the report was created.

If the report was created from a Microsoft Access database, the end user's computer must be able to access the Access database, and it must be in the same path as the computer where the report was created.

If the report was created from an ODBC database source, then the ODBC DSN must be configured the same way as the computer where the report was created

If you are using OLE/DB or native drivers to connect to the database, the user must have the same drivers installed on their computer. You may be able to deploy those by including them when compiling your report package. Or you might need to install them separately using the vendor's installation tool.

Missing DLL   If the report is using a DLL, it is easy to forget to include that DLL in the deployment package. Crystal Reports will provide a message saying that it is unable to find a required DLL. Re-create the deployment package including the missing DLL, and retry the deployment. You may need to do this a few times until it works.

Sometimes if the DLL is part of database connectivity, such as Oracle's SQL*Net, it is better to install the necessary database driver's DLLs, called *middleware*, from the vendor's CD and retry running your report.

We hate to be vague on the issue of testing and troubleshooting; however, it is very difficult to write about all the different problems that can happen. Unfortunately, it comes down to trial and error. That is why we emphasize testing the deployment on one end user's computer before deploying to your whole organization.

NOTE   *The grief involved in testing and debugging on each user's computer is one of the main drivers of Internet deployment. With Internet deployment, you only need to get the report to work on the web server, and all your users need is a web browser. However, this is not feasible for all users, so we still need to deal with installation issues.*

Summary

Once your report is developed, you still are not finished until the end users have the report. Crystal Reports offers many options to deploy the report. Before you can decide how to deploy the report, you need to analyze your end users' needs. Do they require real-time data from the database or will a static report be sufficient? Then you can decide whether you want to deploy the Crystal Report file, export the file to various formats, such as DOC, XLS, PDF, or HTML, place the report on the end user's computer, or have the end user get the report from a file or web server.

If you find that Crystal Reports does not offer you enough deployment options, Crystal Decisions also offers Crystal Enterprise and ePortfolio, which work with Crystal Reports to deploy the report. You can also write custom applications to deploy your report.

Once the end user has the report, you are finished.

Chapter 17

The Crystal Programming Forest

WELCOME TO THE FOREST! In this section we will be looking at Crystal Reports from a completely different point of view. So far we have been using Crystal Reports as an application to write reports. In some ways it is similar to Microsoft Word or Excel, standalone programs you use to build your documents or spreadsheets; in Crystal Reports, you build reports. Crystal Reports has another side to it; you can use Crystal Reports as a component in application development. For example, if you were building an application such as an airline travel system, you would need reporting as part of the application. Instead of doing all the report programming from scratch, you can use Crystal Reports to provide the reporting capabilities and embed Crystal Reports in your application.

> *Business Question: I want to add reports to my business application. How can Crystal Reports fit in?*

In this chapter you will get a bird's-eye view of the various development environments and options where Crystal Reports can be used. Crystal Reports has been around since 1992. Crystal Reports gained popularity in 1993 when it was bundled with Visual Basic, and since then programmers have used Crystal Reports in their applications. In the decade that Crystal has been around, the computer industry has gone through many changes, and Crystal Reports has followed along. In this chapter we will examine the various environments that Crystal Reports works in. This will help you understand how Crystal fits in and what its capabilities are and how you can use it in your environment. Often the number of choices is confusing because Crystal Reports supports many different environments. The following chapters will examine in detail how to program Crystal Reports in those environments.

Featured in this chapter:

- ◆ Exploring the various Crystal Reports development environments

- ◆ Seeing how Crystal Reports fits in with .NET development

- ◆ Using Crystal Reports in your web applications

- ◆ Discovering web services and how Crystal Reports fits in

- ◆ Looking at the skills required to develop in the various environments

Simple Application Example

If you have used Crystal Reports only as report writer, you might be wondering how Crystal Reports can be used with an application. Figures 17.1 and 17.2 display a Crystal Report in a reporting system. This system uses VistaNations travel reports that we created in previous chapters. The application groups management reports in an easy-to-use system where managers can choose the report they would like to see and click the Refresh button to view it. Notice in Figures 17.1 and 17.2 that users can choose to see All countries, North America, or Others. Behind the scenes, the programmer has written code to modify the Crystal Reports selection formula. The end user does not need to know how to use Crystal Reports or even what a selection formula is. The programmer can provide a simple-to-use interface.

The report in our example is displayed in a Windows Forms Viewer for the Windows application and a Web Forms Viewer for the browser application. The viewers are components that display Crystal Reports and are included with Crystal Reports Developer Edition. They can be programmed and controlled in the application as well as in the Crystal report itself.

FIGURE 17.1

A Windows application displaying a Crystal report

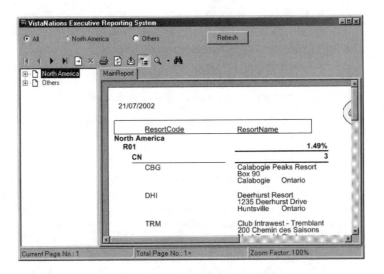

WARNING   *Before you can use Crystal Reports in your custom application, you must have the Developer or Advanced Edition of Crystal Reports. See the section "Licensing Issues" later in this chapter for more details.*

Crystal Reports has been providing report-writing capabilities to custom applications from companies like PeopleSoft, Great Plains Software, ACCPAC International, and over 150 other applications. The developers of these applications focus on the core business functionality of the application and let Crystal Reports focus on the details of the reports. You can use Crystal Reports for your custom applications in the same way as these commercial applications use it.

FIGURE 17.2

A web application displaying a Crystal report

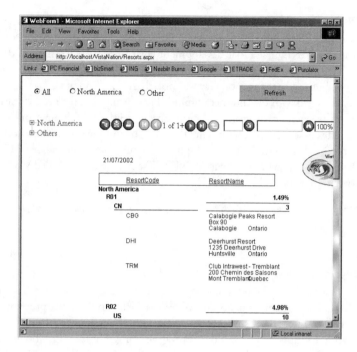

Using Crystal Reports in an Application

Crystal Reports exposes all report-writing functionality to a development language. Anything that you can do with Crystal Reports as an end user you can also do with a development language. In our example in Figures 17.1 and 17.2 we are modifying the selection criteria formula and refreshing the report from the database. You can add groups, modify graphics, etc., through program code, and your application provides a custom user interface to the Crystal functionality. For example, the user is able to change the selection criterion from All to North America and click the Refresh button. The code behind the buttons modifies the selection criteria in Crystal Reports and redisplays the report with the required data. This provides an easy-to-use interface instead of you having to teach all your end users how to write selection criteria in Crystal Reports.

Crystal Development Platforms

Crystal Reports supports the following development platforms: Windows, .NET, and Java.

WINDOWS

By *Windows* we mean an application or program that is installed on the user's (client's) computer and runs inside Microsoft Windows. Sometimes this is referred to as a *thick client* because code has to be installed on the end user's computer. Crystal Reports 9 supports two separate Windows development platforms: legacy Windows and .NET. From an end user's perspective there is no difference; the platforms start and run the application and it behaves like any other Windows application. However, from a developer's perspective they are completely different.

.NET

In spring 2002, Microsoft released a brand-new development platform called .NET (pronounced dot net). They recognized that development environments have changed drastically with the introduction of the Internet. Since 1995, Microsoft has added Internet functionality to development language tools, but Internet functionality was not always well integrated or easy to use because the tools were not designed with the Internet in mind. They recognized the need to clean the white board and redesign an entire environment from an Internet perspective. .NET Framework is that new environment. .NET includes new system components that run in Windows and Microsoft's IIS (Internet Information Server) web servers. A new development language has been created called C# (C Sharp), and Visual Basic has been rewritten to run in .NET. The new version is called VB.NET. Crystal Reports 9 was also written to work in the new .NET environment.

NOTE   *Crystal Report is the only third-party product to be bundled with Microsoft's Visual Studio .NET development environment.*

Legacy Windows

We refer to legacy Windows as any development environment that uses Windows COM (Component Object Model) components and Windows APIs (applications programming interfaces) instead of the .NET Framework. Visual Basic 6 and C++ fall into the legacy category. Crystal Reports 9 is also written to support a COM-based programming interface for VB6 and C++ and any language that uses COM. Both development environments of Crystal Reports 9, .NET and legacy Windows development, offer similar functionality but they run on different platforms.

Over the years Crystal Reports has evolved along with Visual Basic, and a number of programming interfaces have been developed with the evolving technologies. For legacy Windows development as of version 9 of Crystal Reports, the only supported development environment is the Report Designer Component (RDC) introduced in version 8 of Crystal Reports. The RDC is a COM-based interface that replaces all the development environments previously introduced. Chapter 19 is devoted to the RDC. Table 17.1 lists the retired development environments.

TABLE 17.1: RETIRED WINDOWS DEVELOPMENT APIS

API	COMMENTS
Report Engine API	This was called the CRPE API (Crystal Reports Programming Engine API (aka Creepy). It is a Windows DLL-based programming interface. Your program must call DLL subroutines and functions. These are low-level C++ functions that are not easy to work with. The CRPE API is very powerful but also very difficult to use. Initially this was the only way to manage Crystal Reports programmatically.
Report Engine Automation Server	Microsoft developed the COM standard and Crystal Decisions followed with the Report Engine Automation Server. This was an object-oriented programming approach to programming Crystal Reports. It has not been upgraded to version 8 of Crystal Reports.

Continued on next page

TABLE 17.1: RETIRED WINDOWS DEVELOPMENT APIS *(continued)*

API	COMMENTS
ActiveX control	Until the RDC came out, this was the easiest way to manage Crystal Reports in your application. A Visual Basic program would add the Crystal Reports ActiveX control to the VB toolbar and then add it to the form. By setting a few properties, you could easily display Crystal Reports. Because of its simplicity, there was limited functionality.
Design Time Control for Microsoft Visual Interdev	The Design Time Control simplified adding a report to an ASP page in Visual Interdev. (We cover how to manually add a report to an ASP web page in Chapter 20.)
RDC Runtime C Headers	No longer supported as of Crystal Reports 9

WEB-BASED APPLICATIONS

A web application is an application that the end user accesses via a web browser, such as Internet Explorer or Netscape Navigator. This is sometimes called a *thin client application* because no software, or very little software, is installed on the client's computer. Crystal Decisions has two products that can be used in web application development: Crystal Reports and Crystal Enterprise.

Crystal Enterprise is a web-based application that houses and runs Crystal Reports on a web server. Chapter 23 discusses Crystal Enterprise. With Crystal Reports 8.5, Crystal Decisions shipped the standard version of Crystal Enterprise. With version 9 of Crystal Reports, Crystal Decisions ships the Report Application Server (RAS), which is an entry-level version of Crystal Enterprise. You can purchase the standard or professional version for Crystal Enterprise. The RAS server supports a Microsoft and Java development Environment. Chapter 24 discusses programming RAS.

TIP   The Professional, Developer, and Advanced editions of Crystal Reports received the Report Application Server. Refer to Appendix A for the breakdown of versions.

Also, with the release of .NET, Microsoft web applications development has two separate environments: legacy Active Server Pages (ASP) and ASP.NET. Crystal Reports 9 supports both environments.

Are you confused yet? Table 17.2 summarizes the development environments supported.

TABLE 17.2: APPLICATION DEVELOPMENT CHOICES

MICROSOFT ENVIRONMENT AND CRYSTAL APIS	COMMENTS
RDC	Can be used in ASP or legacy Windows applications
RAS	Used for Web applications and provides an easy transition to Crystal Enterprise Standard and Professional
.NET	Fully integrated with ASP.NET and Windows applications

Continued on next page

TABLE 17.2: APPLICATION DEVELOPMENT CHOICES *(continued)*	
JAVA ENVIRONMENT	**COMMENTS**
RAS	Used for Web applications and for web deployment of reports. RAS also provides an easy transition to Crystal Enterprise Standard and Professional editions.

NOTE *It will be interesting to see how .NET evolves over the next decade and whether we will have a long list of technologies to choose from as we do with legacy Windows development or whether the design is good enough to handle a decade of computer changes. Only time will tell. Our bigger concerns now are migration issues from legacy Windows to .NET.*

XML WEB SERVICES

Large-scale, or enterprise, applications have been developed with a three-tier systems development model for years. In that model the system is separated into three parts representing three logical or physical tiers: the client graphical user interface, the business logic and functions, and the database access. The advantages of this design are that the client's graphical user interface can change from a Windows application to a web application or support both Windows and web applications, and there is only one set of business rules on the second tier. Changes in the business tier are automatically reflected in all clients.

The disadvantage to this type of model (apart from being complicated to design) is that the client and business services communicate using proprietary protocols. The two main protocols in the industry are Microsoft's DCOM (Distributed Component Object Model), used in Microsoft's development, and CORBA (Common Object Request Broker Architecture), used in Java development. They do not communicate with each other.

XML web services are the business components in the three-tier application model. They can be accessed via a newly developed Internet protocol, SOAP (Simple Object Access Protocol), that the industry has agreed upon. Microsoft and Java can share components that are written as XML web services. An example of a web service might be where a bank creates a web service program that accepts a credit card number and the amount of the purchase. An application written by a programmer, which follows web services standards, then can call the web service and tell the bank's web service the credit card number and the amount of the purchase. The web service then tells the client program whether the credit card transaction is accepted or declined. Because the web service is using industry standards, it does not matter whether the client program is a Microsoft program or a Java program. A web service is a way of publishing functionality on the Web and letting any client access the functionality no matter which language it is written in.

Crystal Decisions has embraced the web service concept for Crystal Reports. Crystal Reports can be published on the Web as a web service, and any application on the Internet that understands web services can retrieve your report and display it, as shown in Figure 17.3. (Of course, you can add security to prevent just anyone from accessing your report.)

FIGURE 17.3

A web service

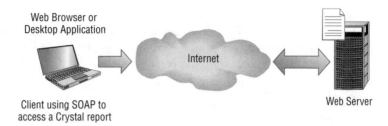

In the following chapters we will see how to implement all these types of applications.

.NET OR VB6?

It is best to consult with your Information Technology department to determine when they are planning to move to .NET. Upgrading an existing VB6 application that uses Crystal Reports 8.*x* RDC's (Report Designer Component) Report designer is not possible because the .NET environment does not support Designers from VB6. Your only option is to rewrite the application for .NET or continue to run the application in VB6. Crystal Reports 9 has components that will work in both environments.

If you access Crystal Reports via RDC's automation server (see Chapter 19 for a complete list of components included with the RDC) and did not use the Report designer, or used the Report Engine API or the ActiveX control, upgrading would be possible. However, we would not recommend it, because the .NET upgrade wizard adds a layer of compatibility code for .NET so it works with legacy components, and this code is not always efficient.

NOTE   Microsoft has recognized that legacy Windows will not go away for a long time because of the huge number of systems in use. They have pledged to support both .NET and COM environments for many years, and Crystal Decisions will support both also.

Development Languages

Because Crystal Reports supports both legacy Windows and .NET, we need to look at language options in both environments. (Who said it was going be easy?)

LEGACY DEVELOPMENT

Crystal Reports' developer components work with Windows development languages such as Visual Basic, C++, and Inprise Delphi. Basically any language that can use a Windows COM component should be able to work with Crystal Reports. In ASP applications you can use VBScript, JavaScript, or JScript.

.NET

The .NET environment was written to be language neutral—you can use any language in the .NET environment. VB.NET and C# are the two main choices. However, other languages are being written for the .NET environment.

JAVA

Crystal also supports Java for the Crystal Report Viewer Java Bean (or Report Viewer Bean). The Java report viewer can be added to an application in any development environment that supports Java version 1.1. Java is also used for the Remote Application Server (RAS).

OUR CHOICE

The most popular development language for Crystal Reports is Visual Basic in legacy applications and VBScript for ASP applications. We are going to use Visual Basic, VBScript, and Visual Basic.NET for our examples in this book.

Licensing Issues

With version 9 of Crystal Reports, Crystal Decisions has introduced two developer licenses: the Developer and Advanced Developer licenses. Licensing has also been broken down depending on which platform the application is running on.

ENVIRONMENT	LICENSE	COMMENT
Windows Applications (.NET and Legacy)	Developer	If you use RDC in your Windows application to display reports, change selection criteria, or modify graphics, you are free to compile Crystal Reports in your application and distribute the application royalty free.
	Advanced	If you are using the RDC to create reports, then you will need to purchase the report creation API license from Crystal Decisions before you deploy your applications.
RDC and .NET	Developer	Can only create a single instance of each component on a single server.
RAS		Intended for testing and development only. Report requests in excess of five simultaneous requests are denied.
RAS	Advanced	Excess requests are queued; can upgrade to multiprocessor or Crystal enterprise for larger user base.

NOTE *For the complete details on licensing, refer to* `license.chm` *in* `C:\Program Files\Crystal Decisions\ Crystal Reports 9\Developer Files\Help\en` *(this is the standard directory; your directory might be different). Refer to "Runtime File Use Restrictions" for a complete list of functions that require the Report Creation License.*

Development Skills Summary

Tables 17.2, 17.3, 17.4, 17.5, 17.6, and 17.7 summarize the technical skills that are required to build Windows or web applications with Crystal Reports and RAS. We cannot possibly teach these technologies in this book. We are summarizing the technologies to help you understand what you need to learn in order to use Crystal Reports to its maximum potential in your applications.

TABLE 17.2: WINDOWS DEVELOPMENT REQUIREMENTS

WINDOWS DEVELOPMENT	COMMENTS
Visual Basic, C++, or Delphi	Visual Basic is the most popular language used to develop Crystal Reports.
Database (SQL, stored procedures)	A good understanding of databases and SQL is necessary. Knowing how to write and use stored procedures is a benefit and will improve the performance of your reports.
ADO (ActiveX Data Objects)	If you are developing reports in a Microsoft environment, understanding ADO will be beneficial because Crystal Reports can report from ADO datasets.

TABLE 17.3: ASP DEVELOPMENT REQUIREMENTS

ASP DEVELOPMENT	COMMENTS
VBScript or JavaScript	ASP Consists of six objects that reside on Microsoft's IIS web server. Dynamic web pages can be programmed using the ASP objects with VBScript or JavaScript. If you are familiar with VB, VBScript will be very easy to understand. If you know JavaScript, there is no need to learn VBScript, since you can use JavaScript to control the ASP objects.
Database (SQL, stored procedures)	See Windows Development above.
ADO	See Windows Development above.
HTML	A good understanding of HTML is required to build web pages.
Internet Information Server (IIS) basic administration	A basic understanding of security and physical and logical directories on IIS is required.

TABLE 17.4: .NET WINDOWS DEVELOPMENT REQUIREMENTS

.NET WINDOWS DEVELOPMENT	COMMENTS
Visual Basic .NET, C#, or any .NET language	VB.NET might be the most popular language for .NET, but C# is the next most popular. You can use any .NET language. If you have VB6 experience, you will find that the VB in VB.NET is completely different. VB6 and VB.NET share similar syntax and the name only; the rest is completely different!
Database (SQL, stored procedures)	See Windows Development above.
ADO	See Windows Development above.

Continued on next page

TABLE 17.4: .NET Windows Development Requirements *(continued)*

.NET Windows Development	Comments
ADO .NET	ADO was designed to be used in a client/server connected environment where the client and the server are always talking to each other. ADO.NET was designed for an Internet disconnected environment. ADO.NET is not a replacement for ADO. Use ADO.NET if your application will work with disconnected record sets.
.NET Framework	.NET Framework is a replacement for all Windows system DLLs. It is important that you understand this framework to be able to program in a .NET language.

TABLE 17.5: .NET Windows Web Development Requirements

.NET Windows Web Development	Comments
Visual Basic, C#, or any .NET language	See .NET Windows Development above.
Database (SQL, stored procedures)	See Windows Development above.
ADO	See Windows Development above.
ADO.NET	See .NET Development above.
.NET Framework	See .NET Development above.
HTML	See ASP Development above.
JavaScript	JavaScript is important in .NET if you are planning to write code that will execute on the client's browser. If your application will perform only server-side processing, then you can use any .NET language.

TABLE 17.6: XML Web Services Development Requirements

XML Web Services Development	Comments
Visual Basic, C#, or any .NET language	See .NET Windows Development above.
XML	XML is a large set of technologies. From a web services point of view, it is important that you understand the structure of an XML file (document), WSDL (Web Services Description Language), and SOAP (Simple Object Access Protocol).

TABLE 17.7: JAVA WEB DEVELOPMENT

JAVA WEB DEVELOPMENT	COMMENTS
Java and Object Oriented Technology	Understanding of the Java language and OO concepts is mandatory.
Database (SQL, stored procedures)	See Windows Development above.
HTML	See .NET development above.
Web Server	Understand how to configure a web server.
Unix or Linux	A good understanding of the Unix or Linux operations systems is mandatory.

Summary

Crystal Reports has a programming interface that allows developers to control Crystal Reports from code. The interface provides all the functionality of the end-user tool but allows a programmer to create a custom application and embed Crystal Reports in the application. This is very powerful because it allows the developer to focus on the functionality of the application and not on the details of writing the report.

Version 9 of Crystal Reports supports two very different development environments: legacy Microsoft COM-based tools, such as Visual Basic 6, Delphi, and C++, and the .NET development environment. Crystal Reports also includes the RAS Server, which provides entry-level Crystal Enterprise services. RAS can run in a Microsoft or Unix environment.

Upgrading a legacy VB application to .NET will only work if you did not use the RDC's Report Designer; otherwise, Microsoft .NET upgrade wizard will upgrade your code, but your code is not guaranteed to work efficiently or upgrade smoothly. We recommend not upgrading. Microsoft and Crystal Decisions will support both environments for years to come. .NET has cleaned up the development environment considerably, but the changes are great and it will take time to get used to them.

Now that we can see the programming forest from the trees, let's begin examining each area in detail in the following chapters.

Chapter 18

The Object-Oriented Primer

CRYSTAL REPORTS IS A very powerful report-development tool. However, its power does not end as a stand-alone report writer. You can use Crystal Reports with a custom application or a web-based application to provide its report-writing power to the application.

Think of the tools in your garage. Each tool, such as hammer or screwdriver, can be used for a certain task, but on its own each is limited. Together the tools can be used to build houses or factories. Crystal Reports is like a toolbox with all the individual tools working together: a tool that connects to databases, a tool that formats sections, a tool that totals and subtotals your report, and a tool that creates graphics. Crystal Reports uses these tools to create the Crystal Report Writer.

Through program code we can access these Crystal Report tools so we can use them in our custom application. These tools are hidden away as objects. To make use of these objects, you will need to know the concepts of object-oriented programming (OOP).

> *Business Question: I need to use Crystal Reports inside a custom application but I don't understand object-oriented concepts, and all the documentation and sample code seem to be object-oriented.*

If you are familiar with OOP concepts, you can skip this chapter and move to the other chapters in this section. If you are not familiar with OOP concepts, this chapter will provide you the foundation you will need to understand OOP concepts so you can use Crystal's objects in your applications. We will start by discussing programming concepts and show how they evolved to OOP concepts, and then we'll show how to apply those concepts to Crystal Reports.

In this chapter, we will examine the following topics:

- ◆ Explore the evolution of creating reusable programs
- ◆ Explore a simplified object model
- ◆ Differentiate among methods, properties, and events
- ◆ Connect object-oriented Programming to Crystal Reports
- ◆ Introduce Crystal Decisions' object models

What Are Objects?

Objects are reusable and shareable programs. Objects are frequently described in abstract terms as entities that have methods, properties, and behaviors. These abstract concepts are difficult to grasp when learning to use objects and dealing with object-oriented programming. Often these abstract concepts are confusing to beginners learning OOP.

Objects contain code and data, the same stuff we use in every formula or program we have ever written. We are going to look at objects through their code and data. We will start with a simple stand-alone program and move to the evolution of objects. Once you understand the mechanics of objects, we can then look at them from a more abstract point of view and define some of the confusing OO terminology.

NOTE   *Entire books have been written about object-oriented programming. The purpose of this chapter is to give you as much information as you need, as quickly as possible, so you can gain the necessary understanding of OOP concepts and then return to the task of using Crystal Reports. We have kept the examples and details as simple so you can concentrate on concepts and not get bogged down in details.*

NOTE   *All or most of Crystal Reports is written in C++, an OOP language. The developers often create their own documentation. If you understand their lingo, you can understand what they are trying to say.*

A Stand-alone Program

When the first computer programs were written, whether on punch cards or old green 3270 monitors or formulas in Crystal Reports, the programs stood alone. They usually read some data, processed the data, saved the data, and maybe printed a report about the data. Listing 18.1 is an example of a simple stand-alone program that adds interest to money borrowed.

LISTING 18.1: STAND-ALONE PROGRAM

```
Dim BorrowAmount As Number
Dim InterestRate As Number
Dim InterestAmount As Number
Dim Total As Number

BorrowAmount = {Customers.BorrowAmount}
InterestRate = {Rates.Interest}
InterestAmount = BorrowAmount * (InterestRate /100 )
Total = BorrowAmount + InterestAmount

Formula = Total
```

NOTE   *The above program is written in Crystal Basic syntax so that you would be familiar with the syntax. However, this program can be written in any language and compiled to run on the computer. This sample is not meant to be compiled; it is simply meant for illustration purposes.*

The program reads the amount borrowed from the Customers table and the interest rate from the Rates table. It stores that information in two variables, *BorrowAmount* and *InterestRate*. It then calculates the interest amount and stores it in the *InterestAmount* variable, and finally it adds the original borrowed amount and calculated interest amount to calculate the total amount. The total amount is the result of the formula.

Listing 18.1 can also be broken down conceptually into two categories:

Data   Variables and data used in the program:

```
Dim BorrowAmount As Number
Dim InterestRate As Number
Dim InterestAmount As Number
Dim Total As Number
```

Code (logic)   Work that the program does using the data:

```
BorrowAmount = {Customers.BorrowAmount}
InterestRate = {Rates.Interest}
InterestAmount = BorrowAmount * (InterestRate /100 )
Total = BorrowAmount + InterestAmount
```

This is a stand-alone program because it does not depend on any other program to do its work. Everything it needs, the data and code, is self-contained.

NOTE   *We've kept the program very simple to illustrate the concepts. In reality, the data and logic sections could be very large and contain thousands of lines of code.*

RUNNING THE PROGRAM

Before this program can be run, it must be compiled to instructions that the computer will understand. The program shown in Listing 18.1 is called *source code*, and both a programmer and the compiler can understand it. A *compiler* is a computer program that takes the code and compiles it to machine instructions that a computer can understand. The output from the compiler is an *executable program*, a file with an .exe extension. Figure 18.1 illustrates this concept.

FIGURE 18.1

Compiling the program

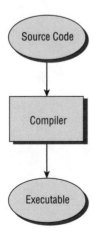

From a reusability point of view, this program is not very flexible. The code section cannot be shared with another program. For example, if another program needed to calculate interest, then that program would need to contain the same logic again. This is an expensive proposition, especially if the logic is complicated because the same logic would need to be rewritten in that program. It also leads to support problems because you must support the same logic in multiple places. If you were to find a bug in one place, you would have to fix it in many places.

Libraries

To get around this problem, computer scientists came up with the concept of *libraries*. Libraries contain sections of code that can be reused in multiple programs. Figure 18.2 illustrates this concept.

FIGURE 18.2

Reusing
program code

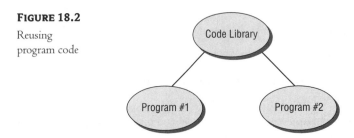

We can rewrite the original loan program to include code from a library and use the same library in a different program. Listing 18.2 shows the interest calculation library.

Listing 18.3 is the same program as Listing 18.1 except that the logic in the program is copied from an external library.

Listing 18.4 uses the same logic as used in Listing 18.3. It is reusing the Listing 18.2 logic. Notice also that Listing 18.4 adds 3% to the total after the total is calculated, showing that a program can use existing logic and add logic as required. This demonstrates how two programs can do different things but share the same core logic. This approach is much more flexible than the Listing 18.1 approach.

LISTING 18.2: INTEREST CALCULATION LIBRARY

```
BorrowAmount = {Customers.BorrowAmount}
InterestRate = {Rates.Interest}
InterestAmount = BorrowAmount * (InterestRate /100 )
Total = BorrowAmount + InterestAmount
```

LISTING 18.3: INTEREST PROGRAM ONE

```
Dim BorrowAmount As Number
Dim InterestRate As Number
Dim InterestAmount As Number
Dim Total As Number
```

```
<<Include Listing 18.2 Interest Calculation Library>>

Formula = Total
```

LISTING 18.4: INTEREST PROGRAM TWO

```
Dim BorrowAmount As Number
Dim InterestRate As Number
Dim InterestAmount As Number
Dim Total As Number

<<Include Listing 18.2 Interest Calculation Library>>
Total = Total * 1.03

Formula = Total
```

NOTE We are using Crystal Basic syntax for clarity. However, Crystal does not support including logic as described above. The purpose of this code is simply to illustrate a concept. This type of code is called pseudo code. We are using the pseudo code to illustrate code techniques that are used.

RUNNING THE PROGRAM

Just as with the stand-alone program, before we can run this program we must compile it. The compiler copies the library of code and uses it in the compilation. Figure 18.3 illustrates this point. Because the compiler copies the code and compiles it, this is called *static linking*. If the library changes, the program will not change until the program is recompiled.

FIGURE 18.3

Compiling the program

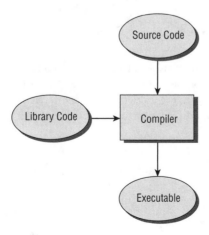

From a reusability point of view, the samples in Listings 18.3 and 18.4 are much more flexible. If a bug is discovered in the library code in Listing 18.2, all you have to do is fix the bug in the library code, and the other two programs will reflect the changes when they are recompiled.

This leads to another problem: If the library code is changed, the changes are not reflected automatically in Program One and Two, Listings 18.3 and 18.4, until those programs are recompiled.

NOTE *Older mainframe computer systems use code libraries extensively. Before the arrival of Y2K (year 2000), programmers needed to find date bugs in libraries and programs and recompile the executable. However, some of the programs were so old that the original source code was lost, making compilation very difficult.*

Compiled Libraries

To get around the limitation of having to compile all the programs that use the same library, computer scientists created dynamic linked libraries (DLL). A DLL is a library that is precompiled and can be used by compiled programs; it does not need to be compiled with your program. Therefore, if the DLL changes, the program will automatically pick up the changes without you having to recompile the original program. Figure 18.4 illustrates this concept.

FIGURE 18.4

Using a DLL

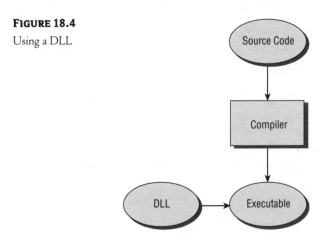

To update the loan program from Listings 18.2 and 18.3 to use a DLL, the first thing we must do is take our library source code and compile it with a DLL compiler, as shown in Figure 18.5. This is the same process as illustrated in Figure 18.1. However, the output file has a `.dll` extension instead of an `.exe` extension. DLL files cannot run by themselves; they must be called and run in another program.

FIGURE 18.5

Compiling the program

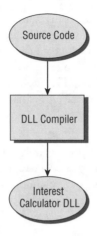

Listings 18.5 and 18.6 show the programs updated to use the DLL file.

LISTING 18.5: INTEREST PROGRAM ONE

```
Dim BorrowAmount As Number
Dim InterestRate As Number
Dim InterestAmount As Number
Dim Total As Number

<<Include InterestCalc.DLL>>

Formula = Total
```

LISTING 18.6: INTEREST PROGRAM TWO

```
Dim BorrowAmount As Number
Dim InterestRate As Number
Dim InterestAmount As Number
Dim Total As Number

<<Include InterestCalc.DLL>>
Total = Total * 1.03

Formula = Total
```

If we find a bug in the DLL, all we have to do is recompile the DLL, and the programs will automatically pick up the changes.

NOTE   *Again, we are using Crystal Basic syntax for clarity. The syntax is for illustration purposes only.*

At this point, you can see the evolution of computer programming architectures and how code can be reused in a computer system. The concept of OOP is based on being able to reuse code. Before we can jump into OOP, we need to look a little deeper into what makes up a DLL.

In Listing 18.2, which shows the library code that we compiled into a DLL, we imply that a DLL contains one block of code that is reused in the program. This is possible; however, in reality a DLL contains many blocks of code, and the programmer using the DLL decides what code to call in the DLL.

Functions and Subroutines

A DLL includes sections of code called *subroutines* or *functions*. Subroutines and functions are blocks of code that are executed when called by the calling program. The only difference between a subroutine and a function is that a function returns a value to the program that called the function. This sounds more complicated than it really is. Let's take a look at an example of subroutines and functions in a stand-alone program; then we will move them to a DLL to see the difference.

To demonstrate this example we need to make our loan program a little more robust. We are going to add a function to our program that calculates interest on borrowed money and a subroutine that prints the calculated amount. Listing 18.7 contains the sample program.

NOTE *Subroutines and functions are created with languages such as Visual Basic or C++. These languages are used to create the inner workings of DLLs; they are also used to create the inner workings of Crystal Reports. If you understand conceptually what is happening under the hood, then using the functionality available to you in Crystal Reports is easier.*

NOTE *The following code examples are created in pseudo code to demonstrate concepts. The concepts can be applied in VB or C++.*

LISTING 18.7: STAND-ALONE EXAMPLE SUBROUTINES AND FUNCTIONS

```
Dim Total As Number
Dim BorrowAmount As Number
BorrowAmount = {Customers.BorrowAmount}
Total = BorrowAmount + CalcInterestAmount(BorrowAmount)
Call PrintTotal
End program


Function CalcInterestAmount(LoanAmount)
   Dim InterestRate As Number
   Dim InterestAmount As Number

   InterestRate = {Rates.Interest}
   CalcInterestAmount = LoanAmount * (InterestRate /100 )
End Sub
```

```
Sub PrintTotal
   Dim prTotal As String

   prTotal = "$" + Total
   Print prTotal
End Sub
```

The program in Listing 18.7 can be broken down into three sections: the main loan program, a function, and a subroutine.

LOAN PROGRAM

The main part of the program is the first six lines of code. It creates two variables, Total and BorrowAmount, reads the Customers.BorrowAmount from the database, and stores that amount in the BorrowAmount variable. Then it adds interest to the BorrowAmount and stores that value in the Total variable.

Notice how interest is calculated by calling the CalcInterestAmount function. The program passes to the function the BorrowAmount in the brackets, and the CalcInterestAmount Function reads that value to calculate the interest amount:

```
Total = BorrowAmount + CalcInterestAmount(BorrowAmount)
```

The program then prints the total amount by calling the PrintTotal subroutine: Notice the subroutine does not return any value it just runs the code in the subroutine.

```
Call PrintTotal
```

FUNCTION

The purpose of this function is to receive the amount of money borrowed and send back to the caller the interest on that amount of money. It receives the amount borrowed through the LoanAmount variable declared in the brackets beside the name of the function, CalcInterestAmount. It then reads the interest rate from Rates.Interest in the database and stores that amount in the InterestRate variable:

```
Function CalcInterestAmount(LoanAmount)
```

The next line calculates the interest amount by multiplying the amount of money borrowed by the interest rate. In the same line it sets the return value of the function by equating the name of the function to a value. This says that the entire function is equal to this value and this value can be used by the calling program:

```
CalcInterestAmount = LoanAmount * (InterestRate /100 )
```

NOTE   *Some programming languages specify the return value of the function by using the keyword* return, *such as* return = LoanAmount * (InterestRate /100).

SUBROUTINE

The `PrintTotal` subroutine reads the total amount of money borrowed, appends a dollar sign to the amount, and prints the amount borrowed with a dollar sign. The subroutine does not return any values; it just runs code.

This coding style is an example of structured coding. The program is broken down into logical sections that make the code easier to debug and maintain. All the logical sections are contained in the same program. This program is also stand-alone.

As we showed previously, we can provide reusability of the function `CalcInterest` and subroutine `PrintTotal` to other programs by moving the subroutine and function code to a separate DLL file. Listing 18.8 demonstrates creating the DLL, and Listing 18.9 demonstrates using methods and functions in the DLL.

LISTING 18.8: CREATING A DLL

```
Function CalcInterestAmount(LoanAmount)
   Dim InterestRate As Number
   Dim InterestAmount As Number


   InterestRate = {Rates.Interest}
   CalcInterestAmount = LoanAmount * (InterestRate /100 )
End Sub


Sub PrintTotal
   Dim PrTotal As String

   PrTotal = "$" + Total
   Print PrTotal
End Sub
```

This program has the same function and subroutine as the stand-alone program in Listing 18.7. The program will be compiled to a DLL and the DLL will be called `CalcInterest.dll`, as shown previously in Figure 18.5.

The bolded lines of code indicate the changes we made to the original loan program. In Listing 18.9 we create a variable named `IntCalc`, which will represent our DLL. We set the `IntCalc` variable equal to `CalcInterest.dll`, and we call the function and subroutine as we did before, but this time we prefix the name with the variable that represents the DLL.

Another program could make a reference to the same DLL and use it as this program does. Because the DLL is compiled, if a bug is found and fixed, when the DLL is recompiled, any program that uses it will automatically get the changes.

LISTING 18. 9: USING METHODS AND FUNCTIONS IN A DLL

```
Dim Total As Number
Dim BorrowAmount As Number
Dim IntCalc
BorrowAmount = {Customers.BorrowAmount}

IntCalc = "CalcInterest.dll"

Total = BorrowAmount + IntCalc.CalcInterestAmount(BorrowAmount)

Call IntCalc.PrintTotal
End Program
```

ARCHITECTURE REVIEW

Let's stop for a moment to review what we have done. Listing 18.1 is the stand-alone program. It has all the logic and data necessary for the program to run. In Listing 18.6 we moved our logic from the program to a separate file called a DLL. The program in Listing 18.9 contains the data, the program variables, and the DLL. Listing 18.8 contains the logic. The DLL contains more than just a block of code; it actually contains a section of code divided into subroutines and sections. The program that is using the DLL can call the section of code that it requires.

APPLICATION PROGRAMMING INTERFACE (API)

This architecture is an example of an Application Programming Interface (API). DLLs are created to provide reusable code, and many programs use the same DLL. Crystal Reports uses this type of API to provide functionality to the report writer. Crystal Reports also contains an object-oriented API.

NOTE   As you can see, this architecture is very powerful but it can lead to problems. A program depends on a DLL for its code, or logic. If the DLL is upgraded from version 1 to version 2, and the programmer who created version 2 removes or changes some of the functionality that was in version 1, then all programs that expect the functionality of the version 1 DLL will fail when the version 2 DLL is installed in the computer. This is exactly why sometimes when you install a program on your Windows computer, suddenly other programs break. The newly installed program updates some shared DLL that was not written to be backward compatible, and the old programs break. This is also affectionately known as "DLL Hell."

Objects

At this point in our design we have separated the logic in a DLL using subroutines and functions. Programs that call the DLL contain the variables and any necessary code to use the code in the DLL. Objects are reusable and shareable programs. An object combines data and code, and a program can use both the data and the code.

NOTE *Objects are compiled into a DLL file. This is the same extension we saw when discussing subroutines and functions. Even though the file extension is the same, the functionality is different. Objects can also be compiled into an* `.exe` *extension. Functionally, they are the same, but memory in the computer is used differently.*

To create an object, we add data to the DLL. Because an object contains both data and code, it has everything a stand-alone program has. However, objects don't run by themselves; they are called by other programs like DLLs, as we discussed previously. We now have the power to be able to reuse code in the DLL, as well as access the data within the object.

TERMINOLOGY CHANGE

Because an object contains data and code like a stand-alone program does, OOP designers felt that it was necessary to use different terminology to identify data and code, hence they came up with the following terms:

♦ Methods (code) are subroutines or functions in an object. These are the same subroutines and functions as in a DLL. Subroutines run code, but functions run code and return a value.

♦ Properties (data) are variables declared in an object. These variables can be used by the object or the calling program.

AN ABSTRACT POINT OF VIEW OF OBJECTS

So far we have examined objects from a coding point of view, observing how programming has evolved from subroutines and functions into objects. However, OO people look at objects from a more abstract point of view. They view an object as something that represents entities in the real world, like employees, bank accounts, or reports. They describe the entities as containing methods and properties.

♦ Methods represent actions that the object or entity can do. Methods are sometimes called *verbs*.

♦ Properties represent characteristics of the object. Properties are sometimes referred to as *adjectives*, describing the object.

This view of objects has merit because it forces the person to think of what the object can do from a "real-world" point of view. This makes it easier to design objects to represent actual work entities such as a report or a customer without getting bogged down in the mechanics of what code will need to be written in the object. After the higher level design is done, the methods and properties still turn into subroutine, functions, and variables. We can design objects better if we focus on what they are, not on how they do things.

OO people often start talking about objects from this abstract point of view of methods and properties without tying objects back to the code and data that a programmer is familiar with. This might be okay for a computer analyst, but for a programmer who has to use someone else's objects, it is important to understand how everything ties together.

Knowing both points of view of an object—the code point of view and the abstract point of view—you will be able to understand the high-level discussion of methods and properties and also understand what is happening under the hood.

It does not matter whether you prefer to understand objects from a code or abstract point of view. The most important thing is to know what they are and what their capabilities are. Let's expand our program that calculates the interest for borrowed money to give it more functionality and to make it object oriented.

OO Point of View

A business analyst identifies the following characteristics of a customer who has a loan and what they do.

Properties:

◆ Customer's name

◆ Borrowed amount

◆ Balance

Methods:

◆ Make payment

Code Point of View

The programmer translates the characteristics of the object into code, as shown in Listing 18.10.

NOTE *These examples of OOP are not meant to be an exhaustive list of techniques. Their purpose is to identify concepts that you need to understand to be able to use objects in Crystal Reports. The coding examples loosely follow Visual Basic 6 code, which is similar to Crystal Basic code.*

LISTING 18.10: LOANCUSTOMER OBJECT

```
Public CustName
Public BorrowAmount
Public Balance

Public Sub MakePayment(PayAmount)
   'Lookup customers balance in DB
   BorrowAmount = {Customers.Balance}

   Balance = Balance - PayAmount + CalcInterestAmount(BorrowAmount)

   'Update the database with new balance
   {Customers.balance} = Balance
End Sub

Private Function CalcInterestAmount(LoanAmount)
   Dim InterestRate As Number
   Dim InterestAmount As Number
```

```
    InterestRate = {Rates.Interest}
    CalcInterestAmount = LoanAmount * (InterestRate /100 )
End Sub

Public Sub PrintTotal
    Dim PrTotal As String

    PrTotal = "$" + Balance
    Print PpTotal
End Sub
```

The loan object has these properties and methods:

Properties:

- CustName contains the names of the customers.

- BorrowAmount contains amount of money borrowed.

- Balance contains the balance of the loan.

Methods:

- MakePayment accepts as input the loan payment amount and updates the database.

- CalcInterest calculates the interest on the loan and accepts as input the balance.

- PrintTotal prints the balance of the loan.

An object can contain public and private methods or properties. Public methods and properties can be called by an outside program. Private methods can be called only by the object itself. This allows the designer of the object to expose only the necessary functionality. When working with Crystal Report objects, you will have access to the public methods and properties.

Listing 18.11 demonstrates using the loan object.

LISTING 18.11: USING THE LOAN OBJECT

```
Dim CustOne As New LoanCustomer
Dim CustTwo As New LoanCustomer

CustOne.CustName = "Gord"
CustTwo.CustName = "Nancy"

CustOne.MakePayment (500)
CustTwo.MakePayment (300)

CustOne.PrintTotal
CustTwo.PrintTotal
```

In this program we create two variables that will each hold one loan object for `CustOne` and `CustTwo`. The program will create two copies of the `LoanCustomer` object, one for each customer.

NOTE *We can also say we have two instances of the loan object.*

We update the `CustName` property for both objects to the customer's name so that each object is identified uniquely.

Then we make payments for 500 and 300 by calling the `MakePayment` method and passing to that method the payment amount. The `MakePayment` method calls the private function `CalcInterestAmount` to calculate the interest and updates the `Balance` property for the loan.

Finally we call the `PrintTotal` method for each customer to print the balance of the loan.

Notice the simplicity of Listing 18.11. The complex code is hidden in the object, shown in Listing 18.10. We create the object and use its methods and properties. The complex work of looking up the database and calculating loan payments is done in the object.

NOTE *Let's tie this abstract discussion back to Crystal Reports. An example of an object in Crystal Reports would be the report object. It represents a report and would contain methods to save and export the report and properties to indicate paper size and page orientation. In your program it would create an instance of the report object and manipulate its methods and properties. We will be doing that in the following chapters.*

COLLECTIONS

As you have seen, objects can represent entities and help hide complex code to make our application easier to write. Computer scientists have added another OOP concept to help design objects to better reflect real-life examples. The concept is a *collection* of objects. A collection is an object that contains a reference to other objects.

If you are familiar with the concept of arrays, through either Crystal formula language or another language, the concept is very similar. A collection usually contains similar objects. The collection object contains the following properties and methods. Notice that the collection is an object, a program that does something.

Properties:

- ◆ `Count` tells how many items are in the collection.
- ◆ `Item` is the actual object inside the collection.

Methods:

- ◆ `Add` is used to add items to the collection.
- ◆ `Remove` is used to remove items from the collection.

This is best explained with an example. Let's continue with our loan discussion.

How many loans can a customer have? Answer: one or more loans. In the previous `LoanCustomer` object, shown in Listing 18.11, the object is limited to one loan per customer. If a customer has multiple loans, we will have to create a `LoanCustomer` object to represent each loan, and the customer's name will be the same for each loan. (Have you ever gone to a bank to change your address and they had to do it in several places?) We can better design loan and customer objects so we have one customer object that can have a multiple loan objects.

Customer Object - OO Point of View

A business analyst identifies the following characteristics of a customer:

Properties:

◆ Customer name

◆ Loans

Methods:

◆ Make payment

◆ Take out a loan

◆ Loan balance

Loan Object - OO Point of View

A business analyst identifies the following characteristic of a loan:

Properties:

◆ Borrow amount

Code Point of View

The programmer translates the characteristics of the objects into code, as shown in Listings 18.12, 18.13, and 18.14.

NOTE   *These examples of OOP are not meant to be an exhaustive list of techniques. Their purpose is to identify concepts that are necessary to be able to use objects in Crystal Reports. The coding examples loosely follow Visual Basic 6 code.*

Lines of code that begin with an apostrophe are comments. Refer to the comments for a description.

LISTING 18.12: CUSTOMER OBJECT

```
Public CustName As String

'Loans represent the entire set of loans
Public Loans As Collection

'ALoan represents one loan in from the set
Private ALoan As Loan

Private LoanID As Number

'The method accepts a payment amount and the loan number to apply it to

Public Sub MakePayment(PayAmount, LoanNumber)
    'An individual loan in a collection can be referred to by its index number,
    in our case the loan number
```

```
    ALoan = Loans(LoanNumber)
    'Read the amount borrowed for this particular loan
    BorrowAmount = ALoan.BorrowAmount

    ALoan(LoanNumber).Balance = BorrowAmount - PayAmount +
    CalcInterestAmount(BorrowAmount)

    'Update the database with new balance
    {Customers.Balance} = Balance, LoanNumber
End Sub

Private Function CalcInterestAmount(LoanAmount, LoanNumber)
    Dim InterestRate As Number
    Dim InterestAmount As Number

    InterestRate = {Rates.Interest}
    CalcInterestAmount = LoanAmount * (InterestRate /100 )
End Sub

Public Function NewLoan(BorrowAmount)
    'Increment the loan ID key so we can keep track of loans
    LoanID = LoanID + 1

    'Add a new loan to the collection of loans
    Loans.AddItem Loan, LoanID

'Set how much was borrowed
    Loans("LoadID").BorrowAmount = BorrowAmount
    NewLoan = LoanID
End Sub

Public Function LoansBalance()
    Dim TotalBalance As Currency
    Dim x As Integer

    'Loop through all the loans in the loan collection
    'the count property of the loans object tells you how
' many loans there are

For x = 1 to Loans.Count
     TotalBalance = TotalBalance + Loans(x).Balance
Next x

    'Set the return value
    LoansBalance = TotalBalance
End Function
```

LISTING 18.13: LOAN OBJECT

```
'The loan object contains only data about the loan
'All the code is done in the customer object

Public LoanNumber As Number
Public BorrowAmount As Currency
Private Balance As Currency
```

LISTING 18.14: USING THE LOAN AND CUSTOMER OBJECTS

```
'Create a new customer
Dim CustOne As New LoanCustomer

'Create an object to represent a loan
Dim ALoan As Loan

'Variable to keep track of a loan
Dim LoanNumber As Number

'Assign the customer name to the name property in the object
CustOne.Name = "John"

'Create a new loan for $500. The method will return the loan number so we can
   refer to it later
LoanNumber = CustOne.NewLoan ("500")

'Make a $300 dollar payment to the new loan
CustOne.MakePayment(300,LoanNumber)

'Find out how much money I owe in all my loans.
'The loan's balance method does all the hard work and it
'returns the total of all the loans
Print "Total Money owed is " & CustOne.LoansBalance
```

As you can see, most of the code is done inside the objects. The application that creates and uses the object has little code. Don't get bogged down on what the code in the objects is doing. The point of this exercise is to show that methods and properties call code and work with data inside an object. When working with the Crystal Reports objects, you will never see the inner workings of the object as we have shown here. We are showing you this so you can have an appreciation of what is happening behind the scenes. This will deepen your knowledge of the Crystal object model.

EVENTS

So far we have shown that a program can create an object and use its methods and properties; the communication has always been from the program that created the object to the object. The object can communicate back to the program using *events*. An event is a way for the object to notify the program that something has occurred.

To continue with our loan example, when a customer makes a loan payment and the balance reaches zero, the object can notify the program that is using this object that this is the last payment. We will modify the MakePayment method in the customer object to cause an event to be raised if the balance reaches zero or less than zero. Listing 18.15 contains the modified method in bold. The remaining code is the same as in Listing 18.12 and is not displayed in Listing 18.15.

LISTING 18.15: CUSTOMER OBJECT

```
Public Sub MakePayment(PayAmount, LoanNumber)
    'An individual loan in a collection can be referred to by its index number,
    in our case the loan number

    ALoan = Loans(LoanNumber)

    'Read the amount borrowed for this particular loan
    BorrowAmount = ALoan.BorrowAmount

    ALoan(LoanNumber).Balance = BorrowAmount - PayAmount +
    CalcInterestAmount(BorrowAmount, LoanNumber)

    'If the balance reaches zero or less than zero
    'notify the program and pass back the loan number that
    'is paid off
    If Balance < = 0 Then
        RaiseEvent BalancePaid(LoanNumber)
    End If

    'Update the database with new balance
    {Customers.Balance} = Balance, LoanNumber
End Sub
```

A program that uses objects that can raise events must create an event subroutine that gets called by the object. The object will run the code in event subroutine. Listing 18.16 contains the modified method in bold. The remaining code is the same as in Listing 18.13 and is not displayed in Listing 18.16.

LISTING 18.16: RESPONDING TO AN EVENT

```
'Make a $300 payment to the new loan
CustOne.MakePayment(300,loanNumber)

'This subroutine will get called by the object if the loan
'balance is zero or less.
Public Sub BalancePaid(LoanNumber)
Print "Congratulations your loan number " $ LoanNumber & "is paid off"
End Sub
```

The customer object calls the `BalancePaid` event if the loan balance is less than zero. In Listing 18.16 the `Sub BalancePaid` is called by the customer object.

THE LOAN OBJECT MODEL

We can continue expanding the customer and loan examples until we have a full-fledged banking system. At this point we would have hundreds of objects representing the various components of a banking system. The number of objects and the relationships among them would be difficult to understand. To help clarify the objects and their relationships, OO designers create an object model to model all the objects and their relationships. The OO object model is similar to a relational database model that was discussed in Chapter 9, "Working with Multiple Tables," in Part 3: "Advanced Reporting." Figure 18.6 represents our customer and loan object model.

FIGURE 18.6

Loan object model

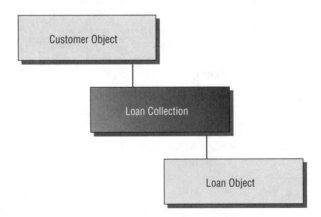

The main object in our model is the customer object and it contains a Loans Collection, which is a container that holds the loan objects for the customer.

CRYSTAL REPORTS AND OBJECTS

We have seen objects from a theoretical point of view. The discussions about methods, properties, events, and collections apply to objects within Crystal Reports. Crystal Reports contains hundreds of objects that represent the functionality of the report writer, and their relationships can be complex. The concepts we discussed in our simple banking application are the same that Crystal has in the Crystal Reports object model. Figure 18.7 contains a partial snapshot of the object model.

FIGURE 18.7

The Crystal Report object model

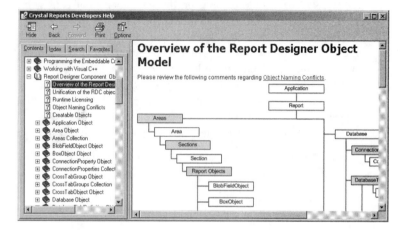

The entire object model and reference to the object's methods and properties can be found in C:\Program Files\Crystal Decisions\Crystal Reports 9\Developer Files\Help\ Crystal-DevHelp.chm. Figure 18.8 shows a partial list of the report object's methods, properties, and events.

FIGURE 18.8

Methods, properties, and events in a Crystal object

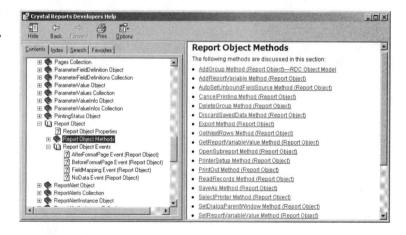

We will look at these objects and their use in detail in the following chapters.

Summary

Over the years since programmers have been writing programs, various techniques have evolved that allowed programmers to write code that can be shared from program to program.

The first type of code sharing was a simple library of code containing common routines that could be copied into programs. This worked well until a bug appeared in the common routine; then all the programs that used that routine needed to be recompiled.

To solve the recompilation issue, dynamic libraries of code were created. The library was precompiled and a program simply referenced the code in the library and used it. If the dynamic library changed, all programs that referenced that library were automatically updated because the code was not statically copied into the program but rather loaded dynamically when the program ran. This type of reuse was limited to code only.

Object-oriented techniques were invented that allowed both code and data to be placed in a reusable object. Since objects contain both data and code, they really have everything a program has and can represent real-life entities like customers or reports.

OO programmers introduced the following terminology to describe entities:

◆ Methods describe what an object can do; methods behind the scene are subroutines and functions in the object.

◆ Properties describe the characteristics of an object; behind-the-scene properties are variables and data in an object.

◆ A special collection object contains references to other objects. Collections can be considered an array of objects.

◆ Object model diagrams illustrate the relationship between one object and another in complex systems.

Crystal Reports exposes it functionally through objects, so it is imperative to understand OOP concepts in order to effectively use Crystal Reports in a custom application.

Chapter 19

Building Windows Applications with the Report Designer Component

IN THIS CHAPTER WE will develop Visual Basic applications that incorporate Crystal Reports 9. As you have seen in Chapter 17, "The Crystal Programming Forest," there are many ways to program Crystal Reports in an application; this chapter focuses on building applications using Visual Basic 6 and the Report Designer Component (RDC). Because of the similarities between the Visual Basic language and VBScript (a subset of the VB language, which is used when developing ASP applications), the RDC examples we include in this chapter can be used in Windows and ASP development. Chapter 20, "ASP Web Applications," focuses on differences when working within a web environment. We will not focus on Visual Basic or Windows development; rather, we will focus on using the RDC. We start by installing the RDC in Visual Basic, and then we will open a report and manipulate it via the RDC.

The RDC is a large object model that exposes all the functionality of Crystal Reports through its objects. We will cover the main components of the RDC and show you techniques for working with it. Once you understand one technique and how the components are organized, you can apply the same technique to other parts of the RDC object model. We will keep our examples straightforward so you can easily use our sample code in your application.

If you are comfortable with working with objects and object-oriented programs, then you can jump right into this chapter. If you are new to object-oriented programming (OOP), we recommend reading Chapter 18, "The Object-Oriented Primer," so you can understand the OO terms and techniques required to program with the RDC. It is also important to understand the functionality of Crystal Reports before working with the RDC because the RDC allows you to control Crystal Reports functionality through code. If you know the capabilities of Crystal Reports, it will be easier to understand how to use the RDC.

In this chapter, we will examine the following topics:

◆ Installing the RDC

◆ Opening existing reports

◆ Changing selection criteria

◆ Modifying group and sort criteria

◆ Setting database logon parameters

◆ Switching databases

◆ Working with graphs and subreports

◆ Modifying the Crystal Viewer

◆ Designing reports in Visual Basic

The code sample in this chapter can be downloaded from the Sybex website at www.sybex.com.

Installing Crystal Reports for Visual Basic

You must first install Visual Basic 6 on your development computer before you can install Crystal Reports. When installing Crystal Reports, choose the Custom installation option, and make sure that you select the Report Designer Component and Visual Basic. Notice in Figure 19.1 that the RDC can be installed for both VB and ASP.

FIGURE 19.1

Installing Crystal developer components

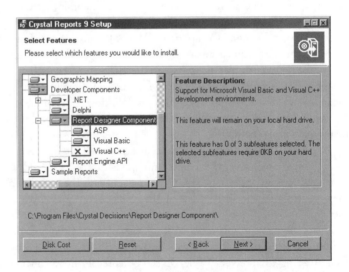

After Visual Basic and Crystal Reports are installed, you still might not see Crystal Reports in VB. If you don't see Crystal Reports 9 listed on the Project menu, start Visual Basic and choose a Standard EXE project. Choose Project ➢ Components and click the Designers tab. Select Crystal Reports 9 to enable it, as shown in Figure 19.2. This enables the Crystal Report Designer; the other components of the RDC are installed and registered on the computer and ready to use.

FIGURE 19.2

Enabling the Crystal Report Designer

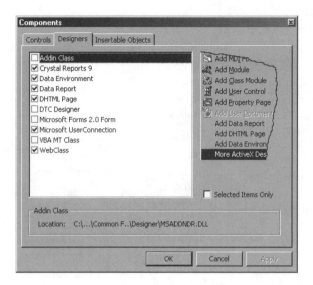

NOTE *Visual Basic 6 is the most popular language for developing Windows applications with Crystal Reports. However, the RDC follows COM standards, so any language such as C++, VBScript in ASP, or Delphi can use COM components and the RDC.*

VISUAL BASIC AND CRYSTAL REPORTS

Version 9 of Crystal Reports is not included with VB 6; as a matter of fact, neither is version 8! Since version 3 of VB, Crystal Reports has always been included with VB. Microsoft made a direction change with version 6 of VB, so all programs follow a common object technology called the Component Object Model (COM) standard. Previous versions of Crystal Reports used older API (Application Programming Interface) technology and as a result were not included with VB 6 (see Chapter 17). After VB 6 was released, Crystal Reports released version 8 of Crystal Reports, which followed a COM programming model with the Crystal RDC (Report Designer Component). Version 9 of Crystal Reports continues to follow the COM standard. To use Crystal Reports version 9 with VB, you need to install Crystal Reports.

To develop applications with Crystal Reports 9, you need at minimum Crystal Reports Developer Edition. In this version of Crystal Reports, Crystal Decisions released two editions of Crystal Reports: Developer Edition and Advanced Edition. The Developer Edition allows you to work with and modify a Crystal Report in an application. The Advanced Edition allows everything that the Developer Edition does and adds the abilities to create a Crystal report directly from code and to define custom data sources for .NET, COM, and Java Beans. Refer to Appendix A for a feature comparison of Crystal Reports.

Crystal Reports is included with Visual Basic .NET; we cover that topic in Chapter 21, ".NET Applications."

Report Designer Component

The RDC is not one component but a set of components. Figure 19.3 shows the components and their relationships.

FIGURE 19.3

The RDC components

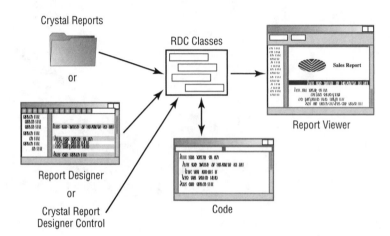

Report Designer   The Report Designer allows the VB developer to create Crystal Reports from a blank report or modify existing Crystal Reports inside VB. You do not need to develop your reports with Crystal Reports and then import them into VB as you had to do previously. Using the Report Designer is like having Crystal Reports inside VB.

Embeddable Crystal Report Designer Control   The Crystal Report Designer control allows the end user of your applications to develop or modify a Crystal report from within your application. With your application you can give users the power of Crystal Reports without installing Crystal Reports on their system. However, the purchase of additional licensing is required.

Automation Server   The Automation Server is the central component in the RDC. This is a COM-based object hierarchy that allows you to control all the functionality of Crystal Reports through code, by manipulating methods and properties of the objects that represent the components of a report. Automation Server is a fancy marketing term; this is a set of objects (a rather large set) with methods and properties that allow you to control Crystal Reports. Two separate Automation Servers are provided with the RDC:

Crystal Reports ActiveX Designer Runtime Library (`craxdrt.dll`)   This library is known as the RDC runtime engine. To access this library in VB, select Project ➤ References and choose Crystal Reports 9 ActiveX Designer Runtime Library. Then you can dimension a variable to access the objects in the object library, shown in Figure 19.4.

Crystal Reports ActiveX Designer Design and Runtime Library (`craxddrt.dll`)   This library is known as the RDC design and runtime engine. To access this library in VB, select Project ➤ References and choose Crystal Reports 9 ActiveX Designer Design And Runtime Library. Figure 19.5 shows the object library.

WARNING   *If you have the Developer Edition and try to use some of the report-creation features of the ActiveX Designer Design and Runtime Library, you will receive a "Creation feature not enabled error" or the application will not run.*

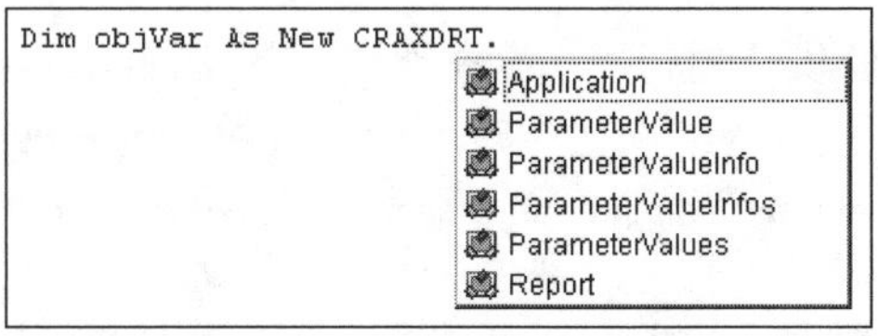

FIGURE 19.4

Crystal Reports
ActiveX Designer
Runtime Library

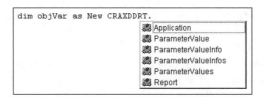

FIGURE 19.5

Crystal Reports
ActiveX Designer
Design and Runtime
Library

Both RDC Automation Servers provide the same manipulation of Crystal Reports. However, the Crystal Reports ActiveX Designer Design Runtime Library provides the additional functionality to create Crystal Reports.

The `craxdrt.dll` can be used in either a VB application or an ASP application. The `craxddrt.dll` (design) should be used only in a Windows VB application because it is not multithreaded for a web environment.

Crystal Report Viewer   Crystal Report Viewer control is similar to the preview window in Crystal Reports. The Report Viewer displays Crystal Reports. Modifications you make to the report in the RDC, via the Report Designer or Automation Server, are displayed in the Report Viewer. There are two viewers available:

ActiveX Viewer   The ActiveX Viewer can be added to any application that supports the ActiveX standard, such as Visual Basic, Delphi, or C++. In VB, the Crystal Report Viewer is added to the VB toolbox and placed on the form. To add the viewer to the VB toolbox, select Project ➤ Components and choose Crystal Report Viewer Control 9.

Report Bean Viewer   The Report Bean Viewer can be added to any development environment that supports Java version 1.1. The viewer gets Crystal Reports from a web server. You set the reportName property to an address for the web server that contains the Crystal report.

Crystal Reports Select Expert   The Select Expert is the Select Expert and Search Expert from Crystal Reports. Using this control you can provide in your application the same Search and Select Expert as in Crystal Reports.

Each of these RDC components has a specific task, such as displaying a report, allowing you to view a report, or building a report either at runtime or design time. You can use the RDC components in any combination. Table 19.1 examines some possibilities.

TABLE 19.1: EXAMPLES OF USING THE RDC COMPONENTS

TASK	RDC COMPONENT
Design a report at design time and modify the report at runtime via code.	Use the Report Designer with the Automation Server.
Design a report at design time, modify the report at runtime via code, and display the report to the users.	Use the Report Designer, Automation Server, and Crystal Report Viewer.
Load an existing report or create a report using code, and view the report.	Use the Automation Server and the Crystal Report Viewer.
Allow your users to develop a report in your application, modify the report at runtime via code, and view the report in the application.	Use the Automation Server, Embeddable Designer, and the Crystal Report Viewer.
Create a report via code; print or export the report.	Use the Automation Server.

TIP *Full Developer documentation, license documentation, and runtime deployment documentation can be found at* `C:\Program Files\Crystal Decisions\Crystal Reports 9\Developer Files\Help\en`, *assuming you installed Crystal Reports in the default directory. The installation CD also contains a* `\Docs` *directory with documentation in Adobe PDF format.*

Adding a Report with the Crystal Report Expert

The Crystal Report Expert is the easiest way to start working with Crystal Reports and Visual Basic. The Report Expert hides some of the complexity of the various RDC components by automatically making project references and adding components to the VB toolbox. Later on in this chapter we will show you how to use Crystal Reports without the expert so you can have the greatest flexibility and understand what the expert does for you. For now, let's examine how to configure VB and take a tour of what the Report Expert does for you.

Start Visual Basic and select a Standard EXE project. Select Project ➤ Add Crystal Report 9. Visual Basic will display the Crystal Report Gallery dialog box, as shown in Figure 19.6. Does this look familiar to you? This is the same interface as in Crystal Reports! The Report Expert will guide you through creating a report, creating a blank report, or opening an existing report.

If you choose Using The Report Expert or As A Blank Report, you will be prompted to choose the data source for the report, as shown in Figure 19.7. You can choose the normal data sources for a Crystal Report; Visual Basic also adds Project Data as a new data source. Project Data is Microsoft's Data Environment that was added to Visual Basic 6. The Data Environment is a graphical interface to ADO (ActiveX Data Objects). This allows Crystal Reports to report from an ADO record set in your application.

FIGURE 19.6

Crystal Report Gallery with VB

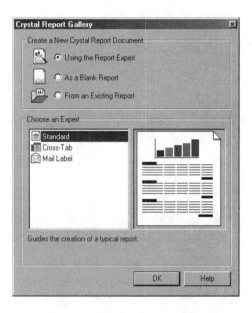

To report from Project Data, add a Data Environment to your VB project by choosing Project ➤ Add Data Environment (if you don't have VB 6 SP 5, then the menu will be Project ➤ More ActiveX Designers ➤ Data Environment) before adding a Crystal report. Configure the Data Environment to connect to an ADO data source by right-clicking Connection1 and choosing Properties. Choose the OLEDB provider for your data source, click the Next button, and then select the database server and database to report from. This creates a connection to the data source. Once that is done, right-click the connection and choose Add Command. The command represents the command you want to send to the database and the data that will be returned to the data environment. The command can be a SQL statement, the name of a database table, or a stored procedure. Right-click the command, and choose Properties to configure the command for the database. (Refer to VB documentation for more details on the data environment.)

Once you've configured a Data Environment, you can add a Crystal Report Designer and choose the Project Data as a source for your report.

NOTE   *Crystal Reports can also report from an ADO record set without using the Data Environment.*

After you have chosen the Crystal report, the Crystal Expert will prompt you to add a Crystal Report Viewer to a VB form and change the VB project properties so that the newly added form is the form that starts when the application runs, as shown in Figure 19.8. If you choose not to add the Crystal Report Viewer at this time, you can add it yourself later. Or, if you select not to change the startup object, you can modify this yourself later in VB.

FIGURE 19.7

Project data using
the Report Expert

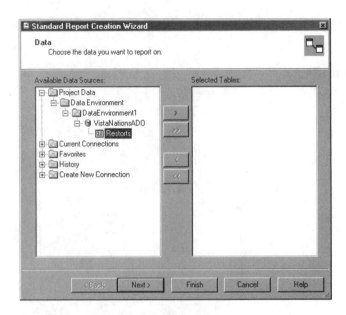

FIGURE 19.8

Crystal Report
Expert

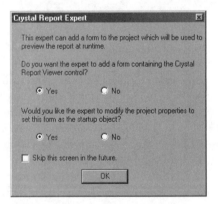

When you click OK in the Crystal Report Expert, you will be presented with the Crystal Report Designer that contains the Crystal report, and `CrystalReport1` will be added to the Project Explorer in VB under the Designers folder. Refer to Figure 19.9 to see the additions and changes to the VB development environment.

The Report Designer provides Crystal Report functionality. Reports can be modified or designed from scratch in the designer. To access the Crystal menus, right-click the white area to the left of the report in the Report Designer; the menus should be familiar Crystal menus. The toolbar is also similar to the one in Crystal Reports. Reports created in the Report Designer are saved as DSR files. DSR files can be opened only by Visual Basic. You can also save reports created in the Report Designer by clicking the Save To Crystal Report icon on the toolbar (seventh from the left).

The Crystal Report Expert will also add the Crystal Report Viewer to a VB form, Form2 in our case. The Report Viewer is used to display the report from the designer.

NOTE   You can add multiple Crystal Reports to your VB project. Each one will be contained in its own designer.

FIGURE 19.9

Visual Basic design environment

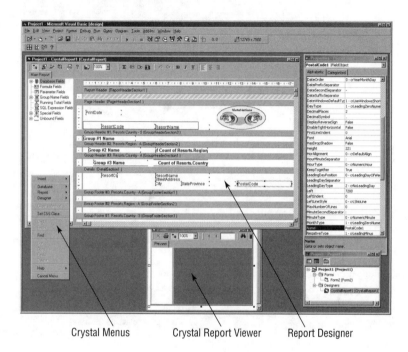

Crystal Menus   Crystal Report Viewer   Report Designer

RDC Object Model

What you don't see in Figure 19.9 is the Automation Server. The Crystal Report Expert automatically made a reference in VB (Project ➤ References) to both Crystal Reports 9 ActiveX Designer Design and Runtime Library and Crystal Reports 9 ActiveX Design Runtime Library. It is not necessary to make a reference to both libraries for a VB project; however, the Crystal Report Expert adds both because it does not know which library you will need. If you are not using the design capabilities of the automation server (refer back our discussion on the Automation Server), you may want to remove the reference to Crystal Reports 9 ActiveX Designer Design and Runtime Library from VB to avoid confusion. Both automation servers have similar methods and properties, and they are only distinguished by one letter—`craxddrt` versus `craxdrt`—so it is easy to make a mistake and add bugs to your project.

The Automation Server has no visual interface; you manipulate it through code. The Automation Server is a set of objects that represent the functionality of Crystal Reports. You need to be familiar with working with objects in order to work with the Automation Server; refer to Chapter 18 if necessary. Figure 19.10 contains a diagram of the Automation Server objects and their relationships, and Figure 19.11 shows the methods for the Application object.

FIGURE 19.10

RDC Object model hierarchy diagram

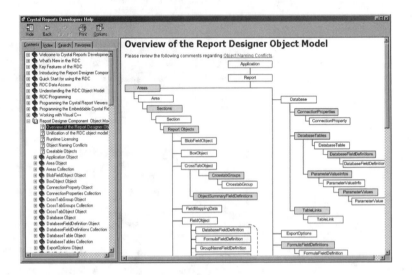

FIGURE 19.11

Methods for the Application object

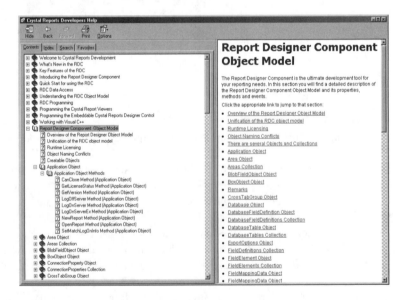

TIP   *For a complete list of all the objects, methods, properties, and events of the RDC, refer to* `CrystalDevHelp.chm` *in* `C:\Program Files\Crystal Decisions\Crystal Reports 9\Developer Files\Help\en`.

The object model looks very complicated, especially when you look at it for the first time, because it represents all the functionality of Crystal Reports. Imagine if we showed you all the menus of Crystal Reports on one page; it would look very complicated too. The main objects of the RDC are as follows:

Application Object   The Application object is the main object in the hierarchy. Think of the Application object as the Crystal Reports application you use to build reports. This object has methods such as `OpenReport` or `NewReport`, which allow you to open and create new reports. The Crystal Expert automatically creates this object when you add the Report Designer to your VB project. You can also create this object manually if you choose not to use the expert. We will discuss this in more detail later in the chapter.

Report Object   The Report object represents a Crystal report and all the objects that can be included in the report. Notice in Figure 19.10 how the Report object contains collections of sections and other Report objects. Each collection contains the actual object that we see in Crystal Reports, such as a Graph object or Field object. The Report object contains methods such as `SaveAs` to save the Crystal report or properties such as `RecordSelectionFormula` to specify the records you would like to see in the report. The Crystal Report Designer is the Report object with a visual interface. You can also access the Report object without the Crystal Report Designer. We will discuss this in more detail later in the chapter.

Database Object   The Database object represents the data sources that are used in the report. It contains a collection of tables and fields within the tables. The Database object contains information about the data sources in the report as well as the connection information to the database, such as the name of the server and the user ID and password required to access the server. Using the Database object you can change data sources and modify user IDs and passwords. We will examine this in more detail later in the chapter.

Sections and Report Objects   Notice back in Figure 19.9 how the report is broken down into sections, and each section contains objects (just like Crystal Reports). Each section has a name: Report Header is called `ReportHeaderSection1`, Page Header is called `PageHeaderSection1`, etc. Each of the Report objects in Crystal also has a name. Notice in the Properties window that the PostalCode object is named `PostalCode1`. Examine the Properties window further and you will see the properties for `PostalCode1`; for example, it has 2 decimal places, a height of 221 twips, and is indented left 7200 twips. Through the Report Designer you can access all the objects in a Crystal Report. You can also access all the methods and properties of the Report object via code and manipulate the report at runtime instead of at design time.

NOTE   *1,440 twips equal one inch, and 567 twips equal one centimeter.*

Visual Basic Code

The last item in our tour is the code that was generated by the Crystal Expert. Listing 19.1 contains all the code generated by the expert.

LISTING 19.1: CRYSTAL EXPERT-GENERATED CODE

```
Dim Report As New CrystalReport1

Option Explicit

Private Sub Form_Load()
    Screen.MousePointer = vbHourglass
    CRViewer91.ReportSource = Report
    CRViewer91.ViewReport
    Screen.MousePointer = vbDefault
End Sub

Private Sub Form_Resize()
    CRViewer91.Top = 0
    CRViewer91.Left = 0
    CRViewer91.Height = ScaleHeight
    CRViewer91.Width = ScaleWidth
End Sub
```

In the first line, a variable called `Report` is created that represents a Crystal Report object. When you added the Crystal Report Designer to VB, VB automatically named it `CrystalReports1`. Remember that the Crystal Report Designer is the Report object in the Automation Server with a visual interface. In this line of code we create a new instance of a Report object and copy `CrystalReport1` into that object. We can then access the methods and properties of the Report object, through the Report object variable.

```
CRViewer91.ReportSource = Report
```

`CRViewer91` is name of Crystal Report Viewer that was added to the form; the `ReportSource` property of the viewer accepts a Report object. Once a Report object is assigned to the report source, the viewer can display the report.

```
CRViewer91.ViewReport
```

The `ViewReport` method tells the Crystal Viewer to display the report in the viewer. The rest of the code that is generated by the expert changes the mouse pointer from an arrow to an hourglass to indicate to the user that something is happening.

The expert adds code in the `Form_Resize` event to resize the Crystal Viewer to the dimensions of the form that contains it. The Crystal Viewer supports the standard `Top`, `Left`, `Height`, and `Width` properties of all objects in VB.

We find that the sample code generated by the Crystal Report Expert can lead to confusion when working with Crystal Reports in VB. For example, the line

```
Dim Report As New CrystalReport1
```

causes VB to create two copies of the same report because of the `New` keyword in this line. You can then access both of them through the variable `CrystalReport1` or `Report` and they both will have methods and properties of the Automation Server Report object. If you always refer to the Crystal report using the `Report` variable, then you will not run into bugs. However, memory is wasted because of two instances of the same report. We find that it is too easy to refer to `CrystalReport1` in one part of your code and `Report` in another part of your code, thinking that you are modifying properties of the same report, and later you spend hours trying to figure out why things are not working.

You can achieve the same results if you don't declare the `Report` variable and just use `CrystalReport1`, the name of the Report Designer. Here the default code is rewritten to use `CrystalReport1` instead of `Report`. We deleted the first `Dim Report` line and assigned `CrystalReport1` to the `ReportSource`; see the bolded line of code:

```
Option Explicit

Private Sub Form_Load()
    Screen.MousePointer = vbHourglass
    CRViewer91.ReportSource = CrystalReport1
    CRViewer91.ViewReport
    Screen.MousePointer = vbDefault
End Sub
```

If you prefer to use the `Report` variable you still can do so, but don't use the `New` keyword to create a new instance of a report. Here is the sample code rewritten so that `Report` is used but two copies of the report are not created. Again the lines that are changed are bolded:

```
Dim Report As CrystalReport1

Option Explicit

Private Sub Form_Load()
    Set Report = CrystalReport1
    Screen.MousePointer = vbHourglass
    CRViewer91.ReportSource = Report
    CRViewer91.ViewReport
    Screen.MousePointer = vbDefault
End Sub
```

Now that you have the basics under your belt, we can start working with the VB and RDC to build Windows applications.

Working with the RDC

Refer back to Figure 19.9 and notice that the PostalCode field is selected. When you select a field in the Report Designer, the properties of that field are displayed in the Properties window. In the Properties window of Figure 19.9, the `Name` property is highlighted. This is the name of the object, and it enables you to access the object from VB code via its name. The other properties of the report are listed in the Properties window; for example, `DecimalPlaces` identifies how many decimal places to display in the field, and `BackColor` identifies the background color of the field. The rest of the properties should look familiar to you because they are report properties that you set in Crystal Reports;

however, they are now available in VB. Using the Properties window, you can change the properties of the objects at design time, or you can modify the properties at runtime using code.

```
CrystalReport1.PostalCode1.BackColor = vbRed
CrystalReport1.PostalCode1.Left = 1000
```

If we place these two lines of code in the Form_Load event, shown in Listing 19.1 above, before we display the report, we will change the background color of the PostalCode field to Red and move it 1,000 twips from the left of the form.

NOTE   *vbRed is a predefined color in Visual Basic. You can also supply the hex value for the color, such as* .backcolor = &HFFFF00, *which will give you teal. The easiest way to determine the color is to click the* BackColor *property in the Properties window, select a color, and then cut and paste the hex value from the Properties window into your program.*

Refer again to Figure 19.9. At the top of the Properties window in the drop-down list is the name of the object you selected, PostalCode1 in our example. Beside the name of the object is the object type, FieldObject in our case. The object type identifies what type of object you are working with and what method and properties are available. Refer back to Figure 19.10, and you can see that the Field object is part of the Report object. In the Developers help file (CrystalDevHelp.chm) search for "Report Designer Component Object Model" to get a complete list of objects and their methods, properties, and events. Figure 19.12 shows the table of methods and properties for the Field object from the help file and a description of each. The Read/Write column indicates whether you can change the property or just read what value it contains from your program.

NOTE   *The figure shows IfieldObject, the "I" indicating that this is the interface for the FieldObject. Interface is a fancy object-oriented term that indicates the methods and properties available in the object.*

FIGURE 19.12

Field object
properties

Crystal Report Events

In general, properties in Visual Basic are accessible at design time or runtime, and you can read, write, or read and write the properties. Crystal Reports adds one more level of accessibility. Because the report engine in Crystal Reports goes through multiple passes, a particular field may not always accessible to your VB code. The Restriction In Event Handler column shown in Figure 19.12 indicates when you can use these events. The Automation Server sends an event to your program to notify you when formatting for a particular area is occurring, and at this time you can modify the properties for that object if it has restrictions. To access the event, from the Project window in Visual Basic, right-click Crystal-Report1 in the Designers folder in the project window and choose View Code. This will take you to the code behind the Report Designer. From there, click the Object drop-down list box (top left) to choose a section of the Crystal report, as shown in Figure 19.13. Visual Basic will automatically create a `Format` event for that section. You can also access the `Initialize` and `Terminate` events for the entire report. These events indicate the beginning and end of the report processing.

FIGURE 19.13

Report section events

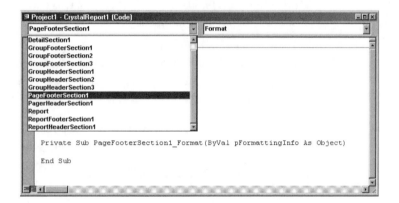

From our previous example, the `Background` and the `Left` properties are accessible from the event; when formatting is idle, you can access these properties from both places. The code below modifies the properties as described above. However, remember that when you are working with objects and properties on a report, if you try to access a variable that is accessible only during event processing, you will receive an "Access denied" error.

```
Private Sub DetailSection1_Format(ByVal pFormattingInfo As Object)
    CrystalReport1.PostalCode1.BackColor = vbRed
    CrystalReport1.PostalCode1.Left = 1000
End Sub
```

If you have a large report that contains many sections and Report objects, the default naming conventions for Crystal Reports, such as `Text1`, `DetailSection1`, etc., will make your code difficult to follow. You can select each section or object that you want to work with and change the name so your code is easier to follow. This is similar to how we changed the default names of objects in VB from `command1` to `cmdPrint`, for example.

Adding a "Continued" Message on Repeating Groups through Events

The Format event for each section receives as input a pFormattingInfo object, as shown in Figure 19.13. This object contains three read-only properties: IsEndOfGroup, IsRepeatedGroupHeader, and IsStartOfGroup. The properties can contain a True or False to indicate group formatting information. You can use these properties to help you create formatting logic in your program. For example, if your report is designed so that groups repeat on a new page, you can check IsRepeatedGroupHeader Is True and update the Text object beside the group name to read "Continued…." To demonstrate this, follow these steps:

1. Insert a Text object beside the Group #1 Name field in the Group section of a report, change the Name property to txtContinuedMsg, and leave the text in the Text object blank.

2. Make sure the group name will repeat in the report. From the Report Designer in VB, right-click Group #1, select Group Expert, click the Options button, and then choose the Options tab.

3. Select Repeat Group Header On Each Page. Now the Group Header will repeat for each page if the whole group can't print on one page.

4. In our code we need to test whether the group is repeated and change the message in our Text object if it is. Add the following code to the GroupHeaderSection1 Format event:

```
Private Sub GroupHeaderSection3_Format(ByVal [AU: Line of code wraps. Insert a
break where desired. LSR As is okay]pFormattingInfo As Object)

    If pFormattingInfo.IsRepeatedGroupHeader Then
        txtContinuedMsg.SetText ".... Continued"
    Else
        txtContinuedMsg.SetText ""
    End If
End Sub
```

NOTE   The Text object we added is a TextObject object type; it has a SetText method that allows you to change the text that it displays.

Using Program Counters

It is common in programs to create counters such as counter = counter + 1 to keep track of events or items in our code. If you need to add a counter to your program, keep in mind that formatting events may be called multiple times by the Crystal Report Engine. If you place program counters in the section event that depends on the event being called once, your counters will not always be correct. If you need to keep track of counters, the Report object has three methods you can use: AddReport-Variable, GetReportVariable, and SetReportVariable, so you can work with counters in the events. The special variables are called Report variables. The Report Engine keeps track of the variables so they don't get incremented many times if the formatting event has to be called multiple times.

The AddReportVariable method creates the Report variable and assigns it a data type. Similarly to the Dim statement in VB, SetReportVariableValue and GetReportVariableValue allow you to read and write the variable, as demonstrated in Listing 19.2.

LISTING 19.2: IMPLEMENTING COUNTERS IN A FORMAT EVENT

```
Private Sub Report_Initialize()
    CrystalReport1.AddReportVariable crRVNumber, "Counter"
End Sub


Private Sub GroupHeaderSection2_Format(ByVal pFormattingInfo As Object)

    CrystalReport1.SetReportVariableValue "Counter", _
    CrystalReport1.GetReportVariableValue("Counter") + 1

End Sub
```

The AddReportVariable must be declared in the Report Initialize event of the report. In GroupHeaderSection2 we read and increment the "Counter" variable. This is an abstract code sample that does nothing with the counter, its purpose is to demonstrate setting up counters; in your program you will need to add code to do something with the counter.

Changing Record and Group Selection

We have created a sample application that will allow users to select whether they want to see only five-star resorts and to change the countries they want to see in the report. Figure 19.14 displays the user interface. We populated the list box with countries from the same data source as the report so the list would match. Let's examine the code in Listing 19.3.

FIGURE 19.14

Resort VB application

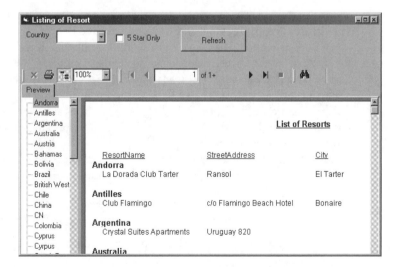

LISTING 19.3: CHANGING RECORD AND GROUP SELECTION

```
Private Sub cboCountries_Click()

    CrystalReport1.GroupSelectionFormula = _
      "{Resorts.Country} = '" & cboCountries.Text & "'"

End Sub

Private Sub chk5Star_Click()
    If chk5Star.Value = 1 Then 'checked
        CrystalReport1.RecordSelectionFormula = _
          " {Resorts.FiveStarRating}"
    Else
        CrystalReport1.RecordSelectionFormula = _
      " not {Resorts.FiveStarRating}"
    End If
End Sub

Private Sub cmdRefresh_Click()
    CrystalReport1.DiscardSavedData
    CRViewer91.Refresh
End Sub
```

In this application we are demonstrating how to set the group selection formula and the record selection formula in a report from Visual Basic. When the user selects a country from the list of countries in the Country combo box, the `cboCountries_Click` event will be generated. In that event we update the `GroupSelectionFormula` property of the Report object. When you set a formula in Crystal Reports via Visual Basic, you must set the formula exactly the same way Crystal Reports would set it. For example, if the user selected Canada in the combo box, the group selection formula would be set to `{Resorts.Country} = 'Canada'`. Notice that we must use single and double quotes in Visual Basic to build the exact formula that Crystal Reports requires.

When a user clicks the 5 Star Only check box, the `chk5Star_Click` event is generated and we do the same thing, except this time we set the record selection formula instead of the group selection formula. In this example we did not have to append any text from VB to build the group selection formula and we simply created a Crystal Report formula. If we did have to add append text, we would have to mix single and double quotes and append strings together as in the group selection formula.

TIP   The easiest way to build Crystal Reports formulas for Visual Basic is to use Crystal Reports and build the formulas using the Formula Workshop. You can then cut and paste the formulas into VB and modify them as required.

When a user clicks the Refresh button, the report will be redisplayed with the new selection criteria. The `CRViewer91.Refresh` method refreshes the report.

The Crystal Viewer has two refresh methods, `Refresh` and `RefreshEx`. The `Refresh` method loads and redisplays the report; the `RefreshEx` method accepts a Boolean parameter, so you specify whether or not to refresh the report from the database. For example, `CRViewer91.RefreshEx False` will refresh the report but not from the data source.

The `RefreshEx` method is not documented in the Crystal Reports Developers help file. Occasionally, the documentation and code are out of sync, and this may be one of those times. The best way to get a list of all the methods and properties for any object you are working with is to view the object with VB's Object Browser (click the F2 button), or select View ➤ Object Browser from the menu. Once the Object Browser opens, select the library you want to view from the top-left drop-down list. The Object Browser interrogates the selected libraries' objects for all the publicly accessible methods, properties, and events and displays them and provides limited help. Figure 19.15 shows the methods, properties, and events for the Crystal Report Viewer via the Object Browser.

TIP Methods are indicated with a thrown block, events with a lightning bolt, and properties with a pointing finger. Sometimes methods properties, and events are collectively known as members of a class. A class is the program that created the object.

FIGURE 19.15

Methods, properties, and events of the Crystal Report Viewer with VB's Object Browser

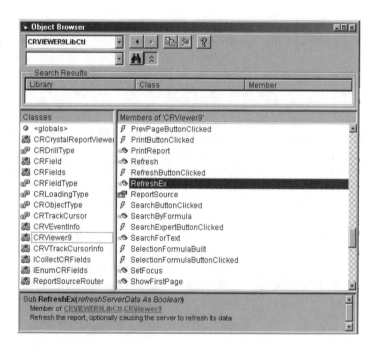

NO DATA EVENT

When you provide a user the ability to modify selection criteria for a report, it is possible that the user will pick criteria such that no data is returned to the report. The Report object in Crystal Report can intercept a no data condition and call a `NoData` event, we can write code to deal with that scenario.

To access the `NoData` event, right-click the Crystal report from the Designers folder in Project window of Visual Basic and choose View Code. In the Code window, select Report from the Object drop-down list on the left; the `NoData` event should be displayed in the Procedure drop-down list on the right. Listing 19.4 shows the code for displaying a message if a report has no data.

LISTING 19.4: DISPLAYING A MESSAGE IF A REPORT HAS NO DATA

```
Private Sub Report_NoData(pCancel As Boolean)

    MsgBox "no data in report"
    pCancel = True

End Sub
```

For our report we have simply added a message that will be displayed if the report has no data. The NoData event has a pCancel argument. If you set this argument to True, as we have done, the report will stop processing and nothing will be displayed in the Crystal Viewer. Otherwise, a blank report will be displayed with report headings and titles.

Working with Pictures in a Report

Crystal Reports has the ability to display pictures that have been stored in a database in a report. Storing pictures in a database is okay for small amounts of data, but it is very inefficient to store many pictures. Pictures are stored as binary large objects (BLOBs) in a database. BLOBs are very inefficient, and some database administrators will not even allow BLOBs to be stored in a database. A better approach would be to store the name and path of the picture in the database and change the picture using code in the report.

To set up the report we added three database fields to the Details section of a report: First Name, Last Name, and File Name. The File Name field contains the name and path of the picture. We added a picture from the hard drive by choosing Insert ➢ Picture from the Crystal Reports menu in the Report Designer. The picture we added was one of the pictures we want to modify via code. This way the Picture object added to the Crystal report will be the same size so we can format our report properly. From the Report Designer we suppressed the File Name field so it is not displayed on the report and changed the Picture Name property to Employee.

For the code, select the Format event for the Details section of the report as we did above in the section "Crystal Report Events". The FormattedPicture property of the Report object contains the picture to be displayed in the report. You set the picture by using the LoadPicture method in VB. The app.path statement gets the current path of the application and appends it to the name of the picture. Listing 19.5 shows show to change a picture at runtime.

WARNING   Modifying the picture must be done during the Format event; otherwise, the application will not work.

LISTING 19.5: CHANGING A PICTURE AT RUNTIME

```
Private Sub DetailSection1_Format(ByVal pFormattingInfo As Object)

    Set CrystalReport1.Employee.FormattedPicture = _
    LoadPicture(app.path & "\" & _      CrystalReport1.FileName.Value)

End Sub
```

TIP *Crystal Reports can also display Word and Excel documents inside a report. You are not limited to just changing pictures as we demonstrated here. Refer to* `C:\Program Files\Crystal Decisions\Crystal Reports 9\ Samples\En\Code\Visual Basic\Change Runtime Location of OLE Object` *for sample code that Crystal Reports provides for manipulating Excel and Word. Your directory structure might be different if you did not install Crystal Reports in the default directory.*

Changing Sort Criteria

We have modified the application we created in Figure 19.14 and added four option buttons (sometimes called radio buttons) so the users can choose the sort order of the report, and we have modified the Refresh command button to change the sort of the report when the report is refreshed.

The property that we need to modify on the Report object to change the sort sequence is the `RecordSortFields` property. However, working with this property is not as straightforward as working with the properties we have used so far. The `RecordSortFields` property is a Collection object that contains a group of fields on which you want the report be sorted. Think back to working with Crystal Reports; when you choose the sort order using the Record Sort Order dialog box, you can choose multiple fields that the report will be sorted on, for example, Sort by Country, then by Region. Each of the fields that you want to sort on is contained in the `RecordSortFields` collection. Listing 19.6 shows how to change the sort criteria.

NOTE *By convention, the names given to Collection objects are usually plural so they can be more easily identified as collections, but this is not always the case.*

LISTING 19.6: CHANGING SORT CRITERIA

```
Private Sub cmdRefresh_Click()
    Dim fd As CRAXDRT.DatabaseFieldDefinition

    If optName.Value = True Then
        Set fd = _ CrystalReport1.Database.Tables.Item(1).Fields(3)
    ElseIf optCity.Value = True Then
        Set fd = _ CrystalReport1.Database.Tables.Item(1).Fields(5)
    ElseIf optState.Value = True Then
        Set fd =  CrystalReport1.Database.Tables.Item(1).Fields(6)
    ElseIf optCountry.Value = True Then
        Set fd = CrystalReport1.Database.Tables.Item(1).Fields(7)
    End If

    CrystalReport1.RecordSortFields.Item(1).Field = fd
    CRViewer91.Refresh

End Sub
```

We tell Crystal Reports on what field we want the report to be sorted in the line before we refresh report viewer, near the end.

```
CrystalReport1.RecordSortFields.Item(1).Field = fd
```

The `RecordSortFields` collection contains the group of Database field objects on which you want the report to be sorted. In our report we have only one sort criteria, so there is only one item in the collection. We access it though the `Item` property of the collection. Collections start at one item. The item in the collection represents a Database object on which you want to sort the report.

You would think you could set an item equal to a database field name such as `CrystalReport1`
`.RecordSortFields.Item(1).Field = "{emp.name}"` but this will *not* work. You have to set the item equal to a Database Field object because that item collection expects a DatabaseFieldDefinition object. At the top of the program we declare a variable called `fd` that will reference a DatabaseFieldDefinition object.

We will assign to the `fd` field a database field on which we want the report sorted. Crystal Reports keeps database fields in the Database object. The Database object contains a collection of tables, and the tables contain a collection of fields that are used in the report.

NOTE *This list of tables and fields is not a complete list of tables and fields in the database; it is all the fields and tables you selected for the report.*

In our program, we check to see which option button the user selected, such as Name or City, and then assign that field to the `fd` variable. Notice that we access the Tables collection the same way we access the RecordSortFields collection—through the item number in the report:

```
Set fd = CrystalReport1.Database.Tables.Item(1).Fields(3)
```

You might be wondering how we know that `Item(1).Fields(3)` represent the Name field in the database. Fortunately there is an easy way to figure it out. The Fields object contains a `Name` property, and you can write a loop to go through all the fields in the collection and determine which field is holding which database field, as we have done in Listing 19.7.

LISTING 19.7: TECHNIQUES FOR LOOPING THROUGH A COLLECTION

```
Private Sub cmdShowNames_Click()

    Dim fds As CRAXDRT.DatabaseFieldDefinitions
    Dim fd As CRAXDRT.DatabaseFieldDefinition

    Dim counter As Integer

    Set fds = CrystalReport1.Database.Tables(1).Fields

    For Each fd In fds
        counter = counter + 1
```

```
    MsgBox counter & " " & fd.Name
Next


' or the same using the For loop

Dim x As Integer

For x = 1 To fds.Count
    MsgBox x & " " & _        CrystalReport1.Database.Tables(1).Fields(x).Name

Next x

End Sub
```

The VB language lets you loop through a collection of objects in two ways: using the For Each or For Next construct. Both constructs do the same thing; however, we find that some people are more comfortable with one or the other, so we are showing you both.

In the For Each construct, we have to declare a variable to represent the collection, fds in our case, and a variable to represent each item in the collection, fd in our case. We assign the collection to our fds variable:

```
Set fds = CrystalReport1.Database.Tables(1).Fields
```

The For Each loop will go through each object in the fds collection and assign each object to fd as it goes through the loop. We then can access the methods and properties of that item in the collection. The fd object has a Name property, and we simply display the name with a message to see which database field each object is holding.

In the For Each loop, we read the Count property of the collection (all collections have a Count property), to determine how many items are in the collection, and access each field through the loop variable X.

If we had multiple tables in our report, we could write similar code to loop through each of the tables.

NOTE   *When working with collections in Visual Basic, you can refer to the object by name or position in the collection. Unfortunately, the Crystal Reports Automation Server allows you to access the objects in a collection by position only.*

We have demonstrated how to change the sort criteria at runtime in VB. However, we also demonstrated the concepts of working with collections and objects in the collection in the RDC. These techniques of working with collections can be used in all places in the RDC where there are collections. If you think about a Crystal report from an object-oriented point of view, you will realize that it is filled with collections, objects, sections, tables, fields, etc.

Working with Parameters

In this section we are going to work with a report that contains parameters and see how to manipulate it with code. The ParameterFieldDefinitions collection and the ParameterFieldDefinition object contain the parameters in the report. Refer back to the discussion on changing sort criteria to see how to work with collections and objects in a collection.

If the Report Designer contains a report with parameters, and you refresh the report, the report will prompt you for the required parameters. This might be how you would like the report to behave; however, you might want to set the parameters for the report via code and avoid prompting the user for the parameters. In that case, you can suppress the prompting for parameters by setting the EnableParameterPrompting property of the Report object to False:

```
CrystalReport1.EnableParameterPrompting = False
```

If we disable parameter prompting, we need to set the parameter values in code, as shown in Listing 19.8.

LISTING 19.8: SETTING REPORT PARAMETERS

```
Private Sub Form_Load()

    Screen.MousePointer = vbHourglass

    CRViewer91.ReportSource = CrystalReport1
    CrystalReport1.ParameterFields(1).SetCurrentValue "UK"
    CrystalReport1.EnableParameterPrompting = False
    Form2.CRViewer91.ViewReport

    Screen.MousePointer = vbDefault

End Sub
```

The setCurrentValue method sets the parameter of the report. In our case we are hard-coding the string "UK" for the parameter value. We then turn off parameter prompting and display the report.

Notice in this example that we are setting the parameters in the report when the form is being loaded, in the Form_Load event. Parameters must be set before you view the report in the Report Viewer. If you reset the report parameters after you view the report and refresh the report, the report will not display. The workaround for this is to add another Crystal Report Viewer to the form and set its Visible property to False. Then when you want to redisplay the report with the new parameters, you need to assign the new parameter values to the report, hide the first viewer, and show the new viewer, which will display the report with the new parameters. In our example we have two viewers, one on Form1 and another on Form2. Listing 19.9 redisplays a report after changing parameter values.

NOTE *To add another viewer to a form, add a form to your VB project and then add the Crystal Report Viewer from the toolbox to the new form.*

LISTING 19.9: REDISPLAYING A REPORT AFTER CHANGING PARAMETER VALUES

```
CrystalReport1.ParameterFields(1).SetCurrentValue "CN"
Form2.CRViewer91.ReportSource = CrystalReport1
Form2.Show
Form2.CRViewer91.ViewReport
Unload Form1
```

By referring to the ParameterField object you can access properties of the parameter, such as its `MaximumValue`, `MinimumValue`, etc. In the example below, we display the name of the parameter; refer to the Report Designer Component Object Model in the help file for a list of all the methods and properties for the ParameterFieldDefinition object.

```
Dim p As CRAXDRT.ParameterFieldDefinition
Set p = CrystalReport1.ParameterFields(1)
MsgBox p.Name
```

As you can see, setting and refreshing a report with parameters is not as straightforward as changing the sort or selection criteria. Report parameters were designed to give Crystal Reports the ability to mimic a simple application by prompting the user for data before displaying the report. If you are designing a report that is going to be used in an application, then you can design the report in such a way as to make working with the report easier in code. Since Visual Basic, or any development environment that supports Crystal Reports, has a much richer interface to get and receive input data from a user, you may want to avoid using parameters in a report for an application and dynamically set the selection criteria by setting record group selection formulas.

While we are on the topic of designing reports for an application, the easiest way to incorporate Crystal Reports into an application is to design the report to include components, such as sorting, grouping, parameters, etc., and modify the objects as we show them. The Automation Server allows you to start with a blank report and add sort criteria or groups to a report using the methods and properties of the various collections. However, it is much easier to work with a prebuilt report from Crystal Reports. Also, if you don't have the Advanced Developer license, you may be unable to add certain objects to your report and you may need to work with a base report.

Exporting a Report

In your application you can give the user the ability to export your report to the various formats that Crystal Reports supports. The simplest approach is to provide the Crystal Report Export dialog box and let the user choose the export format. The following code displays the Crystal Reports Export dialog box, shown in Figure 19.16, and allows the user to choose the export format and the parts of the report to export:

```
Private Sub cmdExportUserDialog_Click()
    CrystalReport1.Export
End Sub
```

FIGURE 19.16

User choosing export format and destination

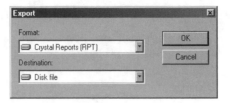

Alternatively, you can programmatically set the options for export in your program and suppress the Export dialog box. In Listing 19.10 we export the entire report to PDF format without prompting the user.

LISTING 19.10: SETTING EXPORT OPTIONS IN CODE TO EXPORT A REPORT TO PDF FORMAT

```
Private Sub cmdExportPDF_Click()

    Dim ex As CRAXDRT.ExportOptions

    Set ex = CrystalReport1.ExportOptions

    ex.DestinationType = crEDTDiskFile
    ex.DiskFileName = "c:\aExport.pdf"
    ex.FormatType = crEFTPortableDocFormat
    ex.PDFExportAllPages = True
    CrystalReport1.Export (False)

End Sub
```

Export options in Crystal Reports are contained in the ExportOption object. To access this object, create a variable that will hold a reference to the ExportOptions object, ex in our case. The ExportOptions property of the Report object contains the reference to the ExportOptions object. Assign the ExportOptions property to the ex variable. Then assign the export options required. You need to set at minimum the Destination, the Export Format Type, and the number of pages to export. Once you set these properties, you pass a False to the Export method to indicate that you do not want to see the dialog box. Listing 19.11 exports the first page of the report to Excel.

WARNING *If you don't specify all the required parameters, the application will prompt you for the missing parameter, or you will get a runtime error.*

LISTING 19.11: SETTING REPORT PARAMETERS

```
Private Sub cmdExportExcelPage1_Click()

    Dim ex As CRAXDRT.ExportOptions
```

```
Set ex = CrystalReport1.ExportOptions

ex.DestinationType = crEDTDiskFile
ex.DiskFileName = "c:\aExport.xls"
ex.FormatType = crEFTExcel70
ex.PDFExportAllPages = False
ex.ExcelFirstPageNumber = 1
ex.ExcelLastPageNumber = 1
CrystalReport1.Export (False)

End Sub
```

Setting other export destinations and formats is very similar; refer to the Export Options object in the help file for the additional formats.

Working with Formulas

Previously in this chapter we worked with Database Field Definition objects to change the sort criteria in a report. Working with formulas is very similar. The formulas in a report are contained in a FormulaFieldDefinitions collection, and you can access the formulas via the FormulaFieldDefinition object. In this example, our report has two formulas: one created using Crystal syntax and the other created using Basic syntax. Listing 19.12 shows how to change report formulas at runtime.

LISTING 19.12: CHANGING REPORT FORMUALS AT RUNTIME

```
Private Sub cmdFormula_Click()

    Dim frs As CRAXDRT.FormulaFieldDefinitions
    Dim fs As CRAXDRT.FormulaFieldDefinition

    Set frs = CrystalReport1.FormulaFields

    'figure out the location of each formula, remove this
    'code when we go to production
    dim x as integer
    x = x + 1
    For Each fs In frs
        MsgBox x & " = " & fs.Name
        X = x + 1
    Next

    'set the syntax to Crystal
    CrystalReport1.FormulaSyntax = crCrystalSyntaxFormula

    Set fs = frs.Item(1)
    fs.Text = "'Owner = ' + {Owners.OwnerLastName} + ' ' + {Owners.OwnerFirstName}"
```

```
'Set the syntax to Basic
CrystalReport1.FormulaSyntax = crBasicSyntaxFormula

Set fs = frs.Item(2)
fs.Text = "formula =  {Owners.OwnerLastName}"

CRViewer91.Refresh

End Sub
```

Each formula added to a report is added to the FormulaFieldDefinitions collection. As with sort fields, we need to reference the formula by its position in the collection. To determine which formula is in which position, we create a loop to go through all the formulas and view their names.

We then assign the formula from the collection to a Field Definition object and modify the formula by setting the Text property. Notice that we need to identify the syntax we are using by setting the FormulaSyntax property of the report before setting the formula. Make sure your formula syntax is correct or your report will have runtime errors.

Working with Graphs

Giving the user the ability to dynamically change a graph in an application at runtime is a very powerful feature. In this sample we have a report that was created with a bar graph in the Report Header. The user will be able to click a button in VB to change the graph from a bar graph to a pie graph. Listing 19.13 shows how to change a graph at runtime.

LISTING 19.13: CHANGING A GRAPH AT RUNTIME

```
Private Sub cmdPieGraph_Click()

    CrystalReport1.Graph1.GraphType = crRegularPieGraph
    CRViewer91.RefreshEx False

End Sub
```

Notice in the code that we simply reference the Graph object in the Crystal Designer by name and change the graph type. We then refresh the report without hitting the database.

The Graph object contains a large number of properties that allow you to configure the graph's appearance. Figure 19.17 shows the properties in the Properties window of VB; you can also refer to the project Graph object in the developer's help file. In our example we changed only one of the properties. As with working with graphs in Crystal Reports, you may need to experiment with the various options available before you find the right settings to make your graph look good.

FIGURE 19.17

Graph properties

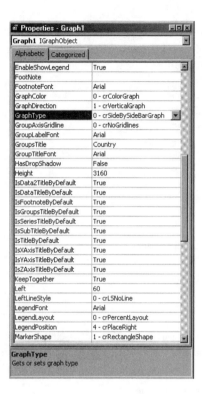

Working with Sections

A Crystal report contains various sections: Page Header, Report Footer, etc. Each of these sections in the Automation Server is an object that can be manipulated to control the appearance of your report. When working with sections in Crystal Reports, typical requirements would be to suppress a section or to go to a new page after a section. The following code sample demonstrates working with the Page Header section:

```
Private Sub cmdModifyPageHeader_Click()
    CrystalReport1.ReportHeaderSection1.Suppress = True
    CrystalReport1.ReportHeaderSection1.NewPageAfter = True
    CRViewer91.RefreshEx False
End Sub
```

You can treat a report section as an individual object as we did; however, a section is also a collection. A section contains Crystal Reports objects, such as database fields, text objects, or graphs that make up the contents of that section. In the sample code in Listing 19.14 we are going to change the graph from a bar graph to a pie graph as we did previously. However, we will access chart by looping though the objects in the sections. You may be wondering why we would do this if we can simply change the graph in one line of code as we did above. As your reports become more complex, having the ability to loop through objects in a section will prove to be very useful. This technique allows you to also work with different objects in a section without having to access them by name in the Report Designer.

LISTING 19.14: LOOPING THROUGH THE OBJECTS IN A SECTION

```
Private Sub cmdLineGraph_Click()
    Dim sc As CRAXDRT.Section
    Dim gr As CRAXDRT.GraphObject
    Dim obj As Object

    Set sc = CrystalReport1.Sections(1)
    For Each obj In sc.ReportObjects
        If obj.Kind = crGraphObject Then
            Set gr = obj
            Exit For
        End If
    Next obj

    gr.GraphType = crStackedLineGraph
    CRViewer91.RefreshEx False

End Sub
```

In this example we declare a Report Section object, a Graph object, and a generic object. We need to declare a generic object because a section can contain many different kinds of objects. We then assign one of the sections to the Section object so we can work with it.

```
Set sc = CrystalReport1.Sections(1)
```

We then build a loop to go through all the objects in that section. Since `obj` is declared as a generic object, we can assign any object to it. All objects in the Automation Server have a `Kind` property that allows us to identify what type of object we are looking at so that we then know which methods and properties are available to use. In our case we are looking for a Graph object. When we find the Graph object, we assign it to the `gr` object variable and manipulate its methods and properties.

NOTE   You can argue that assigning the generic obj object to `gr` is not necessary and that we also manipulate the graph with the `obj` variable. Yes, this is correct, but if we assign a generic object to a specific object, it makes our code easier to read and leads to fewer bugs.

Working with Subreports

Subreports are similar to sections when you deal with them in the Automation Server. A subreport can be considered another object in the report. However, a subreport is also a full report on its own, with all the objects that we have been working with so far.

In this example we are treating the report as single object and suppressing it.

```
Private Sub cmdSupressSubreport_Click()
    CrystalReport1.Subreport1.Suppress = True
End Sub
```

In the following example in Listing 19.15, we are accessing the subreport as a full report. Notice how we declare sRpt as a report variable that will reference a Report object. We then assign the subreport to sRpt by using the OpenSubreport method of the Report object. At this point, the sRpt object has all the methods and properties of the regular report, and we can manipulate the subreport's methods and properties. To demonstrate this, we change the subreport's RecordSelectionFormula using the same techniques previously used in the main report earlier in the chapter, and refresh the report.

LISTING 19.15: ACCESSING A SUBREPORT

```
Private Sub cmdChangeSubReport_Click()

    Dim sRpt As Report

    Set sRpt = CrystalReport1.Subreport1.OpenSubreport

    sRpt.RecordSelectionFormula = "{Regions.RegionCode} = 'R02'"
    CRViewer91.Refresh

End Sub
```

So far in the chapter we have been working with our report through the Report Designer, Crystal-Report1. However, in this case we have created an object variable that represents a report. The Crystal Report Designer is an object that represents a report, and it has a visual interface. In this example we still have an object that represents the report, but sRpt does not have a visual interface. We still have access to all the methods, properties, and collections of the report, but we need to access them via code instead of clicking them in the Report Designer. In working with sections we demonstrated how to loop through the objects in a section of a report to identify what kind of object it is and then manipulate the object via code. That technique would be very useful when working with a subreport because we don't have a visual interface to work with and would need a way to access the objects.

The example in Listing 19.16 is a continuation of the code above. In this example we loop through all the sections of the report and all the objects in the sections.

LISTING 19.16: LOOPING THROUGH SECTIONS IN A REPORT

```
Private Sub cmdSubReportSections_Click()

    Dim sRpt As Report
    Dim obj As Object
    Dim oSec As CRAXDRT.Section

    Set sRpt = CrystalReport1.Subreport1.OpenSubreport
    For Each oSec In sRpt.Sections
        MsgBox oSec.Name

        For Each obj In oSec.ReportObjects
```

```
        MsgBox obj.Kind & " " & obj.Name

    Next obj
  Next oSec

End Sub
```

Using this technique we are able to identify which section we are working with and what kind of object we are referencing in a section. This code is very powerful if you need to access or change many objects in a report.

Logging into a Database

Crystal Reports can connect to multiple tables for a report, and those tables can each have different connection information. To be able to deal with multiple connections, each table has a `Connection` property and `Connection` property collection that holds all the required information for a database connection. Think back to establishing a connection to a data source such as Microsoft's SQL Server or Oracle. You needed to provide Crystal Reports information, the name of the database server, the name of the database to connect to on the server, the protocol used to connect to the database, your user ID, your password, etc. All of this information is contained in the `Connection` property. In Listing 19.17 we have a report that is connected to one table, and we print the connection information for that report.

LISTING 19.17: DISPLAYING CONNECTION INFORMATION

```
Private Sub cmdViewConnectionInfo_Click()

    Dim tables As CRAXDRT.DatabaseTables
    Dim csProp As CRAXDRT.ConnectionProperties
    Dim cs As CRAXDRT.ConnectionProperty

    Set tables = CrystalReport1.Database.tables
    Set csProp = tables.Item(1).ConnectionProperties

    'if you try to print the password you will get a write only error.
    'move the debug pointer to next to continue
    For Each cs In csProp
    Debug.Print cs.Name & " = " & cs.Value
    Next

End Sub
```

Figure 19.18 displays the output of the connection information. In this example we are connecting to Microsoft's SQL Server and the sample pubs database. You can see all the connection information to the database except the password. The password is a write-only property, and if you try to print it you will get an error.

FIGURE 19.18

Connection information to SQL Server

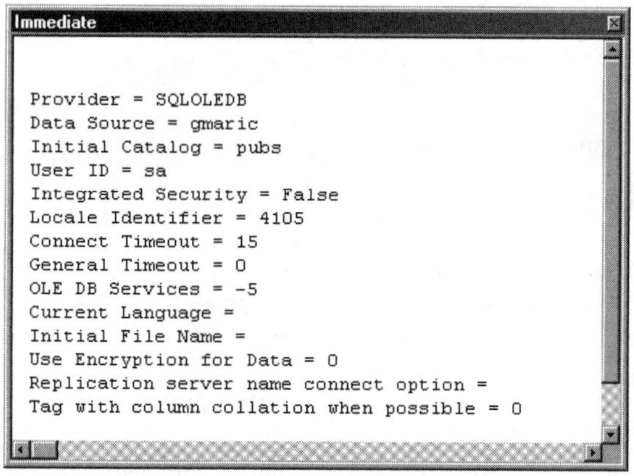

```
Immediate                                            [X]
────────────────────────────────────────────────────────
  Provider = SQLOLEDB
  Data Source = gmaric
  Initial Catalog = pubs
  User ID = sa
  Integrated Security = False
  Locale Identifier = 4105
  Connect Timeout = 15
  General Timeout = 0
  OLE DB Services = -5
  Current Language =
  Initial File Name =
  Use Encryption for Data = 0
  Replication server name connect option =
  Tag with column collation when possible = 0
────────────────────────────────────────────────────────
```

The Connection property object is called a property bag type object. This means that it contains a set of name and value pairs for each connection. Look back to Figure 19.19, and you can see the name and the value for each item. Because each data source requires different connection information, the Connection Property object was designed as a property bag so it can contain different name and value pairs for different data sources.

You can access each of the values in the Connection object through its name. In the sample in Listing 19.18, we are prompting the user for a user ID and password before displaying the report.

LISTING 19.18: DISPLAYING A REPORT ONLY AFTER A USER ENTERS A USER ID AND PASSWORD

```
Private Sub cmdSetLogon_Click()

    Dim tables As CRAXDRT.DatabaseTables
    Dim csProp As CRAXDRT.ConnectionProperties
    Dim cs As CRAXDRT.ConnectionProperty

    Set tables = CrystalReport1.Database.tables

    Set csProp = tables.Item(1).ConnectionProperties


    csProp.Item("User ID") = InputBox("ID")
    csProp.Item("Password") = InputBox("Password")
    CRViewer91.ReportSource = CrystalReport1
    CRViewer91.ViewReport

End Sub
```

Switching Data Sources

You can also modify other properties for the Connection properties. In Listing 19.19, we are modifying the Datasource property, which identifies the database server, and the Initial Catalog property, which identifies the database to report from. This allows us to switch to a different SQL Server, perhaps from a test server to a production server.

LISTING 19.19: SWITCHING DATABASES

```
Private Sub cmdSwitchDB_Click()

    Dim tables As CRAXDRT.DatabaseTables
    Dim csProp As CRAXDRT.ConnectionProperties
    Dim cs As CRAXDRT.ConnectionProperty

    Set tables = CrystalReport1.Database.tables

    Set csProp = tables.Item(1).ConnectionProperties

    csProp.Item("Data Source") = "gmaric"
    csProp.Item("Initial Catalog") = "pubs1"

    csProp.Item("User ID") = InputBox("ID")
    csProp.Item("Password") = InputBox("Password")

    CRViewer91.ReportSource = CrystalReport1
    CRViewer91.ViewReport

End Sub
```

In this example we worked with Microsoft's SQL Server; different databases will keep different connection information in the connection property bag. We find that the easiest way to work with and identify this information is to create a Crystal report and establish all the connection information in the report through the Designer. Crystal Reports will add all the necessary information to the Connection property, and we can then loop through the names and value pairs as demonstrated above and modify them as required.

NOTE *The example above will work only if you are switching databases for the same server type, for example, from one Oracle database to another Oracle database, which is the most common requirement. If you need to switch from SQL Server to Oracle, for example, then you will need to build the appropriate connection information and identify to Crystal Reports which driver and DLL to use. Refer to the Developer help file and search for "How to connect" in the Developer documentation.*

Manually Working with the RDC and Visual Basic

So far we have been loading our Crystal report using the Report Designer. As you have seen, the Designer provides an easy way to load Crystal Reports in VB. The Designer is good if you need to modify a Crystal report from within VB. If your Crystal report is already finished and you don't need to design it in VB, then you can avoid using the Designer and load the report via code. Another advantage is that you can choose which report to load at runtime instead of choosing the report at design time in VB. We are now going to duplicate what the Crystal Expert does for us so we can get a better understanding of the RDC components and have more flexibility in our application.

NOTE   If you are going to work with Crystal Reports using ASP to develop a web page, then you will need to take this manual approach. The ASP environment does not support the Crystal Expert and Report Designer. We will cover Crystal Reports and ASP in the next chapter.

Loading a Report without the Report Designer

Before you can work with Crystal Reports, you need to make a reference to the Crystal Report libraries. Start Visual Basic and start a new standard application. From the Project menu select References and choose the Crystal Reports 9 ActiveX Designer Run Time Library. Remember that there are two Automation Server libraries: Crystal Reports 9 ActiveX Designer Runtime Library and Crystal Reports 9 ActiveX Designer Design and Runtime library. We are going to open an existing Crystal report, so we require the Crystal Report 9 ActiveX Designer Runtime Library. You would use the other library if you were going to build a report via code.

Remember back in our discussion of the RDC objects that we said the main object in the hierarchy is the Application object; however, we have not used it yet. Actually we have—Crystal Expert created the Application object automatically for us via the Report Designer. We can create this object ourselves, as shown here:

```
Dim crApp As New CRAXDRT.application
Dim Report As Report

Set Report = _
  crApp.OpenReport(App.Path & "\" & "ResortList.rpt")
```

The first line of code creates the Crystal Report Application object; notice that we used the `New` keyword to build the object. The second line of code creates a variable that will reference a Crystal report. Notice that we don't use the `New` keyword this time because the `OpenReport` method of the Application object will create the report and pass back a reference to the report.

At this point we have a report in memory, and we can access all its methods and properties via the Report object. We could repeat the samples we previously discussed, such as changing the Field object or the sort sequence by accessing the report via the Report object variable instead of `CrystalReport1` variable, which is the name of the designer. The Report Designer gave us access to the Crystal Report via `CrystalReport1`, but we now have access to it via the `Report` variable. It does not matter how you get access to the report, as long as you have are reference to the Crystal Report, you can manipulate it via code. That why all of our example above still apply. An advantage of accessing a Crystal report without the Report Designer is that you can choose which report to load at runtime. You can provide a Windows Common dialog box so your users can choose the Crystal report, as shown in Listing 19.20. If you were using the Report Designer, you would have to preload all the reports.

LISTING 19.20: CHOOSING A REPORT TO OPEN AT RUNTIME

```
Private Sub cmdChooseReport_Click()

    Dim crApp As New CRAXDRT.Application
    Dim Report As Report
    Dim strRptPath As String

    CommonDialog1.Filter = _
      "Reports (*.rpt)|*.rpt|All files|*.*"
    CommonDialog1.ShowOpen

    If CommonDialog1.FileName <> "" Then
        strRptPath = CommonDialog1.FileName
        Set Report = crApp.OpenReport(strRptPath)
        CRViewer91.ReportSource = Report
        CRViewer91.ViewReport
    Else
        MsgBox "Select a report"
    End If

End Sub
```

At this point we have a report in memory that we can manipulate via code. If your application only needs to print or export the report and does not need to display it, then you don't need to load the Crystal Report Viewer.

Displaying the Report

If you want to display the report in the application, you need to add the Crystal Report Viewer to a VB form. From the Project menu choose Components and select Crystal Report Viewer 9. Then from the VB toolbox add the Crystal Report Viewer to the form. All you need to do now is tell the viewer which report to display.

```
CRViewer91.ReportSource = Report
CRViewer91.ViewReport
```

When you add a Report Viewer manually to the form, you will need to manually add the viewer resize code if you want the Report Viewer to resize with your form. The Report Expert did this for us automatically:

```
Private Sub Form_Resize()

  CRViewer91.Top = 0
  CRViewer91.Left = 0
```

```
CRViewer91.Height = ScaleHeight
CRViewer91.Width = ScaleWidth

End Sub
```

By manually controlling the components of the RDC, we are using memory efficiently in our application. The Crystal Expert provides an easy way to start with VB and Crystal, but this approach is preferable.

Embeddable Crystal Reports Designer Component

So far we have shown how to view and manipulate a report. The RDC includes a Report Designer Component that allows you to provide Crystal Report design capabilities in your application. Figure 19.20 shows a Visual Basic application using the Report Designer. Notice how you can provide the user the same capabilities as Crystal Reports has in a custom application.

The Report Designer Component is an ActiveX control that you must add to the VB toolbox before it can be used. To add the component, select Project ➤ Components and choose Embedded Crystal Reports 9 Designer Control.

In our application we will give the user the ability to open an existing report, create a new report, and modify designer options using the buttons we added to the top of our form, shown in Figure 19.19.

FIGURE 19.19

Report Designer
Component

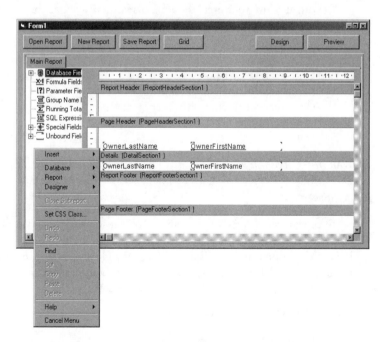

To work with the Report Designer, you must make a reference to the Crystal Reports ActiveX Designer Design and Runtime Library. Select Project ➤ References and choose Crystal Reports 9

ActiveX Designer Design and Runtime Library. In the following code example, notice that when we dimensioned the Application object and the Report object, we prefixed the object with CRXDDRT, as opposed to CRXDRT. We have been using the Crystal Reports 9 ActiveX Designer Runtime Library, CRXDRT, until now. Crystal Reports 9 ActiveX Designer Design and Runtime Library allows you to create and modify reports at runtime.

```
Dim crApp As New CRAXDDRT.Application
Dim crRep As CRAXDDRT.Report
```

To open a report we use the OpenReport method of the Application object and set the Report variable to the newly open report. In this example we hard-code a report name to keep it simple; we could have also used a Common dialog box like we did in the previous example. Once a report is created, to display the report in the Report Designer you must assign the Report object property to the object variable that is referencing the Crystal report.

```
Private Sub cmdOpenReport_Click()

Set crRep = _
  crApp.OpenReport(App.Path & "/" & _ "design.rpt")
CRDesignerCtrl1.ReportObject = crRep
End Sub
```

You can also give your users the ability create a new report by using the NewReport method of the Application object and setting the Report variable to the new report:

```
Private Sub cmdNewReport_Click()

    Set crRep = Nothing
    Set crRep = crApp.NewReport
    CRDesignerCtrl1.ReportObject = crRep

End Sub
```

WARNING *This code will run only if you have the Advanced Developer Edition of Crystal Reports. The Regular Developer Edition does not allow report creation. If you run this code without the correct license, you will get a "Creation feature not enabled" error.*

To provide report preview capabilities you need to add the Crystal Report Viewer to your application. From the Project menu choose Components and select Crystal Report Viewer 9. We added the Report Viewer on top of the Report Designer and set the Visible property of the viewer to False so it can't be seen. When the user clicks the Preview button, shown in Figure 19.20, we show the Report Viewer and assign to the viewer's ReportSource property the object variable referencing the report.

```
Private Sub Form_Load()

    CRViewer91.Visible = False

End Sub
```

```
Private Sub cmdPreview_Click()

    CRViewer91.Visible = True
    CRViewer91.ReportSource = crRep
    CRViewer91.Refresh
    CRViewer91.ViewReport

End Sub
```

When the user wants to go back to Report Design mode, we simply hide the Report Viewer again.

```
Private Sub cmdDesign_Click()

    CRViewer91.Visible = False

End Sub
```

FIGURE 19.20

Previewing a report from the Report Designer

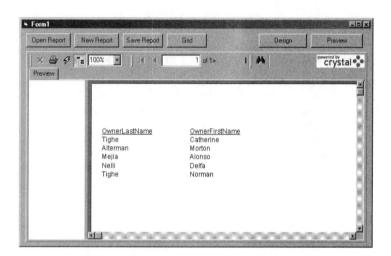

Reports created in the Report Designer can be saved to Crystal Report files, as shown here:

```
Private Sub cmdSaveReport_Click()

    CRDesignerCtrl1.SaveReport ("c:/test.rpt")

End Sub
```

You can provide your users the same options that are in Crystal Reports to modify the Report Designer. In this case we are toggling the grid in the Report Designer:

```
Private Sub cmdDisplayGrid_Click()

    If CRDesignerCtrl1.DisplayGrid = True Then
        CRDesignerCtrl1.DisplayGrid = False
```

```
        Else
            CRDesignerCtrl1.DisplayGrid = True
        End If

    End Sub
```

NOTE   *Refer to the Developers help file for "Embeddable Crystal Reports Designer Control Object Model" for the complete set of methods and properties for the Report Designer.*

Crystal Report Viewer

Throughout this chapter we have modified the Crystal Report Viewer's Top, Left, Height, and Width properties in the Form_Resize event so that the Report Viewer will resize with the form in which it is displayed. The Crystal Report Viewer has many methods and properties that allow you to fully control the viewer at runtime. In Listing 19.21 we turn off all the features of the viewer so we can maximize the amount of the report we see in the form, as shown in Figure 19.21.

LISTING 19.21: MODIFYING THE CRYSTAL REPORT DESIGNER

```
    Private Sub cmdModifyViewer_Click()

        CRViewer91.DisplayBackgroundEdge = False
        CRViewer91.DisplayTabs = False
        CRViewer91.DisplayToolbar = False
        CRViewer91.DisplayGroupTree = False

    End Sub
```

You can also enable and disable viewer functionality by setting properties. For example, to disable printing set the EnablePrintButton property to False:

```
    CRViewer91.EnablePrintButton = False.
```

Refer to the help file for a full list of methods, properties, and events for the viewer.

The Crystal Report Viewer will also fire events to your VB application like other Windows controls, so you know what users are doing in your application and can fully control it. Figure 19.22 displays the Crystal Viewer events.

FIGURE 19.21

The customized
Crystal Report
Viewer

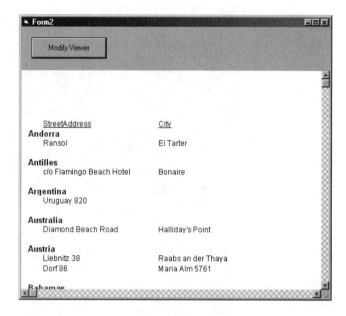

FIGURE 19.22

Report Viewer events

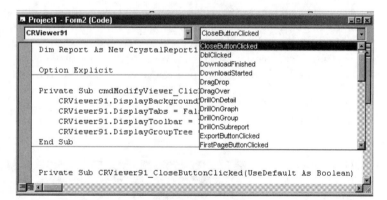

Deploying Your Applications

Once your application is written and tested, you need to deploy it to your users. The easiest way to deploy your application is to create a `setup.exe` installation package using the Package and Deployment Wizard from Microsoft Visual Basic. Compile your completed Visual Basic application and choose the Start ➤ Programs ➤ Microsoft Visual Studio 6.0 ➤ Microsoft Visual Studio Tools ➤ Package & Deployment Wizard to start the wizard. In the first screen of the wizard, choose the VBP project file for your application and click the Package button, as shown in Figure 19.23.

FIGURE 19.23

Package and
Deployment
Wizard

The Package and Deployment Wizard will analyze your VB project and determine which DLLs will need to be deployed with the application. Figure 19.24 shows the list of DLLs required for an application and in particular the RDC Automation Server DLL. Click the Next button, and choose the destination for the `setup.exe` program and the CAB file. Continue clicking Next and indicate where to install the your application on the Start menu. After you answer a number of questions, the wizard will create three files: `setup.exe` and two files that are named the same as your project with `.cab` and `.1st` extensions. To deploy your application, copy those three files to your user's computer or to network drive where your user can access the files and run `setup.exe`.

TIP   CAB files contain your program and the DLLs required by your program. The `setup.exe` program extracts the contents from the CAB files when installing your application on the remote user's computer.

FIGURE 19.24

RDC Automation
Server DLL

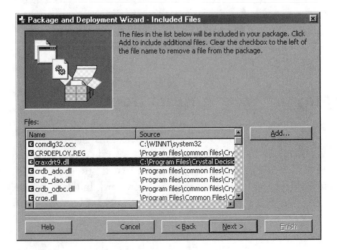

The setup program will install your application as well as the Automation Server, Crystal Report Viewer, and any other components you used in your application. Test your application on a user's machine to make sure everything works as expected.

Keep these things in mind when deploying your application:

◆ Your users must have the same database software and connectivity setup configured as on your development computer. If they don't, the reports in your application will fail or you will need to dynamically configure the database the report is using via the Automation Server; refer back to "Switching Data Sources" in this chapter. Make sure everything works on one user's computers before doing a widespread deployment.

◆ If your users have other Visual Basic applications that use Crystal Reports, make sure those applications still work as expected. During the installation process you installed shared DLLs, such as the Automation Server, and it is possible that you installed a newer version of a DLL when another application expects the older version of the DLL. Your application may work fine, but you may have broken the other application in the process.

TIP   *In addition to the samples we provided in this chapter, Crystal Reports includes samples in the following directory:* `C:\Program Files\Crystal Decisions\Crystal Reports 9\Samples\En\Code\Visual Basic`.

Summary

Building an application that uses Crystal Reports requires working with the different components of the RDC. The RDC consists of Report Viewers, Report Designers, and Automation Server objects. Each of these fulfills a specific task for Crystal Reports, such as designing the report in VB or viewing the report in your application.

The heart of the RDC is the Automation Server, which contains all the objects and collections that represent Crystal Reports. The Application object refers to the Crystal report and allows you to create and open reports. The Report object refers to a Crystal report, and the Database object refers to the data sources the report is using. Using these objects, you can manipulate every aspect of Crystal Reports via code and provide your users a custom application that contains Crystal Reports.

The RDC Automation Server can be used in a VB application as well as in any development environment that supports COM-based objects, such as ASP or Delphi.

Chapter 20

ASP Web Applications

IN CHAPTER 19, "BUILDING Windows Applications with the Report Designer Component," we showed you how to use the RDC in a Windows application; now we are going to discuss how to use the RDC in an ASP application. Setting up an ASP application is little more work; fortunately, once it is done you can reuse your code. As we explained in Chapter 17, "The Crystal Programming Forest," there are many ways to do the same thing. In this chapter we are going to focus on the RDC, and we will cover the Remote Application Server (RAS) in Chapter 24, "Report Application Server."

> *Business Question: I need to develop a web-based reporting system that serves up data dynamically and in a manner that's easy to use. What's the best way to do that?*

The main benefit of a web-reporting solution is that you skip all of the installation hassles of software on end-user machines. The Crystal viewer of your choice is delivered automatically from the web server into the end user's Internet cache and becomes available for all the reports that the user views.

Two Main Technologies

With Crystal Reports 9, there are two main technologies to focus on when considering web reporting. The first of these technologies is called the Report Design Component, or RDC. The RDC comprises a complete, web-ready COM wrapper around the Crystal reporting engine and allows for full control over the loading and displaying of reports. New features in Crystal 9 make the RDC even more powerful and easy to use.

A handy reference to the RDC can be found in the file `TechRef.pdf`, located in the `DOCS` folder of your Crystal CD, or in `C:\Program Files\Crystal Decisions\Crystal Reports 9\Developer Files\Help\en\ CrystalDevHelp.chm`.

The second technology available to you for web reporting is called the Report Application Server, or RAS. This technology is brand new to Crystal Reports version 9. It is a COM (and/or Java) technology designed explicitly for the Web. RAS can be used to customize the standard web viewers to the point where they can exist on web pages with other information, so, for example, a chart could be displayed in the corner of a web page from a Crystal report. You can learn more about RAS in Chapter 24.

An explanation providing a nice overview of the two technologies can be found in the file DevGuide.pdf, located DOCS folder of your Crystal CD.

NOTE   The PDF files in the DOCS folder are not copied to your hard drive during the installation, so you'll need to go back to your Crystal CD to find these handy guides.

Report Design Component Programming

We will use some of the reports from previous chapters in this book to put together the beginnings of a web application that contains Crystal Reports. One particular focus of these examples will be to create some *reusable* Active Server Page code, so that once a basic reporting engine is in place, putting a new report in your library becomes an easier task.

The first step (after successfully installing Crystal Reports 9 on your web server) is to create an application in IIS and point it to a virtual directory on your network. Then you should copy the files listed in Table 20.1 from your local Crystal 9 installation to that directory.

TABLE 20.1: FILES FROM CRYSTAL 9 INSTALLATION

FILE	DESCRIPTION
Cleanup.asp	Removes instances of RDC objects in memory, for both licensing and resource reasons.
framepage.asp	Used by the HTML viewer to set up frames.
htmstart.asp	Contains the start page of the HTML viewer.
rptserver.asp	Holds shared code that interfaces the viewers to the RDC.
SmartViewerActiveX.asp	Contains the ActiveX viewer component (IE).
ActiveXPluginViewer.asp	Contains the ActiveX viewer component (Netscape).
SmartViewerJava.asp	Contains the Java viewer component (IE).
JavaPluginViewer.asp	Contains the Java viewer component (Netscape).
toolbar.asp	Used by the HTML viewer.

NOTE   These files, assuming you installed Crystal 9 in its default location, can be found in folder C:\Program Files\Crystal Decisions\Crystal Reports 9\Samples\En\Code\Web\Report Designer Component.

Next you should hunt down some sample code that Crystal Decisions provides online. The file is called aspxmps8.exe and can be found by going to http://support.crystaldecisions.com and searching for that filename. There are dozens of examples in this download, but for the time being we're interested only in two files with the following names:

◆ AlwaysRequiredSteps.asp

◆ MoreRequiredSteps.asp

These two files are located multiple times, in many of the folders created by the download, so you should have no trouble finding them. Copy these two files into the IIS application virtual directory with the other files from above.

Now that you've stolen code from multiple places for your own evil purposes, it's time to write some code yourself. Create a new file named GenericReportViewer.asp in the same virtual directory folder with all the other files, and fill it with the code from Listing 20.1 (either in Visual Interdev, Notepad, or the ASP editor of your choice).

LISTING 20.1: GENERICREPORTVIEWER.ASP<% LANGUAGE="VBSCRIPT" %>

```
<% Response.Expires = 0 %>

<html>

<head>
<title>Report Viewer</title>
</head>

<%
    ReportName = Request.QueryString("rpt")
    cCom       = Request.QueryString("com")
    cSel       = Request.QueryString("sel")

    Server.ScriptTimeOut = 180

%>

<!-- #include file="AlwaysRequiredSteps.asp" -->

<%
    session("oRpt").ReportComments = cCom
    session("oRpt").RecordSelectionFormula = cSel
%>

<!-- #include file="MoreRequiredSteps.asp" -->
<!-- #include file="SmartViewerActiveX.asp" -->
</body>
</html>
```

Note that this code makes use of the include file capabilities of Active Server Pages. Three ASP files are included in this one listing. The first two, AlwaysRequiredSteps.asp and MoreRequired-Steps.asp, are the ones you swiped from the example code found online. The last one, SmartViewer-ActiveX.asp, places the ActiveX Report Viewer on this web page.

You should be ready to see your first report online. Place an RPT file in your virtual folder, and then type the following URL into your web browser:

`http://localhost/crystal/GenericReportViewer.asp?rpt=CH02.rpt`

Your URL will vary based on the name of your web server, the name you gave your web application in IIS (the one above is named `crystal`), and the name of the report that you wish to view. Assuming all is well, you should see something like the Report Viewer shown in Figure 20.1.

WARNING *Remember that the report contains the connection information and that the server that is running this report needs the same connectivity information for the report to run. When you first test, we suggest copying the VistaNation's database to the virtual directory and building a report from that database. That way you can concentrate on getting the ASP instead of connectivity. We will show you how to go to other databases later.*

FIGURE 20.1

Report Viewer

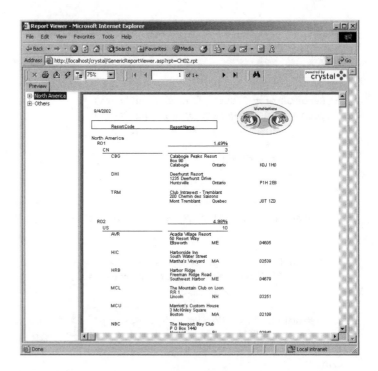

Note that you included the name of the report to display in the query string of the URL. This means that you could display virtually any Crystal report using this same code simply by changing the query string. This second query string displays a different report:

`http://localhost/crystal/GenericReportViewer.asp?rpt=CH7.rpt`

How It All Works

You just cobbled together a web-reporting solution using ASP files from several different sources, so some explanation might be in order as to how these files work together.

The top of the `GenericReportViewer.asp` program, shown in Listing 20.1, is pretty standard for a web page. The first actual lines of ASP code set three variables named *ReportName*, *cCom*, and *cSel*.

The *ReportName* variable is referenced in the file `AlwaysRequiredSteps.asp`, a portion of which is shown here (with the comments removed):

```
Path = Request.ServerVariables("PATH_TRANSLATED")
   While (Right(Path, 1) <> "\" And Len(Path) <> 0)
   iLen = Len(Path) - 1
   Path = Left(Path, iLen)
Wend
If IsObject(session("oRpt")) then
   Set session("oRpt") = nothing
End if
On error resume next
Set session("oRpt") = session("oApp").OpenReport(path & reportname, 1)
```

The purpose of this block of code is to retrieve the physical path in which the current ASP resides and to initialize the session-level variable named *oRpt* by opening the Crystal report having the name stored in variable *ReportName*. The *oRpt* variable is the Report object part of the RDC, as you saw previously in Chapter 19. Likewise, the *oApp* variable is an instance of the RDC Application object. The rest of `AlwaysRequiredSteps.asp` does some error checking to make sure the Report object was created successfully, sets a few properties on the Report object, and then discards any data that might have been saved with the report:

```
If Err.Number <> 0 Then
  Response.Write "Error Occurred creating Report Object: " & _
Err.Description
  Set Session("oRpt") = nothing
  Set Session("oApp") = nothing
  Session.Abandon
  Response.End
End If

session("oRpt").MorePrintEngineErrorMessages = False
session("oRpt").EnableParameterPrompting = False
session("oRpt").DiscardSavedData
```

This marks the end of the `AlwaysRequiredSteps.asp` file, so code execution resumes in `GenericReportViewer.asp`, where two properties of the Report object are set based on values retrieved at the top of this page:

```
session("oRpt").ReportComments = cCom
session("oRpt").RecordSelectionFormula = cSel
```

You'll see the purpose of these properties a bit later in this chapter. Next comes the execution of `MoreRequiredSteps.asp`, shown here in its entirety:

```
<%
'================================================================
' Retrieve the Records and Create the "Page on Demand" Engine Object
'================================================================
On Error Resume Next

session("oRpt").ReadRecords

If Err.Number <> 0 Then
  Response.Write "Error Occurred Reading Records: " & Err.Description
  Set Session("oRpt") = nothing
  Set Session("oApp") = nothing
  Session.Abandon
  Response.End
Else
  If IsObject(session("oPageEngine")) Then
     set session("oPageEngine") = nothing
  End If
  set session("oPageEngine") = session("oRpt").PageEngine
End If
%>
```

This code is responsible for reading the records out of the database and into the report and checking to determine whether this read was successful. The code also initializes the `PageEngine` variable, used later. The `PageEngine` class is also part of the RDC—it is the object that generates each page of the report and sends it to the client.

Finally, `SmartViewerActiveX.asp` is included:

```
<HTML>
<HEAD>
<TITLE>Crystal Reports ActiveX Viewer</TITLE>
</HEAD>
<BODY BGCOLOR=C6C6C6 ONUNLOAD="CallDestroy();" leftmargin=0 topmargin=0
rightmargin=0 bottommargin=0>

<OBJECT ID="CRViewer"
   CLASSID="CLSID:2DEF4530-8CE6-41c9-84B6-A54536C90213"
   WIDTH=100% HEIGHT=100%
   CODEBASE="/viewer9/activeXViewer/activexviewer.cab#Version=9,2,0,442"
VIEWASTEXT>
<PARAM NAME="EnableRefreshButton" VALUE=1>
<PARAM NAME="EnableGroupTree" VALUE=1>
<PARAM NAME="DisplayGroupTree" VALUE=1>
<PARAM NAME="EnablePrintButton" VALUE=1>
<PARAM NAME="EnableExportButton" VALUE=1>
<PARAM NAME="EnableDrillDown" VALUE=1>
```

```
<PARAM NAME="EnableSearchControl" VALUE=1>
<PARAM NAME="EnableAnimationControl" VALUE=1>
<PARAM NAME="EnableZoomControl" VALUE=1>
</OBJECT>

<SCRIPT LANGUAGE="VBScript">
<!--
Sub Window_Onload
    On Error Resume Next
    Dim webBroker
    Set webBroker = CreateObject("WebReportBroker9.WebReportBroker")
    if ScriptEngineMajorVersion < 2 then
        window.alert "IE 3.02 users on NT4 need to get the latest version of VBScript
or install IE 4.01 SP1. IE 3.02 users on Win95 need DCOM95 and latest version of
VBScript, or install IE 4.01 SP1. These files are available at Microsoft's web site."
    else
        Dim webSource
        Set webSource = CreateObject("WebReportSource9.WebReportSource")
        webSource.ReportSource = webBroker
        webSource.URL = "rptserver.asp"
        webSource.PromptOnRefresh = True
        CRViewer.ReportSource = webSource
    end if
    CRViewer.ViewReport
End Sub
-->
</SCRIPT>

<script language="javascript">
function CallDestroy()
{
    window.open("Cleanup.asp");
}
</script>

</BODY>
</HTML>
```

This client-side script instantiates an instance of the ActiveX Crystal Report Viewer. The `Object` tag defines which ActiveX object we're instantiating. ActiveX controls are differentiated by their ClassID. This long hexadecimal number is called a GUID (globally unique identifier) and is unique for every ActiveX control. Internet Explorer automatically determines whether the client machine has this ActiveX control installed at runtime and, if not, downloads it from the specified source. This is exactly why web-based reporting is so easy from the standpoint of client installs —because IE does it automatically.

NOTE   *A separate include file, named* `ActiveXPluginViewer.asp`, *should be used for Netscape clients.*

The various PARAM tags configure the ActiveX viewer. Most of the buttons on the viewer can be made visible or invisible. The standard include file as shown above leaves all buttons and the group tree visible.

Finally, an instance of the WebReportSource9.WebReportSource object is created and is set to point to the file rptserver.asp. This last ASP file is quite large and does all the actual report rendering. You don't need to understand the contents of this file to comprehend how the basic components of your RDC web-reporting server function.

NOTE   *Keep in mind that the first time users try to use the ActiveX viewer they will be prompted to download the viewer. If the security settings are set high in IE, this download may be prevented.*

Changing the Database Connection String

The two report examples shown earlier use the VistaNations Access database and reports found earlier in this book. They both assume that the web server can "see" the Access MDB file in the same physical location as when the report was developed (on the root of the C: drive). If the Access database is not found, you may see this error when you attempt to view the report in your browser.

```
Error Occurred Reading Records: Logon failed. Details: DAO Error Code:
 0xbd0 Source: DAO.Workspace Description: Could not find file
 'C:\VistaNations.mdb'.
```

Of course, you could fix this by copying the Access database to the root of the C: drive of your web server, but your network manager may hit you with something. She probably doesn't want "stuff" mucking up the C: drives of her servers. Clearly, you're going to need a way to dynamically change the location of the database in the report.

The code you'll need to write depends on exactly where the database is going to be located. If the database is going to be in a known, "hard-coded" location on the server, you can do something like the following:

```
<%
   cDB = "D:\Database\VistaNations.mdb"
   for each t in session("oRpt").Database.Tables
      t.Location = cDB
   next
%>
```

Note how the code loops through all of the tables in the report and sets their location to the location specified by variable *cDB*. If the database is located in the same folder as the rest of the files, then the following code will retrieve the name of that folder and set all the tables in the report to that location.

```
<%
   Path = Request.ServerVariables("PATH_TRANSLATED")
   While (Right(Path, 1) <> "\" And Len(Path) <> 0)
      iLen = Len(Path) - 1
      Path = Left(Path, iLen)
   Wend
```

```
    for each t in session("oRpt").Database.Tables
        t.Location = Path & "VistaNations.mdb"
    next
%>
```

This code is similar to the prior one but uses the *PATH_TRANSLATED* variable available in Active Server Page code to get the physical path of the current page.

The code examples above would be placed in the `GenericReportViewer.asp` application, between the `include` commands for `AlwaysRequiredSteps.asp` and `MoreRequiredSteps.asp`.

SQL Server Database Connections

Setting Microsoft SQL Server connection information is done much differently than for Access connections:

```
svr = "MyServer"
usr = "MyUser"
pwd = "MyPwd"
db = "MyDB"

session("oApp").LogonServer  "PDSSQL.DLL", cStr(svr), cStr(db),cStr(usr), cStr(pwd)
```

This code is explicit to Microsoft SQL Server because of the `PDSSQL.DLL` parameter used as the first parameter to the `LogonServer` method. Logging onto different servers is done with different DLL names.

NOTE *You won't find a* PDSSQL.DLL *if you look for it on your PC. The parameter, although it looks like a filename, no longer corresponds to the actual name of the DLL containing the SQL Server connection code. Refer to the help file for the other driver names for different databases.*

The method shown is also different than the `PropertyBag` method used in Chapter 19, but both methods serve an equivalent purpose.

This `LogonServer` call on the RDC Application object (stored in session variable *oApp*) is necessary before the call to `ReadRecords`, which can be found in the `MoreRequiredSteps.asp` file. The example above shows hard-coded SQL Server credentials. You would more commonly put this information in session variables in the `global.asa` file or some other more easily accessible place. Your environment may also require the dynamic retrieval of the SQL Server logon parameters based on the current intranet user if your SQL Server uses its own security logins or mixed-mode authentication.

Changing Selection Criteria

The example so far can load and display any report and dynamically change the database location. Another useful ability is to dynamically change the selection criteria of the report so that it can display records for a certain date range or location in the alphabet or whatever other selection criteria that make sense for your report.

The `GenericReportViewer` ASP code listed earlier already supports changing the selection criteria on the fly. All that needs to be done is to pass the criteria in the query string, like so:

```
http://localhost/crystal/GenericReportViewera.asp?rpt=CH02.rpt&sel={Resorts.
StateProvince}='NV'
```

You should be greeted with the filtered report shown in Figure 20.2.

FIGURE 20.2

Filtered report

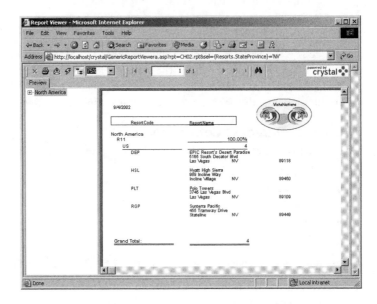

The key to this functionality is that the selection criteria are pulled off the query string and into the variable *cSel*:

```
cSel        = Request.QueryString("sel")
```

The criteria are later placed into the `RecordSelectionForumula` property of the RDC Report object:
```
session("oRpt").RecordSelectionFormula = cSel
```

TIP   *Once we have our ASP environment set up, we can focus on the RDC objects and manipulate their methods and properties. Chapter 19 provides further RDC examples.*

NOTE   *We are passing the selection string on the address line for simplicity; ideally you would build an interface where users can choose the selection criteria and build the selection string behind the scenes, as shown later in this chapter.*

Report Comments

The Report Comment field in a Crystal Report (found in Special Fields) can be used in any section of a report. One common use for the Report Comment is in the Page Header to serve as a subtitle, often explaining in plain text to readers of the report which records are selected.

In the `GenericReportViewer` example listed above, report comments are handled in the identical way as record selection criteria. A third query string, named `com`, supports the entry of a comment field:

```
http://localhost/crystal/GenericReportViewera.asp?rpt=CH02.rpt&sel={Resorts.
StateProvince}='NV'&com=Resorts%20in%20NV
```

This field is extracted from the query string and later placed into the `ReportComments` property of the RDC Report object:

```
cCom  = Request.QueryString("com")
.
<code removed>
.
session("oRpt").ReportComments = cCom
```

We are setting the RDC `ReportComments` property with the `com` value from the URL. You can see the Report Comment at the top of the report in Figure 20.3.

FIGURE 20.3

Report comment

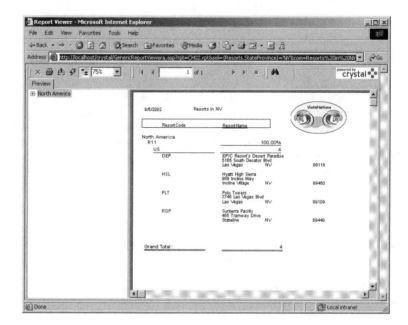

Form Posting

The method of setting up a report by passing query string information in the URL can handle many different reporting cases, but it's sometimes difficult for a programmer to build that long of a query string. The super-long query strings are also a bit more unsightly. Fortunately, there is another, more robust method to send information from one web page to another, and that's by using an Active Server Page form on one page and posting that information to the second page.

Consider the following Active Server Page, named `CH7Params.asp`, which sets up a simple data entry form:

```
<%@ LANGUAGE="VBSCRIPT" %>

<html>
```

```
<head>
<meta NAME="GENERATOR" Content="Microsoft FrontPage 3.0">
<title>Resort Report</title>
</head>

<body bgColor=lightyellow>
<font face=Tahoma>
<p><font size=4>Select Letter that Resort Begins With</font></p>

<hr>
<form  name="fFRM" method="post" action="GenericReportViewer.asp">

<table>
<tr><td>Enter the Start of the Resort Code</td></tr>
<tr><td><INPUT type="TEXT" name=tbStart></td></tr>

</table>
<p>
<input type="submit" value="Submit" name="cbGo"></P>
<input type="hidden" name="hCom"  value=" ">
<input type="hidden" name="hRpt"  value="CH7.rpt">
<input type="hidden" name="hSel"  value=" ">
</FORM>

<script LANGUAGE="VBSCRIPT">

Sub cbGo_OnClick

   cLet  = fFRM.tbStart.Value

   cSel = "{Resorts.ResortCode} startswith '" & cLet & "'"

   fFRM.hSel.Value = cSel
   fFRM.hCom.Value = "Resorts Beginning with Letter '" & cLet & "'"
   fFRM.Submit

end sub

</script>
</FONT>
</body>
</html>
```

This code creates a form with four input elements (only one of which is visible), as shown in Figure 20.4.

The visible input element is a text box that the end user can type into. The three hidden elements represent the Report Name (hRpt), the Selection Criteria (hSel), and the Report Comments (hCom). Note how the Report Name element is prefilled with the name of the report we will display (this element could be changed on the fly based on elements the user selects; for example, you could set up a Summary Report Only check box that would change the report displayed).

FIGURE 20.4

Form with four input elements

The client-side VBScript procedure cbGo_OnClick is processed when the user clicks the Submit button. This code takes the contents of the text box and places it in both the selection criteria and the report comment variables and then submits the form. The form is programmed to post to your old friend, GenericReportViewer.asp. This web page still needs a bit more modification, however. It is currently designed to retrieve the three important variables from the URL, or query string. It needs to be modified to retrieve the variables from the preceding page's form. Instead of creating an almost identical page except for this retrieval method, it is easy to combine both methods into one page:

```
<%
    'report information can come via form OR querystring
    'check form first

    ReportName = Request.Form("hRpt")
    cCom       = Request.Form("hCom")
    cSel       = Request.Form("hSel")
    if len(trim(ReportName)) = 0 then
        ReportName = Request.QueryString("rpt")
        cCom       = Request.QueryString("com")
        cSel       = Request.QueryString("sel")
    end if


    Server.ScriptTimeOut = 180

%>

<!-- #include file="AlwaysRequiredSteps.asp" -->
```

This code first looks for variables on a posted form having the names *hRpt*, *hCom*, and *hSel* (the exact names of the three hidden elements on page CH7Params.asp). If the *hRpt* variable is not found or is empty, then the query string (the data on the address line of the browser, like we saw above) is parsed for the same information (this page will not work without a valid Crystal report name specified, so it is assumed that if the *hRpt* variable is blank, then the query string method is being used to send the data to the page).

The GenericReportViewer has just gained quite a bit of functionality. You can pass necessary information to display any report, with any selection criteria, along with comments, as a URL string. Alternatively, you can set up a "parameters" Active Server Page with user interface elements so that the user can specify date ranges, partial search strings, or any other elements, and these values can easily be posted over to the generic viewer as the selection criteria for any Crystal report. The data received from the parameters page can be used to modify the selection criteria or the group selection criteria of the RDC Report object.

Choosing a Different Viewer

Not content to provide only one way to view a report when three or four can do it better, Crystal Decisions provides different types of web-enabled viewers. Actually, because of the evolving web-browser market, they had no choice. The samples above use the ActiveX viewer. In addition, there are a Java-based viewer and a frame-based HTML-only viewer. The ActiveX viewer provides the closest rendition of the report in a browser but will work only with Internet Explorer. The Java viewer is the next best choice for rendering your report but requires a Java-compatible browser. Both viewers will download code to your browser, and your users will receive warning messages that a viewer will be installed. The HTML and HTML frames viewer will work on all browsers, but your report will lose formatting. You can base your choice on what technology works best for your environment.

To change viewers, modify the last line in GenericReportViewer.asp. To use the ActiveX viewer, the line should appear as one of the following:

```
<!-- #include file="SmartViewerActiveX.asp" -->
<!-- #include file="JavaPluginViewer.asp" -->
<!-- #include file="FramePage.asp" -->
```

Screenshots of the Java viewer and the HTML viewer are shown in Figure 20.5 and Figure 20.6.

NOTE *The Java runtime environment must be present on your machine in order to use the Java viewer. You will be prompted to download it automatically the first time you attempt to use the Java viewer (assuming you have a valid Internet connection).*

FIGURE 20.5

The Java viewer

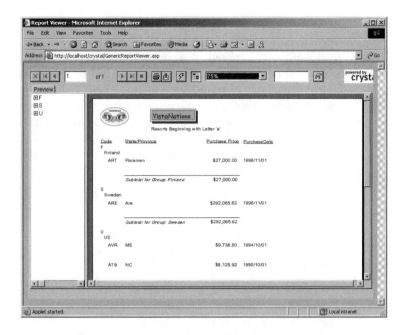

FIGURE 20.6

The HTML viewer

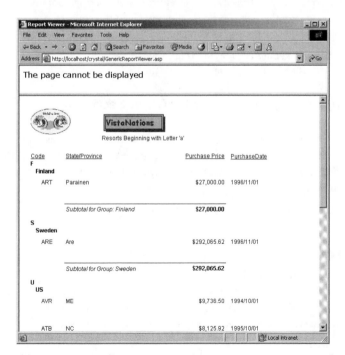

Reports with Parameters

The previous sections give enough examples to put together a generic, web-based Crystal viewer that can show multiple reports and allow for the changing of selection criteria and report comments at runtime. Of course, we have access to the entire RDC from Active Server Page code, and we can design any kind of application we would like.

One such feature is the use of report parameters. These are often used in conjunction with report-selection criteria to limit the data shown in a report. Parameters are a bit more difficult to use in Active Server Page code, only because the report's parameters are exposed as a collection, and this collection must be looped through in order to find a certain parameter by name and set it by value. Here is an example of some Active Server Page code that does that:

```
For Each oParam in session("oRpt").ParameterFields
    Select Case oParam.ParameterFieldName
        Case "pShowallValues"
            iValue = Request.QueryString("Show")
            oParam.SetCurrentValue Clng(iValue)
    End Select
Next
```

This loop looks for a parameter named pShowallValues and, if/when found, sets that value to the value in the Show portion of the query string.

Of course, if you know that your report has only a single parameter, then this loop is not necessary—you can specify the first (and only) parameter in the collection:

```
Set oParam = session("oRpt").ParameterFields(1)
iValue = Request.QueryString("Show")
oParam.SetCurrentValue Clng(iValue)
```

Suppressing Detail Lines (or Other Sections)

Another useful property exposed by the RDC is the Suppress property on the Section object. Using this, you can dynamically suppress any section in a report. This might be useful for offering the option of a detail or a summary only by using a single Crystal report file, with a check box on the Options page selecting whether to suppress or not. The line below shows the suppression of Section number 3 in a report:

```
session("oRpt").Sections(3).Suppress = true
```

Summary

Writing Active Server Page code to interface with Crystal Reports is not much different than writing standard Visual Basic code from the standpoint that the developer has access to the entire RDC for the dynamic display of reports. The developer nevertheless must be aware of the architectural differences between a synchronous client/server environment and an asynchronous web-based environment. The web interface gives the developer an almost zero client install footprint (depending on the viewer chosen) on the end-user machine, and the developer can put together a few simple web pages for the creation of a generic reporting interface that can handle the display of many different types of Crystal Reports.

Chapter 21

.NET Applications

IN LATE 2001, MICROSOFT changed all the rules by introducing their new application development framework, known collectively as .NET (pronounced "dot net"). This object-oriented programming platform consists of a set of classes, known as the .NET Framework, as well as several new programming languages that build upon the Framework. .NET can be used to develop traditional desktop applications, as well as Internet/intranet applications (using the new flavor of Active Server Pages called ASP .NET). This chapter will familiarize you with the display of Crystal Reports from several different .NET program types.

The chapter assumes that the reader is not brand new to .NET development and has at least some experience writing applications in the new platform.

Desktop Applications

The traditional desktop application is not dead, even if many trends in development point to browser and Intranet-based development. In fact, the .NET Framework hopes to bring about more of a sort of hybrid application—one that relies on an Intranet backbone for data transferring but uses Windows forms as the primary user interface.

Crystal Reports can be viewed from the standard Windows Forms app in several different ways, with each way having its own pros and cons. You'll see demonstrations of each method here.

Report Embedding

The first way to include a Crystal report in your application is to "embed" it right into the project and therefore the final executable. The advantage to this method is that you no longer have to distribute separate RPT files with your program. Follow the steps below to see a sample application that embeds a report into a Windows application:

1. Create a new Windows Forms application in either Visual Basic or C#.

2. Add a `CrystalReportViewer` control to the default form (you will need to scroll down in the toolbox to find it). Set the `Dock` property to `Fill` so that the viewer's size expands as the form expands. Resize the form to a decent size so that most of parts of the Crystal Report Viewer are visible.

3. From the Solution Explorer, right-click the project name and select Add ➢ Add Existing Item. In the Add Existing Windows dialog, change the file type to Crystal Reports and navigate on your hard drive to the location of an RPT file and select it. You should see the RPT file in your project and be able to edit the report using the Crystal Report Designer built into Visual Studio .NET.

NOTE *Adding a Crystal report to your project in this way copies the RPT file from the location you specify into the project folder, so you will still have an unaltered copy of the report in its original location.*

4. The act of adding the report to the project also created a wrapper class for the report. If you wish to see this class, click the Show All Files button at the top of Solution Explorer, and the Crystal Report node in the Treeview will be shown with a child node on it. Opening this node will reveal a VB or CS file with the same name as the Crystal report. Figure 21.1 shows the Solution Explorer with the embedded report and the generated class under it.

FIGURE 21.1

Solution Explorer

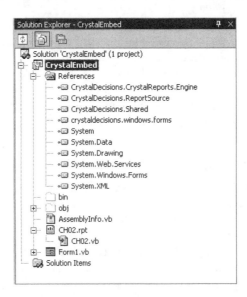

WARNING *You can look at the code in this file to see how Visual Studio .NET generates a class wrapper around the report, but you cannot edit this code because your changes will continually get overwritten as changes are made to the report and saved.*

5. Add a `ReportDocument` instance to your project. This class is found in the Components tab of the toolbox. After you drag this class to your form (you can drop it on the Form Viewer that

takes up the whole form), the Choose A ReportDocument dialog, shown in Figure 21.2, asks you to choose one of the report classes to tie to this `ReportDocument` object. This is an easy choice in this sample project, as only one report has been added to the project so far.

FIGURE 21.2

Choose A Report-Document dialog

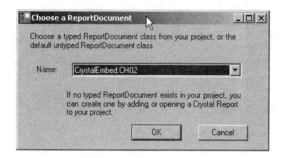

6. Select the `CrystalReportViewer` object on your form and set the `ReportSource` property to the bound `ReportDocument` instance you just created. Figure 21.3 shows how this will appear in the Property Inspector.

FIGURE 21.3

Property Inspector

7. Run the project. All the hookups should be complete. Running the project should show you the desired Crystal report in the viewer, as shown in Figure 21.4.

FIGURE 21.4

Report Viewer

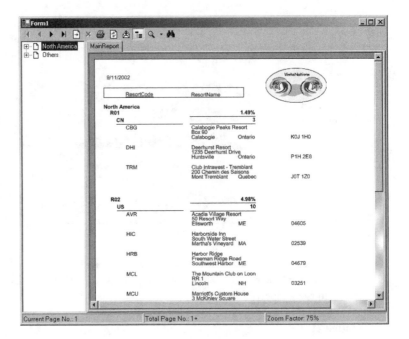

CUSTOMIZING THE REPORT

Okay, you've embedded a report into a Windows Forms project. Usually, for a report to be useful, you must do some measure of runtime customization. For example, you often need to set the report selection criteria to specify a date range or otherwise limit the data displayed. Further customization is also possible, like suppressing detail sections to give the option of a summary-only report.

You can gain access to the Report objects through the `ReportDocument` object that you placed in the project. For example, this snippet of code sets the report-selection criteria:

```
cH021.RecordSelectionFormula = "{Resorts.ResortCode}='CBG'"
aViewer.ReportSource = cH021
```

NOTE   *The formula we pass to the `RecordSelectionFormula` is the same syntax we use in Crystal Reports.*

Note that the second line of code rebinds the *ReportDocument* variable cH021 to the Crystal Viewer. This is a required step when doing any runtime manipulation to the Report object, even if you have already bound the `ReportSource` property to this *ReportDocument* variable at runtime.

Logging into a secure database is also done via the `ReportDocument` object. The following code snippet loops through all the tables in a report and sets the login credentials to the values found in four variables (possibly loaded from a CONFIG file, INI file, or the Registry):

```
Dim oTable As Table
Dim oLogonInfo As TableLogOnInfo
For Each oTable In cH021.Database.Tables
   oLogonInfo = oTable.LogOnInfo
```

```
    With oLogonInfo
        .ConnectionInfo.ServerName = FSQLServer
        .ConnectionInfo.DatabaseName = FSQLDatabase
        .ConnectionInfo.UserID = FSQLUser
        .ConnectionInfo.Password = FSQLPassword
    End With
    oTable.ApplyLogOnInfo(oLogonInfo)
Next
```

You also have access to each individual report element in your report. For example, suppose you want to change the font of the report dynamically to match a user-selected font in your application. To do this, you would have to loop through every Report object and change the font. This is actually much easier than it sounds:

```
Imports CrystalDecisions.CrystalReports.Engine
Imports CrystalDecisions.Shared

Private Sub cbFontClick(ByVal sender As System.Object, _
    ByVal e As System.EventArgs) Handles cbFont.Click


Dim oSec As Section
Dim o As ReportObject
Dim f As New Font("Arial", 8, FontStyle.Italic)

For Each oSec In cHO21.ReportDefinition.Sections
    For Each o In oSec.ReportObjects
        Select Case o.Kind
            Case ReportObjectKind.FieldObject
                With CType(o, FieldObject)
                    .Color = Color.Red
                    .ApplyFont(f)
                End With
            Case ReportObjectKind.TextObject
                With CType(o, TextObject)
                    .Color = Color.Red
                    .ApplyFont(f)
                End With
        End Select
    Next
Next
aViewer.ReportSource = cHO21

End Sub
```

This code loops through every object in every section of the *ReportDocument* variable, which is named ch021 (this is the default name given to a variable of class ch02, which is the name of the wrapper class generated around the RPT file we imported into the project earlier). It looks for all of the `FieldObjects` and `TextObjects` in each section and, when found, changes their font to red, italic, 8 point, Arial.

The object model within the `ReportDocument` object gives you access to every element within the report, including all of the fields, sections, formulas, parameters, summary information, database connectivity information, and printer options. See the online help for the `ReportDocument` object for a complete reference to customizing the report at runtime.

CUSTOMIZING THE VIEWER

You can also customize the `CrystalReportViewer` control itself in a number of ways. Each of the buttons at the top of the report, as well as the group tree to the left of the viewer, can be shown or hidden. The following code example shows or hides all of the buttons at the top of the viewer and the toolbar based on the value of a check box:

```
'checkbox reading "bare bones viewer". When checked, turn stuff off
Dim bShow = Not cbViewer.Checked

With aViewer
    .DisplayToolbar = bShow
    .DisplayGroupTree = bShow
End With
```

You also have access to each individual button on the tool. If you wanted to prevent the user from being able to export or print from the viewer, for example, then you can simply turn those two buttons off:

```
With aViewer
    .ShowExportButton = false
    .ShowPrintButton = false
End With
```

HANDLING EVENTS

The viewer fires off a number of events that allow you to create interactivity with it. The complete list of events is `Drill`, `DrillDownSubreport`, `HandleException`, `Navigate`, `ReportRefresh`, `Search`, and `ViewZoom` (see the Visual Studio .NET online help for an explanation of what each event does).

The short event handler below updates a label named `lbPage` with the current page number in the viewer. It also plays a trick on the user of the program in that it prevents the user from navigating to page 3 of the report by setting the `Handled` property to `True`. Setting the *Handled* variable to `True` tells the Crystal Report Viewer that you have handled the `Navigate` event yourself, so it should not continue performing this function.

```
Private Sub aViewer_Navigate(ByVal source As Object, _
    ByVal e As CrystalDecisions.Windows.Forms.NavigateEventArgs) _
    Handles aViewer.Navigate

If e.NewPageNumber = 3 Then
    e.Handled = True
```

```
    Else
        lbPage.Text = "Page " & e.NewPageNumber
    End If
End Sub
```

Loading Reports on the Fly

There are definite benefits to embedding all of the Crystal Reports into an application, but there are drawbacks as well. Many times, an end user will ask for a simple change to a report (such as adding an underline or changing a font). This change can be done very quickly in a freestanding Crystal report, but making a change to an embedded report would require a recompile of the application.

The alternative to embedding the reports in an application is to leave the RPT files loose and load them into a `CrystalReportViewer` object at runtime. This has the disadvantage of not being able to edit your reports directly in Visual Studio .NET, but some might argue that the Report Editor that comes with Crystal Reports 9 is easier to use anyway.

Crystal Reports 9 comes with a sample .NET project that demonstrates the dynamic loading of reports in this way. The project is called `Simple` and by default is located in the folder `C:\Program Files\Crystal Decisions\Crystal Reports 9\Samples\En\Code\.NET\WinForms\VB` or `C:\ Program Files\Crystal Decisions\Crystal Reports 9\Samples\En\Code\.NET\WinForms\C#` (choose your favorite language).

The project consists of a `CrystalReportViewer` on a form, with a single button. The code behind the button is shown in Listing 21.1 and is the only code in the application.

LISTING 21.1: SIMPLE.SLN

```
Private Sub btnSelectReport_Click(ByVal sender As _
    System.Object, ByVal e As System.EventArgs) _
    Handles btnSelectReport.Click

    Dim dlg As New OpenFileDialog()
    dlg.Title = "Select Crystal Reports file"
    dlg.Filter = "Crystal Reports (*.rpt)|*.rpt|All Files (*.*)|*.*"
    dlg.InitialDirectory = "C:\Program Files\Microsoft Visual
    ➥Studio.NET\Crystal Reports\Samples\Reports"

    If (dlg.ShowDialog() = DialogResult().OK) Then
        Me.Cursor = Cursors.WaitCursor
        crystalReportViewer().ReportSource = dlg.FileName
        Me.Cursor = Cursors.Default
    End If
End Sub
```

This code displays a common dialog box and prompts the user to locate an RPT file on disk, and then it displays the report in the viewer by setting the viewer's `ReportSource` property. Could it be any easier?

If the report being loaded from disk needs no further modification, then loading the report using this method works perfectly well. If the report does need runtime modifications like those demonstrated above, the method of loading shown here bypasses the use of the `ReportDocument` object. While the code above gets the report shown on the screen, it makes it a bit more difficult to customize the report later using all of the techniques described in the previous section. By changing the above example very little, we can achieve the same result but use a `ReportDocument` object so we can have access to all of the cool customization features. Listing 21.2 shows the modified code.

LISTING 21.2: A BIT LESS SIMPLE.SLN

```
Private Sub Button1_Click(ByVal sender As _
    System.Object, ByVal e As System.EventArgs) _
    Handles Button1.Click

Dim dlg As New OpenFileDialog()
Dim oDoc As ReportDocument

dlg.Title = "Select Crystal Reports file"
dlg.Filter = "Crystal Reports (*.rpt)|*.rpt|All Files (*.*)|*.*"
dlg.InitialDirectory = "C:\Program Files\Microsoft Visual
➥Studio.NET\Crystal Reports\Samples\Reports"

If (dlg.ShowDialog() = DialogResult().OK) Then
    Me.Cursor = Cursors.WaitCursor
    Try
        oDoc = New ReportDocument()
        oDoc.Load(dlg.FileName, OpenReportMethod.OpenReportByTempCopy)

        crystalReportViewer.ReportSource = oDoc
    Finally
        Me.Cursor = Cursors.Default
    End Try
End If

End Sub
```

There are really only two lines that differ, with a `Try..Except` exception-handling block thrown in for good measure. The *oDoc* variable is of the coveted `ReportDocument` type, and this variable is loaded with the report chosen by the user in the `OpenFileDialog`. The *ReportDocument* variable is then passed as the `ReportSource` of the viewer. By performing this intermediate step, you now have access to all of the customization abilities shown in the previous section.

Application Deployment

Once you've created a Windows Forms application, you often need to create a Setup project in order to deploy it on end-user machines. .NET applications are much easier to deploy than previous Visual Basic projects, but there are still some "gotchas" that you need to look out for.

The first thing to obviously make sure of is that you include any RPT files in your setup application that your program may load on the fly. Embedded reports need not be considered because, by definition, they are embedded in the application.

There are also some specific dependencies for Crystal Reports that must be installed on the end-user machine. These dependencies are called *merge modules* and are part of a Setup and Deployment project. To create a Setup and Deployment project, first open the Windows Forms solution that you wish to deploy, then select Add Project from the File menu. Navigate to Setup And Deployment Projects in the Project Types list, and select Setup Project from the Templates list, as shown in Figure 21.5. Give your project an appropriate name and click OK.

FIGURE 21.5

Creating a Setup and Deployment project

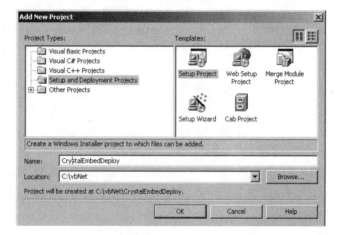

Once you've created the Setup and Deployment project, right-click the project name and select Add ➤ Merge Module, as shown in Figure 21.6.

FIGURE 21.6

Adding merge modules

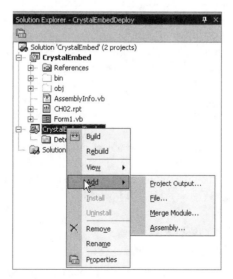

From the dialog that comes up, select the following merge modules:

`Managed.msm`

`Database_Access.msm`

`Database_Access_enu.msm`

`Regwiz.msm.`

When you add this last merge module, you will be prompted to type in your Crystal Reports license key if you have not done so in a previous project. Once you've entered these merge modules, along with all the other application-specific files you wish to deploy in this project, you can build the Setup project (choose Rebuild Solution or Rebuild <projectname> from the Build menu), and all of the runtime libraries required for your program to display Crystal Reports properly will be created for you. Figure 21.7 shows the final output of the Setup project: a `Setup.exe` file, an MSI file, and some other support files.

FIGURE 21.7

Setup project output

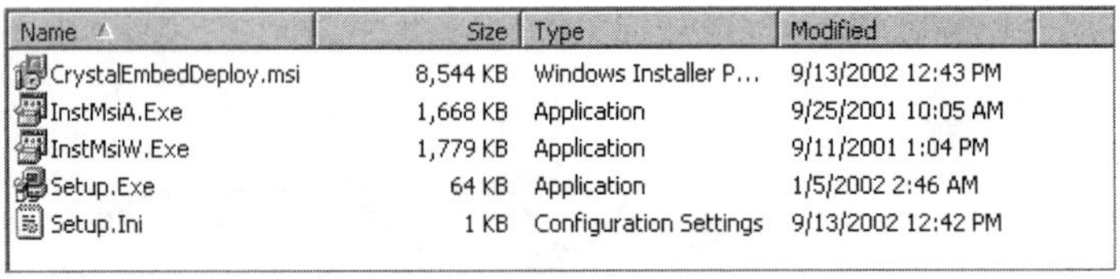

Name △	Size	Type	Modified	
CrystalEmbedDeploy.msi	8,544 KB	Windows Installer P...	9/13/2002 12:43 PM	
InstMsiA.Exe	1,668 KB	Application	9/25/2001 10:05 AM	
InstMsiW.Exe	1,779 KB	Application	9/11/2001 1:04 PM	
Setup.Exe	64 KB	Application	1/5/2002 2:46 AM	
Setup.Ini	1 KB	Configuration Settings	9/13/2002 12:42 PM	

Running `Setup.exe` on an end user's machine will make your application available for use on that computer.

ASP .NET Applications

Microsoft didn't stop with changing Visual Basic and creating the new language C# when they introduced the .NET Framework—they also greatly enhanced the Active Server Page platform and integrated it into the .NET language family. You can now choose to develop web code in any of the .NET languages, whether you are a VB syntax guru or a C# type of coder.

The method of developing web applications is also much easier and is similar to desktop application development. You can now design web pages by dragging user interface elements onto a canvas, sizing and positioning them dynamically, and setting properties in the Visual Studio Property Browser, much like Windows Forms applications are designed.

The Web Forms version of the Crystal Report Viewer does behave a bit differently than its Windows counterpart but is every bit as functional. Also, as is the case in other aspects of ASP .NET versus desktop .NET development, the underlying object model for interfacing with Crystal Reports is identical under both platforms, meaning the end of learning two APIs. Since you've already become familiar with the `ReportDocument` class in .NET desktop development, you have a big head start on hooking up Crystal Reports in the ASP .NET world.

Adding a Report to a Web Page

To embed a report onto a web page, follow the steps below:

1. Create a new ASP .NET application. Select your favorite .NET language.

2. Open the default page in the application, named `WebForm1.aspx`.

3. Drag a `CrystalReportViewer` control onto the web page. You should see a gray descriptive box, as shown in Figure 21.8.

FIGURE 21.8

Adding a Crystal
Viewer to a web page

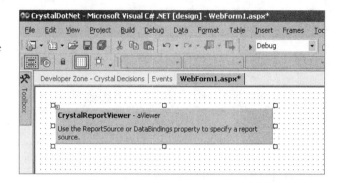

4. To bind the viewer to a report, click the button next to the `Databindings` property in the Property Inspector. You will see a dialog like the one shown in Figure 21.9. Select the `Report-Source` property from the Bindable Properties list, click the Custom Binding Expression button on the lower right, and then type in the name and location of the desired RPT file on your hard drive. Make sure that the web server has rights to the folder you specify and that you include double quotes around the name. Also note that the screenshot below uses double back-slashes in the filename because this is a C# example. You would not double the backslashes if your project were a VB .Net project.

FIGURE 21.9

Binding a report to
the viewer

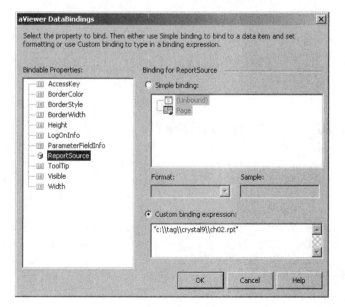

If you specify the report filename successfully, you should see the actual report data in the viewer, while still in Design mode, as shown in Figure 21.10.

FIGURE 21.10

Viewing the report data

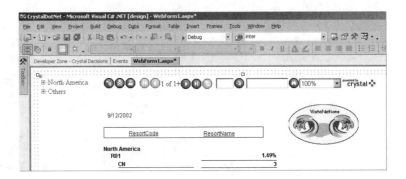

To complete the viewer code, go into the code-behind file for WebForm1.ascx, find the OnInit method call (you may have to expand the Visual Studio-generated code), and add a DataBind method to the end of the routine. The completed routine should look like this:

```
override protected void OnInit(EventArgs e)
    {
    //
    // CODEGEN: This call is required by the ASP.NET Web Form Designer.
    //
        InitializeComponent();
        base.OnInit(e);
        DataBind();
    }
```

You can now compile and run your application and see the report in your web browser.

NOTE   *In a Visual Basic .NET project, you would add the* Databind *method to the existing* Page_Init *procedure, as opposed to* OnInit.

Loading Web Reports on the Fly

As with Windows applications, embedding the report name in the web page is handy, but loading the report on the fly could be even more so. As you can imagine, like the ASP-based generic report viewer that we created in Chapter 19, "Building Windows Applications with the Report Designer Component," it would be pretty easy to create a similar reporting engine in ASP .NET code.

One of the best parts about ASP .NET development is that the object model between Windows Forms and Web Forms is often identical, meaning that if you've learned how to do something on one platform, then there's a good chance that you can do it on the other platform as well.

Listing 21.3 shows a piece of C# code that loads a report into a web-based CrystalReportViewer control at runtime.

LISTING 21.3: C# LOADING OF A CRYSTAL REPORT AT RUNTIME

```csharp
using System;
using System.Collections;
using System.ComponentModel;
using System.Data;
using System.Drawing;
using System.Web;
using System.Web.SessionState;
using System.Web.UI;
using System.Web.UI.WebControls;
using System.Web.UI.HtmlControls;
using CrystalDecisions.CrystalReports.Engine;

namespace CrystalDotNet
{
    /// <summary>
    /// Summary description for OnTheFly.
    /// </summary>
    public class OnTheFly : System.Web.UI.Page
    {
        protected CrystalDecisions.Web.CrystalReportViewer aViewer;
        protected ReportDocument oDoc;

        private void Page_Load(object sender, System.EventArgs e)
        {
            // Put user code to initialize the page here
            ReportDocument oDoc = new ReportDocument();
            oDoc.Load("c:\\tag\\crystal9\\ch02.rpt");
            aViewer.ReportSource = oDoc;
        }

        … Visual Studio auto-generated code removed…
    }
}
```

Other than the syntax, this should look very similar to the desktop examples shown earlier. A *Report-Document* variable is declared and a report is loaded into it. That variable then becomes the `ReportSource` value for the viewer. One useful implementation of this technique might be to create a menu of available reports that are loaded dynamically as the user selects the desired report from the menu.

If you're thinking ahead, you might already be asking if this `ReportDocument` object is customizable in the same ways that it was in the Windows Forms world. The answer is yes!

CUSTOMIZING THE REPORT AT RUNTIME

The `ReportDocument` object that was used in the previous section is the same `ReportDocument` object used in the Windows Forms examples, meaning that the coder can use it to customize the Crystal report at runtime using all the same methods. Listing 21.4 shows the ASP .NET, C# version of the code shown earlier to turn all of the `FieldObject` and `TextObject` elements in the report to an italic, red font.

LISTING 21.4: RUNTIME REPORT OBJECT CUSTOMIZATION

```csharp
using System
using System.Collections;
using System.ComponentModel;
using System.Data;
using System.Drawing;
using System.Web;
using System.Web.SessionState;
using System.Web.UI;
using System.Web.UI.WebControls;
using System.Web.UI.HtmlControls;
using CrystalDecisions.CrystalReports.Engine;
using CrystalDecisions.Shared;

namespace CrystalDotNet
{
    /// <summary>
    /// Summary description for OnTheFly.
    /// </summary>
        public class OnTheFly : System.Web.UI.Page
        {
            protected CrystalDecisions.Web.CrystalReportViewer aViewer;
            protected ReportDocument oDoc;

    private void Page_Load(object sender, System.EventArgs e)
            {
                // Put user code to initialize the page here
                oDoc = new ReportDocument();
                oDoc.Load("c:\\tag\\crystal9\\ch02.rpt");
                MakeItRed();
                aViewer.ReportSource = oDoc;
            }

    private void MakeItRed()
            {
                Font f = new Font("Arial", 8, FontStyle.Italic);

                foreach (Section oSec in oDoc.ReportDefinition.Sections)
                    foreach (ReportObject o in oSec.ReportObjects)
                    {
                        switch (o.Kind)
                        {
                        case ReportObjectKind.FieldObject:
                            (o as FieldObject).Color = Color.Red;
                    (o as FieldObject).ApplyFont(f);
                    break;
                        case ReportObjectKind.TextObject:
```

```
                        (o as TextObject).Color = Color.Red;
                    (o as TextObject).ApplyFont(f);
                    break;
                      }
                }

            }
            … Visual Studio auto-generated code removed…
        }
    }
```

Other than the preponderance of curly braces, this code should look pretty familiar. It takes the `ReportDocument` object and loops through each section, and each `ReportObject` within each section, hunting down `FieldObject` and `TextObject` instances, and changes the font and color of each one.

REPORT CACHING

Crystal Reports can take advantage of the caching mechanism built into ASP .NET projects, meaning that you can improve the reports used by many users. To take advantage of this caching ability, however, the report must be brought directly into your project. Let's see how to do this.

Just as in Windows Forms applications, you can add any RPT file to your ASP .NET project. Simply right-click the project name in the Solution Explorer, select Add ➤ Add Existing Item, and navigate to an available RPT file. The report will then be shown in the Solution Explorer as part of the project. If you then click Show All Files at the top of the Solution Explorer, you will see that a CS file (or a VB file, depending on what language your project is based on) has been automatically generated. An examination of this file will show that two wrapper classes have been created based on the report, as shown here:

```
public class CH7 : ReportClass { ... }

public class CachedCH7 : Component, ICachedReport { ... }
```

The details of this class are not important, as you cannot change any of the code in this auto-generated module. What is important to see is how the second class implements the `ICachedReport` interface, meaning that it has provided ASP .NET caching functionality.

This second, cacheable class is the one that you will use in your web page. An instance of this class can be used as the `ReportSource` for a `CrystalReportViewer`, as shown in Listing 21.5.

LISTING 21.5: USING A CACHED REPORT CLASS IN A VIEWER

```
using System;
using System.Collections;
using System.ComponentModel;
using System.Data;
using System.Drawing;
using System.Web;
```

```
using System.Web.SessionState;
using System.Web.UI;
using System.Web.UI.WebControls;
using System.Web.UI.HtmlControls;

namespace CrystalDotNet
{
   /// <summary>
   /// Summary description for CachedReport.
   /// </summary>
   public class CachedReport : System.Web.UI.Page
   {
   protected CrystalDecisions.Web.CrystalReportViewer aViewer;
   protected System.Web.UI.WebControls.Label lbNote;

   protected   CachedCH7 oRpt;

      private void Page_Load(object sender, System.EventArgs e)
      {
         // Put user code to initialize the page here
         oRpt = new CachedCH7();
         aViewer.ReportSource = oRpt;
      }

      … Visual Studio auto-generated code removed…

   }
}
```

INTERACTIVITY WITH THE REPORT VIEWER

The Viewer control provides a number of events that you can use to enhance the interactivity of report navigation. Two such event examples are shown below. The Drill event is fired whenever the user drills down into the report. The parameters passed into the Drill event allow you to determine exactly where the user is drilling. The event code below updates a label control's contents with the name and level of the group the user just clicked on:

```
private void aViewer_Drill(object source, CrystalDecisions.Web.DrillEventArgs e)
   {
      string s;

      s = "you clicked on group " + e.NewGroupName;
      s += ", level " + e.NewGroupLevel;
      lbOut.Text = s;
   }
```

Another event available in the viewer is the `ViewZoom` event, called whenever the user changes the Zoom level. The simple example below updates a label with the old and new zoom levels if the zoom is 50 percent or above and prevents the user from zooming below 50 percent:

```
private void aViewer_ViewZoom(object source, CrystalDecisions.Web.ZoomEventArgs e)
    {
      if (e.NewZoomFactor < 50)
      {
        lbOut.Text = "zooming too small disallowed";
         e.Handled = true;
      } else
        lbOut.Text = "zoomed from " + e.CurrentZoomFactor + " to " +
e.NewZoomFactor;
    }
```

Summary

The .NET world is brand new, and there are numerous options for hooking up Crystal Reports into the different types of available .NET applications. A wide range of report runtime customization and interactivity is available in all of the different reporting methods. The examples shown here should give you a number of techniques for serving all your corporate reports to your end users, as we've shown you how to embed a report into both a web-based and traditional desktop application or to load the RPT file on the fly.

You've seen how to access the `ReportDocument` class so you can customize the report at runtime. You've also seen how to handle events sent from the viewer and how to make your ASP .NET reports perform quickly via caching. This should give you enough options to provide a multifunctional, reusable reporting engine in your .NET applications.

Chapter 22

XML Web Services

THE INTERNET HAS MATURED over the last few years to where we are starting to use it for more than simple web browsing. The Internet is beginning to be used for business-to-business communications, where one company's system communicates with another company's system across the Internet to exchange information. Crystal Reports provides a web service that allows your company to provide reports to other companies' applications across the Internet.

> *Business Question: I want my customers to be able to use my Crystal Reports in their applications over the Internet or an intranet. How can I do that?*

Covered in this chapter:

◆ What web services are

◆ Technology standards for web services

◆ Building a Crystal report as a web service

◆ Displaying a Crystal report from a web service

What Are Web Services?

Web services are an evolution of object-oriented technologies that we are already using. In the previous object-oriented chapter, Chapter 18, "The Object-Oriented Primer," we took a look at the evolution of programming to object-oriented programming (OOP). We saw how common computer routines (computer code) evolved into objects and how those objects then became reusable components in different applications. In the previous three chapters, we used the Crystal Reports objects to add reports to our custom applications.

If we step back from the details of the Crystal objects and examine the architecture, we can see that the Crystal objects are installed on the same computer as our application. If we wanted to write another application on a different computer, we would have to install the objects on that computer before we could use them. This leads to the same objects being installed in multiple places. A drawback to this type of design is that each application must have the same set of objects installed on each computer for the application to work. If we needed to upgrade an object to fix a bug, we would have to upgrade it in multiple places. Wouldn't it be nice if we did not have to install these objects on each computer and could instead install them on a central object server? We could then use those objects from that server in many applications. If we needed to upgrade our objects, we could ensure that all our clients received the update by upgrading those objects on the server.

There are a number of technologies that allow objects to reside on a server and clients to call and use those objects. The technologies are Microsoft's Distributed Component Object Model (DCOM), Java's Remote Method Invocation (RMI), and Common Object Request Broker Architecture (CORBA). Essentially these technologies do similar things. They allow a client to communicate with a remote server and use the objects on the remote server. The downside to these technologies is they are not compatible with one another. A DCOM component can't be used with a client that expects a CORBA object. You have the benefit of distributing objects and centralized object management. However, you are tied to a particular technology or vendor because the different technologies are not compatible.

The Internet has necessitated the creation of standards that allow computers with different operating systems and web servers to communicate. When you surf to a computer and get a web page, you don't know, or care, if the computer is running Microsoft's IIS (Internet Information Server) web server or Apache's web server on Linux. You simply receive a web page with the information you requested. For different browsers and web servers to communicate, the various vendors have agreed on standards such as TCP/IP (Transport Control Protocol/Internet Protocol) and HTML (Hypertext Markup Language) so everybody can share information no matter what operating system or language they are using.

A set of Internet standards has been created so objects can be placed on a web server and then used by any application. Web services are those objects. Web services allow any application to call them across the Internet and use the methods in those web services.

NOTE   *Internet standards are governed by the World Wide Web Consortium at* www.w3c.org.

Web Service Example

Before we look at the Crystal Reports web services, let's examine a simple web service so we can see how they work. Web services can be written in any language as long as they follow the standards; we will examine those standards later in the chapter. First we will create a very simple web service that accepts two numbers, adds the numbers, and then sends back the result. We will build our web service using Microsoft's Visual Studio .NET and call it AddMe.

BUILDING A SIMPLE WEB SERVICE

Designing and building a web service is not much different from building an object. You decide what methods and properties need to be created for the object and then build the code. The pseudocode for our AddMe web service would look like this:

```
Public Function AddMe(x As Integer, y As Integer) As Long
    Return x + y
End Function
```

To write this web service in Visual Studio .NET, start Visual Studio .NET and create a new Visual Basic Project, ASP.NET web service project by clicking File ➤ New Project as shown in Figure 22.1. In the Location text box, type the name of the web server and virtual directory that will contain the web service. Visual Studio .NET will create the virtual directory specified and a set of projects files for your web server.

FIGURE 22.1

Creating a web service project in Visual Studio .NET

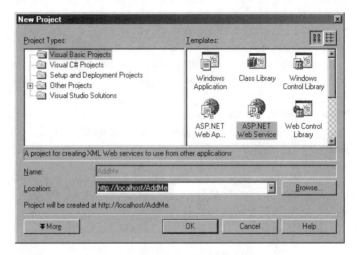

From the Solution Explorer in Visual Studio, right-click `Service1.asmx` and choose View Code. `Service1.asmx` contains the code for our web service. In the Service1 class, write the following code, as shown in Figure 22.2:

```
<WebMethod()> Public Function AddMe(ByVal x As Integer, ByVal y As Integer) As Long
    Return x + y
End Function
```

FIGURE 22.2

Creating the AddMe web method

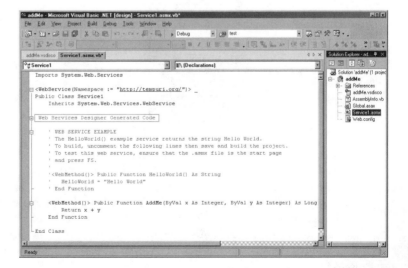

If you have written object-oriented code before, this will look very familiar. If not, we are creating a method called `AddMe` that accepts two integers. It then adds the two integers and returns the result. Notice the `<WebMethod>` in front of the function declaration. In Visual Studio .NET, this is called an *attribute*. The `<WebMethod>` attribute tells Visual Studio .NET to make any methods prefixed with `<WebMethod>` accessible via the web server as a web service. The file `Service1.asmx` can contain multiple methods; we are adding only one.

To make the web service available, all we need to do now is save and build the project. To build the project, click Build ➢ Build Solution.

USING THE WEB SERVICE

We are going to use our AddMe web service in Microsoft's Visual Studio .NET Windows application using VB.NET code. We could have also used the web service in ASP.NET, ASP, VB6, C++, Java, or any language that understands how to call a web service.

To build a client, start a new Visual Studio .NET project and create a new Windows application by clicking File ➢ New Project and choosing Visual Basic Projects ➢ Windows Applications. Name this project WinWebServiceClient From the toolbox, drag a command button and three textboxes onto the Windows form. Then set the following properties:

1. Set the Text property of TextBox1 to 5.

2. Set the Text property of TextBox2 to 6.

3. Set the Text property of TextBox3 to blank.

You application should look similar to Figure 22.3.

FIGURE 22.3

Web service client
interface

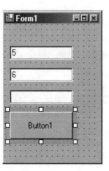

From the Solution Explorer in Visual Studio .NET, right-click References and choose Add Web Reference. In the Address box of the Add Web Reference dialog box, enter the URL to the web service, `http://localhost/AddMe/service1.asmx`, and press the Enter key or click the green arrow beside the URL address. `Service1.asmx` is the class where we built the AddMe web service. `Localhost` is the name of the web server that contains the web service. In our case it's on the same computer, but it could be anywhere on the Internet. The Add Web Reference dialog box will query the web service and display the methods that are available; our `AddMe` method is displayed, as shown in Figure 22.4. Click the Add Reference button at the bottom to add the reference to Visual Studio.

FIGURE 22.4

Adding a web reference

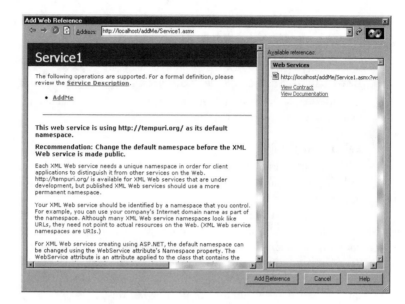

Once you have set up a reference to a web service, using it is just like using any other object, as we have done in the previous chapters; you dimension a variable that will hold a reference to an object and then use the object's methods and properties. We are going to call the web service when the user clicks the command button and pass the web service the numbers entered into textbox1 and textbox2. The web service will add the numbers, and we will put the result in textbox3. Here is the code for the Click event of the button.

```
Private Sub Button1_Click(ByVal sender As System.Object, ByVal e As
System.EventArgs) Handles Button1.Click

Dim ws As New localhost.Service1()

'change cursor to hourglass
Me.Cursor.Current = Cursors.WaitCursor

'call the addme web method.
TextBox3.Text = ws.AddMe(TextBox1.Text, TextBox2.Text)

'change cursor back to arrow
Me.Cursor.Current = Cursors.Default

   End Sub
```

Run the application by clicking the Start toolbar button in Visual Studio. The top two textboxes contain the values 5 and 6. Click the button on the form and those values are passed to the AddMe web service. The web service then adds the numbers and places the result in the last textbox. Try entering different values in the top two textboxes, and click the button again on the form.

Any client who understands how to call a web service can use the AddMe web service. It seems too easy? Visual Studio .NET does a great job of hiding the complexity behind calling web services. Let's take a look at what is happening behind the scenes.

Behind the Scenes of Web Services

To understand how and why web services work, it is necessary to understand some Internet standards that have evolved to make web services possible.

XML PRIMER

XML is standard way of representing data. Period. Nothing more. XML documents contain data and information about the data. Let's look at an example of how XML can be used and why it is so important.

If we were designing a system that accepts purchase orders, the first thing we would have to figure out is the format for our purchase order; that is, should it be comma-separated values, fixed-length columns, or an Excel file? The problem with any of those choices is that there are no standards for creating the file, and we would have to advise our customers how we want to receive the file. If we choose an XML format, it allows us to represent the data in an industry-standard way. Using XML, our purchase order would look something like this:

```
<PO number="123">
    <Customer>
        <FirstName>Gizmo</FirstName>
        <LastName>Capper</LastName>
        <Address>21 Harcourt Park Dr.</Address>
        <City>Toronto</City>
    </Customer>
    <OrderLine Product="23423" Qty="6"/>
    <OrderLine Product="342" Qty="1"/>
    <OrderLine Product="7886t" Qty="3"/>
</PO>
```

XML represents data in text format. Text is the lowest common denominator across all systems. It is easy to work with, it cannot carry viruses, and it is very easy to send across the Internet and to and from web servers.

An XML file contains the data and information about the data. Every piece of data, like the customer's first name or quantity ordered, is identified. This makes reading and using XML data very easy, either visually by humans or through program code.

XML allows you to represent data in two ways: as elements or attributes. Element data is always enclosed in element tags. An example of element data in our purchase order document is `<FirstName>Gizmo</FirstName>`. The `<FirstName>` and `</FirstName>` are the opening and closing tags. Attribute data is part of an element tag; in our example `Product` and `Qty` are attribute data.

XML follows a strict syntax to represent data:

◆ One root element—PO in our case.

◆ No spaces in the element or attribute names.

◆ All elements must be correctly nested.

◆ XML is case-sensitive.

◆ All attributes are enclosed in quotes.

So what's the big deal—all we have is a way to represent data? Why all the hype about XML? The big deal is that since everybody in the computer industry has agreed to represent data in a standard way (an agreement that represents a huge feat), we can build tools to read and write data in common ways. This solves the problem of having to tell your customers in what format you would like the data. With XML, you simply say that you are sending them an XML document. You don't care what tools they are using to read the document or what operating system they are using, because all XML tools follow the same syntax standards.

XML syntax solves the problem of representing data; however, we still have to solve the problem of telling our customers what tags we would like to see in a purchase order document. For example, the document needs to start with a `<PO>` tag, and the `<PO>` tag must contain an attribute called `Number` that represents the purchase order number. If we could take our simple purchase order and get everybody in the world to agree on the elements and attributes for a purchase order system, then it would be very easy to exchange purchase orders with anybody. When you establish a set of tags and rules for what tags you are allowing in a particular XML document, you have created a *vocabulary* for that type of XML document. As long as everybody agrees to use XML and follow the established vocabulary, then it becomes very easy for any system to exchange data with any other system.

That is the hype and the big deal of XML. XML allows you to build standard ways of representing data and the allowable elements and attributes for a particular vocabulary. If we can agree on vocabularies to represent data for purchase orders—or any document—then sending information between computer systems becomes easier.

NOTE *Organizations like* `www.rosettanet.org` *are working to create XML standard vocabularies for XML documents.*

NOTE *The XML world has two standards that describe the allowable elements and attributes in an XML document; Document Type Definitions (DTD), and XML Schemas. DTDs are text documents that are not written in XML syntax; DTDs are limited and are being replaced by XML Schemas. XML Schemas are written in XML syntax and contain a vocabulary for describing the allowable elements and attributes in an XML file.*

HTML is a vocabulary of XML! Let's examine a simple HTML document:

```
<html>
<head>
   <title>Simple HTML file</title>
</head>
<body>
   <h1>Hello World</h1>
</body>
</html>
```

An HTML file looks very much like an XML file, except the elements and attributes are predefined (HTML has its own vocabulary). For example, the browser knows when it sees a piece of data wrapped in an `<h1>` tag to display it in a large bold font. That is the reason why, when we surf the web, it does not matter if we get our HTML documents from a Unix server or a Windows server; they both give us HTML, which is a common format, and the browser can interpret it.

NOTE *HTML does not have to strictly follow the XML rules mentioned above. Browsers are written to deal with inconsistencies. If an HTML author creates an HTML document that follows the stricter XML rules, the HTML document is called XHTML.*

SOAP

SOAP, the Simple Object Access Protocol, is an XML vocabulary. It allows you to specify, in an XML document, what objects or program you would like to access on a remote computer, what data you are passing to the object or program, and what is returned.

WSDL

Web Services Description Language (WSDL) is an XML vocabulary that describes the services that are available, the methods that are available, and the expected input and output parameters. If you are a programmer, you can think of WSDL as an XML-based type library.

TIP *For complete details on SOAP, WSDL, XML, DTD, XML Schemas, and other Internet standards, visit* www.w3c.org.

PUTTING IT ALL TOGETHER

In our example, we used Visual Studio to build the web service and the client that uses the web service; however, we did not see WSDL, SOAP, or XML. Visual Studio .NET does a great job of hiding the complexity of SOAP, WSDL, and XML. Figure 22.5 shows what is happening behind the scenes.

FIGURE 22.5

Web service architecture

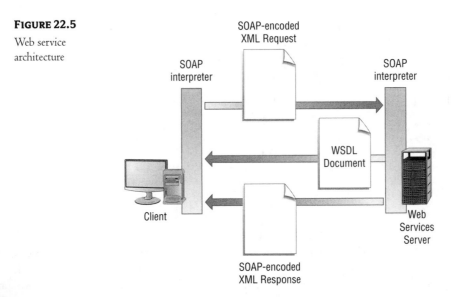

When we created our Windows client and made a web reference to `http://localhost/AddMe/service1.asmx`, we received from the web service a WSDL document describing the web services that are available. Open your Windows client and make a web reference to our web service again. Refer back to "Using the Web Service" and Figure 22.4. From the Add Web Reference dialog box, you can see that the `AddMe` method is identified as an available service. Visual Studio received this information from the WSDL document. If you click the Service Description link above the `AddMe` method, you can see the WSDL document describing the web service, shown in Figure 22.6.

FIGURE 22.6

WSDL document

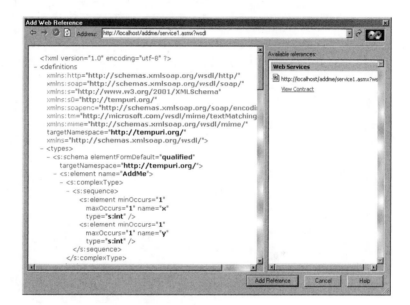

To use a web service, a client must build a SOAP request document, identifying what method it would like to call and the data it will pass to those methods, and then send the SOAP document to the web server running the web service. The web server reads the SOAP XML document to determine what services the client would like run. It then calls and runs the requested program. When the program has completed, the web server builds a SOAP response document and sends it back to the client that made the request. Click the `AddMe` web method and Visual Studio will show you a sample of the SOAP request and the response that will be sent back to the client from the server, as shown in Figure 22.7.

When you make a web reference, Visual Studio allows you to test the web service. Above the SOAP request and response, you can see a sample client that Visual Studio built for AddMe. Specify the values for the x and y parameters, click the Invoke button, and Visual Studio will build a SOAP request to call the web service and display the SOAP response returned. Figure 22.8 displays the SOAP response.

FIGURE 22.7

SOAP request and response using Visual Studio's test client

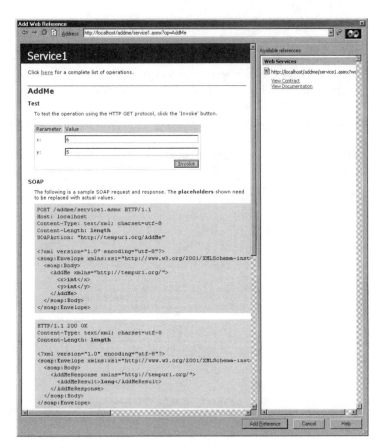

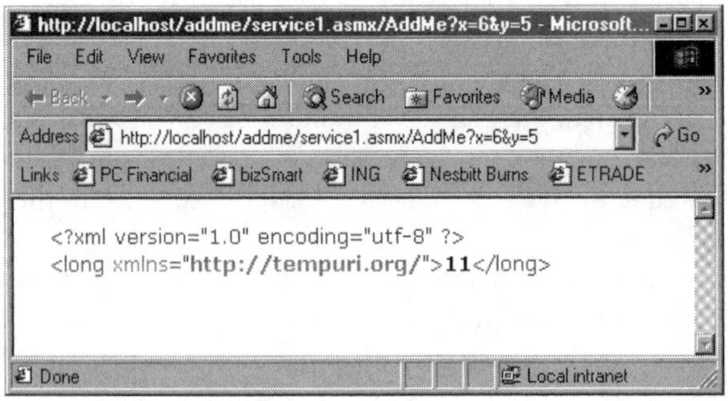

FIGURE 22.8

SOAP response from the AddMe web service

Crystal Reports Web Services

Crystal reports can be built as web services and accessed by any application using the Windows Form Viewer in a .NET Windows application or the Web Form Viewer in an ASP.NET application. By exposing your Crystal report, you allow your customers to use your reports in their applications. Your customers do not need to have access to your database or copy the reports to their systems; all you have to provide is a Crystal report as a web service, and they can use the report from your web server in their applications.

Creating a Crystal Report Web Service

Building a Crystal report web service is a simple process. As we demonstrated in building the AddMe web service, the complexity of SOAP, WSDL, and XML have been hidden by Visual Studio.

1. Start Visual Studio .NET, and create a new Visual Basic ASP.NET web service project. Call it CrWebService.

2. In the Solution Explorer, right-click the `Service1.asmx` file and delete it. We will replace the `Service1.asmx` file with a Crystal report web service.

3. Copy the Crystal report that you want to publish to your web server directory. We are doing this so the web server will have access to the report file. This is an easy way to make sure we have access to the report. The web server may not have access to the report file if it is in a different directory, alternatively you can change the permission in your web server.

4. Back in Visual Studio, in the Solution Explorer, right-click the project name, choose Add Existing Item, and add the report that you copied to the web server. You will have to change the file type to display the Crystal report. We are going to add our report called `resorts.rpt`.

5. Right-click the report you added and select Publish As Web Service, as shown in Figure 22.9. That's all there is to making a Crystal report web service. Visual Studio will create a source code file that will publish the web service. The name of the source file will be the name of the report with `Service.asmx` appended to it. In our case, the report was called `resorts.rpt`. Visual Studio created `resortsService.asmx`. If you click the Show All icon in the Solution Explorer, you will see the files that are generated.

6. Right-click the source file that was generated, `resortsService.asmx` in our case, and choose Set As Start Page. This will allow you to test the web service without having to build a client to make sure the report has been published as a web service.

7. Save and build your application.

8. Start the web service application by pressing F5. Visual Studio will display your web service page with a list of the methods that are exposed by the web service, as shown in Figure 22.10. You can click the various web methods to view the SOAP request and response.

WARNING *You will not be able to invoke these methods directly. The Crystal web service requires a Crystal Report Viewer to call these methods.*

FIGURE 22.9

Publishing a Crystal report as a web service

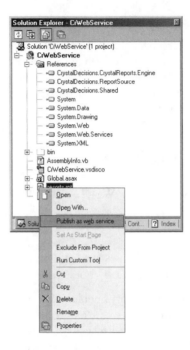

FIGURE 22.10

Crystal web service methods available to the Crystal Viewer

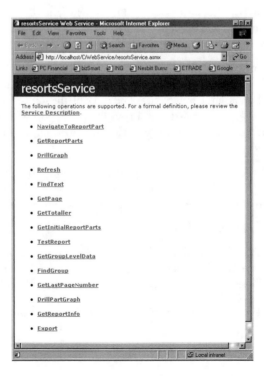

Using the Web Service

The Crystal web service report can be accessed by either the Windows Form Viewer in a .NET Windows application or a Web Form Viewer in an ASP.NET application. Either way, the steps to view the Crystal reports are the same.

Start Visual Studio .NET and create a Windows application or an ASP.NET web application. From the toolbox, drag the Crystal Report Viewer and a command button to the form.

NOTE *The Crystal Report Viewer is called a Windows Form Viewer in a Windows application and the Web Form Viewer in an ASP application.*

To display the web service report, all we need to do is bind the Report Viewer to the web service. There are two ways to bind the viewer to the report:

Directly   To bind the Report Viewer to the report service, simply set the `ReportSource` property of the viewer to the report web service:

```
Private Sub Button1_Click(ByVal sender As System.Object,
    ByVal e As System.EventArgs) Handles Button1.Click

CrystalReportViewer1.ReportSource =
"http://localhost/crwebservice/resortsservice.asmx"

    End Sub
```

TIP *In the URL above,* `localhost` *represents the name of your web server and* `crwebservice` *is the virtual directory where you build you web service application. These may be different in your environment.*

Web Reference   Alternatively, you can create a web reference, as we did in the AddMe web service client. Visual Studio will build a proxy class to call the web service. To add a web reference, right-click the project in the Solution Explorer and choose Add Web Reference; then add the URL of the web service in the Address line. In our case, it is `http://localhost/crwebservice/resortsservice.asmx CH01Service.asmx`.

```
Private Sub Button1_Click(ByVal sender As
    System.Object, ByVal e As System.EventArgs) Handles
    Button1.Click

        Dim wsResorts As New localhost.resortsService()
        CrystalReportViewer1.ReportSource = wsResorts

    End Sub
```

In either case, when you click Button1, the Crystal Report Viewer will call the web service and display the reports. All the SOAP, WSDL, and XML documents are automatically taken care of. Figure 22.11 displays the report from the web service.

NOTE *If you are publishing your reports as a web service, you may need to secure the reports so that only authorized users can access the report. Microsoft's Internet Information Server (IIS) web server provides a number of techniques for securing access and encrypting communication via Secure Sockets Layer (SSL or https). Refer to IIS documentation or your web administrator for more information.*

FIGURE 22.11

Displaying the web
service report

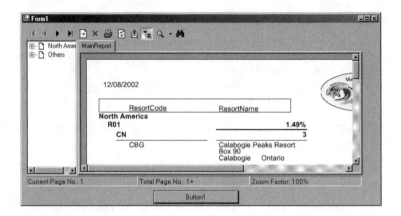

CHANGING SELECTION CRITERIA

Once a report is bound to a report viewer, whether it is bound directly as we did in the previous chapters or though a web service, you can manage the report by working with the methods in the Crystal Report Viewer. The following example sets the selection criteria of the report so that we receive only "US" countries from the web service:

```
CrystalReportViewer1.SelectionFormula =
"{Resorts.Country} = 'US'"

CrystalReportViewer1.ReportSource =
"http://localhost/crwebservice/resortsservice.asmx"
```

Summary

Object-oriented programming has evolved to where objects can be stored on a central object server so that various applications can share and use the services of those objects. This architecture is very beneficial because it allows for centralized object management. However, distributed object technologies such as DCOM, CORBA, and RMI do not communicate with one another, meaning that object sharing is available only if you are using the same platform.

The web standards have evolved to allow objects to be shared, no matter which operating system or platform they were written in. These standards include XML as a standard way of representing data; SOAP, a defined set of XML elements and attributes that specifies which methods to run on a remote server; and WSDL, a defined set of XML elements and attributes that allows a client to discover what methods are available on the remote sever and how to call them.

With Visual Studio .NET, Crystal Reports allows a Crystal report to be published as a web service by simply adding the report to a web service project and choosing to publish the report from a menu. Any client who uses a Crystal Report Viewer can set the report source to be the Crystal web service and view the report.

Part 5

Enterprise Reporting

Chapter 23

Crystal Enterprise

So far we have seen that Crystal Reports is a very capable report-writing tool and can be used in web or Windows applications. Crystal Reports is used as the basis for Crystal Enterprise, a web-based application that manages Crystal Reports, allowing you to schedule, archive, and distribute reports to your organization.

> *Business Question: I have many reports and users. I need to manage and distribute the reports.*
> *I also need to administer the system. How can I do this with Crystal Reports?*

Featured in this chapter:

◆ Examining the Enterprise Report solutions offered by Crystal Decisions

◆ Installing Crystal Enterprise

◆ Exploring the architecture of Crystal Enterprise

◆ Expanding Crystal Enterprise to handle a large user base

What Is Crystal Enterprise?

Crystal Decisions recognized the need for a company-wide reporting system that manages reports, is secure, and has the ability to schedule reports, archive old reports, easily deploy to users, and give the users the ability to view reports online or offline. Crystal Enterprise is that system.

The heart of Crystal Enterprise is Crystal Reports. Any Crystal Report that you create can be published to Crystal Enterprise. Crystal Enterprise can also handle Crystal Analysis Reports.

NOTE *Crystal Decisions has another report-writing tool called Crystal Analysis that specializes in Online Analytical Processing (OLAP) reports.*

Crystal Enterprise can be used on a single computer for a small company or department as a central reporting system, or it can be installed on many computers that handle thousands of users in a large corporate-wide reporting system. By installing Crystal Enterprise on many computers the system can be configured for fault tolerance. If one computer fails, the other computers will take over, providing reliability in the reporting system.

Flavors of Crystal Enterprise

Crystal Enterprise comes in three editions: Report Application Server, Standard, and Professional.

Crystal Enterprise Report Application Server is the entry-level edition of Crystal Enterprise, and it is included with the Crystal Reports Developer and Advanced Editions. It can be installed on only a single computer, but it does allow up to five concurrent user connections. However, much of the functionality found in the Standard and Professional Editions is disabled, but you can provide a simple web-based reporting application. Its intended purpose is to give developers a basic platform for Crystal Enterprise development with the idea that eventually they will upgrade their applications to one of the more full-featured editions of Crystal Enterprise. For more details, see Chapter 24, "Report Application Server."

The Standard Edition of Crystal Enterprise is a step up from the Report Application Server, but it too has some of the Professional-level features disabled. The primary features that are missing are security and the ability to distribute report processing across multiple computers. You will need to purchase an upgrade to the Professional Edition if you want to take Crystal Enterprise to a larger user base in your organization.

Crystal Enterprise Professional Edition is the full-featured version that has all of the enterprise-wide reporting capabilities enabled. It is this version that we will be discussing in this section of the book.

NOTE   *Version confusion: The current version of Crystal Enterprise is 8.5, released in May 2002. Unfortunately, Crystal Enterprise 8.5 is not compatible with Crystal Reports 9.0, although the Report Application Server that ships with some of the Crystal Reports 9.0 editions is compatible. According to a whitepaper posted on the Crystal Decisions website at* `http://www.crystaldecisions.com/products/crystalreports/downloads/cr9_ras.pdf`, *a newer version of Crystal Enterprise should be available in late 2002. It is certain that this newer version of Crystal Enterprise will be compatible with Crystal Reports 9.0.*

Crystal Enterprise Components

Let's take a look at the components that make up Crystal Enterprise 8.5. We can be fairly confident that these will be the same components that make up Crystal Enterprise 9. (Of course, more features will be added to version 9.) This will give you a good idea of what makes up Crystal Enterprise and help you decide if you would like to upgrade to version 9 when it is released. If your company has version 8.5 of Crystal Enterprise, this will explain what you have and how to configure it.

Crystal Enterprise is a large application that consists of many components. The components include applications that the end users or administrators of the system use and services/daemons (programs) that run on the server. Figure 23.1 is a diagram of all the components of Crystal Enterprise. Before we discuss installing Crystal Enterprise, you need a better understanding of what it includes.

FIGURE 23.1

Crystal Enterprise architecture

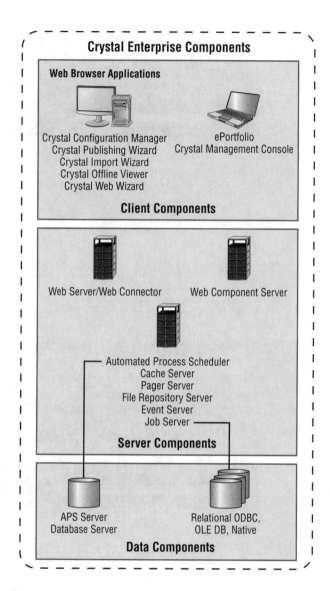

WEB BROWSER APPLICATIONS

The web browser components are the most visible part of Crystal Enterprise. They include an end-user application and an administrative application:

ePortfolio   ePortfolio is the end-user application, allowing users to access, schedule, and view reports from a web browser. Figure 23.2 shows the main ePortfolio page, which displays a list of reports and folders available to users.

FIGURE 23.2

ePortfolio main page

The list shows the sample reports that are included with Crystal Enterprise. If we select the Inventory Report (By Category) option, we are presented with a menu to view the latest instance, to schedule a report, or to view the historical report, as shown in Figure 23.3.

FIGURE 23.3

Report Options menu

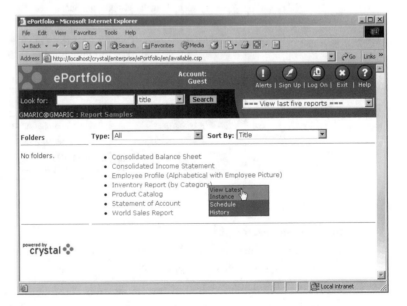

If we choose to view the latest instance, we are presented with that report in a Crystal Report Viewer, as shown in Figure 23.4.

FIGURE 23.4

Viewing a report
from Crystal
Enterprise

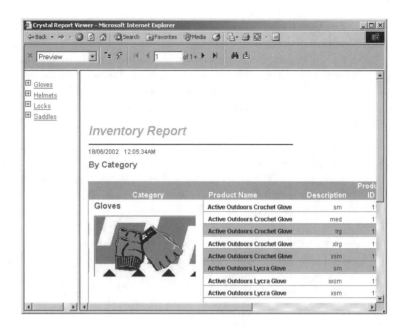

Crystal Management Console   Crystal Management Console is a web-based Crystal Enterprise
administration application. Administrators can set up users, folders, and groups and manage the
Crystal Enterprise services with this tool. Figure 23.5 displays the main menu of the Crystal
Management Console.

FIGURE 23.5

Crystal Management
Console main menu

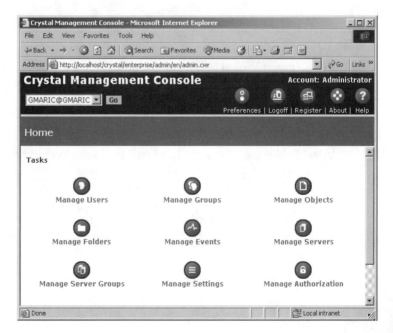

CLIENT COMPONENTS

Most users will not need anything installed on their computers because Crystal Enterprise is designed as a web-based application. However, it includes the following tools that can be installed on a client's computer if required. The tools are mostly used by administrators of the Crystal Enterprise environment or users who need to view reports offline. When you install Crystal Enterprise, these tools are available by choosing Start ➤ Program Files ➤ Crystal Enterprise. They can be selectively installed as needed.

Crystal Configuration Manager   This is an administration tool used to configure, start, and stop Crystal Enterprise server services. Crystal Configuration Manager is similar to the Windows 2000 Services administration tool located in the Administrative Tools folder off the Windows Start menu. Figure 23.6 displays Crystal Configuration Manager with all the Crystal Enterprise services running. We will use this tool later in the chapter to configure Crystal Enterprise.

FIGURE 23.6

Crystal Enterprise Configuration Manager

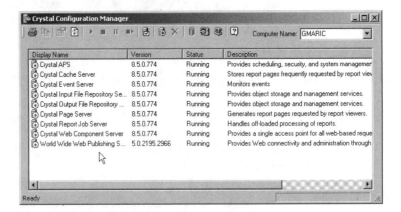

Crystal Import Wizard   Crystal Enterprise is the second-generation enterprise-reporting tool offered by Crystal Decisions; the first one was called Seagate Info. See the sidebar, "Crystal Enterprise versus Seagate Info," later in this chapter. The Crystal Import Wizard is an administrative tool that migrates a Seagate Info configuration to Crystal Enterprise or vice versa. Figure 23.7 displays the Crystal Import Wizard.

Crystal Publishing Wizard   The Crystal Publishing Wizard allows you to move Crystal Reports into Crystal Enterprise. The wizard walks you through the steps of selecting a report or reports and choosing which folder you would like to add them to in Crystal Enterprise, as shown in Figure 23.8. The wizard also allows you to configure database logon information and to configure parameter information before it is copied into the Crystal Enterprise environment. Crystal Reports can also be published to Crystal Enterprise using the Crystal Management Console and via Crystal Reports.

FIGURE 23.7

Crystal Import
Wizard

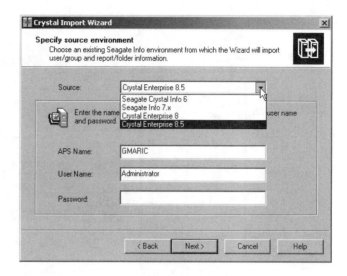

FIGURE 23.8

Adding a Crystal
report to a Crystal
Enterprise folder

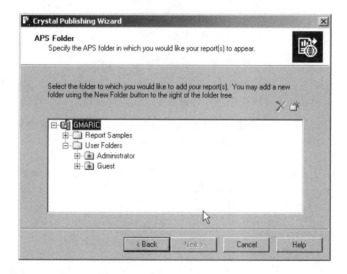

Crystal Offline Viewer   The Crystal Offline Viewer opens Crystal Reports saved on your local computer. The viewer is similar to the Compiled Report Viewer discussed in Chapter 16, "Deploying Your Report"; it allows saving, printing, sorting, and filtering of the report data. Figure 23.9 displays a sample report in the viewer. Later in the chapter we will examine installing and using the Offline Viewer.

FIGURE 23.09

Crystal Offline
Viewer

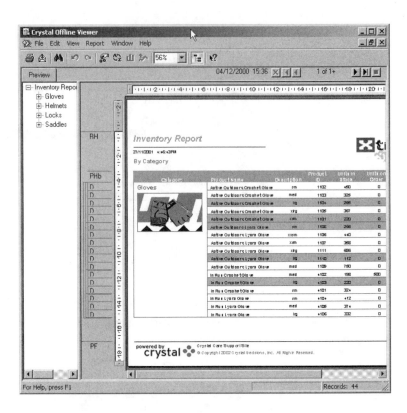

Crystal Web Wizard ePortfolio is a sample web application developed by Crystal Decisions that uses the services of Crystal Enterprise. The Crystal Enterprise services have an Application Programming Interface (API), such as Crystal Reports with the RDC, as we have seen previously. Programmers can use the services and APIs of Crystal Enterprise to develop custom web-reporting applications. The Crystal Web Wizard builds a base Crystal Enterprise web application that can be customized by a developer.

SERVER COMPONENTS

The main working components of Crystal Enterprise are Windows services or Unix daemons that run Crystal reports, handle requests from web browsers, manage security, and schedule reports. Crystal Enterprise server components can be installed on Windows, Solaris, and Linux servers. (Linux is supported only for the web connector.) Refer back to Figure 23.1 to refresh your memory of the services.

The services that are implemented in Crystal Enterprise are as follows:

Web Server Crystal Enterprise requires a web server. It will work with following web servers.

◆ Microsoft Internet Information Server (IIS) 5.0, 4.0

◆ iPlanet Web Server Enterprise Edition 6.0, 4.1 SP8

◆ Apache 1.3.20

◆ Lotus Domino 5.0.8

Web Connector   The web connector is loaded on the web server. The web connector recognizes when a user requests a Crystal Report from Crystal Enterprise, and it communicates and sends Crystal Enterprise requests to the Web Component Server. In a large environment, if multiple copies of the Web Component Server are running, then the web connector will send the requests to the least-busy Web Component Server.

Web Component Server   The Web Component Server (WCS) accepts requests from the web connector, processes those requests, and passes them to the appropriate components in the Crystal Enterprise server environment. It will handle report prompts and database logins, and it will convert reports to HTML if the user requests an HTML format.

The WCS can also accept a request for a Crystal Report file (an RPT file) from a web browser address, and it will run and send back the report. This is similar to the Web Reports Server in previous versions of Crystal Reports.

Automated Process Scheduler   The Automated Process Scheduler (APS) maintains the Crystal Enterprise database that contains information about the published reports in Crystal Enterprise, users, groups, folders, and security. Other components query the APS database.

The APS components role can be broken down into three main tasks:

Security   Manages the database of users and their rights. It also enforces security.

Reports   Manages the reports that are in Crystal Enterprise and their location on the server. It communicates with the Job Server to instruct it to run scheduled reports.

Server   The APS frequently queries the other server components in Crystal Enterprise and keeps track of their state. As a result, if a component is not busy, the next report request can be handed to that component.

File Repository Server   When you publish a report to Crystal Enterprise, that report is placed in the Input File Repository. When you run a report, Crystal Enterprise keeps a copy of it in the Output File Repository. The Output File Repository also keeps historical reports. The File Repository Server is responsible for managing all the reports in the Crystal Enterprise environment.

The default location on the Crystal Enterprise server for the files that Crystal Enterprise manages is `C:\Program Files\Crystal Decisions\Enterprise\FileStore`. If you look in that directory, you will find a confusing set of directories and subdirectories. If you dig deep enough, you will find Crystal Reports. The good news is you needn't worry about this directory structure; the APS and the File Repository Server manage all this and provide a simple list of reports that are in Crystal Enterprise. It is best not to touch this directory.

Cache Server   When a user requests a report from Crystal Enterprise, the Cache Server checks to see if it has that report page in its cache. If it does, it passes the page back to the WCS to show it to the users. If it is not cached, it passes the request to the Page Server to run the report.

Page Server   The Page Server receives requests from the Cache Server for a report page. It then either connects to the database to generate the report or retrieves the last copy of the report that ran, depending on whether the user requested the latest information from the database or the last-run report. The Page Server then creates a special page called an Encapsulated Page Format (EPF) page, which contains a Crystal report page, and passes it to the Cache Server.

Job Server   The Job Server runs scheduled reports, as requested by the APS. The Job Server keeps track of the older copies of the report by referring to the APS database and noting the version information.

Event Server   In previous versions of Crystal Enterprise, the only way to run a report was by scheduling a time to run it via the APS. In the current version, you can now schedule a report though a file event. The Event Server polls (looks) for a particular file to show up in a directory, and when the file appears, the Event Server notifies the APS to start the report processing.

As you can see, Crystal Enterprise is a sophisticated environment designed to manage Crystal Reports and many users. Let's take a look at how all the services work together when a user requests a report and when a user schedules a report.

In ePortfolio, when the user requests a report, the request is sent to the web server and then to the web connector. The web connector passes the request to the Web Component Server. The WCS passes the request to the Cache Server. The Cache Server checks to see if it has the requested pages cached. If the requested page is in the cache, the Cache Server checks with the APS to see if the user has rights to view the report. If so, the Cache Server sends the report pages (EPF files) to the WCS. If a cached version is not available, the Cache Server requests the files from the Page Server. The Page Server either retrieves the last copy of the report from the File Repository Server or runs the report against the database.

When the user schedules a report, the request is sent first to the web server and then to the web connector. The web connector passes the request to the Web Component Server. The WCS passes the request to the APS server. The APS server checks to see if the user has rights to schedule the report. If so, the APS server schedules the report to run at the requested time. When that time arrives, the APS passes the request to the Job Server; the Job Server then retrieves the report from the Input File Repository Server and runs the report against the database. After the report is run, the Job Server saves the latest copy of the report to the Output File Repository Server and informs the APS that it has finished. The APS updates the database with the latest report.

DEVELOPER COMPONENTS: SOFTWARE DEVELOPMENT KIT

Just like Crystal Reports, Crystal Enterprise exposes its functionality through a programming interface so developers can use its services in their custom applications. Crystal Enterprise exposes its functionality through Microsoft's Component Object Model (COM), as well as through a Java interface. Developers can develop either specific client applications or administration applications to manage the Crystal Enterprise environment.

ePortfolio and the Crystal Management Desk are written using the Crystal Enterprise Software Development Kit (SDK). You can customize and change those applications as required.

NOTE   *As of this writing, Crystal Decisions has not released the Java SDK; it is currently in beta. They expect it to be released in the fourth quarter of 2002. However, the RAS server shipped with Crystal Reports 9 does provide support for Java; see Appendix C for more information.*

TIP   *Installation, administration, and development documentation can be found on the* \docs *folder on the installation CD.*

Installing Crystal Enterprise

The Crystal Enterprise services can be installed on a single computer or on multiple computers for reliability and scalability. At a minimum, your Unix or Windows server should have 256 megabytes of RAM and 700 megabytes of hard drive space. Crystal Enterprise supports the following server environments:

♦ Microsoft Windows 2000 Server SP2, NT4 Server SP6a

♦ Sun Solaris Sparc 8, Sparc 7

♦ Linux: Red Hat 7.1, 6.2 (Apache web connector only)

♦ Linux: SuSE 7.2, 6.4 (Apache web connector only)

Crystal Enterprise requires a database to store information about the reports and users. The database can be on the same computer as Crystal Enterprise or on a separate computer. Crystal Enterprise supports the following databases:

For APS on Solaris:

♦ Oracle 9i, 8i (8.1.7), 8.0.6

♦ IBM DB2 UDB 7.2 (native)

For APS on Windows:

♦ Microsoft SQL Server 2000 SP1, Server 7 SP3

♦ Oracle 8i (8.1.7), 8.0.6

♦ IBM DB2 UDB 7.2

♦ Sybase Adaptive Server 12.5

♦ Informix Dynamic Server 2000 v 9.21

♦ Microsoft Data Engine (MSDE) or the SQL Server 2000 Desktop Engine

When you install Crystal Enterprise on a Windows platform, it will automatically check for SQL Server, or MSDE, and create a database. If a database is not available, it will install MSDE, which is the core SQL Server engine licensed to be used with Crystal Enterprise.

On a Unix platform, before you install Crystal Enterprise you must create a new, empty database.

TIP   *Refer to* \platforms.txt *on the Crystal Enterprise installation CD for a complete list of supported databases, firewalls, web servers, etc.*

Windows Installation on a Single Computer

The simplest installation is one where all the components are located on a single computer. This is a good way to get started and get used to the tools, and then you can grow the Crystal Enterprise environment as needed. Make sure your Windows server has a web server loaded and running for a single-computer installation.

Log on to the Windows server with an ID that has administrator privileges. Insert the CD in the CD drive; you should then see a Crystal Enterprise screen. Click Install Crystal Enterprise to start the installation. If the CD does not autostart, you can run \setup.exe on the CD. In the Installation Type screen, shown in Figure 23.10, click the New option and then click Next. Follow the prompts to install Crystal Enterprise.

FIGURE 23.10

Installing Crystal Enterprise

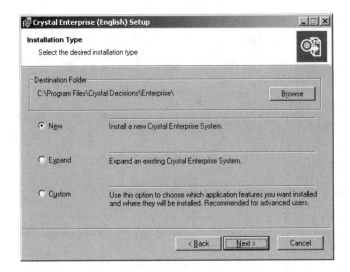

After Crystal Enterprise is installed, start a web browser and go to http://localhost/crystal/ enterprise, where localhost is the name of your server. This will start the Crystal Enterprise Launchpad, as shown in Figure 23.11. Crystal Enterprise Launchpad is the main website for Crystal Enterprise; it has links to ePortfolio, the Crystal Management Console, documentation, and application samples.

Choose Start ➢ Programs ➢ Crystal Enterprise ➢ Crystal Configuration Manager to start the Configuration Manager, shown previously in Figure 23.6. In this window you should see all the server services running on your computer.

Scaling Crystal Enterprise

Running Crystal Enterprise on a single computer is okay to start with, but as the complexity of your reporting needs increases and the user base grows, your Crystal Enterprise system may run out of steam. You can add extra memory and CPUs to it to give it more life, but eventually you will need to migrate to multiple computers to scale Crystal Enterprise.

The Crystal Enterprise environment can be broken down into three logical processes: the APS database, the Crystal Enterprise services, and the web server. Each of these processes can run on a separate computer, and we can also separate the Crystal Enterprise services into separate computers. Let's examine some of the installation scenarios that will give you a very robust Crystal Enterprise environment.

FIGURE 23.11

Crystal Enterprise
Launchpad

SEPARATING THE WEB SERVER FROM CRYSTAL ENTERPRISE

To separate the web server from Crystal Enterprise, you must dedicate a server where Crystal Enterprise will be installed. Without installing a web server on that server, run the Crystal Enterprise `setup.exe` program from the installation CD. Select a New install, click Next to continue, and follow the prompts. Crystal Enterprise will eventually complain with the message `No Compatible Web Server Found`; click Next to continue with the install. This means that a web connector will not be installed on that computer. You will need to install the web connector on the other computer that will run the web server.

On the web server computer, run the Crystal Enterprise `setup.exe` program from the installation CD. Select a Custom install. In the Select Features dialog box, select the Web Server Connectors and Help Files options and disable all the remaining components, as shown in Figure 23.12.

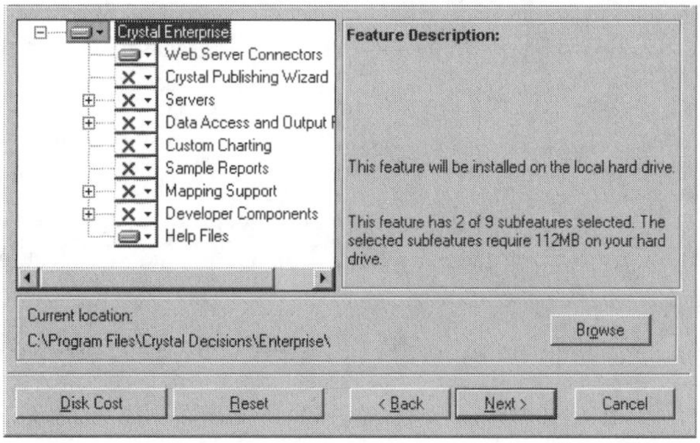

FIGURE 23.12

Installing a web
connector only

Click Next; you are then prompted to enter a Web Component Server Name. Type the name of the machine where you installed Crystal Enterprise, which is running the Web Component Server. Remember, the web connector talks to the WCS. Continue clicking Next until the installation starts.

If the web server on the web server computer is Microsoft IIS, iPlanet Enterprise Server, or Lotus Domino, the setup configures the Crystal Enterprise Web Connector automatically. Refer to \platforms .txt on the installation CD for a list of supported web servers.

You can access Crystal Enterprise by typing http://webserver/crystal/enterprise/ to start Launchpad. Notice that we are now accessing Crystal Enterprise through the web server. From there choose to run ePortfolio or the Crystal Management Console. The web connector installed on the web server communicates with the WCS on the Crystal Enterprise computer.

This scenario is also viable if you are running a Unix web server and want to install a Windows-based Crystal Enterprise environment.

SEPARATING THE CRYSTAL ENTERPRISE SERVICES FROM THE APS DATABASE

If the APS database and the Crystal Enterprise services run on the same computer, they can put a large load on the server if there is a lot of activity. We can move the database processing to a separate computer to lighten the load on the Crystal Enterprise computer.

To separate Crystal Enterprise from the database, we need to copy the existing APS database and configure the APS so it points to the new database server. Start by configuring another server with one of the supported databases such as SQL Server or Oracle. See \platforms.txt on the installation CD for a complete list.

Next, start the Crystal Configuration Manager (choose Start ➤ Program Files ➤ Crystal Enterprise ➤ Crystal Configuration Manager) and then follow these steps to copy the database. Refer back to Figure 23.6.

1. Click Crystal APS in the services list, and then click the Stop button on the toolbar. The status of the APS will change from Running to Stopped.

2. Click the Specify APS Data Source icon on the toolbar (fourth from the left), and then choose Copy Data From Another Data Source in the APS Database Setup dialog, as shown in Figure 23.13. Click OK.

3. The Specify Data Source dialog will be displayed. Click the Specify button and select the current APS database. In the case of Windows SQL Server, the APS is connected via ODBC and the DSN name is CE85.

4. Click the Browse button and select the new APS database server.

5. Click OK to start copying the database. You will be notified when it is done.

Now we need to tell the APS to point to the new database:

1. Back in the Crystal Configuration Manager, click the Specify APS Data Source icon on the toolbar (fourth from the left). This time, choose Select A Data Source (refer back to Figure 23.13) and click OK.

2. Choose the connection method to the newly copied database and click OK.

3. Click the Start button on the toolbar to restart the APS.

Now you are using three separate computers to run Crystal Enterprise: a database server, a web server, and a Crystal Enterprise server.

FIGURE 23.13

Copying the APS database

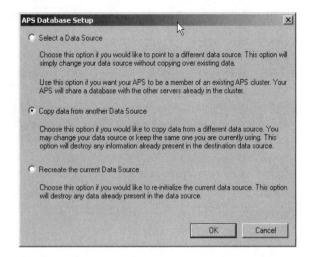

SEPARATING CRYSTAL ENTERPRISE SERVICES

We can continue to expand Crystal Enterprise to handle more users by separating the Crystal Enterprise services that run on the server. Think back to the services that make up Crystal Enterprise; there is a logical grouping of the services. For example, the WCS always talks to the Cache Server to ask if the report page has been processed. The Page Server, Job Server, and File Repository Server all work to build a report. Table 23.1 shows how the Crystal Enterprise services should be broken out by server.

TABLE 23.1: LOGICAL GROUPING OF CRYSTAL ENTERPRISE SERVICES

LOGICAL GROUPING	CRYSTAL ENTERPRISE SERVICE	COMMENT
Report scheduling	APS Event Server	The Event Server should be installed on the computer where it is monitoring the file events. If the file monitoring is done on the same computer as the APS, then combining them is fine.
Request processing	WCS Cache Server	Crystal Decisions calls this grouping the *intelligence tier*.
Report processing	APage Server Job Server File Repository Server	Crystal Decisions calls this grouping the *processing tier*.

To separate the Crystal Enterprise services as described in Table 23.1, you will need three separate computers with the required OS: Windows NT, Windows 2000, or Solaris.

Run the Crystal Enterprise `setup.exe` program from the installation CD. Select the Expand options, and click Next to continue. Figure 23.14 displays the Expand Options dialog box.

FIGURE 23.14

Adding Crystal
Enterprise services
to another server

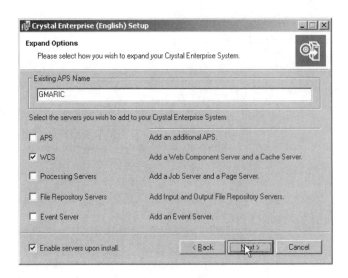

In the Existing APS Name field, type the name of the server that is currently running as your APS, and then select the services that you want to add to the server.

NOTE *Crystal Decisions has grouped the common servers options together; for example, when you select WCS, it installs both the WCS and a Cache Server. You can choose individual services if you choose the Custom option in the opening setup dialog.*

If you choose to add another APS, you will be prompted for database login information. Click Next to continue the setup.

Repeat the above procedure to add the remaining services for the other two computers, as grouped in Table 23.1. If you are expanding an existing single Crystal Enterprise server system, you will have to stop the services running on a single Crystal Enterprise server using the Crystal Configuration Manager. At this point we are using five computers—three dedicated to Crystal Enterprise, one web server, and one database server, as shown in Figure 23.15.

RUNNING MULTIPLE CRYSTAL ENTERPRISE SERVICES ON THE SAME COMPUTER

We have shown how you can run separate Crystal Enterprise services on different computers. You can also run duplicate services on the same computer, for example, two Page Servers or Job Servers. This provides software redundancy and fault tolerance; if one service fails, the other will continue working.

To run multiple services on the same computer, start Crystal Configuration Manager (refer back to Figure 23.06), click the Add Server toolbar button (sixth from the left), click the Next button, and choose the services you would like to add. If you are adding another APS, then you will be prompted for the APS database connection and logon information. If you are adding other services, you will be prompted for the name of the server running the APS. You can use the Crystal Enterprise configuration on three computers as described above and run multiple services on each computer, as shown in Figure 23.16.

FIGURE 23.15

Three computers dedicated to Crystal Enterprise and separate database and web servers

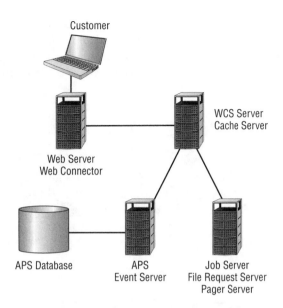

TIP According to the Crystal Decisions technical support department, in the configuration shown in Figure 23.16, if each computer has four CPUs and 2GB of RAM, the system will be able to handle 280 simultaneous user requests.

WARNING Do not run multiple services on the same computer unless you have more than one CPU; two or four would be better. If you run multiple services on a single CPU, you will actually have lower performance because the OS will spend more time managing the multiple services than running your reports.

FIGURE 23.16

Hardware and software redundancy

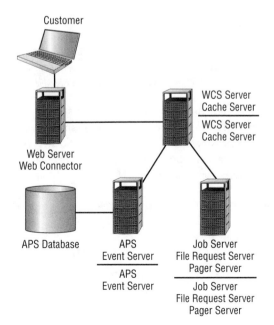

To modify this configuration for the largest system you will probably ever need, we can add three more computers to our three-computer system and duplicate the Crystal Enterprise services on each computer, the same way we did above. This provides hardware redundancy as well as software redundancy and fault tolerance, so if software or hardware breaks, the system will continue to run, as shown in Figure 23.17.

FIGURE 23.17

Hardware and software redundancy and fault tolerance

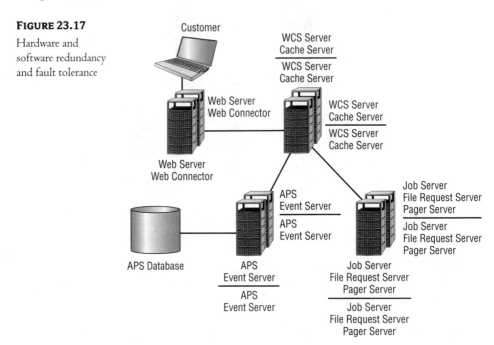

TIP   *According to the Crystal Decisions technical support department, in a configuration like the one shown in Figure 23.18, if each computer has four CPUs and 2GB of RAM, the system will be able to handle 580 simultaneous user requests.*

To give you even more scalability (or confusion), the services don't all have to run on a Windows platform or Unix servers. You can mix and match; for example, you can run an Apache web server with an Apache database connection, an Oracle database on a Solaris server, the APS on a Windows 2000 Server, and the other Crystal Enterprise services on another Solaris server or Windows servers. All that is required is that all servers communicate via TCP/IP.

TIP   *Refer to the administrator's guide and installation guide in* \docs *on the installation CD for other configuration options.*

CRYSTAL ENTERPRISE VERSUS SEAGATE INFO

If you have been around Crystal Reports for a while, you will have heard, or maybe even used, a product called Seagate Info or Crystal Info. Crystal Info came out in approximately the mid-1990s and was the first-generation enterprise-reporting tool offered by Crystal Decisions (Seagate Software at the time). Crystal Info offered almost the same functionality as Crystal Enterprise, but it was built using a client/server model, which was popular at the time. Each user was required to load a Crystal Info client that provided functionality similar to that of the web client that Crystal Enterprise now uses. The rest of the underlying technical architecture was similar to Crystal Enterprise.

Crystal Decisions reorganized the movement to the web and migrated Crystal Info to Crystal Enterprise. Crystal Info is still available as a product, but Crystal Decisions no longer promotes it. (As a matter of fact, it's a tiny link at the bottom of their products section in their web page). They obviously want you to move to Crystal Enterprise.

If you are using Crystal Info, you can use a wizard to migrate your users and folders to Crystal Enterprise. After installing Crystal Enterprise, choose Start ➤ Programs ➤ Crystal Enterprise ➤ Crystal Import Wizard. The following graphic shows the sources of data that you can import from:

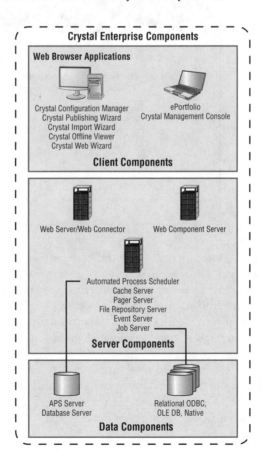

Continued on next page

CRYSTAL ENTERPRISE VERSUS SEAGATE INFO *(continued)*

Notice that the source of data can be Crystal Enterprise. You can actually import from Crystal Info to Crystal Enterprise. When the Crystal Import Wizard screen first appears, click the Help button; it provides details about the limitations of migrating data between the two systems.

Crystal Enterprise Offline Viewer

To view a report from Crystal Enterprise offline, you must download the report and save it on your local computer. To download a report from Crystal Enterprise, click the Export toolbar button. Choose to export the report to Crystal Reports format, and then click the link Click Here To Start Download Of Exported Report, as shown in Figure 23.18.

FIGURE 23.18

Downloading a
Crystal Report

Once the report is saved on your computer, go to the folder where the report was downloaded and double-click the report. The report will open in the Crystal Offline Viewer.

If you already have Crystal Reports installed on your computer, it is not necessary to install the Offline Viewer. When you export a Crystal Report from Crystal Enterprise, you are exporting the entire Crystal Report with the data. Crystal Reports can open the report.

The Offline Viewer installation file is located on the Crystal Enterprise computer in the `C:\Program Files\Crystal Decisions\viewers\Offline\en\cvwsetup.exe` directory. Run `cvwsetup.exe` on the computer where you want to install the Crystal Offline Viewer. A link to the Offline Viewer is available from the Crystal Enterprise Launchpad, which is the main website for Crystal Enterprise. You can also access the Launchpad by choosing Start ➢ Program Files ➢ Crystal Enterprise on the computer where Crystal Enterprise is installed, and you will see a link to the Offline Viewer.

Summary

Crystal Enterprise provides a report-management and web-based distribution application. Using Crystal Enterprise, you can schedule, archive, secure, and distribute reports to a small or large group of users. The services on the Crystal Enterprise server—APS, Event Server, WCS, Job Server, Page Server, and Cache Server—all provide functionality to manage the Crystal Reports. These Crystal Enterprise services can be installed on a single server or on multiple servers to allow for growth and fault tolerance.

Crystal Enterprise provides ePortfolio, an end-user web-based sample application that can be used to view and schedule reports. Crystal Enterprise also provides management tools such as the Crystal Management Console and Crystal Configuration Manager so administrators can administer the environment.

The Crystal Enterprise environment can also be programmed and its services can be used in custom applications.

Chapter 24

Report Application Server

CRYSTAL DECISIONS' REPORT APPLICATION Server (RAS) is an enterprise-level reporting product that can be used to distribute Crystal Reports within an organization using a web server for report distribution, web browsers for report consumption, and programmatic interfaces for report creation. As mentioned in Chapter 23, "Crystal Enterprise," enterprise reporting involves taking the reports created with Crystal Reports and sharing them throughout an organization by using a centralized reporting system—namely, Crystal Enterprise.

While Crystal Enterprise is the high-end, full-featured system for company-wide report distribution and management, the Report Application Server is the entry-level version of Crystal Enterprise that is designed for developers who want to integrate Crystal Reports into custom report-distribution applications, and it serves as a stepping-stone to Crystal Enterprise, as you can later upgrade it once your distribution needs grow.

Featured in this chapter:

◆ Understanding the Report Application Server

◆ Installing the Report Application Server

◆ Investigating the Report Application Server's capabilities and limitations

◆ Launching and using ePortfolio Lite

◆ Programming the Report Application Server

◆ Understanding the upgrade path to Crystal Enterprise

Understanding the Report Application Server

The first step in understanding the Report Application Server is to understand the architecture that it uses. There are four primary components used in a Report Application Server–based application: the RAS Server, the RAS Software Development Kit (SDK), the web server, and a web browser. These four primary components of the Report Application Server's architecture are shown in Figure 24.1.

FIGURE 24.1

Crystal Enterprise
Report Application
Server architecture

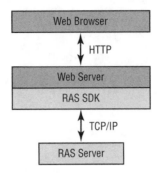

In addition, there is a collection of web-reporting viewers that are used when developing custom, web-based reporting applications. All of the RAS components are described in detail in the following sections.

RAS Server

The Report Application Server is a multi-threaded report-processing engine that provides the ability to build, customize, and view reports. It is a service that runs on the web server, and custom applications can access this service through the RAS Software Development Kit.

The Report Application Server makes use of the Crystal Reports Print Engine (CRPE) for handling reports, and it processes them in a first-in, first-out method (in Crystal terminology this is known as *on-demand mode*). As requests for reports are received, the report processing engine processes them immediately. If more requests come in than can be handled at one time, the engine creates a queue of reports and processes them in the order that they were received, once some processor time becomes available.

Another feature of the report-processing engine is server-side caching, which is the ability to speed up the processing of reports that are frequently requested. Imagine a scenario in which a particular report is viewed by many different departments within a company, all on the same day and within a relatively short period of time. If this report was requested about a hundred times within a one-hour period, and it had to be re-created and distributed by the server each time it was requested—well, you get the picture. The amount of network bandwidth and processor time used to create and distribute the report would be wasteful, not to mention the number of calls that the internal support team may have to field!

Server-side caching alleviates this problem by keeping a report open after it has been processed. It is kept open on the web server for a specific (and configurable) amount of time so that subsequent requests for it can be processed more rapidly.

NOTE   *You may recall from Chapter 23 that Crystal Enterprise implements a Cache Server service. We suspect that it is this same technology that is implemented in the Report Application Server for providing server-side caching of reports. This is one example of how the Report Application Server is based on a subset of Crystal Enterprise functionality. We'll discuss the capabilities and limitations of the Report Application Server further in the section "Capabilities and Limitations of the Report Application Server."*

RAS Software Development Kit

The Report Application Server Software Development Kit (RAS SDK) is a set of Application Programming Interfaces (APIs) that can be used to access the functionality of the RAS Server. These APIs form a library of programmatic interfaces that can be used to create custom web-based applications that allow users to not only view reports but to create and modify them as well.

NOTE *The Report Application Server comes with Component Object Model (COM)–based APIs and Java-based APIs. In this chapter, we will focus on the COM-based APIs. For more information about the Java-based APIs, see Appendix C, "Crystal Reports and Java."*

The RAS SDK is based on three conceptual areas:

Models   The data contained in a report

Controllers   Programmatic interfaces used to manipulate the data contained in a model

Views   The graphical presentation of the data contained in a model

Using these three areas, the RAS SDK allows users to create and modify Report objects such as tables, charts, and fields. More details of the RAS SDK will be covered in the section "Programming the Report Application Server."

Web Server

The web server is the central processing location of any custom application that makes use of the Report Application Server. It may take the form of a personal computer used by a developer within a small team or a central server used by a company at large. In any case, the web server acts as the primary processing source of custom applications that make use of the Report Application Server, and it plays a key role in that application as it serves as the interface between the user requesting a report and the RAS Server that processes the request for it.

Web Browser

Web browsers serve as the client-side graphical user interface to custom applications developed with the Report Application Server. Web browsers make requests of the web server using the Hypertext Transfer Protocol (HTTP), and in turn, the web server communicates with the RAS SDK to make requests of the Report Application Server.

The Report Application Server supports the following web browsers:

◆ Microsoft Internet Explorer 6.0, 5.5

◆ Netscape 6.2, 4.78

NOTE *Other web browsers may also be able to use the reports served up from the Report Application Server, but you will need to experiment with the report viewers and those browsers to make sure. We suggest trying the Report Page Viewer (also known as the HTML Page Viewer) first since it is mostly likely to work with nonsupported browsers. The report viewers are covered in the next section.*

Components for Custom Web-Based Reporting

In addition to the four primary components of the Report Application Server shown in Figure 24.1, there is another set of components provided with RAS that can be used in custom web-based reporting applications. These other components take the form of web-reporting viewers, and they are provided to allow users to view and interact with Crystal Reports using a web browser.

The four web-reporting viewers are listed in Table 24.1.

TABLE 24.1: RAS WEB-REPORTING VIEWERS

VIEWER	DESCRIPTION
Report Page Viewer	A thin-client viewer that provides the most basic web-reporting functionality and is used to render reports on a page-by-page basis.
Interactive Viewer	A thin-client viewer that provides advanced web-reporting functionality including the ability to search the data saved in a report and export the results of the search into a Microsoft Word or Excel document.
Report Parts Viewer	A thin-client viewer that provides the ability to view individual report parts, or objects, in HTML.
ActiveX Viewer	A thick-client viewer that provides the ability to view reports through any browser that supports Microsoft ActiveX technology.

Excluding the ActiveX Viewer, all of these viewers belong to what is known as the Crystal Reports Web Reporting Type Library, which is essentially an object model that is used to instantiate and manipulate the different viewers in scripting code contained in an Active Server Page (ASP). The Web Reporting Type Library is implemented using Microsoft COM technology.

The objects contained in the Web Reporting Type Library expose properties that can be used to control various report viewer features such as displaying buttons, the group tree, a page, or a toolbar. They also support event handling, exporting, printing, displaying multiple viewers in the same page, and both automatic and developer-specified prompting for database or parameter information. More details of the Web Reporting Type Library will be provided in the section "Programming the Report Application Server."

In addition to the report viewers that are part of the Web Reporting Type Library, the Report Application Server also ships with a Java report viewer that can be used in Java Server Pages (JSP).

Installing the Report Application Server

Installing the Report Application Server is a similar process to that of installing Crystal Reports itself, but it is a separate installation program from Crystal Reports so it requires its own product key code, which is supplied with the Report Application Server CD, contained in the Web Reporting Launch kit, included with Crystal Reports.

Since the Report Application Server is designed to be used by developers for creating web-based reporting applications, it is important that it be installed on a computer that has a version of Microsoft

Internet Information Server (IIS) installed and running. RAS supports the following Microsoft Windows platforms:

◆ Windows NT Workstation 4.0 (SP6a)

◆ Windows NT Server 4.0 (SP6a)

◆ Windows 2000 Professional (SP2)

◆ Windows 2000 Server (SP2)

◆ Windows 2000 Advanced Server

◆ Windows XP Professional

NOTE   *Windows 98, 98 Second Edition, and Millennium (Me) operating systems are not supported.*

To launch the installation program, insert the Report Application Server CD into your CD drive; you should then be presented with a Crystal Enterprise Report Application Server Setup screen. Click Next to start the installation process. If the CD does not autostart, you can run `setup.exe` on the CD.

After you read and accept the license agreement and enter your product key code, the Installation Type screen appears, as shown in Figure 24.2. Choose Full and then click Next to install all of the Report Application Server components.

FIGURE 24.2

Selecting the Report Application Server installation type

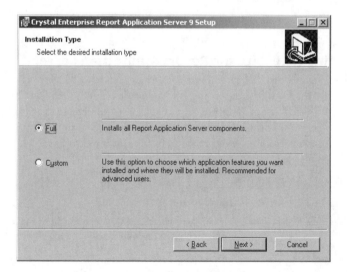

After the installation of the Report Application Server is completed, a new program group titled Crystal Enterprise 9 will appear on the Programs menu. You can access this program group by selecting Start ➤ Programs ➤ Crystal Enterprise 9. Selecting the Crystal Enterprise 9 program group will expand a menu of items; these are listed in Table 24.2.

TABLE 24.2: REPORT APPLICATION SERVER MENU ITEMS

MENU ITEM	DESCRIPTION
Documentation	This menu item contains other menu items that can be used to access help files for the COM Viewer SDK Help, Java RAS SDK Help, Java Viewer SDK Help, and the RAS User's Guide. These and other help files will be discussed in the section "Getting Help with the Report Application Server."
Tools	This menu item contains another menu item that is used to launch the RAS Configuration Manager. The RAS Configuration Manager is discussed in the section "Configuring the Report Application Server."
Crystal Registration Wizard	This menu item is used to register the Report Application Server product with Crystal Decisions.
Report Application Server Launchpad	This menu item is used to open the Report Application Server Launchpad. The Report Application Server Launchpad will be discussed in the section "Using the Report Application Server Launchpad."

NOTE   The installation procedure discussed above is based on the version of the Report Application Server that ships with Crystal Reports 9.0 Developer Edition upgrade. If you have some other edition of Crystal Reports, your installation procedure and the components that it installs may be different.

Getting Help with the Report Application Server

There are a number of help files that are installed with the Report Application Server, and these help files take the form of either compiled Microsoft HTML help files (files with a .chm extension) or pure HTML files. There are four primary sets of help files that are installed by default with the Report Application Server, and these files can be accessed through Start ➢ Programs ➢ Crystal Enterprise 9 ➢ Documentation. These four sets of help files are listed in Table 24.3.

TABLE 24.3: REPORT APPLICATION SERVER HELP FILES

HELP FILE	DESCRIPTION
COM Viewer SDK Help	This help file covers the Component Object Model (COM) web-reporting viewers implemented in the Web Reporting Type Library and the ActiveX Viewer.
Java RAS SDK Help	This help file covers the Java RAS Software Development Kit, which is used to create and modify reports on a Java platform.
Java Viewer SDK Help	This help file covers the Java Viewer Software Development Kit, which is used to create reporting functionality on a Java platform.
RAS User's Guide	The help file covers using the Report Application Server, including installation and administration.

In addition to the four default help files that are installed with the Report Application Server, there is one other important help file that is included on the installation CD but is not installed by the Report Application Server installation program. This file is named RAS_SDK.chm and it can be found on the installation CD in the D:\doc folder.

The Report Application Server Software Development Kit help file contains general information about RAS, its architecture, and its programmatic interfaces.

TIP   It is not clear to us why the RAS_SDK.chm file is not installed by default along with the other RAS help files as it contains very important information about RAS and how to write applications using it. We suggest copying this file to your hard drive in the C:\Program Files\Crystal Decisions\Report Application Server 9\Help\En folder and then creating a shortcut to it in the Crystal Enterprise 9 Documentation program menu. This will make it easier to access this help content.

Configuring the Report Application Server

The tool that is used to configure the Report Application Server is called the Report Application Server Configuration Manager, and it can be opened by selecting Start ➢ Programs ➢ Crystal Enterprise 9 ➢ Tools ➢ RAS Configuration Manager. It is shown in Figure 24.3.

FIGURE 24.3

Report Application Server Configuration Manager

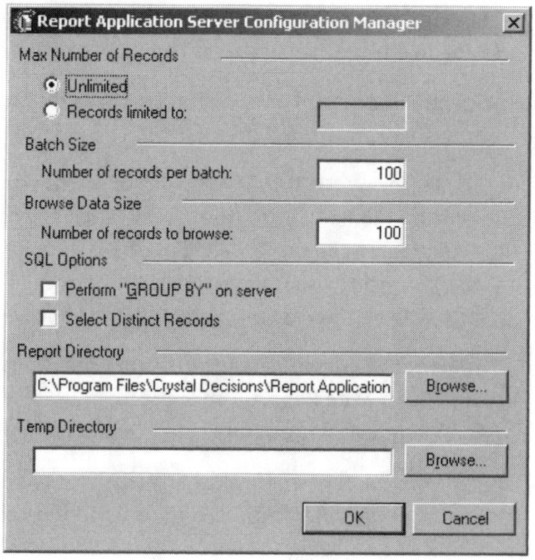

The RAS Configuration Manager is used to administer the Report Application Server by setting various database properties that affect the way that database records are processed on the server, and it is used to set the default report and temporary files directories that are used by the server. If you make a change to one of the settings in the RAS Configuration Manager, you must stop and then restart the Report Application Server for the settings to take effect.

RESTARTING THE REPORT APPLICATION SERVER

Restarting the Report Application Server is a simple, three-step process:

1. In the Windows Control Panel, click Administrative Tools, and then click Services.

2. Scroll down until you find the Report Application Server service.

3. Right-click the service and then select Restart from its shortcut menu.

RAS CONFIGURATION MANAGER SETTINGS

As mentioned previously, the settings available in the RAS Configuration Manager are used to configure how the Report Application Server processes database records and to set the directory locations for report and temporary files. Each of the settings that can be used is listed in Table 24.4.

TABLE 24.4: RAS CONFIGURATION MANAGER SETTINGS

SETTING	DESCRIPTION
Max Number of Records	Specifies the maximum number of records that are returned from the database. It can be set to either Unlimited or a specific number of records. The default value is Unlimited.
Batch Size	Specifies the number of records that are returned in each batch of records that are returned from the database. The default value is 100.
Browse Data Size	Specifies the number of distinct records that are returned from the database when browsing through a field's values. The default value is 100.
SQL Options	The Perform "GROUP BY" On Server setting specifies that group processing of records is to be done on the server. This setting is applied only when a new report is created on the server. The Select Distinct Records setting specifies that only distinct records should be retrieved from the database. This setting is also applied only when a new report is created on the server.
Report Directory	Specifies the default report directory that is used for storing the reports that are accessed by the Report Application Server. The default report directory is C:\Program Files\Crystal Decisions\Report Application Server 9\ Reports.
Temp Directory	Specifies the default directory for temporary files. By default this setting is left blank.

Using the Report Application Server Launchpad

The Report Application Server Launchpad is a web portal that is used to provide links to the ePortfolio Lite sample web-reporting application and to provide links to external websites that contain extra information about Crystal Reports in general. To open the Report Application Server Launchpad, select Start ➢ Programs ➢ Crystal Enterprise 9 ➢ Report Application Server Launchpad. The RAS Launchpad is shown in Figure 24.4.

FIGURE 24.4

Report Application
Server Launchpad

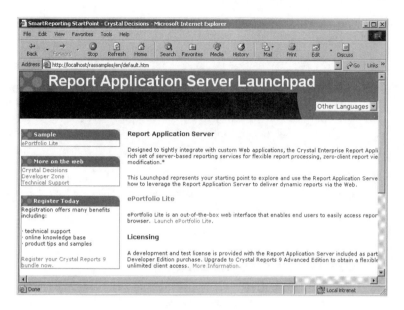

TIP   You can also open the Report Application Server Launchpad with your web browser by entering `http://`
`localhost/rassamples/en/default.htm` *as the address, using the name of your web server in place of* `localhost`.

Capabilities and Limitations of the Report Application Server

When you compare the functionality of the Report Application Server with that of the other two
editions of Crystal Enterprise (Standard and Professional), you will quickly realize that the Report
Application Server is very limited in what it can do for you. Much of the enterprise-level functionality
such as multiserver deployment, scheduling, and security has been removed. What you are left with is a
server that processes reports only on demand, a set of report viewers that allow report viewing and
modification, and a limited set of APIs for building custom web-based reporting applications. In
addition, the Report Application Server does not contain any functionality for managing reports,
folders, users, or permissions.

NOTE   For more details about the features of Crystal Enterprise, see Chapter 23.

In addition to the limited functionality that is available in the Report Application Server, its
licensing limits the number of users that can access it at any one time to five, and it cannot ever be
deployed on more than one web server unless extra licenses are purchased from Crystal Decisions.
You are also prohibited from including it in a custom installation program.

TIP *Trying to understand the ins and outs of Crystal Decisions' licensing scheme for the Report Application Server can be a bit daunting. You can try it for yourself by viewing the license agreement in the* `license.rtf` *file that is in the root directory of the Report Application Server installation CD.*

Since the Report Application Server is so seemingly limited, you may be wondering exactly what it can be used for. The answer is that it can be used for creating a custom, web-based reporting system that will give users the ability to view their reports using a web browser. It also serves as a development platform in that custom applications developed on it can easily be migrated to the more full-featured editions of Crystal Enterprise.

NOTE *We don't mean to sound negative about the Report Application Server: It is a fine platform for small departmental use and for use as a development tool. But you will need to upgrade to Crystal Enterprise Standard or Professional as your reporting environment and enterprise-wide reporting requirements grow.*

Using ePortfolio Lite

When you install the Report Application Server, a sample web reporting application called ePortfolio Lite is also installed. This sample application is used to demonstrate how you can build a user interface on the web-reporting features within the Report Application Server, primarily through the use of the web-reporting viewers.

You can open the ePortfolio Lite application by selecting Start ➢ Programs ➢ Crystal Enterprise 9 ➢ Report Application Server Launchpad and then clicking the Launch ePortfolio Lite link. When ePortfolio Lite opens, you are presented with the user interface shown in Figure 24.5.

FIGURE 24.5

ePortfolio Lite

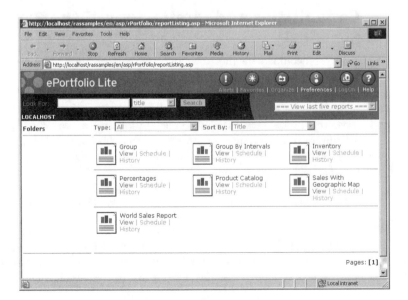

TIP   You can also open ePortfolio Lite directly from your web browser by entering `http://localhost/rassamples/` `en/asp/rPortfolio/reportListing.asp` *as the address, using the name of your web server in place of* `localhost`.

This first thing you may notice about ePortfolio Lite is the number of features that are disabled—items like Search, Alerts, Favorites, Organize, Logon, Folders, and Report Schedule And History. This is where the "Lite" portion of the name comes from. A more full-featured web-reporting sample application that has these ePortfolio Lite-disabled features enabled ships with the Standard and Professional Editions of Crystal Enterprise and is simply called ePortfolio.

Setting ePortfolio Lite Preferences

One of the features of ePortfolio Lite that is enabled is the setting of preferences. Clicking the Preferences button in the upper-right portion of the ePortfolio Lite interface opens the User Preferences window, as shown in Figure 24.6.

FIGURE 24.6

ePortfolio Lite
Preferences

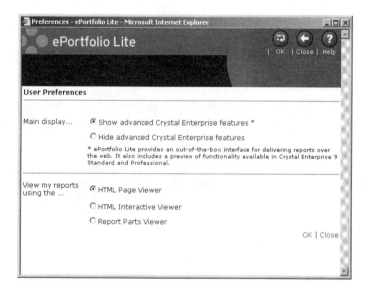

If you select the Main Display option of Hide Advanced Crystal Enterprise Features and then click OK, the ePortfolio Lite user interface is updated with all of the disabled features removed, as shown in Figure 24.7.

Viewing Reports in ePortfolio Lite

You can view a report by selecting the View link that is next to one of the sample reports included with ePortfolio Lite. Clicking the View link next to the Product Catalog sample report results in a new web browser window opening with the report displayed, as shown in Figure 24.8.

FIGURE 24.7

ePortfolio Lite
without the disabled
features

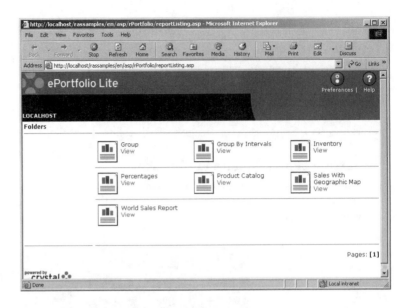

FIGURE 24.8

Product Catalog
report

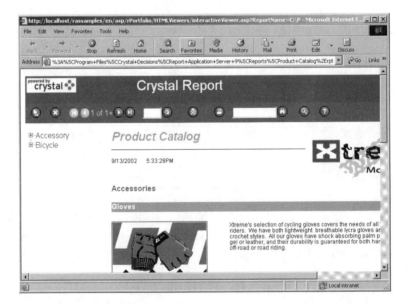

The default web-reporting viewer used for ePortfolio Lite is the Interactive Viewer, and it is this viewer that is displayed in Figure 24.8. However, you can change the default viewer used to display a report by setting the View My Reports Using The… option in the User Preferences window, as shown previously in Figure 24.6.

If you change the report viewer preference to HTML Page Viewer, you will get a much simpler view of the report. The Product Catalog sample report as seen using the HTML Page Viewer is shown in Figure 24.9.

FIGURE 24.9

Product Catalog Report using the HTML Page Viewer

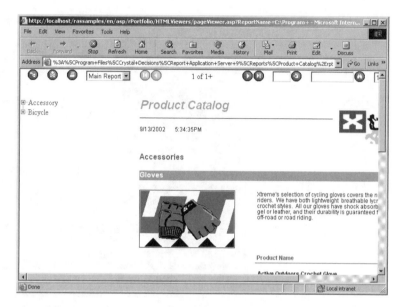

If you change the report viewer preference to Report Parts Viewer, you will get a view of the report that is based solely on the highest level of data it contains, which in most cases is the group level. The Product Catalog sample report as seen using the Report Parts Viewer is shown in Figure 24.10.

FIGURE 24.10

Product Catalog Report using the Report Parts Viewer

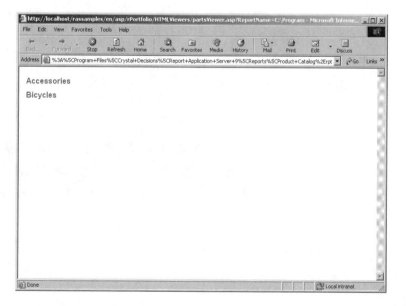

Notice that viewing the Product Catalog report through the Report Parts Viewer displays only the grouping levels of Accessories and Bicycles. If you click the link for the Accessories group level, the Product Catalog detail data for that group is displayed, as shown in Figure 24.11.

FIGURE 24.11

Product Catalog
Report using
the Report
Parts Viewer
Detail view

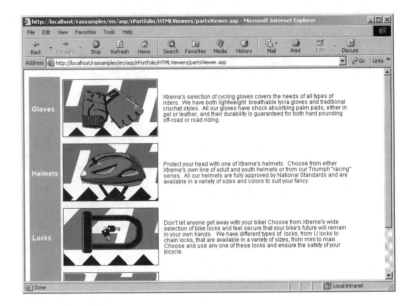

Using the Web-Reporting Viewers

Depending on which web-reporting viewer is selected for viewing reports, certain report-viewing features may or may not be available. Report-viewing features include drill down, page navigation, exporting, printing, searching, zooming, and advanced searching.

INTERACTIVE VIEWER

The Interactive Viewer is by far the most robust of the web-reporting viewers as it has the most end-user features available. You can access the features of the Interactive Viewer from the toolbar in the top portion of the report viewing interface, as shown in Figure 24.12.

FIGURE 24.12

Interactive Report
Viewer toolbar

One feature that is very useful is the ability to export reports to the following formats:

◆ Crystal Reports (RPT)

◆ Acrobat Format (PDF)

- Microsoft Word (DOC)

- Microsoft Excel 97-2000 (XSL)

- Microsoft Excel 97-2000 (Data Only)

- Rich Text Format (RTF)

To export a report, click the Export This Report button from the Interactive Viewer toolbar. This will display a window that allows you to specify the export format and the range of pages to be exported. The Export The Report window is shown in Figure 24.13.

FIGURE 24.13

Export The Report window

Another useful feature of the Interactive Viewer is printing, and the print feature can be used by clicking the Print This Report button from the Interactive Viewer toolbar. This will display a window that allows you to specify the range of pages to print. An interesting twist to the way that the Interactive Viewer implements print functionality is that it does not use the print features of the web browser but instead uses the print features of the Adobe Acrobat Reader. It does this by first converting the report into the PDF format that the Acrobat Reader uses. The Print The Report window is shown in Figure 24.14.

One other feature of the Interactive Viewer that is worth noting is the Advanced Search Wizard. This wizard can be used to search the fields contained in a report using Boolean and comparison (also known as *logical*) operators. You can use the Advanced Search Wizard by selecting the Show/Hide Advanced Search Wizard button from the Interactive Viewer toolbar. This will lower the toolbar and place the interface for the wizard above it, as shown in Figure 24.15.

FIGURE 24.14

Print The Report window

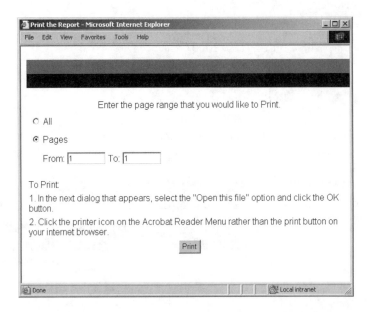

FIGURE 24.15

Advanced Search Wizard

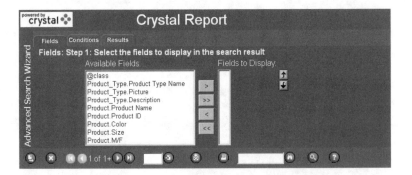

NOTE   In this section we have only highlighted the major features of the Interactive Report Viewer. For a thorough overview of all of its report-viewing features and a comparison of the features of each report viewer, see the COM Viewer SDK help file that was discussed in the previous section, "Getting Help with the Report Application Server."

REPORT PAGE VIEWER

The Report Page Viewer is an HTML-based viewer that implements nearly all of the same features as the Interactive Report Viewer, with the exception of the Advanced Search Wizard. You can access the features of the Report Page Viewer from the toolbar in the top portion of the report-viewing interface, as shown in Figure 24.16.

FIGURE 24.16

Report Page Viewer toolbar

REPORT PARTS VIEWER

The Report Parts Viewer is used to view individual report parts or objects, such as charts, text, fields, and group levels. The Report Parts Viewer has no toolbar and does not support the robust report-viewing features that are included in the Interactive and Report Page Viewers. Examples of the Report Parts Viewer can be seen in Figures 24.10 and 24.11 in the previous section, "Viewing Reports in ePortfolio Lite."

NOTE *The ePortfolio Lite sample web-reporting application makes use of only the three COM-based web-reporting viewers, so those are the only viewers that will be covered in this section. The ActiveX and Java web-reporting viewers will not be covered, although you can read the Report Application Server documentation to learn how to implement and use them.*

Programming the Report Application Server

Programming the Report Application Server involves using a web-development tool like Microsoft's Visual Studio 6.0 or Visual Studio .NET and creating Active Server Pages (or in the case of ASP .NET, webforms) that use programming code to work with the RAS SDK and web-reporting viewers. Perhaps the easiest way to learn how to program with the Report Application Server is to use the sample web-reporting application, ePortfolio Lite.

Creating an ASP Project with ePortfolio Lite

The first step in customizing the ePortfolio Lite sample application is to create a new ASP web project and then import all of the ePortfolio project files into the new project. The following step-by-step procedure uses Microsoft Visual InterDev 6.0, which is a component of Visual Studio 6.0, to create a new ASP web project.

1. Open Visual InterDev, and in the New Project dialog, shown in Figure 24.17, choose New Web Project, name the project **WebReporter**, enter a location for the project files, and then click Open to launch the Web Project Wizard.

2. In step 1 of the Web Project Wizard, select the server that is hosting the Report Application Server and then click Next. (In most cases, this is probably your local machine if that is where you installed the Report Application Server.)

3. In step 2 of the Web Project Wizard, make sure that the Create A New Web Application option is selected and that the name of the project is WebReporter and then click Next. (You can also uncheck the Create Search.htm To Enable Full Text Search check box to cut down on the number of files that Visual InterDev generates.)

4. In step 3 of the Web Project Wizard, click Finish.

FIGURE 24.17

New Project dialog

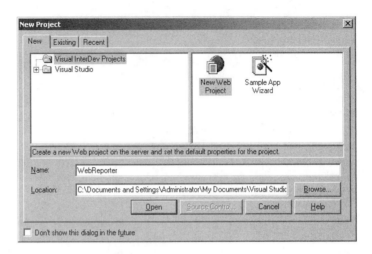

5. Copy the ePortfolio Lite source files into the directory that you specified as the project location in step 1. The ePortfolio Lite source files can be found at `C:\Program Files\Crystal Decisions\ Report Application Server 9\Samples\En\ASP\rPortfolio`. The following is the list of files and folders to copy.

   ◆ `rPortfolio`: Copy the files from this folder to the root project folder.

   ◆ `HTMLViewers`: Copy this folder and the files that it contains to the project folder.

   ◆ `Include`: Copy this folder and the files that it contains to the project folder.

6. Add the files and folders that you just copied to the project using the Project Explorer. In the Project Explorer, right-click the project name and then select Add ➢ Add Item from the context menu. This will open the Add Item dialog, as shown in Figure 24.18.

FIGURE 24.18

Add Item dialog

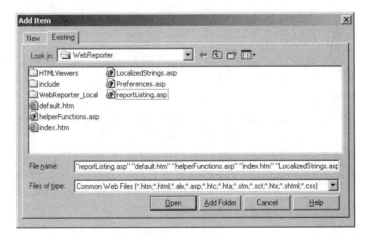

7. Click the Existing tab, select All Files (*.*) in the Files Of Type drop-down list, select all of the ePortfolio Lite files and folders listed, and then click Add Folder. Once the files and folders have been imported into the WebReporter project, your Project Explorer window should look similar to Figure 24.19.

FIGURE 24.19

Project Explorer with ePortfolio Lite files imported

8. Right-click the `default.htm` file in the Project Explorer, and on the context menu, select Set As Start Page.

9. Save your project.

10. Right-click the `default.htm` file and choose View In Browser to run the WebReporter project.

After running your project, you should see ePortfolio Lite open in the web browser and it should appear as it did in Figure 24.5 in the previous section except that this time, the path shown in the Address field of the web browser reads `http://localhost/WebReporter/reportListing.asp`.

Notice that the default page is not named `default.htm` but is instead named `reportListing.asp`. This is because the code in the `default.htm` file makes a call to the `location.replace` method to redirect processing to the `reportListing.asp` file. The code for the `default.htm` file is shown in Listing 24.1.

LISTING 24.1: THE *DEFAULT.HTM* CODE

```
<HTML>
<HEAD>

<SCRIPT language="javascript">
location.replace ( "reportListing.asp" );
</SCRIPT>

</HEAD>
</HTML>
```

Modifying the User Interface

One of the first things that you may want to customize in the ePortfolio Lite application is the user interface. This could include removing the Crystal graphics and replacing them with your own, changing the color scheme, or modifying the buttons in the toolbar.

One of the easiest changes to make is to remove the Powered By Crystal logo that appears in the lower-left portion of the ePortfolio Lite interface. To remove this logo, all you need to do is comment out a portion of the code found in the reportListing.asp file using the <!-- and --> comment tags. The code snippet that can be commented out to accomplish this is shown here:

```
<!--
</DIV>
<DIV align=left>
<a href="http://www.crystaldecisions.com/">
<img alt="<%= L_POWEREDBYCRYSTAL %>"
src="include/pb_blue_sml.gif" border="0" WIDTH="108"
HEIGHT="30">
</a>
</DIV>
-->
```

Modifying the Default Preferences

When users first open ePortfolio Lite, they will immediately notice all of the reporting features that are disabled. While they can click the Preferences button to open the Preferences window and choose to remove these disabled features from the interface, it would be better if they never saw them in the first place.

Changing the default view in the interface is another easy modification to make. Open the default .inc file and replace the value of the *mainDefaultView* variable with **MinimalView**. Listing 24.2 shows the code for the default.inc file with the change already made.

LISTING 24.2: DEFAULT VIEW CODE

```
<%
' Set the Defaults for a new user
const CEView = "0"
const MinimalView = "1"

const ActiveXViewer = "0"
const HTMLPageViewer = "1"
const interactiveViewer = "2"
const javaViewer = "3"
const HTMLPartsViewer = "4"

Dim mainViewDefault, viewerDefault
mainViewDefault = MinimalView
viewerDefault = interactiveViewer
%>
```

Programming the Web-Reporting Viewers

The ePortfolio Lite web-reporting application contains code for displaying reports in the three COM-based report viewers. Table 24.5 lists the ASP files that are used for each of the report viewers.

TABLE 24.5: REPORT VIEWER ASP FILES

ASP FILE	REPORT VIEWER
interactiveViewer.asp	Contains code for using the Interactive Report Viewer.
pageViewer.asp	Contains code for using the Report Page Viewer.
partViewer.asp	Contains code for using the Report Parts Viewer.

The complete code for the interactiveViewer.asp file is shown in Listing 24.3.

LISTING 24.3: INTERACTIVE VIEWER CODE

```
<%@ Language=VBScript CodePage=65001
ENABLESESSIONSTATE = False %>
<% Option Explicit
' Note - the CodePage=65001 is needed to display Unicode
' text correctly in the viewer
'   if Session is null for ProcessHttpRequest
Dim objectFactory
Set objectFactory =
CreateObject("CrystalReports.ObjectFactory.2")

Response.ExpiresAbsolute = Now() - 1

Dim viewer
Set viewer =
objectFactory.CreateObject("CrystalReports.CrystalReportInteractiveViewer")
viewer.Name = "page"
viewer.IsOwnForm = true
viewer.IsOwnPage = true

Dim theReportName
theReportName = Request.Form("ReportName")
if theReportName = "" then
theReportName = Request.QueryString("ReportName")
viewer.URI = "interactiveViewer.asp?ReportName=" +
Server.URLEncode(theReportName)

Dim clientDoc
Set clientDoc =
objectFactory.CreateObject("CrystalClientDoc.ReportClientDocument")
```

```
clientDoc.Open theReportName
viewer.ReportSource = clientDoc.ReportSource

Dim BooleanSearchControl
Set BooleanSearchControl =
objectFactory.CreateObject("CrystalReports.BooleanSearchControl")
BooleanSearchControl.ReportDocument = clientDoc
viewer.BooleanSearchControl = BooleanSearchControl
viewer.ProcessHttpRequest Request, Response, Null
' ReportClientDocument will be automatically closed when
' clientDoc is released
%>
```

As you can see from Listing 24.3, the ASP code uses three primary Crystal objects for displaying a report using the Interactive Report Viewer: `ObjectFactory`, `CrystalReportInteractiveViewer`, and `CrystalClientDoc`. Each of these objects, along with their properties, methods, and events, is documented in the Report Application Server Software Development Kit help file.

Upgrading to Crystal Enterprise

When deciding whether to upgrade your Report Application Server application to Crystal Enterprise, there are a number of factors to consider. The first is whether the more advanced and expensive versions of Crystal Enterprise meet the needs of your business organization or client.

When faced with the need to expand an existing application's functionality, it often comes down to a "buy or build" scenario. If the modifications are minor, and there are development resources available to do the work, building your own application may be the best choice. But if you are limited in development resources and the functionality needed is great, it may be better to purchase an existing application that best meets your requirements and then modify it as needed.

In addition to the "buy or build" scenario, there are also a number of technical issues that should be considered when deciding on the upgrade path for a custom web-based reporting system. In particular, there are a number of scenarios in which upgrading to Crystal Enterprise might make the most sense considering the functionality needed. Table 24.6 lists some of the technical advantages to moving to a more full-featured edition of Crystal Enterprise.

Ultimately, whether or not you choose to upgrade to Crystal Enterprise should be based on careful consideration of time, costs, available resources, and your particular business requirements. For a more thorough discussion of Crystal Enterprise and its various features, see Chapter 23.

TIP Crystal Decisions has put together a brief white paper that discusses the Report Application Server and how it fits into the Crystal Enterprise product line. You can download this white paper from the Crystal Decisions website at `http://www.crystaldecisions.com/products/crystalreports/downloads/cr9_ras.pdf`.

TABLE 24.6: CRYSTAL ENTERPRISE FEATURES

FEATURE	DESCRIPTION
Report processing	Ability to process larger and more complex reports
Scheduling	Ability to schedule when report processing occurs
Load balancing	Ability to run report processing on multiple servers, thereby distributing the workload
Clustering	Ability to group servers together as one logical unit for increased processing power
Fail over	Ability to use other servers as backups in case the main server goes down
Report management	Ability to manage a repository of reports including storage and versioning
Security	Ability to control user access to reports and operations
Analytics	Ability to work with reports generated from Crystal Analysis
Ad hoc reporting	Ability to create and modify reports

Summary

The Report Application Server is an entry-level version of Crystal Decisions' report-distribution and management tool—Crystal Enterprise. It can be used to implement a custom web-based reporting application using a mixture of the Report Application Server Software Development Kit and web-reporting viewers.

The Report Application Server ships with a sample web-based reporting application called ePortfolio Lite, which can be used as a starting point for developing a custom application. Using a web-development tool such as Microsoft Visual Studio 6.0, you can customize the ePortfolio Lite application to meet your own requirements.

Upgrading from the Report Application Server to one of the other more full-featured editions of Crystal Enterprise should be based on careful consideration of time, costs, available resources, and your particular business requirements.

Appendices

In this section you will find:

Appendix A

Crystal Reports Editions

Edition Key:

S = Standard
P = Professional
D = Developer
A = Advanced
N = Crystal Report

CRYSTAL REPORT EDITION *	S	P	D	A	N
REPORT CREATION					
Report Designer	X	X	X	X	X
Templates	X	X	X	X	
Repository		X	X	X	
Custom functions		X	X	X	
THICK-CLIENT (WINDOWS) APPLICATION INTEGRATION AND DISTRIBUTION					
Free runtime license			X	X	X
Report-viewing and modification APIs			X	X	X
Report-creation APIs (add-on licenses required)			X	X	

Crystal Report Edition *	S	P	D	A	N
Data Connectivity					
PC-based ODBC/OLE DB	X	X	X	X	X
SQL commands	X	X	X	X	
Unicode support	X	X	X	X	X
XML (Extensible Markup Language)		X	X	X	
OLAP (Online Analytical Processing)		X	X	X	
Enterprise database servers (ODBC, native)		X	X	X	X
User-defined custom data sources (.NET, JavaBeans, and COM)				X	X
Report Application Server (RAS)					
ePortfolio Lite, web-reporting deployment interface		X	X	X	
Report sharing via Microsoft Smart Tags and Office XP		X	X	X	
Report access via RIM Blackberry, Compaq iPAQ, and WML phones		X	X	X	
Report-viewing SDKs (Java, .NET, and COM)			X	X	X
Report-creation and modification SDKs (Java, .NET, and COM)				X	X
Licensing					
Develop and test		X	X		X
Deployment				X	

Developer Reference Documentation

Crystal Reports Documentation

FILE	DEFAULT LOCATION	FILE CONTENTS
CrystalDevHelp.chm	C:\Program Files\Crystal Decisions\Crystal Reports 9\ Developer Files\Help\En	Main developer's help file for RDC
Legacy.chm	C:\Program Files\Crystal Decisions\Crystal Reports 9\ Developer Files\Help\En	Retired API reference
License.chm	C:\Program Files\Crystal Decisions\Crystal Reports 9\ Developer Files\Help\En	Licensing Information
Runtime.chm	C:\Program Files\Crystal Decisions\Crystal Reports 9\ Developer Files\Help\En	Runtime file requirements and dependencies
Techref.pdf	Installation CD \Docs folder	Same as CrystalDevhelp.chm but in PDF format
DevGuide.pdf	Installation CD \Docs folder	General overview of development environment; Crystal Viewer summary
License.pdf	Installation CD \Docs folder	License agreement
UserGde.pdf	Installation CD \Docs folder	Crystal Reports end user documentation
WhatsNew.pdf	Installation CD \Docs folder	Overview of new Crystal Reports 9 features

Report Application Server (RAS)

Administration and Setup

FILE	DEFAULT LOCATION	FILE CONTENTS
RAS_User.chm	C:\Program Files\Crystal Decisions\Report Application Server 9\Help\En	Administration and user documentation

COM-Based Development

FILE	DEFAULT LOCATION	FILE CONTENTS
RAS_SDK.chm	CD\Program Files\Crystal Decisions\Report Application Server 9\Help\En or CD \Docs folder Note that this file is not installed by default; you must copy it manually from the CD.	COM-based web-development documentation

Java-Based Development

FILE	DEFAULT LOCATION	FILE CONTENTS
Report_Viewers.chm	C:\Program Files\Crystal Decisions\Report Application Server 9\Help\En	COM web-reporting viewers, ActiveX Viewer, and the Crystal Report Viewer for Java documentation
RAS JavaDocs in HTML format	C:\Program Files\Crystal Decisions\Report Application Server 9\Help\En\JavaDocs\RAS Index.html, or Index_all.html to start	For Java-based web-development documentation
RAS Java Development Viewer JavaDocs in HTML format	C:\Program Files\Crystal Decisions\Report Application Server 9\Help\En\JavaDocs\Viewer	The API reference documentation for the Java Viewer APIs

Crystal Reports in Visual Studio .NET

Crystal Reports documentation for Visual Studio .NET is located in the Microsoft Developers Network (MSDN) that comes with Visual Studio. There are two ways to access MSDN. The first is to choose Contents from the Help menu; this will open a window in the top right of Visual Studio and display help. The second way to access MSDN is to select Start ➤ Program Files ➤ Microsoft Visual Studio .NET ➤ Microsoft Visual Studio .NET Documentation. This will open the same documentation but in a help window separate from the Visual Studio .NET development environment.

There are two locations for help with Crystal Reports. If you have just Visual Studio .NET installed, Crystal Reports documentation is located in Visual Studio .NET ➤ Developing with Visual Studio .NET ➤ Designing Distributed Applications➤ Crystal Reports. If you installed Crystal Reports 9 on the same computer as Visual Studio .NET, the documentation will be located in the section already mentioned. Crystal Reports 9 also installs a top-level Crystal Reports 9 documentation in the root of MSDN. Both help files contain similar information, but the second, the Crystal Reports 9 documentation, is more up-to-date because the help files have been updated since Visual Studio .NET was released. Figure B.1 displays both help files. The version installed with Crystal Report 9 is selected, the version installed with Visual Studio .NET is displayed in the expanded tree.

FIGURE B.1

Crystal Reports 9 documentation

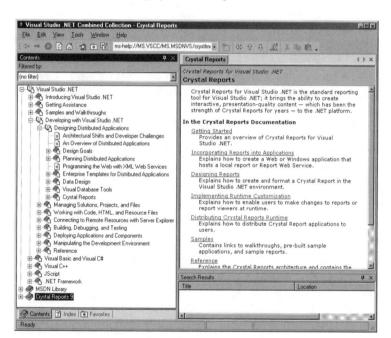

Supported Platforms

Refer to \platforms.txt on the installation CD for a list of platforms that Crystal Reports, RAS, and the development tools have been tested with. You can also refer to http://support.crystal-decisions.com/library/kbase/articles/c2011814.asp for the list online.

Online References

Websites

URL	COMMENTS
`http://support.crystaldecision.com`	Main support website for all products
`http://support.crystaldecisions.com/library/kbase.asp`	Bug fixes and articles
`http://support.crystaldecisions.com/library/`	White papers and discussions
`http://support.crystaldecisions.com/forums/`	Newsgroup discussions
`http://www.crystaldecisions.com/products/dev_zone/`	Home page for developers

News Groups

NEWSGROUP	COMMENTS
Microsoft.public.vb.crystal	General discussion about using Crystal and VB

Appendix C

Crystal Reports and Java

CRYSTAL REPORTS HAS ALWAYS been known as a Microsoft tool. Actually, some people are surprised to find out that Crystal Reports is not a Microsoft product at all but from an independent company. The mistaken impression that Crystal Reports is a Microsoft tool is not surprising because Crystal Reports has been bundled with Visual Basic for a very long time, and it is the only third-party product to be bundled with Microsoft's Visual Studio .NET development environment. Crystal Decisions is now moving into the Java world. Crystal Decisions previously had and still has Java web browser viewers for Crystal Reports. They are moving into server-side processing with the Report Application Server (RAS) and Crystal Enterprise. RAS is essentially the entry-level edition of Crystal Enterprise that ships with Crystal Reports 9. RAS and Crystal Enterprise support both a COM platform and a Java platform. See Chapter 23 for more details on Crystal Enterprise or Chapter 24 for more details on RAS.

With the RAS Software Development Kit (SDK) you can create reports via code; open existing reports; add and remove sections, fields, and charts; manipulate report parameters and formulas; and apply design templates. These are the same features we discussed in Chapters 19, 20, and 21, using COM and .NET.

Crystal Reports 9 also includes a JavaBean data source driver, which supports receiving data from a custom-built Java class. With this driver, developers can write their own Java Data Provider.

WARNING   *The RAS Server is the entry-level edition of Crystal Enterprise. Crystal Enterprise includes two other editions, Standard and Professional, that provide more features and the ability to grow your report deployment environment to a larger audience. Not all features are supported in the entry-level RAS and Crystal Enterprise Standard environments.*

The Crystal Report Writer is still only a Windows product; the RAS Server can open Crystal Reports created in Windows, in this version and previous versions. (See the Introduction for a list of other products available from Crystal Decisions for reporting and report deployment.)

The RAS Environment

The RAS environment consists of the RAS Server components, Crystal Reports that are run by RAS, and the RAS Java SDK. All can reside on the same computer or on separate computers.

The RAS Server has access to a directory and subdirectory, which can contain Crystal Reports. The default location of the directory that RAS has access to is the directory where the sample report files is the located. To publish a report to RAS, simply copy a report to this directory to give RAS access to it. This folder and its subfolders are the only ones that RAS has access to. To change the default location of this directory, use the Configuration Manager installed with RAS. It is recommended for efficiency to keep Crystal Reports on the same RAS Server instead of a separate machine. If the reports are on a different machine, you can access them by using the `rassdk://` prefix when opening a report via the SDK.

The RAS APIs and RAS Server are installed by default on the same computer. The JAR files that contain the APIs can be found in `C:\Program Files\Common Files\Crystal Decisions\2.0\jars\`.

The `clientSDKOptions.xml` file is configuration file that contains a server attribute that specifies the location of the RAS server. You can manipulate this file manually or modify it programmatically. This file is located by default in `C:\Program Files\Common Files\Crystal Decisions\2.0\jars\` and the server attribute is set to the local machine. If you move the JAR files to another computer, you must modify this file to indicate the location of the RAS Server. Listing C.1 shows the `client-SDKOptions.xml` file. If you have multiple RAS Servers, you can add multiple server attribute entries in `clientSDKOptions.xml`.

LISTING C.1: CLIENTSDKOPTIONS.XML

```
<CrystalReports.clientSDKOptions
xmlns:xsi="http://www.w3.org/1999/XMLSchema-instance" version="2"
xsi:type="CrystalReports.ClientSDKOptions">
<ServerInfos version="2" xsi:type="CrystalReports.ServerInfos" id="1">
<ServerInfo version="2" xsi:type="CrystalReports.ServerInfo" id="2">
  <Server>GMARIC</Server>
  <Adapter>TCPIP</Adapter>
  </ServerInfo>
  </ServerInfos>
</CrystalReports.ClientSDKOptions>
```

The `clientSDKOptions` files needs to be set in the `classPath` to enable the API to find it. However, you can define the location of the `clientSDKOptions.xml` file in code. In your JSP or Java files, you can use the Java method `setProperty` from the `System` class with the `ras.config` key for specifying this file. To specify the path, add the following line to your code:

```
system.setProperty("ras.config", "c:/temp")
```

This specifies that the `clientSDKOptions.xml` file used to specify the RAS Server location is in the local `C:/temp` directory.

Packages

Table C.1 lists the Java packages that make up the RAS Software Development Kit.

TABLE C.1: JAVA PACKAGES IN THE RAS SDK

PACKAGE	DESCRIPTION
com.crystaldecisions.sdk.occa.report.application	This package controls the manipulation of supported Report Application Server documents.
com.crystaldecisions.sdk.occa.report.data	This package is used to provide a definition for the report's data.
com.crystaldecisions.sdk.occa.report.definition	This package is used to manipulate the appearance of the report objects that you see on the report.
com.crystaldecisions.sdk.occa.report.document.	This package controls the manipulation of supported Report Application Server documents.
com.crystaldecisions.sdk.occa.report.exportoptions.	This package allows you to specify the export format of a report document.
com.crystaldecisions.sdk.occa.report.lib.	This package is a general utility that provides exception and container classes.
com.crystaldecisions.sdk.occa.report.template.	This package enables you to apply a custom template to a report.

Appendix D

Crystal Reports Custom Functions

Custom Date Functions

The Date functions provided in the Crystal Repository allow you to do date arithmetic for specific tasks. You can calculate the weekends and holidays in a workweek, figure out when the Easter holiday is, or determine the first and last days of the month or the quarter.

cdDateAddSkipWeekends   Given a number of workdays and a start date, returns a due date that doesn't include weekend days.

cdDateDiffSkipHolidays   Given a number of workdays and a start date, returns a due date that doesn't include weekends or statutory holidays.

cdDateDiffSkipWeekends   Given a start date and end date, returns the number of workdays between them, excluding weekends.

cdDateSkipAddSkipHolidays   Given a number of workdays and a start date, returns a due date that accounts for weekends and statutory holidays.

cdEasterDate   Given a four-digit year, calculates the date Easter falls on in that year.

cdFirstDayOfMonth   Given the current date, returns the first day of the month.

cdFirstDayOfQuarter   Given the current date, returns the first day of the quarter.

cdLastDayOfMonth   Given the current date, returns the last day of the month.

cdLastDayOfQuarter   Given the current date, returns the last day of the quarter.

CdSpecialDateRange   Given a date and a text parameter, returns a data range that meets the criteria; the text parameters are accounting phrases like "Aged0to30Days" and "Aged31to60Days."

cdStatutoryHolidays   Returns an array of 10 standard holidays in the United States and Canada.

Custom Finance Function

Crystal Reports ships with one finance function. Detach and modify the function to change the rate.

cdConvertUSToCanadian   Converts the U.S. dollar to the Canadian dollar based on an exchange rate of 1.48.

Custom Formatting Functions

Crystal provides an enormous number of built-in formatting options for dates, times, numbers, and strings. Sometimes, though, you just need to do your own thing! The custom formatting functions in the repository can help you do tasks like format date values, currency values, and string values in specialized ways:

cdFormatCurrencyUsingScaling   Given a currency value, a decimal places value, a thousands symbol, and a millions symbol, returns a text string that represents the currency using the symbols.

cdFormatDateRange   Given a date range, converts to a text string and returns a formatted string that includes phrases like "less than."

cdFormatDateRangeArray   Given a date range, returns a formatted list of text dates separated by carriage return linefeeds (new lines).

cdFormatNumberRange   Given a range of numbers, converts to a text string and returns a formatted string that includes phrases like "less than."

cdFormatNumberRangeArray   Given a range of numbers, converts to a text string and returns a list of text numbers separated by carriage return linefeeds (new lines).

cdFormatNumberUsingScaling   Given a number value, a decimal places value, a thousands symbol, and a millions symbol, returns a text string that represents the number using the symbols.

cdFormatStringRange   Given a range of string data, returns a formatted string that includes phrases like "less than."

cdFormatStringRangeArray   Given a range of strings, returns a list of text separated by carriage return linefeeds (new lines).

cdFormatTimeInterval   Given a numeric time interval, a base unit string, a rounding string, a days symbol string, an hours symbol string, and a minutes symbol string, returns a string that formats the time interval using the input parameters.

Custom Geographic Functions

When geographic data is stored in a database, it is often stored in abbreviated format. Use these functions to expand the abbreviation to its full-text equivalent. Modify the functions to handle data beyond the United States and Canada.

cdExpandRegionAbbreviation   Given a region abbreviation and a country, returns the full text of the region; supplied function handles Canada and United States only.

cdExpandRegionAbbreviationCanada   Given a Canadian abbreviation like "AB," returns the full text of a phrase like "Alberta."

cdExpandRegionAbbreviationUSA   Given a United States state abbreviation like "NY," returns the full text of a phrase like "New York."

Custom Math Functions

The built-in math custom functions focus on calculations to increase a value by a certain percentage as well as calculate the percent difference. A scenario for using these types of functions is to create a report for the sales team showing them what the quotas or future sales numbers need to be if everyone increases their sales by 2.3 percent.

cdIncreaseCurrencyByAPercentage   Given a currency value to increase and a percentage to increase it by, returns the resulting currency value after the increase.

cdIncreaseNumberByAPercentage   Given a number value to increase and a percentage to increase it by, returns the resulting number value after the increase.

cdPercentageDifference   Given a currency value and its updated currency value, returns the percentage difference as a number.

Appendix E

Crystal Reports Built-in Functions

Control Functions

There are several categories of functions that act above and beyond the actual data in a metadata way. These functions act on the report as a whole and often affect the processing and result of data.

Evaluation Time

Not every built-in function can be used at every point in report processing. In fact, Crystal's report-processing model governs the order in which formulas execute (see Chapter 14, "The Report Engine Processing Model," for more details). There are three passes through the data in the processing model, and if you use a function at the wrong point, you'll get a general error message that says something like "The function cannot be used because it must be evaluated later." For instance, you might get this message if you tried to use a function that is evaluated in the second pass in a record-selection formula because record-selection processing is a first-pass activity.

Crystal Reports handles the evaluation time of Report objects automatically. However, you may use a formula in the wrong place or get unexpected results because of the evaluation time mode. Operations such as record selection (which happen on the first pass through the data) cannot contain any functions that are not available until the second pass through the data. This includes the following special fields and functions: GroupNumber, PageNumber, RecordNumber, Previous, and Next. In addition, you cannot create running total fields using any functions that are evaluated on the second pass through the data.

Several built-in statements allow you to control when your formula executes. Add these statements to the beginning of your formula to control when the formula will run:

BeforeReadingRecords   Use this statement to process a formula when constants are being evaluated; it cannot combine with database fields. In the example here, a global variable is set; since it doesn't involve database fields, it can be processed before data is read from the data source:

```
BeforeReadingRecords;
Global numberVar annualQuota = 500000;
```

WhileReadingRecords This statement forces evaluation during the first pass through the data. It can be used to create a formula field to create a second group on a field that is already used in a group in the report. First create the field with following formula and then create a group on the formula field:

```
WhileReadingRecords;
{Resorts.Country};
```

WhileReadingRecords cannot be combined with any functions that are not in the second data pass, including the following:

DistinctCount	NextIsNull	TotalPageCount
WhilePrintingRecords	GroupNumber	Average
TotalPageCount	Previous	PageNofM
Next	PageNumber	OnFirstRecord
RecordNumber	PreviousIsNull	OnLastRecord

WhilePrintingRecords Use this statement to guarantee that the formula executes as database records are being retrieved from the data source. The following formula could be used to suppress the Details section on the first page of a report:

```
WhilePrintingRecords;
PageNumber<>1
```

EvaluateAfter(x) Use this function to force one formula to execute after another. X represents the name of a formula.

Print State/Print Time

Crystal precalculates several pieces of information for you and makes it available in formulas for use in any report. The following functions are evaluated at print time, which is during the second pass through the data.

DrillDownGroupLevel When drilling down through groups in a report, returns a 0 for the top-level group, a 1 for the next level down, and so on.

GroupNumber Each group has a number; use this function in selection formulas to include or exclude groups.

GroupSelection Returns a text string representing the group-selection criteria in effect for the report.

InRepeatedGroupHeader Returns a True value if a Group Header section appears on multiple pages.

IsNull({table.field}) This function checks to see if a Null value is stored in a database field. When used in a formula, it can be used by itself or in combination with other conditions. The

IsNull function must be the first condition in the statement, as demonstrated in the following if-then-else statement, which prints five asterisks in the report if the resort has a five-star rating or prints nothing if the value in the database is either Null or No:

```
If IsNull({Resorts.FiveStarRating}) or
➡{Resorts.FiveStarRating}) = "No" Then
    ""
Else
    "*****"
Next({table.field})
```

When used in the Details section, returns the value of the given field in the next record.

NextIsNull({table.field})   When used in the Details section, checks to see if the field in the previous record has a Null value; returns True or False.

OnFirstRecord   Use this function when formatting a report and wanting to apply or negate special formatting on the first record retrieved from the data source.

OnLastRecord   Use this function when formatting a report and wanting to apply or negate special formatting on the last record retrieved from the data source. The following example prints a "Continued on next page…" message when this formula is placed in the Details section and when the current record's ResortCode is the same as the ResortCode in the next record:

```
If OnLastRecord Then
  //do nothing
Else If {Resorts.ResortCode} = Next({Resorts.ResortCode}) Then
    "Continued on next page…";
```

PageNofM   Returns the current page and the total page in a text string separated by the word "of"; e.g., 7 of 10.

PageNumber   Returns the current page number.

Previous({table.field})   When used in the Details section, returns the value of the given field in the previous record:

```
If Previous({table.field}) = {table.field} Then
  "This value is the same as previous."
Else
  "This value has changed!"
PreviousIsNull({table.field})
```

When used in the Details section, checks to see if the given field in the previous record has a Null value; returns True or False.

RecordNumber   Returns the number of the current database record being processed.

RecordSelection   Returns a text string representing the record-selection criteria in effect for the report.

TotalPageCount   Returns the total number of pages in a report.

Document Properties

Functions in the Document Properties category return information about the report as a whole. Each of the document properties functions maps directly to the Special Fields category of the Field Explorer.

DataDate   Returns the date when the data was last retrieved from the data source.

DataTime   Returns the timestamp for when the data was last retrieved from the data source.

FileAuthor   Returns a field with the name of the author of the report.

FileCreationDate   Returns a field with the date the report was created.

Filename   Returns a field with the external filename of the report.

ModificationDate   Returns the date the report was last modified.

ModificationTime   Returns the timestamp for when the report was last modified.

PrintDate   Returns the date the report was last printed or displayed.

PrintTime   Returns the date the report was last printed or displayed.

ReportComments   Returns the value of the Comments field in the document properties assigned using File ➤ Summary Info.

ReportTitle   Returns the value of the ReportTitle field in the document properties assigned using File ➤ Summary Info.

Report Alerts

Report alerts are messages that pop up when a report first opens to indicate that a value that has been flagged has reached a threshold. For instance, if MonthlySales < 10,000, a message will pop up. Use the Report Alerts functions to determine the state of the alerts.

IsAlertEnabled(alertName)   Returns True if the named alert is active, False otherwise.

IsAlertTriggered(alertName)   Returns True if the named alert has been triggered on the current set of data, False otherwise.

AlertMessage(alertName)   Returns the string message associated with the named alert.

Math Functions

The built-in math functions for Basic Syntax and Crystal Syntax allow some fairly sophisticated mathematic calculations. Use these functions in formula fields, conditional statements, and in other functions.

Abs(x)   Returns a positive value for x.

Atn (number)   Returns the angle whose tangent is the argument to the function.

Cos (number)   Returns the cosine of an angle that was specified in radians.

Exp (number)   Returns e (approximately 2.718282) raised to a power.

Fix (number), Fix (number, #places)   Returns a truncated value.

Log (number)   Returns a natural logarithm.

Pi   Returns 3.14159265…

Remainder (number1, number2)   Returns an integer that is left over after number1 is divided by number2. The following Basic Syntax function can be used to control formatting in the Details section and set each even record number background to green and each odd number background to white:

```
If Remainder( recordNumber, 2) = 0 Then
    crGreen
Else
    crWhite
End If
```

Rnd, Rnd (seed)   Returns a random number optionally based on a starting seed value.

Round (x), Round (x, #places)   Returns a number rounded down to the nearest integer.

Sin (number)   Returns the sine of an angle that was specified in radians.

Sqr (number)   Returns the square root of a number.

Tan (number)   Returns the tangent of an angle that was specified in radians.

Truncate (x), Truncate (x, #places)   Returns a truncated value.

Summary Functions

The arguments to summary functions are fields from the report or the data source. These functions gather statistics and summarize data values. Some functions allow an array of values to be passed to a summarization function. These functions are often used with groups.

Average({table.field})   Returns the average for the given field value for however many records were processed in the Details section. This function can also accept the name of an array in place of the {table.field} argument.

Correlation   Returns a number that represents how well the variation of one value can be predicted from the variation of another.

Count   Returns the number of occurrences of a field. This function can also accept the name of an array in place of the {table.field} argument.

Covariance   Returns a number that represents the tendency of two variables to move in tandem to one another.

DistinctCount   Returns the number of unique occurrences of a value in a field. This function can also accept the name of an array in place of the {table.field} argument.

Maximum   Returns the maximum value in a set of values (e.g., all the records for a given field). This function can also accept the name of an array in place of the {table.field} argument.

Median   Returns the middle number in a set of values by dividing numerically ordered data into two equal parts.

Minimum   Returns the minimum value in a set of values (e.g., all the records for a given field). This function can also accept the name of an array in place of the {table.field} argument.

Mode   Returns the data value that occurred the most often in the set of values.

NthLargest   Where N is any positive integer, returns the N largest data values.

NthMostFrequent   Where N is any positive integer, returns the N most frequently occurring data value.

NthSmallest   Where N is any positive integer, returns the N smallest data values.

PercentOfAverage   Returns the average of values in a group relative to the percentage of all values.

PercentOfCount   Returns the count of values in a group relative to the count of all values.

PercentOfDistinctCount   Returns the count of distinct values in a group relative to the count of all distinct values.

PercentOfMaximum   Returns the maximum of values in a group relative to the maximum of all values.

PercentOfMinimum   Returns the minimum of values in a group relative to the minimum of all values.

PercentOfSum   Returns the sum of values in a group relative to the sum of all values.

Population Variance   Returns a number representing the dispersion in the values of a given population of data.

PopulationStdDev   This function can also accept the name of an array in place of the {table.field} argument.

PthPercentile   Returns the value associated with the specified percentile for the given field.

StdDev   Standard deviation measures the spread of a distribution about the mean in a set of data values. This function can also accept the name of an array in place of the {table.field} argument.

Sum   Adds the values in a field or set of values. This function can also accept the name of an array in place of the {table.field} argument.

Variance   Returns a number measuring the amount of change between values in a set of data. This function can also accept the name of an array in place of the {table.field} argument.

WeightedAverage   Returns an average that accounts for a dependent variable.

Financial Functions

Crystal Reports 9 contains over 50 financial functions, with more than 40 of them being new in this release. The functions calculate values like internal rates of return, net present value, amortization, depreciation, coupon settlement information, annual percentage rates, and many more of similar nature to financial spreadsheet analysis and statistical financial software. Many of the functions are heavily used by third-party tools that ship with Crystal Reports, such as accounting systems. You can use one of these functions to get a single answer or you can combine functions, treating each as building block, to generate answers to complex financial reporting problems.

ACCRINT   Returns accrued interest for a security that pays interest periodically.

ACCRINTM   Returns accrued interest for a security that pays interest at maturity.

AmorDEGRC   Returns depreciation on an asset for a given year.

AmorLINC   Returns linear depreciation on an asset for a given year.

CoupDayBS   Returns the number of days between the latest coupon date before the settlement and the actual settlement date.

CoupDays   Returns the number of days in the coupon period containing the settlement date.

CoupDaysNC   Returns the number of days between the settlement date and the next coupon date after the settlement date.

CoupNCD   Returns the date of the next coupon after the settlement date.

CoupNum   Returns the number of coupon periods between the settlement date and the maturity date.

CoupPCD   Returns the date of the last coupon before the settlement date.

CumIPMT   Returns the total interest paid on a loan for a given period.

CumPrinc   Returns the total money paid toward the principal on a loan for a given period.

Days360   Returns the number of days between two dates using 30 days for a month and 360 days for year.

DB   Returns a number representing the depreciation on an asset in a time period using the fixed-declining balance method.

DDB   Returns a number representing the depreciation on an asset in a time period using the double-declining balance method.

DISC   Returns the discount rate for a security based on settlement and maturity dates.

DollarDE   Returns a currency value expressed as a decimal given a currency value expressed as a fraction.

DollarFR   Returns a currency value expressed as a fraction given a currency value expressed as a decimal.

Duration   Returns a number representing the weighted average of the present value of cash flows.

Effect Returns the effective annual interest rate given a specific interest rate and number of compounding periods.

FV Returns the future value of an annuity.

FVSchedule Returns the future value of an investment given interest rates for several periods.

IntRate Returns the interest rate for a fully invested security.

IPmt Returns a number representing the interest payment on an annuity.

IRR Returns the internal rate of return for cash flow in a period.

ISPMT Returns the interest paid during a given period.

MDuration Returns a number representing the modified duration of a bond.

MIRR Returns the modified internal rate of return for cash flow in a period.

Nominal Returns the nominal annual interest rate given the effective interest rate.

NPer Returns the number of periods for an annuity.

NPV Returns the net present value of an investment.

OddFPrice Returns the price of a security that pays interest periodically but has an odd first period.

OddFYield Returns the yield of a security that pays interest periodically but has an odd first period.

OddLPrice Returns the price of a security that pays interest periodically but has an odd last period.

OddLYield Returns the yield of a security that pays interest periodically but has an odd last period.

Pmt Returns the payment amount for an annuity with fixed payments and fixed interest.

PPmt Returns the principal payment amount for an annuity with fixed payments and fixed interest.

Price Returns the price of a security paying interest periodically per $100 of face value.

PriceDisc Returns the price of a discounted security per $100 of face value.

PriceMat Returns the price of a security that pays interest at maturity per $100 of face value.

PV Returns the present value of an annuity.

Rate Returns the interest rate for an annuity period.

Received Returns the amount received for a fully invested security at maturity.

SLN Returns the straight-line depreciation on an asset.

SYD Returns the sum-of-years' digits depreciation on an asset.

TBillEq Returns the bond-equivalent yield for a Treasury bill.

TBillPrice   Returns the price per $100 face value for a Treasury bill.

TBillYield   Returns the yield for a Treasury bill.

VDB   Returns the depreciation of an asset for a given period using the double-declining balance method.

XIRR   Returns the internal rate of return for nonperiodic cash flows.

XNPV   Returns the net present value for nonperiodic cash flows.

YearFrac   Returns a fractional value representing the percentage of a year between two given dates.

Yield   Returns the yield on a security paying periodic interest.

YieldDisc   Returns the annual yield for a discounted security.

YieldMat   Returns the annual yield of a security that pays its interest at maturity.

String Functions

String data is character or textual data. It is common to parse or manipulate text values for presentation purposes in a report. The built-in string functions provide many formatting options.

Asc   Returns the ASCII code for the first character in a given string.

AscW   Returns the Unicode value for the first character in a given string.

Chr   Returns a character given an ASCII code.

ChrW   Returns a Unicode character given an ASCII code.

Filter   Searches an array for a given value.

InStr   Searches a string for a given value.

InStrRev   Searches a string for a given value by starting at the last character in the string and searching down to the first.

Join   Converts a list of multiple elements to a single string containing all the element values.

Left   Returns the leftmost characters in a given string for the number of characters specified.

Length   When Basic Syntax is used, Len(x) is also acceptable usage.

LowerCase   Converts a value to lowercase.

Mid   Extracts part of a string based on a starting position in the string and a given number of characters to extract.

NumericText   Returns True if the content of a text string is a valid number.

ProperCase (string)   Returns a string with initial capitalization on each word.

Replace   Returns a string that has had values replaced based on a pattern passed to this function.

ReplicateString   Make a specified number of copies of a text string.

Right   Returns the rightmost characters in a given string for the number of characters specified.

Roman   Returns a Roman numeral corresponding to an integer value.

Space   Returns a specified number of blank spaces.

Split   Converts the words in a string into a list of multiple elements.

StrCmp   Compares two strings to one another.

StrReverse   Reverses the characters in a string.

ToNumber   Converts a given value to a double value.

ToText   Converts a given value to a text string; the following example truncates a number to 0 decimals and then converts it to a text string:

```
ToText({Table.Field},00,"")
```

ToWords   Converts a number to a text string with an opportunity to handle decimal conversion.

Trim   Removes leading and trailing blanks from a string.

TrimLeft   Removes blanks at the beginning of a string (leading) from the string.

TrimRight   Removes blanks at the end of a string (trailing) from the string.

UpperCase   Converts a value to uppercase.

Val   Extracts a numeric value from the text string in which it is embedded.

Date and Time-Related Functions

The functions in this section help you format information and set values based on date ranges, calendar ranges, aging information, and other types of date time information. These formulas are typically used in conditional statements to set values or formatting in a report.

Aged0To30Days   Given a date, determines if the date is 0 to 30 days in the past; the following Basic Syntax code example, when placed in the Background Color formatting formula for a Details section, will change the color of the Detail row based on the age of a date:

```
Select Case ({Invoice.PaymentDueDate})
  Case Aged0To30Days
    Formula = crWhite
  Case Aged31to60Days
    Formula = crGreen
  Case Aged61to90Days
    Formula = crBlue
  Case Else
    Formula = crRed
End Select
```

Aged31to60Days   Given a date, determines if the date is 31 to 60 days in the past.

Aged61to90Days   Given a date, determines if the date is 61 to 90 days in the past.

AllDatesFromToday   Given a date, determines if the date is in the future starting with today's date.

AllDatesFromTomorrow   Given a date, determines if the date is in the future starting with tomorrow's date.

AllDatesToToday   Given a date, determines if the date is in the past including today's date.

AllDatesToYesterday   Given a date, determines if the date is in the past up to yesterday's date.

Calendar1stHalf   Given a date, determines if the date is within the period January 1 through June 30, inclusive.

Calendar1stQtr   Given a date, determines if the date is within the period January 1 through March 31, inclusive.

Calendar2ndHalf   Given a date, determines if the date is within the period July 1 through December 31, inclusive.

Calendar2ndQtr   Given a date, determines if the date is within the period April 1 through June 30, inclusive.

Calendar3rdQtr   Given a date, determines if the date is within the period July 1 through September 30, inclusive.

Calendar4thQtr   Given a date, determines if the date is within the period October 1 through December 31, inclusive.

CurrentDate   Returns the current date in date format as read from the underlying operating system.

CurrentDateTime   Returns the current date and time in date time format as read from the underlying operating system.

CurrentTime   Returns the current time in time format as read from the underlying operating system.

Date   Converts a number, string, or date time to a date type; valid in Crystal Syntax only.

DateAdd   Increments a date by passing in a starting date and a number of years, months, days, weeks, etc., to be added.

DateDiff   Decrements a date by passing in a starting date and a number of years, months, days, weeks, etc., to be subtracted.

DatePart   Given a date, extracts the year, quarter, month, day, etc.

DateSerial   Returns a date given three integer parameters or integer expressions representing the year, month, and day.

DateTime   Converts a number, string, or date time to a date time type; valid in Crystal Syntax only.

DateTimeValue   Converts a number, string, or date time to a date time type.

DateValue   Converts a number, string, or date time to a date type.

Day   Given a date value, returns the day component as an integer from 1 to 31.

DayOfWeek   Given a date, returns an integer representing the day of the week the date occurs, where 1 is Sunday and 7 is Saturday.

Hour   Given a date time value, returns the hour component as an integer from 0 to 23.

IsDate   Returns True if the given value is of the date data type or can be successfully converted to the date data type.

IsDateTime   Returns True if the given value is of the date time data type or can be successfully converted to the date time data type.

IsTime   Returns True if the given value is of the time data type or can be successfully converted to the time data type.

Last4WeeksToSun   Given a date, determines if the date is in the four weeks prior to the previous Sunday date.

Last7Days   Given a date, determines if the date is in the last seven days.

LastFullMonth   Given a date, determines if the date is in the previous calendar month.

LastFullWeek   Given a date, determines if the date is in the previous Sunday-through-Saturday week.

LastYearMTD   Given a date, determines if the date is in the prior year for the current month to the current date in that year.

LastYearYTD   Given a date, determines if the date is in the prior year to the current date in that year.

Minute   Given a time value, returns the minute component in the format 0 to 59.

Month   Given a date or date time value, returns the month component in the format 1 to 12.

MonthName   Given a date or date time value, returns the month component in the format January to December or Jan to Dec.

MonthToDate   Given a date, determines if the date is in the current month up until the current date.

Next30Days   Given a date, determines if the date is within the next 30 days counting today.

Next31To60Days   Given a date, determines if the date is within the next 31 to 60 days counting today.

Next61To90Days   Given a date, determines if the date is within the next 61 to 90 days counting today.

Next91DaysTo365Days   Given a date, determines if the date is within the next 91 days to 365 days including today.

Over90Days   Given a date, determines if the date is more than 90 days later than the date.

Second   Given a time value, returns the second component in the format 0 to 59.

Time   Converts a number, string, date time, or HH, MM, SS value to a valid time data type.

Timer   Returns the number of seconds elapsed since midnight.

TimeSerial   Returns a time given three integer parameters or integer expressions representing hours, minutes, and seconds.

TimeValue   Converts a number, string, or date time to a time type.

WeekDay   Given a date, returns an integer representing the day of the week the date occurs, where 1 is Sunday and 7 is Saturday.

WeekdayName   Given a date, returns a text string integer representing the day of the week the date occurs in the format Sunday to Saturday or Sun to Sat.

WeekToDateFromSun   Given a date, determines if the date is in the current week prior to today and up to last Sunday.

Year   Given a date, extracts the year component of the date.

YearToDate   Given a date, determines if the date falls in the range of the current calendar year up to the current date.

Data Type Conversion Functions

Data type conversion functions change a value from one data type to another. If the conversion is not possible given the type of data value provided and the conversion being attempted, an error message is presented.

CBool   Returns True if a given number is positive or negative; returns False if it is 0.

CCur   Converts a given value to a currency value.

CDbl   Converts a given value to a double value.

CStr   Converts a given value to a string value.

CDate   Converts a given value to a date value.

CTime   Converts a given value to a time value.

CDateTime   Converts a given value to a date timestamp value.

Index

Note to the Reader: Page numbers in **bold** indicate the principle discussion of a topic or the definition of a term. Page numbers in *italic* indicate illustrations.

C

G

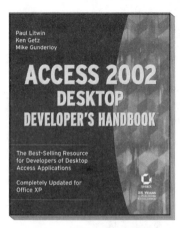
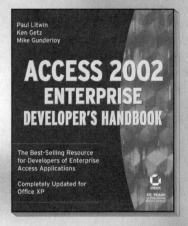

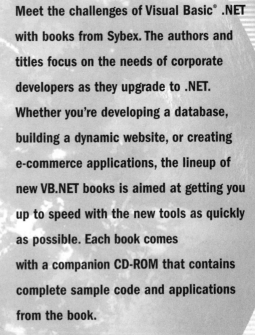